Traditions & Encounters

Volume I
From the Beginning
to 1500

SEVENTH EDITION

Traditions & Encounters

Volume I
From the Beginning to 1500

Jerry H. Bentley
UNIVERSITY OF HAWAI'I

Herbert F. Ziegler
UNIVERSITY OF HAWAI'I

Heather E. Streets-Salter
NORTHEASTERN UNIVERSITY

Craig Benjamin
GRAND VALLEY STATE UNIVERSITY

McGraw Hill

TRADITIONS & ENCOUNTERS: VOLUME 1 FROM THE BEGINNING TO 1500, SEVENTH EDITION

Published by McGraw Hill Education, 2 Penn Plaza, New York, NY 10121. Copyright ©2021 by McGraw Hill Education. All rights reserved. Printed in the United States of America. Previous editions ©2015, 2011, and 2008. No part of this publication may be reproduced or distributed in any form or by any means, or stored in a database or retrieval system, without the prior written consent of McGraw Hill Education, including, but not limited to, in any network or other electronic storage or transmission, or broadcast for distance learning.

Some ancillaries, including electronic and print components, may not be available to customers outside the United States.

This book is printed on acid-free paper.

1 2 3 4 5 6 7 8 9 LWI 24 23 22 21 20

ISBN 978-1-264-08814-0 (bound edition)
MHID 1-264-08814-0 (bound edition)
ISBN 978-1-264-08809-6 (loose-leaf edition)
MHID 1-264-08809-4 (loose-leaf edition)

Senior Portfolio Manager: *Jason Seitz*
Marketing Manager: *Rasheité Calhoun*
Content Project Managers: *Sandy Wille; Vanessa McClune*
Product Development Manager: *Dawn Groundwater*
Senior Buyer: *Laura Fuller*
Lead Designer: *David W. Hash*
Senior Content Licensing Specialists: *Brianna Kirschbaum*
Compositor: *Aptara®, Inc.*
Cover Image: *Arp 273: Egyptian Studio/Shutterstock; finger: chaoss/Shutterstock; fern fiddlehead: Zoonar GmbH/ Alamy Stock Photo; Cave of Hands painting: Eduardo Rivero/Shutterstock; shell pattern: andreahast/123RF; Egyptian Rosetta Stone: Photos.com/Getty Images; marble inlay: Glow Images; textile fragment: The Metropolitan Museum of Art, New York, Gift of Henry G. Marquand, 1882; fish mosaics: Lissa Harrison; tunic: The Walters Art Museum, Baltimore, Gift of Georgia and Michael de Havenon, 2016; Greek vase: Digital image courtesy of the Getty's Open Content Program; mosaic of triangles: Alfredo Venturi/Alamy; Roman mosaic: neil harrison/iStock/Getty Images; Ardabil carpet: LACMA -Los Angeles County Museum of Art; Pont du Gard: Bertl123/Shutterstock; Jameh Mosque: Andrea Ricordi, Italy/Moment/Getty Images; Moroccan tile: AlxeyPnferov/iStock/Getty Images; Celtic knot tombstone: Robin Bath/Alamy; Buddhist mani stone: Egmont Strigl/Imagebroker RF/age footstock; bowl: The Metropolitan Museum of Art; New York, The Michael C. Rockefeller Memorial Collection, Purchase, Nelson A. Rockefeller Gift; Vitruvian Man: Janaka Dharmasena/Shutterstock; Romanian carpet; Europeana Collections / INP - National Heritage Institute, Bucharest; dot painting: Paul Pegler/E+/Getty Images; distemper on cloth: The Metropolitan Museum of Art, New York, Purchase, Lita Annenberg Hazen Charitable Trust Gift, 1987; barkcloth: LACMA - Los Angeles County Museum; Moroccan tiles: AlxeyPnferov/iStock/Getty Images; mosaic floor: Digital image courtesy of the Getty's Open Content Program; Pair of Parfleches: The Metropolitan Museum of Art, New York, Ralph T. Coe Collection, Gift of Ralph T. Coe Foundation for the Arts, 2011; Moroccan tile: AlxeyPnferov/iStock/Getty Images; fabric pattern: ADELART/Shutterstock; El Castillo: Kitti Boonnitrod/Getty Images; Buddhist temple: Melba Photo Agency/Alamy; tile: LACMA - Los Angeles County Museum of Art; fan patterns: Jenny Dettrick/Moment/Getty Images; molecules: McGraw Hill; spiral staircase: Rob Tilley/Spaces Images/Blend Images LLC; ceremonial skirt: The Metropolitan Museum of Art, Rogers Fund, 2004; Fleur-de-lis: Exactostock/ SuperStock; Saint Basil's Cathedral: Dave and Les Jacobs/Blend Images LLC; Japanese maple leaf pattern: Photosindia.Com, Llc/Glow Images; DNA: Jezper/Shutterstock; farming village: KingWu/iStockphoto; silk sari: jayk7/Getty Images; bark cloth: Yale University Art Gallery, Photo Credit: Christopher Gardner; silk brocade: Kevin McNeill/iStock/360/Getty Images; Lozenge composition: The Art Institute of Chicago, Gift of Edgar Kaufmann, Jr.; blue technology background: SkillUp/Shutterstock*

All credits appearing on page or at the end of the book are considered to be an extension of the copyright page.

The Internet addresses listed in the text were accurate at the time of publication. The inclusion of a website does not indicate an endorsement by the authors or McGraw Hill Education, and McGraw Hill Education does not guarantee the accuracy of the information presented at these sites.

mheducation.com/highered

Brief Contents

Contents

Maps

Power of Process for
Primary Sources

Sources from the Past

Connecting the Sources

Preface

How do the themes of traditions and encounters continue to help make sense of the entire human past in the twenty-first century?

As Jerry Bentley and Herb Zeigler noted in their original Preface to this book, world history is about both diversity and connections. They began this text with a simple goal: to help our students understand the unique histories of the world's rich variety of peoples, while at the same time allowing them to see the long histories of connections and interactions that have shaped all human communities for millennia. To do this, the authors wrote a story around the dual themes of traditions and encounters to highlight the many different religions and customs embraced by the world's peoples while also exploring the encounters with other cultures that brought about inevitable change.

It is the interaction of these traditions and encounters that continues to provide the key to making sense of our past. Human communities furthered themselves not by remaining isolated, but by interacting with others and exploring the benefits and risks of reaching out. The vitality of history—and its interpretation—lies in understanding the nature of individual cultural traditions and the scope of encounters that punctuated every significant event in human history.

This Seventh Edition of *Traditions & Encounters: A Global Perspective on the Past* provides a genuinely global vision of history that is increasingly meaningful in the shrinking world of the twenty-first century. The theme of *traditions* draws attention to the formation, maintenance, and sometimes collapse of so many distinctive, individual societies. Because the world's peoples have also interacted regularly with one another since the earliest days of human history, the theme of *encounters* directs attention to communications, interactions, networks, and exchanges that have linked individual societies to their neighbors and others in the larger world. Despite many changes in the way world historians have tried to conceptualize the past and present since the appearance of the first edition of *Traditions and Encounters* decades ago, the twin themes of traditions and encounters remain at the heart of every chapter in the text, no matter how extensive revisions might have been. They provide a lens through which to interpret the affairs of humankind and the pressures that continue to shape history. All aspects of the text support these themes—from the organization of chapters, engaging stories of the world's peoples, to the robust map program, updated primary sources, and critical-thinking features that permeate the text.

Some of the changes authors Heather Streets-Salter and Craig Benjamin have introduced to the Seventh Edition of *Traditions and Encounters* include the following:

We have worked hard to eliminate any gendered or out-of-date language throughout the book, in line with most historical writing being done today.

We decided to eliminate the Part Openers and Part Closers to help provide a more seamless narrative and to downplay the somewhat compartmentalized and episodic structure that was more common when earlier editions were prepared.

We have changed the old Eyewitness feature to *Zooming in on Traditions* or *Zooming in on Encounters* to further emphasize the key organizational lens of the book. And we have streamlined the opening stories featured in these *Zooming* features to give greater voice to the many individuals from the past they include. We have also separated these stories from a new *Chapter Overview* that helps better prepare readers for the contents of the chapter that follows.

We have changed the titles of a number of chapters to reflect recent thinking within the field and, in some cases, to be more geographically and politically inclusive. We have also made numerous changes to headers and subheaders throughout, both to reflect new interpretations of how we should "label" various peoples and historical processes and also to make the structure of each chapter clearer.

We have replaced and updated a number of sources in the *Sources from the Past* and *Connecting the Sources* features and have also selected many new images to better illustrate the text. We have added in-line comprehension questions to the sources and also updated reflection questions on most sources, maps, and images to help students practice both their comprehension and analytical thinking skills.

We have changed the old *Reverberations* feature to *How the Past Shapes the Future*, both to further enhance the flow of historical processes and also to more clearly emphasize the continuing relevance of each of the themes explored to the global world of today.

We have changed the old *Summary* feature to a *Conclusion* and modified the language in each to more succinctly sum up the developments described in the chapter. We have also moved the *Chronology* section earlier in the chapter and updated it to incorporate recent date revisions by historians and added new and more relevant secondary courses to the *For Further Reading* section at the end of each chapter.

New to this edition, we have added a feature called *What's Left Out?* to call attention to issues most texts do not usually have space to discuss. Its purpose is to remind students that history is far more complicated and nuanced than any brief narrative can provide. For example, in chapter 9 the authors explore the little-known role of the Kushan King Kanishka the Great in promoting Mahayana Buddhism and helping facilitate its spread into China, enriching the standard account of its transmission by missionaries. In chapter 27 the authors give greater context on non-elite women in Southwest Asia because most textbooks focus on elite women associated with the imperial harem, while in chapter 37 they help students understand that the rivalries of the Cold War in fact originated much earlier in the interwar period.

CHAPTER-BY-CHAPTER CHANGES

The following is a chapter-by-chapter list of topics that are new to this edition or elements that have been substantially revised or updated.

Chapter 1: Early Human History

- Changed title to reflect recent reinterpretations of the Paleolithic and Neolithic eras.
- Reconceptualized the period originally considered as "pre-history" but now better understood as early human history.
- Added information on *Homo habilis* to discussion of *Homo genus*.
- Added information in text and on maps concerning recent hominid discoveries.
- Replaced *hunting and gathering* with *foraging* throughout as a more accurate description of Paleolithic lifeways.
- Updated information about Neandertals, including their contribution to European *Homo sapiens* gene pool.
- Updated several dates for the emergence of agriculture in the Americas.
- Added a "What's Left Out?" about Gobekli Tepe and how its construction by foraging peoples seems to be a so-far-unexplained exception to the challenges of monumental architecture construction by foraging peoples.

Chapter 2: The Emergence of Complex Societies in Southwest Asia and Encounters with Indo-European-Speaking Peoples

- Changed title to emphasize "complex" societies and bring it into line with subsequent chapter titles.
- Updated "Zooming in on Traditions" to more clearly explain the significance of the *Epic of Gilgamesh*.
- Changed text to emphasize key theme of "traditions and encounters."
- Added language throughout to reflect long-term influence of achievements of Mesopotamian peoples on subsequent cultures and civilizations.
- Added recent genetic information on origin of Phoenicians.
- Added a "What's Left Out?" about the possible place of origin of pastoralism: Dereivka in Ukraine.

Chapter 3: The Emergence of Complex Societies in Africa and the Bantu Migrations

- Changed title to emphasize "complex" societies and bring it into line with other chapter titles.

- Added definition of *pharaoh*.
- Added updated information about the Pyramid of Khufu, and the workers who constructed it, based on recent archaeological discoveries of pyramid workers' tombs.
- Updated information in Bantu Migrations section to reflect recent interpretations.
- Added a "What's Left Out?" about the recent discovery of a Mitanni palace on the banks of the Tigris; Mitanni fought with the Egyptians during the reign of Tuthmosis III.

Chapter 4: The Emergence of Complex Societies in South Asia

- Changed title to emphasize "complex" societies and bring it into line with other chapter titles.
- Changed "India" to "South Asia" throughout to reflect political sensibilities and reality that ancient South Asia included regions that are now part of the modern nations of India, Pakistan, Sri Lanka, and Bangladesh.
- Changed several section headers and subheaders to reflect current interpretations (in particular, replaced Harrapan Society/Civilization with Indus Society/Civilization).
- Also changed "Aryans" to more accurate "Indo-Aryans."
- Added language that emphasizes the role of the environment in the collapse of Indus Civilization.
- Replaced Rig-Veda source with extracts from the Laws of Manu, with emphasis on gender relations.
- Deleted any controversial discussion of the practice of Suti.
- Added a "What's Left Out?" about recent genetic discoveries that confirm the Indo-Aryan migrations and why this has become a politically controversial topic in modern India.

Chapter 5: The Emergence of Complex Society in Mainland East Asia

- Changed title to emphasize "complex" societies and bring it into line with other chapter titles.
- Changed language to reflect recent archaeological discoveries of Xia and Shang dynasty artifacts.
- Updated some dates throughout to reflect more recent interpretations.
- Emphasized influence of nomadic military strategies on early Chinese armies.
- Added "What's Left Out?" on the ambiguity of the tomb of, and oracle bone references to, Lady Fu Hao in the context of gender relations in early Chinese society.

Chapter 6: Early Societies in the Americas and Oceania

- Changed "Mayan" to "Maya" throughout chapter, except when used as an adjective.

- Updated dates throughout to reflect current thinking (particularly concerning human migration to the Americas).

- Updated discussion of role of Olmecs (mother or sister culture?) to reflect current thinking.

- Updated discussion of origins of agriculture in South America, pushing dates of early evidence back several thousand years.

- Updated discussion of Chavin de Huantar culture to reflect recent interpretations (and also changed descriptor from "cult" to "culture").

- Changed "Mochica" to "Moche" throughout.

- Added qualifier to early adoption of agriculture in New Guinea.

- Added "What's Left Out?" about environmental impact of Polynesian migrations to New Zealand and other Pacific islands.

Chapter 7: The Empires of Persia

- Changed several section headers and subheaders to reflect current interpretations (e.g., "Sasanid" to "Sasanian" and eliminated all references to "classical era").

- Added artist's impression of Persepolis at its peak.

- Modified some maps to more accurately reflect geopolitical reality, such as adding border between Parthian/Sasanian empires and Roman Empire.

- Added language that reflects intentional emphasis on political continuity among Achaemenids, Parthians, and Sasanians to reinforce legitimacy of the founders of these later Persian empires.

- Updated captions to some images in response to reviewers' suggestions, increasing caption specificity and accuracy.

- Added "What's Left Out?" on references in Persian sources like the Avesta to the role of women in the Persian Empire, including powerful regents and managers of work groups.

Chapter 8: The Unification of China

- Updated language regarding Qin Shi Huangdi's oppression of Confucianism.

- Edited and improved questions in "Connecting the Sources," emphasizing ambiguity of Ban Zhao's "Lessons for Women."

- Added language emphasizing the critical importance of the history of Sima Qian to our understanding of this period of Chinese history.

- Added "What's Left Out?" on Cai Lun and the invention of paper in the Later Han Dynasty.

Chapter 9: State, Society, and the Quest for Salvation in South Asia

- Changed title from "Indian" to "South Asia"—and changed "India" to "South Asia" throughout this chapter—to reflect political sensibilities and reality that ancient South Asia included regions that are now part of the modern nations of India, Pakistan, Sri Lanka, and Bangladesh.

- Added references in text to more closely bring students' attention to maps.

- Added geographical terminology throughout to help students better understand where these ancient states were located in relation to modern nations.

- Updated language about the Kushan Empire.

- Added superb image of double-sided gold coin of Kanishka to show how it can be used as both political and religious evidence.

- Added new, more cautious language about the difficulty of interpreting classics like the Ramayana and Mahabharata as evidence of attitudes toward women.

- Added a "What's Left Out?" about the role of Kushan King Kanishka in the spread of Mahayana Buddhism.

Chapter 10: Civilizations of the Mediterranean Basin: The Greeks

- Changed title to match other chapter titles on Mediterranean-based civilizations to emphasize the role of the environment of the Mediterranean Basin in those civilizations' formation and success.

- Eliminated all references to "classical" throughout, in line with recent thinking.

- Updated discussion of Alexander.

- More clearly defined terms like *satrapies* and *atom*.

- Eliminated superfluous language about Platonic philosophy.

- Added a "What's Left Out?" about the reign of Pericles in Athens and the cost of constructing the Parthenon.

Chapter 11: Civilizations of the Mediterranean Basin: The Romans

- Changed title to match other chapter titles on Mediterranean-based civilizations to emphasize the role of the environment of the Mediterranean Basin in those civilizations' formation and success.

- Eliminated all references to "classical" throughout, in line with recent thinking.

- Added further discussion to the section on gender relations, including discussion of elite Roman women's public response to passing of the Lex Oppia in 215 B.C.E.

- Changed language to a more nuanced discussion of slavery.

- Updated language in discussion of Mithraism and worship of Isis (e.g., eliminated references to "cults" that might be confusing for students).

■ Added a "What's Left Out?" on recent evidence about the origins and roles of gladiators in the Roman state.

Chapter 12: Cross-Cultural Exchanges on the Silk Roads

■ Changed title to eliminate reference to classical and eliminated references to "classical" throughout, in line with recent thinking.

■ Updated language in discussion of the Periplus of the Erythrian Sea.

■ Added language and headers to emphasize different eras of the Silk Roads (First, Second, etc.).

■ Updated information concerning geographical routes and regions of the Silk Roads (and also modified maps to reflect this).

■ Replaced "India" with "South Asia" throughout.

■ Expanded "How the Past Shapes the Future" to emphasize long-term historical ramifications of spread of epidemic diseases along the Silk Roads.

■ Added a "What's Left Out?" on the origins and significance of the cache of high-value trade goods discovered near Kabul in Afghanistan in the 1930s, the so-called Begram Hoard.

Chapter 13: The Resurgence of Empire in South Asia

■ Updated geographical locations throughout (e.g., of Xuanzang's journey).

■ Added language to emphasize continuity of certain Tang and Song social practices into modern Chinese society.

■ Defined religious terms like *scriptoria* and *stupa*.

■ Included reference to female ruler of Korean Silla state, Queen Seondeok.

■ Included references to Soga in discussion of Japanese clans.

■ Added a "What's Left Out?" on history and evolution of role of concubines in Chinese society.

Chapter 14: The Expansive Realm of Islam

■ Added definitions and clarifications of various Islamic and Arabic terms (*ibn*, *hadith*, *jihad*, etc.).

■ Added language to help clarify the disagreements over succession following the death of the Prophet Muhammad.

■ Added some language to provide a more nuanced discussion of attitudes toward women, including role of female Sufis.

■ Added language throughout to emphasize continuing relevance of the expansion of Islam to the modern world.

■ Added a "What's Left Out?" about why an otherwise obscure and out-of-the way trading town named Mecca became so central to the Islamic faith, as well as the relevance of Ka'ba.

Chapter 15: India and the Indian Ocean Basin

■ Added more careful descriptors of relevant groups such as White Huns (Hephthalites), Turkic-Mongols, Turkic-Iranian, etc.

■ Added new phrasing about climatic causes of monsoon winds.

■ Added language reminding readers that Indian Ocean Basin trade had also flourished back in the First Silk Roads Era.

■ Defined terms such as *emporia*.

■ Added language emphasizing how religious developments during the first millennium C.E. are still influencing South Asia today.

■ Added new sources to provide a more balanced view of trade and exchange in the Indian Ocean Basin and Southeast Asia during the era, including Chinese observations of Nanhai trade, Chinese reports on a wealthy Javanese commercial kingdom, and Marco Polo on the flourishing port of Quanzhou (Zaiton).

■ Added a "What's Left Out?" on Queen Pwa Saw, the power behind the throne in Myanmar in the thirteenth century.

Chapter 16: Eastern and Western Europe in the Early Medieval Period

■ Changed chapter title to reflect more recent thinking and emphasize continuing relevance today of the emergence of "two Europes" during the first millennium C.E.

■ Through new subheaders and language, added further emphasis of the different ways of comparing the two halves of Europe using different lenses—political, economic, cultural, etc.

■ Added General Belisarius to discussion of Justinian's attempts to reconstitute the Roman Empire; added reference to Saracens.

■ Added a "What's Left Out?" on Anna Comnena and Hildegard of Bingen as a final way of comparing the two halves of early Medieval Europe—this time through the lives of elite women.

Chapter 17: Nomadic Empires and Eurasian Integration

■ Streamlined and updated the opening story.

■ Updated the introductory paragraphs for both "Sources from the Past."

■ Added a "What's Left Out?" about problems of language and translation in Mongol sources.

■ Updated information on the controversial legacies of Mongol invasions.

Chapter 18: States and Societies in Sub-Saharan Africa

■ Updated and streamlined the opening story based on new information about Sundiata.

■ Replaced the term *Bantu-speaking peoples* throughout to reflect updated scholarly understanding.

■ Updated information on kin-based societies to reflect current scholarly understanding.

■ Moved the section on Islamic Kingdoms and Empires so that it now follows the section on African Society and Cultural Development to improve the flow of the chapter.

■ Updated the section on gender to more accurately reflect current scholarship.

■ De-emphasized exoticism of African religions throughout.

■ Added a "What's Left Out?" on academic contributions to stereotypes about Africa's pre-colonial past.

Chapter 19: The Increasing Integration of Europe with the Wider World

■ Changed title to emphasize Europe's outlier position in world history at the time.

■ Added a "What's Left Out?" on the everyday lives of peasants in medieval Europe.

■ Added a new "Sources from the Past" on Margery Kempe to emphasize the role of women.

■ Clarified the origins of the Holy Roman Empire.

■ Clarified events regarding the Norman conquest of England.

Chapter 20: Worlds Apart: The Americas and Oceania

■ Deleted long quote in-text by Bernal Diaz.

■ Streamlined and clarified the section on Mexica.

■ Widened discussion on Mexica religion and Mexica culture.

■ Changed language in subhead from Inca Gods to Inca Religion.

■ Deleted information on Easter Island because it is now disputed by scholars.

■ Added a "What's Left Out?" about the difficulties of interpreting Nahuatl sources sponsored by Spanish conquerors.

Chapter 21: Expanding Horizons of Cross-Cultural Interaction

■ Streamlined opening vignette.

■ Added a "What's Left Out?" about the motivations behind becoming a eunuch.

■ Clarified and streamlined section on the slave trade.

PRIMARY SOURCES HELP STUDENTS THINK CRITICALLY ABOUT HISTORY

Power of Process for Primary Sources Primary sources help students think critically about history and expose them to contrasting perspectives of key events. The Seventh Edition of *Traditions & Encounters* provides four different ways to use primary source documents:

Power of Process for Primary Sources Power of Process is a critical thinking tool for reading and writing about primary sources. As part of Connect History, McGraw Hill's learning platform, Power of Process contains a database of more than 400 searchable primary sources in addition to the capability for instructors to upload their own sources. Instructors can then select a series of strategies for students to use to analyze and comment on a source. The Power of Process framework helps students develop essential academic skills such as understanding, analyzing, and synthesizing readings and visuals such as maps, leading students toward higher-order thinking and writing.

The Power of Process landing page makes it easy for instructors to find pre-populated documents or to add their own.

Sources from the Past These features showcase a significant primary source document of the period, such as a poem, journal account, religious writing, or letter. Thought-provoking questions prompt readers to analyze key issues raised in the document.

Connecting the Sources This feature helps students recognize that historiography is based on scholars' interpretation of historical information. It focuses on two documents or images, asking students to think critically about the different ways information can be interpreted.

McGraw Hill Create Because no two history courses are the same, you can select primary sources that meet the unique needs of your course. Using McGraw Hill's Create allows you to quickly and easily create custom course materials with cross-disciplinary content. Here's what you can do:

- Choose your own content: Create a book that contains only the chapters you want, in the order you want. Create will even renumber the pages for you!

- Add readings: Add readings from our collection or add your own original content such as syllabus or history major requirements.

- Choose your format: Print or ebook? Softcover, spiral, or loose-leaf? Black-and-white or color?

- Customize your cover: Pick your own cover image and include your name and course information right on the cover. Students will know they're purchasing the right book—and using everything they purchase!

- Review your creation: When you are all done, you'll receive a free PDF to review in just minutes. To get started, go to create.mheducation.com and register today.

SMARTBOOK 2.0 TAILORS CONTENT TO THE INDIVIDUAL STUDENT

SMARTBOOK Available within Connect History, SmartBook has been updated with improved learning objectives to ensure that students gain foundational knowledge, while also learning to make connections to help them formulate a broader understanding of historical events. SmartBook 2.0 personalizes learning to individual student needs, continually adapting to pinpoint knowledge gaps and focus learning on topics that need the most attention. Study time is more productive, and as a result, students are better prepared for class and coursework. For instructors, SmartBook 2.0 tracks student progress and provides insights that can help guide teaching strategies.

WRITING ASSIGNMENT

McGraw Hill's new Writing Assignment Plus tool delivers a learning experience that improves students' written communication skills and conceptual understanding with every assignment. Assign, monitor, and provide feedback on writing more efficiently and grade assignments within McGraw Hill Connect® and McGraw Hill Connect Master® 2.0. Writing Assignment Plus gives you time-saving tools with a just-in-time basic writing and originality checker.

Features include:

- Grammar/writing checking with McGraw Hill learning resources.

- Originality checker with McGraw Hill learning resources.

- Writing stats.

- Rubric building and scoring.

- Ability to assign draft and final deadline milestones.

- Tablet ready and tools for all learners.

CONTEXTUALIZE HISTORY

Help students experience history in a whole new way with our new Podcast Assignments. We've gathered some of the most interesting and popular history podcasts currently available and built assignable questions around them. These assignments allow instructors to bring greater context and nuance to their courses while engaging students through the storytelling power of podcasts.

APPLICATION-BASED ACTIVITIES

New to this edition, McGraw Hill's Application-Based Activities are highly interactive, automatically graded, online learn-by-doing exercises that provide students a safe space to apply their knowledge and problem-solving skills in class and in everyday life. Skill-based activities focus on topics such as "How to Read Primary Sources" and "Analyzing Audience" and map activities such as "Roman Imperial Expansion."

INSTRUCTOR RESOURCES

Traditions & Encounters offers an array of instructor resources for the world history course:

Instructor's Manual The Instructor's Manual provides a wide variety of tools and resources for presenting the course, including learning objectives and ideas for lectures and discussions.

Test Bank By increasing the rigor of the test bank development process, McGraw Hill has raised the bar for student assessment. Each question has been tagged for level of difficulty, Bloom's taxonomy, and topic coverage. Organized by chapter, the questions are designed to test factual, conceptual, and higher order thinking.

Test Builder New to this edition and available within Connect, Test Builder is a cloud-based tool that enables instructors to format tests that can be printed and administered within a Learning Management System. Test Builder offers a modern, streamlined interface for easy content configuration that matches course needs, without requiring a download.

Test Builder enables instructors to:

- Access all test bank content from a particular title.
- Easily pinpoint the most relevant content through robust filtering options.
- Manipulate the order of questions or scramble questions and/or answers.
- Pin questions to a specific location within a test.
- Determine your preferred treatment of algorithmic questions.
- Choose the layout and spacing.
- Add instructions and configure default settings.

PowerPoint The PowerPoint presentations highlight the key points of the chapter and include supporting visuals. New to this edition, all slides are WCAG compliant.

About the Authors

Jerry H. Bentley was professor of history at the University of Hawai'i and editor of the *Journal of World History*. His research on the religious, moral, and political writings of the Renaissance led to the publication of *Humanists and Holy Writ: New Testament Scholarship in the Renaissance* (Princeton, 1983) and *Politics and Culture in Renaissance Naples* (Princeton, 1987). More recently, his research concentrated on global history and particularly on processes of cross-cultural interaction. His book *Old World Encounters: Cross-Cultural Contacts and Exchanges in Pre-Modern Times* (New York, 1993) examines processes of cultural exchange and religious conversion before the modern era, and his pamphlet *Shapes of World History in Twentieth-Century Scholarship* (1996) discusses the historiography of world history. His most recent publication is *The Oxford Handbook of World History* (Oxford, 2011), and he served as a member of the editorial team preparing the forthcoming *Cambridge History of the World*. Jerry Bentley passed away in July 2012, although his legacy lives on through his significant contributions to the study of world history. The World History Association recently named an annual prize in his honor for outstanding publications in the field.

Herbert F. Ziegler is an associate professor of history at the University of Hawai'i. He has taught world history since 1980; he previously served as director of the world history program at the University of Hawai'i as well as book review editor of the *Journal of World History*. His interest in twentieth-century European social and political history led to the publication of *Nazi Germany's New Aristocracy: The SS Leadership, 1925–1939* (Princeton, 1990) and to his participation in new educational endeavors in the history of the Holocaust, including the development of an upper-division course for undergraduates. He is at present working on a study that explores from a global point of view the demographic trends of the past ten thousand years, along with their concomitant technological, economic, and social developments. His other current research project focuses on the application of complexity theory to a comparative study of societies and their internal dynamics.

Heather Streets-Salter is Professor and Director of World History Programs at Northeastern University in Boston, Massachusetts. She is the author of *World War One in Southeast Asia: Colonialism and Anticolonialism in an Era of Global Conflict* (Cambridge University Press, 2017); *Martial Races: The Military, Martial Races, and Masculinity in British Imperial Culture, 1857–1914* (Manchester University Press, 2004); and *Empires and Colonies in the Modern World* (Oxford University Press, 2015) with Trevor Getz. Her next book is called *The Chill Before the Cold War: Communism and Anti-Communism in Colonial Southeast Asia in the Interwar Period*.

Craig Benjamin is a Professor of History in the Frederik J. Meijer Honors College at Grand Valley State University in Michigan. He is the author of *The Yuezhi: Origin, Migration and the Conquest of Northern Bactria* (Brepols, 2007); *Empires of Ancient Eurasia. The First Silk Roads Era 100 BCE–250 CE* (Cambridge University Press, 2018); and *Big History: Between Nothing and Everything* (McGraw-Hill, 2014) with David Christian and Cynthia Stokes Brown. He is the editor of Volume 4 of the *Cambridge History of the World* (Cambridge University Press, 2015) and *The Routledge Companion to Big History* (Routledge, 2019) with Esther Quaedackers and David Baker. His next book is called *Eurasia Reconnected. The Second Silk Roads Era 600–1000 CE*.

Acknowledgments

Many individuals have contributed to this book, and the authors take pleasure in recording deep thanks for all the comments, criticism, advice, and suggestions that helped to improve the work. The editorial, marketing, and production teams at McGraw Hill did an outstanding job of seeing the project through to publication. Special thanks go to Jason Seitz, Stephanie Ventura, and Sandy Wille, who provided crucial support by helping the authors work through difficult issues and solve the innumerable problems of content, style, and organization that arise in any project to produce a history of the world. Many colleagues at the University of Hawai'i at Mānoa, most notably Professor Margot A. Henriksen, and elsewhere aided and advised the authors on matters of organization and composition. Finally, we would like to express our appreciation for the advice of the following individuals, who read and commented on the Seventh Edition, as well as previous editions of *Traditions & Encounters*.

Brian C. Black, *Pennsylvania State University*
Beau Bowers, *Central Piedmont Community College*
Erika Briesacher, *Worcester State University*
Stanley Burstein, *California State University, Los Angeles*
David Eaton, *Grand Valley State University*
David Fahey, *Miami University of Ohio*
Amy Forss, *Metropolitan Community College, Omaha*
Melissa Gayan, *Georgia Southern University*
Aimee Harris-Johnson, *El Paso Community College*
Matthew Herbst, *University of California San Diego*
Mark Lee, *University of Nebraska*
Emily G. Miller, *University of Indianapolis*
William Plants, *University of Rio Grande*
Annie Tracy Samuel, *University of Tennessee at Chattanooga*
Pamela Sayre, *Henry Ford Community College*
William Schell Jr., *Murray State University*
Scott Seagle, *University of Tennessee at Chattanooga*
David Simonelli, *Youngstown State University*
Adam Stanley, *University of Wisconsin at Platteville*
Ryan Thompson, *Cleveland State Community College*

Special thanks and gratitude to the McGraw Hill Academic Integrity Board of Advisors who were instrumental in providing guidance on chapter content, illustration program, and language and conventions. Our advisors include:

Susan Bragg, *Georgia Southwestern State University*
Jennifer Epley Sanders, *Texas A & M*
Eileen Ford, *California State University, Los Angeles*
Nicholas Fox, *Houston College*
Rudy Jean-Bart, *Broward Community College*
Darnell Morehand-Olufade, *University of Bridgeport*
Sharon Navarro, *University of Texas at San Antonio*
Jeffrey Ogbar, *University of Connecticut*
Andrea Oliver, *Tallahassee Community College*
Birte Pfleger, *California State University, Los Angeles*
Linda Reed, *University of Houston*

Traditions & Encounters

Volume I
From the Beginning
to 1500

Early Human History

ZOOMING IN ON ENCOUNTERS
Lucy and the Archaeologists

Throughout the evening of 30 November 1974, a tape player in an Ethiopian desert blared the Beatles' song "Lucy in the Sky with Diamonds" at top volume. The site was an archaeological camp at Hadar, a remote spot about 320 kilometers (200 miles) northeast of Addis Ababa. The music helped fuel a spirited celebration: earlier in the day, archaeologists had discovered the skeleton of a female hominid who died 3.2 million years ago. Scholars refer to this skeleton as AL 288-1, but the female herself has become by far the world's best-known prehistoric individual under the name Lucy.

At the time of her death, from unknown causes, Lucy was age twenty-five to thirty. She stood just over 1 meter (about 3.5 feet) tall and probably weighed about 25 kilograms (55 pounds). After she died, sand and mud covered Lucy's body, hardened gradually into rock, and entombed her remains. By 1974, however, rain waters had eroded the rock and exposed Lucy's fossilized skeleton. The archaeological team that first encountered Lucy and her companions at Hadar eventually found 40 percent of Lucy's bones, which together form one of the most complete and best-preserved skeletons of any early human ancestor. Later searches at Hadar turned up bones belonging to perhaps as many as sixty-five additional individuals, although no other collection of bones from Hadar rivals Lucy's skeleton for completeness.

Analysis of Lucy's skeleton and other bones found at Hadar demonstrates that the earliest ancestors of modern humans walked upright on two feet. Erect walking is crucial for humans because it frees their arms and hands for other tasks. Lucy and her contemporaries did not possess large or well-developed

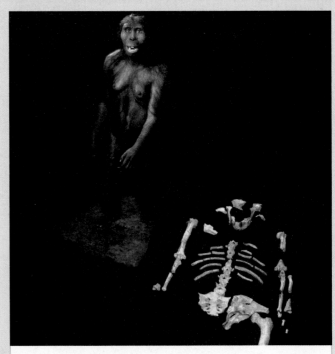

Reconstruction of the female Australopithecine hominid "Lucy", made from the bones discovered by archaeologists in the Omo Valley in 1974.
Philippe Plailly & Atelier Daynes/Science Source

brains—Lucy's skull was about the size of a small grapefruit—but unlike the neighboring apes, which used their forelimbs for locomotion, Lucy and her companions could carry objects with their arms and manipulate tools with their dexterous hands. Those abilities enabled Lucy and her companions to survive better than many other species. As the brains of our hominid ancestors grew larger and more sophisticated—a process that occurred over a period of several million years—humans learned to take even better advantage of their arms and hands and established flourishing communities throughout the world.

CHAPTER OVERVIEW

According to geologists the earth came into being about 4.5 billion years ago. The first living organisms made their appearance hundreds of millions of years later. In their wake came increasingly complex creatures such as fish, birds, reptiles, and mammals. About forty million years ago, short, hairy, monkeylike animals began to populate tropical regions of the world. Humanlike cousins to these animals began to appear only four or five million years ago, and our species, *Homo sapiens,* about two hundred and fifty thousand years ago.

Even the most sketchy review of the earth's natural history clearly shows that human society has not developed in a vacuum, but has rather been shaped by an array of encounters with other species. The earliest humans inhabited a world already well stocked with flora and fauna, a world shaped for countless eons by natural rhythms that governed the behavior of all the earth's creatures. Humans made a place for themselves in this world, and over time they demonstrated remarkable ingenuity in devising ways to take advantage of the earth's resources. Indeed, it has become clear in recent years that the human animal has exploited the natural environment so thoroughly that the earth has undergone irreversible changes.

A discussion of such early times is of fundamental importance to a book that is mostly focused on the history of human societies, their origins, development, and interactions. For some conventional historians, the period of human history before the invention of writing is termed *prehistory*, whereas the term *history* is used to describe the period following the invention of writing. It is certainly true that the availability of written documents enhances the ability of scholars to understand past ages, but recent research by archaeologists and evolutionary biologists has provided substantial evidence of the physical and social development of early humans. It is now clear that long before the invention of writing, humans made a place for their species in the natural world and laid the social, economic, and cultural foundations on which their successors built increasingly complex societies.

CHRONOLOGY

4 million–1 million years ago	Era of *Australopithecus*
3.2 million years ago	Era of Lucy
2.5 million–200,000 years ago	Era of *Homo habilis* and *Homo erectus*
250–200,000 B.C.E.	Early evolution of *Homo sapiens*
400,000–30,000 B.C.E.	Era of the Neandertals
13,500–10,500 B.C.E.	Natufian society
10,000–8000 B.C.E.	Early experimentation with agriculture
14,000–1000 B.C.E.	Jomon society
8000 B.C.E.	Appearance of agricultural villages
4000–3500 B.C.E.	Appearance of cities
3000 B.C.E.–1850 C.E.	Chinook society

THE EVOLUTION OF *HOMO SAPIENS*

During the past century or so, archaeologists, evolutionary biologists, and other scholars have vastly increased the understanding of human origins and the lives our distant ancestors led. Their work has done much to clarify the relationship between humans and other animal species. On one hand, researchers have shown that humans share some remarkable similarities with the large apes. This point is true not only of external features, such as physical form, but also of the basic elements of genetic makeup and body chemistry—DNA, chromosomal patterns, life-sustaining proteins, and blood types. In the case of some of these elements, scientists have been able to observe a difference of only 1.6 percent between the DNA of humans and that of chimpanzees. Biologists therefore place humans in the order of primates, along with monkeys, chimpanzees, gorillas, and the various other large apes.

Yet humans clearly stand out as the most distinctive of the primate species. Small differences in genetic makeup and body chemistry have led to enormous differences in levels of intelligence and ability to exercise control over the natural world. Humans developed an extraordinarily high order of intelligence, which enabled them to devise tools, technologies, language skills, and other means of communication and cooperation. Whereas other animal species adapted physically and genetically to their natural environment, or made small changes to it, humans drastically altered the natural environment to suit their needs and desires—a process that began in remote prehistory and continues in the present day. Over the long term, too, intelligence endowed humans with immense potential for social and cultural development.

Hominids

A series of spectacular discoveries in east Africa, and more recently in south Africa and Eurasia, has thrown valuable light on the evolution of the human species. At numerous sites across Africa and Eurasia, archaeologists have unearthed bones and tools of human ancestors going back about five million years. The Olduvai Gorge in Tanzania and Hadar in Ethiopia have yielded especially rich remains of individuals like the famous Lucy. These individuals probably represented several different species belonging to the genus *Australopithecus* ("the southern ape"), which flourished in east Africa during the long period from about four million to one million years ago.

Australopithecus In spite of its name, *Australopithecus* was not an ape but, rather, a hominid—a creature belonging to the family **Hominidae,** which includes human and human-like species. Evolutionary biologists recognize *Australopithecus* as a genus standing alongside *Homo* (the genus in which biologists place modern humans) in the family of hominids. Compared with our species, *Homo sapiens,* Lucy and other australopithecines would seem short, hairy, and limited in intelligence. They stood something over 1 meter (3 feet) tall, weighed 25 to 55 kilograms (55 to 121 pounds), and had a brain size of about 500 cubic centimeters. (The brain size of modern humans averages about 1,400 cc.)

Compared with other ape and animal species, however, australopithecines were sophisticated creatures. They walked upright on two legs, which enabled them to use their arms independently for other tasks. They had well-developed hands with opposable thumbs, which enabled them to grasp tools and perform intricate operations. They almost certainly had some ability to communicate verbally, although analysis of their skulls suggests that the portion of the brain responsible for speech was not very large or well developed.

The intelligence of australopithecines was sufficient to allow them to plan complex ventures. They often traveled deliberately—over distances of 15 kilometers (9.3 miles) and more—to obtain the particular kinds of stone that they needed to fashion tools. Chemical analyses show that the stone from which australopithecines made tools was often available only at sites distant from the camps where archaeologists discovered the finished tools. Those tools included choppers, scrapers, and other implements for food preparation. With the aid of their tools and intelligence, australopithecines established themselves securely throughout most of eastern and southern Africa.

Fossilized footprints preserved near Olduvai Gorge in modern Tanzania show that hominids walked upright some 3.5 million years ago. These prints are striking evidence that australopithecines were bipedal.

John Reader/Science Source

Homo erectus By about one million years ago, australopithecines had disappeared as new species of hominids possessing greater intelligence evolved and displaced their predecessors. The new species belonged to the genus *Homo* and thus represented creatures considerably different from the australopithecines. The two most important of the early *Homo* genus were *Homo habilis,* which systematically manufactured stone tools and flourished from about 2.4 to 1.5 million years ago, and ***Homo erectus***—"upright-walking human"—who flourished from about two million to two hundred thousand years ago. *Homo erectus* possessed a larger brain than the australopithecines—the average capacity was about 1,000 cc—and fashioned more sophisticated tools as well. To the australopithecine choppers and scrapers, *Homo erectus* added cleavers and hand axes, which not only were useful in food preparation but also provided protection against predators. *Homo erectus* also learned how to start and tend fires, which furnished the species with a means to cook food, a defense against large animals, and a source of artificial heat.

Even more important than tools and fire were intelligence and the ability to communicate complex ideas. *Homo erectus* individuals did not have the physiological means to enunciate the many sounds that are essential for sophisticated language, but they were able to devise plans, convey their intentions, and coordinate their activities. Archaeologists have found many sites that served as camps where *Homo erectus* groups congregated and collected food. They came together at these sites, bringing meat from small animals that they hunted as well as the plants and nuts that they gathered. They probably also scavenged the meat of large animals that had fallen prey to lions and other predators. The large quantities of food remains that archaeologists have excavated at these sites indicate that *Homo erectus* individuals had the ability to organize their activities and communicate plans for obtaining and distributing food.

Migrations of *Homo erectus* With effective tools, fire, intelligence, and communication abilities, *Homo erectus* gained increasing control over the natural environment and introduced the human species into widely scattered regions. Whereas australopithecines and *Homo habilis* had not ventured beyond eastern and southern Africa, *Homo erectus* migrated

---

Australopithecus (ah-strah-loh-PITH-uh-kuhs)
Hominidae (HAW-mih-nihd-ee)

to north Africa and the Eurasian landmass. Almost two million years ago, *Homo erectus* groups moved to southwest Asia and beyond to Europe, south Asia, east Asia, and southeast Asia. By two hundred thousand years ago, they had established themselves throughout the temperate zones of the eastern hemisphere, where archaeologists have unearthed many specimens of their bones and tools.

Homo sapiens

Like *Australopithecus,* though, *Homo erectus* faded with the arrival of more intelligent and successful human species. ***Homo sapiens*** ("consciously thinking human") evolved about two hundred thousand years ago and has skillfully adapted to the natural environment ever since. Early *Homo sapiens* already possessed a large brain, more or less the same size as human brains today. More important than size, however, is the structure of the brain; *Homo sapiens'* brains are especially well developed in the frontal regions, where conscious and reflective thought takes place. This physical feature provided *Homo sapiens* with an enormous advantage. Although not endowed with great strength and not equipped with natural means of attack and defense—claws, beaks, fangs, shells, venom, and the like—*Homo sapiens* possessed a remarkable intelligence that provided a powerful edge in the contest for survival. It enabled individuals to understand the structure of the world around them, to organize more efficient methods of exploiting natural resources, and to communicate and cooperate on increasingly complex tasks.

Language Furthermore, between about one hundred thousand and fifty thousand years ago, *Homo sapiens* evolved a combination of physiological traits that was unique among animal species—a throat with vocal cords and a separate mouth cavity with a tongue, which enabled them to enunciate hundreds of distinct sounds. Over time, *Homo sapiens* articulated those sounds into spoken languages that were endlessly flexible and that enabled individuals to communicate messages that were far more complex, more detailed, and more precise than those of *Homo erectus* and other human species. High intelligence and flexible language made for a powerful combination that enhanced the ability of *Homo sapiens* to share and pool knowledge and manipulate the world around them in a way that no other species could.

Migrations of *Homo sapiens* Intelligence and language enabled *Homo sapiens* to adapt to widely varying environmental conditions and to establish the species securely throughout the world. Beginning about ninety thousand years ago, communities of *Homo sapiens* spread throughout the eastern hemisphere and populated the temperate lands of Africa, Europe, and Asia, where they encountered *Homo erectus* and other early human groups that had inhabited those regions for several hundred thousand years. *Homo sapiens* soon moved beyond the temperate zones, though, and established

communities in progressively colder regions—migrations that were possible because their intelligence allowed *Homo sapiens* to fashion warm clothes from animal skins and to build effective shelters against the cold.

Between sixty thousand and fifteen thousand years ago, *Homo sapiens* extended the range of human population even further. The most recent ice age cooled the earth's temperature during that period, resulting in the concentration of water in massive glaciers, the lowering of the world's sea levels, and the exposure of land bridges that linked Asia with regions of the world previously uninhabited by humans. Small bands of individuals crossed those bridges and established communities in the islands of Indonesia and New Guinea, and some of them went farther to cross the temporarily narrow straits of water separating southeast Asia from Australia.

The Peopling of the World *Homo sapiens* arrived in Australia about sixty thousand years ago, perhaps even earlier. Somewhat later, beginning as early perhaps as twenty-five thousand years ago, other groups took advantage of land bridges linking Siberia with Alaska and established human communities in North America. From there they migrated throughout the western hemisphere. By about fifteen thousand years ago, communities of *Homo sapiens* had appeared in almost every habitable region of the world.

This peopling of the world was a remarkable accomplishment. No other animal or plant species has autonomously made its way to all habitable parts of the world. Some species, such as rats and roaches, have tagged along with humans and established themselves in distant homes. Other animals and plants—dogs and horses, for example, and wheat and potatoes—have found their way to new lands because humans intentionally transported them. Only *Homo sapiens,* however, has been able to make a home independently in all parts of the world.

The Natural Environment Their intellectual abilities enabled members of the *Homo sapiens* species to recognize problems and possibilities in their environment and then to take action that favored their survival. At sites of early settlements, archaeologists have discovered increasingly sophisticated tools that reflect *Homo sapiens'* progressive control over the environment. In addition to the choppers, scrapers, axes, and other tools that earlier species possessed, *Homo sapiens* used knives, spears, and bows and arrows. Individuals made dwellings for themselves in caves and in hutlike shelters fabricated from wood, bones, and animal skins. In cold regions *Homo sapiens* warmed themselves with fire and cloaked themselves in the skins of animals. Mounds of ashes discovered at their campsites show that in especially cold regions, they kept fires burning continuously during the winter months. *Homo sapiens* used superior intelligence, sophisticated tools, and language to exploit the natural world more efficiently than any other species the earth had seen.

Indeed, intelligent, tool-bearing humans competed so successfully in the natural world that they brought tremendous pressure to bear on other species they encountered. As the

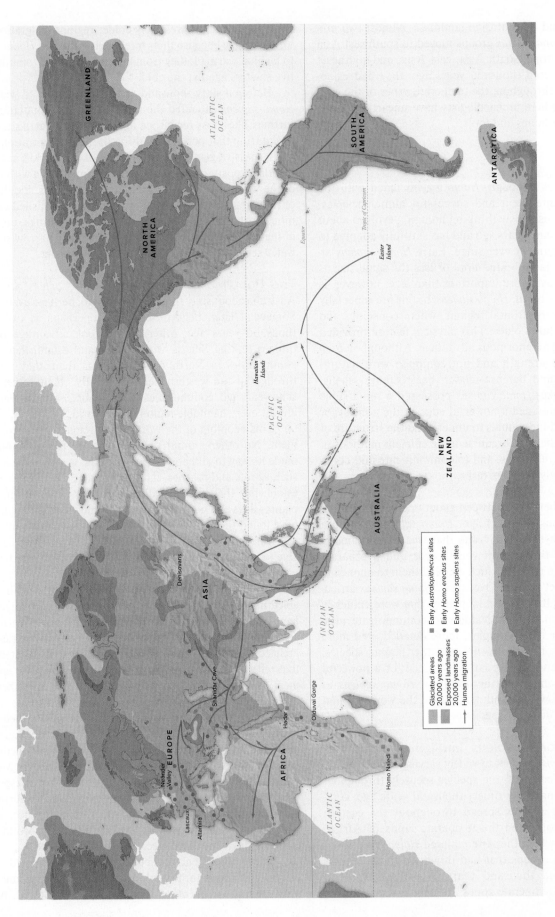

MAP 1.1 Global migrations of *Homo erectus* and *Homo sapiens*.

On the basis of the sites indicated, compare the extent of *Homo erectus* and *Homo sapiens* migrations out of Africa.

How can you explain the wider range of Homo sapiens migrations?

population of *Homo sapiens* increased, large mammal species in several parts of the world became extinct. Mammoths and the woolly rhinoceros disappeared from Europe; giant kangaroos from Australia; and mammoths, mastodons, and horses from the Americas. Archaeologists believe that changes in the earth's climate altered the natural environment enough to harm those species. In most cases, however, human hunting probably helped push large animals into extinction. Thus, from their earliest days on earth, members of the species *Homo sapiens* became effective and efficient competitors in the natural world—to the point that they threatened the very survival of other large but less intelligent species.

THE PALEOLITHIC ERA

By far the longest portion of the human experience on earth is the period historians and archaeologists call the **paleolithic** era, the "old stone age." The principal characteristic of the paleolithic era was that humans foraged for their food: they scavenged meat killed by predators or hunted wild animals or gathered edible products of naturally growing plants. The paleolithic era extended from the evolution of the first hominids until about twelve thousand years ago, when groups of *Homo sapiens* in several parts of the world began to transition to the use of domesticated plants and animals to feed themselves.

Foraging Lifeways

In the absence of written records, scholars have drawn inferences about paleolithic economy and society from other kinds of evidence. Archaeologists have excavated many sites that open windows on paleolithic life, and anthropologists have carefully studied hunting and gathering societies in the contemporary world. In the Amazon basin of South America, the tropical forests of Africa and southeast Asia, the deserts of Africa and Australia, and a few other regions as well, small communities of hunters and gatherers follow the ways of our common paleolithic ancestors. Although contemporary foraging communities reflect the influence of the modern world—they are by no means exact replicas of paleolithic societies—they throw important light on the economic and social dynamics that shaped the experiences of prehistoric foragers. In combination, then, the studies of both archaeologists and anthropologists help to illustrate how the foraging economy decisively influenced all dimensions of the human experience during the paleolithic era.

Relative Social Equality A foraging economy virtually prevents individuals from accumulating private property and basing social distinctions on wealth. To survive, most foragers must follow the animals that they stalk, and they must move with the seasons in search of edible plant life. Given their

mobility, it is easy to see that, for them, the notion of private, landed property has no meaning at all. Individuals possess only a few small items such as weapons and tools that they can carry easily as they move. In the absence of accumulated wealth, hunters and gatherers of paleolithic times, like their contemporary descendants, probably lived a relatively egalitarian existence. Social distinctions no doubt arose, and some individuals became influential because of their age, strength, courage, intelligence, fertility, force of personality, or some other trait. But personal or family wealth could not have served as a basis for permanent social differences.

Relative Gender Equality Some scholars believe that this relative social equality during the Paleolithic Era extended even further, to relations between the sexes. All members of a paleolithic group made important contributions to the survival of the community. Men traveled on sometimes distant hunting expeditions in search of large animals while women and children gathered edible plants, roots, nuts, and fruits from the area near the group's camp. Meat from the hunt was the most highly prized item in the paleolithic diet, but plant foods were essential to survival. Anthropologists calculate that in modern hunting and gathering societies, women contribute more calories to the community's diet than do the men. As a source of protein, meat represents a crucial supplement to the diet. But plant products sustain the men during hunting expeditions and feed the entire community when the hunt does not succeed. Because of the thorough interdependence of the sexes from the viewpoint of food production, paleolithic society probably did not encourage the domination of one sex by the other—certainly not to the extent that became common later.

A foraging economy has implications not only for social and sexual relations but also for community size and organization. The foraging lifestyle of hunters and gatherers dictates that they mostly live in small bands, which today include about thirty to fifty members. Larger groups could not move efficiently or find enough food to survive over a long period. During times of drought or famine, even small bands have trouble providing for themselves. Individual bands certainly have relationships with their neighbors—agreements concerning the territories that the groups exploit, for example, or arrangements to take marriage partners from each other's groups—but the immediate community is the focus of social life.

The survival of foraging bands depends on a sophisticated understanding of their natural environment. In contemporary studies, anthropologists have found that foraging peoples do not wander aimlessly about hoping to find a bit of food. Instead, they exploit the environment systematically and efficiently by timing their movements to coincide with

paleolithic (pey-lee-oh-LITH-ik)

the seasonal migrations of the animals they hunt and the life cycles of the plant species they gather.

Big-Game Hunting Archaeological remains show that early peoples also went about hunting and gathering in a purposeful and intelligent manner. Although it was relatively easy to take a small, young, or wounded animal, the hunting of big game posed special challenges. Large animals such as elephant, mastodon, rhinoceros, bison, and wild cattle were not only strong and fast but also well equipped to defend themselves and even attack their human hunters. *Homo sapiens* fashioned special tools, such as sharp knives, spears, and bows and arrows, and devised special tactics for hunting these animals. The hunters wore disguises such as animal skins and coordinated their movements so as to attack game simultaneously from several directions. They sometimes even started fires or caused disturbances to stampede herds over cliffs, or into swamps or enclosed areas where hunters could kill them more easily. Paleolithic hunting was a complicated venture. It clearly demonstrated the capacity of early human communities to pool their uniquely human traits—high intelligence, ability to make complicated plans, and sophisticated language and communications skills—to exploit the environment.

Paleolithic Settlements In regions where food resources were especially rich, a few peoples in late paleolithic times abandoned the nomadic lifestyle and established semi-permanent settlements. The most prominent paleolithic settlements were those of Natufian society in the eastern Mediterranean (modern-day Israel and Lebanon), Jomon society in central Japan, and Chinook society in the Pacific northwest region of North America (including the modern states of Oregon and Washington and the Canadian province of British Columbia). As early as 13,500 B.C.E., Natufians

Statue of a Neandertal man based on the study of recently discovered bones. How does his knifelike tool compare with the tools used by *Homo erectus*?
Damian Andrus/Maxwell Museum, University of New Mexico

collected wild wheat and took animals from abundant antelope herds. From 10,000 to 300 B.C.E., Jomon settlers harvested wild buckwheat and developed a productive fishing economy. Chinook society emerged after 3000 B.C.E. and flourished until the mid-nineteenth century C.E., principally on the basis of wild berries, acorns, and massive salmon

Diorama of a Neanderthal family eating outside of their dwelling.
dpa picture alliance archive/ Alamy Stock Photo

runs in local rivers. Paleolithic settlements had permanent dwellings, sometimes in the form of longhouses that accommodated several hundred people, but often in the form of smaller structures for individual families. Many settlements had populations of several hundred or more individuals. As archaeological excavations continue, it is becoming increasingly clear that paleolithic peoples organized complex societies with specialized rulers and craftsmen in many regions where they found abundant food resources.

Paleolithic Culture

Neandertal Peoples Paleolithic individuals did not limit their creative thinking to strictly practical matters of subsistence and survival. Instead, they reflected on the nature of human existence and the world around them. The earliest evidence of reflective thought comes from sites associated with **Neandertal** peoples, named after the Neander valley in western Germany where their remains first came to light. Neandertal peoples flourished in Europe and southwest Asia between about two hundred thousand and thirty-five thousand years ago. Most scholars regard Neandertal peoples as members of a distinct human species known as *Homo neandertalensis.* For about fifteen millennia, from forty-five thousand to thirty thousand years ago, Neandertal groups inhabited some of the same regions as *Homo sapiens* communities, and members of the two species sometimes lived in close proximity to each other. DNA analysis suggests that some interbreeding occurred between the two species, and recent research demonstrates that the DNA of most Europeans alive today contains about 2 percent Neandertal DNA. Archaeological evidence also shows that individual humans and Neandertals facilitated trade between their communities and also that some Neandertals imitated the more complex technologies and crafts of human communities they encountered.

At several Neandertal sites, archaeologists have discovered signs of careful, deliberate burial accompanied by ritual observances. Perhaps the most notable is that of Shanidar cave, located about 400 kilometers (250 miles) north of Baghdad in modern-day Iraq, where survivors laid the deceased to rest on beds of freshly picked wildflowers and then covered the bodies with shrouds and garlands of other flowers. At other Neandertal sites in France, Italy, and central Asia, survivors placed flint tools and animal bones in and around the graves of the deceased. It is impossible to know precisely what Neandertal peoples were thinking when they buried their dead in that fashion. Possibly they simply wanted to honor the memory of the departed, or perhaps they wanted to prepare the dead for a new dimension of existence, a life beyond the grave. Whatever their intentions, Neandertal peoples apparently recognized a significance in the life and death of individuals that, according to the evidence we have available, none of their hominid ancestors had apparently appreciated. They had developed a capacity for emotions and feelings, and they cared for one

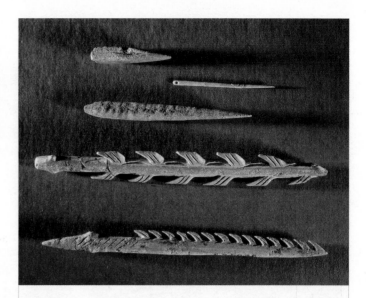

Tools (including a sewing needle) fashioned from animal bones about fifteen thousand years ago.
Gianni Dagli Orti/Shutterstock

another even to the extent of preparing elaborate resting places for the departed.

The Creativity of *Homo sapiens* *Homo sapiens* was much more intellectually inventive and creative than *Homo neandertalensis.* Many scholars argue that *Homo sapiens* owed much of the species's intellectual prowess to the ability to construct powerful and flexible languages for the communication of complex ideas. With the development of languages, humans were able both to accumulate knowledge and to transmit it precisely and efficiently to new generations. Thus it was not necessary for every individual human to learn from trial and error or from direct personal experience about the nature of the local environment or the best techniques for making advanced tools. Rather, it was possible for human groups to pass large and complex bodies of information along to their offspring, who then were able to make immediate use of it and furthermore were in a good position to build on inherited information by devising increasingly effective ways of satisfying human needs and desires.

From its earliest days on the earth, *Homo sapiens* distinguished itself as a creative species. At least 200,000 years ago, *Homo sapiens* was producing stone blades with long cutting edges. By 140,000 years ago, early humans had learned to supplement their diet with shellfish from coastal waters, and they had developed networks with neighbors that enabled them to trade high-quality obsidian stone over

Cave painting from Lascaux in southern France, perhaps intended to help hunters gain control over the spirits of large game animals. To what extent do you think a painting can "capture" an animal?

The Picture Art Collection/Alamy Stock Photo

distances sometimes exceeding 300 kilometers (185 miles). By 110,000 years ago, they had devised means of catching fish from deep waters. By 100,000 years ago, they had begun to fashion sharp tools, such as sewing needles and barbed harpoons, out of animal bones. Somewhat later they invented spear-throwers—small slings that enabled hunters to hurl spears at speeds upwards of 160 kilometers per hour (100 miles per hour). About 50,000 to 40,000 years ago, they were fabricating ornamental beads, necklaces, and bracelets, and shortly thereafter they began painting images of human and animal subjects. About 10,000 years ago, they invented the bow and arrow, a weapon that dramatically enhanced the power of humans with respect to other animal species.

Paleolithic Art The most visually impressive creations of early *Homo sapiens* are the Venus figurines and cave paintings

found at many sites of early human habitation. Archaeologists use the term *Venus figurines*—named after the Roman goddess of love—to refer to small sculptures of women, usually depicted with exaggerated sexual features. Most scholars believe that the figures reflect a deep interest in fertility. The prominent sexual features of the Venus figurines suggest that the sculptors' principal interests were fecundity and the generation of new life—matters of immediate concern to paleolithic societies. Some interpreters speculate that the figures had a place in ritual observances intended to increase fertility.

Paintings in caves frequented by early humans are the most dramatic examples of prehistoric art. The known examples of cave art date from about thirty-four thousand to twelve thousand years ago, and most of them are in caves in southern France and northern Spain. In that region alone, archaeologists have discovered more than one hundred

Venus figurine from southern France. This image, carved on a cave wall about twenty-five thousand years ago, depicts a woman of ample proportions. The exaggerated sexual features suggest that paleolithic peoples fashioned this and similar figurines out of an interest in fertility.
Apic/Hulton Archive/Getty Images

caves bearing prehistoric paintings. The best-known are Lascaux and Chauvet in France and Altamira in Spain. There, prehistoric peoples left depictions of remarkable sensitivity and power. Most of the subjects were animals, especially large game such as mammoth, bison, and reindeer, although a few human figures also appear.

As in the case of the Venus figurines, the explanation for the **cave paintings** involves a certain amount of educated guesswork. It is conceivable that early artists sometimes worked for purely aesthetic reasons—to beautify their living quarters. But many examples of cave art occur in places that are almost inaccessible to humans deep within remote chambers, for example, or at the end of long and constricted passages. Paintings in such remote locations presumably had some other purpose. Most analysts believe that the prominence of game animals in the paintings reflects the artists' interest in successful hunting expeditions. Thus cave paintings may have represented efforts to exercise sympathetic magic—to gain control over subjects (in this case, game animals) by capturing their spirits (by way of accurate representations of their physical forms). Although not universally accepted, this interpretation accounts

Cave painting produced five to six thousand years ago to illustrate the different roles played by men and women in the early days of agriculture. Here women harvest grain.
DPK-Photo/Alamy Stock Photo

reasonably well for a great deal of the evidence and has won widespread support among scholars.

Whatever the explanation for prehistoric art, the production of the works themselves represented conscious and purposeful activity of a high order. Early artists compounded pigments and manufactured tools. They made paints from minerals, plants, blood, saliva, water, animal fat, and other available ingredients. They used mortar and pestle for grinding pigments and mixing paints, which they applied with moss, frayed twigs and branches, or primitive brushes fabricated from hair. The simplicity and power of their representations have left deep impressions on modern critics ever since the early twentieth century, when their works became widely known. The display of prehistoric artistic talent clearly testifies once again to the remarkable intellectual power of the human species.

THE NEOLITHIC ERA AND THE TRANSITION TO AGRICULTURE

A few societies of hunting and gathering peoples inhabit the contemporary world, although most of them do not thrive because agricultural and industrial societies have taken over environments best suited to a foraging economy. Demographers estimate that current hunters and gatherers make up only a tiny fraction of the world's human population of more than seven billion. The vast majority of the world's peoples, however, have crossed an economic threshold of immense significance. When humans brought plants under cultivation and animals under domestication, they dramatically altered the natural world and steered human societies in new directions.

The Origins of Agriculture

Neolithic Era   The term *neolithic era* means "new stone age," in contrast to the old stone age of the paleolithic. Archaeologists first used the term **neolithic** because of refinements in toolmaking techniques: they found polished stone tools in neolithic sites rather than the chipped implements characteristic of paleolithic sites. Gradually, however, archaeologists became aware that something more fundamental than tool production distinguished the neolithic from the paleolithic era. Polished stone tools occurred in sites where peoples relied on cultivation, rather than foraging, for their subsistence. Today the term *neolithic era* refers to the early stages of agricultural society, from about twelve thousand to six thousand years ago.

Global Climate Change   Agriculture was almost impossible and indeed inconceivable until about fifteen thousand years ago. During the last ice age, the earth was much colder and

drier than it is today; furthermore, it experienced wild fluctuations of temperature and rainfall. In any given year, sun and rain might have brought abundant harvests, but frigid and arid conditions might ruin crops for the next decade or more. Thus agriculture would have been an unreliable and even foolhardy venture. After the end of the last ice age, the earth entered an era of general warming, increased rainfall, and more stable climatic conditions. Neolithic peoples took advantage of those conditions by encouraging the growth of edible plants and domesticating previously wild animals.

Gender Relations and Agriculture   Many scholars believe that women most likely began the systematic care of plants. As the principal gatherers in foraging communities, women became familiar with the life cycles of plants and noticed the effects of sunshine, rain, and temperature on vegetation. Hoping for larger and more reliable supplies of food, women in neolithic societies probably began to nurture plants instead of simply collecting available foods in the wild. Meanwhile, instead of just stalking game with the intention of killing it for meat, neolithic men began to capture animals and domesticate them by providing for their needs and supervising their breeding. Over a period of centuries, those practices gradually led to the formation of agricultural economies.

Independent Inventions of Agriculture   Agriculture—including both the cultivation of crops and the domestication of animals—emerged independently in several different parts of the world. The earliest evidence of agricultural activity discovered so far dates to the era after 9000 B.C.E., when peoples of southwest Asia (modern-day Iraq, Syria, and Turkey) cultivated wheat and barley while domesticating sheep, goats, pigs, and cattle. Between 9000 and 7000 B.C.E., African peoples inhabiting the southeastern margin of the Sahara desert (modern-day Sudan) domesticated cattle, sheep, and goats while cultivating sorghum. Between 8000 and 6000 B.C.E., peoples of sub-Saharan west Africa (in the vicinity of modern Nigeria) also began independently to cultivate yams, okra, and black-eyed peas. In east Asia, residents of the Yangzi River valley began to cultivate rice as early as 6500 B.C.E., and their neighbors to the north in the Yellow River valley raised crops of millet and soybeans after 5500 B.C.E. East Asian peoples also kept pigs and chickens from an early date, perhaps 6000 B.C.E., and they later added water buffaloes to their domesticated stock. In southeast Asia the cultivation of taro; yams; coconut; breadfruit; bananas; and citrus fruits, including oranges, lemons, limes, tangerines, and grapefruit, dates from probably 3000 B.C.E. or earlier.

Peoples of the western hemisphere also turned independently to agriculture. Inhabitants of Mesoamerica (central Mexico) cultivated maize (corn) from at least 4000 B.C.E. and probably several millennia earlier, and they later added a range of additional food crops, including beans, peppers,

---

neolithic (nee-uh-LITH-ik)

squashes, and tomatoes. Residents of the central Andean region of South America (modern Peru) cultivated potatoes after 5000 B.C.E., and they later added maize and beans to their diets. It is possible that the Amazon River valley was yet another site of independently invented agriculture, this one centering on the cultivation of manioc, sweet potatoes, and peanuts. Domesticated animals were much less prominent in the Americas than in the eastern hemisphere. Paleolithic peoples had hunted many large species to extinction: mammoths, mastodons, and horses had all disappeared from the Americas by 7000 B.C.E. (The horses that have figured so prominently in the modern history of the Americas all descended from animals reintroduced to the western hemisphere during the past five hundred years.) With the exception of llamas, alpacas, and guinea pigs of the Andean regions, most American animals were not well suited to domestication.

The Early Spread of Agriculture Once established, agriculture spread rapidly, partly because of the methods of early cultivators. One of the earliest techniques, known as slash-and-burn cultivation, involved frequent movement on the part of farmers. To prepare a field for cultivation, a community would slash the bark on a stand of trees in a forest and later burn the dead trees to the ground. The resulting weed-free patch was extremely fertile and produced abundant harvests. After a few years, however, weeds invaded the field, and the soil lost its original fertility. The community then moved to another forest region and repeated the procedure.

Migrations of slash-and-burn cultivators helped spread agriculture throughout both eastern and western hemispheres. By 6000 B.C.E., for example, agriculture had spread from its southwest Asian homeland to the eastern shores of the Mediterranean and the Balkan region of eastern Europe, and by 4000 B.C.E. it had spread farther to western Europe north of the Mediterranean.

While agriculture radiated out from its various places, foods originally cultivated in only one region also spread widely, as merchants, migrants, or other travelers carried knowledge of those foods to agricultural lands that previously had relied on different crops. Wheat, for example, spread from its original homeland in southwest Asia to Iran and northern India after 5000 B.C.E. and farther to northern China perhaps by 3000 B.C.E. Meanwhile, rice spread from southern China to southeast Asia by 3000 B.C.E. and to the Ganges River valley in India by 1500 B.C.E. African sorghum reached India by 2000 B.C.E., while southeast Asian bananas took root in tropical lands throughout the Indian Ocean basin. In the western hemisphere, maize spread from Mesoamerica to the southwestern part of the United States by 1200 B.C.E. and farther to the eastern woodlands region of North America by 100 C.E.

Agriculture involved long hours of hard physical labor—clearing land, preparing fields, planting seeds, pulling weeds, and harvesting crops. Indeed, agriculture probably required more work than paleolithic foraging: anthropologists calculate that modern hunting and gathering peoples spend about four hours per day in providing themselves with food and other

Men herd domesticated cattle in the early days of agriculture. This painting and the one on page 11 are both in a cave at Tassili n'Ajjer in modern-day Algeria. George Halton/Science Source

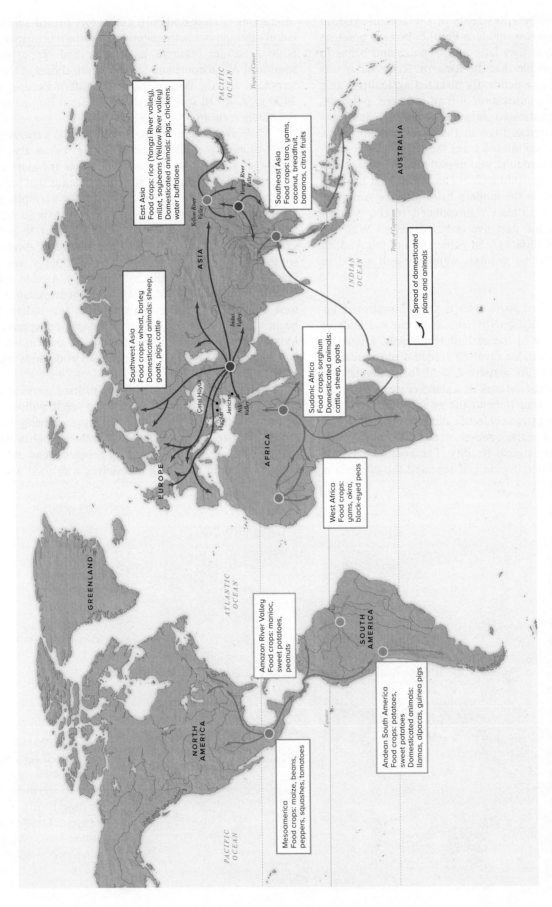

MAP 1.2 Origins and early spread of agriculture.

After 9000 B.C.E. peoples in several parts of the world independently began to cultivate plants and domesticate animals that were native to their regions. Agriculture and animal husbandry spread quickly to neighboring territories and eventually also to distant lands.

East Asia
Food crops: rice (Yangzi River valley),
millet, soybeans (Yellow River valley)
Domesticated animals: pigs, chickens,
water buffaloes

Southeast Asia
Food crops: taro, yams,
coconut, breadfruit,
bananas, citrus fruits

Southwest Asia
Food crops: wheat, barley
Domesticated animals: sheep,
goats, pigs, cattle

Sudanic Africa
Food crops: sorghum
Domesticated animals:
cattle, sheep, goats

West Africa
Food crops:
yams, okra,
black-eyed peas

Spread of domesticated
plants and animals

Mesoamerica
Food crops: maize, beans,
peppers, squashes, tomatoes

Amazon River Valley
Food crops: manioc,
sweet potatoes,
peanuts

Andean South America
Food crops: potatoes,
sweet potatoes
Domesticated animals:
llamas, alpacas, guinea pigs

PACIFIC OCEAN
ATLANTIC OCEAN
PACIFIC OCEAN
INDIAN OCEAN

GREENLAND
NORTH AMERICA
SOUTH AMERICA
EUROPE
AFRICA
ASIA
AUSTRALIA

Tropic of Cancer
Equator
Tropic of Capricorn

Yellow River Valley
Yangzi River Valley
Indus Valley
Nile Valley
Jericho
Çatal Hüyük
Hacilar

necessities, devoting the remainder of their time to rest, leisure, and social activities. Yet over time agriculture made possible the production of abundant food supplies. Eventually agriculture spread widely, influencing the lives and experience of almost all humans.

Early Agrarian Societies

In the wake of agriculture came a series of social and cultural changes that transformed human history. Perhaps the most important change associated with early agriculture was a significant increase in human population in those regions where agriculture had emerged. Spread thinly across the earth in paleolithic times, the human species multiplied prodigiously after agriculture increased the supply of food. Historians estimate that before agriculture, about 10,000 B.C.E., the earth's human population was four million. By 5000 B.C.E., when agriculture had appeared in a few world regions, human population had risen to about five million. Estimates for later dates demonstrate eloquently the speed with which, thanks to agriculture, human numbers increased:

Year	Human Population
3000 B.C.E.	14 million
2000 B.C.E.	27 million
1000 B.C.E.	50 million
500 B.C.E.	100 million

Emergence of Villages and Towns Their agricultural economy and rapidly increasing numbers encouraged neolithic peoples to adopt new forms of social organization. Because they devoted their time to cultivation rather than foraging, neolithic peoples did not continue the migratory life of their paleolithic predecessors but, rather, settled near their fields in permanent villages. One of the earliest known neolithic villages was Jericho, site of a freshwater oasis north of the Dead Sea in present-day Israel, which came into existence before 8000 B.C.E. Even in its early days, Jericho may have had two thousand residents—a vast crowd compared with a paleolithic foraging band. The residents farmed mostly wheat and barley with the aid of water from the oasis. During the earliest days of the settlement, they kept no domesticated animals, but they added meat to their diet by hunting local game animals. They also engaged in a limited amount of trade, particularly in salt and obsidian, a hard, volcanic glass from which ancient peoples fashioned knives and blades. About 7000 B.C.E., the residents surrounded their circular mud huts with a formidable wall and moat—which some archaeologists have interpreted as suggesting that the wealth concentrated at Jericho had begun to attract the interest of human predators.

Specialization of Labor The concentration of large numbers of people in villages encouraged specialization of labor. Most people in neolithic villages cultivated crops or kept animals. Many also continued to hunt and forage for wild plants. But a surplus of food enabled some individuals to concentrate their time and talents on enterprises that had nothing to do with the production of food. The rapid development of specialized labor is apparent from excavations carried out at one of the best-known neolithic settlements, **Çatal Hüyük.** Located in south-central Anatolia (modern-day Turkey), Çatal Hüyük was occupied continuously from 7250 to 5400 B.C.E., when residents abandoned the site. Originally a small and undistinguished neolithic village, Çatal Hüyük grew into a bustling town, accommodating about five thousand inhabitants. Archaeologists have uncovered evidence that residents manufactured pots, baskets, textiles, leather, stone and metal tools, wood carvings, carpets, beads, and jewelry, among other products. Çatal Hüyük became a prominent village partly because of its close proximity to large obsidian deposits. The village probably was a center of production and trade in obsidian tools: archaeologists have discovered obsidian that originated near Çatal Hüyük at sites throughout much of the eastern Mediterranean region.

Three early craft industries—pottery, metallurgy, and textile production—illustrate the potential of specialized labor in neolithic times. Neolithic craftsmen were not always the original inventors of the technologies behind those industries: the Jomon society of central Japan produced the world's first known pottery, for example, about 10,000 B.C.E. But neolithic craftsmen expanded dramatically on existing practices and supplemented them with new techniques to fashion natural products into useful items. Their enterprises reflected the conditions of early agricultural society: either the craft industries provided tools and utensils needed by cultivators, or they made use of cultivators' and herders' products in new ways.

Pottery The earliest of the three craft industries to emerge was pottery. Paleolithic foragers had no use for pots. They did not store food for long periods of time, and in any case lugging heavy clay pots around as they moved from one site to another would have been inconvenient. A food-producing society, however, needs containers to store surplus foods. By about 7000 B.C.E., neolithic villagers in several parts of the world had discovered processes that transformed malleable clay into fire-hardened, waterproof pottery capable of storing dry or liquid products. Soon thereafter, neolithic craftsmen discovered that they could etch designs into their clay that fire would harden into permanent decorations and

Çatal Hüyük (chat-l hoo-yook)

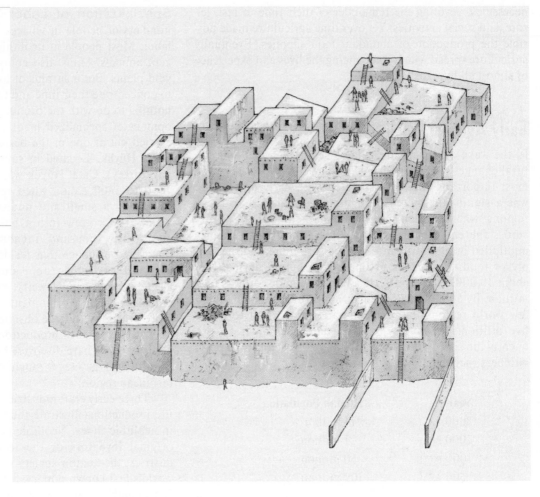

Artist's conception of Çatal Hüyük, one of the world's first cities. Çatal Hüyük had no streets and no ground-level doors or windows that might have provided easy access for predators and invaders. Residents entered their homes from rooftops and pulled ladders up behind them.
Dorling Kindersley/Getty Images

furthermore that they could color their products with glazes. As a result, pottery became a medium of artistic expression as well as a source of practical utensils.

Metalworking Metallurgy soon joined pottery as a neolithic industry. The earliest metal that humans worked with systematically was copper. In many regions of the world, copper occurs naturally in relatively pure and easily malleable form. By hammering the cold metal, it was possible to turn it into jewelry and simple tools. By 6000 B.C.E., though, neolithic villagers had discovered that they could use heat to extract copper from its ores and that, when heated to high temperatures, copper became much more workable. By 5000 B.C.E., they had raised temperatures in their furnaces high enough to melt copper and pour it into molds. With the technology of smelting and casting copper, neolithic communities were able to make not only jewelry and decorative items but also tools such as knives, axes, hoes, and weapons. Moreover, copper metallurgy served as a technological foundation on which later neolithic craftsmen

developed expertise in the working of gold, bronze, iron, and other metals.

Textile Production Because natural fibers decay more easily than pottery or copper, the dating of textile production is not certain, but fragments of textiles survive from as early as 6000 B.C.E. As soon as they began to raise crops and keep animals, neolithic peoples experimented with techniques of selective breeding. Before long they had bred strains of plants and animals that provided long, lustrous, easily worked fibers. They then developed technologies for spinning the fibers into threads and weaving the threads into cloth. The invention of textiles was probably the work of women, who were able to spin thread and weave fabrics at home while nursing and watching over small children. Textile production quickly became one of the most important enterprises in agricultural society.

Social Distinctions and Social Inequality The concentration of people into permanent settlements and the increasing specialization of labor provided the first opportunity

The Role of Urbanization in the Creation of Patriarchy

Some events or processes in the global past are so momentous that they produce social, political, economic, or environmental changes for centuries—even in places thousands of miles from their points of origin. In other words, we can see how processes in the distant past shaped the future in multiple places and at multiple times long after they first occurred. Understanding the spectrum of consequences spurred by such momentous events and processes can help us trace the historical connections between the world's people and places, even when such connections may not have been obvious to people living at the time.

Urbanization and Patriarchy

The creation of the first cities in human history was one of these momentous processes. Between 4000 and 3500 B.C.E., urban settlements emerged in some of the areas where agriculture had taken hold, such as Çatal Hüyük. In Mesopotamia (chapter 2), Sumerians built large city-states that dominated ever-larger regions, which spread the values and practices of these urban centers across Mesopotamia, Anatolia, and Egypt. Soon after this, peoples in North Africa (chapter 3), India (chapter 4), and east Asia (chapter 5) also built cities independently beginning in about 3100 B.C.E., 3000 B.C.E., and 2200 B.C.E., respectively. Near the turn of the first millennium C.E., large-scale agriculture similarly led to the development of cities in Central and South America (chapter 6). In all these locations, early urbanization involved the establishment of states that localized power in the hands of a small group of people, organized military protection, made laws to control large populations, oversaw the development of large-scale infrastructure such as irrigation, and exerted control over the surrounding countryside. Also in all these locations, urbanization appears to have resulted in the decline of women's status over time and in the creation of **patriarchy,** or the institutional domination of men over women.

Why Patriarchy?

Scholars believe the emergence of patriarchy was closely linked to early urbanization. Although evidence from the deep human past is limited, many historians and archaeologists believe that urbanization created a set of similar pressures that led societies to develop patriarchal practices in many different areas. Once established, these practices and traditions spread as cities and city-states increased their influence over surrounding regions—with long-lasting and profound effects on the development of human societies for thousands of years.

Scholars suggest a variety of reasons why urbanization might have encouraged the development of patriarchy. Some argue that the transition to intensive agriculture characteristic of early cities led to practices that emphasized women's roles as producers of children, who could provide

Hammurabi's Laws. Hammurabi's Code of Laws demonstrate that women already occupied a subordinate legal and social position in ancient Mesopotamia nearly four thousand years ago.
Universal Images Group/Getty Images

the workforce necessary for such large-scale agriculture. At the same time, this emphasis on producing large numbers of children may have led women to have less time and energy for heavy agricultural work—particularly once plows had been introduced. Other scholars argue that increased militarization of agricultural societies—in order to protect resources from outside invaders—led to a decline in women's status because pregnancy and child-rearing tended to prevent most women from soldiering. In fact, some scholars speculate that this may be why the status of women in the early cities of the Nile River valley (chapter 3) and the Indus River valley (chapter 4) was higher than in the cities of Mesopotamia and east Asia (chapters 2 and 5): since early cities in the former two areas were more militarily secure—and thus less militarized—than their counterparts in Mesopotamia and east Asia, they also may have been less patriarchal. Still other scholars argue that as power and wealth grew concentrated in the hands of a small class of elites, the desire to keep such power and wealth within particular families led to increased anxieties about ensuring the lineage of all family members. Since it was impossible for men to ensure the paternity of their children, paternity was increasingly ensured by controlling women's movements, morality, and access to other men through the assumption of political control, laws, veiling, and seclusion.

Patriarchy did not develop overnight in ancient urban areas, and it seems clear that gender stratification was already developing among farming villages by the time cities first emerged. However, by 1000 B.C.E. patriarchal practices, enshrined in both cultural traditions and law, had become a way of life for urbanized peoples in Mesopotamia, the Nile, the Indus River valley, and east Asia. In the Americas, patriarchal practices also seem to have emerged in early cities, although evidence of their particular shape is quite limited. For these reasons, many scholars view the development of patriarchy as an integral part of the development of urbanization. When reading subsequent chapters, consider the effects patriarchal structures have had on societies around the world over the very long term.

for individuals to accumulate considerable wealth. Individuals could trade surplus food or manufactured products for gems, jewelry, and other valuable items. The institutionalization of privately owned landed property—which occurred at an uncertain date after the introduction of agriculture—enhanced the significance of accumulated wealth. Because land was (and remains) the ultimate source of wealth in any agricultural society, ownership of land carried enormous economic power. When especially successful individuals managed to consolidate wealth in their families' hands and kept it there for several generations, clearly defined social classes emerged. Already at Çatal Hüyük, for example, differences in wealth and social status are clear from the quality of interior decorations in houses and the value of goods buried with individuals from different social classes.

Neolithic Culture

Quite apart from its social effects, agriculture left its mark on the cultural dimension of the human experience. Because their lives and communities depended on the successful

Statuette of a Mother Goddess from Çatalhöyük, created between 5500 and 6000 B.C.E. Museum of Anatolian Civilizations in Ankara, Turkey.
Gianni Dagli Orti/Shutterstock

cultivation of crops, neolithic farmers closely observed the natural world around them and noted the conditions that favored successful harvests. In other words, they developed a kind of early applied science. From experience accumulated over the generations, they acquired an impressive working knowledge of the earth and its rhythms. Agricultural peoples had to learn when changes of season would take place: survival depended on the ability to predict when they could reasonably expect sunshine, rain, warmth, and freezing temperatures. They learned to associate the seasons with the different positions of the sun, moon, and stars. As a result, they accumulated a store of knowledge concerning relationships between the heavens and the earth, and they made the first steps toward the elaboration of a calendar, which would enable them to predict with tolerable accuracy the kind of weather they could expect at various times of the year.

Religious Values The workings of the natural world also influenced neolithic religion. Paleolithic communities had already honored, and perhaps even worshiped, Venus figurines in hopes of ensuring fertility. Neolithic religion reflected the same interest in fertility, but it celebrated particularly the rhythms that governed agricultural society—birth, growth, death, and regenerated life. Archaeologists have unearthed thousands of neolithic representations of gods and goddesses in the form of clay figurines, drawings on pots and vases, decorations on tools, and ritual objects.

The neolithic gods included not only the life-bearing, Venus-type figures of paleolithic times but also deities associated with the cycle of life, death, and regeneration. A pregnant goddess of vegetation, for example, represented neolithic hopes for fertility in the fields. Sometimes neolithic worshipers associated these goddesses with animals such as frogs or butterflies that dramatically changed form during the course of their lives, just as seeds of grain sprouted, flourished, died, and produced new seed for another agricultural cycle. Meanwhile, young male gods associated with bulls and goats represented the energy and virility that participates in the creation of life.

Some deities were associated with death: many neolithic goddesses possessed the power to bring about decay and destruction. Yet physical death was not an absolute end. The procreative capacities of gods and goddesses resulted in the births of infant deities who represented the regeneration of life—freshly sprouted crops, replenished stocks of domestic animals, and infant humans to inaugurate a new biological cycle. Thus neolithic religious thought clearly reflected the natural world of early agricultural society.

The Origins of Urban Life

Over the millennia that followed its initial appearance, agriculture gradually but profoundly transformed the face of the earth. Humans multiplied prodigiously, congregated in

What's Left Out?

Although this chapter has argued that it was only after the transition to agriculture that human communities acquired the necessary material and labor resources to build villages, towns, and cities with monumental architecture, there are some exceptions that are difficult for historians to explain. One such exception is the monumental structure uncovered by archaeologists at the site of Gobekli Tepe in modern Turkey. The oldest structures at the site were erected between 9000 and 8000 B.C.E., well before the appearance of agriculture. This means that it must have been foraging peoples who erected more than two hundred massive pillars carved from limestone, each up to 6 meters (20 feet) tall, and weighing an average of 10 tons. Many of the pillars are decorated with carvings of abstract symbols or animals. These extraordinary structures predate pottery, the discovery of metallurgy, the invention of writing, and the entire Neolithic Revolution. Somehow the foraging communities living in this area were able to quarry and erect these heavy pillars after transporting them a considerable distance. Archaeologists believe this is the oldest temple in the world, and historians can only speculate on what motivated these small populations of foragers to undertake this extraordinary operation.

Source: K. Schmidt, 2000b, "Göbekli Tepe, Southeastern Turkey. A Preliminary Report on the 1995–1999 Excavations." In: *Palèorient* CNRS Ed., Paris 2000: 26.1, 45–54, ISSN 0153-9345.

Photograph of some of the limestone pillars at the site of Göbekli Tepe, Turkey. The pillars were erected by unknown peoples sometime between 9000 and 8000 B.C.E.

serkan senturk/Shutterstock

densely populated quarters, placed the surrounding lands under cultivation, and domesticated several species of animals. Besides altering the physical appearance of the earth, agriculture transformed the lives of humans. Even a modest neolithic village dwarfed a paleolithic band of a few dozen hunters and gatherers. In larger villages and towns, such as Jericho and Çatal Hüyük, with their populations of several thousand people, their specialized labor, and their craft industries, social relationships became more complex than would have been conceivable during paleolithic times. Gradually, dense populations, specialized labor, and complex social relations gave rise to an altogether new form of social organization—the city.

Emergence of Cities Like the transition from foraging to agricultural society, the development of cities and complex societies organized around urban centers was a gradual process rather than a well-defined event. Because of favorable location, some neolithic villages and towns attracted more people and grew larger than others. Over time, some of those settlements evolved into cities. What distinguished early cities from their predecessors, the neolithic villages and towns?

Even in their early days, cities differed from neolithic villages and towns in two principal ways. In the first, cities were larger and more complex than neolithic villages and towns. Çatal Hüyük featured an impressive variety of specialized crafts and industries. With progressively larger populations, cities fostered more intense specialization than any of their predecessors among the neolithic villages and towns. Thus it was in cities that large classes of professionals emerged—individuals who devoted all their time to efforts other than the production of food. Professional craft workers refined existing technologies, invented new ones, and raised levels of quality and production. Professional managers also appeared—governors, administrators, military strategists, tax collectors, and the like—whose services were necessary to the survival of the community. Cities also gave rise to professional cultural specialists such as priests, who maintained their communities' traditions, transmitted their values, organized public rituals, and sought to discover meaning in human existence.

In the second, whereas neolithic villages and towns served the needs of their inhabitants and immediate neighbors, cities decisively influenced the political, economic, and cultural life of large regions. Cities established marketplaces that attracted buyers and sellers from distant parts. Brisk trade, conducted over increasingly longer distances, promoted economic integration on a much larger scale than was possible in neolithic times. To ensure adequate food supplies for their large populations, cities also extended their claims to authority over their hinterlands, thus becoming centers of political and military control as well as economic influence. In time, too, the building of temples and schools in neighboring regions enabled the cities to extend their cultural traditions and values to surrounding areas.

The earliest known cities grew out of agricultural villages and towns in the valleys of the Tigris and Euphrates rivers in modern-day Iraq. These communities crossed the urban threshold during the period about 4000 to 3500 B.C.E. and soon dominated their regions. During the following centuries, cities appeared in several other parts of the world, including Egypt, northern India, northern China, central Mexico, and the central Andean region of South America. Cities became the focal points of public affairs—the sites from which leaders guided human fortunes, supervised neighboring regions, and organized the world's earliest complex societies.

CONCLUSION

In many ways the world of prehistoric humans seems remote and even alien. Yet the evolution of the human species and the development of human society during the paleolithic and neolithic eras have profoundly influenced the lives of all the world's peoples during the past six millennia. Paleolithic peoples enjoyed levels of intelligence that far exceeded those of other animals, and they invented tools and languages that enabled them to flourish in all regions of the world. Indeed, they thrived so well that they threatened their sources of food. Their neolithic descendants began to cultivate food to sustain their communities, and the agricultural societies that they built transformed the world. Human population rose dramatically, and human groups congregated in villages, towns, and eventually cities. There they engaged in specialized labor and launched industries that produced pottery, metal goods, and textiles as well as tools and decorative items. Thus intelligence, language, reflective thought, agriculture, urban settlements, and craft industries all figure in the legacy that early humans left for their descendants. These remarkable human abilities and developments would lead, over the centuries that followed, to the appearance of increasingly complex states and civilizations, each of which developed unique traditions that were tested and reshaped as these states encountered each other through trade and warfare.

STUDY TERMS

Australopithecus (4)	Neandertal (9)
Çatal Hüyük (15)	neolithic (12)
cave paintings (11)	paleolithic (7)
Hominidae (4)	patriarchy (17)
Homo erectus (4)	*Venus figurines* (10)
Homo sapiens (5)	

FOR FURTHER READING

Peter Bellwood. *First Farmers: The Origins of Agricultural Societies.* Oxford, 2005. A comprehensive and comparative review of early agriculture and its effects.

David Christian. *Maps of Time: An Introduction to Big History.* Berkeley, 2004. A brilliant study that considers human history in the context of natural history since the big bang.

R. Dale Guthrie. *The Nature of Paleolithic Art.* Chicago, 2005. Examines paleolithic art in the context of human physiology and argues that much paleolithic art reflected interests in food and sex.

Donald C. Johanson and Maitland A. Edey. *Lucy: The Beginnings of Humankind.* New York, 1981. Fascinating account of the discovery of Lucy and the scholarly controversies that ensued.

Richard G. Klein. *The Dawn of Human Culture.* New York, 2002. Places the development of human consciousness in the context of evolutionary history.

James Mellaart. *Çatal Hüyük: A Neolithic Town in Anatolia.* New York, 1967. Discussion of Çatal Hüyük by its excavator.

Susan Meyer. *The Neolithic Revolution.* New York: Rosen Publishing Group, 2016. An up-to-date account of the transition from foraging to farming, incorporating some of the more recent theories and evidence that have been proposed to explain it.

L. Ristvet. *In the Beginning: World History from Human Evolution to the First States.* New York: McGraw-Hill, 2007. A succinct and very readable overview of the earliest periods in human history.

William Ruddiman. *Plows, Plagues, and Petroleum: How Humans Took Control of Climate,* Princeton, NJ: Princeton University Press, 2005. An extraordinary deep historical overview of the relationship between humans and the environment from the earliest periods of human history through to the present.

Chris Scarre, ed. *The Human Past: World Prehistory and the Development of Human Societies.* London: Thames & Hudson, 2005. A superb collection of chapters by leading specialists on the paleolithic and neolithic eras of human history.

Nicholas Wade. *Before the Dawn: Recovering the Lost History of Our Ancestors.* New York, 2006. Excellent synthesis of studies on human evolution.

The Emergence of Complex Societies in Southwest Asia and Encounters with Indo-European-Speaking Peoples

The Quest for Order
  Mesopotamia: "The Land between the Rivers"
  The First Empires
  Later Mesopotamian Empires

The Formation of Sophisticated Social and Cultural Traditions
  Economic Specialization and Trade
  The Emergence of a Stratified Patriarchal Society
  The Development of Written Cultural Traditions

The Broader Influence of Mesopotamian Society
  Hebrews, Israelites, and Jews
  The Phoenicians

Indo-European Migrations
  Indo-European Origins
  Indo-European Expansion and Its Effects

ZOOMING IN ON TRADITIONS
Gilgamesh: The Man and the Myth

By far the best-known individual of ancient Mesopotamian society was a ruler named **Gilgamesh.** According to historical sources, Gilgamesh was the fifth king of the city of Uruk. He ruled Uruk sometime between 2800 and 2500 B.C.E., and records from the nearby city of Kish suggest Gilgamesh may have led his people in conflicts with that city. However, historical records record few additional details about Gilgamesh's life and deeds.

After his death, Gilgamesh was deified and went on to become a key figure in the legendary myths of Mesopotamian society. He was the subject of numerous poems and legends, and Mesopotamian bards made him the central figure in a cycle of stories known collectively as the *Epic of Gilgamesh.* By the Old Babylonian Period (1830–1530 B.C.E.), Gilgamesh had become the greatest heroic figure in all of Mesopotamia, and his exploits were woven into the traditions of all the complex societies that emerged in southwest Asia. According to the stories, the gods granted Gilgamesh a perfect body and endowed him with superhuman strength and courage. He was "the man to whom all things were known," a supremely wise individual who "saw mysteries and knew secret things." The legends declare that he constructed the massive city walls of Uruk as well as several of the city's magnificent temples to Mesopotamian deities.

A wall relief from an Assyrian palace of the eighth century B.C.E. depicts Gilgamesh as a heroic figure holding a lion.
Album/Prisma/SuperStock

The stories that make up the *Epic of Gilgamesh* recount the adventures of this hero and his cherished friend Enkidu as they sought fame. They killed an evil monster, rescued Uruk from a ravaging bull, and matched wits with the gods. In spite of their heroic deeds, Enkidu offended the gods and fell under a sentence of death. His loss profoundly affected Gilgamesh, who sought some way to cheat death and gain eternal life. He eventually found a magical plant that had the power to confer immortality, but a serpent stole the plant and carried it away, forcing Gilgamesh to recognize that death is the ultimate fate of all humans. Thus, while focusing on the activities of Gilgamesh and Enkidu, the stories explored themes of friendship, loyalty, ambition, fear of death, and longing for something that only the gods possessed—immortality. In doing so they reflected the interests, concerns, and traditions of the complex, urban-based society that had recently emerged in Mesopotamia.

CHAPTER OVERVIEW

Productive agricultural economies supported the development of the world's first complex societies, in which sizable numbers of people lived in cities and extended their political, social, economic, and cultural influence over large regions. The earliest urban societies so far known emerged during the early fourth millennium B.C.E. in southwest Asia, particularly in Mesopotamia, establishing social and cultural traditions that would resonate widely through the region over the centuries that followed.

As people congregated in cities, they needed to find ways to resolve disputes—sometimes between residents within individual settlements, other times between whole settlements themselves—that inevitably arose as individual and group interests conflicted. In search of order, settled agricultural peoples recognized political authorities and built states throughout Mesopotamia. The establishment of states encouraged the creation of empires, as some states sought to extend their power and enhance their security by imposing their rule on neighboring lands.

Apart from stimulating the establishment of states, urban society in Mesopotamia also promoted the emergence of social classes, thus giving rise to increasingly complex social and economic structures. Cities fostered specialized labor, and the resulting efficient production of high-quality goods in turn stimulated trade. Furthermore, early Mesopotamia also developed distinctive cultural traditions as Mesopotamians invented a system of writing and supported organized religions.

But Southwest Asia did not exist in a geographical vacuum, which meant that Mesopotamians regularly encountered peoples of different customs and traditions. Indeed, Mesopotamian prosperity attracted numerous migrants, such as the ancient Hebrews, who settled in the region's cities and adopted Mesopotamian traditions. Merchants such as the Phoenicians, who also embraced Mesopotamian society, built extensive maritime trade networks that linked southwest Asia with lands throughout the Mediterranean basin. Some Indo-European peoples also had direct encounters with their Mesopotamian contemporaries, with effects crucial for both Indo-European and Mesopotamian societies. Other Indo-European peoples probably never heard of Mesopotamia, but they employed Mesopotamian inventions such as wheels and metallurgy when undertaking extensive migrations that profoundly influenced historical development throughout much of Eurasia from western Europe to India and beyond. Even in the earliest periods of complex urban life, Eurasia was the site of frequent encounters between different peoples, which profoundly shaped and modified the traditions already established by these different societies.

CHRONOLOGY

3200–2350 B.C.E.	Era of Sumerian dominance in Mesopotamia
3000 B.C.E.–1000 C.E.	Era of Indo-European migrations
2350–1600 B.C.E.	Era of Babylonian dominance in Mesopotamia
2334–2315 B.C.E.	Reign of Sargon of Akkad
1792–1750 B.C.E.	Reign of Hammurabi
1700–1200 B.C.E.	Era of Hittite dominance in Anatolia
1000–612 B.C.E.	Era of Assyrian dominance in Mesopotamia
1000–970 B.C.E.	Reign of Israelite King David
970–930 B.C.E.	Reign of Israelite King Solomon
722 B.C.E.	Assyrian conquest of the kingdom of Israel
605–562 B.C.E.	Reign of Nebuchadnezzar
600–550 B.C.E.	New Babylonian empire
586 B.C.E.	New Babylonian conquest of the kingdom of Judah

THE QUEST FOR ORDER

During the fourth millennium B.C.E., human population increased rapidly in Mesopotamia. Inhabitants had few precedents to guide them in the organization of a large-scale society. At most they inherited a few techniques for keeping order in the small agricultural villages of neolithic times. By experimentation and adaptation, however, they created states and governmental machinery that brought political and social order to their territories. Moreover, effective political and military organization enabled them to build regional empires and extend their authority to neighboring peoples.

Mesopotamia: "The Land between the Rivers"

The place-name *Mesopotamia* comes from two Greek words meaning "the land between the rivers," and it refers specifically to the fertile valleys of the Tigris and Euphrates rivers in modern-day Iraq. This was one of four river valley regions in which the first ancient civilizations were established. Each shared important geographic features, including dry soils, an environment that was slowly drying and warming following the end of the last ice age, and seasonally flooding rivers that

---

Euphrates (yoo-FRAY-tees)
Sumerian (soo-MEHR-ee-un)
Semitic (suh-MIHT-ikh)
Phoenician (fi-NEE-shin)

made irrigation agriculture possible. So, although Mesopotamia received little rainfall, the Tigris and Euphrates brought large volumes of freshwater to the region. Early cultivators realized that by tapping these rivers, building reservoirs, and digging canals, they could irrigate fields of barley, wheat, and peas. Small-scale irrigation began in Mesopotamia soon after 6000 B.C.E.

Sumer Artificial irrigation led to increased food supplies, which in turn supported a rapidly increasing human population while also attracting migrants from other regions. Human numbers grew especially fast in the land of Sumer in the southern half of Mesopotamia. It is possible that the people known as the **Sumerians** already inhabited this land in the sixth millennium B.C.E., but it is perhaps more likely that they were later migrants attracted to the region by its agricultural potential. In either case, by about 5000 B.C.E. the Sumerians were constructing elaborate irrigation networks that helped them realize abundant agricultural harvests. By 3000 B.C.E. the population of Sumer was approaching one hundred thousand—by far the densest concentration of humans seen anywhere in the world to this point in history—and the Sumerians were the dominant people of Mesopotamia.

Semitic Migrants While supporting a growing population, the wealth of Sumer also attracted migrants from other regions. Most of the new arrivals were **Semitic** peoples—so called because they spoke tongues in the Semitic family of languages, including Akkadian, Aramaic, Hebrew, and **Phoenician.** (Semitic languages spoken in the world today include Arabic

MAP 2.1 Early Mesopotamia, 3000–2000 B.C.E.

Note the locations of Mesopotamian cities in relation to the Tigris and Euphrates rivers.

In what ways did the environment of Southwest Asia facilitate the emergence of complex societies in the region?

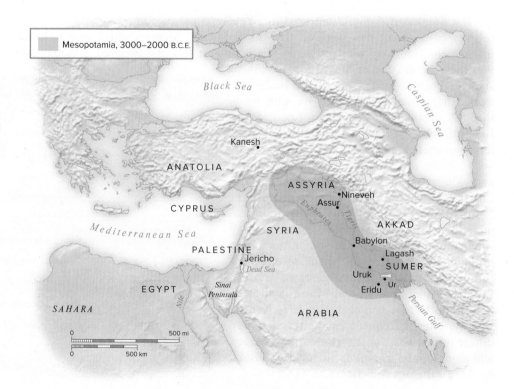

Mesopotamia, 3000–2000 B.C.E.

Rising more than 30 meters (100 feet), the massive temple of the moon god Nanna-Suen (sometimes known as Sin) dominated the Sumerian city of Ur. Constructing temples of this size required a huge investment of resources and thousands of laborers. As some of the largest human-built structures of the time, what role might such temples have played in the social and religious traditions of the Mesopotamian peoples?

Georg Gerster/Science Source

and Hebrew, and African peoples speak many other languages related to Semitic tongues.) Semitic peoples were nomadic herders who went to Mesopotamia from the Arabian and Syrian deserts to the south and west. They often intermarried with the Sumerians, and they largely adapted to Sumerian traditions.

Beginning around 4000 B.C.E., as human numbers increased in southern Mesopotamia, the Sumerians built the world's first cities. These cities differed markedly from the neolithic villages that preceded them. Unlike the earlier settlements, the Sumerian cities were centers of political and military authority, and their jurisdiction extended into the surrounding regions. Moreover, bustling marketplaces that drew buyers and sellers from near and far turned the cities into economic hubs as well. The cities also served as cultural centers where priests maintained organized religions and scribes developed traditions of writing and formal education.

Sumerian City-States For almost a millennium, from 3200 to 2350 B.C.E., a dozen Sumerian cities—Eridu, Ur, Uruk (the city ruled by King Gilgamesh), Lagash, Nippur, Kish, and others—dominated public affairs in Mesopotamia. These cities all experienced internal and external pressures that prompted them to establish states—formal governmental institutions that wielded authority throughout their territories. Internally, the cities needed to maintain order and ensure that inhabitants cooperated on community projects. With their expanding populations, the cities also needed to prevent conflicts between urban residents from escalating into serious civic disorder. Moreover, because agriculture was crucial to the welfare of urban residents, the cities all became city-states: they not only controlled public life within the city walls but also extended their authority to neighboring territories and oversaw affairs in surrounding agricultural regions.

While preserving the peace, government authorities also organized work on projects of value to the entire community. Palaces, temples, and defensive walls dominated all the Sumerian cities, and all were the work of laborers recruited and coordinated by government authorities such as Gilgamesh, whom legendary accounts credit with the building of city walls and temples at Uruk. Particularly impressive were the **ziggurats**—distinctive stepped pyramids that housed temples and altars to the principal local deity. In the city of Uruk, a massive ziggurat and temple complex was constructed about 3200 B.C.E. to honor the fertility goddess Inanna. Scholars have calculated that its construction required the services of fifteen hundred laborers working ten hours per day for five years. Ziggurats and temple complexes were at the heart of all the great Mesopotamian cities, which were essentially constructed around these religious complexes.

Even more important than buildings were the irrigation systems that supported productive agriculture and urban society. As their population grew, the Sumerians expanded their networks of reservoirs and canals. The construction, maintenance, and repair of the irrigation systems required the labor of untold thousands of probably coerced workers. Only recognized government authorities had the standing to draft workers for this difficult labor and order them to participate in such large-scale projects. Even when the irrigation systems functioned perfectly, recognized authority was still necessary to ensure equitable distribution of water and to resolve disputes.

In addition to their internal pressures, the Sumerian cities faced external problems. The wealth stored in Sumerian cities attracted the interest of peoples outside the cities. Mesopotamia is a mostly flat land with few natural geographic barriers. It was a simple matter for raiders to attack the Sumerian cities and take their wealth. The cities responded to that threat by building defensive walls and organizing military forces. The need to recruit, train, equip, maintain, and deploy military forces created another demand for recognized authority.

Sumerian Kings

The earliest Sumerian governments were probably assemblies of prominent men who made decisions on behalf of the whole community. When crises arose, assemblies yielded their power to individuals who possessed full authority during the period of emergency. These individual rulers gradually usurped the authority of the assemblies and established themselves as monarchs. By about 3000 B.C.E. all Sumerian cities had kings (known as *lugals*—a word that literally means

"big man" in Sumerian) who claimed absolute authority within their realms. In fact, however, the kings generally ruled in cooperation with local nobles, who came mostly from the ranks of military leaders who had displayed special valor in battle. By 2500 B.C.E. city-states dominated public life in Sumer, and city-states such as Assur and Nineveh had also begun to emerge in northern Mesopotamia.

The First Empires

Once they had organized effective states, Mesopotamians ventured beyond the boundaries of their societies. As early as 2800 B.C.E., conflicts between city-states often led to war, as aggrieved or ambitious kings sought to punish or conquer their neighbors. Sumerian accounts indicate that the king of Kish, a city-state located just east of Babylon, extended his rule to much of southern Mesopotamia after 2800 B.C.E., for example, and Sumerian poems praised King Gilgamesh for later liberating Uruk from Kish's control. In efforts to move beyond constant conflicts, a series of conquerors worked to establish order on a scale larger than the city-state by building empires that supervised the affairs of numerous subject cities and peoples. After 2350 B.C.E. Mesopotamia fell under the control of several powerful regional empires.

Sargon of Akkad These regional empires emerged as Semitic peoples such as the Akkadians and the Babylonians of northern Mesopotamia began to overshadow the Sumerians. The creator of the first empire in Mesopotamia was **Sargon of Akkad,** a city near Kish and Babylon whose precise location has so far eluded archaeologists. A talented administrator and brilliant warrior, Sargon (r. 2334–2284 B.C.E.) began his career as a minister to the king of Kish. About 2334 B.C.E. he organized a coup against the king, recruited an army, and went on the offensive against the Sumerian city-states. He conquered the cities one by one, destroyed their defensive walls, and placed them under his governors and administrators. As Sargon's conquests mounted, his armies grew larger and more professional, and no single city-state could withstand his forces.

Bronze bust of a Mesopotamian king often thought to represent Sargon of Akkad. The sculpture dates to about 2350 B.C.E. and reflects high levels of expertise in the working of bronze.
Iraq Museum, Baghdad/Hirmer Fotoarchiv

Empire: A New Form of Political Organization Sargon's empire represented a historical experiment, as the conqueror worked to devise ways and means to hold his possessions together. He relied heavily on his personal presence to maintain stability throughout his realm. For much of his reign, he traveled with armies, which sometimes numbered more than five thousand, from one Mesopotamian city to another. The resulting experience was quite unpleasant for the cities he visited, because their populations had to provide food, lodging, and financial support whenever Sargon and his forces descended upon them. That inconvenience naturally generated considerable resentment of the conqueror and frequently sparked local rebellions. In a never-ending search for funds to support his army and his government, Sargon also seized control of trade routes and supplies of natural resources such as silver, tin, and cedar wood. By controlling and taxing trade, Sargon obtained financial resources to maintain his military juggernaut and transform his capital of Akkad into the wealthiest and most powerful city in the world. At the high point of his reign, his empire embraced all of Mesopotamia, and his armies had ventured as far afield as the Mediterranean and the Black Sea.

For several generations Sargon's successors maintained his empire. Gradually, though, it weakened, partly because of chronic rebellion in city-states that resented imperial rule, partly also because of invasions by peoples hoping to seize a portion of Mesopotamia's fabulous wealth. By about 2150 B.C.E. Sargon's empire had collapsed altogether. Yet the memory of his deeds, recorded in legends and histories as well as in his works of propaganda, inspired later conquerors to follow his example.

Hammurabi and the Babylonian Empire Most prominent of the later conquerors was the Babylonian Hammurabi (reigned 1792–1750 B.C.E.), who styled himself "king of the four quarters of the world." The Babylonian empire dominated Mesopotamia until about 1600 B.C.E. Hammurabi improved on Sargon's administrative techniques by relying on centralized bureaucratic rule and regular taxation. Instead of traveling from city to city with an army both large and hungry, Hammurabi and his successors ruled from Babylon (located near modern Baghdad) and stationed deputies in the territories they controlled. Instead of confiscating supplies and other wealth in the unfortunate regions their armies visited, Hammurabi and later rulers instituted less ruinous but more regular taxes collected by their officials. By these means Hammurabi developed a more efficient and predictable government than his predecessors and also spread its costs more evenly over the population, thus establishing a model for the maintenance of empire that would influence subsequent conquerors.

Hammurabi's Laws Hammurabi also sought to maintain his empire by providing it with a code of law. Sumerian rulers had promulgated laws perhaps as early as 2500 B.C.E., and

Hammurabi borrowed liberally from his predecessors in compiling the most extensive and most complete Mesopotamian law code. In the prologue to his laws, Hammurabi proclaimed that the gods had chosen him "to promote the welfare of the people, . . . to cause justice to prevail in the land, to destroy the wicked and evil, [so] that the strong might not oppress the weak, to rise like the sun over the people, and to light up the land." Hammurabi's laws established high standards of behavior and stern punishments for violators. They prescribed death penalties for murder, theft, fraud, false accusations, sheltering of runaway slaves, failure to obey royal orders, adultery, and incest. Civil laws regulated prices, wages, commercial dealings, marital relationships, and the conditions of slavery.

The code relied heavily on the principle of *lex talionis,* a Latin phrase that means the "law of retaliation," whereby offenders suffered punishments resembling their violations. But the code also took account of social standing when applying this principle. It provided, for example, that a noble who destroyed the eye or broke the bone of another noble would have his own eye destroyed or bone broken, but if a noble destroyed the eye or broke the bone of a commoner, the noble merely paid a fine in silver. Local judges did not always follow the prescriptions of **Hammurabi's Code:** indeed, they frequently relied on their own judgment when deciding cases that came before them. Nevertheless, Hammurabi's laws established a set of standards that lent some degree of cultural unity to the far-flung Babylonian empire.

Despite Hammurabi's administrative efficiencies and impressive law code, the wealth of the Babylonian empire attracted invaders, particularly the Indo-European-speaking Hittites, who had built a powerful empire in Anatolia (modern-day Turkey), and about 1595 B.C.E. the Babylonian empire crumbled before Hittite assaults. For several centuries after the fall of Babylon, southwest Asia was a land of considerable turmoil, as regional states competed for power and position while migrants and invaders struggled to establish footholds for themselves in Mesopotamia and neighboring regions.

Later Mesopotamian Empires

Imperial rule returned to Mesopotamia with the **Assyrians,** a formidable people from northern Mesopotamia who had built a compact state in the Tigris River valley during the nineteenth century B.C.E. Taking advantage of their location on trade routes running both north-south and east-west, the Assyrians built flourishing cities at Assur and Nineveh. They built a powerful and intimidating army by organizing their forces into standardized units and placing them under the command of professional officers. The Assyrians appointed

---

Hammurabi (hahm-uh-RAH-bee)

lex talionis (lehks tah-lee-oh-nihs)

Assyrians (uh-SEER-ee-uhns)

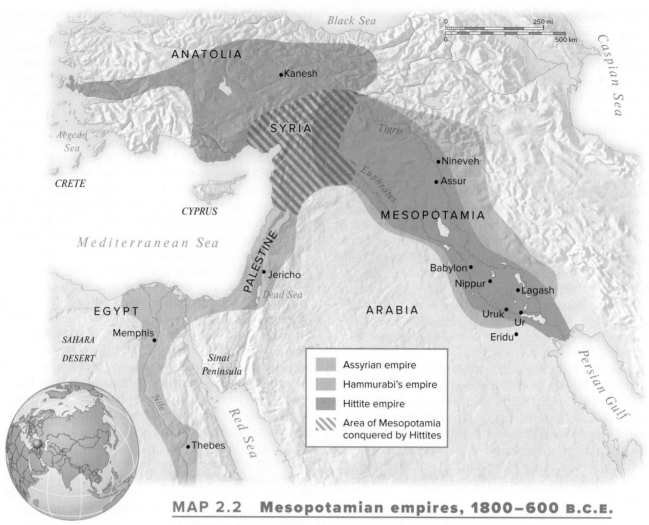

MAP 2.2 Mesopotamian empires, 1800–600 B.C.E.

Mesopotamian empires facilitated encounters between peoples from different societies.

How did the environment of the region influence the types of interactions that occurred between different societies during the second and first millennia B.C.E.?

these officers because of merit, skill, and bravery rather than noble birth or family connections. They supplemented infantry with cavalry forces and light, swift, horse-drawn chariots, which they borrowed from the Hittites. These chariots were devastating instruments of war that allowed archers to attack their enemies from rapidly moving platforms. Waves of Assyrian chariots stormed their opponents with a combination of high speed and withering firepower that unnerved the opponents and left them vulnerable to the Assyrian infantry and cavalry forces.

The Assyrian Empire

After the collapse of the Babylonian empire, the Assyrian state was one among many jockeying for power and position in northern Mesopotamia. After about 1300 B.C.E. Assyrians gradually extended their authority to much of southwest Asia. They made use of recently invented iron weapons to strengthen their army, which sometimes numbered upwards of fifty thousand troops who

pushed relentlessly in all directions. At its high point, during the eighth and seventh centuries B.C.E., the Assyrian empire embraced not only Mesopotamia but also Syria, Palestine, much of Anatolia, and most of Egypt. King Assurbanipal, whose long reign (668–627 B.C.E.) coincided with the high tide of Assyrian domination, went so far as to style himself not only "king of Assyria" but also, grandiosely, "king of the universe."

Like most other Mesopotamian peoples, the Assyrians relied on the administrative techniques pioneered by their Babylonian predecessors, and they followed laws much like those enshrined in the code of Hammurabi. They also preserved a great deal of Mesopotamian literature in huge libraries maintained at their large and lavish courts. At his magnificent royal palace in Nineveh, for example, King Assurbanipal maintained a vast library that included thousands of literary scholarly texts as well as diplomatic correspondence and administrative records. Indeed, Assurbanipal's library

SOURCES FROM THE PAST

The Flood Story from the *Epic of Gilgamesh*

The Epic of Gilgamesh *is the oldest surviving epic poem in history, dating from about 2500 B.C.E. The epic poem tells us a great deal about social and cultural life in Mesopotamia. As part of his adventures, Gilgamesh seeks the secret of immortality from a wise man named Ut-napishtim. During the visit, Ut-napishtim tells him how the god Ea alerted him to a plot by the gods to destroy humankind by a massive flood. Here, Ut-napishtim recounts the story to Gilgamesh.*

In its circuit (the boat measured) 14 measures
I placed its roof on it (and) I enclosed it
I rode in it, for the sixth time;
I (rode in it) for the seventh time into the restless deep.
Its planks the waters within it admitted,
I saw breaks and holes.
Three measures of bitumen I poured over the outside,
Three measures of bitumen I poured over the inside.
The men carrying its baskets . . . fixed an altar;
I unclosed the altar for an offering.
The material of the ship (was) completed;
Reeds I spread above and below.
All I possessed I collected it, all I possessed I collected of silver,
All I possessed I collected of gold,
All I possessed I collected of the seed of life, the whole.
I caused to go up into the ship, all my male and female servants,
The beasts of the field, the animals of the field,
And the sons of the army all of them, I caused to go up. —————

> What sort of cargo does Ut-napishtim load into his boat?

A flood Shamas made, and he spoke saying in the night,
'I will cause it to rain from heaven heavily;
Enter to the midst of the ship, and shut thy door.'
A flood he raised, and he spoke saying in the night,
'I will cause it to rain from heaven heavily.' —————

> Why is he building a boat?

In the day that I celebrated his festival, the day that he had appointed; fear I had.
I entered to the midst of the ship, and shut my door . . .
The raging of a storm in the morning arose,
From the horizon of heaven extending and wide . . .
The bright earth to a waste was turned;
The surface of the earth (was) swept.
It destroyed all life, from the face of the earth.
The strong tempest over the people, reached to heaven.
Brother saw not his brother, it did not spare the people . . .
Six days and nights passed, the wind tempest and storm overwhelmed.
On the seventh day in its course, was calmed the storm, and all the tempest which had
    destroyed like an earthquake, quieted.
The sea he caused to dry, and the wind and tempest ended.
I was carried through the sea.
The doer of evil, and the whole of mankind who turned to sin, like reeds their corpses floated.
I opened the window and the light broke in, over my refuge it passed . . .
On the seventh day . . . I sent forth a dove, and it left.
The dove went and searched and a resting place it did not find, and it returned.
I sent forth a swallow, and it left.
The swallow went and searched and a resting place it did not find, and it returned.

(Continued)

I sent forth a raven, and it left.
The raven went, and the corpses on the waters it saw,
And it did eat, it swam, and wandered away, and did not return.
I sent the animals forth to the four winds;
I poured out a libation;
I built an altar on the peak of the mountain.

> **What happens on the seventh day of the flood?**

For Further Reflection

■ What is similar and what is different between this flood account included in the story of Gilgamesh and the account of Noah and the flood in the Old Testament?

■ How might we account for these similarities and differences?

■ What does this tell us about the influence of Mesopotamian cultures on the ideas and cultures of subsequent regional states and peoples?

Source: Thomas Sanders et al. *Encounters in World History: Sources and Themes from the Global Past,* Vol. I. Boston: McGraw-Hill, 2006, pp. 40–41.

preserved most of the Mesopotamian literature that has survived to the present day, including the *Epic of Gilgamesh.* Through all these activities, the Assyrians ensured that the cultural, political, and legal traditions established by the Sumerians were preserved and passed on to subsequent regional states and empires.

The Assyrian empire brought wealth, comfort, and sophistication to the Assyrian heartland, particularly the cities of Assur and Nineveh, but elsewhere Assyrian domination was extremely unpopular. Assyrian rulers faced intermittent rebellion by subjects in one part or another of their empire, the very size of which presented enormous administrative challenges. Ultimately, a combination of internal unrest and external assault brought their empire down in 612 B.C.E.

Nebuchadnezzar and the New Babylonian Empire

For half a century, from 600 to 550 B.C.E., Babylon once again dominated Mesopotamia during the New Babylonian empire, sometimes called the Chaldean empire. King **Nebuchadnezzar** (reigned 605–562 B.C.E.) lavished wealth and resources on his capital city. Babylon occupied some 850 hectares (more than 2,100 acres), and the city's defensive walls were reportedly so thick that a four-horse chariot could turn around on top of them. Within the walls there were enormous palaces and 1,179 temples, some of them faced with gold and decorated with thousands of statues. When one of the king's wives longed for flowering shrubs from her mountain homeland, Nebuchadnezzar had them planted in terraces above the city walls, and the hanging gardens of Babylon have symbolized the city's luxuriousness ever since, although recent research suggests that these gardens may actually have been in the nearby city of Nineveh.

By that time, however, peoples beyond Mesopotamia had acquired advanced weapons and experimented with techniques of administering large territories. By the mid-sixth century B.C.E., Mesopotamians largely lost control of their affairs, as foreign conquerors absorbed them into their empires.

Artist's illustration of an Assyrian stone relief depicting the forces of King Tiglath-Pileser III (r. 745–727 B.C.E.) besieging a city, possibly Nineveh. A siege engine and slain enemy troops can be seen in the background.
Quagga Media/Alamy Stock Photo

Nebuchadnezzar (neb-uh-kud-NEZ-er)

THE FORMATION OF SOPHISTICATED SOCIAL AND CULTURAL TRADITIONS

With the emergence of cities and the congregation of dense populations in urban spaces, specialized labor proliferated. The Mesopotamian economy became increasingly diverse, and trade linked the region with distant peoples. Clearly defined social classes emerged, as small groups of people concentrated wealth and power in their hands, and Mesopotamia developed into a patriarchal society that vested authority largely in adult males. While building a complex society, Mesopotamians also allocated some of their resources to individuals who worked to develop sophisticated cultural traditions. They invented systems of writing that enabled them to record information for future retrieval. Writing soon became a foundation for education, science, literature, and religious reflection.

Economic Specialization and Trade

When large numbers of people began to congregate in cities and work at tasks other than agriculture, they vastly expanded the stock of human skills. Craftsmen refined techniques inherited from earlier generations and experimented with new ways of doing things. Pottery, textile manufacture, woodworking, leather production, brick making, stonecutting, and masonry all became distinct occupations in the world's earliest cities.

Bronze Metallurgy Metallurgical innovations ranked among the most important developments that came about because of specialized labor. Already in neolithic times, craftsmen had fashioned copper into tools and jewelry. In pure form, however, copper is too soft for use as an effective weapon or as a tool for heavy work. Sometime in the mid-fourth millennium B.C.E., Mesopotamian metalworkers discovered that if they alloyed copper with tin, they could make much harder and stronger implements. Experimentation with copper metallurgy thus led to the invention of bronze. Because both copper and tin were relatively rare and hence expensive, most people could not afford bronze implements. But bronze had an immediate impact on military affairs, as craftsmen turned out swords, spears, axes, shields, and armor made of the recently invented metal. Over a longer period, bronze also had an impact on agriculture. Mesopotamian farmers began to use bronze knives and bronze-tipped plows instead of tools made of bone, wood, stone, or obsidian.

Iron Metallurgy After about 1000 B.C.E. Mesopotamian craftsmen began to manufacture effective tools and weapons with iron as well as bronze. Experimentation with iron metallurgy began as early as the fourth millennium B.C.E., but early efforts resulted in products that were too brittle for heavy-duty uses. About 1300 B.C.E. craftsmen from Hittite society in Anatolia (discussed later in this chapter) developed techniques of forging exceptionally strong iron tools and weapons. Iron metallurgy soon spread throughout Anatolia, Mesopotamia, and other regions as well, and Assyrian conquerors made particularly effective use of iron weapons in building their empire. Because iron deposits are much cheaper and more widely available than copper and tin, the ingredients of bronze, iron quickly became the metal of choice for weapons and tools.

Depictions of onager-drawn carts and chariots on the Sumerian "battle standard of Ur" (dated to c. 2500 B.C.E.).
Kamira/Shutterstock

The Wheel While some craftsmen refined the techniques of bronze and iron metallurgy, others devised efficient means of transportation based on wheeled vehicles and sailing ships, both of which facilitated long-distance trade. The wheel appears to have been invented in the mid-fifth millennium B.C.E. as an aid to pottery manufacturing, but by the mid-third millennium there is widespread evidence of the use of wheeled carts for transportation. Wheeled carts and wagons enabled people to haul heavy loads of bulk goods—such as grain, bricks, or metal ores—over much longer distances than human porters or draft animals could manage. The wheel rapidly diffused from Sumer to neighboring lands, and within a few centuries it was in common use throughout Mesopotamia and beyond both for commercial and military purposes.

Shipbuilding Sumerians also experimented with technologies of maritime transportation. By 3500 B.C.E. they had built watercraft that allowed them to venture into the Persian Gulf. By 2300 B.C.E. they were trading regularly with merchants of the Indus civilization in modern Pakistan (discussed in chapter 4), which they reached by sailing through the Persian Gulf and the Arabian Sea. Until about 1750 B.C.E. Sumerian merchants shipped woolen textiles, leather goods, sesame oil, and jewelry to India in exchange for copper, ivory, pearls, and semiprecious stones. During the time of the Babylonian empire, Mesopotamians traded extensively with peoples in all directions: they imported silver from Anatolia, cedar wood from Lebanon, copper from Arabia, gold from Egypt, tin from Persia, lapis lazuli from Afghanistan, and semiprecious stones from northern India.

Trade Networks Archaeological excavations have shed bright light on one Mesopotamian trade network in particular. During the early second millennium B.C.E., Assyrian merchants traveled regularly by donkey caravan some 1,600 kilometers (1,000 miles) from their home of Assur in northern Mesopotamia to Kanesh (modern Kültepe) in Anatolia. Surviving correspondence shows that during the forty-five years from 1810 to 1765 B.C.E., merchants transported at least 80 tons of tin and one hundred thousand textiles from Assur and returned from Kanesh with no less than 10 tons of silver. The correspondence also shows that the merchants and their families operated a well-organized business. Merchants' wives and children manufactured textiles in Assur and sent them to male members of their families who lived in trading colonies at Kanesh. The merchants responded with orders for textiles in the styles desired at Kanesh.

The Emergence of a Stratified Patriarchal Society

Social Classes Agriculture enabled human groups to accumulate wealth, and distinctions between the more and less wealthy had already appeared in much earlier neolithic settlements such as Jericho and Çatal Hüyük. With increasingly specialized labor and long-distance trade, however, cities provided many more opportunities for the accumulation of wealth. Social distinctions in Mesopotamia became much more sharply defined than those of neolithic villages.

In early Mesopotamia the ruling classes consisted of kings and nobles who won their positions because of their valor and success as warriors. The early kings of the Sumerian cities made such a deep impression on their contemporaries that legends portrayed them as offspring of the gods. According to many legends, for example, Gilgamesh of Uruk, the son of a goddess and a king, was two-thirds divine and one-third human. Some legends recognized him as a full-fledged god. Large-scale construction projects ordered by the kings and the lavish decoration of capital cities also reflected the high status of the Mesopotamian ruling classes. All the Mesopotamian cities boasted massive city walls and imposing public buildings.

Temple Communities Closely allied with the ruling elites were priests and priestesses, many of whom were younger relatives of the rulers. The principal role of the priestly elites was to intervene with the gods to ensure good fortune for their communities. In exchange for those services, priests and priestesses lived in temple communities and received offerings of food, drink, and clothing from city inhabitants. Temples also generated income from vast tracts of land that they owned and large workshops that they maintained. One temple community near the city of Lagash employed six thousand textile workers between 2150 and 2100 B.C.E. Other temple communities cultivated grains; herded sheep and goats; and manufactured leather, wood, metal, and stone goods. Because of their wealth, temples provided comfortable livings for their inhabitants, and they also served the needs of the larger community. Temples functioned as banks where individuals could store wealth, and they helped underwrite trading ventures to distant lands. They also helped those in need by taking in orphans, supplying grain in times of famine, and providing ransoms for community members captured in battle.

Apart from the ruling and priestly elites, Mesopotamian society included less privileged classes of free commoners, dependent clients, and slaves. Free commoners mostly worked as peasant cultivators in the countryside on land owned by their families, although some also worked in the cities as builders, craftsmen, or professionals, such as physicians or engineers. Dependent clients had fewer options than free commoners because they possessed no property. Dependent clients usually worked as agricultural laborers on estates owned by others, including the king, nobles, or priestly communities, and they owed a portion of their production to the landowners. Free commoners and dependent clients all paid taxes—usually in the form of surplus agricultural production—that supported the ruling classes, military forces, and temple

The Royal Standard of Ur, produced about 2700 B.C.E., depicts diners at an elaborate banquet with musicians (top rank) as well as common folk who bring fish, goats, sheep, cattle, and agricultural produce for the affair. What do the depictions of these people and their animals tell us about social life in Sumerian cities?

CM Dixon/age fotostock

communities. In addition, when conscripted by ruling authorities, free commoners and dependent clients also provided labor services for large-scale construction projects involving roads, city walls, irrigation systems, temples, and public buildings.

Slaves Slaves came from three main sources: prisoners of war, convicted criminals, and heavily indebted individuals who sold themselves into slavery to satisfy their obligations. Some slaves worked as agricultural laborers on the estates of nobles or temple communities, but most were domestic servants in wealthy households. Many masters granted slaves their freedom, often with a financial gift, after several years of good service. Slaves with accommodating masters sometimes even engaged in small-scale trade and earned enough money to purchase their freedom.

Patriarchal Society While recognizing differences of rank, wealth, and social status, Mesopotamians also built a patriarchal society that vested authority over public and private affairs in adult men. Within their households men decided the work that family members would perform and made marriage arrangements for their children as well as any others who came under their authority. Men also dominated public life. Men ruled as kings, and decisions about policies and public affairs rested almost entirely in men's hands.

Hammurabi's laws throw considerable light on gender relations in ancient Mesopotamia. The laws recognized men as heads of their households and entrusted all major family decisions to their judgment. Men even had the power to sell their wives and children into slavery to satisfy their debts. In the interests of protecting the reputations of husbands and the legitimacy of offspring, the laws prescribed death by drowning as the punishment for adulterous wives, as well as for their partners, while permitting men to engage in consensual sexual relations with concubines, slaves, or prostitutes without penalty.

Women's Roles In spite of their subordinate legal status, women made their influence felt in Mesopotamian society. At ruling courts women sometimes advised kings and their governments. A few women wielded great power as high priestesses who managed the enormous estates belonging to their temples. Others obtained a formal education and worked as scribes—literate individuals who prepared administrative and legal documents for governments and private parties. Women also pursued careers as midwives, shopkeepers, brewers, bakers, tavern keepers, and textile manufacturers. There are no records of women serving as rulers or holding high-level administrative positions, although some of the most powerful Mesopotamian deities were female.

During the second millennium B.C.E., Mesopotamian men progressively tightened their control over the social and sexual behavior of women. To protect family fortunes and guarantee the legitimacy of heirs, Mesopotamians insisted on the virginity of brides at marriage, and they forbade casual socializing between married women and men outside their family. By 1500 B.C.E. and probably even earlier, upper-class women in Mesopotamian cities had begun to wear veils when they ventured beyond their own households to discourage the attention of men from other families. This tradition of designating women as being of subordinate status and putting in place various practices to control women's social and sexual behavior spread throughout much of southwest Asia and the Mediterranean basin, where it reinforced patriarchal social structures.

The Development of Written Cultural Traditions

The world's earliest known writing came from Mesopotamia. Sumerians invented a system of writing late in the fourth millennium B.C.E. to keep track of commercial transactions and tax collections. They first experimented with pictographs representing animals, agricultural products, and trade items—such as sheep, oxen, wheat, barley, pots, and fish—that figured prominently in tax and commercial transactions. By 3100 B.C.E. conventional signs representing specific words had spread throughout Mesopotamia.

Cuneiform Writing A writing system that depends on pictures is useful for purposes such as keeping records, but it is a cumbersome way to communicate abstract ideas. Beginning about 2900 B.C.E. the Sumerians developed a more flexible system of writing that used graphic symbols to represent sounds, syllables, and ideas as well as physical objects. By combining pictographs and other symbols, the Sumerians created a powerful writing system.

When writing, a Sumerian scribe used a stylus fashioned from a reed to impress symbols on wet clay. Because the stylus left lines and wedge-shaped marks, Sumerian writing is known as *cuneiform,* a term that comes from two Latin words meaning "wedge-shaped." When dried in the sun or baked in an oven, the clay hardened and preserved a permanent record of

Sumerian inscription in monumental archaic style, dated to c. 2600 B.C.E. A master scribe has impressed symbols into wet clay which has hardened to preserve a permanent record of gifts donated to a high temple priestess.
The Picture Art Collection/Alamy Stock Photo

the scribe's message. Babylonians, Assyrians, and other peoples later adapted the Sumerians' script to their languages, and the tradition of cuneiform writing continued for more than three thousand years. Thousands of clay tablets with cuneiform writing survive to the present day. Although it entered a period of decline in the fourth century B.C.E. after the arrival of Greek alphabetic script, in which each written symbol represents a distinct, individual sound, scribes continued to produce cuneiform documents into the early centuries C.E.

Education Most education in ancient times was vocational instruction designed to train individuals to work in specific trades and crafts. Yet Mesopotamians also established formal school because it required a great deal of time and concentrated effort to learn cuneiform writing. Most of those who learned to read and write became scribes or government officials. A few pursued their studies further and became priests, physicians, or professionals such as engineers and architects. Formal education was by no means common, but already by 3000 B.C.E., literacy was essential to the smooth functioning of Mesopotamian society.

Though originally invented for purposes of keeping records, writing clearly had potential that went far beyond the purely practical matter of storing information. Mesopotamians relied on writing to communicate complex ideas about the world, the gods, humans, and their relationships with one another. Indeed, writing made possible the emergence of a distinctive cultural tradition that shaped Mesopotamian values for almost three thousand years.

Astronomy and Mathematics Literacy led to a rapid expansion of knowledge. Mesopotamian scholars devoted themselves to the study of astronomy and mathematics—crucial sciences for agricultural societies. Knowledge of astronomy helped them prepare accurate calendars, which in turn enabled them to chart the rhythms of the seasons and determine the appropriate times for planting and harvesting crops. They used their mathematical skills to survey agricultural lands and allocate them to the proper owners or tenants. Some Mesopotamian conventions persist to the present day: Mesopotamian scientists divided the year into twelve months, for example, and they divided the hours of the day into sixty minutes, each composed of sixty seconds.

cuneiform (KYOO-ni-form)

SOURCES FROM THE PAST

Hammurabi's Laws on Family Relationships

By the time of Hammurabi, Mesopotamian marriages had come to represent important business and economic relationships between families. Hammurabi's laws reflect a concern to ensure the legitimacy of children and to protect the economic interests of both marital partners and their families. While placing women under the authority of their fathers and husbands, the laws also protected women against unreasonable treatment by their husbands or other men.

[128] If a man take a woman to be his wife, but has no intercourse with her, this woman is no wife to him.

[129] If a man's wife be surprised having sexual relations with another man, both shall be tied and thrown into the water, but the husband may pardon his wife and the king may spare her.

[130] If a man violates the wife (betrothed or child-wife) of another man, who has never known a man, and still lives in her father's house, and sleeps with her and be surprised, this man shall be put to death, but the wife is blameless.

[131] If a man brings a charge against his wife, but she is not surprised with another man, she must take an oath and then may return to her house.

[138] If a man wishes to separate from his wife who has borne him no children, he shall give her the amount of her purchase money and the dowry which she brought from her father's house, and let her go.

[139] If there was no purchase price he shall give her one mina of gold as a gift of release.

[140] If he be a freed man he shall give her one-third of a mina of gold.

[141] If a man's wife, who lives in his house, wishes to leave it, plunges into debt, tries to ruin her house, neglects her husband, and is judicially convicted: if her husband offer her release, she may go on her way, and he gives her nothing as a gift of release. If her husband does not wish to release her, and if he takes another wife, she shall remain as servant in her husband's house.

[142] If a woman quarrels with her husband, and says: "You are not congenial to me," the reasons for her prejudice must be presented. If she is guiltless, and there is no fault on her part, but he leaves and neglects her, then no guilt attaches to this woman, she shall take her dowry and go back to her father's house.

[143] If she is not innocent, but leaves her husband, and ruins her house, neglecting her husband, this woman shall be cast into the water.

What are the differences in punishments for a man and a woman for the crime of adultery?

What is the punishment for rape?

What is the process for separation or divorce, according to the laws?

For Further Reflection

■ What family relationship is the main focus of these laws?
■ What do these laws suggest about the complexity of married life in ancient Babylon?
■ Do these laws seem to favor one gender over another?

Source: James B. Pritchard, ed. Ancient Near Eastern Texts Relating to the Old Testament. Princeton: Princeton University Press, 1955, pp. 171–72.

THE BROADER INFLUENCE OF MESOPOTAMIAN SOCIETY

While building cities and regional states, Mesopotamians deeply influenced the development and experiences of peoples living far beyond Mesopotamia. Often their wealth and power attracted the attention of neighboring peoples. Sometimes Mesopotamians projected their power to foreign lands and imposed their ways by force. Occasionally migrants left Mesopotamia and carried their inherited traditions to new lands. Mesopotamian influence did not completely transform other peoples and turn them into carbon copies of Mesopotamians. On the contrary, other peoples adopted Mesopotamian ways selectively and adapted them to their needs and interests. Yet the broader impact of Mesopotamian society shows that, even in early times, complex agricultural societies organized around

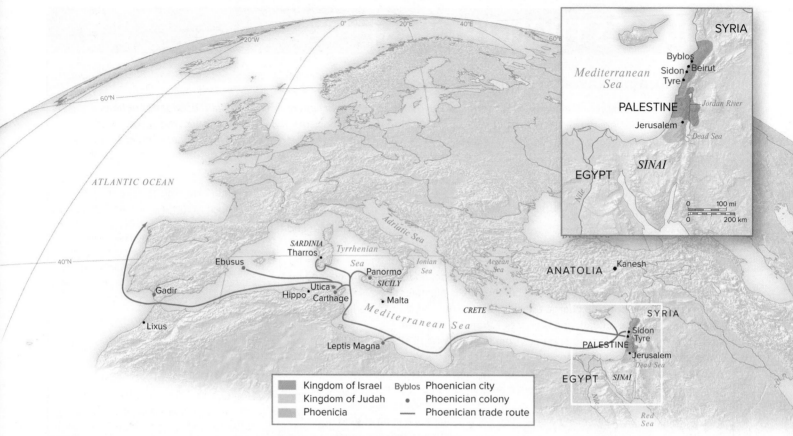

MAP 2.3 Israel and Phoenicia, 1500–600 B.C.E.

Note the location of Israel and Phoenicia with respect to Mesopotamia, Egypt, and the Mediterranean Sea.

How might the geographical location of Israel and Phoenicia have influenced their commercial relationships with regional neighbors?

cities had strong potential to influence the development of distant human communities.

Hebrews, Israelites, and Jews

The best-known cases of early Mesopotamian influence involved **Hebrews, Israelites,** and **Jews,** who preserved memories of their historical experiences in an extensive collection of sacred writings. Hebrews were speakers of the ancient Hebrew language. Israelites formed a branch of Hebrews who settled in Palestine (modern-day Israel) after 1200 B.C.E. Jews descended from southern Israelites who inhabited the kingdom of Judah. For more than two thousand years, Hebrews, Israelites, and Jews interacted constantly with Mesopotamians and other peoples as well, with profound consequences for the development of their societies.

The Early Hebrews The earliest Hebrews were pastoral nomads who inhabited lands between Mesopotamia and Egypt during the second millennium B.C.E. As Mesopotamia prospered, some Hebrews settled in the region's cities. According to the Hebrew scriptures (the Old Testament of the Christian Bible), the Hebrew patriarch Abraham came from the Sumerian city of Ur, but he migrated to northern Mesopotamia about 1850 B.C.E., perhaps because of disorder in Sumer. Abraham's

descendants continued to recognize many of the deities, values, and customs common to Mesopotamian peoples. Hebrew law, for example, borrowed the principle of *lex talionis* from Hammurabi's code. The Hebrews also told the story of a devastating flood that had destroyed all early human society. Their account was a variation on similar flood stories related from the earliest days of Sumerian society. One early version of the story made its way into the *Epic of Gilgamesh.* The Hebrews altered the story and adapted it to their own interests and purposes, but their familiarity with the flood story shows that they participated fully in the larger society of Mesopotamia.

Migrations and Settlement in Palestine The Hebrew scriptures do not offer reliable historical accounts of early times, but they present memories and interpretations of Hebrew experience from the perspectives of later religious leaders who collected oral reports and edited them into a body of writings after 800 B.C.E. According to those scriptures, some Hebrews migrated to Egypt during the eighteenth century B.C.E. About 1300 B.C.E., however, this branch of the Hebrews departed under the leadership of Moses and went to Palestine. Organized into a loose federation of twelve tribes, these Hebrews, known as the Israelites, fought bitterly with other inhabitants of Palestine and carved out a territory for themselves. Eventually the Israelites abandoned their inherited tribal structure in favor of a Mesopotamian-style monarchy that brought the twelve tribes under unified rule. According to the scriptures, during the reigns of King David (1000–970 B.C.E.) and King Solomon (970–930 B.C.E.), Israelites dominated the territory between Syria and the Sinai Peninsula. Israelites dominated the territory between Syria and the Sinai peninsula. They built an elaborate and cosmopolitan capital city at Jerusalem and entered into diplomatic and commercial relations with Mesopotamians, Egyptians, and Arabian peoples.

Moses and Monotheism The Hebrew scriptures also teach that after the time of Moses, the religious beliefs of the Israelites developed along increasingly distinctive lines. The early Hebrews had recognized many of the same gods as their Mesopotamian neighbors: they believed that nature spirits inhabited trees, rocks, and mountains, for example, and they honored various deities as patrons or protectors of their clans. Moses, however, embraced **monotheism:** he taught that there was only one god, known as **Yahweh,** who was a supremely powerful deity, the creator and sustainer of the world. All other gods, including the various Mesopotamian deities, were impostors—figments of the human imagination rather than true and powerful gods. When the kings of the Israelites established their capital at Jerusalem, they did not build a ziggurat, which they associated with false Mesopotamian gods but, rather, a magnificent, lavishly decorated temple in honor of Yahweh.

Although he was the omnipotent creator of the universe, Yahweh was also a personal god. He expected his followers to worship him alone, and he demanded that they observe high moral and ethical standards. In the Ten Commandments, a set of religious and ethical principles that Moses announced to the Israelites, Yahweh warned his followers against destructive and antisocial behaviors such as lying, theft, adultery, and murder. A detailed and elaborate legal code prepared after Moses's death instructed the Israelites to provide relief and protection for widows, orphans, slaves, and the poor. Between about 800 and 400 B.C.E., the Israelites' religious leaders compiled their teachings in a set of holy scriptures known as the Torah (Hebrew for "doctrine" or "teaching"), which laid down Yahweh's laws and outlined his role in creating the world and guiding human affairs. The Torah taught that

Yahweh would reward individuals who obeyed his will and punish those who did not. It also taught that Yahweh would reward or punish the whole community collectively, according to its observance of his commandments.

Historical and archaeological records tell a less colorful story than the account preserved in the Hebrew scriptures. Archaeological evidence shows that Israelites maintained communities in the hills of central Palestine after 1200 B.C.E. and that they formed several small kingdoms in the region after 1000 B.C.E. There are signs of intermittent conflicts with neighboring peoples, but there is no indication that Israelites conquered all of Palestine. On the contrary, they interacted and sometimes intermarried with other peoples of the region. Like their neighbors, they learned to use iron to fabricate weapons and tools. They even honored some of the deities of other Palestinian peoples: the Hebrew scriptures themselves mention that the Israelites worshiped gods other than Yahweh. The recognition of Yahweh as the only true god seems to have emerged about the eighth century B.C.E. rather than in the early days of the Hebrews' history.

Assyrian and Babylonian Conquests The Israelites placed increasing emphasis on devotion to Yahweh as they experienced a series of political and military setbacks. Following King Solomon's reign, tribal tensions led to the division of the community into a large kingdom of Israel in the north and a smaller kingdom of Judah in the land known as Judea to the south. During the ninth century B.C.E., the kingdom of Israel came under pressure from the expanding Assyrian empire and even had to pay tribute to Assyrian rulers. In 722 B.C.E. Assyrian forces conquered the northern kingdom and deported many of its inhabitants to other regions. Most of

Yahweh (YAH-way)

An Assyrian relief sculpture depicts King Jehu of Israel paying tribute to King Shalmaneser III of Assyria about the middle of the ninth century B.C.E.
Zev Radovan/BibleLandPictures/Alamy Stock Photo

these exiles assimilated into other communities and lost their identity as Israelites. The kingdom of Judah retained its independence only temporarily: founders of the New Babylonian empire toppled the Assyrians, then looked south, conquered the kingdom of Judah, and destroyed Jerusalem in 586 B.C.E. Again, the conquerors forced many residents into exile. Unlike their cousins to the north, however, most of these Israelites maintained their religious identity, and many of the deportees eventually returned to Judea, where they became known as Jews.

Ironically, perhaps, the Israelites' devotion to Yahweh intensified during this era of turmoil. Between the ninth and sixth centuries B.C.E., a series of prophets urged the Israelites to rededicate themselves to their faith and obey Yahweh's commandments. These prophets were moral and social critics who blasted their compatriots for their materialism, their neglect of the needy, and their interest in the fertility gods and nature deities worshiped by neighboring peoples. The prophets warned the Israelites that unless they mended their ways, Yahweh would punish them by sending conquerors to humiliate and enslave them. Many Israelites took the Assyrian and Babylonian conquests as proof that the prophets accurately represented Yahweh's mind and will.

The Early Jewish Community The exiles who returned to Judea after the Babylonian conquest did not abandon hope for a state of their own, and indeed they organized several small Jewish states as tributaries to the great empires that dominated southwest Asia after the sixth century B.C.E. But the returnees also built a distinctive religious community based on their conviction that they had a special relationship with Yahweh, their devotion to Yahweh's teachings as expressed in the Torah, and their concern for justice and righteousness. These elements enabled the Jews to maintain a strong sense of identity as a people distinct from Mesopotamians and others, even as they participated fully in the development of a larger complex society in southwest Asia. Over the longer term, Jewish monotheism, scriptures, and moral concerns also profoundly influenced the development of Christianity and Islam.

The Phoenicians

North of the Israelites' kingdom in Palestine, the Phoenicians occupied a narrow coastal plain between the Mediterranean Sea and the Lebanon Mountains. They spoke a Semitic language, referring to themselves as Canaanites and their land as Canaan. (The term *Phoenician* comes from early Greek references.)

A relief sculpture from an Assyrian palace depicts Phoenician ships transporting cedar logs, both by towing them and by hauling them on top of the boats.
CM Dixon/Print Collector/ Hulton Archive/Getty Images

The Early Phoenicians Ancestors of the Phoenicians, who both ancient and more recent scholarship suggests may have come from the region of modern Bahrain in the Persian Gulf, migrated to the Mediterranean coast and built their first settlements sometime after 3000 B.C.E. They did not establish a unified monarchy but, rather, organized a series of independent city-states ruled by local kings. The major cities—Tyre, Sidon, Beirut, and Byblos—had considerable influence over their smaller neighbors, and during the tenth century B.C.E. Tyre dominated southern Phoenicia. Generally speaking, however, the Phoenicians showed more interest in pursuing commercial opportunities than in state building or military expansion. Indeed, Phoenician cities were often subject to imperial rule from Egypt or Mesopotamia.

Phoenician Trade Networks Though not a numerous or militarily powerful people, the Phoenicians influenced societies throughout the Mediterranean basin because of their maritime trade and communication networks. Their meager lands did not permit development of a large agricultural society, so after about 2500 B.C.E. the Phoenicians turned increasingly to industry and trade. They traded overland with Mesopotamian and other peoples, and they provided much of the cedar timber, furnishings, and decorative items that went into the Israelites' temple in Jerusalem. Soon the Phoenicians ventured onto the seas and engaged also in maritime trade. They imported food and raw materials in exchange for high-quality metal goods, textiles, pottery, glass, and works of art that they produced for export. They enjoyed a special reputation for brilliant red and purple textiles colored with dyes extracted from several species of mollusc that were common in waters near Phoenicia. Indeed the Greek word for the Phoenicians can also be translated as "crimson or purple from Tyre," one of the major Phoenician cities, which demonstrates the crucial role these dyes played in Phoenician commerce. They also supplied Mesopotamians and Egyptians with cedar logs from the Lebanon Mountains for construction and shipbuilding.

The Phoenicians were excellent sailors, and they built the best ships of their times. Between 1200 and 800 B.C.E., they dominated Mediterranean trade. They established commercial colonies in Rhodes, Cyprus, Sicily, Sardinia, Spain, and north Africa. They sailed far and wide in search of raw materials such as copper and tin, which they used to make bronze, as well as more exotic items such as ivory and semiprecious stones, which they fashioned into works of decorative art. Their quest for raw materials took them well beyond the Mediterranean: Phoenician merchant ships visited the Canary Islands, coastal ports in Portugal and France, and even the distant British Isles, and adventurous Phoenician mariners made exploratory voyages to the Azores Islands and down the west coast of Africa as far as the Gulf of Guinea.

Like the Hebrews, the Phoenicians largely adapted Mesopotamian cultural traditions to their own needs. Their gods, for example, mostly came from Mesopotamia. The Phoenicians' most prominent female deity was Astarte, a fertility goddess known to the Sumerians as Inanna, and in Babylon and Assyria as Ishtar. Like the Mesopotamians, the Phoenicians associated other deities with mountains, the sky, lightning, and other natural phenomena. Yet the Phoenicians did not blindly follow Mesopotamian examples: each city built temples to its favored deities and devised rituals and ceremonies to honor them.

Alphabetic Writing The Phoenicians' tradition of writing also illustrates their creative adaptation of Mesopotamian practices to their own needs. For a millennium or more, they relied on cuneiform writing to preserve information, and they compiled a vast collection of religious, historical, and literary writings. (Most Phoenician writing has perished, although some fragments have survived.) After 2000 B.C.E. Syrian, Phoenician, and other peoples began experimenting with simpler alternatives to cuneiform. By 1500 B.C.E. Phoenician scribes had devised an early alphabetic script consisting of twenty-two symbols representing consonants—the Phoenician alphabet had no symbols for vowels. Learning twenty-two letters and building words with them was much easier than memorizing the hundreds of symbols employed in cuneiform. Because alphabetic writing required much less investment in education than did cuneiform writing, more people were able to become literate than ever before.

| NORTH SEMITIC | | | GREEK | | ETRUSCAN | LATIN | |
Early Phoenician	Early Hebrew	Phoenician	Early	Classical	Early	Early	Classical
K	K	⋡	◁	A	A	A	A
9	9	9	8	B	B		B
1	1	1	1	Γ	1		C
△	△	◁	△	△	◁	◁	D

Phoenician, Greek, Hebrew, and Roman letters.

Alphabetic writing spread widely as the Phoenicians traveled and traded throughout the Mediterranean basin. About the ninth century B.C.E., for example, Greeks modified the Phoenician alphabet and added symbols representing vowels. Romans later adapted the Greek alphabet to their language and passed it along to their cultural heirs in Europe. In later centuries alphabetic writing spread to central Asia, south Asia, southeast Asia, and ultimately throughout most of the world.

INDO-EUROPEAN MIGRATIONS

After 3000 B.C.E. Mesopotamia was a prosperous, productive region where peoples from many different communities mixed and mingled. But Mesopotamia was only one region in a much larger world of interaction and exchange. Mesopotamians and their neighbors all dealt frequently with peoples they encountered from regions far beyond southwest Asia. Among the most influential of these peoples in the third and second millennia B.C.E. were those who spoke various Indo-European languages. Their migrations throughout much of Eurasia profoundly influenced historical development in both southwest Asia and the larger world as well.

Indo-European Origins

Indo-European Languages During the eighteenth and nineteenth centuries, linguists noticed that many languages of Europe, southwest Asia, and India featured remarkable similarities in vocabulary and grammatical structure. Ancient languages displaying these similarities included Sanskrit (the sacred language of ancient India), Old Persian, Greek, and Latin. Modern descendants of these languages include Hindi and other languages of northern India, Farsi (the language of modern Iran), and most European languages, excepting only a few, such as Basque, Finnish, and Hungarian. Because of the geographic regions where these tongues are found, scholars refer to them as **Indo-European** languages. Major subgroups of

the Indo-European family of languages include Indo-Iranian, Greek, Balto-Slavic, Germanic, Italic, and Celtic. English belongs to the Germanic subgroup of the Indo-European family of languages.

After noticing linguistic similarities, scholars sought a way to explain the close relationship between the Indo-European languages. It was inconceivable that speakers of all these languages independently adopted similar vocabularies and grammatical structures. The only persuasive explanation for the high degree of linguistic coincidence was that speakers of Indo-European languages were all descendants of ancestors who spoke a common tongue and migrated from their original homeland widely across much of Eurasia. As migrants established separate communities and lost touch with one another, their languages evolved along different lines, adding new words and expressing ideas in different ways. Yet they retained the basic grammatical structure of their original speech, and they also kept much of their ancestors' vocabulary, even though they often adopted different pronunciations (and consequently different spellings) of the words they inherited from the earliest Indo-European language.

The Indo-European Homeland The original homeland of Indo-European speakers was probably the steppe region of modern-day Ukraine and southern Russia, the region just north of the Black Sea and the Caspian Sea. The earliest Indo-European speakers built their society there between about 4500 and 2500 B.C.E. They lived mostly by herding cattle, sheep, and goats, while cultivating barley and millet in small quantities. They also hunted horses, which flourished in the vast grasslands of the Eurasian steppe stretching from Hungary in the west to Mongolia in the east.

Horses Because they had observed horses closely and learned the animals' behavioral patterns, Indo-European speakers were able to domesticate horses about 4000 B.C.E. They probably used horses originally as a source of food, but they also began to ride them soon after domesticating them.

TABLE 2.1	Similarities in Vocabulary Indicating Close Relationships between Select Indo-European Languages				
English	**German**	**Spanish**	**Greek**	**Latin**	**Sanskrit**
father	vater	padre	pater	pater	pitar
one	ein	uno	hen	unus	ekam
fire	feuer	fuego	pyr	ignis	agnis
field	feld	campo	agros	ager	ajras
sun	sonne	sol	helios	sol	surya
king	könig	rey	basileus	rex	raja
god	gott	dios	theos	deus	devas

A stone carving from about 1200 B.C.E. depicts a Hittite chariot with spoked wheels during a lion hunt. A horse pulls the chariot bearing one driver and one archer.

Archiv Gerstenberg/ullstein bild/Getty Images

By 3000 B.C.E. Sumerian knowledge of bronze metallurgy and wheels had spread north to the Indo-European homeland, and soon thereafter Indo-European speakers devised ways to hitch horses to carts, wagons, and chariots. The earliest Indo-European language had words not only for cattle, sheep, goats, and horses, but also for wheels, axles, shafts, harnesses, hubs, and linchpins—all of the latter learned from Mesopotamian examples.

The possession of domesticated horses vastly magnified the power of Indo-European speakers. Once they had domesticated horses, Indo-European speakers were able to exploit the grasslands of southern Russia, where they relied on horses and wheeled vehicles for transport and on cattle and sheep for meat, milk, leather, and wool. Horses also enabled them to develop transportation technologies that were much faster and more efficient than alternatives that relied on cattle, donkey, or human power. Furthermore, because of their strength and speed, horses provided Indo-European speakers with a tremendous military advantage over peoples they encountered. It is perhaps significant that many groups of Indo-European speakers considered themselves superior to other peoples: the terms *Aryan, Iran,* and *Eire* (the official name of the modern Republic of Ireland) all derive from the Indo-European word *aryo,* meaning "nobleman" or "lord."

Indo-European Expansion and Its Effects

The Nature of Indo-European Migrations Horses also provided Indo-European speakers with a means of expanding far beyond their original homeland. As they flourished in southern Russia, Indo-European speakers experienced a population explosion, which prompted some of them to move into the sparsely inhabited eastern steppe or even beyond the grasslands altogether. The earliest Indo-European society began to break up about 3000 B.C.E., as migrants took their horses and other animals and made their way to new lands. Intermittent migrations of Indo-European peoples continued until about 1000 C.E. Like early movements of other peoples, these were not mass migrations so much as gradual and incremental processes that resulted in the spread of Indo-European languages and ethnic communities, as small groups of people established settlements in new lands, which then became foundations for further expansion.

The Hittites Some of the most influential Indo-European migrants in ancient times were the **Hittites.** About 1900 B.C.E. the Hittites migrated to the central plain of Anatolia, where they imposed their language and rule on the region's inhabitants. During the seventeenth and sixteenth centuries B.C.E., they built a powerful kingdom and established close relations with Mesopotamian peoples. They traded with Babylonians and Assyrians, adapted cuneiform writing to their Indo-European language, and accepted many Mesopotamian deities into their pantheon. In 1595 B.C.E. the Hittites toppled the mighty Babylonian empire, and for several centuries thereafter they were the dominant power in southwest Asia. Between 1450 and 1200 B.C.E., their authority extended to eastern Anatolia, northern Mesopotamia, and Syria down to Phoenicia. After 1200 B.C.E. the unified Hittite state dissolved, as waves of invaders attacked societies throughout the eastern Mediterranean region. Nevertheless, a Hittite identity survived, along with the Hittite language, throughout the era of the Assyrian empire and beyond.

War Chariots The Hittites were responsible for two technological innovations—the construction of light, horse-drawn **war chariots** and the refinement of iron metallurgy—that greatly strengthened their society and influenced other peoples throughout much of the ancient world. Sumerian armies had sometimes used heavy chariots with solid wooden wheels, but they were so slow and cumbersome that they had limited military value. About 2000 B.C.E. Hittites fitted chariots with recently invented spoked wheels, which were much lighter and more maneuverable than Sumerian wheels. The Hittites' speedy chariots were crucial in their campaign to establish a state in Anatolia. Following the Hittites' example, Mesopotamians soon added chariot teams to their armies, and Assyrians made especially effective use of chariots in building their empire. Indeed, chariot warfare was so effective—and its techniques spread so widely—that charioteers became the elite strike forces in armies throughout much of the ancient world, from Rome to China.

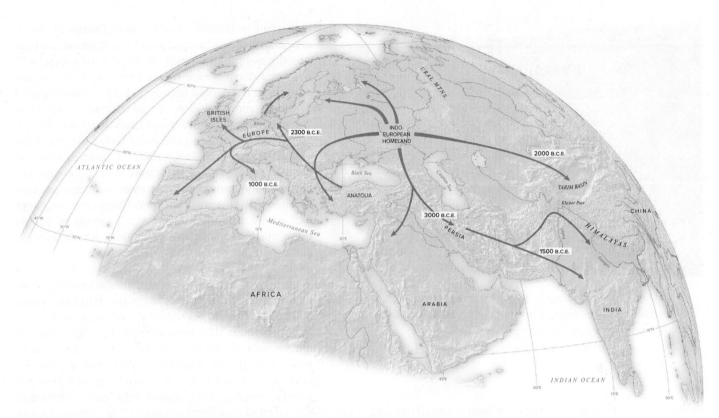

MAP 2.4   Indo-European migrations, 3000–1000 B.C.E.

Consider the vast distances over which Indo-European migrants established communities.

What technological and ecological advantages made it possible for Indo-European speakers to spread so widely across Eurasia?

Iron Metallurgy After about 1300 B.C.E. the Hittites also refined the technology of iron metallurgy, which enabled them to produce effective weapons cheaply and in large quantities. Other peoples had tried casting iron into molds, but cast iron was too brittle for use as tools or weapons. Hittite craftsmen discovered that by heating iron in a bed of charcoal, then hammering it into the desired shape, they could forge strong, durable implements. Hittite methods of iron production diffused rapidly—especially after the collapse of their kingdom in 1200 B.C.E. and the subsequent dispersal of Hittite craftsmen—and eventually spread throughout all of Eurasia. (Peoples of sub-Saharan Africa, and also probably China, independently invented iron metallurgy.) Hittites were not the original inventors either of horse-drawn chariots or of iron metallurgy: in both cases they built on Mesopotamian precedents. But in both cases they clearly improved on existing technologies and introduced innovations that other peoples readily adopted.

Indo-European Migrations to the East While the Hittites were building a state in Anatolia, other Indo-European speakers migrated from the steppe to different regions. Some

went east into central Asia, venturing as far as the Tarim Basin (now western China) by 2000 B.C.E. Stunning evidence of those migrations came to light in the 1980s when archaeologists excavated burials of individuals with European features in China's **Xinjiang** province. Because of the region's extremely dry atmosphere, the remains of some deceased individuals are so well preserved that their fair skin, light hair, and brightly colored garments are still clearly visible. Descendants of these migrants survived in central Asia and spoke Indo-European languages until well after 1000 C.E., but most of them were later absorbed into societies of Turkic-speaking peoples.

Indo-European Migrations to the West Meanwhile, other Indo-European migrants moved west. One wave of migration took Indo-European speakers into Greece after 2200 B.C.E., with their descendants moving into central Italy by 1000 B.C.E. Another migratory wave established an Indo-European presence farther to the west. By 2300 B.C.E. some Indo-European speakers had made their way from southern Russia into central Europe (modern Germany and Austria), by 1200 B.C.E. to western Europe (modern France), and shortly thereafter to the British Isles, the Baltic region, and the Iberian peninsula. These migrants depended on a pastoral and agricultural economy: none of them built cities or organized large states. For most of the first millennium B.C.E.,

Xinjiang (shin-jyahng)

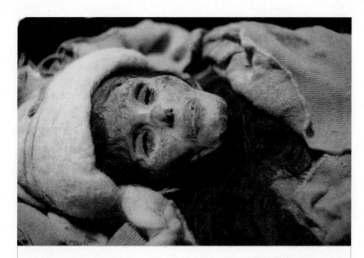

Remains of a deceased person found in the Tarim Basin in western China. The person was probably buried about three thousand years ago and was remarkably well preserved in the dry desert atmosphere of the region. What do this deceased person's facial features suggest about the extent of Indo-European migrations?

Jae C. Hong/AP Images

however, Indo-European Celtic peoples largely dominated Europe north of the Mediterranean, speaking related languages and honoring similar deities throughout the region. They recognized three principal social groups: a military ruling elite, a small group of priests, and a large class of commoners. Most of the commoners tended herds and cultivated crops, but some also worked as miners, craftsmen, or producers of metal goods. Even without large states, Celtic peoples traded copper, tin, and handicrafts throughout much of Europe.

Indo-European Migrations to the South Yet another, later wave of migrations established an Indo-European presence in Iran and India. About 1500 B.C.E. the Medes and Persians migrated into the Iranian plateau, while peoples sometimes called the Indo-Aryans began filtering into northern India. Like the Indo-European Celts in Europe, the Medes, Persians, and Aryans herded animals, cultivated grains, and divided themselves into classes of rulers, priests, and commoners. Unlike the Celts, though, the Medes, Persians, and Aryans soon built powerful states (discussed in later chapters) on the basis of their horse-based military technologies and later their possession also of iron weapons.

What's Left Out?

Although we know a great deal about the impact of Indo-European languages, and also about the various migrations of Indo-European-speaking peoples across the steppe, there is a lot we do not know about the origins of the lifeway pursued by the original Indo-Europeans: pastoral nomadism. It looks as though pastoralism first emerged as a viable lifeway around five thousand years ago when some human communities learned that it was possible to survive and even live well by using the "secondary products" of domesticated animals such as sheep, cattle, goats, camels, and horses. One possible site where this may have first occurred is at Dereikva in Ukraine, where archaeologist have discovered early horse-riding technologies, suggesting that farmers became increasingly dependent on domesticated herds of horses. Although the origins of pastoral nomadism remain obscure, there is no doubt that the mobility of groups such as the original Indo-Europeans, and their interactions with virtually every complex state and agrarian civilization across Eurasia over thousands of years, were crucial to the way history unfolded within that enormous world zone.

Source: C. Benjamin, *Empires of Ancient Eurasia. The First Silk Roads Era 100 B.C.E.–250 C.E.*, Cambridge: Cambridge University Press, 2018, chapter 1.

CONCLUSION

Building on neolithic traditions Mesopotamian peoples constructed societies that were much more complex, powerful, and influential than those of their predecessors. Through the city-states, kingdoms, and regional empires they established, Mesopotamians created formal institutions of government that extended the authority of ruling elites to all corners of their states, and they occasionally mobilized forces that projected their power to distant lands. They generated several distinct social classes. Specialized labor fueled productive economies and encouraged the establishment of long-distance trade networks. They devised systems of writing, which enabled them to develop sophisticated cultural traditions. They deeply influenced other peoples, such as the Hebrews and the Phoenicians, throughout southwest Asia and the eastern Mediterranean basin. They had frequent encounters also with Indo-European peoples. Although Indo-European society emerged far to the north of Mesopotamia, speakers of Indo-European languages migrated widely and established societies throughout much of Eurasia. Sometimes they drew inspiration from Mesopotamian traditions, and sometimes they developed new practices that influenced Mesopotamians and others as well. Thus, already in remote antiquity, the various peoples of the world profoundly influenced one another through cross-cultural encounters and exchange.

STUDY TERMS

Assyrians (27)	monotheism (37)
cuneiform (34)	Nebuchadnezzar (30)
Gilgamesh (22)	Phoenician (24)
Hammurabi's Code (27)	Sargon of Akkad (26)
Hebrews (36)	Semitic (24)
Hittites (41)	Sumerians (24)
Indo-European (40)	war chariots (41)
Israelites (36)	Xinjiang (42)
Jews (36)	Yahweh (37)
lex talionis (27)	ziggurats (26)
Mesopotamia (24)	

FOR FURTHER READING

David W. Anthony. *The Horse, the Wheel, and Language: How Bronze-Age Riders from the Eurasian Steppes Shaped the Modern World.* Princeton, 2007. Brilliant study of early Indo-European speakers and the uses they made of domesticated horses.

Elizabeth Wayland Barber. *Women's Work: The First 20,000 Years.* New York, 1994. Fascinating study of ancient textiles, which the author argues was a craft industry dominated by women from the earliest times.

Trevor Bryce. *The Kingdom of the Hittites.* New ed. Oxford, 2005. A solid, scholarly account of Hittite history, with an emphasis on political issues.

Israel Finkelstein and Neil Asher Silberman. *The Bible Unearthed: Archaeology's New Vision of Ancient Israel and the Origin of Its Sacred Texts.* New York, 2001. Interprets the Hebrew scriptures and early Israelite history in light of numerous archaeological discoveries.

Andrew George, trans. *The Epic of Gilgamesh.* London, 1999 (Reprinted with revisions 2003). A careful study and fresh translation of the best-known Mesopotamian literary work prepared on the basis of recently discovered texts.

Gwendolyn Leick. *Mesopotamia: The Invention of the City,* London, 2004. A refreshing look at ancient Mesopotamia through the lens of its major cities.

J. P. Mallory. *In Search of the Indo-Europeans.* London, 1991. Classic investigation of the probable origins and migrations of the Indo-Europeans.

J. P. Mallory and Victor H. Mair. *The Tarim Mummies: Ancient China and the Mystery of the Earliest Peoples from the West.* London, 2000. A cautious analysis of the Indo-European migrants to the Tarim Basin, drawing heavily on linguistic evidence.

Hans J. Nissen and Peter Heine. *From Mesopotamia to Iraq: A Concise History.* Chicago, 2009. An authoritative discussion of ancient Mesopotamia viewed in the context of the longer history of Iraq.

Michael Roaf. *Cultural Atlas of Mesopotamia and the Ancient Near East.* New York, 1990. Richly illustrated volume with well-informed essays on all dimensions of Mesopotamian history.

Marc van de Mieroop. *A History of the Ancient Near East, ca. 3000–323 B.C.* Oxford, 2004. A concise and readable history of ancient Mesopotamia and neighboring societies.

Chapter 3

The Emergence of Complex Societies in Africa and the Bantu Migrations

ZOOMING IN ON TRADITIONS

Herodotus and the Making of a Mummy

For almost three thousand years, Egyptian embalmers preserved the bodies of deceased individuals through a process of mummification. Egyptian records rarely mention the techniques of mummification, but the Greek historian Herodotus, who may have traveled in Egypt about 450 B.C.E., briefly explained the craft. The embalmer first used a metal hook to draw the brain of the deceased out through a nostril and then removed the internal organs through an incision made alongside the abdomen, soaked them in palm wine, and sealed them with preservatives in stone vessels. Next, the embalmer washed the body, filled it with spices and aromatics, and covered it for about two months with natron, a naturally occurring salt substance. When the natron had extracted all moisture from the body, the embalmer cleansed it again and wrapped it with strips of fine linen covered with resin. Adorned with jewelry, the preserved body then went into a coffin bearing a painting or sculpted likeness of the deceased.

Careful preservation of the body was only a part of the funerary ritual for prominent Egyptians. Ruling elites, wealthy individuals, and sometimes common people as well laid their deceased to rest in expensive tombs equipped with furniture, tools, weapons, and ornaments that the departed

Anubis, the jackal-headed Egyptian god of mummification, prepares the mummy of a deceased worker for burial. This painting comes from the wall of a tomb built about the thirteenth century B.C.E.
Werner Forman Archive/E. Strouhal/Heritage Image Partnership Ltd/ Alamy Stock Photo

would need in their next lives. Relatives periodically brought food and wine to nourish the deceased, and archaeologists have discovered soups, beef ribs, pigeons, quail, fish, bread, cakes, and fruits among those offerings. Artists decorated some tombs with elegant paintings of family members and servants, whose images accompanied the departed into a new dimension of existence.

Egyptian funerary traditions were reflections of not only deeply held religious beliefs, but also of a prosperous agricultural society. Food offerings consisted mostly of local agricultural products, and scenes painted on tomb walls often depicted workers preparing fields or cultivating crops. Moreover, bountiful harvests explained the accumulation of wealth that supported elaborate funerary practices, and they also enabled some individuals to devote their efforts to specialized tasks such as embalming. Agriculture even influenced religious beliefs. Egyptians believed fervently in a life beyond the grave, and they likened the human experience of life and death to the agricultural cycle in which crops grow, die, and come to life again in another season.

CHAPTER OVERVIEW

As Mesopotamians built a productive agricultural society in southwest Asia and as Indo-European peoples introduced domesticated horses to much of Eurasia, cultivation and herding also transformed African societies. African agriculture first took root in the Sudan, then moved into the Nile River valley and eventually to most parts of sub-Saharan Africa. Agriculture flourished particularly in the fertile Nile valley, and abundant harvests soon supported fast-growing populations. This exceptional agricultural productivity was fundamental to the emergence of complex society in Egypt, where one of the most powerful and prosperous states of the ancient world was established, and also in Nubia, Egypt's neighbor to the south.

Distinctive Egyptian and Nubian societies began to take shape in the valley of the Nile River during the late fourth millennium B.C.E., shortly after the emergence of complex society in Mesopotamia. Like their Mesopotamian counterparts, Egyptians and Nubians drew on agricultural surpluses to organize formal states, support specialized laborers, and develop distinctive cultural traditions. Like Mesopotamians again, Egyptian and Nubian residents of the Nile valley had regular encounters with peoples from other societies. They drew inspiration for political and social organization both from Mesopotamia and from their African neighbors to the south. Egyptian merchants also traded actively with Mesopotamians, Phoenicians, Africans, and other regional neighbors. Political and economic competition sometimes led to military conflicts with peoples of other societies: on several occasions when they enjoyed great wealth and power, both Egyptians and Nubians embarked on campaigns of imperial conquest, but when their power waned, they found themselves intermittently under attack from the outside.

Indeed, like their counterparts in Mesopotamia, Egyptian and Nubian societies developed within a larger world of interaction and exchange. Just as Mesopotamians, Hittites, Hebrews, and Phoenicians influenced one another in southwest Asia, inhabitants of the Nile valley mixed and mingled with Mesopotamians, Phoenicians, and other peoples from the eastern Mediterranean, southwest Asia, and sub-Saharan Africa. Just as Indo-European peoples migrated to new lands and established communities that transformed much of Eurasia, Bantu peoples migrated from their original homeland in west Africa and established settlements that brought profound change to much of sub-Saharan Africa. By no means were Egypt and Nubia isolated centers of social development. Like Mesopotamia, Egypt in particular was a spectacularly prosperous society, but like Mesopotamia again, Egypt was only one part of a much larger world of interacting societies.

CHRONOLOGY	
9000 B.C.E.	Origins of Sudanic herding
7500 B.C.E.	Origins of Sudanic cultivation
3100 B.C.E.	Unification of Egypt
3100–2660 B.C.E.	Archaic Period of Egyptian history
3000 B.C.E.	Beginnings of Bantu migrations
2660–2160 B.C.E.	Egyptian Old Kingdom
2600–2500 B.C.E.	Era of pyramid building in Egypt
2500–1450 B.C.E.	Early kingdom of Kush with capital at Kerma
2050–1550 B.C.E.	Egyptian Middle Kingdom
1550–1070 B.C.E.	Egyptian New Kingdom
1479–1425 B.C.E.	Reign of Pharaoh Tuthmosis III
1473–1458 B.C.E.	Reign of Queen Hatshepsut (coruler with Tuthmosis III)
1353–1335 B.C.E.	Reign of Pharaoh Amenhotep IV (Akhenaten)
1000 B.C.E.	Invention of iron metallurgy in sub-Saharan Africa
760 B.C.E.	Conquest of Egypt by King Kashta of Kush

EARLY AGRARIAN SOCIETIES IN AFRICA

Egypt was the most prominent of early African societies, but it was by no means the only agricultural society, nor even the only complex, city-based society of ancient Africa. On the contrary, Egypt emerged alongside Nubia and other agricultural societies in sub-Saharan Africa. Evidence suggests that agricultural crops and domesticated animals reached Egypt from sub-Saharan Africa by way of Nubia as well as from southwest Asia. Favorable geographic conditions enabled Egyptians to build an especially productive agricultural economy that supported a powerful state, while Nubia became home to a somewhat less prosperous but nonetheless sophisticated society. After taking shape as distinctive societies, Egypt had regular encounters with both eastern Mediterranean and southwest Asian peoples, and Nubia linked Egypt and the eastern Mediterranean basin with the peoples and societies of sub-Saharan Africa.

The Emergence of Agriculture in Africa

African agriculture emerged in the context of gradual but momentous changes in climatic conditions. About 10,000 B.C.E.,

after the end of the last ice age, the area now occupied by the Sahara desert was mostly a grassy steppe land with numerous lakes, rivers, and streams. Saharan climatic and geographic conditions were much like the extensive transition zone of savanna and grassland that stretches across the African continent today between the Sahara to the north and the tropical rain forest to the south. Grasses and cattle flourished in that environment. Many human inhabitants of the region lived by hunting wild cattle and collecting wild grains, while others subsisted on fish and aquatic resources from the region's waters.

Early Sudanic Agriculture After about 9000 B.C.E., peoples of the eastern Sudan domesticated cattle and became nomadic herders while continuing to collect wild grains. After 7500 B.C.E. they established permanent settlements and began to cultivate sorghum, a grain still widely grown in Africa for human and animal consumption. Meanwhile, after about 8000 B.C.E., inhabitants of the western Sudan began to cultivate yams in the region between the Niger and Congo rivers. Sudanic agriculture became increasingly diverse over the following centuries: sheep and goats arrived from southwest Asia after 7000 B.C.E., and Sudanic peoples began to cultivate gourds, watermelons, and cotton after 6500 B.C.E.

Agricultural productivity enabled Sudanic peoples to organize small-scale states. By about 5000 B.C.E. many Sudanic peoples had formed small monarchies ruled by kings who were viewed as divine or semidivine beings. For several thousand years, when Sudanic peoples buried their deceased kings, they also routinely executed a group of royal servants and entombed them along with the king so that they could continue to meet their master's needs in another life. Sudanic peoples also developed religious beliefs that reflected their agricultural society. They recognized a single divine force as the source of good and evil, and they associated it with rain—a matter of concern for any agricultural society.

Climatic Change After 5000 B.C.E. the northern half of Africa entered a period of long-term climatic change that profoundly influenced social organization and agriculture throughout the region. Although there was considerable fluctuation, the climate generally became much hotter and drier than before. The Sahara desert, which as late as

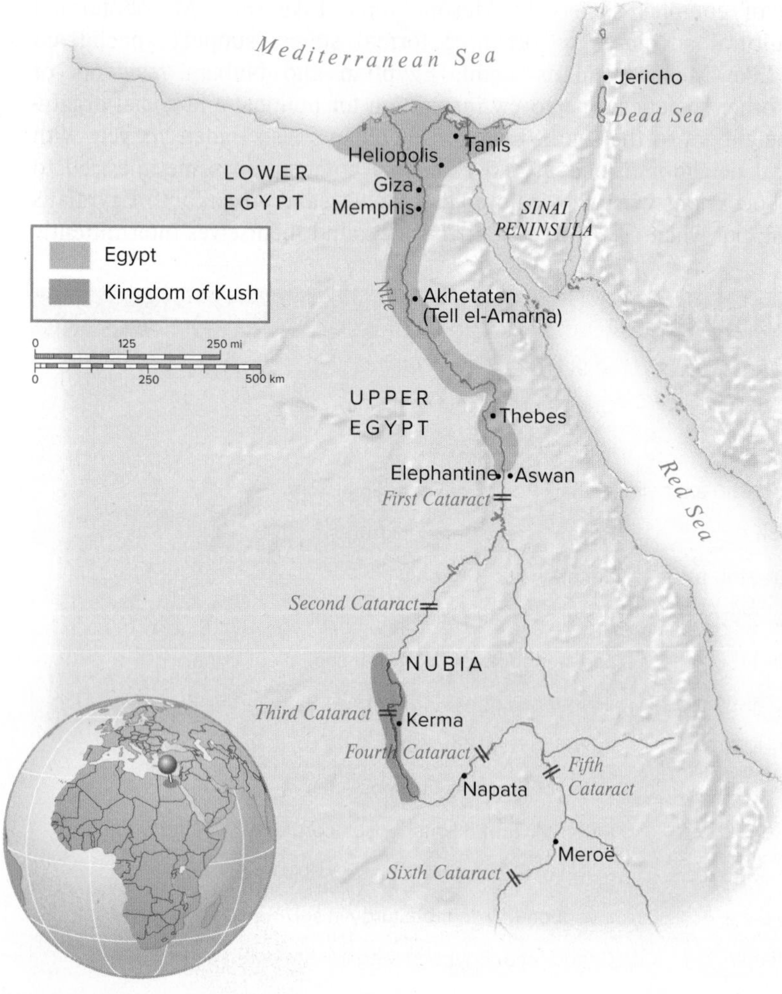

MAP 3.1 The Nile valley, 3000–2000 B.C.E.

Note the difference in size between the kingdom of Egypt and the kingdom of Kush.

In what ways did the geography of the Nile River valley influence the development of complex states in Egypt and Nubia?

5000 B.C.E. had been cool and well watered enough to support humans, animals, and crops, became increasingly arid and uninhabitable. This process of desiccation turned rich grasslands into barren desert, and it drove humans and animals to more hospitable regions. Many Sudanic cultivators and herders gathered around remaining bodies of water such as Lake Chad. Some moved south to the territory that is now northern Uganda. Others congregated in the valley of the **Nile River,** the principal source of water flowing through north Africa.

The Nile River Valley Fed by rain and snow in the high mountains of east Africa, the Nile, which is the world's longest river, flows some 6,695 kilometers (4,160 miles) from its source at Lake Victoria to its outlet through the delta to the Mediterranean Sea. Each spring, rain and melting snow swell the river, which surges north through the Sudan and Egypt. Until the completion of the high dam at Aswan in 1968, the Nile's accumulated waters annually flooded the plains downstream. When the waters receded, they left behind a layer of rich, fertile alluvial deposits that supported a remarkably productive agricultural economy throughout the Nile River valley.

Egypt and Nubia: "Gifts of the Nile"

Agriculture transformed the entire Nile River valley, with effects that were most dramatic in Egypt. In ancient times, Egypt referred not to the territory embraced by the modern state of Egypt but, rather, to the ribbon of land bordering the lower third of the Nile between the Mediterranean and the river's first cataract (an unnavigable stretch of rapids and waterfalls) near Aswan. Egypt enjoyed a much larger floodplain than most of the land to the south known as Nubia, the middle stretches of the Nile valley between the river's first and sixth cataracts. As the Sahara became increasingly arid, cultivators flocked to the Nile valley and established societies that depended on intensive agriculture. Because of their broad floodplains, Egyptians were able to take better advantage of the Nile's annual floods than the **Nubians** to the south, and they turned Egypt into an especially productive agricultural region that was capable of supporting a much larger population than Nubia. Because of its prosperity, the Greek historian Herodotus—the same historian who described the process of mummification earlier in this chapter—proclaimed Egypt the "gift of the Nile." If he had known more about Nubia, Herodotus might well have realized that it, too, was a gift of the Nile, even if it was less prosperous.

A painting from the tomb of a priest who lived about the fifteenth century B.C.E. depicts agricultural workers plowing and sowing crops in southern Egypt.
Zev Radovan/Alamy Stock Photo

Early Agriculture in the Nile Valley Geography ensured that both Egypt and Nubia would come under the influence of the Mediterranean basin to the north and sub-Saharan Africa to the south because the Nile River links the two regions. About 10,000 B.C.E., migrants from the Red Sea hills in northern Ethiopia traveled down the Nile valley and introduced to Egypt and Nubia the practice of collecting wild grains. They also introduced a language ancestral to Coptic, the language of ancient Egypt, to the lower reaches of the Nile valley. After 5000 B.C.E., as the African climate grew hotter and drier, Sudanic cultivators and herders moved down the Nile, introducing Egypt and Nubia to African crops such as gourds and watermelons as well as animals domesticated in the Sudan, particularly cattle and donkeys. About the same time, wheat and barley from Mesopotamia reached Egypt and Nubia by traveling up the Nile from the Mediterranean.

By c. 5000 B.C.E. both Egyptians and Nubians were heavily dependent on agriculture. Egyptian cultivators went into the floodplains in the late summer, after the recession of the Nile's annual flood, sowed their seeds without extensive preparation of the soil, allowed their crops to mature during the cool months of the year, and harvested them during the winter and early spring. With less extensive floodplains, Nubians relied more on prepared fields and irrigation by waters diverted from the Nile. As in Mesopotamia, high agricultural productivity led to a rapid increase in population throughout the Nile valley. Demographic pressures soon forced Egyptians in particular to develop more intense and sophisticated methods of agriculture. Cultivators moved beyond the Nile's immediate floodplains and began to grow crops on higher ground that required plowing and careful preparation. They built dikes to protect their fields from floods and catchment basins to store water for irrigation. By 4000 B.C.E. agricultural villages dotted the Nile's shores from the Mediterranean in the north to the river's fourth cataract in the south.

Political Organization As in Mesopotamia, dense human population in Egypt and Nubia brought a need for formal organization of public affairs. Neither Egypt nor Nubia faced the external dangers that threatened Mesopotamia because the Red Sea, the Mediterranean Sea, and hostile deserts discouraged foreign invaders. Nevertheless, the need to maintain order and organize community projects led both Egyptians and Nubians to create states and recognize official authorities. By 4000 B.C.E. agricultural villages along the Nile were trading regularly with one another and cooperating in building irrigation networks.

The earliest Egyptian and Nubian states were small kingdoms much like those instituted in the Sudan after 5000 B.C.E. It is likely that the notion of divine or semidivine rulers reached Egypt and Nubia from the eastern and central Sudan, where rulers had earlier founded small kingdoms to govern their agricultural and herding communities. In any case, small kingdoms appeared first in southern Egypt and Nubia after 4000 B.C.E. During the following centuries, residents living farther down the Nile (to the north) founded similar states, so that by 3300 B.C.E. small local kingdoms existed throughout Egypt as well as Nubia. As in the earlier Sudanic states, royal servants in these Nile kingdoms routinely accompanied deceased rulers to their graves.

Great Pyramid of the Pharaoh Khufu, completed around 2560 B.C.E. At 481 feet (146.5 meters) high, this was the tallest manmade structure on earth for the next 3800 years.

Photov.com/Pixtal/age fotostock

servants with them to the grave. Egyptians associated the early pharaohs with Horus, the sky god, and they often represented the pharaohs together with a falcon or a hawk, the symbol of Horus. Later they viewed rulers as offspring of Amon, a sun god, so that the pharaoh was a son of the sun. They considered the ruling pharaoh a human sun overseeing affairs on the earth, just as Amon was the sun supervising the larger cosmos, and they believed that after his death the pharaoh actually merged with Amon. Artistic representations also depict pharaohs as enormous figures towering over their human subjects.

The Unification of Egypt

Menes After 3100 B.C.E. Egypt followed a path quite different from those of the smaller Nubian kingdoms. Drawing on agricultural and demographic advantages, Egyptian rulers forged all the territory between the Nile delta and the river's first cataract (a shallow area of whitewater rapids in a river) into a unified kingdom much larger and more powerful than any other Nile state. Tradition suggests that unified rule came to Egypt about 3100 B.C.E. in the person of a conqueror named **Menes** (who was possibly the same man as another early Egyptian ruler called Narmer). Menes was an ambitious minor official from southern Egypt (known as Upper Egypt because the Nile flows north) who rose to power and extended his authority north and into the delta (known as Lower Egypt). According to tradition, Menes founded the city of Memphis, near modern Cairo, which stood at the junction of Upper and Lower Egypt. Memphis served as Menes' capital and eventually became the cultural as well as the political center of ancient Egypt.

Menes and his successors built a centralized state ruled by the pharaoh, the Egyptian king. The title *pharoah* comes from two Egyptian words—*per-ao*—which means "great house." The early pharaohs claimed to be gods living on the earth in human form, the owners and absolute rulers of all the land. In that respect, they continued the tradition of divine kingship inherited from the early agricultural societies of the Sudan. Indeed, as late as 2600 B.C.E., deceased pharaohs took royal

The Archaic Period and the Old Kingdom The power of the pharaohs was greatest during the first millennium of Egyptian history—the eras known as the **Archaic Period** (3100–2660 B.C.E.) and the **Old Kingdom** (2660–2160 B.C.E.). The most enduring symbols of their authority and divine status are the massive pyramids constructed during the Old Kingdom as royal tombs, most of them during the century from 2600 to 2500 B.C.E. These enormous monuments stand today at Giza, near Cairo, as testimony to the pharaohs' ability to marshal Egyptian resources. The largest is the pyramid of Khufu (also known as Cheops), which involved the precise cutting and fitting of 2.3 million limestone blocks weighing up to 15 tons each, with an average weight of 2.5 tons. Scholars estimate that construction of Khufu's pyramid required the services of some eighty-four thousand laborers working eighty days per year (probably during the late fall and winter, when the demand for agricultural labor was light) for twenty years. Recent discoveries of the tombs of many of these workers suggests that the labor force was actually paid for its work rather than coerced. Apart from the laborers, hundreds of architects, engineers, craftsmen, and artists also contributed to the construction of the pyramids.

Relations between Egypt and Nubia Even after the emergence of the strong pharaonic state that took Egypt on a path different from those followed by other Nile societies, the fortunes of Egypt and Nubia remained closely intertwined. Egyptians had strong interests in Nubia for both political and commercial reasons: they were wary of Nubian kingdoms that might threaten Upper Egypt, and they desired products such as gold, ivory, ebony, and precious stones that were available only from southern lands. Meanwhile, Nubians had equally strong interests in Egypt: they wanted to protect

Menes (mee-neez)

Nubian mercenary soldiers in marching formation. Nubian mercenaries were prominent in Egyptian armies and often married Egyptian wives.

Art Media/Heritage Images/The Print Collector/Alamy Stock Photo

their independence from their large and powerful neighbor to the north, and they sought to profit by controlling trade down the Nile.

The Early Kingdom of Kush Tensions led to frequent violence between Egypt and Nubia throughout the Archaic Period and the Old Kingdom. The early **pharaohs** organized at least five military campaigns to Nubia between 3100 and 2600 B.C.E. Pharaonic forces destroyed the Nubian kingdom of Ta-Seti soon after the unification of Egypt, leading to Egyptian domination of Lower Nubia (the land between the first and second cataracts of the Nile) for more than half a millennium, from about 3000 to 2400 B.C.E. That Egyptian presence in the north forced Nubian leaders to concentrate their efforts at political organization farther to the south in Upper Nubia. By about 2500 B.C.E. they had established a powerful kingdom, called **Kush,** with a capital at Kerma, about 700 kilometers (435 miles) south of Aswan. Though not as powerful

as united Egypt, the kingdom of Kush was a formidable and wealthy state that dominated the upper reaches of the Nile and occasionally threatened southern Egypt.

In spite of constant tension and frequent hostilities, numerous diplomats and explorers traveled from Egypt to Nubia in search of political alliances and commercial relationships, and many Nubians sought improved fortunes in Egypt. Around 2300 B.C.E., for example, the Egyptian explorer Harkhuf made four expeditions to Nubia. He returned from one of his trips with a caravan of some three hundred donkeys bearing exotic products from tropical Africa, as well as a dancing dwarf, and his cargo stimulated Egyptian desire for trade with southern lands (see *Sources from the Past* on p. 54). Meanwhile, Nubian peoples looked for opportunities to pursue in Egypt. By the end of the Old Kingdom, Nubian mercenaries were quite prominent in Egyptian armies. Indeed, they often married Egyptian women and assimilated into Egyptian society.

What's Left Out? ▮▮ ▮▮ ▮ ▮ ▮

Because of extensive tomb inscriptions, we know quite a lot about the age of Egyptian Imperialism, particularly during the reign of Tuthmosis III (r. 1479–1425 B.C.E.), who created the largest Egyptian Empire of all. But there is still much we don't know about some of the peoples and empires that Egyptian armies fought against and conquered during this period. One such empire was that of the mysterious Mitanni, who dominated large regions of northern Mesopotamia and Syria. Recently archaeologists have uncovered the ruins of a substantial Mitanni palace, built close to the banks of the Tigris River. The palace was occupied for perhaps four hundred years and was decorated with colorful murals. Archaeologists hope that excavations will reveal much more about the politics, economy, and social structure of the Mitanni. A severe drought led to the drying up of this section of the dammed Tigris River, allowing archaeologists an unprecedented opportunity to gain deeper insight into the world of the Mitanni. This was a powerful state that Tuthmosis III was apparently so determined to crush that he became the first pharaoh to lead Egyptian forces across the Euphrates River to do so, and the Euphrates is a long way away from the heartland of ancient Egypt.

Source: https://www.sciencealert.com/archaeologists-uncover-a-grand-mysterious-palace-on-the-tigris-river.

Turmoil and Empire

The Hyksos After the Old Kingdom declined, Egyptians experienced considerable and sometimes unsettling change. A particularly challenging era of change followed from their encounters with a Semitic people whom Egyptians called the **Hyksos** ("foreign rulers"). Little information survives about the Hyksos, but it is clear that they were horse-riding nomads. Indeed, they probably introduced horses to Egypt, and their horse-drawn chariots, which they learned about from Hittites and Mesopotamians, provided them with a significant military advantage over Egyptian forces. They enjoyed an advantage also in their weaponry: the Hyksos used bronze weapons and bronze-tipped arrows, whereas Egyptians relied mostly on wooden weapons and arrows with stone heads. About 1674 B.C.E. the Hyksos captured Memphis and levied tribute throughout Egypt, bringing to an end the Middle Kingdom Period of Egyptian history.

Hyksos rule provoked a strong reaction especially in Upper Egypt, where disgruntled nobles organized revolts against the foreigners. They adopted horses and chariots for their own military forces. They also equipped their troops with bronze weapons. Working from Thebes and later from Memphis, Egyptian leaders gradually pushed the Hyksos out of the Nile delta and founded a powerful state known as the New Kingdom (1550–1070 B.C.E.).

The New Kingdom Pharaohs of the New Kingdom presided over a prosperous and productive

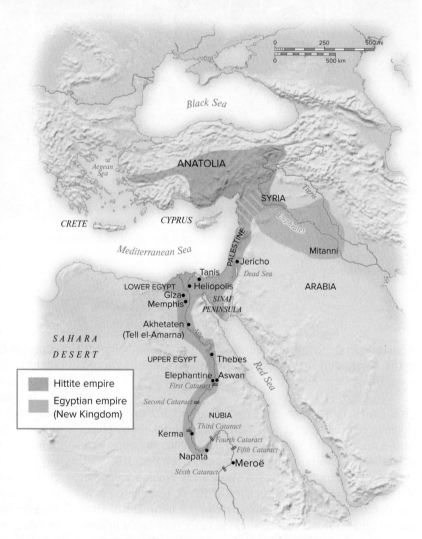

MAP 3.2 Imperial Egypt, 1400 B.C.E.

Compare the territory ruled by the New Kingdom with the earlier kingdom of Egypt as represented in Map 3.1.

What environmental and political factors help explain the difference in size between the Old and New Kingdoms?

A wall painting from the tomb of an Egyptian imperial official in Nubia depicts a delegation of Nubians bringing tribute in the forms of exotic beasts, animal skins, and rings of gold. Why might these unusual gifts have been welcome tribute for Egyptians?
Robert B. Partridge (1951–2011)/Peartree Publishing and Design, Manchester UK

society. Agricultural surpluses supported a population of perhaps four million people as well as an army and an elaborate bureaucracy that divided responsibilities among different offices. One department oversaw the court and royal estates, for example, while others dealt with military forces, state-recognized religious cults, the treasury, agricultural affairs, local government, and the administration of conquered territories. Pharaohs of the New Kingdom did not build enormous pyramids as did their predecessors of the Old Kingdom, but they erected numerous temples, palaces, and monumental statues to demonstrate their power and authority.

Egyptian Imperialism Pharaohs of the New Kingdom also worked to extend Egyptian authority well beyond the Nile valley and the delta. After expelling the Hyksos, they sought to prevent new invasions by seizing control of regions that might pose threats in the future. Most vigorous of the New Kingdom pharaohs was **Tuthmosis III** (reigned 1479–1425 B.C.E.). After seventeen campaigns that he personally led to Palestine and Syria, Tuthmosis dominated the coastal regions of the eastern Mediterranean as well as north Africa. Rulers of the New Kingdom also turned their attention to the south and restored Egyptian dominance in Nubia. Campaigning as far south as the Nile's fifth cataract, Egyptian armies destroyed Kerma, the capital of the kingdom of Kush, and crushed a series of small Nubian states that had

arisen during the period of Hyksos rule. Thus for half a millennium Egypt was an imperial power throughout much of the eastern Mediterranean basin and southwest Asia as well as most of the Nile River valley.

After the New Kingdom, Egypt entered a long period of political and military decline. Just as Hyksos rule provoked a reaction in Egypt, Egyptian rule provoked reactions in the regions subdued by pharaonic armies. Local resistance drove Egyptian forces out of Nubia and southwest Asia, then Kushite and Assyrian armies invaded Egypt itself.

The Revived Kingdom of Kush By 1100 B.C.E. Egyptian forces were in full retreat from Nubia. After they vacated the region, about the tenth century B.C.E., Nubian leaders organized a new kingdom of Kush with a capital at Napata, located just below the Nile's fourth cataract. By the eighth century B.C.E., rulers of this revived kingdom of Kush were powerful enough to invade Egypt, which at the time was in the grip of religious and factional disputes. **King Kashta** conquered Thebes about 760 B.C.E. and founded a Kushite dynasty that ruled Egypt for almost a century. Kashta's successors consolidated Kushite authority in Upper Egypt, claimed the title of pharaoh, and eventually extended their rule to the Nile delta and beyond.

Tuthmosis (tuh-MOE-sis)

SOURCES FROM THE PAST

Harkhuf's Expeditions to Nubia

Many Egyptians wrote brief autobiographies that they or their descendants had carved into their tombs. One of the most famous autobiographies from the Old Kingdom is that of Harkhuf, a royal official who became governor of Upper Egypt before 2300 B.C.E. The inscriptions in his tomb mention his four expeditions to Nubia to seek valuable items and report on political conditions there. The inscriptions also include the text of a letter from the boy-pharaoh Neferkare expressing his appreciation for Harkhuf's fourth expedition and his desire to see the dancing dwarf that Harkhuf brought back from Nubia.

Pharaoh Mernera, my Lord, sent me with my father Ara to the Nubian region of Amam, to open up a road into this country. I completed the journey in seven months. I brought back gifts of all kinds from that place and received great praise for this. The Pharaoh sent me a second time by myself. I came back after eight months and brought back very large quantities of offerings from the country . . . there was very great praise to me for it. His Majesty sent me a second time by myself . . . I came back . . . in a period of eight months . . . and I brought very large quantities of offerings from this country. Never were brought such things to this land . . . His Majesty sent me a third time to Amam . . . I came back . . . with three hundred asses laden with incense, ebony, heknu, grain, panther skins, ivory . . . and valuable products of every kind.

> What do you think Mernera means by the word "offerings" here?

[The letter from Pharaoh Nefekare to Harkuf]: Royal despatch to the . . . governor of the caravan, Herkhuf. I have understood the words of this letter, which you have written to the king in his chamber to make him to know that you have returned in peace from Amam, together with the soldiers who were with thee. You say in this . . . letter that there have been brought back . . . beautiful offerings of all kinds . . . like the pygmy whom the seal-bearer of the god Baurtet brought back from Punt in the time of Assa. Thou say to [my] Majesty, "The like of him has never been brought back by any other person who has visited Amam."

Behold, every year you perform what thy Lord wishes and praises. Behold, you pass your days and nights meditating about doing what thy Lord orders, wishes, and praises. And His Majesty will confer on you so many splendid honors, which shall give renown to your grandson for ever, that all the people shall say when they have heard what [my] Majesty hath done for thee, "Was there ever anything like this that has been done for . . . Harkhuf when he came back from Amam because of the attention . . . he displayed in doing what his Lord commanded, and wished for, and praised?"

> Why does the Pharaoh want to award such splendid honors to Mernera?

Come down the river at once to the Capital. Bring with you this pygmy whom you have brought from the Land of the Spirits, alive, strong, and healthy, to dance the dance of the god, and to cheer and gratify the heart of the King of the South and North . . . When he comes down with you in the boat, cause trustworthy men to be about him on both sides of the boat, to prevent him from falling into the water. When he is asleep at night cause trustworthy men to sleep by his side on his bedding.

See [that he is there] ten times [each] night. [My] Majesty wishes to see this pygmy more than any offering of the countries of Ba and Punt. If when you arrive at the Capital, this pygmy who is with you is alive, and strong, and in good health, [My] Majesty will confer upon you a greater honor than that which was conferred upon the bearer of the seal Baurtet in the time of Assa, and as great is the wish of [My] Majesty to see this pygmy orders have been brought to . . . the overseer of the priests, the governor of the town . . . to arrange that rations for him shall be drawn from every station of supply, and from every temple that has not been exempted.

For Further Reflection

■ Why would pharaohs have sent Harkhuf on the expeditions described in the first paragraph?

■ What valuable item in particular is the boy-pharaoh Neferkare most interested in?

■ What do these inscriptions tell us about the relationship between Egypt and Nubia and the ways in which Egyptians increased their knowledge of Nubia?

Source: E. A. Wallis Budge, *The Literature of the Ancient Egyptians.* London, 1914; J. M. Dent & Sons Limited, Aldine House, Bedford Street, W. C. Project Guttenberg.

Updated with modern language by the textbook authors.

Meanwhile, as Kushites pushed into Egypt from the south, Assyrian armies equipped with iron weapons bore down from the north. During the mid-seventh century B.C.E., while building their vast empire, the Assyrians invaded Egypt, campaigned as far south as Thebes, drove out the Kushites, and subjected Egypt to Assyrian rule. After the mid-sixth century B.C.E., like Mesopotamia, Egypt fell to a series of foreign conquerors who built vast empires throughout southwest Asia and the eastern Mediterranean region, including Egypt and north Africa.

THE FORMATION OF COMPLEX SOCIETIES AND SOPHISTICATED CULTURAL TRADITIONS

As in Mesopotamia, cities and the congregation of dense populations encouraged the emergence of specialized labor in the early agricultural societies of Africa. This development was particularly noticeable in Egypt, but specialized labor was a prominent feature also of societies in the southern Nile River valley. Clearly defined social classes emerged throughout the Nile valley, and both Egyptians and Nubians built patriarchal societies that placed authority largely in the hands of adult males. The Egyptian economy was especially productive and, because of both its prosperity and its geographic location, Egypt figured as a center of trade, linking lands in southwest Asia, the eastern Mediterranean, and sub-Saharan Africa. Meanwhile, as in the river valleys of southwest Asia, the Nile valley was a site of sophisticated cultural development. Writing systems appeared in both Egypt and Nubia, and writing soon became a principal medium of literary expression and religious reflection as well as a means for preserving governmental records and commercial information.

The Emergence of Cities and Stratified Societies

Cities of the Nile Valley: Egypt Cities were not as prominent in early societies of the Nile River valley as they were in ancient Mesopotamia. In the Nile valley, populations clustered mostly in numerous agricultural villages that traded regularly with their neighbors up and down the river. Nevertheless,

Ancient pyramids and modern reconstructions at the site of the Nubian capital of Meroe.
hecke61/Shutterstock

several major cities emerged and guided affairs in both Egypt and Nubia. According to tradition, the conqueror Menes founded Memphis as early as 3100 B.C.E. Located at the head of the Nile delta, Memphis was a convenient site for a capital: Menes and many later pharaohs ruled over a unified Egypt from Memphis. Besides the capital, other cities played important roles in Egyptian affairs. Thebes, for example, was a prominent political center even before the unification of Egypt. After unification, Thebes became the administrative center of Upper Egypt, and several pharaohs even took the city as their capital. Heliopolis, meaning "City of the Sun," was the headquarters of a sun cult near Memphis and a principal cultural center of ancient Egypt. Founded about 2900 B.C.E., Heliopolis reached the height of its influence during the New Kingdom, when it was the site of an enormous temple to the sun god Re. Yet another important city was Tanis on the Nile delta. At least by the time of the Middle Kingdom, and perhaps even earlier, Tanis was a bustling port and Egypt's gateway to the Mediterranean.

Cities of the Nile Valley: Nubia Nubian cities are not as well known as those of Egypt, but written records and archaeological excavations both make it clear that powerful and prosperous cities emerged in the southern Nile valley as well as in Egypt. The most prominent Nubian cities of ancient times were Kerma, Napata, and Meroë. Kerma, located just above the Nile's third cataract, was the capital of the earliest kingdom of Kush. For a millennium after its foundation about 2500 B.C.E., Kerma dominated both river and overland routes between Egypt to the north and Sudanic regions to the south. The fortunes of Kerma waxed and waned as Egypt and Kush contended with each other for power in Nubia, but it remained an influential site until its destruction about 1450 B.C.E. by the aggressive armies of Egypt's expansive New Kingdom. About the tenth century B.C.E., Napata emerged as the new political center of Nubia. Located just below the Nile's fourth cataract, Napata was more distant from Egypt than Kerma and hence less vulnerable to threats from the north. After King Kashta and his successors conquered Egypt, Napata enjoyed tremendous prosperity because of the wealth that flowed up the Nile to the Kushite capital. About the middle of the seventh century B.C.E., after Assyrian forces expelled the Kushites and asserted imperial control in Egypt, the capital of Kush moved farther south, this time to Meroë, located between the Nile's fifth and sixth cataracts about 1,600 kilometers (1,000 miles) from the southern border of Egypt. Meroë presided over a flourishing kingdom of Kush that enjoyed great prosperity because of its participation in Nile trade networks until its gradual decline after about 100 C.E.

Social Classes In Egypt and Nubia alike, ancient cities were centers of considerable accumulated wealth, which encouraged the development of social distinctions and hierarchies. Like the Mesopotamians, ancient Egyptians recognized a series of well-defined social classes. Egyptian peasants and slaves played roles in society similar to those of their Mesopotamian counterparts: they supplied the hard labor that made complex agricultural society possible. The organization of the ruling classes, however, differed considerably between Mesopotamia and Egypt. Instead of a series of urban kings, as in Mesopotamia, Egyptians recognized the pharaoh as a supreme central ruler. Because the pharaoh was theoretically an absolute ruler, Egyptian society had little room for a noble class like that of Mesopotamia. Instead of depending on nobles who owed their positions to their birth, Egypt relied on professional military forces and an elaborate bureaucracy of administrators and tax collectors who served the central government. Thus, in Egypt much more than in Mesopotamia, individuals of common birth could attain high positions in society through government service.

Surviving information illuminates Egyptian society much better than Nubian, but it is clear that Nubia also was the site of a complex, hierarchical society in ancient times. Meroë, for example, was home to government officials, priests, craftsmen, merchants, laborers, and slaves. Cemeteries associated with Nubian cities clearly reveal social and economic distinctions. Tombs of wealthy and powerful individuals were often elaborate structures—comfortable dwelling places tastefully decorated with paintings and filled with expensive goods such as gold jewelry, gems, fine furniture, and abundant supplies of food. In keeping with the ancient traditions of Sudanic kingship, many royal tombs became the final resting places also of servants ritually executed so that they could tend to the needs of their master in death. Graves of commoners were much simpler, although they often contained jewelry, pottery, personal ornaments, and other goods to accompany the departed.

Patriarchal Society Like their Mesopotamian counterparts, both Egyptian and Nubian peoples built patriarchal societies that vested authority over public and private affairs in their men. Women of upper elite classes oversaw the domestic work of household servants. Below the level of the upper elites, even in wealthy households, women routinely performed domestic work, which included growing vegetables, grinding grain, baking bread, brewing beer, spinning thread, and weaving textiles. Elite men enjoyed comfortable positions as scribes or government officials, while men of lower classes worked as agricultural laborers, potters, carpenters, craftsmen, or fishermen. Both men and women were able to accumulate property, including slaves, and pass wealth along to their children. Men alone, however, were the governors of households and the larger society as a whole. With rare exceptions men were the rulers in both Egyptian and Nubian states, and decisions about government policies and public affairs rested mostly in men's hands.

Women's Influence in Egypt and Nubia Yet women made their influence felt in ancient Egyptian and Nubian societies much more than in contemporary Mesopotamia. In Egypt, women of the royal family frequently served as regents for young rulers. Many royal women also used their status to influence policy, sometimes going so far as to participate in plots to manipulate affairs in favor of their sons or even in palace rebellions seeking to unseat a pharaoh. In one notable case, a woman took power as pharaoh herself: **Queen Hatshepsut** (reigned 1473–1458 B.C.E.) served as coruler with her stepson Tuthmosis III. The notion of a female ruler was unfamiliar and perhaps somewhat unsettling to many Egyptians. In an effort to present her in unthreatening guise, a monumental statue of Queen Hatshepsut depicts her wearing the stylized beard traditionally associated with the pharaohs. In Nubia, in contrast, there is abundant evidence of many women rulers in the kingdom of Kush, particularly during the period when Meroë was the capital. Some ruled in their own right, others reigned jointly with male kings, and many governed also in the capacity of a regent known as the *kandake* (root of the name Candace). Meanwhile, other women wielded considerable power as priestesses in the numerous religious cults observed in Egypt and Nubia. A few women also obtained a formal education and worked as scribes who prepared administrative and legal documents for governments and private parties.

Economic Specialization and Trade

With the formation of complex, city-based societies, peoples of the Nile valley were able to draw on a rapidly expanding stock of human skills. Bronze metallurgy made its way from Mesopotamia to both Egypt and Nubia, and Sudanic peoples independently developed a technology of iron production that eventually spread to most parts of sub-Saharan Africa. Pottery, textile manufacture, woodworking, leather production, stonecutting, and masonry all became distinct occupations in cities throughout the Nile valley. Specialized labor and the invention of efficient transportation technologies encouraged the development of trade networks that linked the Nile valley to a much larger world.

Bronze Metallurgy Nile societies were much slower than their Mesopotamian counterparts to adopt metal tools and weapons. Whereas the production of bronze flourished in Mesopotamia by 3000 B.C.E., use of bronze implements became widespread in Egypt only after the seventeenth century B.C.E., when the Hyksos used bronze weapons to impose their authority on the Nile delta. After expelling the Hyksos, Egyptians equipped their forces with bronze weapons, and the imperial armies of Tuthmosis and other pharaohs of the New Kingdom carried up-to-date bronze weapons like those used in Mesopotamia and neighboring lands. As in Mesopotamia and regions of ancient Eurasia, the high cost of copper and tin kept bronze out of the hands of most people. Royal workshops closely monitored supplies of the valuable metal: officers weighed the bronze tools issued to workers at royal tombs, for example, to ensure that craftsmen did not shave slivers off them and divert expensive metal to personal uses.

Iron Metallurgy Bronze was even less prominent in Nubian societies than in Egypt. Nubia produced little bronze because the region was poor in copper and tin and so relied on imports from the north. During the centuries after 1000 B.C.E., however, the southern Nile societies made up for their lack of

---

Hatshepsut (hat-SHEP-soot)

A wall painting produced about 1300 B.C.E. shows Egyptian goldsmiths fashioning jewelry and decorative objects for elite patrons. Early experience with gold metallurgy prepared craftsmen to work with bronze and iron when knowledge of those metals reached Egypt. DEA/G. DAGLI ORTI/De Agostini/ Getty Images

Connecting the Sources

Thinking about non-elites in the ancient Egyptian past

In order to write about the past, historians must find and interpret **primary sources**. Primary sources can include material objects, archaeological evidence, oral traditions, texts (including official documents, letters, accounts, newspapers), or images. They provide the evidence on which historical narratives rest. This exercise highlights some of the challenges of interpreting original primary sources by asking you to consider the kinds of contextual information you might need in order to interpret such documents accurately and by asking you to consider what individual documents can and cannot tell you.

The problem   Writing about the ancient past poses multiple problems for historians. Among these is the problem of *preservation* because many potential sources for historical documentation simply have not survived over thousands of years. For textual sources there is also the problem of *language and script* because ancient societies used languages and forms of writing very different from our own. In addition, even when sources have been preserved and historians are able to decipher ancient texts, there is the problem of *selectivity*—meaning that the sources most likely to have been preserved were those generated by elites.

Fortunately for historians, ancient Egyptian peoples left many textual, material, and archaeological sources behind. The arid climate helped to preserve many textual sources written on papyrus, while the use of stone allowed many monuments to withstand thousands of years of exposure to the elements. Despite the abundance of primary sources, however, much less is known about the lives of everyday Egyptians than is known about Egyptian monarchs, nobles, political elites, and religious authorities. Historians know that most Egyptians were farmers, but few surviving sources tell their story from their own perspective. In the following two documents, which were generated centuries apart, think about what historians can and cannot infer about the lives of non-elites in ancient Egypt.

The documents   Read the documents below, and consider carefully the questions that follow.

Document 1:

Stela (inscribed stone) from the tomb of a man named Mentuhotep, from the 11th Dynasty (2133–1991 B.C.E.). On the original Stela Mentuhotep is depicted with his parents, children and servants. The inscription reads as follows:

(1) *O ye who live and are upon the earth and who shall pass by this tomb, who love life and hate death, say ye: "May Osiris, head of the Westerners [people of the underworld], glorify Mentuhotep."*

(2) *Now I was first among my contemporaries, the foreman of my gang [man of the people], one who discovered the statement about which he had been asked, and answered (it) appropriately,*

(3) *cool(-headed), one who obtained bread in its (due) season, one whose (own) counsel replaced for him a mother at home, a father making the family fortune (??), and a son of good disposition, one whom his (own) nature instructed as (it were) a child growing up with its father.*

(4) *Now although I was become an orphan, I acquired cattle and got oxen (?) and developed my business in goats; I built a house and excavated a (garden-) pond, the priest Mentuhotep.*

> To what does Mentuhotep mostly attribute his success in life?

Translated by Alan Gardiner. From W. M. F. Petrie, *Tombs of the Courtiers and Oxyrhynkhos*, 1922.

Document 2:

The following comes from a declaration freeing slaves, from the 20th Dynasty (1185–1070 B.C.E.).

Year 28, 1st month of Inundation, day 10, under the Majesty of the King of Upper and Lower Egypt, Ramesses (XI). On this day, declaration made by the stable-master Neb-nufe and his wife the musician of Seth of Spermeru Rennufe, to wit:

"We purchased the female slave Dini-huiry and she gave birth to these three children, one male and two female, in all three. And I [i.e., Rennufe] took them and nourished them and brought them up, and I have reached this day with them without their doing evil towards me, but they dealt well with me, I having no son or daughter except them. And the stable-master Padiu entered my house and took Ta-Amon-no, their elder sister, to wife, he being related to me and being my younger brother. And I accepted him for her and he is with her at this day.

"Now behold, I have made her a freewoman of the land of Pharaoh, and if she bears either son or daughter, they shall be freemen of the land of Pharaoh in exactly the same way, they being with the stable-master Padiu, this younger brother of mine. And the children shall be with their elder sister in the house of Padiu, this stable-master, this younger brother of mine, and today I make him a son of mine exactly like them."

And she said: "As Amun endures, and the Ruler endures, I (hereby) make the people whom I have put on record freemen of the land of Pharaoh,

"And if I have fields in the country, or if I have any property in the world, or if I have merchants (?), these shall be divided among my four children, Padiu being one of them. And as for these matters of which I have spoken, they are entrusted in their entirety to Padiu, this son of mine, who dealt well with me when I was a widow and when my husband had died."

Before many and numerous witnesses . . . (both men and women). ————————

> Why does Rennufe want to free the three slaves she owns?

Alan H. Gardiner, Adoption Extraordinary, *JEA* 26 (1940) 23–29. Used with permission.

Questions

1. What can these sources definitively tell you about the lives of the people who produced them? What facts can be gleaned from these sources?
2. In Document 1, does the inscription indicate that the social mobility described by Mentuhotep was common or uncommon during the 11th Dynasty?
3. Also in Document 1, do the figures on the right offer clues about the daily lives of people in Mentuhotep's household?
4. Does Document 2 offer any clues about the experience of slavery in Egypt during the 20th Dynasty?
5. Also in Document 2, does this document allow speculation about the status of women in Egypt during the 20th Dynasty? If so, in what ways?
6. Taking both documents together, what can they tell us about the experience of non-elites in ancient Egypt? What kinds of additional contextual information would you need in order to answer this question more fully?

   Sources such as these can give historians tantalizing evidence about the lives of everyday people, even in the ancient past. To understand them accurately, however, historians must place individual sources in their larger historical context in order to decide whether they represent broad trends or historical exceptions.

Source Website: **Document 1:** http://www.reshafim.org.il/ad/egypt/texts/mentuhotep_stela.htm. **Document 2:** http://www.reshafim.org.il/ad/egypt/texts/adoption_papyrus.htm

A wooden model found in a tomb shows how Egyptians traveled up and down the Nile River. Produced about 2000 B.C.E., this sculpture depicts a relatively small boat with a mast, sail, rudder, and poles to push the vessel through shallow waters as the figure in front gauges the water's depth. Many wall and tomb paintings confirm the accuracy of this model.
Werner Forman Archive/British Museum, London/Heritage Image Partnership Ltd/Alamy Stock Photo

bronze with the emergence of large-scale production of iron. The Hittites had developed techniques for forging iron in Anatolia about 1300 B.C.E., but **iron metallurgy** in Africa may have arisen independently from local experimentation with iron ores, which are plentiful in sub-Saharan Africa. The earliest traces of African iron production discovered by archaeologists date from about 1000 B.C.E., in the Nok culture of modern Nigeria, then soon after 900 B.C.E. in the Great Lakes region of east Africa (modern-day Burundi and Rwanda), and also on the southern side of Lake Chad (in modern-day Cameroon). It is possible that African peoples produced iron before 1000 B.C.E., although the evidence for this is ambiguous and controversial. During the first millennium B.C.E. iron metallurgy quickly spread throughout most of sub-Saharan Africa. Furnaces churned out iron implements both in Nubia and in west Africa at least by 500 B.C.E. Meroë in particular became a site of large-scale iron production. Indeed, archaeologists who excavated Meroë in the early twentieth century C.E. found enormous mounds of slag still remaining from ancient times.

Transportation   Nile craftsmen also worked from the early days of agricultural society to devise efficient means of transportation. Within Egypt, the Nile River greatly facilitated transportation, and Egyptians traveled up and down the river before 3500 B.C.E. Because the Nile flows north, boats could

ride the currents from Upper to Lower Egypt. Meanwhile, prevailing winds blow almost year-round from the north, so that by raising a sail, boats could easily make their way upriver from Lower to Upper Egypt. Soon after 3000 B.C.E. Egyptians sailed beyond the Nile into the Mediterranean, and by about 2000 B.C.E. they had thoroughly explored the waters of the Red Sea, the Gulf of Aden, and the western portion of the Arabian Sea. Egyptians also made use of Mesopotamian-style wheeled vehicles for local transport, and they relied on donkey caravans for transport between the Nile valley and ports on the Red Sea.

In Nubia, navigation on the Nile was less convenient than in Egypt because unnavigable cataracts made it necessary to transport goods overland before continuing on the river. Moreover, sailing ships heading upriver found it difficult to negotiate a long stretch of the Nile around the fourth cataract because winds blow the same direction as the currents. Thus, although Nubian societies were able to make some use of the Nile for purposes of transportation, they had to rely more than Egyptians on overland transport by wheeled vehicles and donkey caravan.

Trade Networks   In both Egypt and Nubia, specialized labor and efficient means of transportation encouraged the development of long-distance trade. Egypt was in special need of trade because the land enjoys few natural resources other

A drawing of a painting that was found in the tomb of Queen Hatshepsut, c. 1450 B.C.E. The illustration shows a superbly designed commercial vessel with workers carrying exotic trade goods from the Land of Punt onboard, ready to be taken back to Egypt.
INTERFOTO/History/Alamy Stock Photo

than the waters of the Nile. Irregular exchanges of goods between Egypt and Nubia took place in early times, perhaps 4000 B.C.E. or even before. By the time of the Old Kingdom, trade flowed regularly between Egypt and Nubia. The cities of Aswan and Elephantine at the southern border of Egypt reflected that trade in their very names: Aswan took its name from the ancient Egyptian word *swene,* meaning "trade," and Elephantine owed its name to the large quantities of elephant ivory that passed through it while traveling down the Nile from Nubia to Egypt. Apart from ivory, exotic African goods such as ebony, leopard skins, ostrich feathers, gemstones, gold, and slaves went down the Nile in exchange for pottery, wine, honey, and finished products from Egypt. Among the most prized Egyptian exports were fine linen textiles woven from the flax that flourished in the Nile valley as well as high-quality decorative and ornamental objects such as boxes, furniture, and jewelry produced by skilled artisans. Commerce linked Egypt and Nubia throughout ancient times, even when tensions or hostilities complicated relations between the two societies.

Egyptian merchants looked north as well as south. They traded with Mesopotamians as early as 3500 B.C.E., and after 3000 B.C.E. they were active throughout the eastern Mediterranean basin. Egyptian commerce in the Mediterranean sometimes involved enormous cargoes of goods. Since Egypt has few trees, for example, all wood came from abroad. Pharaohs especially prized aromatic cedar for their tombs, and Egyptian ships regularly imported huge loads from Lebanon. One record of about 2600 B.C.E. mentions an expedition of forty ships hauling cedar logs. In exchange for cedar Egyptians offered gold, silver, linen textiles, leather goods, and dried foods such as lentils.

Maritime Trade: Egypt and Punt After the establishment of the New Kingdom, Egyptians also traded through the Red Sea and the Gulf of Aden with an east African land they called **Punt**—probably located somewhere in modern-day Somalia and Ethiopia. From Punt they imported gold, ebony, ivory, cattle, aromatics, and slaves. The tomb of Queen Hatshepsut bears detailed illustrations of a trading expedition to Punt about 1450 B.C.E. Paintings in the tomb show large Egyptian ships bearing jewelry, tools, and weapons to Punt and then loading the exotic products of the southern land, including apes, monkeys, dogs, a panther, and myrrh trees with their roots carefully bound in bags. Thus, as was the case in Mesopotamia, specialization of labor and efficient technologies of transportation not only quickened the economies of complex societies in Egypt and Nubia but also encouraged their interaction with peoples of distant lands.

Early Writing in the Nile Valley

Hieroglyphic Writing Writing appeared in Egypt at least by 3200 B.C.E., possibly as a result of Mesopotamian influence. As in Mesopotamia, the earliest Egyptian writing was pictographic, but Egyptians soon supplemented their pictographs with symbols representing sounds and ideas. Early

Greek visitors to Egypt marveled at the large and handsome pictographs that adorned Egyptian monuments and buildings. Since the symbols were particularly prominent on temples, the visitors called them **hieroglyphs,** from two Greek words meaning "holy inscriptions." Quite apart from monument inscriptions, hieroglyphic writing survives on sheets of papyrus, a paper-like material fashioned from the insides of papyrus reeds, which flourish along the Nile River. The hot, dry climate of Egypt has preserved not only mummified bodies but also large numbers of papyrus texts bearing administrative and commercial records as well as literary and religious texts.

Hieroglyphs from the tomb of New Kingdom Pharaoh Seti I (r. 1290–1279 B.C.E.).
Peter Horree/Alamy Stock Photo

Although striking and dramatic, hieroglyphs were also somewhat cumbersome. Egyptians went to the trouble of using hieroglyphs for formal writing and monument inscriptions, but for everyday affairs they commonly relied on the **hieratic** ("priestly") script, a simplified, cursive form of hieroglyphs. Hieratic appeared in the early centuries of the third millennium B.C.E., and Egyptians made extensive use of the script for more than three thousand years, from about 2600 B.C.E. to 600 C.E. Hieratic largely disappeared after the middle of the first millennium C.E., when Egyptians adapted the Greek alphabet to their language and developed alphabetic scripts known as the demotic ("popular") and Coptic ("Egyptian") scripts. Hieratic, demotic, and Coptic scripts all survive mostly in papyrus texts but occasionally also in inscriptions.

Education Formal education and literacy brought handsome rewards in ancient Egypt. The privileged life of a scribe comes across clearly in a short work known as "The Satire of the Trades." Written by a scribe exhorting his son to study diligently, the work detailed all the miseries associated with eighteen different professions: metalsmiths stunk like fish; potters grubbed in the mud like pigs; fishermen ran the risk of sudden death in the jaws of the Nile's ferocious crocodiles. Only the scribe led a comfortable, honorable, and dignified life.

Nubian peoples spoke their own languages, although many individuals were fully conversant in Egyptian as well as their native tongues, but all early writing in Nubia was Egyptian hieroglyphic writing. Indeed, over the centuries Egypt wielded great cultural influence in Nubia, especially during times when Egyptian political and military influence was strong in southern lands. Egyptian political and military officials often erected monuments and inscribed them with accounts in hieroglyphics

of their deeds in Nubia. Similarly, Egyptian priests traveled regularly to Nubia, organized temples devoted to Egyptian gods, and promoted their beliefs in hieroglyphics. Egyptian influence was very strong in Nubia also during the eighth and seventh centuries B.C.E. when the kings of Kush ruled Egypt as pharaohs and sponsored extensive trade, travel, and communication between Egypt and Nubia.

Meroitic Writing Nubian inscriptions continued to appear in Egyptian hieroglyphic writing as late as the first century C.E. After about the fifth century B.C.E., however, Egyptian cultural influence declined noticeably in Nubia. After the transfer of the Kushite capital from Napata to Meroë, Nubian scribes even devised an alphabetic script for the **Meroitic** language. They borrowed Egyptian hieroglyphs but used them to represent sounds rather than ideas and so created a flexible writing system. Many Meroitic inscriptions survive, both on monuments and on papyrus. To date, however, scholars have not been able to understand Meroitic writing. Although they have ascertained the sound values of the alphabet, the Meroitic language itself is so different from other known languages that no one has been able to decipher Meroitic texts.

Religion in Egypt and Nubia

Amon and Re Like their counterparts in other world regions, Egyptians and Nubians believed that deities played prominent roles in the world and that proper cultivation of the gods was an important community responsibility. The principal gods revered in ancient Egypt were Amon and Re. **Amon** was originally a local Theban deity associated with the sun, creation, fertility, and reproductive forces, and **Re** was a sun god worshiped at Heliopolis. During the Old Kingdom, priests associated the two gods with each other and honored them in the combined cult of Amon-Re. At Heliopolis, a massive temple complex supported priests who tended to the cult of Amon-Re and studied the heavens for astronomical purposes. When Egypt became an imperial power during the New Kingdom, some devotees suggested that Amon-Re might even be a universal god who presided over all the earth.

Aten and Monotheism For a brief period the cult of Amon-Re faced a monotheistic challenge from the god **Aten,** another deity associated with the sun. Aten's champion was Pharaoh Amenhotep IV (reigned 1353–1335 B.C.E.), who changed his name to Akhenaten in honor of his preferred deity. Akhenaten considered Aten the world's "sole god, like

hieroglyph (heye-ruh-GLIF)
Akhenaten (ahk-eh-NAH-ton)

SOURCES FROM THE PAST

Hymn to Osiris

According to myth, Osiris was murdered by his evil brother Seth, and his dismembered body was scattered throughout the land. Osiris' wife retrieved the parts and gave her husband a proper burial, an act that so impressed the gods they bestowed upon Osiris an immortal life as a god of the underworld. The Cult of Osiris worshipped him as the source of the Nile and also as the judge of human souls after death. The Hymn to Osiris demonstrates the respect the gods, particularly Ra, had for Osiris, and also his role in ensuring that the Nile continued to flow, so that Egyptians could continue to enjoy the fruits of its bounty.

"Praise be unto you, you who extends your arms, who lies asleep on your side, who lies on the sand, the Lord of the earth, the divine mummy. . . . You are the Child of the Earth Serpent, of great age. Ra . . . shines upon your body, when you lie on your bed in the form of Seker, so that he may drive away the darkness that shrouds you, and may infuse light in your two eyes. He passes a long period of time shining upon you, and sheds tears over you. The earth rests upon your shoulders, and its corners rest upon you as far as the four pillars of heaven. If you move yourself, the earth quakes, for you are great . . . The Nile appears out of the sweat of your two hands. You breathe forth the air that is in your throat into the nostrils of men; divine is that thing whereon they live. Through your nostrils subsist the flowers, the herbage, the reeds, the barley, the wheat, and the plants whereon men live. If canals are dug and houses and temples are built, and great statues are dragged along, and lands are ploughed up, and tombs and funerary monuments are made, they all rest upon you. It is you who makes them. They are upon your back. They are more than can be described in writing. There is no vacant space on your back, they all lie on your back, and yet you do not say "I am over weighted." You are the father and mother of men and women, they live by your breath, they eat the flesh of your members. Primeval God is your name."

> What does this passage suggest about the importance of the Nile River to the Egyptians?

> What does this passage tell us about the importance of agriculture to the Egyptians?

For Further Reflection

■ What is the relationship between Osiris and Ra, as described in the passage?

■ What is the relationship between Osiris and the Nile River, whose annual flood was crucial to the success of Egyptian civilization?

■ What is the role of humans in ensuring the success of the annual flood?

Source: E. A. Wallis Budge, *The Literature of the Ancient Egyptians.* London, 1914; J. M. Dent & Sons Limited, Aldine House, Bedford Street, W. C. Project Guttenberg.

Updated with modern language by the textbook authors.

---

whom there is no other." Thus, unlike the priests of Amon-Re, most of whom viewed their god as one among many, Akhenaten and others devoted to Aten considered their deity the one and only true god. Their faith represented one of the world's earliest expressions of monotheism—the belief that a single god rules over all creation.

Akhenaten built a new capital city called Akhetaten ("Horizon of Aten," located at modern Tell el-Amarna), where broad streets, courtyards, and open temples allowed unobscured vision and constant veneration of the sun. He also dispatched agents to all parts of Egypt with instructions to encourage the worship of Aten and to chisel out the names of Amon, Re, and other gods from inscriptions on temples and public buildings. As long as Akhenaten lived, the cult of Aten flourished. But when Akhenaton died, traditional priests mounted a fierce counterattack, restored the cult of Amon-Re

to privileged status, and nearly annihilated the worship and even the memory of Aten.

Mummification Whereas Mesopotamians believed with Gilgamesh that death brought an end to an individual's existence, many Egyptians believed that death was not an end so much as a transition to a new dimension of existence. The deeply held belief in the possibility of immortality helps to explain the Egyptian practice of mummifying the dead, which we explored at the beginning of this chapter. During the Old Kingdom, Egyptians believed that only the ruling elites would survive the grave, so they mummified only pharaohs and their close relatives. Later, however, other royal officials and wealthy individuals merited the posthumous honor of mummification. During the New Kingdom, Egyptians came to think of eternal life as a condition available to normal mortals as well as to

Osiris, Egyptian god of the underworld (seated at right), receives a recently deceased individual, while attendants weigh the heart of another individual against a feather to determine if the person is deserving of immortality. This illustration comes from a papyrus copy of the *Book of the Dead* that was buried with a royal mummy.

Hulton Fine Art Collection/Heritage Images/Getty Images

members of the ruling classes. By the time the Greek historian Herodotus described the process of mummification in the fifth century B.C.E., many wealthy families were able to help their deceased relatives attain immortality by preserving their bodies. Mummification never became general practice in Egypt, but with or without preservation of the body, a variety of religious cults promised to lead individuals of all classes to immortality.

Cult of Osiris The cult of **Osiris** had a particularly strong following in ancient Egypt. According to the myths surrounding the cult, Osiris's evil brother Seth murdered him and scattered his dismembered parts throughout the land, but the victim's loyal wife, Isis, retrieved his parts and gave her husband a proper burial. Impressed by her devotion, the gods restored Osiris to life—not to physical human life among mortals, however, but to a different kind of existence as god of the underworld, the dwelling place of the departed. Because of his death and resurrection, Egyptians associated Osiris with the Nile (which flooded, retreated, and then flooded again the following year) and with their crops (which grew, died, and then sprouted and grew again).

Egyptians also associated Osiris with immortality and honored him through a religious cult that demanded observance of high moral standards. As lord of the underworld, Osiris had the power to determine who deserved the blessing of immortality and who did not. Following their deaths,

individual souls faced the judgment of Osiris, who had their hearts weighed against a feather symbolizing justice. Those with heavy hearts carrying a burden of evil and guilt did not merit immortality, whereas those of pure heart and honorable deeds gained the gift of eternal life. Thus Osiris's cult held out hope of eternal reward for those who behaved according to high moral standards, and it passed on its message in language and symbols easily understood by the farmers who made up the bulk of the Egyptian population.

Nubian Religious Beliefs Nubian peoples observed their own religious traditions, some of which they probably inherited from the early agricultural societies of the Sudan, but little written information survives about their religious beliefs. The most prominent of the Nubian deities was the lion-god Apedemak, often depicted with a bow and arrows, who served as war god for the kingdom of Kush. Another deity, Sebiumeker, was a creator god and divine guardian of his human devotees.

Alongside native traditions, Egyptian religious cults were quite prominent in Nubia, especially after the aggressive pharaohs of the New Kingdom imposed Egyptian rule on Nubia. Nubian peoples did not mummify the remains of their deceased, but they built pyramids similar to those of Egypt, although smaller, and they embraced several Egyptian gods. Amon was the preeminent Egyptian deity in Nubia as in Egypt itself: many Nubian temples honored Amon, and the kings of

Kush portrayed themselves as champions of the Egyptian god. Osiris was also popular in Nubia, where he sometimes appeared in association with the native deity Sebiumeker. In the early days after their introduction, Egyptian cults were most prominent among the Nubian ruling classes. Gradually, however, Egyptian gods attracted a sizable following, and they remained popular in Nubia until the sixth century C.E. They did not displace native gods so much as they joined them in the Nubian pantheon. Indeed, Nubians often identified Egyptian gods with their own deities or endowed the foreign gods with traits important in Nubian society.

BANTU MIGRATIONS AND EARLY AGRICULTURAL SOCIETIES OF SUB-SAHARAN AFRICA

Like their counterparts in southwest Asia, Egyptian and Nubian societies participated in a much larger world of interaction and exchange. Mesopotamian societies developed under the strong influences of long-distance trade, diffusions of technological innovations, the spread of cultural traditions, and the far-flung migrations of Semitic and Indo-European peoples. Similarly, quite apart from their dealings with southwest Asian and Mediterranean peoples, Egyptian and Nubian societies developed in the context of widespread interaction and exchange in sub-Saharan Africa. The most prominent processes unfolding in sub-Saharan Africa during ancient times were the migrations of Bantu-speaking peoples and the establishment of agricultural societies in regions where Bantu speakers settled. Just as Sudanic agriculture spread to the Nile valley and provided an economic foundation for the development of Egyptian and Nubian societies, it also spread to most other regions of Africa south of the Sahara and supported the emergence of distinctive agricultural societies.

The Dynamics of Bantu Expansion

The Bantu Among the most influential peoples of sub-Saharan Africa in ancient times were those who spoke **Bantu** languages. The original Bantu language was one of many related tongues in the larger Niger-Congo family of languages widely spoken in west Africa after 4000 B.C.E. The earliest Bantu speakers inhabited a region embracing the eastern part of modern Nigeria and the southern part of modern Cameroon. Members of this community referred to themselves as *bantu*

An elaborate gold ring from a tomb at Meroë, dating probably to the third century C.E., depicts the Nubian god Sebiumeker. Although often associated with Osiris, Sebiumeker was a Meroitic god with no exact counterpart in Egypt. INTERFOTO/Fine Arts/Alamy Stock Photo

(meaning "persons" or "people"). The earliest Bantu speakers settled mostly along the banks of rivers, which they navigated in canoes, and in open areas of the region's forests. They cultivated yams and oil palms, which first came under cultivation by early agricultural peoples in the western Sudan, and in later centuries they also adopted crops that reached them from the eastern and central Sudan, particularly millet and sorghum. They also kept goats and raised guinea fowl. They lived in clan-based villages headed by chiefs who conducted religious rituals and represented their communities in dealings with neighboring villages. They traded regularly with hunting and gathering peoples who inhabited the tropical forests. Formerly called pygmies, these peoples are now referred to as forest peoples. Bantu cultivators provided these forest peoples with pottery and stone axes in exchange for meat, honey, and other forest products.

Bantu Migrations Unlike most of their neighbors, the Bantu displayed an early readiness to migrate to new territories. By 3000 B.C.E. they were slowly spreading south into the west African forest, and after 2000 B.C.E. they expanded rapidly to the south toward the Congo River basin and east toward the Great Lakes, absorbing local populations of hunting, gathering, and fishing peoples into their agricultural societies. Over the centuries, as some groups of Bantu speakers settled and others moved on to new territories, their languages differentiated into more than five hundred distinct but related tongues. (Today, hundreds of millions of people speak Bantu languages, which collectively constitute the most prominent family of languages in sub-Saharan Africa.) Like the Indo-European migrations discussed in chapter 2, the Bantu migrations were not mass movements of peoples. Instead, they were intermittent and incremental processes that resulted in the gradual spread of Bantu languages and ethnic communities, as small groups moved to new territories and established settlements, which then became foundations for further expansion. By 1000 C.E. Bantu-speaking peoples occupied most of Africa south of the equator.

The precise motives of the early Bantu migrants remain unclear but it seems likely that population pressures drove the migrations. Two features of Bantu society were especially important for the earliest migrations. First, Bantu peoples made effective use of canoes in traveling the networks of the Niger, Congo, and other rivers. Canoes enabled

MAP 3.3 Bantu migrations, 2000 B.C.E.–1000 C.E.

Note that Bantu migrations proceeded to the south and east of the original homeland of Bantu-speaking peoples.

What environmental factors explain the direction and extent of Bantu migrations?

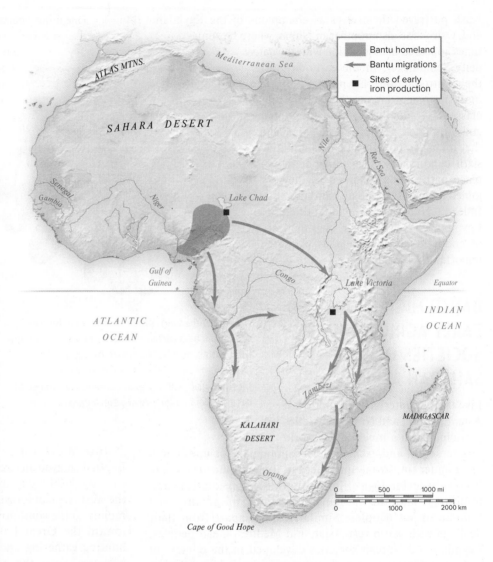

Bantu to travel rapidly up and down the rivers, bypassing existing villages and establishing new ones at inviting spots on riverbanks. Second, agricultural surpluses enabled the Bantu population to increase more rapidly than the populations of hunting, gathering, and fishing peoples whom they encountered as they moved into new regions. When settlements grew uncomfortably large and placed strains on available resources, small groups left their parent communities and moved to new territories. Sometimes they moved to new sites along the rivers, but they often moved inland as well, encroaching on territories occupied by forest peoples. Bantu migrants placed pressures on the forest dwellers, and they most likely clashed with them over land resources. They learned a great deal about local environments from the forest peoples, however, and they also continued to trade regularly with them. Indeed, they often intermarried and absorbed forest peoples into Bantu agricultural society.

Iron and Migration Around the middle of the first millennium B.C.E., the pace of Bantu migrations quickened, as Bantu peoples began to produce iron tools and weapons. Iron tools enabled Bantu cultivators to clear land and expand the zone of agriculture more effectively than before, and iron weapons strengthened the hand of Bantu groups against adversaries and competitors for lands or other resources. Thus iron metallurgy supported rapid population growth among the Bantu while also lending increased momentum to their continuing migrations, which in turn facilitated the spread of iron metallurgy throughout most of sub-Saharan Africa.

Early Agrarian Societies in Sub-Saharan Africa

Several smaller migrations took place alongside the spread of Bantu peoples in sub-Saharan Africa. Between 3500 and 1000 B.C.E., southern Kushite herders pushed into parts of east Africa (modern-day Kenya and Tanzania), while Sudanese cultivators and herders moved into the upper reaches of the Nile River (now southern Sudan and northern Uganda). Meanwhile, Mande-speaking peoples who cultivated African rice established communities along the Atlantic estuaries of west Africa, and other peoples speaking Niger-Congo languages spread the cultivation of okra from forest regions throughout much of west Africa.

Spread of Agriculture Among the most important effects of Bantu and other migrations was the establishment of agricultural societies throughout most of sub-Saharan Africa. Between 1000 and 500 B.C.E., farmers extended the cultivation of yams and grains deep into east and south Africa (modern-day Kenya, Malawi, Mozambique, Zimbabwe, and South Africa), while herders introduced sheep and cattle to the region. About the same time, Bantu and other peoples speaking Niger-Congo languages spread the intensive cultivation of yams, oil palms, millet, and sorghum throughout west and central Africa while also introducing sheep, pigs, and cattle to the region. By the late centuries B.C.E., agriculture had reached almost all of sub-Saharan Africa except for densely forested regions and deserts.

As cultivation and herding spread throughout sub-Saharan Africa, agricultural peoples built distinctive societies and cultural traditions. Most Bantu and other peoples as well lived in communities of a few hundred individuals led by chiefs. Many peoples recognized groups that anthropologists later named age sets, or age grades, consisting of individuals born within a few years of one another. Members of each age set jointly assumed responsibility for tasks appropriate to their levels of strength, energy, maturity, and experience. During their early years, for example, members of an age set might perform light public chores. At maturity, members jointly underwent elaborate initiation rites that introduced them to adult society. Older men cultivated fields and provided military service, while women tended to domestic duties and sometimes traded at markets. In later years, members of age sets served as community leaders and military officers.

Religious Beliefs African cultivators and herders also developed distinctive cultural and religious traditions. Both Sudanic and Niger-Congo peoples (including Bantu speakers), for example, held monotheistic religious beliefs by 5000 B.C.E. Sudanic peoples recognized a single, impersonal divine force that they regarded as the source of both good and evil. They believed that this divine force could take the form of individual spirits, and they often addressed the divine force through prayers to intermediary spirits. The divine force itself, however, was ultimately responsible for rewards and punishments meted out to humans. For their part, Niger-Congo peoples recognized a single god originally called Nyamba who created the world and established the principles that would govern its development and then stepped back and allowed the world to proceed on its own. Individuals did not generally address this distant creator god directly but, rather, offered their prayers to ancestor spirits and local territorial spirits believed to inhabit the world and influence the fortunes of living humans. Proper attention to these spirits would ensure good fortune, they believed, whereas their neglect would bring punishment or adversity from disgruntled spirits.

Individual communities did not always hold religious beliefs in these precise forms, however. Rather, they frequently borrowed elements from other communities and adapted their beliefs to changing circumstances or fresh understandings of the world. Migrations of Bantu and other peoples in particular resulted in a great deal of cultural mixing and mingling, and religious beliefs often spread to new communities in the wake of population movements. After 1000 B.C.E., for example, as they encountered Sudanic peoples and their reverence of a single divine force that was the source of good and evil, many Bantu peoples associated the god Nyamba with goodness. As a result, this formerly distant creator god took on a new moral dimension that brought him closer to the lives of individuals. Thus, changing religious beliefs sometimes reflected widespread interactions among African societies.

CONCLUSION

Like other world regions, Africa was a land of encounters in which peoples of different societies regularly traded, communicated, and interacted with one another from ancient times. The traditions of African agriculture and herding first emerged in the Sudan, then spread both to the Nile River valley and to arable lands throughout sub-Saharan Africa. Agricultural crops and domesticated animals from southwest Asia soon made their way into the Nile valley. With its broad floodplains, Egypt became an especially productive land, while Nubia supported a smaller but flourishing society. Throughout the Nile valley, abundant agricultural surpluses supported dense populations and supported the construction of prosperous societies with sophisticated cultural traditions. Elsewhere in sub-Saharan Africa, populations were less dense, but the migrations of Bantu and other peoples facilitated the spread of agriculture, and later iron metallurgy as well, throughout most of the region. Meanwhile, the Nile River served as a route of trade and communication linking Egypt and the Mediterranean basin to the north with the Sudan and sub-Saharan Africa to the south. Only in the context of migration, trade, communication, and interaction is it possible to understand the early development of African societies.

STUDY TERMS

Amon (62)	Meroitic (62)
Archaic Period (50)	Nile River (49)
Aten (62)	Nubians (49)
Bantu (65)	Old Kingdom (50)
hieratic (62)	Osiris (64)
hieroglyphs (62)	pharaohs (51)
Hyksos (52)	primary sources (58)
iron metallurgy (60)	Punt (61)
King Kashta (53)	Queen Hatshepsut (57)
Kush (51)	Re (62)
Menes (50)	Tuthmosis III (53)

FOR FURTHER READING

Kathryn A. Bard. *An Introduction to the Archaeology of Ancient Egypt,* London, 2015. A student-friendly guide to the history and scope of Egyptian archaeology from archaic times to the Greco-Roman period.

Stanley M. Burstein, ed. *Ancient African Civilizations: Kush and Axum.* 2nd ed., Princeton: Markus Wiener, 2009.

Basil Davidson. *Lost Cities of Africa.* Rev. ed. Boston, 1970. Popular account with discussions of Kush and Meroë.

Christopher Ehret. *The Civilizations of Africa: A History to 1800.* Charlottesville, 2001. An important contribution that views Africa in the context of world history.

John L. Foster. *Ancient Egyptian Literature: An Anthology.* Austin, 2001. A useful and readily accessible selection of literary works from ancient Egypt.

Zahi Hawass. *Silent Images: Women in Pharaonic Egypt.* New York, 2000. A prominent archaeologist draws on both textual and artifactual evidence in throwing light on women's experiences in ancient Egypt.

Barry J. Kemp. *Ancient Egypt: Anatomy of a Civilization.* New York, 2006. Wide-ranging and reflective analysis emphasizing Egyptian identity.

Roderick James McIntosh. *The Peoples of the Middle Niger: The Island of Gold.* Oxford, 1998. Fascinating volume emphasizing the environmental context of west African history.

Catharine H. Roehrig, Renée Dreyfus, and Cathleen A. Keller, eds. *Hatshepsut: From Queen to Pharaoh.* New York, 2005. Brilliantly illustrated volume focusing on the reign of the New Kingdom's female pharaoh.

Jan Vansina. *Paths in the Rainforests: Toward a History of Political Tradition in Equatorial Africa.* Madison, 1990. A brilliant synthesis concentrating on central Africa by one of the world's foremost historians of Africa.

Derek A. Welsby. *The Kingdom of Kush: The Napatan and Meroitic Empires.* London, 1996. Draws on both written and archaeological sources in tracing the development of ancient Nubia and charting its relationship with Egypt.

Chapter 4

The Emergence of Complex Societies in South Asia

The Indus Civilization
    Foundations of the Indus Civilization
    Indus Society and Culture

Indo-Aryan Migrations and Early Vedic India
    The Indo-Aryans and India
    Origins of the Caste System
    The Development of Patriarchal Society

Religion in the Vedic Age
    Indo-Aryan Religion
    The Blending of Indo-Aryan and Dravidian Values

ZOOMING IN ON ENCOUNTERS
Indra, War God of the Indo-Aryans

For a god, **Indra** was quite a force of nature. According to the stories told about him by the Indo-Aryans, Indra had few if any peers in fighting, feasting, or drinking. The Indo-Aryans were a herding people who spoke an Indo-European language and who migrated to South Asia in large numbers after 1500 B.C.E. In the early days of their migrations they took Indra as their chief deity. The Indo-Aryans told dozens of stories about Indra and sang hundreds of hymns in his honor.

One story had to do with a war between the gods and the demons. When the gods were tiring, they appointed Indra as their leader, and soon they had turned the tide against their enemies. Another story, a favorite of the Indo-Aryans, had to do with Indra's role in bringing rain to the earth—a crucial concern for any agricultural society. According to this story, Indra did battle with a dragon who lived in the sky and hoarded water in the clouds. Indra first slaked his thirst with generous drafts of *soma,* a hallucinogenic potion consumed by Indo-Aryan priests, and then attacked the dragon, by hurling thunderbolts at it. The dragon's heavy fall caused turmoil both on earth and in the atmosphere, but afterward the rains filled seven rivers that flowed through northern India and brought life-giving waters to inhabitants of the region.

The Indo-Aryans took Indra as a leader against earthly as well as heavenly foes. They did not mount a planned invasion of India, but as they migrated in sizable numbers into South Asia, they encountered and often came into conflict with Dravidian and other peoples already living there. When they clashed with these original inhabitants, the Indo-Aryans took the belligerent Indra as their guide. Indo-Aryan hymns praised Indra as the military hero who trampled enemy forces and opened the way for the migrants to build a new society.

The so-called Pashupati Seal, depicting a seated figure, surrounded by animals. The seal was discovered at Mohenjo-Daro and some scholars identify the figure as an Indus deity.
The History Collection/Alamy Stock Photo

For all his contributions, Indra did not survive permanently as a prominent deity. As Indo-Aryan and Dravidian peoples mixed, mingled, interacted, and intermarried, tensions between them subsided. Memories of the stormy and violent Indra receded into the background, and eventually they faded almost to nothing. For a thousand years and more, however, Indo-Aryans looked upon the rowdy, raucous war god as a ready source of inspiration as they sought to build a society in an already occupied land.

CHAPTER OVERVIEW

Tools excavated by archaeologists show that South Asia was a site of human occupation at least two hundred thousand years ago, long before the Indo-Aryans introduced Indra to South Asia. Between 8000 and 5000 B.C.E., cultivators built an agrarian society west of the Indus River, in the region bordering on the Iranian plateau, probably as a result of Mesopotamian influence. By 7000 B.C.E. agriculture had taken root in the Indus River valley. Thereafter agriculture spread rapidly, and by about 3000 B.C.E. neolithic communities had been established throughout much of the Indian subcontinent. The earliest neolithic settlers cultivated wheat, barley, and cotton, and they also kept herds of cattle, sheep, and goats. Agricultural villages were especially numerous in the valley of the Indus River. As the population of the valley swelled and as people interacted with increasing frequency, some of those villages evolved into bustling cities, which served as the organizational centers of South Asian society.

Early cities in South Asia stood at the center of an impressive political, social, and cultural order built on the foundation of an agricultural economy. The earliest urban society in India, known today as the Indus Civilization brought wealth and power to the Indus River valley. Eventually, however, it fell into decline, possibly because of environmental problems, just as large numbers of Indo-European migrants moved into India from central Asia and built a very different society. For half a millennium, from about 1500 to 1000 B.C.E., the Indian subcontinent was a site of turmoil as the migrants struggled with Dravidian peoples and other early residents of the subcontinent for control of the land and its resources. Gradually, however, stability returned with the establishment of numerous agricultural villages and regional states. During the centuries after 1000 B.C.E., Indo-Aryan and Dravidian peoples increasingly interacted and intermarried, and their combined legacies led to the development of a distinctive society and a rich cultural tradition.

THE INDUS CIVILIZATION

Like early agricultural societies in Mesopotamia and Egypt, the Indus Civilization was established in the valley of a major river, the Indus, whose waters allowed for large-scale irrigation. As agricultural yields increased, the population also grew rapidly, and by about 3000 B.C.E. neolithic villages were evolving into thriving cities.

Unfortunately, it is impossible to follow the development of Indus society in detail for two reasons. One is that many of the earliest Indus physical remains are inaccessible. Silt deposits have raised the level of the land in the Indus valley, and the water table has risen correspondingly. Because the earliest Indus remains lie below the water table, archaeologists cannot excavate them or study them systematically. The earliest accessible remains date from about 2500 B.C.E., when Indus society was already well established. As a result, scholars have learned something about the Indus Civilization at its high point, but little about the circumstances that brought it into being or the conditions of life during its earliest days.

A second problem that handicaps scholars who study Indus society is the lack of deciphered written records. Indus

CHRONOLOGY	
8000–7000 B.C.E.	Beginnings of agriculture in South Asia
2500–2000 B.C.E.	High point of Indus society
1900 B.C.E.	Beginning of Indus decline
1500 B.C.E.	Beginning of Indo-Aryan migration to India
1500–500 B.C.E.	Vedic age
1400–900 B.C.E.	Composition of the *Rig Veda*
1000 B.C.E.	Early Indo-Aryan migrations into the Ganges River valley
1000 B.C.E.	Emergence of *varna* distinctions
1000–500 B.C.E.	Formation of regional kingdoms in northern India
800–400 B.C.E.	Composition of the principal Upanishads
750 B.C.E.	Establishment of first Indo-Aryan cities in the Ganges valley
500 B.C.E.	Early Indo-Aryan migrations to the Deccan Plateau

had a system of writing that used about four hundred symbols to represent sounds and words, and archaeologists have discovered thousands of clay seals, copper tablets, and other artifacts with Indus inscriptions. Some scholars have theorized that the language might have been related to Dravidian, a language spoken today mostly in southern India, but they have not yet succeeded in deciphering the script. As a result, the details of Indus life remain hidden behind the veil of an elaborate pictographic script. The understanding of Indus society depends entirely on the study of material remains that archaeologists have uncovered since the 1920s.

Foundations of the Indus Civilization

The Indus River If the Greek historian Herodotus, who we met in the previous chapter discussing the practice of mummification in Egypt, had known of Harappan society, he might have called it the "gift of the Indus." Like the Nile, the **Indus River** draws its waters from rain and melting snow in towering mountains—in this case, the Hindu Kush and the Himalayas, the world's highest peaks. As the waters charge downhill, they pick up enormous quantities of silt, which they carry for hundreds of kilometers. Like the Nile again, the Indus then deposits its burden of rich soil as it courses through lowlands and loses its force. Today, a series of dams has largely tamed the Indus, but for most of history it spilled its waters annually over a vast floodplain, sometimes with devastating effect. Much less predictable than the Nile, the Indus has many times left its channel altogether and carved a new course to the sea.

Despite its occasional ferocity, the Indus made agricultural society possible in the northern regions of South Asia. The most important food crops and domesticated animals came to the region from Mesopotamia. Early cultivators in the Indus River valley sowed wheat and barley in September, after the flood receded, and harvested their crops the following spring. Inhabitants of the valley supplemented their harvests of wheat and barley with meat from herds of cattle, sheep, and goats. Their diet also included poultry: cultivators in the Indus valley kept flocks of the world's first domesticated chickens. Indus valley inhabitants cultivated cotton probably before 5000 B.C.E., and fragments of dyed cloth dating to about 2000 B.C.E. testify to the existence of a cotton textile industry.

As in Mesopotamia and Egypt, agricultural surpluses in the Indus Valley vastly increased the food supply, stimulated population growth, and supported the establishment of cities

Harappan (huh-RUHP-puhn)

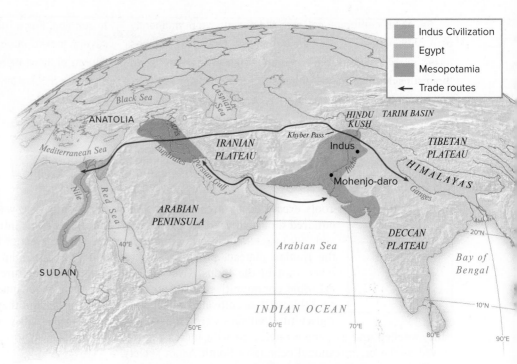

MAP 4.1   The Indus Civilization and its neighbors, ca. 2000 B.C.E.

Compare Indus society with its Mesopotamian and Egyptian contemporaries with respect to size.

In what way did the geography of the region influence the nature of trade and exchange between Egypt, Mesopotamia, and the Indus?

and specialized labor. Between 3000 and 2500 B.C.E., a complex society emerged that dominated the Indus River valley until its decline after 1900 B.C.E. The agricultural surplus of the Indus valley fed two large cities, Harappa and **Mohenjo-daro,** as well as numerous other cities and a vast agricultural hinterland. Archaeologists have excavated about seventy Harappan settlements along the Indus River. Harappan society embraced much of modern-day Pakistan and part of northern India as well—a territory about 1.3 million square kilometers (502,000 square miles)—much larger than either Mesopotamian or Egyptian society.

Political Organization Little evidence survives concerning the Indus political system. Archaeological excavations have turned up no evidence of a royal or imperial authority. It is possible that, like the early Sumerian city-states, the Indus cities were economic and political centers for their own regions. Because of their large size, however, Harappa and Mohenjo-daro were especially prominent in Indus society even if they did not dominate the Indus valley politically or militarily. Both Mohenjo-daro and Harappa supported populations of about 40,000 people, so these were very large cities. Archaeologists have discovered the sites of about 1,500 Indus settlements, but none of the others approached the size of Harappa or Mohenjo-daro.

Excavations at the Indus Civilization city of Mohenjo-Daro. What does the layout of the city suggest about the way Indus urban planners approached the design of their cities?

SM Rafiq Photography/Moment Open/Getty Images

Harappa and Mohenjo-Daro Both Harappa and Mohenjo-daro had city walls, a fortified citadel, and a large granary, suggesting that they served as centers of political authority and sites for the collection and redistribution of taxes paid in the form of grain. The two cities represented a considerable investment of human labor and other resources: both featured marketplaces, temples, public buildings, extensive residential districts, and broad streets laid out on a carefully planned grid so that they ran north-south or east-west. Mohenjo-daro also had a large pool, perhaps used for religious or ritual purposes, with private dressing rooms for bathers.

The two cities clearly established the patterns that shaped the larger society: weights, measures, architectural styles, and even brick sizes were consistent throughout the land, even though Indus society stretched almost 1,500 kilometers (932 miles) from one end to the other. This standardization no doubt reflects the prominence of Harappa and Mohenjo-daro as powerful and wealthy cities whose influence touched all parts of Indus society. The high degree of standardization was possible also because the Indus River facilitated trade, travel, and communications among the far-flung regions of Indus society.

Specialized Labor and Trade Like all complex societies in ancient times, Harappa depended on a successful agricultural economy. But Indus peoples also engaged in trade, both domestic and foreign. Pottery, tools, and decorative items produced in Harappa and Mohenjo-daro found their way to all corners of the Indus valley. From neighboring peoples in Persia and the Hindu Kush mountains, Indus merchants obtained gold, silver, copper, lead, gems, and semiprecious stones. During the period about 2300 to 1750 B.C.E., they also traded with Mesopotamians, exchanging Indian copper, ivory, beads, and semiprecious stones for Sumerian wool, leather, and olive oil. Some of that trade may have gone by land over the Iranian plateau, but most of it probably traveled by ships that followed the coastline of the Arabian Sea between the mouth of the Indus River and the Persian Gulf.

Indus Society and Culture

Like societies in Mesopotamia and Egypt, Indus society generated considerable wealth. Excavations at Mohenjo-daro show that at its high point, from about 2500 to 2000 B.C.E., the city was a thriving economic center with a population of about forty thousand. Goldsmiths, potters, weavers, masons, and architects, among other professionals, maintained shops that lined Mohenjo-daro's streets. Other cities also housed communities of jewelers, artists, and merchants.

Social Distinctions The wealth of Indus society, like that in Mesopotamia and Egypt, encouraged the formation of social distinctions. Indus peoples built no pyramids, palaces, or magnificent tombs, but their rulers wielded great authority from the citadels at Harappa and Mohenjo-daro. It is clear from Indus dwellings that rich and poor lived in very different styles. In Mohenjo-daro, for example, many people lived in one-room tenements in barrackslike structures, but there were also individual houses of two and three stories with a dozen rooms and an interior courtyard, as well as a few large houses with several dozen rooms and multiple courtyards. Most of the larger houses had their own wells and built-in brick ovens. Almost all houses had private bathrooms with toilets that drained into city sewage systems. The water and sewage systems of Mohenjo-daro were among the most sophisticated of the ancient world, and they represented a tremendous investment of community resources.

Seal depicting a nude male deity with three faces, seated in yogic position on a throne, wearing bangles on both arms and an elaborate headdress. What does this image suggest about the influence of Indus beliefs on subsequent Indian religious attitudes?
World History Archive/Alamy Stock Photo

A bronze statuette produced at Mohenjo-daro between 3000 and 1500 B.C.E. depicts a lithe dancing girl.
Angelo Hornak/Alamy Stock Photo

In the absence of deciphered writing, Indus beliefs and values are even more difficult to interpret than politics and society. Archaeologists have discovered samples of Harappan writing dating as early as 3300 B.C.E., and they have recovered hundreds of seals bearing illustrations and written inscriptions. Scholars have been able to identify several symbols representing names or words, but not enough to understand the significance of the texts. Even without written texts, however, material remains shed some tantalizing light on Indus society. A variety of statues, figurines, and illustrations carved onto seals reflect a tradition of representational art as well as expertise in gold, copper, and bronze metallurgy. A particularly striking statue is a bronze figurine of a dancing girl discovered at Mohenjo-daro. Provocatively posed and clad only in bracelets and a necklace, the figure expresses a remarkable suppleness and liveliness.

Fertility Cults The religion of the Indus Civilization reflected a strong concern for fertility. Like other early agricultural societies, Indus peoples venerated gods and goddesses whom they associated with creation and procreation. They recognized a mother goddess and a horned fertility god, and they held trees and animals sacred because of their associations with vital forces. For lack of written descriptions, it is impossible to characterize Indus religious beliefs more specifically. Many scholars believe, however, that some Indus deities survived the collapse of the larger society and found places later in the Hindu pantheon. Fertility and procreation are prominent concerns in popular Hinduism, and scholars have often noticed similarities between Indus and Hindu deities associated with those values.

Decline of the Indus Civilization Sometime after 1900 B.C.E., Indus society entered a period of decline. Unlike the situation with most other ancient civilizations, there is no evidence to suggest that this decline was caused by political turmoil or military conflict. One prominent theory holds that ecological degradation was a major cause of decline. It is possible that Indus peoples deforested the Indus valley to clear land for cultivation and to obtain firewood. Deforestation led to erosion of topsoil and also to reduced amounts of rainfall. Over hundreds of years—perhaps half a millennium or more—most of the Indus valley became a desert, and agriculture is possible there today only with the aid of artificial irrigation. Those climatic and ecological changes reduced agricultural yields, and Indus society faced a subsistence crisis during the centuries after 1900 B.C.E.

It is also likely that natural catastrophes—periodic flooding of the Indus River or earthquakes—weakened Indus society. Archaeologists found more than thirty unburied human skeletons scattered about the streets and buildings of Mohenjo-daro. No sign of criminal or military violence accounts for their presence, but a sudden flood or earthquake could have trapped some residents who were unable to flee the impending disaster. In any case, by about 1700 B.C.E., the populations of Harappa and Mohenjo-daro had abandoned the cities as mounting difficulties made it impossible to sustain complex urban societies. Some of the smaller, subordinate cities outlived Harappa and Mohenjo-daro, but by about 1500 B.C.E., Indus cities had almost entirely collapsed.

Decline of the cities, however, did not mean the total disappearance of Indus social and cultural traditions. In many ways, Indus traditions survived the decline of the cities because peoples from other societies adopted Indus ways for their own purposes. Cultivation of wheat, barley, and cotton continued to flourish in the Indus valley long after the decline of Indus society. Indus deities and religious beliefs intrigued migrants to India and found a home in new societies. Eventually, cities themselves returned to South Asia, and, in some cases, Indus urban traditions may even have inspired the establishment of new cities.

INDO-ARYAN MIGRATIONS AND EARLY VEDIC INDIA

During the second millennium B.C.E., as the Indus Civilization declined, bands of outside peoples filtered into the Indian subcontinent and settled throughout the Indus valley and beyond. Most prominent were nomadic and pastoral peoples speaking Indo-European languages who called themselves **Indo-Aryans** ("noble people"). By 1500 B.C.E. or perhaps somewhat earlier, they had begun to file through the passes of the Hindu Kush mountains and establish small herding and agricultural communities throughout northern India.

These migrations appear to have taken place over several centuries: by no means did the arrival of the Indo-Aryans constitute an invasion or an organized military campaign. It is likely that Indo-Aryan migrants clashed with **Dravidians** and other peoples they encountered who were already settled in India, but there is no indication that the Indo-Aryans conquered or destroyed Indus society. By the time the Indo-Europeans entered India, internal problems had already brought Indus society to the point of collapse. During the centuries after 1500 B.C.E., Dravidian and Indo-Aryan peoples intermarried, interacted, and laid social and cultural foundations that would influence South Asian society to the present day.

The Indo-Aryans and India

The Early Indo-Aryans When they entered India, the Indo-Aryans practiced a limited amount of agriculture, but they depended much more heavily on a pastoral economy. They kept sheep and goats, but they especially prized their horses and herds of cattle. Horses were quite valuable because of their expense and relative rarity: horses do not breed well in the tropical environment of South Asia, so it was necessary for Indo-Aryans to replenish their supplies of horseflesh by importing animals from central Asia. Like their Indo-European cousins to the north, the Indo-Aryans harnessed horses to carts and wagons to facilitate transportation, and they also hitched them to chariots, which proved to be devastating war machines when deployed against peoples who made no use of horsepower. Meanwhile, cattle became the principal measure of wealth in early Indo-Aryan society. The Indo-Aryans consumed both dairy products and beef—cattle did not become sacred, protected animals (as they are today among Hindus) until many centuries after the Indo-Aryans' arrival—and they often calculated prices in terms of cattle. Wealthy individuals in early Indo-Aryan society usually owned extensive herds of cattle.

The Vedas The early Indo-Aryans did not use writing, but they composed numerous poems and songs. Indeed, they preserved extensive collections of religious and literary works by memorizing them and transmitting them orally from one generation to another in their sacred language, Sanskrit. (For everyday communication, the Indo-Aryans relied on a related but less formal tongue known as Prakrit, which later evolved into Hindi, Bengali, Urdu, and other languages currently spoken in northern India.) The earliest of those orally transmitted works were the **Vedas,** which were collections of hymns, songs, prayers, and rituals honoring the various gods of the Indo-Aryans. There are four Vedas, the earliest and most important of which is the *Rig Veda,* a collection of 1,028 hymns addressed to Indo-Aryan gods. Indo-Aryan priests compiled the *Rig Veda* between about 1400 and 900 B.C.E., and they committed it to writing, along with the three later Vedas, about 600 B.C.E.

The Vedas represent a priestly perspective on affairs: the word *veda* means "wisdom" or "knowledge" and refers to the knowledge that priests needed to carry out their functions. While transmitting religious knowledge, however, the Vedas also shed considerable light on early Indo-Aryan society in India. In view of their importance as historical sources, scholars refer to Indian history during the millennium between 1500 and 500 B.C.E. as the Vedic age.

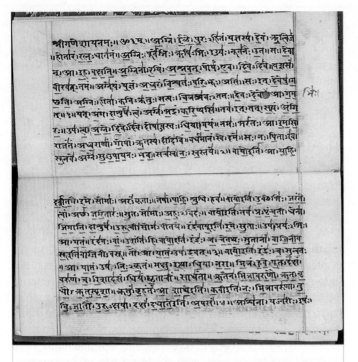

Early 19th century manuscript of the Rig Veda in Devanagari script, which is closely related to the original Brahmi script that the Vedas were first written in c. 600 B.C.E.

FLHC 39/Alamy Stock Photo

great significance because the Indo-Aryans regarded cattle as the chief form of wealth in their society. Occasionally, too, ambitious chiefs sought to extend their authority by conquering neighbors and dominating the regions surrounding their communities.

Indo-Aryan Migrations in South Asia During the early centuries of the Vedic age, Indo-Aryan groups settled in the Punjab, the upper Indus River valley that straddles the modern-day border between northern India and Pakistan. These migrations were some of the most prominent waves in the larger process of early Indo-European migrations (discussed in chapter 2). After establishing themselves in the Punjab, Indo-Aryan migrants spread east and south and established communities throughout much of the Indian subcontinent. After 1000 B.C.E. they began to settle in the area between the Himalayan foothills and the Ganges River. About that same time they learned how to make iron tools, and with axes and iron-tipped plows they cleared forests and established agricultural communities in the Ganges valley. Iron implements enabled them to cultivate more land, produce more food, and support larger communities, which in turn encouraged them to push deeper into the Ganges River valley. There they began to cultivate rice rather than the wheat and barley that were staple crops in the Punjab. Since rice is a highly productive crop, it provided food for rapidly expanding populations. By about 750 B.C.E., populations had increased

The Vedic Age The Vedas reflect a violent society in which the Indo-Aryans clashed repeatedly with the Dravidians and other peoples already living in India. The Vedas refer frequently to conflicts between Indo-Aryans and indigenous peoples whom the Indo-Aryans called *dasas,* meaning "enemies" or "subject peoples." The Vedas identify Indra, the Indo-Aryan war god and military hero, that we met at the start of the chapter as one who ravaged citadels, smashed dams, and destroyed forts the way age consumes cloth garments. These characterizations suggest that the Indo-Aryans clashed frequently with the Dravidians; but it is clear that Indo-Aryans also often had friendly relations with Dravidian peoples. They learned about the land, for example, and adopted Dravidian agricultural techniques when they settled in villages. Nevertheless, competition over land and resources fueled intermittent conflict between Indo-Aryan and Dravidian peoples.

The Indo-Aryans also fought ferociously among themselves. They did not have a state or common government but, rather, formed hundreds of chiefdoms organized around herding communities and agricultural villages. Most of the chiefdoms had a leader known as a *raja*—a **Sanskrit** term related to the Latin word *rex* ("king"), which reminds us of the influence of proto-Indo-European on so many languages of Eurasia—who governed in collaboration with a council of village elders. Given the large number of chiefdoms, there was enormous potential for conflict in Indo-Aryan society. The men of one village often raided the herds of their neighbors—an offense of

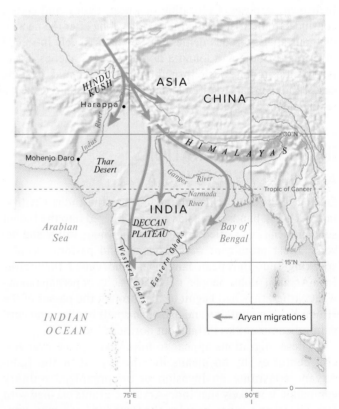

MAP 4.2 Indo-Aryan Migrations into India, 1500–250 B.C.

enough that Indo-Aryans had established the first small cities in the Ganges River valley. Indeed, population became so dense in northern India that some Indo-Aryans decided to move along and seek their fortunes elsewhere. By 500 B.C.E. Indo-Aryan groups had migrated as far south as the northern Deccan, a plateau region in the southern cone of the Indian subcontinent about 1,500 kilometers (950 miles) south of the Punjab.

Changing Political Organization As they settled into permanent communities and began to rely more on agriculture than herding, the Indo-Aryans gradually lost the tribal political organization that they had brought into India and evolved more formal political institutions. In a few places, especially in the isolated hilly and mountainous regions of northern India, councils of elders won recognition as the principal sources of political authority. They directed the affairs of small republics—states governed by representatives of the citizens. In most places, though, chiefdoms developed into regional kingdoms. Between 1000 and 500 B.C.E., tribal chiefs worked increasingly from permanent capitals and depended on the services of professional administrators. They did not build large imperial states: not until the fourth century B.C.E. did an Indian state embrace as much territory as Harappan society. But they established regional kingdoms as the most common form of political organization throughout most of the subcontinent.

Origins of the Caste System

Although they did not build a large-scale political structure, the Indo-Aryans constructed a well-defined social order. Indeed, in some ways their social hierarchy served to maintain the order and stability that states and political structures guaranteed in other societies, such as Mesopotamia, Egypt, and, China. The Indo-Aryan social structure rested on sharp hereditary distinctions between individuals and groups, according to their occupations and roles in society. Those distinctions became the foundation of the caste system, which largely determined the places that individuals and groups occupied in society.

The term *caste* comes from the Portuguese word *casta*, and it refers to a social class of hereditary and usually unchangeable status. When Portuguese merchants and mariners visited India during the sixteenth century C.E., they noticed the sharp, inherited distinctions between different social groups, which they referred to as castes. Scholars have employed the term *caste* ever since in reference to the Indian social order.

Caste and *Varna* Caste identities developed slowly and gradually as the Indo-Aryans established settlements throughout India. When the Indo-Aryans first entered India, they probably had a fairly simple society consisting of herders and cultivators led by warrior-chiefs and priests. As they settled in India, however, growing social complexity and interaction with Dravidian and other peoples prompted them to refine their social distinctions. The Indo-Aryans used the term *varna*, a Sanskrit word meaning "color," to refer to the major social classes. This terminology suggests that social distinctions arose partly from differences in complexion between the Indo-Aryans, who referred to themselves as "wheat-colored," and the darker-skinned Dravidians. Over time Indo-Aryans and Dravidians mixed, mingled, interacted, and intermarried to the point that distinguishing between them was impossible. Nevertheless, in early Vedic times differences between the two peoples probably prompted Indo-Aryans to base social distinctions on Indo-Aryan or Dravidian ancestry.

Social Distinctions in the Late Vedic Age After about 1000 B.C.E. the Indo-Aryans increasingly recognized four main *varnas: **brahmins*** (priests), ***kshatriyas*** (warriors and aristocrats), ***vaishyas*** (cultivators, artisans, and merchants), and ***shudras*** (landless peasants and serfs). Some centuries later, probably about the end of the Vedic age, they added the category of the ***untouchables***—people who performed dirty or unpleasant tasks, such as butchering animals or handling dead bodies, and who theoretically became so polluted from their work that their very touch could defile individuals of higher status. A late hymn of the *Rig Veda*, composed probably around 1000 B.C.E., offers a priestly perspective on *varna* distinctions. According to the hymn, the gods created the four *varnas* during the early days of the world and produced brahmins and kshatriyas as the most honorable human groups that would lead their societies. Thus during the late Vedic age the recognition of *varnas* and theories of their origins had the effect of enhancing the status and power of priestly and aristocratic classes.

Subcastes and *Jati* Until about the sixth century B.C.E., the four *varnas* described Vedic society reasonably well. Because they did not live in cities and did not yet pursue many specialized occupations, the Indo-Aryans had little need for a more complicated social order. Over the longer term, however, a much more elaborate scheme of social classification emerged. As Vedic society became more complex and generated increasingly specialized occupations, the caste system served as the umbrella for a complicated hierarchy of subcastes known as ***jati***. Occupation largely determined an individual's *jati:* people working at the same or similar tasks in a given area belonged to the same subcaste, and their offspring joined them in both occupation and *jati* membership. By the eighteenth and nineteenth centuries C.E., in its most fully articulated form, the system featured several thousand *jati,* which prescribed individuals' roles in society in minute detail. Brahmins alone divided themselves into some 1,800 *jati*. Even untouchables belonged to *jati,* and some of them looked down upon others as far more miserable and polluted than themselves.

---

brahmins (BRAH-minz)
kshatriyas (SHUHT-ree-uhs)
vaishyas (VEYESH-yuhs)
shudras (SHOO-druhs)

SOURCES FROM THE PAST

Extract from the *Laws of Manu:* CHAPTER III.

The Laws of Manu *were written by an anonymous author in the first century B.C.E. (or perhaps earlier). The following extracts from Chapter III concern the choosing of a wife for a man who has undergone the rigorous training and become a Brahmin (a twice-born man) and also for the subsequent relationship between husband and wife. The Brahmins were the highest caste in the Varna system that first emerged during the Vedic Age.*

1. Having bathed, with the permission of his teacher, and performed according to the rule the Samavartana (the rite on returning home), a twice-born man shall marry a wife of equal caste who is endowed with auspicious (bodily) marks.

2. In connecting himself with a wife, let him carefully avoid the ten following families, be they ever so great, or rich in kine, horses, sheep, grain, or (other) property,

   > What types of families are to be avoided by a Brahmin when choosing a wife?

3. One which neglects the sacred rites, one in which no male children (are born), one in which the Veda is not studied, one (the members of) which have thick hair on the body, those which are subject to hemorrhoids, phthisis, weakness of digestion, epilepsy, or white or black leprosy.

4. Let him not marry a maiden (with) reddish (hair), nor one who has a redundant member, nor one who is sickly, nor one either with no hair (on the body) or too much, nor one who is garrulous or has red (eyes),

   > Why would women with certain types of names also need to be avoided?

5. Nor one named after a constellation, a tree, or a river, nor one bearing the name of a low caste, or of a mountain, nor one named after a bird, a snake, or a slave, nor one whose name inspires terror.

6. Let him wed a female free from bodily defects, who has an agreeable name, the (graceful) gait of a Hamsa or of an elephant, a moderate (quantity of) hair on the body and on the head, small teeth, and soft limbs.

7. For the first marriage of twice-born men (wives) of equal caste are recommended; but for those who through desire proceed (to marry again) the following females, (chosen) according to the (direct) order (of the castes), are most approved.

8. It is declared that a Sudra woman alone (can be) the wife of a Sudra, she and one of his own caste (the wives) of a Vaisya, those two and one of his own caste (the wives) of a Kshatriya, those three and one of his own caste (the wives) of a Brahmana.

9. Twice-born men who, in their folly, wed wives of the low (Sudra) caste, soon degrade their families and their children to the state of Sudras.

10. A Brahmana who takes a Sudra wife to his bed, will (after death) sink into hell; if he begets a child by her, he will lose the rank of a Brahmana.

11. The voluntary union of a maiden and her lover one must know (to be) the Gandharva rite, which springs from desire and has sexual intercourse for its purpose.

12. Let (the husband) approach his wife in due season, being constantly satisfied with her (alone); he may also, being intent on pleasing her, approach her with a desire for conjugal union (on any day) excepting the Parvans.

13. Sixteen (days and) nights (in each month), including four days which differ from the rest and are censured by the virtuous, (are called) the natural season of women.

14. Women must be honoured and adorned by their fathers, brothers, husbands, and brothers-in-law, who desire (their own) welfare.

15. In that family, where the husband is pleased with his wife and the wife with her husband, happiness will assuredly be lasting.

16. For if the wife is not radiant with beauty, she will not attract her husband; but if she has no attractions for him, no children will be born.

For Further Reflection

■ In what ways do the *Laws of Manu* reinforce the rigid caste system of Vedic South Asia?
■ In what ways do the laws reinforce the patriarchal social structure that emerged in Vedic South Asia?
■ In what ways do the laws offer protections for women?

Source: George Bühler, trans. *The Laws of Manu* (*Sacred Books of the East, Volume 25*). Internet Sacred Text Archive, https://www.sacred-texts.com/hin/manu.htm

Updated with modern language by the textbook authors.

Castes and subcastes deeply influenced the lives of individual Indians through much of history. Members of a *jati* ate with one another and intermarried, and they cared for those who became ill or fell on hard times. Elaborate rules dictated forms of address and specific behavior appropriate for communication between members of different castes and subcastes. Violation of *jati* rules could result in expulsion from the larger group. That penalty was serious because an outcaste individual could not function well and sometimes could not even survive when shunned by all members of the larger society.

Caste and Social Mobility The caste system never functioned in an absolutely rigid or inflexible manner but, rather, operated so as to accommodate social change. Indeed, if the system had entirely lacked the capacity to change and reflect new social conditions, it would have disappeared. Individual vaishyas or shudras occasionally turned to new lines of work and prospered on the basis of their initiative, for example, and individual brahmins or kshatriyas sometimes fell on hard times, lost their positions of honor, and moved down in the social hierarchy. More often, however, social mobility came about as the result of group rather than individual efforts, as members of *jati* improved their condition collectively. Achieving upward mobility was not an easy matter—it often entailed moving to a new area or at least taking on a new line of work—but the possibility of improving individual or group status helped to dissipate tensions that otherwise might have severely tested Indian society.

The caste system also enabled foreign peoples to find a place in Indian society. The Indo-Aryans were by no means the only foreigners to cross the passes of the Hindu Kush and enter South Asia. Many others followed them over the course of the centuries and, upon arrival, sooner or later organized themselves into well-defined groups and adopted caste identities.

By the end of the Vedic age, caste distinctions had become central traditions in Indo-Aryan India. Whereas in other lands, states and empires maintained public order, in India the caste system served as a principal foundation of social organization. Individuals have often identified more closely with their *jati* than with their cities or states, and castes have played a large role in maintaining social discipline in India.

The Development of Patriarchal Society

While building an elaborate social hierarchy on the foundations of caste and *varna* distinctions, the Indo-Aryans also constructed a strongly patriarchal social order on the basis of gender

A Vedic Era sculpture in schist stone illustrating the relationship between a mother and her child. LACMA-Los Angeles County Museum of Art

distinctions. At the time of their migrations into India, men already dominated Indo-Aryan society. All priests, warriors, and tribal chiefs were men, and the Indo-Aryans recognized descent through the male line. Women influenced affairs within their families but enjoyed no public authority. By maintaining and reinforcing gender distinctions, the Indo-Aryans established a patriarchal social order that stood alongside the caste system and *varna* hierarchy as a prominent feature of their society.

As the Indo-Aryans settled in agricultural communities throughout India, they maintained a thoroughly patriarchal society. Only males could inherit property, unless a family had no male heirs, and only men could preside over family rituals that honored departed ancestors. Because they had no priestly responsibilities, women rarely learned the Vedas, and formal education in Sanskrit remained almost exclusively a male preserve.

The *Laws of Manu* The patriarchal spokesmen of Vedic society sought to place women explicitly under the authority of men. During the first century B.C.E. or perhaps somewhat later, an anonymous sage prepared a work and attributed it to Manu, founder of the human race according to Indian mythology. Much of the work, known as the *Laws of Manu,* dealt with proper moral behavior and social relationships, including sex and gender relationships. Although composed after the Vedic age, the *Laws of Manu* reflected the society constructed earlier under Indo-Aryan influence. The author advised men to treat women with honor and respect, but he insisted that women remain subject to the guidance of the principal men in their lives—first their fathers, then their husbands, and, finally, if they survived their husbands, their sons. The *Laws of Manu* also specified that the most important duties of women were to bear children and maintain wholesome homes for their families. Thus, like Mesopotamian, Egyptian, and other early agricultural societies, Vedic India constructed and maintained a deeply patriarchal social order.

RELIGION IN THE VEDIC AGE

As the caste system emerged and helped to organize Indian society, distinctive cultural and religious traditions also took shape. The Indo-Aryans entered India with traditions and beliefs that met the needs of a mobile and often violent society. During the early centuries after their arrival in India, those inherited traditions served them well as they fought to establish a place for themselves in the subcontinent. As they spread throughout India and mixed with the Dravidians, however, the Indo-Aryans encountered new religious ideas that they considered intriguing and persuasive. The resulting fusion of Indo-Aryan traditions with Dravidian beliefs and values laid the foundation for Hinduism, a faith immensely popular in India and parts of southeast Asia for more than two millennia.

Indo-Aryan Religion

As in Mesopotamia, Egypt, and other ancient civilizations, religious values in India reflected the larger society. During the early centuries following their migrations, for example, the Indo-Aryans spread through the Punjab and other parts of India, often fighting with the Dravidians and even among themselves. The hymns, songs, and prayers collected in the *Rig Veda* throw considerable light on Indo-Aryan values during this period.

Indo-Aryan Gods The chief deity of the *Rig Veda* was Indra, the boisterous and often violent character who was fond of both fighting and strong drink. Indra was primarily a war god. The Indo-Aryans portrayed him as the wielder of thunderbolts who led them into battle against their enemies. The Indo-Aryans also associated Indra with the weather and especially with the coming of rain to water the crops and the land. The Indo-Aryans also recognized a host of other deities, including gods of the sun, the sky, the moon, fire, health, disease, dawn, and the underworld. The preeminence of Indra, however, reflects the instability and turbulence of early Vedic society.

Although the Aryans accorded high respect to Indra and his military leadership, their religion did not neglect ethics. They believed that Varuna presided over the sky from his heavenly palace, where he oversaw the behavior of mortals and preserved the cosmic order. Varuna and his helpers despised lying and evil deeds of all sorts, and they afflicted wrongdoers with severe punishments, including disease and death. They dispatched the souls of serious evildoers to the subterranean House of Clay, a dreary and miserable realm of punishment, while allowing souls of the virtuous to enter the Indo-Aryan heaven known as the World of the Fathers.

Ritual Sacrifices Yet that ethical concern was a relatively minor aspect of Indo-Aryan religion during early Vedic times. Far more important from a practical point of view was the proper performance of ritual sacrifices by which the Indo-Aryans hoped to win the favor of the gods. By the time the Indo-Aryans entered India, those sacrifices had become complex and elaborate affairs. They involved the slaughter of dozens and sometimes even hundreds of specially prepared animals—cattle, sheep, goats, and horses from the Indo-Aryans' herds—as priests spoke the sacred and mysterious chants and worshipers partook of soma, a hallucinogenic concoction that produced sensations of power and divine inspiration. The Indo-Aryans believed that during the sacrificial event their gods visited the earth and joined the worshipers in ritual eating and drinking. By pleasing the gods with frequent and large sacrifices, the Indo-Aryans expected to gain divine support that would ensure military success, large families, long life, and abundant herds of cattle. But those rewards required constant attention to religious ritual: proper honor for the gods called for households to have brahmins perform no fewer than five sacrifices per day—a time-consuming and expensive obligation.

Spirituality Later in the Vedic age, Indo-Aryan religious thought underwent a remarkable evolution. As the centuries passed, many Indo-Aryans became dissatisfied with the sacrificial cults of the Vedas, which increasingly seemed like mechanical rituals rather than a genuine means of communicating with the gods. Even brahmins sometimes became disenchanted with rituals that did not satisfy spiritual longings. Beginning about 800 B.C.E. many men seeking enlightenment left their villages and retreated to the forests of the Ganges valley, where they lived as hermits and reflected on the relationships between human beings, the world, and the gods. They contemplated the Vedas and sought mystical understandings of the texts, and they attracted disciples who also thirsted for a spiritually fulfilling faith.

These mystics drew inspiration from the religious beliefs of Dravidian peoples, who often worshiped nature spirits that they associated with fertility and the generation of new life. Dravidians also believed that human souls took on new physical forms after the deaths of their bodily hosts. Sometimes souls returned as plants or animals, sometimes in the bodily shell of newborn humans. The notion that souls could experience transmigration and reincarnation—that an individual soul could depart one body at death and become associated with another body through a new birth—intrigued thoughtful people and a remarkable tradition of religious thinking emerged.

Indra, chief deity of the Rig Veda, rides an elephant that carries him through the clouds.
Alistair Laming/Alamy Stock Photo

SOURCES FROM THE PAST

The *Mundaka Upanishad* on the Nature of Brahman

Indan commentators often spoke of the Mundaka Upanishad *as "the shaving Upanishad" because, like a razor, it cut off errors arising in the mind. Its purpose was to teach knowledge of Brahman, which it held was not accessible through sacrifices, rites, or even worship. Only proper instruction would bring understanding of Brahman.*

This knowledge of Brahman which Brahma taught to Atharva, Atharva taught first to Angir; Angir taught it to Satyavah Bharadwaja; and Bharadwaja taught it in due succession to the sage Angiras.

Now there was a man named Shaunaka, the great householder, who approached the sage Angiras with fitting humility, and asked of him: What is that, O Bhagavan (revered master), which being known, all else becomes known?

The Sage replied: There are two kinds of knowledge to be known, so we are told by the knowers of Brahman – higher knowledge and lower knowledge.

Lower knowledge consists of the Rig Veda, Yajur Veda, Sama Veda, Artharva Veda, phonetics, ceremony, grammar, etymology, meter, and astronomy. Higher knowledge is that by which the Imperishable (Brahman) is known.

He that cannot be seen, which cannot be seized, which has no origin and no attributes, no eyes or ears, no hands nor feet; he that is eternal, diversely manifesting, all-pervading, extremely subtle; that Imperishable One the wise regard as the Source of all created things.

As the spider spins its thread, as herbs spring from the earth, as hair grows on the living body, likewise does the universe come forth from the Imperishable.

> What is the author's purpose in comparing spiders and plants to the path toward eternal salvation?

Through Tapas (the power of meditation), Brahman expands; from this food is produced; from food comes Prana (energy), mind, the elements, the worlds, good works and their immortal fruit.

From that Spirit, the One who is all-perceiving and all-knowing, whose Tapas consists of wisdom, are born Brahma (the Creator), name, form and food.

This is the Truth: the sacrificial rites which the sages found in the hymns are described variously in the three Vedas. Perform them faithfully, O ye seekers of truth; this is the path that leads to the world of good deeds . . . .

> How do you understand the relationship between the spirit Brahman and the god Brahma?

This is the truth. As from the blazing fire burst forth thousands of sparks like unto fire, so also, gentle youth, do the various beings spring forth from the Imperishable and return thither again.

That Being is without form; He exists both without and within; He is unborn; without Breath and without mind; pure, higher than the High Imperishable.

From Him are born Prana (the life force), mind, all the sense organs, ether, air, fire, water and the earth, support of all.

Fire is His head, sun and moon are His eyes, the four quarters are His ears, the revealed Vedas are His words, His breath is the air, His heart is the universe, and from His feet came forth the earth. He is the inner self of all living beings.

From Him comes the fire, whose fuel is the sun; from the moon come the clouds (rain); from the earth come all herbs; the male places the seed in the female, thus many beings are born from the Purusha (the Great Being).

From Him are born all oceans, mountains and diverse rivers. From Him come all herbs and juices, by which the inner self subsists, together with the great elements.

For Further Reflection

■ How was knowledge of Brahman passed on to humans?
■ What are some aspects of the lower kind of wisdom?
■ What is the ultimate aim of the higher kind of wisdom?
■ What practice in particular helps in attaining the higher kind of wisdom?
■ What similarities do you see between the power and role of Brahman and the creator gods of other religions?

Source: Brahma was the first of the Devas, the Creator of the universe, the Protector of the world. He taught his oldest son Atharva the knowledge of Brahman (the Supreme), which is the foundation of all knowledge. Swami Paramanande, trans. *The Upanishads. Boston,* Mass., 1919.

The Blending of Indo-Aryan and Dravidian Values

The Upanishads Traces of that tradition appear in the Vedas, but it achieved its fullest development in a body of works known as the **Upanishads,** which began to appear late in the Vedic age, about 800 to 400 B.C.E. (Later Upanishads continued to appear until the fifteenth century C.E., but the most important were those composed during the late Vedic age.) The word *upanishad* literally means "a sitting in front of," and it refers to the practice of disciples gathering before a sage for discussion of religious issues. Most of the disciples were men, but not all. Gargi Vakaknavi, for example, was a woman who drove the eminent sage Yajnavalkya to exasperation because he could not answer her persistent questions. The Upanishads often took the form of dialogues that explored the Vedas and the religious issues that they raised.

Brahman, the Universal Soul The Upanishads taught that individual human beings in fact are not separate and autonomous creatures. Instead, each person forms a small part of a universal soul, known as **Brahman.** Whereas the physical world is a theater of change, instability, and illusion, Brahman is an eternal, unchanging, permanent foundation for all things that exist—hence the only genuine reality. The authors of the Upanishads believed that individual souls were born into the physical world not once, but many times: they believed that souls appeared most often as humans but

sometimes as animals and possibly even occasionally as plants or other vegetable matter. The highest goal of the individual soul, however, was to escape this cycle of birth and rebirth and enter into permanent union with Brahman.

Teachings of the Upanishads The Upanishads developed several specific doctrines to explain this line of thought. One was the doctrine of *samsara,* which held that upon death, individual souls go temporarily to the World of the Fathers and then return to earth in a new incarnation. Another was the doctrine of *karma,* which accounted for the specific incarnations that souls experienced. The *Brhadaranyaka Upanishad* offers a succinct explanation of the workings of karma: "Now as a man is like this or like that, according as he acts and according as he behaves, so will he be: a man of good acts will become good, a man of bad acts, bad. He becomes pure by pure deeds, bad by bad deeds." Thus individuals who lived virtuous lives and fulfilled all their duties could expect rebirth into a purer and more honorable existence—for example, into a higher and more distinguished caste. Those who accumulated a heavy burden of karma, however, would suffer in a future incarnation by being reborn into a difficult existence, or perhaps even into the body of an animal or an insect.

Even under the best of circumstances, the cycle of rebirth involved a certain amount of pain and suffering that inevitably accompany human existence. The authors of the Upanishads sought to escape the cycle altogether and attain the state of (*moksha*), which they characterized as a deep, dreamless sleep that came with permanent liberation from physical incarnation. That goal was difficult to reach because it entailed severing all ties to the physical world and identifying with the ultimate reality of Brahman, the universal soul.

Upanishads (oo-PAHN-ee-shahds)
moksha (mōkshə)

A cave painting from an undetermined age, perhaps several thousand years ago, shows that early inhabitants of India lived in close company with other residents of the natural world.

Dinodia Photos/Alamy Stock Photo

The two principal means to *moksha* were asceticism and meditation. By embarking on a regime of extreme asceticism—leading extremely simple lives and denying themselves all pleasure—individuals could purge themselves of desire for the comforts of the physical world. By practicing yoga, a form of intense and disciplined meditation that probably dates back to the Indus Civilization, they could concentrate on the nature of Brahman and its relationship to their souls. Diligent efforts, then, would enable individuals to achieve *moksha* by separating themselves from the physical world of change, illusion, and incarnation. Then their souls would merge with Brahman, and they would experience eternal, peaceful ecstasy.

Religion and Vedic Society Just as brahmin theories about the origins of *varna* distinctions reflected Indo-Aryan society about 1000 B.C.E., so the religious views of the Upanishads dovetailed with the social order of the late Vedic age. Some modern commentators have interpreted the worldview of the Upanishads—particularly the doctrines of samsara and karma—as a cynical ideology designed to justify the social inequalities imposed by the caste system. The doctrines of samsara and karma certainly reinforced the Vedic social order: they explained why individuals were born into their castes—because they had behaved virtuously or badly during a previous incarnation—and they encouraged individuals to observe their caste duties in hopes of enjoying a more comfortable and honorable incarnation in the future.

It would be overly simplistic, however, to consider these doctrines merely efforts of a hereditary elite to justify its position and maintain its hegemony over other classes of society. The sages who gave voice to these doctrines were conscientiously attempting to deal with genuine spiritual and intellectual problems. To them the material world seemed supremely superficial—a realm of constant change and illusion offering no clear sign as to the nature of ultimate reality. It seemed logical to suppose that a more real and substantial world stood behind the one that they inhabited. Greek philosophers, Christian theologians, and many others have arrived at similar positions during the course of the centuries. It could thus be argued that the authors of the Upanishads sought ultimate truth and certain knowledge in an ideal world that transcends our own. Their formulation of concepts such as samsara and karma represented efforts to characterize the relationship between the world of physical incarnation and the realm of ultimate truth and reality.

The Upanishads not only influenced Indian thought about the nature of the world but also called for the observance of high ethical standards. They discouraged greed, envy, gluttony, and all manner of vice because those traits indicated excessive attachment to the material world and insufficient concentration on union with the universal soul. The Upanishads advocated honesty, self-control, charity, and mercy. Most of all, they encouraged the cultivation of personal integrity—a self-knowledge that would incline individuals naturally toward both ethical behavior and union with Brahman. The Upanishads also taught respect for all living things, animal as well as human. Animal bodies, after all, might well hold incarnations of unfortunate souls suffering the effects of a heavy debt of karma. Despite the evil behavior of these souls in their earlier incarnations, devout individuals would not want to cause them additional suffering or harm. A vegetarian diet thus became a common feature of the ascetic regime.

What's Left Out? ▬▬ ▬▬ ▬▬ ▬▬ ▬▬

One of the most controversial and divisive questions in the history of ancient South Asia has been whether there was or was not a major migration of Indo-Aryan peoples into the subcontinent sometime between 2000 and 1500 B.C.E., as this chapter has argued. For some time many Indian scholars had argued that there had not been a significant migration of outside peoples into the subcontinent, and thus the very notion of a genetic divide between Dravidian and Aryan peoples was a myth. Early genetic evidence seemed to support this in that studies using matrilineal DNA (transmitted only from mothers to daughters) did not show evidence of any significant external infusion into the gene pool over the past twelve thousand five hundred years. However, more recent genetic research focusing on Y-chromosomes (transmitted through the male line) has shown that there was indeed a significant flow of external genes from Central Asia to South Asia roughly four thousand years ago, indicating that mostly male Indo-Aryan migrants had then intermarried with native females. This Y-chromosome evidence strikingly supports the impact of Indo-Aryan migrations on South Asian history, although the issue has become so controversial that there remains considerable resistance to this new evidence.

Source: "A Genetic Chronology for the Indian Subcontinent Points to Heavily Sex-Biased Dispersals," 16 scientists led by Prof. Martin P. Richards of the University of Huddersfield, UK, 2017. See also Tony Joseph, "How Genetics Is Settling the Aryan Migration Debate," *The Hindu,* June 16, 2017.

CONCLUSION

Like sub-Saharan African and other regions of Eurasia, South Asia was a land of cross-cultural interaction and exchange even in ancient times. Knowledge of agriculture made its way to the Indian subcontinent as early as 7000 B.C.E., probably from southwest Asia, and a productive agricultural economy made possible the construction of a sophisticated society in the Indus River valley that established trade relations with peoples as far away as Mesopotamia. The arrival of Indo-Aryan migrants led to intense interactions between peoples of markedly different social and cultural traditions. Although they often engaged in conflicts, they also found ways of dealing with one another and living together in a common land. By the end of the Vedic age, the merging of Indo-Aryan and Dravidian traditions had generated a distinctive Indian society. Agriculture and herding had spread to most parts of the Indian subcontinent. Regional states maintained order over substantial territories and established kingship as the most common form of government. The caste system not only endowed social groups with a powerful sense of identity but also helped to maintain public order. A distinctive set of religious beliefs explained the world and the role of human beings in it, and the use of writing facilitated further reflection on spiritual and intellectual matters.

STUDY TERMS

Brahman (82)	Mohenjo-daro (72)
brahmins (77)	moksha (82)
caste (77)	*raja* (76)
dasas (76)	*samsara* (82)
Dravidians (75)	Sanskrit (76)
Indo-Aryans (75)	*shudras* (77)
Indra (70)	*untouchables* (77)
Indus River (72)	Upanishads (82)
jati (77)	*vaishyas* (77)
karma (82)	*varna* (77)
kshatriyas (77)	Vedas (75)
Laws of Manu (79)	

FOR FURTHER READING

Ainslie T. Embree, ed. *Sources of Indian Tradition.* 2 vols. 2nd ed. New York, 1988. An important collection of primary sources in translation.

Irfan Habib and Vijay Thakur, *The Vedic Age.* Thulika Books, New Delhi, 2016. This first volume in the multi-volume *People's History of India* offers a detailed account of various aspects of the development of South Asian culture and beliefs during the Vedic Age.

J. P. Mallory. *In Search of the Indo-Europeans: Language, Archaeology, and Myth.* London, 1989. Carefully reviews modern theories about early Indo-European speakers in light of both the linguistic and the archaeological evidence.

Juan Mascaró, trans. *The Upanishads.* London, 1965. A superb English version of selected Upanishads by a gifted translator.

Shereen Ratnagar. *Trading Encounters: From the Euphrates to the Indus in the Bronze Age.* New Delhi, 2004. Relies on archaeological discoveries in examining commercial relations between Harappan society and Mesopotamia.

Charles River, *Mohenjodaro: The History and Legacy of the Ancient Settlement of the Indus Valley Civilization.* Charles Rivers Editors, 2016. An up to date account of the archaeology and cultural legacy of the Indus Civilization.

Andrew Robinson, *Indus. Lost Civilization.* Reaktion Books, London, 2016. A well-illustrated and well-written account of the rise and fall of the Indus Civilization.

Romila Thapar. *Early India: From the Origins to A.D. 1300.* Berkeley, 2003. A fresh view by one of the leading scholars of early Indian history.

Stanley Wolpert. *A New History of India.* 7th ed. New York, 2004. A concise and readable survey of Indian history.

The Emergence of Complex Society in Mainland East Asia

ZOOMING IN ON TRADITIONS

King Yu and the Taming of the Yellow River

Ancient Chinese histories tell the stories of heroic figures who invented agriculture, domesticated animals, taught people to marry and live in families, created music, introduced the calendar, and instructed people in the arts and crafts. Most important of these heroes were three sage-kings—Yao, Shun, and Yu—who, according to ancient Chinese historian Sima Qian, laid the foundations of Chinese society. King Yao was a towering figure, sometimes associated with a mountain, who was extraordinarily modest, sincere, and respectful. Yao's virtuous influence brought harmony to his family, the larger society, and ultimately all the states of China. King Shun succeeded Yao and continued his work by ordering the four seasons of the year and instituting uniform weights, measures, and units of time.

Most dashing of the sage-kings was Yu, a vigorous and tireless worker who rescued China from the raging waters of the flooding Yellow River. Before Yu, according to the stories, experts tried to control the Yellow River's floods by building dikes to contain its waters. The river was much too large and strong for the dikes, however, and when it broke through them it unleashed massive floods. Yu abandoned the effort to dam the Yellow River and organized two alternative strategies. He dredged the river to deepen its channel and minimize the likelihood of overflows, and he dug canals parallel to the river

Bronze battle axe of the Shang Dynasty. The axe depicts a fearsome face symbolizing power and military prowess and was probably used in battle by an important Shang elite warrior.

Archive PL/Alamy Stock Photo

so that floodwaters would flow harmlessly to the sea without devastating the countryside.

According to Sima Qian, Yu worked on the river for thirteen years without ever returning home. Because he tamed the Yellow River and made it possible to cultivate rice and millet, Yu became a popular hero. Poets praised the man who protected fields and villages from deadly and destructive floods. Historians such as Sima Qian reported that he led the waters to the sea in a manner as orderly as lords proceeding to a formal reception. Eventually, Yu succeeded King Shun as leader of the Chinese people, and according to Sima Qian, he founded the Xia dynasty, which many believe to have been the first ruling house of ancient China.

The legends of Yao, Shun, and Yu no doubt exaggerated the virtues and deeds of the sage-kings. Agriculture, arts, crafts, marriage, family, government, and means of water control developed over an extended period of time, and no single individual was responsible for introducing them into China. Yet legends about early heroic figures reflected the interest of a people in the traditions that defined their society. At the same time, the moral thinkers who transmitted the legends used them to advocate values they considered beneficial for their society. By exalting Yao, Shun, and Yu as exemplars of virtue, Chinese moralists promoted the values of social harmony and selfless, dedicated work that the sage-kings represented.

CHAPTER OVERVIEW

Groups of the hominid species *Homo erectus* made their way to east Asia almost two million years ago. They and the *Homo sapiens* who followed used stone tools and relied on a hunting and gathering economy like their counterparts in other regions of the earth. As in Mesopotamia, Egypt, and India, however, population pressures in east Asia encouraged communities to experiment with agriculture. Peoples of southern China and southeast Asia domesticated rice after about 7000 B.C.E., and by 5000 B.C.E. neolithic villages throughout the valley of the Yangzi River (Chang Jiang) depended on rice as the staple item in their diet. During the same era, millet came under cultivation farther north, in the valley of the Yellow River (Huang He), where neolithic communities flourished by 5000 B.C.E. In later centuries wheat and barley made their way from Mesopotamia to northern China, and by 2000 B.C.E. they supplemented millet as staple foods of the region.

Agricultural surpluses supported numerous neolithic communities throughout east Asia. During the centuries after 3000 B.C.E., residents of the Yangzi River and Yellow River valleys lived in agricultural villages and communicated and traded with others throughout the region. During the second millennium B.C.E., they began to establish cities, build large states, and construct distinctive social and cultural traditions. Powerful dynastic states based in the Yellow River valley brought much of China under their authority and forged many local communities into a larger unified society. Sharp social distinctions emerged in early Chinese society, and patriarchal family heads exercised authority in both public and private affairs. A distinctive form of writing supported the development of sophisticated cultural traditions. Meanwhile, Chinese cultivators had frequent encounters with peoples from other societies, particularly with nomadic herders inhabiting the grassy steppes of central Asia. Migrating frequently on the steppes, nomadic peoples linked China with lands to the west. As in early Mesopotamia, Egypt, and India, then, complex society in east Asia promoted the development of distinctive social and cultural traditions in the context of cross-cultural interaction and exchange.

POLITICAL ORGANIZATION IN EARLY CHINA

As agricultural populations expanded, villages and towns flourished throughout the **Yellow River** and **Yangzi River** valleys. Originally, those settlements looked after their own affairs and organized local states that maintained order in small territories. By the late centuries of the third millennium B.C.E., however, much larger regional states began to emerge. Among the most important were perhaps those of the Xia, and certainly the powerful Shang and Zhou dynasties, which progressively brought much of China under their authority and laid a political foundation for the development of a distinctive Chinese society.

CHRONOLOGY	
5000–3000 B.C.E.	Yangshao society
2100–1600 B.C.E.	Xia dynasty
1600–1050 B.C.E.	Shang dynasty
1050–256 B.C.E.	Zhou dynasty
480–221 B.C.E.	Period of the Warring States

Yangzi (YAHNG-zuh)

Xia (SHYAH)

Zhou (JOH)

Early Agricultural Society and the Xia Dynasty

The Yellow River Like the Indus, the Yellow River is boisterous and unpredictable. It rises in the mountains bordering the high plateau of Tibet, and it courses almost 4,700 kilometers (2,920 miles) before emptying into the Yellow Sea. It takes its name, Huang He, meaning "Yellow River," from the vast quantities of light-colored loess soil that it picks up along its route. Loess is an extremely fine, powderlike soil that was deposited on the plains of northern China, as well as in several other parts of the world, after the retreat of the glaciers at the end of the last ice age, about twelve thousand to fifteen thousand years ago. So much loess becomes suspended in the Yellow River that the water turns yellow and the river takes on the consistency of a soup. The soil gradually builds up, raising the riverbed and forcing the water out of its established path. The Yellow River periodically unleashes a tremendous flood that devastates fields, communities, and anything else in its way. The Yellow River has altered its course many times and has caused so much destruction that it has earned the nickname "China's Sorrow."

Yet geographic conditions have also supported the development of complex society in China. During most years, there is enough rainfall for crops, so early cultivators had no need to build complex irrigation systems like those of Mesopotamia. They invested a great deal of labor, however, in dredging the river and building dikes, in a partially successful effort to limit the flood damage. Loess soil is extremely fertile and easy to work, so even before the introduction of metal tools, cultivators using wooden implements could bring in generous harvests.

Yangshao Society and Banpo Village
Abundant harvests in northern China supported the development of several neolithic societies during the centuries after 5000 B.C.E. Each developed its own style of pottery and architecture, and each likely had its own political, social, and cultural traditions. Yangshao society, which flourished from about 5000 to 3000 B.C.E. in the middle region of the Yellow River valley, is especially well known from the discovery in 1952 of an entire neolithic village at Banpo, near modern Xi'an. Excavations at Banpo, and many other sites discovered more recently, have unearthed a large quantity of fine painted pottery and bone

Pottery bowl from the early Yangshao era excavated at Banpo, near modern Xi'an. The bowl is fine red pottery decorated with masks and fishnets in black.
Lou-Foto/Alamy Stock Photo

tools used by early cultivators in the sixth and fifth millennia B.C.E.

As the human population increased, settlements like that at Banpo cropped up throughout much of China, in the valley of the Yangzi River as well as the Yellow River. In east Asia, as in other parts of the world, the concentration of people in small areas brought a need for recognized authorities who could maintain order, resolve disputes, and organize public works projects. Village-level organization sufficed for purely local affairs, but it did little to prevent or resolve conflicts between villages and did not have the authority to organize large-scale projects in the interests of the larger community.

Chinese legends and early historians such as Sima Qian speak of three ancient dynasties—the Xia, the Shang, and the Zhou—that arose before the Qin and Han dynasties brought China under unified rule in the third century B.C.E. The Xia, Shang, and Zhou dynasties were hereditary states that extended their control over progressively larger regions, although none of them embraced all the territory claimed by later Chinese dynasties. Large numbers of written accounts survive to throw light on the Zhou dynasty, which scholars have long recognized as a historical ruling house. Until the twentieth century, however, information about the Xia and Shang dynasties came only from legendary accounts that scholars mostly did not trust. As a result, many historians dismissed reports of the Xia and the Shang dynasties as mythical fantasies. Only in the twentieth century did archaeological excavations turn up evidence that certainly the Shang, and perhaps the Xia, were indeed historical dynasties rather than figments of ancient imaginations.

The Xia Dynasty
Archaeological study of the **Xia dynasty** has made significant progress over recent years. Archaeological discoveries now more strongly support the idea that the Xia dynasty made one of the first efforts to organize public life in China on a large scale. Although it was not the only early state in China, the Xia appears to have been one of the more vigorous of its time. The dynasty perhaps came into being about 2100 B.C.E. in roughly the same region as the Yangshao society. By extending formal control over this region, the Xia dynasty established a precedent for hereditary monarchical rule in China.

Ancient legends, many based on the words of Han Dynasty historian Sima Qian, credit the dynasty's founder, the sage-king Yu, with the organization of effective flood-control projects: thus here, as in Mesopotamia and Egypt, the need to

MAP 5.1 The Xia, Shang, and Zhou dynasties, 2100–256 B.C.E.

Note that the three dynasties extended their territorial reach through time.

What role did technology play in the increasing size of early Chinese states?

organize large-scale public works projects helped to establish recognized authorities and formal political institutions. Although little information survives about the political institutions of the Xia, the dynasty's rulers may have exercised power throughout the middle Yellow River valley by controlling the leaders of individual villages. The dynasty encouraged the founding of cities and the development of metallurgy because the ruling classes needed administrative centers and bronze weapons to maintain their control. The excavated city of Erlitou, near Luoyang, might well have been the capital of the Xia dynasty. Excavations have shown that the city featured a large, palace-type structure as well as more modest houses, pottery workshops, and a bronze foundry.

The Shang Dynasty

According to Sima Qian the last Xia king was an oppressive despot who lost his realm to the founder of the **Shang dynasty.** In fact, the Xia state did not entirely collapse and did not disappear so much as it gave way gradually before the Shang, which arose in a region to the south and east of the Xia realm. Tradition assigns the Shang dynasty to the period 1766

to 1122 B.C.E., although recent archaeological studies suggest that the Shang probably ruled from roughly 1600 to 1050 B.C.E. Because the Shang dynasty left written records as well as material remains, the basic features of early Chinese society come into much clearer focus than they did during the Xia.

Bronze Metallurgy and Horse-Drawn Chariots

Technology helps to explain the rise and success of the Shang dynasty. Bronze metallurgy transformed Chinese society during Shang times and probably enabled Shang rulers to displace the Xia dynasty. Some scholars believe metallurgy went to China from southwest Asia. They argue that this and other technologies traveled to China as well as India with the early Indo-European migrants (discussed in chapter 2), some of whom made their way to the Tarim Basin (now Xinjiang province in western China) as early as 2000 B.C.E. Other scholars dispute this and argue that Chinese people independently invented these technologies as the need for them arose.

Bronze metallurgy reached China before the Shang dynasty, and indeed the Xia dynasty had already made use of bronze tools and weapons. But Shang ruling elites managed to monopolize the production of bronze in the Yellow River valley by controlling access to copper and tin ores. They also dramatically expanded production by employing government craftsmen to turn out large quantities of bronze axes, spears, knives, and arrowheads exclusively for the Shang rulers and their armies. Control over bronze production strengthened Shang military forces and provided them with arms far superior to stone, wood, and bone weapons wielded by their rivals.

Shang nobles also used bronze to make fittings for their horse-drawn chariots, which began to appear in China between about 1500 and 1200 B.C.E. Like the Aryans in India and Assyrians in Mesopotamia, Shang warriors used these vehicles to devastating effect against adversaries who lacked horses and chariots. With their arsenal of bronze weapons, Shang armies had little difficulty imposing their rule on agricultural villages and extending their influence throughout much of the Yellow River valley. Meanwhile, because the ruling elites did not permit free production of bronze, potential rebels or competitors had little hope of resisting Shang forces and even less possibility of displacing the dynasty.

Shang kings extended their rule to a large portion of northeastern China centered on the modern-day province of Henan. Like state builders in other parts of the world, the kings claimed a generous portion of the surplus agricultural production from the regions they controlled and then used that surplus to support military forces, political allies, and others who could help them maintain their rule. Shang rulers

Xinjiang (shin-jyahng)

A tomb from the early Zhou dynasty containing the remains of horses and war chariots, which transformed military affairs in ancient China. Survivors sacrificed the horses and buried them along with the chariots for use by the tomb's occupant after his death.

akg/Bildarchiv Steffens/Newscom

clearly had abundant military force at their disposal. Surviving records mention armies of 3,000, 5,000, 10,000, and even 13,000 troops, and one report mentions the capture of 30,000 enemy troops. Although those numbers are probably exaggerated, they still suggest that Shang rulers maintained a powerful military machine.

Shang Political Organization Like their Xia predecessors, Shang rulers also relied on political alliances. They did not rule a highly centralized state. Rather, their authority rested on a vast network of walled towns whose local rulers recognized the authority of the Shang kings. During the course of the dynasty, Shang kings may have controlled one thousand or more towns. Apart from local rulers of those towns, others who shared the agricultural surplus of Shang China included advisers. Ministers, craftsmen, and metalsmiths, who in their various ways helped Shang rulers shape policy or spread their influence throughout their realm.

Shang society revolved around several large cities, the first cities to appear anywhere in East Asia. According to tradition, the Shang capital moved six times during the course of the dynasty. Though originally chosen for political and military reasons, in each case the capital also became an important social, economic, and cultural center—the site not only of administration and military command but also of bronze foundries, arts, crafts, trade, and religious observances.

The Shang Capital at Ao Excavations at two sites have revealed much about the workings of the Shang dynasty. The Shang named one of its earliest capitals **Ao,** and archaeologists have found its remains near modern Zhengzhou. The most remarkable feature of this site is the city wall, which originally stood at least 10 meters (33 feet) high, with a base some 20 meters (66 feet) thick. The wall consisted of layer upon layer of pounded earth—soil packed firmly between wooden forms and then pounded with mallets until it reached rocklike hardness before the addition of a new layer of soil on top. This building technique, still used in the countryside of northern China, can produce structures of tremendous durability. Even today, for example, parts of the wall of Ao survive to a height of 3 to 4 meters (10 to 13 feet). The investment in labor required to build this wall testifies to the ability of Shang rulers to mobilize their subjects: modern estimates suggest that the wall required the services of ten thousand laborers working for at least ten and perhaps as many as twenty years.

The Shang Capital at Yin Even more impressive than Ao is the site of Yin, near modern Anyang, which was the capital during the last two or three centuries of the Shang dynasty. Archaeologists working at Yin have identified a complex of royal palaces; archives with written documents; several residential neighborhoods; two large bronze foundries; several workshops used by potters, woodworkers, bone carvers, and other craftsmen; and scattered burial grounds.

Eleven large and lavish tombs constructed for Shang kings, as well as other, more modest tombs, have received

Zhengzhou (jeng-joh)

particular attention. Like the resting places of the Egyptian pharaohs, most of these tombs attracted grave robbers soon after their construction. Enough remains, however, to show that the later Shang kings continued to command the high respect enjoyed by their predecessors at Ao. The graves included thousands of objects—chariots; weapons; bronze goods; pottery; carvings of jade and ivory; cowry shells (which served both as money and as exotic ornamentation); and sacrificial victims, including dogs, horses, and scores of sacrificed humans intended to serve the deceased royals in another existence. One tomb alone contained skeletons of more than three hundred sacrificial victims—probably wives, servants, friends, and hunting companions—who joined the Shang king in death.

The Tomb of Lady Fu Hao

Most important of the tombs at Yin is that of **Fu Hao,** one of sixty-four consorts (wives) of the Shang king Wu Ding, who ruled in the thirteenth century B.C.E. Fu Hao's resting place is the only tomb at Yin to escape the notice of grave robbers—perhaps because it was located in the Shang palace rather than in the cemetery that held other royal tombs. In any case, after her burial about 1250 B.C.E., Fu Hao's tomb remained undisturbed for more than three thousand years until Chinese archaeologists discovered it and excavated it in 1976.

Fu Hao was King Wu Ding's favorite consort, and her tomb reflected her status. It contained 468 bronze objects, including 130 weapons, 23 bells, and 4 mirrors. The bronze items in her tomb weighed about 1,600 kilograms (3,500 pounds) in total. Metalsmiths would have required 11 tons of ore to produce these objects. In an age when bronze was extremely expensive and hence rare, Fu Hao and the Shang royal family were conspicuous consumers of that valuable commodity. Quite apart from bronzewares, Fu Hao's tomb contained 755 jade carvings, 564 bone carvings, 5 finely carved ivory cups, 11 pottery objects, and 6,900 cowry shells that were probably used as money during the Shang. The tomb also held

The tomb of Lady Fu Hao as it was discovered by archaeologists, now displayed in the Yinxu natural history garden Anyang Henan China Exhibition

Liu Xiaoyang/China Images/Alamy Stock Photo

the remains of six dogs and the skeletons of sixteen humans—sacrificial victims buried with Fu Hao to guard her and attend to her needs after death. Fu Hao's unlooted tomb has thrown valuable light on the Shang dynasty and the resources that were available to residents of the royal court.

Beyond the Yellow River Valley   Like the Xia state, the Shang realm was only one of many that organized public life in ancient China. Legendary and historical accounts paid special attention to the Xia and Shang dynasties because of their location in the Yellow River valley, where the first Chinese imperial states later appeared. But archaeological excavations are making it clear that similar states dominated other regions at the same time the Xia and Shang ruled the Yellow River valley. Recent excavations, for example, have unearthed evidence of a very large city at Sanxingdui in modern-day Sichuan province (southwestern China). Occupied about 1700 to 1000 B.C.E., the city was roughly contemporaneous with the Shang dynasty, and it probably served as capital of a regional kingdom. Like their Xia and Shang counterparts, tombs at Sanxingdui held large quantities of bronze, jade, stone, and pottery objects, as well as cowry shells and elephant tusks, that indicate close relationships with societies in the valleys of both the Yangzi River and the Yellow River.

The Zhou Dynasty

Little information survives to illustrate the principles of law, justice, and administration by which Shang rulers maintained order. They did not promulgate law codes such as those issued in Mesopotamia but, rather, ruled by proclamation or decree, trusting their military forces and political allies to enforce their will. The principles of ancient Chinese politics and statecraft become more clear in the practices of the **Zhou dynasty,** which succeeded the Shang as the ruling dynasty of northern China. Dwelling in the Wei River valley of northwestern China (modern Shaanxi province), the Zhou were a formidable people who battled Shang forces in the east and nomadic raiders from the steppes in the west. Eventually, the Zhou allied with the Shang and won recognition as kings of the western regions. Because they organized their allies more effectively than the Shang, however, they gradually eclipsed the Shang dynasty and ultimately displaced it altogether.

Bronze mask with gold leaf, discovered in a tomb at Sanxingdui in Southern China.
Bill Perry/Shutterstock

Rise of the Zhou   Shang and Zhou ambitions collided in the eleventh century B.C.E. According to Zhou accounts, the last Shang king was a criminal fool who gave himself over to wine, women, tyranny, and greed. As a result, many of the towns and political districts subject to the Shang transferred their loyalties to the Zhou. After several unsuccessful attempts to discipline the Shang king, Zhou forces seized the Shang capital of Yin, beheaded the king, and replaced his administration with their own state sometime around 1050 B.C.E. The new rulers allowed Shang heirs to continue governing small districts but reserved for themselves the right to oversee affairs throughout the realm. The new dynasty ruled most of northern and central China, at least nominally, until 256 B.C.E.

The Mandate of Heaven   In justifying the deposition of the Shang, some two centuries after the event, spokesmen for the Zhou dynasty articulated a set of principles that have influenced Chinese thinking about government and political legitimacy through to the twentieth century C.E. The Zhou theory of politics rested on the assumption that earthly events were closely related to heavenly affairs. More specifically, heavenly powers granted the right to govern—the **mandate of heaven**—to an especially deserving individual known as the "son of heaven." The ruler then served as a link between heaven and earth. He had the duty to govern conscientiously, observe high standards of honor and justice, and maintain order and harmony within his realm. As long as he did so, the heavenly powers would approve of his work, the cosmos would enjoy a harmonious and well-balanced stability, and the ruling dynasty would retain its mandate to govern. If a ruler failed in his duties, however, chaos and suffering would afflict his realm, the cosmos would fall out of balance, and the displeased heavenly powers would withdraw the mandate to rule and transfer it to a more deserving candidate. On the basis of that reasoning, later Zhou spokesmen explained the fall of the Shang and the transfer of the mandate of heaven to the Zhou. From that time until the twentieth century, Chinese ruling houses routinely invoked the doctrine of the mandate of heaven to justify their rule, and emperors habitually took the title "son of heaven."

Political Organization The Zhou state was much larger than the Shang. In fact, it was so extensive that a single central court could not rule the entire land effectively, at least not with the transportation and communication technologies available at that time. As a result, Zhou rulers relied on a decentralized administration: they entrusted power, authority, and responsibility to subordinates who in return owed allegiance, tribute, and military support to the central government.

During the early centuries of the dynasty, that system worked reasonably well. The conquerors continued to rule the Zhou ancestral homeland from their capital at Hao, near modern Xi'an, but they allotted possessions in conquered territories to relatives and other allies. The subordinates ruled their territories with limited supervision from the central government. In return for their political rights, they visited the Zhou royal court on specified occasions to demonstrate their continued loyalty to the dynasty, they delivered taxes and tribute that accounted for the major part of Zhou finances, and they provided military forces that the kings deployed in the interests of the Zhou state as a whole. When not already related to their subordinates, the Zhou rulers sought to arrange marriages that would strengthen their ties to their political allies.

Weakening of the Zhou Despite their best efforts, however, the Zhou kings could not maintain control indefinitely over this decentralized political system. Subordinates gradually established their own bases of power: they ruled their territories not only as allies of the Zhou kings but also as long-established and traditional governors. They set up regional bureaucracies, armies, and tax systems, which allowed them to consolidate their rule and exercise their authority. They promulgated law codes and enforced them with their own forces. As they became more secure in their rule, they also became more independent of the Zhou dynasty itself. Subordinates sometimes ignored their obligations to appear at the royal court or deliver tax proceeds. Occasionally, they refused to provide military support or even turned their forces against the dynasty in an effort to build up their regional states.

The Eastern Zhou dynasty saw the development of weapons technology that resulted in stronger and more lethal weapons. Bronze and iron weapons such as those depicted here contributed to political instability and chronic warfare during the late Zhou dynasty.
G. DAGLI ORTI/Getty Images

Iron Metallurgy Technological developments also worked in favor of subordinate rulers. The Shang kings had largely monopolized the production of bronze weapons by controlling the sources of copper and tin, but because of technological changes, Zhou rulers were unable to control metal production as closely as their predecessors. During the first millennium B.C.E., the technology of iron metallurgy emerged in China and gradually made bronze weapons obsolete. Because iron ores are cheaper, more abundant, and more widely distributed than copper and tin, Zhou kings were unable to control access to them. Their subordinates moved quickly to establish ironworks and outfit their forces with iron weapons that were just as effective as those employed by Zhou armies. Thus iron weapons enabled subordinates to resist the central government and pursue their own interests.

In the early eighth century B.C.E., the Zhou rulers faced severe problems that brought the dynasty to the point of collapse. In 771 B.C.E. nomadic peoples, along with disaffected allies of the Zhou, invaded China from the west. They came during the rule of a particularly ineffective king who did not enjoy the respect of his political allies. When subordinates refused to support the king, the invaders overwhelmed the capital at Hao. Following that disaster, the royal court moved east to Luoyang in the Yellow River valley, which served as the Zhou capital until the end of the dynasty.

In reality, political power had now passed from the Zhou kings to their subordinates, and the royal court never regained its authority. During the fifth century B.C.E., territorial princes ignored the central government and used their resources to build, strengthen, and expand their states. They fought ferociously with one another in hopes of establishing themselves as leaders of a new political order. So violent were the last centuries of the Zhou dynasty that they are known as the **Period of the Warring States** (480–221 B.C.E.). In 256 B.C.E. the Zhou dynasty ended when the last king abdicated his position under pressure from his ambitious subordinate the king of Qin. Only with the establishment of the Qin dynasty in 221 B.C.E. did effective central government return to China.

MAP 5.2 China during the Period of the Warring States, 480–221 B.C.E.

Early Zhou rulers used iron tools and weapons to create a sizable kingdom. As knowledge of iron production spread, however, political and military leaders were able to establish several regional states that ended up locked in bitter conflict during the aptly named "Warring States" period.

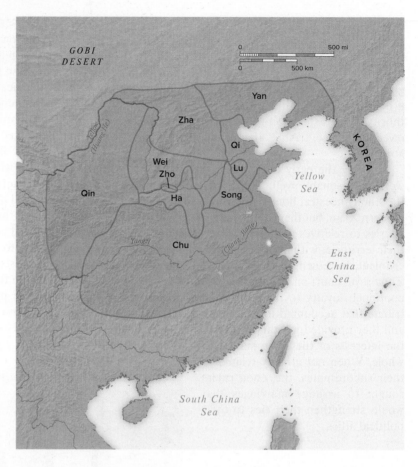

SOCIETY AND FAMILY IN ANCIENT CHINA

In China, as in other parts of the ancient world, the introduction of agriculture enabled individuals to accumulate wealth and preserve it within their families. Social distinctions began to appear during neolithic times, and during the reigns of the Xia, Shang, and Zhou dynasties the distinctions became even sharper. Throughout China the patriarchal family emerged as the institution that most directly influenced individuals' lives and their roles in the larger society.

The Social Order

Ruling Elites Already during the Xia dynasty, but especially under the Shang and the early Zhou, the royal family and allied noble families occupied the most honored positions in Chinese society. They resided in large, palatial compounds made of pounded earth, and they lived on the agricultural surplus and taxes delivered by their subjects. Because of the high cost of copper and tin, bronze implements were beyond the means of all but the wealthy, so the conspicuous consumption of bronze by ruling elites clearly set them apart from less privileged classes. Ruling elites possessed much of the bronze weaponry that ensured military strength and political hegemony, and through their subordinates and retainers they controlled most of the remaining bronze weapons available in northern China. They also supplied their households with cast-bronze utensils—pots, jars, wine cups, plates, serving dishes, mirrors, bells, drums, and vessels used in ritual ceremonies—which were beyond the means of less privileged people. These utensils, which can be found in many of the great museums of the world today, often featured elaborate, detailed decorations that indicated remarkable skill on the part of the artisans

who built the molds and cast the metal. Expensive bronze utensils bore steamed rice and rich dishes of fish, pheasant, poultry, pork, mutton, and rabbit to royal and aristocratic tables, whereas less privileged classes relied on clay pots and consumed much simpler fare, such as vegetables and porridges made of millet, wheat, or rice. Ruling elites consumed bronze in staggering quantities: the tomb of Marquis Yi of Zeng, a provincial governor of the late Zhou dynasty, contained a collection of bronze weapons and decorative objects that weighed almost 11 tons.

A privileged class of hereditary aristocrats rose from the military allies of Shang and Zhou rulers. Aristocrats possessed extensive landholdings, and they worked at administrative and military tasks. By Zhou times many of them lived in cities where they obtained at least an elementary education, and their standard of living was much more refined than that of the commoners and slaves who worked their fields and served their needs. Manuals of etiquette from Zhou times instructed the privileged classes in decorous behavior and outlined the proper way to carry out rituals. When dining in polite company, for example, the cultivated aristocrat should show honor to the host and refrain from gulping down food, swilling wine, making unpleasant noises, picking teeth at the table, and playing with food by rolling it into a ball.

The delicate design of this bronze wine vessel displays the high level of craftsmanship during the late Shang dynasty. What was the attraction of objects such as this to members of the elite class?

Werner Forman/Universal Images Group/Getty Images

Specialized Labor A small class of free artisans and craftsmen plied their trades in the cities of ancient China. Some, who worked almost exclusively for the privileged classes, enjoyed a reasonably comfortable existence. During the Shang dynasty, for example, bronzesmiths often lived in sturdy houses built of pounded earth. Jewelers, jade workers, embroiderers, and manufacturers of silk textiles also benefited socially because of their importance to the ruling elites.

Merchants and Trade There is little information about merchants and trade in ancient China until the latter part of the Zhou dynasty, but archaeological discoveries show that

long-distance trade routes may have reached China during the Shang dynasty. Despite the high mountain ranges and forbidding deserts that stood between China and complex societies in India and southwest Asia, small-scale trade networks linked China with lands to the west and south early in the third millennium B.C.E. Jade in Shang tombs came from modern Xinjiang in far western China, while Shang bronzesmiths worked with tin that came from the Malay peninsula in southeast Asia, and cowry shells came through southeast Asia from Burma and the Maldive Islands in the Indian Ocean. Archaeologists have unearthed a few pieces of Shang pottery from Mohenjo-daro and other Indus Civilization sites, suggesting that pottery may have been the most important trade item exported from China.

Meanwhile, Chinese mariners began to probe nearby waters for profitable sea routes. Legendary accounts credit King Yu, the supposed founder of the Xia dynasty, with the invention of sails. There is no archaeological indication of Chinese sails before about 500 B.C.E., but there is abundant evidence that Chinese mariners used large oar-propelled vessels before 2000 B.C.E. These watercraft supported fishing and trade with offshore islands even before the emergence of the first dynasties. By the time of the Shang dynasty, Chinese ships were traveling across the Yellow Sea to Korea. During the Zhou dynasty, shipbuilding emerged as a prominent business all along coastal China, and mariners had discovered how to navigate their vessels by the stars and other heavenly bodies.

Peasants Back on the land, a large class of peasants populated the Chinese countryside. They owned no land but provided agricultural, military, and labor services for their lords in exchange for plots to cultivate, security, and a portion of the harvest. They lived like their neolithic predecessors in small subterranean houses excavated to a depth of about 1 meter (3 feet) and protected from the elements by thatched walls and roofs. Women's duties included mostly indoor activities such as wine making, weaving, and cultivation of silkworms, whereas men spent most of their time outside working in the fields, hunting, and fishing.

Agricultural tools were primitive before the late Zhou dynasty. Farmers mostly relied on wooden digging sticks and spades with bone or stone tips, which were strong enough to cultivate the powdery loess soil of northern China; bronze tools were too expensive for peasant cultivators. Beginning about the sixth century B.C.E., however, iron production increased dramatically in China, and iron plows, picks, spades, hoes, sickles, knives, and rakes all came into daily use in the countryside.

Slaves There was also a sizable class of slaves, most of whom were enemy warriors captured during battles between the many competing states of ancient China. Slaves performed hard labor, such as the clearing of new fields or the building of

SOURCES FROM THE PAST

Peasants' Protest

Peasants in ancient China mostly did not own land. Instead, they worked as tenants on plots allotted to them by royal or aristocratic owners, who took sizable portions of the harvest. The following poem is from the Book of Songs, *a collection of verses dating from Zhou times.*

Large rats! Large rats!
Do not eat our millet.
Three years have we had to deal with you.
And you have not been willing to show any regard for us.
We will leave you,
And go to that happy land.
Happy land! Happy land!
There shall we find our place.

> Who are the people described as "large rats" in the poem?

Large rats! Large rats!
Do not eat our wheat.
Three years have we had to deal with you.
And you have not been willing to show any kindness to us.
We will leave you,
And go to that happy state.
Happy state! Happy state!
There shall we find ourselves aright.

> What is the happy state (or happy land) the author keeps referring to?

Large rats! Large rats!
Do not eat our springing grain!
Three years have we had to deal with you,
And you have not been willing to think of our toil.
We will leave you,
And go to those happy lands.
Happy lands! Happy lands!
Who will there make us always to groan?

For Further Reflection

■ What does this poem tell us about the lives of peasants in Zhou Dynasty China?
■ What does the poem tell us about the attitudes of elites toward peasants in Zhou Dynasty China?
■ Given that the peasants were illiterate, and that this poem must have been written by an educated person, how reliable a source do you think it is about the lives of peasants and elites in Zhou Dynasty China?

Source: James Legge, trans. *The Chinese Classics,* 5 vols. London: Henry Frowde, 1893, 4:171–72.

Updated with modern language by the textbook authors.

city walls, that required a large workforce. During the Shang dynasty, but rarely thereafter, hundreds of slaves also figured among the victims sacrificed during funerary, religious, and other ritual observances.

Family and Patriarchy

Throughout human history the family has served as the principal institution for the socialization of children and the preservation of cultural traditions. In China the extended family emerged as a particularly influential institution during neolithic times, and it continued to play a prominent role in the shaping of both private and public affairs after the appearance of the first dynasties, which largely ruled their territories through family and kinship groups.

Veneration of Ancestors One reason for the pronounced influence of the Chinese family is the veneration of ancestors, a practice with roots in neolithic times. In those early days agricultural peoples in China diligently tended the graves and memories of their departed ancestors. They believed that spirits of their ancestors passed into another realm of existence from which they had the power to support and protect their surviving families if the descendants displayed proper respect and ministered to the spirits' needs. Survivors buried tools, weapons, jewelry, and other material goods along with their dead. They also offered sacrifices of food and drink at the graves of departed relatives. The strong sense of ancestors' presence and continuing influence in the world led to an equally strong ethic of family solidarity. A family could expect to prosper only if all its members—the dead as well as the living—worked cooperatively toward common interests. The family became an institution linking departed generations to the living

and even to those yet unborn—an institution that wielded enormous influence over both the private and the public lives of its members.

In the absence of organized religion or official priesthood in ancient China, the patriarchal head of the family presided at rites and ceremonies honoring ancestors' spirits. As mediator between the family's living members and its departed relatives, the family patriarch possessed tremendous authority. He officiated not only at ceremonies honoring ancestors of his household but also at memorials for collateral and subordinate family branches that might include hundreds of individuals.

Patriarchal Society Chinese society vested authority principally in elderly males who headed their households. Like its counterparts in other regions, Chinese society took on a strongly patriarchal character—one that intensified with the emergence of large states. During neolithic times Chinese men wielded public authority, but they won their rights to it by virtue of the female line of their descent. Even if it did not vest power and authority in women, this system provided solid reasons for a family to honor its female members. As late as Shang times, two queens posthumously received the high honor of having temples dedicated to their memories.

Women's Influence Women occasionally played prominent roles in public life during Shang times. Fu Hao, for example, the consort of King Wu Ding whose tomb has thrown important light on Shang royal society, ventured beyond the corridors of the Shang palace to play a prominent role in public life. Documents from her tomb indicate Fu Hao supervised her estate and presided over sacrificial ceremonies that were usually the responsibility of men who were heads of their households. She even served as general on several military campaigns and once led thirteen thousand troops in a successful operation against a neighboring state. But see *What's Left Out* (see p. 99), for a further discussion of Lady Hao and the complexity of attitudes about gender in the Zhou Dynasty.

During the later Shang and Zhou dynasties, however, women came to live increasingly in the shadow of men. Large states brought the military and political contributions of men into sharp focus. The ruling classes performed elaborate ceremonies publicly honoring the spirits of departed ancestors, particularly males who had guided their families and led especially notable lives. Gradually, the emphasis on men became so intense that Chinese society lost its matrilineal character. After the Shang dynasty, not even queens and empresses merited temples dedicated exclusively to their memories: at most, they had the honor of being remembered in association with their illustrious husbands.

A Chinese lacquered coffin with dragon and bird decoration from the Chu state, 4th century B.C.E. (Hubei Provincial Museum, Wuhan, China)
Pictures from History/Newscom

SOURCES FROM THE PAST

Family Solidarity in Ancient China

A poem from the Book of Songs *illustrates clearly the importance of family connections in ancient China.*

The flowers of the cherry tree—
Are they not gorgeously displayed?
Of all the men in the world
There are none equal to brothers.

> Why is the author comparing brothers to flowers on a cherry tree?

On the dreaded occasions of death and burial,
It is brothers who greatly sympathize.
When fugitives are collected on the heights and low grounds,
They are brothers who will seek one another out.

There is the wagtail on the level height—
When brothers are in urgent difficulties,
Friends, though they may be good
Will only heave long sighs.

Brothers may quarrel inside the walls [of their own home],
But they will oppose insult from without,
When friends, however good they may be,
Will not afford help.

When death and disorder are past,
And there are tranquillity and rest,
Although they have brothers,
Some reckon them not equal to friends.

> What is the author implying about the attitude of friends during times of trouble and peace?

Your dishes may be set in array,
And you may drink to satiety.
But it is when your brothers are all present
That you are harmonious and happy, with child-like joy.

Loving union with wife and children
Is like the music of lutes.
But it is the accord of brothers
That makes the harmony and happiness lasting.

For the ordering of your family,
For the joy in your wife and children,
Examine this and study it—
Will you not find that it is truly so?

For Further Reflection

■ Why do you think this poem emphasizes the relationship between brothers as being most important for family solidarity?
■ List some of the ways in which brothers are expected to support each other.
■ How would you compare the relationship between brothers and that between a husband and his wife and children?
■ What does this poem tell us about the nature of gender relations in ancient China?

Source: James Legge, trans. *The Chinese Classics,* 5 vols. London: Henry Frowde, 1893, 4:250–53. (Translation slightly modified.)

EARLY CHINESE WRITING AND CULTURAL DEVELOPMENT

Organized religion did not play as important a role in ancient China as it did in other early societies. Early Chinese myths and legends explained the origins of the world, humans, agriculture, and the various arts and crafts. But Chinese thinkers saw no need to organize those ideas into systematic religious traditions. They often spoke of an impersonal heavenly power—*tian* ("heaven"), the agent responsible for bestowing and removing the mandate of heaven on rulers—but they did not recognize a personal supreme deity who intervened in human affairs or took special interest in human behavior. Nor did ancient China support a large class of priests like those of Mesopotamia, Egypt, and India who mediated between humans and the gods. A few priests conducted ritual observances in honor of royal ancestors at royal courts, but for the most part family patriarchs represented the interests of living generations to the spirits of departed ancestors.

In that environment, then, writing served as the foundation for a distinctive secular cultural tradition in ancient China. Chinese scribes may have used written symbols to keep simple records during Xia times, but surviving evidence suggests that writing came into extensive use only during the Shang dynasty. As in other lands, writing in east Asia quickly became an indispensable tool of government as well as a means of expressing ideas and offering reflections on humans and their world.

Oracle Bones and Early Chinese Writing

In Mesopotamia and India, administrators and merchants pioneered the use of writing. In China, however, the earliest known writing served the interests of rulers. Writing in China goes back at least to the early part of the second millennium (approximately 2000 through 1001) B.C.E. Surviving records indicate that scribes at the Shang royal court kept written accounts of important events on strips of bamboo or pieces of silk. Unfortunately, almost all those materials have perished, along with their messages. Yet one medium employed by ancient Chinese scribes has survived the ravages of time to prove beyond doubt that writing figured prominently in the political life of the Shang dynasty. Recognized just over a century ago, inscriptions on so-called oracle bones have thrown tremendous light both on the Shang dynasty and on the early stages of Chinese writing.

Oracle Bones Oracle bones were the principal instruments used by fortune-tellers in ancient China. In other early societies, specialists forecast the future by examining the entrails of sacrificed animals, divining the meaning of omens or celestial events such as eclipses, studying the flight of birds, or interpreting weather patterns. In China, diviners used specially prepared broad bones, such as the shoulder blades of oxen or turtle shells. They inscribed a question on the bone and then subjected it to heat, either by placing it into a fire or by scorching it with an extremely hot tool. When heated, the bone developed networks of splits and cracks. The fortune-teller then studied the patterns and determined the answer to the question inscribed on the bone. Often the diviner recorded the answer on the bone, and later scribes occasionally added further information about the events that actually came to pass.

During the nineteenth century C.E., peasants working in the fields around Anyang discovered many oracle bones bearing inscriptions in archaic Chinese writing. They did not recognize the writing, but they knew they had found an unusual and valuable commodity. They called their finds "dragon bones" and sold them to druggists, who ground them into powder that they resold as an especially potent medicine. Thus an untold number of oracle bones went to the relief of aches, pains, and ills before scholars recognized their true nature. During the late 1890s dragon bones came to the attention of historians and literary scholars, who soon determined that the inscriptions represented an early and previously unknown form of Chinese writing. Since then,

What's Left Out? ▰ ▰ ▰ ▰ ▰

In this chapter we have discussed the tomb of Lady Fu Hao, which was found by archaeologists in 1976 and contained an astonishing array of valuable artifacts. Lady Fu Hao is also mentioned in several oracle bone inscriptions in contexts that suggest she was an extraordinary woman in this age of patriarchy. She supervised state rituals; had her own estate outside the capital; and personally led several military campaigns, including an army of thirteen thousand troops sent against militarized nomads in the west. Yet, despite the lady's wealth and eminence, what should we make of the meaning of one of the oracle inscriptions about Lady Fu Hao, which notes that she was unlucky in childbirth because she gave birth to a girl?

This is how the oracle bone inscription describes her bad luck: "Lady Hao shall have a fortunate birth. The King prognosticated saying, if she gives birth on a *ding* day it shall be fortunate; if on a *geng* day, it shall be greatly auspicious. On the thirty-third day Lady Hao gave birth. It was not fortunate; it was a girl."

fragments of hundreds of thousands of oracle bones have come to light.

Most of the oracle bones have come from royal archives, and the questions posed on them clearly reveal the day-to-day concerns of the Shang royal court. Will the season's harvest be abundant or poor? Should the king attack his enemy or not? Would it please the royal ancestors to receive a sacrifice of animals—or perhaps of human slaves? During the reign of King Wu Ding, no fewer than 1,300 oracle bones recorded questions about the prospects for rain. Information preserved on the oracle bones has allowed historians to piece together an understanding of the political and social order of Shang times.

Early Chinese Writing Even more important, the oracle bones offer the earliest glimpse into the tradition of Chinese writing. The earliest form of Chinese writing, like Sumerian and Egyptian writing, was the pictograph—a conventional or stylized representation of an object. To represent complex or abstract notions, the written language often combined various pictographs into an ideograph. Thus, for example, the combined pictographs of a mother and child mean "good" in written Chinese. Unlike most other languages, written Chinese did not include an alphabetic or phonetic component.

The characters used in contemporary Chinese writing are direct descendants of those used in Shang times. Scholars have identified more than two thousand characters inscribed on oracle bones, most of which have a modern counterpart. (Contemporary Chinese writing regularly uses about five thousand characters, although thousands of additional characters are also used for technical and specialized purposes.) Over the centuries, written Chinese characters have undergone considerable modification: generally speaking, they have become more stylized, conventional, and abstract. Yet the affinities between Shang and later Chinese written characters are apparent at a glance.

Thought and Literature in Ancient China

The political interests of the Shang kings may have accounted for the origin of Chinese writing, but once established, the technology was available for other uses. Because Shang writing survives only on oracle bones and a small number of bronze inscriptions—all products that reflected the interests of the ruling elite that commissioned them—evidence for the expanded uses of writing comes only from the Zhou dynasty and later times.

A few oracle bones survive from Zhou times, along with a large number of inscriptions on bronze ceremonial utensils that the ruling classes used during rituals venerating their ancestors. Apart from those texts, the Zhou dynasty also produced books of poetry and history, manuals of divination and ritual, and essays dealing with moral, religious, philosophical, and political themes. Best known of these works are the reflections of Confucius and other late Zhou thinkers (discussed in chapter 8), which served as the intellectual foundation of classical Chinese society. But many other less famous works show that Zhou writers, mostly anonymous, were keen observers of the world and subtle commentators on human affairs.

Zhou Literature Several writings of the Zhou dynasty won recognition as works of high authority, and they exercised deep influence because they served as textbooks in Chinese schools. Among the most popular of these works in ancient times was the *Book of Changes,* which was a manual instructing diviners in the art of foretelling the future. Zhou

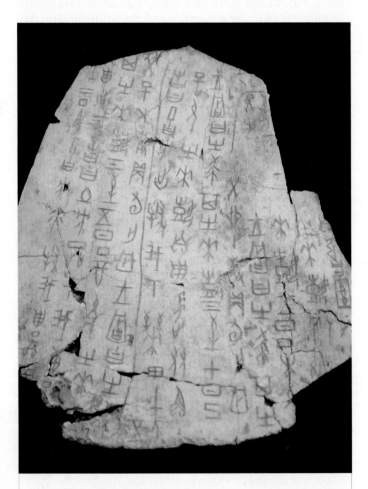

An oracle bone from Shang times has an inscribed question and numerous cracks caused by exposure of the bone to fire. Fortune-tellers answered the inscribed question by interpreting the cracks.

Zens photo/Moment Open/Getty Images

ruling elites also placed great emphasis on the *Book of History,* a collection of documents that justified the Zhou state and called for subjects to obey their overlords. Zhou aristocrats learned the art of polite behavior and the proper way to conduct rituals from the *Book of Etiquette,* also known as the *Book of Rites.*

The *Book of Songs* Most notable of the classic works, however, was the ***Book of Songs,*** also known as the *Book of Poetry* and the *Book of Odes,* a collection of verses on themes both light and serious. Though compiled and edited after 600 B.C.E., many of the 311 poems in the collection date from a much earlier period and reflect conditions of the early Zhou dynasty. Some of the poems had political implications because they recorded the illustrious deeds of heroic figures and ancient sage-kings, and others were hymns sung at ritual observances. Yet many of them are charming verses about life, love, family, friendship, eating, drinking, work, play, nature, and daily life that offer reflections on human affairs without particular concern for political or social conditions. One poem, for example, described a bride about to join the household of her husband:

> The peach tree is young and elegant;
> Brilliant are its flowers.
> This young lady is going to her future home,
> And will order well her chamber and house.
>
> The peach tree is young and elegant;
> Abundant will be its fruit.
> This young lady is going to her future home,
> And will order well her house and chamber.
>
> The peach tree is young and elegant;
> Luxuriant are its leaves.
> This young lady is going to her future home,
> And will order well her family.

Destruction of Early Chinese Literature The *Book of Songs* and other writings of the Zhou dynasty offer only a small sample of China's earliest literary tradition, for most Zhou writings have perished. Those written on delicate bamboo strips and silk fabrics have deteriorated: records indicate that the tomb of one Zhou king contained hundreds of books written on bamboo strips, but none of them survive. Other books fell victim to human enemies. When the imperial house of Qin ended the chaos of the Period of the Warring States and brought all of China under tightly centralized rule in 221 B.C.E., the victorious emperor ordered the destruction of all writings that did not have some immediate utilitarian value. He spared works on divination, agriculture, and medicine, but he condemned those on poetry, history, and philosophy, which he feared might

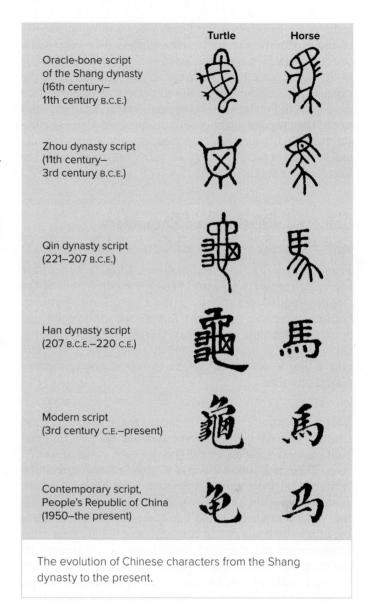

	Turtle	Horse
Oracle-bone script of the Shang dynasty (16th century–11th century B.C.E.)		
Zhou dynasty script (11th century–3rd century B.C.E.)		
Qin dynasty script (221–207 B.C.E.)		
Han dynasty script (207 B.C.E.–220 C.E.)		
Modern script (3rd century C.E.–present)		
Contemporary script, People's Republic of China (1950–the present)		

The evolution of Chinese characters from the Shang dynasty to the present.

inspire doubts about his government or encourage an independence of mind. Only a few items escaped, hidden away for a decade or more until scholars and writers could once again work without fear of persecution. These few survivors represent the earliest development of Chinese literature and moral thought.

ANCIENT CHINA AND THE LARGER WORLD

Towering mountains, forbidding deserts, and turbulent seas stood between China and other early societies of the eastern hemisphere. These geographic features did not entirely prevent communication between China and other lands, but they hindered the establishment of direct long-distance trade relations such as those linking Mesopotamia with Harappan

India or those between the Phoenicians and other peoples of the Mediterranean basin. Nevertheless, like other early societies, ancient China developed in the context of a larger world of interaction and exchange. Trade, migration, and the expansion of Chinese agricultural society all ensured that peoples of the various east Asian and central Asian societies would have regular dealings with one another. Chinese cultivators had particularly intense relations—sometimes friendly and sometimes hostile—with their neighbors to the north, the west, and the south.

Chinese Cultivators and Encounters with Nomadic Peoples of Central Asia

From the valley of the Yellow River, Chinese agriculture spread to the north and west. The dry environment of the steppes limited expansion in these directions, however, because harvests progressively diminished to the point that agriculture became impractical. During the Zhou dynasty, the zone of agriculture extended about 300 kilometers (186 miles) west of Xi'an, to the eastern region of modern Gansu province.

A glazed ceramic figurine of a mounted horse archer. This dates from the slightly later Han Dynasty.
Gift of Mrs. John Marriott, Mrs. John Barry Ryan, Gilbert W. Kahn, Roger Wolfe Kahn (children of Addie W. Kahn), 1949/Metropolitan Museum of Art

Steppe Nomads As they expanded to the north and west, Chinese cultivators encountered nomadic peoples who had built pastoral societies in the grassy steppe lands of central Asia. These lands were too arid to sustain large agricultural societies, but their grasses supported large herds of horses, cattle, sheep, goats, and yaks. After Indo-European peoples in the western steppes began to ride domesticated horses late in the fifth millennium, B.C.E., they were able to herd their other animals more effectively and push deeper into the steppes. By the late third millenium B.C.E., after learning the techniques of bronze metallurgy, they had introduced heavy wagons into the steppes, and by 2200 B.C.E. their wagons were increasingly prominent in the steppe lands east of the Ural Mountains. After about 1000 B.C.E. several clusters of nomadic peoples organized powerful, militarized herding societies on the Eurasian steppes.

Nomadic Society Nomadic peoples did little farming because the arid steppe did not reward efforts at cultivation. Instead, the nomads concentrated on herding their animals, driving them to regions where they could find food and water. The herds provided meat and milk as well as skins and bones from which the nomads fashioned clothes and tools. Because nomadic peoples ranged widely over the grassy steppes of central Asia, they served as links between agricultural societies to the east and west. They were prominent intermediaries in trade networks spanning central Asia. Nomadic peoples depended on agricultural societies for grains and finished products, such as textiles and metal goods, which they could not readily pro-

duce for themselves. In exchange for these products, they offered horses, which flourished on the steppes, and their services as links to other societies.

Despite this somewhat symbiotic arrangement, Chinese and nomadic peoples often had tense relations. Indeed, they often engaged in bitter wars because the relatively poor but hardy nomads frequently raided the rich agricultural society at their doorstep and sought to seize its wealth. At least from the time of the Shang dynasty, and probably from the Xia as well, nomadic raids posed a constant threat to the northern and western regions of China. The Zhou state grew strong enough to overcome the Shang partly because Zhou military forces honed their skills waging campaigns against nomadic peoples to the west and also adopted some of the military technologies and strategy of the nomads. Later, however, the Zhou state almost crumbled under the pressure of nomadic incursions compounded by disaffection among Zhou allies and subordinates.

Nomadic peoples did not imitate Chinese ways. The environment of the steppe prevented them from cultivating crops, and the need to herd their animals made it impossible for them to settle permanently in towns or to build cities. Nomadic peoples did not adopt Chinese political or social traditions but, rather, organized themselves into clans under the leadership of charismatic warrior-chiefs. Nor did they use writing until about the seventh century C.E. Yet pastoral nomadism was a highly successful economic and social adaptation to agricultural society: the grains and manufactured goods available from agricultural lands enabled nomadic peoples to take advantage of the steppe environment by herding animals.

The Southern Expansion of Chinese Society

The Yangzi Valley Chinese influence spread to the south as well as to the north and west. There was no immediate barrier to cultivation in the south: indeed, the valley of the Yangzi River supports even more intensive agriculture than is possible in the Yellow River basin. Known in China as the Chang Jiang ("Long River"), the Yangzi carries enormous volumes of water: 6,300 kilometers (3,915 miles) from its headwaters in the lofty Qinghai mountains of Tibet to its mouth near the modern Chinese cities of Nanjing and Shanghai, where it empties into the East China Sea. The moist, subtropical climate of southern China lent itself readily to the cultivation of rice: ancient cultivators sometimes raised two crops of rice per year.

There was no need for King Yu to tame the Yangzi River, which does not bring devastating floods like those of the Yellow River. But intensive cultivation of rice depended on the construction and maintenance of an elaborate irrigation system that allowed cultivators to flood their paddies and release the waters at the appropriate time. The Shang and Zhou states provided sources of authority that could supervise a complex irrigation system, and harvests in southern China increased

rapidly during the second and first millennia B.C.E. The populations of cultivators' communities surged along with their harvests.

As their counterparts did in lands to the north and west of the Yellow River valley, the indigenous peoples of southern China responded in two ways to the increasing prominence of agriculture in the Yangzi River valley. Many became cultivators themselves and joined Chinese agricultural society. Others continued to live by hunting and gathering: some moved into the hills and mountains, where conditions did not favor agriculture, and others migrated to Taiwan or southeast Asian lands such as Vietnam and Thailand, where agriculture was less common.

The State of Chu Agricultural surpluses and growing populations led to the emergence of cities, states, and complex societies in the Yangzi as well as the Yellow River valley. During the late Zhou dynasty, the powerful state of **Chu,** situated in the central region of the Yangzi, governed its affairs autonomously and challenged the Zhou for supremacy. By the end of the Zhou dynasty, Chu and other states in southern China were in regular communication, and often conflict, with their counterparts in the Yellow River valley. They adopted Chinese political and social traditions as well as Chinese writing, and they built societies closely resembling those of the Yellow River valley. Although only the northern portions of the Yangzi River valley fell under the authority of the Shang and Zhou states, by the end of the Zhou dynasty all of southern China formed part of an emerging larger Chinese society.

CONCLUSION

As in Mesopotamia, Egypt, and India, peoples in east Asia built complex societies based on agriculture. Particularly in the valleys of the Yellow River and the Yangzi River, early Chinese cultivators organized powerful states, developed social distinctions, and established sophisticated cultural traditions. However, their language, writing, beliefs, and values differed considerably from those of their contemporaries in other societies, and these cultural elements lent a distinctiveness to Chinese society. In spite of formidable geographic obstacles in the form of deserts, mountain ranges, and extensive bodies of water, inhabitants of ancient China managed to trade and communicate with peoples of other societies, although on a much smaller scale than in western Eurasia. Early Chinese societies had regular encounters with groups of pastoral nomads who had established communities to the north of China that were dependent on the domestication of various animal species. Often the encounters between Chinese farming societies and

the nomads were peaceful and commercial in nature, but at other times their encounters were tense and violent. Thus, in east Asia as in other parts of Afro-Eurasia agriculture demonstrated its potential to provide a foundation for large-scale social organization and to support interaction and exchange between peoples of different societies.

STUDY TERMS

Ao (90)	Shang dynasty (89)
Book of Songs (101)	Xia dynasty (88)
Chu (103)	Yangzi River (87)
Fu Hao (91)	Yellow River (87)
mandate of heaven (92)	Zhou dynasty (92)
oracle bones (99)	
Period of the	
Warring States (93)	

FOR FURTHER READING

Kwang-chih Chang. *The Archaeology of Ancient China.* 4th ed. New Haven, 1986. Brings the results of archaeological excavations to bear on ancient Chinese history.

Nicola di Cosmo. *Ancient China and Its Enemies: The Rise of Nomadic Power in East Asian History.* Cambridge, 2002. An insightful study analyzing the emergence of pastoral nomadism and relations between Chinese cultivators and nomadic peoples in ancient times.

R. Drews. *Early Riders. The Beginning of Mounted Warriors in Asia and Europe.* New York and London, 2004. An analysis of the origins of militarized nomadic confederations in Eurasia.

Patricia Ebrey. *The Cambridge Illustrated History of China.* Cambridge, 2000. A splendid collection of images and superb text makes this one of the finest resources available on Chinese history and culture.

Li Feng. *Early China. A Social and Cultural History.* Cambridge, 2013. Readable and authoritative study of the emergence of complex states in China, including the first dynasties.

Victor H. Mair, Nancy S. Steinhardt, and Paul R. Goldin, eds. *Hawai`i Reader in Traditional Chinese Culture.* Honolulu, 2005. An imaginative selection of primary sources in English translation.

Conrad Schirokauer et al. *A Brief History of Chinese and Japanese Civilizations.* 3rd ed. New York, 2006. Written by a team of experts, this is a sweeping overview of the history of Chinese and Japanese culture, with a particular emphasis on art, religion, philosophy, and literature.

R. Thorp. *China in the Early Bronze Age: Shang Civilization.* Philadelphia: 2006. Superb introduction to the Shang Dynasty and its extraordinary contribution to the emergence of a unique Chinese culture.

ZOOMING IN ON TRADITIONS

Chan Bahlum Spills Blood to Honor the Gods

Mayan Temple at Chichen Itza, known as El Castillo today.
Kitti Boonnitrod/Getty Images

In early September of the year 683 C.E., a Mayan prince named Chan Bahlum grasped a sharp obsidian knife and cut three deep slits into the skin of his penis. He inserted into each slit a strip of paper made from beaten tree bark so as to encourage a continuing flow of blood. His younger brother Kan Xul performed a similar rite, while other members of his family also drew blood from their bodies.

These bloodletting observances were political and religious rituals, acts of deep piety performed as Chan Bahlum presided over funeral services for his recently deceased father, Pacal, king of the Mayan city of Palenque in the Yucatan peninsula. The Maya believed that the shedding of royal blood was essential to the world's survival. Thus, as Chan Bahlum prepared to succeed his father as king of Palenque, he let his blood flow copiously.

Throughout Mesoamerica, Maya and other peoples performed similar rituals for a millennium and more. Mayan rulers and their family members regularly spilled their blood by opening wounds with obsidian knives, stingray spines, or sharpened bones. Men commonly drew blood from the penis, like Chan Bahlum, and women often drew from the tongue. Both sexes occasionally drew blood also from the earlobes, lips, or cheeks, and they sometimes increased the flow by pulling long, thick cords through their wounds.

This shedding of blood was so crucial to Mayan rituals because of its association with rain and agriculture. According to Mayan religious beliefs the gods had shed their blood to water the earth and nourish crops of maize, and they expected humans to honor them by imitating their sacrifice. By spilling human blood the Maya hoped to please the gods and ensure that life-giving waters would bring bountiful harvests to their fields. By inflicting painful wounds not just on their enemies but on their own bodies as well, the Maya demonstrated their conviction that bloodletting rituals were essential to the coming of rain and the survival of their agricultural society.

CHAPTER OVERVIEW

Early societies in the Americas and Oceania developed independently and differed considerably from their counterparts in Afro-Eurasia. Human migrants reached both regions long after human groups had established populations in most other world regions. In fact, migrations to the Americas and Oceania represented some of the last episodes in the long process by which *Homo sapiens* peopled the earth.

Human foragers reached the Americas, Australia, and New Guinea during the last ice age when glaciers locked up much of the earth's water, causing sea levels all over the world to decline precipitously—sometimes by as much as 300 meters (984 feet). For thousands of years, temporary land bridges linked regions that both before and after the ice ages were separated by the seas. One land bridge linked Siberia with Alaska. Another joined the continent of Australia with the island of New Guinea, while low sea levels also exposed large stretches of land connecting Sumatra, Java, and other Indonesian islands to the peninsula of southeast Asia. The temporary land bridges enabled human migrants to walk right into, or make short sea voyages to, previously unpopulated regions and start new communities.

The establishment of human populations in the Pacific islands was a much later development. Only about three thousand five hundred years ago did the ancestors of the Polynesians invent highly maneuverable sailing canoes and build a body of nautical expertise that allowed them to populate the islands of the vast Pacific Ocean. By about 700 C.E. these remarkable sailors had found their way to virtually every speck of land in the world's largest ocean, which covers one-third of the earth's surface.

Oceans separated the Americas and Oceania from Afro-Eurasia and from each other. By no means, however, did the early human inhabitants of the Americas and Oceania lead completely isolated lives. To the contrary, there were frequent and sometimes regular interactions between peoples of different societies within the Americas and within Oceania. Moreover, there were sporadic but significant contacts between Asian peoples and Pacific islanders and also between Pacific islanders and native peoples of the Americas. It is likely that at least fleeting encounters took place as well between peoples of the eastern and western hemispheres, although little evidence survives on the nature of encounters in early times. Yet even as they dealt with peoples of other societies, the first inhabitants of the Americas and Oceania established distinctive societies of their own, like their counterparts in Afro-Eurasia.

Indeed, despite their different origins and their distinctive political, social, and cultural traditions, peoples of the Americas and Oceania built societies that in some ways resembled those of Afro-Eurasia. Human communities independently discovered agriculture in several regions of North America and South America, and migrants introduced cultivation to the inhabited Pacific islands as well. With agriculture came increasing populations, settlement in towns, specialized labor, formal political authorities, hierarchical social orders, long-distance trade, and organized religious traditions. The Americas also generated large, densely populated societies featuring cities, monumental public works, imperial states, and traditions of writing as well. Thus, like their counterparts in the Afro-Eurasian world zone the earliest societies of the Americas and Oceania reflected a common human tendency toward the development of increasingly complex social structures.

EARLY SOCIETIES OF MESOAMERICA

Much is unclear about the early settlement of the Americas by human communities. The first large wave of migration from Siberia to Alaska probably took place about 15,000 B.C.E. But small numbers of migrants may have crossed the Bering land bridge earlier, and it is also quite likely that some migrants reached the western hemisphere by watercraft, sailing or drifting with the currents from northeast Asia down the west coast of North America. In the view of some scholars, it is also possible that some migrants crossed the Atlantic Ocean and established communities on the eastern coast of North America. Several archaeological excavations at widely

CHRONOLOGY	
AMERICAS	
15,000 B.C.E.	Human migration to North America from Siberia
9000 B.C.E.	Origins of agriculture in South America
8000–7000 B.C.E.	Origins of agriculture in Mesoamerica
4300 B.C.E.	Origins of maize cultivation in Mesoamerica
1200–100 B.C.E.	Olmec society
1000–300 B.C.E.	Chavín culture
200 B.C.E.–750 C.E.	Teotihuacan society
300–1100 C.E.	Mayan society
300–700 C.E.	Mochica society
OCEANIA	
60,000 B.C.E.	Human migration to Australia and New Guinea
5000 B.C.E.	Origins of agriculture in New Guinea
3000 B.C.E.	Austronesian migrations to New Guinea
1600–500 B.C.E.	Lapita society
1500 B.C.E.–700 C.E.	Austronesian migrations to Pacific islands

scattered sites in both North America and South America have yielded remains that scholars date to 15,000 B.C.E. or earlier. In any case, after 15,000 B.C.E. migrants arrived in large numbers, and they quickly populated all habitable regions of the Americas. By 9500 B.C.E. they had reached the southernmost part of South America, more than 17,000 kilometers (10,566 miles) from the Bering land bridge.

The earliest human inhabitants of the Americas lived exclusively by hunting and gathering. Beginning about 8,000 B.C.E., however, it became increasingly difficult for them to survive by foraging. Large game animals became scarce, partly because they did not adapt well to the rapidly warming climate and partly because of overhunting by expanding human communities. By 7500 B.C.E. many species of large animals in the Americas were well on the road to extinction. Some human communities relied on fish and small game to supplement foods that they gathered. Others turned to agriculture, and they gave rise to the first complex societies in the Americas.

The Olmecs

Early Agriculture in Mesoamerica By 8000 to 7000 B.C.E., the peoples of **Mesoamerica**—the region from the central portion of modern Mexico to Honduras and El Salvador—had begun to experiment with the cultivation of squashes, manioc, beans, chili peppers, avocados, and gourds. By 4000 B.C.E. they had discovered the agricultural potential of **maize**, which

Mesoamerica (mez-oh-uh-MER-i-kuh)

soon became the staple food of the region. Later they added tomatoes to the crops they cultivated. Agricultural villages appeared soon after 3000 B.C.E., and by 2000 B.C.E. agriculture had spread throughout Mesoamerica.

Early Mesoamerican peoples had a diet rich in cultivated foods, but they did not keep as many animals as their counterparts in the eastern hemisphere. Their domesticated animals included turkeys and small, barkless dogs, both of which they consumed as food. They had no cattle, sheep, goats, or swine, so far less animal protein was available to them than to their counterparts in the eastern hemisphere. In addition, most large animals of the western hemisphere were not susceptible to domestication, so Mesoamericans were unable to harness the energy of animals such as horses and oxen that were prominent in the eastern hemisphere. Human laborers prepared fields for cultivation, and human porters carried trade goods on their backs. Mesoamericans had no need for wheeled vehicles, which would have been useful only if draft animals were available to pull them.

Ceremonial Centers Toward the end of the second millennium B.C.E., the tempo of Mesoamerican life quickened as elaborate ceremonial centers with monumental pyramids, temples, and palaces arose alongside the agricultural villages. The first of these centers were not cities like those of early societies in the eastern hemisphere. Permanent residents of the ceremonial centers included members of the ruling elite, priests, and a few artisans and craftsmen who tended to the needs of the ruling and priestly classes. Large numbers of people gathered in the ceremonial centers on special occasions to

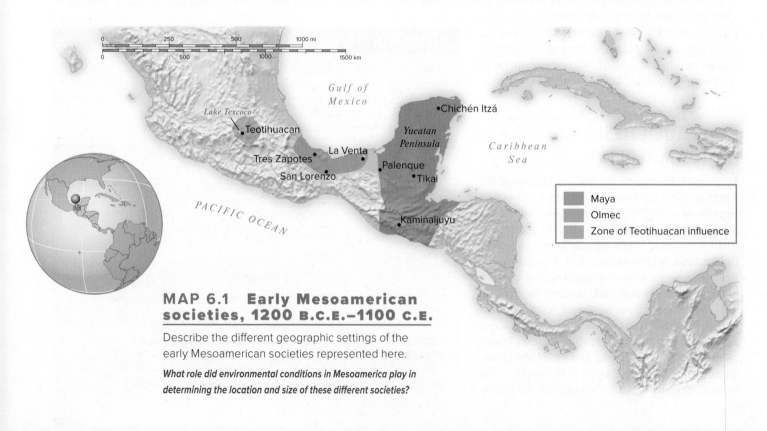

MAP 6.1 Early Mesoamerican societies, 1200 B.C.E.–1100 C.E.

Describe the different geographic settings of the early Mesoamerican societies represented here.

What role did environmental conditions in Mesoamerica play in determining the location and size of these different societies?

observe rituals or on market days to exchange goods, but most people then returned to their homes in neighboring villages and hamlets.

Olmecs: The "Rubber People"

Agricultural villages and ceremonial centers arose in several regions of Mesoamerica. The earliest known and the most thoroughly studied of them appeared on the coast of the Gulf of Mexico, near the modern Mexican city of Veracruz. Historians and archaeologists have systematically studied Olmec society only since the 1940s, and many questions about the **Olmecs** remain unanswered. Even their proper name is unknown: the term *Olmec* (meaning "rubber people") did not come from the ancient people themselves but derives instead from the rubber trees that flourish in the region they inhabited. Nevertheless, the basic features of Olmec society are now better understood, allowing some historians to argue that their influence was so profound that the Olmec should be regarded as the "Mother Culture" of Mesoamerica, while others believe their impact was more limited, like a "Sister Culture" to the other complex states of the region.

The first Olmec ceremonial center arose about 1200 B.C.E. and it served as their capital for some four hundred years. When the influence of San Lorenzo waned, leadership passed to new ceremonial centers at La Venta (800–400 B.C.E.) and Tres Zapotes (400–100 B.C.E.). These sites defined the heartland of Olmec society, where agriculture produced rich harvests. The entire region receives abundant rainfall, so there was no need to build extensive systems of irrigation. Like the peoples of the Indus Civilization, however, the Olmecs constructed elaborate drainage systems to divert waters that otherwise might have flooded their fields or destroyed their settlements. Some Olmec drainage construction remains visible and effective today.

Olmec Society

Olmec society was probably authoritarian in nature. Untold thousands of laborers participated in the construction of the ceremonial centers at San Lorenzo, La Venta, and Tres Zapotes. Each of the principal Olmec sites featured an elaborate complex of temples, pyramids, altars, stone sculptures, and tombs for rulers. Farmers delivered a portion of their harvests for the maintenance of the elite classes living in the ceremonial centers and provided labor for the various large-scale construction projects.

Indeed, common subjects labored regularly on behalf of the Olmec elite—not only in building drainage systems and ceremonial centers but also in providing appropriate artistic adornment for the capitals. The most distinctive artistic creations of the Olmecs were **colossal human heads**—possibly likenesses of rulers—sculpted from basalt rock. The largest of these sculptures stands 3 meters (almost 10 feet) tall and weighs some 20 tons. In the absence of draft animals and wheels, human laborers dragged enormous boulders from quarries, floated them on rafts to points near their destinations, dragged

Colossal Olmec head carved from basalt rock between 1000 and 600 B.C.E. and discovered at La Venta. Olmecs carved similar heads for their ceremonial centers at San Lorenzo and Tres Zapotes. Why might Olmecs have taken the trouble to carve and move such massive sculptures?

Andrew Rakaczy/Science Source

them to their intended sites, and then positioned them for the sculptors. The largest sculptures required the services of about one thousand laborers. Apart from the colossal heads, the Olmec capitals featured many other large stone sculptures and monumental buildings that required the services of laborers by the hundreds and thousands. Construction of the huge pyramid at La Venta, for example, required some eight hundred thousand man-days of labor.

Trade in Jade and Obsidian

Olmec influence extended to much of the central and southern regions of modern Mexico and beyond that to modern Guatemala and El Salvador. The Olmecs spread their influence partly by military force, but trade was a prominent link between the Olmec heartland and the other regions of Mesoamerica. The Olmecs produced large numbers of decorative objects from jade, which they had to import. In the absence of any metal technology, they also made extensive use of obsidian, from which they fashioned knives and axes with wickedly sharp cutting edges. Like jade, obsidian came to the Gulf Coast from distant regions in the interior of Mesoamerica. In exchange for the imports, the Olmecs traded small works of art fashioned from jade, basalt, or ceramics and perhaps also local products such as animal skins.

Among the many mysteries surrounding the Olmecs, one of the most perplexing concerns the decline and fall of their society. The Olmecs systematically destroyed their ceremonial centers at both San Lorenzo and La Venta and then deserted the sites. Archaeologists studying these sites found statues broken and buried, monuments defaced, and the capitals themselves burned. Although intruders may have ravaged the ceremonial centers, many scholars believe that the Olmecs deliberately destroyed their capitals, perhaps because of civil conflicts or doubts about the effectiveness and legitimacy of the ruling classes. In any case, by about 400 B.C.E. Olmec society had fallen on hard times, and soon thereafter societies in other parts of Mesoamerica eclipsed it altogether.

Nevertheless, Olmec traditions deeply influenced later Mesoamerican societies. Olmecs made astronomical observations and created a calendar to help them keep track of the seasons. They invented a system of writing, although unfortunately little of it survives beyond calendrical inscriptions. They also carried out rituals involving human sacrifice and invented a distinctive ball game. Later Mesoamerican peoples adopted all these Olmec traditions as well as their cultivation of maize and their construction of ceremonial centers with temple pyramids. The later and better-known societies of Mesoamerica were clearly influenced by Olmec traditions.

The Maya

During the thousand years following the Olmecs' disappearance about 100 B.C.E., complex societies arose in several Mesoamerican regions. Human population grew dramatically, and ceremonial centers cropped up at sites far removed from the Olmec heartland. Some of them evolved into genuine cities: they attracted large populations of permanent residents, embarked on ambitious programs of construction, maintained large markets, and encouraged increasing specialization of labor. Networks of long-distance trade linked the new urban centers and extended their influence to all parts of Mesoamerica. Within the cities themselves, priests devised written languages and compiled a body of astronomical knowledge. In short, Mesoamerican societies developed in a manner roughly parallel to their counterparts in the eastern hemisphere.

Mayan Settlements One of the best known of these were the **Maya,** who created a remarkable society in the region now occupied by southern Mexico, Guatemala, Belize, Honduras, and El Salvador. The highlands of Guatemala offer fertile soil and excellent conditions for agriculture. Permanent villages began to appear there during the third century B.C.E. The most

Olmec ceremonial axe head carved from jade sometime between 800 and 400 B.C.E.
Peter Horree/Alamy Stock Photo

prominent of them was Kaminaljuyú, located on the site of modern Guatemala City. Like the Olmec capitals, Kaminaljuyú was a ceremonial center rather than a true city, but it dominated the life of other communities in the region. Some twelve thousand to fifteen thousand laborers worked to build its temples, and its products traveled the trade routes as far as central Mexico. During the fourth century C.E., Kaminaljuyú fell under the economic and perhaps also the political dominance of the much larger city of **Teotihuacan** in central Mexico and lost much of its influence in Mayan society.

After the fourth century, Mayan society flourished mostly in the poorly drained Mesoamerican lowlands, where thin, tropical soils quickly lost their fertility. To enhance the agricultural potential of the region, the Maya built terraces designed to trap silt carried by the numerous rivers passing through the lowlands. By artificially retaining rich earth, they dramatically increased the agricultural productivity of their lands. They harvested maize in abundance, and they also cultivated cotton from which they wove fine textiles highly prized both in their own society and by trading partners in other parts of Mesoamerica. Mayan cultivators also raised cacao, the large bean that is the source of chocolate. Cacao was a precious commodity consumed mostly by nobles in Mayan society. They whisked powdered cacao into water to create a stimulating beverage, and they sometimes even ate the bitter cacao beans as snacks. The product was so valuable that the Maya used cacao beans as money.

Tikal From about 300 to 900 C.E., the Maya built more than eighty large ceremonial centers in the lowlands—all with pyramids, palaces, and temples—as well as numerous smaller settlements. Some of the larger centers attracted dense populations and evolved into bona fide cities. Foremost among them was **Tikal,** the most important Mayan political center between the fourth and the ninth centuries C.E. At its height, roughly 600 to 800 C.E., Tikal was a wealthy and bustling city with a population of some 50,000 people, with another 50,000 living in the hinterland around the city. It boasted enormous paved plazas and scores of temples, pyramids, palaces, and public buildings. The Temple of the Giant Jaguar, a stepped pyramid rising sharply to a height of 47 meters (154 feet), dominated the skyline and represented Tikal's control over the surrounding region, which had a population of about five hundred thousand.

The Maya organized themselves politically into scores of small city-kingdoms. Tikal was probably the largest, but Palenque and Chichén Itzá also were sizable states. The smaller kingdoms had populations between ten thousand and thirty thousand. Mayan kings often bore menacing names such as Curl Snout, Smoking Frog, and Stormy Sky. Especially popular were names associated with the jaguar, the most dangerous predator of the Mesoamerican forests. Prominent Mayan kings included Great Jaguar Paw, Shield Jaguar, Bird Jaguar, and Jaguar Penis (meaning the progenitor of other jaguar-kings).

Mayan Warfare Dazzled by Mayan architecture and sculpture, scholars of earlier generations thought these kingdoms were peaceful states that promoted artistic and scientific endeavors. Since the 1970s, however, historians and archaeologists have deciphered thousands of previously unreadable inscriptions that have dramatically transformed understanding of Mayan politics. Combined with fresh archaeological discoveries, these sources make it clear that the Mayan kingdoms fought constantly with one another. Victors generally destroyed the peoples they defeated and took over their ceremonial centers, but the purpose of Mayan warfare was not so much to kill enemies as to capture them in hand-to-hand combat on the battlefield. Warriors won enormous prestige when they brought back important captives from neighboring kingdoms. They stripped captives of their fine dress and symbols of rank, and sometimes they kept high-ranking captives alive for years, displaying them as trophies. Ultimately, however, most captives ended their lives either as slaves or as sacrificial victims to Mayan gods. High-ranking captives in particular often underwent ritual torture and sacrifice in public ceremonies on important occasions.

Chichén Itzá Bitter conflicts between small kingdoms were sources of constant tension in Mayan society. Only about the ninth century C.E. did the state of **Chichén Itzá** in the northern Yucatan peninsula seek to dampen hostile instincts and establish a larger political framework for Mayan society. The rulers of Chichén Itzá preferred to absorb captives and integrate them into their own society rather than annihilate them or offer them up as sacrificial victims. Some captives refused the opportunity and went to their deaths as proud warriors, but many agreed to recognize the authority of Chichén Itzá and participate in the construction of a larger society. Between the ninth and eleventh centuries C.E., Chichén Itzá organized a loose empire that brought a measure of political stability to the northern Yucatan.

Decline of the Maya By about 800 C.E., however, most Mayan populations had begun to desert their cities. Within a century Mayan society was in full decline everywhere except the northern Yucatan, where Chichén Itzá continued to flourish. Historians have suggested many possible causes of the decline, including invasion by foreigners from Mexico, internal dissension and civil war, failure of the system of water control leading to diminished harvests and demographic collapse, ecological problems caused by destruction of the forests, the spread of epidemic diseases, and natural catastrophes

Temple of the Giant Jaguar at Tikal, which served as a funerary pyramid for Lord Cacao, a prominent Mayan ruler of the late sixth and early seventh centuries C.E. Why might a Mayan ruler want to associate himself with a jaguar?
Paul C. Pet/Corbis/Getty Images

such as earthquakes. Possibly several problems combined to destroy Mayan society. It is likely that debilitating civil conflict and excessive siltation of agricultural terraces caused particularly difficult problems for the Maya. In any case, the population declined, the people abandoned their cities, and long-distance trade with central Mexico came to a halt. Meanwhile, the tropical jungles of the lowlands encroached upon human settlements and gradually smothered the cities, temples, pyramids, and monuments of a once-vibrant society.

Mayan Society and Religion

Apart from the kings and ruling families, Mayan society included a large class of priests who maintained an elaborate calendar and transmitted knowledge of writing, astronomy, and mathematics. A hereditary nobility owned most land and cooperated with the kings and priests by organizing military forces and participating in religious rituals. Mayan merchants came from the ruling and noble classes. Their travels had strong political overtones because they served not only as traders but also as ambassadors to neighboring lands and allied peoples. Moreover, they traded mostly in exotic and

Chichén Itzá (chee-CHEN eet-SAH)

A vivid mural from a temple in the small Mayan kingdom of Bonampak (in the southern part of modern Mexico) depicts warriors raiding a neighboring village to capture prisoners who will become sacrificial victims.
agefotostock/Alamy Stock Photo

luxury goods, such as rare animal skins, cacao beans, and finely crafted works of art, which rulers coveted as signs of special status. Apart from the ruling and priestly elites, Mayan society generated several other distinct social classes. Professional architects and sculptors oversaw construction of large monuments and public buildings. Artisans specialized in the production of pottery, tools, and cotton textiles. Large classes of peasants and slaves fed the entire society and provided physical labor for the construction of cities and monuments.

The Maya expanded upon the cultural achievements of their Olmec predecessors. Mayan priests studied astronomy and mathematics, and they devised both a sophisticated calendar and an elaborate system of writing. They understood the movements of heavenly bodies well enough to plot planetary cycles and predict eclipses of the sun and moon. The Maya were one of a handful of ancient peoples to invent the concept of zero and used a symbol to represent zero mathematically, which facilitated their manipulation of large numbers. By combining their astronomical observations and mathematical reasoning, Mayan priests calculated the length of the solar year at 365.242 days—about seventeen seconds shorter than the figure reached by modern astronomers.

The Mayan Calendar Mayan priests constructed the most elaborate calendar of the ancient Americas. Its complexity reflected a powerful urge to identify meaningful cycles of time and to understand human events in the context of those cycles. The Mayan calendar interwove two kinds of year: a solar year of 365 days governed the agricultural cycle, and a

ritual year of 260 days governed daily affairs by organizing time into twenty "months" of thirteen days apiece. The Mayan believed that each day derived certain specific characteristics from its position in both the solar and the ritual calendar and that the combined attributes of each day would determine the fortune of activities undertaken on that day. It took fifty-two years for the two calendars to work through all possible combinations of days and return simultaneously to their respective starting points, so 18,980 different combinations of characteristics could influence the prospects of an individual day. Mayan priests carefully studied the various opportunities and dangers that would come together on a given day in hopes that they could determine which activities were safe to initiate. Apart from calculating the prospects of individual days, the Mayan attributed especially great significance to the fifty-two-year periods in which the two calendars ran.

Mayan Writing Mayan priests also focused on the development of written inscriptions and, indeed, they created the most flexible and sophisticated of all the early American systems of writing. The Mayan script contained both ideographic elements (like Chinese characters) and symbols for syllables. Scholars have begun to decipher this script only since the 1960s, and it has become clear that writing was just as important to the Mayan as it was to early complex societies in the eastern hemisphere. Mayan scribes wrote works of history, poetry, and myth, and they also kept genealogical, administrative, and astronomical records. Most Mayan writing survives today in the form of inscriptions on temples and monuments, but scribes produced untold numbers of books written on paper

SOURCES FROM THE PAST

The Creation of Humanity According to the Popol Vuh

The Popol Vuh, a Mayan creation myth, describes how, after several failed attempts, the Mayan gods finally created humans out of maize and water. The following excerpt from the myth concludes by naming the first four humans, describing them as "our first mothers and fathers." The version of the work that survives today dates from the mid-sixteenth century, but it reflects beliefs of a much earlier era.

THIS, then, is the beginning of the conception of humanity, when that which would become the flesh of mankind was sought. Then spoke they who are called She Who Has Borne Children and He Who Has Begotten Sons, the Framer and the Shaper, Sovereign and Quetzal Serpent:

> Who or what are the characters being referred to in this paragraph?

"The dawn approaches, and our work is not successfully completed. A provider and a sustainer have yet to appear—a child of light, a son of light. Humanity has yet to appear to populate the face of the earth," they said.

Thus they gathered together and joined their thoughts in the darkness, in the night. They searched and they sifted. Here they thought and they pondered. Their thoughts came forth bright and clear. They discovered and established that which would become the flesh of humanity. This took place just a little before the appearance of the sun, moon, and stars above the heads of the Framer and the Shaper.

It was from within the places called Paxil and Cayala that the yellow ears of ripe maize and the white ears of ripe maize came.

THESE were the names of the animals that obtained their food—fox and coyote, parakeet and raven. Four, then, were the animals that revealed to them the yellow ears of maize and the white ears of maize. They came from Paxil and pointed out the path to get there.

Thus was found the food that would become the flesh of the newly framed and shaped people. Water was their blood. It became the blood of humanity. The ears of maize entered into their flesh by means of She Who Has Borne Children and He Who Has Begotten Sons.

Thus they rejoiced over the discovery of that excellent mountain that was filled with delicious things, crowded with yellow ears of maize and white ears of maize. It was crowded as well with pataxte and chocolate, with countless zapotes and anonas, with jocotes and nances, with matasanos and honey. From within the places called Paxil and Cayala came the sweetest foods in the citadel. All the small foods and great foods were there, along with the small and great cultivated fields. The path was thus revealed by the animals.

> What is the path that has been revealed to humans in this paragraph?

The yellow ears of maize and the white ears of maize were then ground fine with nine grindings by Xmucane. Food entered their flesh, along with water to give them strength. Thus was created the fatness of their arms. The yellowness of humanity came to be when they were made by they who are called She Who Has Borne Children and He Who Has Begotten Sons, by Sovereign and Quetzal Serpent.

Thus their frame and shape were given expression by our first Mother and our first Father. Their flesh was merely yellow ears of maize and white ears of maize. Mere food were the legs and arms of humanity, of our first fathers. And so there were four who were made, and mere food was their flesh.

These are the names of the first people who were framed and shaped: the first person was Balam Quitze, the second was Balam Acab, the third was Mahucutah, and the fourth was Iqui Balam. These, then, were the names of our first mothers and fathers.

For Further Reflection

■ According to the text, what was the origin of the foods the Maya depended on?
■ What was the relationship between food and humans?
■ How might this account of creation have influenced the religious beliefs and rituals that emerged in Mayan society?

Source: Alan J. Chistenson, *Popol Vuh: The Sacred Book of the Maya.* Originally published by O Books, Alresford, Hants, U.K. Copyright 2003 by Allen Christenson. Oklahoma edition published 2007 by the University of Oklahoma Press. Reprinted by permission. All rights reserved.

made from beaten tree bark or on vellum made from deerskin. When Spanish conquerors and missionaries arrived in Mayan lands in the sixteenth century C.E., however, they destroyed all the books they could find in hopes of undermining native religious beliefs. Today only four books of the ancient Maya survive, all dealing with astronomical and calendrical matters.

Mayan Creation Myths Surviving inscriptions and other writings shed considerable light on Mayan religious and cultural traditions. The **Popol Vuh,** a Mayan creation myth, taught that the gods had created humans out of maize and water, the ingredients that became human flesh and blood. Thus Mayan religious thought reflected the fundamental role of agriculture in their society, much like religious thought in early complex societies of the eastern hemisphere. Mayan priests also taught that the gods kept the world going and maintained the agricultural cycle in exchange for honors and sacrifices performed for them by humans.

Bloodletting Rituals The most important of those sacrifices involved the shedding of human blood, which the Maya believed would prompt the gods to send rain to water their crops of maize. Some **bloodletting rituals** centered on war captives. Before sacrificing the victims by decapitation, their captors cut off the ends of their fingers or lacerated their bodies so as to cause a copious flow of blood in honor of the gods. Yet the Maya did not look upon those rituals simply as opportunities to torture their enemies. The frequent and voluntary shedding of royal blood, as in the case of Chan Bahlum's self-sacrifice at Palenque, described at the beginning of the chapter, testifies to the depth of Mayan convictions that they inhabited a world created and sustained by deities who expected honor and reverence from their human subjects.

The Mayan Ball Game Apart from the calendar and sacrificial rituals, the Maya, like the Olmecs, played a distinctive ball game. The game sometimes pitted two men against each other, but it often involved teams of two to four members—mostly men, although there is evidence that women sometimes played the game as well. The object of the game was for players to

In this stone relief sculpture, a Mayan king from Yaxchilán (between Tikal and Palenque in the southern Yucatan peninsula) holds a torch over a woman from the royal family as she draws a thorn-studded rope through a hole in her tongue and thus shed her blood in honor of the Mayan gods.

Justin Kerr

score points by propelling a rubber ball through a ring or onto a marker without using their hands. The Maya used a ball about 20 centimeters (8 inches) in diameter. Made of solid baked rubber, the ball was both heavy and hard—a blow to the head could easily cause a concussion—and players needed great dexterity and skill to maneuver it accurately using only their feet, legs, hips, torso, shoulders, or elbows. The game was extremely popular: almost all Mayan ceremonial centers, towns, and cities had stone-paved courts on which players performed publicly.

The Maya played the ball game for several reasons. Sometimes individuals competed for sporting purposes, and sometimes players or spectators laid bets on the outcome of contests between professionals. The ball game figured also in Mayan political affairs as a ritual that honored the conclusion of treaties. High-ranking captives often engaged in forced public competition in which the stakes were their very lives: losers became sacrificial victims and faced torture and execution immediately following the match. Alongside some ball courts were skull racks that bore the severed heads of losing players. Thus Mayan concerns to please the gods by shedding human blood extended even to the realm of sport.

Teotihuacan

While the Maya flourished in the Mesoamerican lowlands, a different society arose to the north in the highlands of Mexico. For most of human history, the valley of central Mexico, situated some two kilometers (more than a mile) above sea level, was the site of several large lakes fed by the waters coming off the surrounding mountains. Most of the lakes have disappeared during the past two or three centuries as a result of environmental changes and deliberate draining of their waters. In earlier times, however, their abundant supplies of fish and waterfowl attracted human settlers. The lakes also served as sources of freshwater and as transportation routes linking communities situated on their shores.

The earliest settlers in the valley of Mexico did not build extensive irrigation systems, but they channeled some of the waters from the mountain streams into their fields and established a productive agricultural society. Expanding human population led to the congregation of people in cities and the emergence of a complex society in the Mesoamerican highlands. The earliest center of that society was the large and bustling city of Teotihuacan, located about 50 kilometers (31 miles) northeast of modern Mexico City.

The City of Teotihuacan

Teotihuacan was probably a large agricultural village by 500 B.C.E. It expanded rapidly after about 200 B.C.E., and by the end of the millennium its population approached fifty thousand. By the year 100 C.E., the city's two most prominent monuments, the colossal pyramids of the sun and the moon, dominated the skyline. The Pyramid of the Sun is the largest single structure in Mesoamerica. It occupies nearly as much space as the pyramid of Khufu in Egypt, though it stands only half as tall. At its high point, about 400 to 600 C.E., Teotihuacan was home to almost two hundred thousand inhabitants, a thriving metropolis with scores of temples, several palatial residences, neighborhoods with small apartments for the masses, busy markets, and hundreds of workshops for artisans and craftsmen.

The organization of a large urban population, along with the hinterland that supported it, required a recognized source of authority. Although Teotihuacan generated large numbers of books and records that perhaps would have shed light on the character of that authority, they unfortunately perished when the city itself declined. Paintings and murals suggest that Teotihuacan was a theocracy of sorts. Priests figure prominently in the works of art, and scholars interpret many figures as representations of deities. Priests were crucial to the survival of the society because they kept the calendar and ensured that planting and harvesting took place at the appropriate seasons. Thus it would not have been unusual for them to govern Teotihuacan in the name of the gods or at least to cooperate closely with a secular ruling class.

The Society of Teotihuacan

Apart from rulers and priests, Teotihuacan's population included cultivators, artisans, and merchants. Perhaps as many as two-thirds of the city's inhabitants worked during the day in fields surrounding Teotihuacan and returned to their small apartments in the city at night. Artisans of Teotihuacan were especially famous for their obsidian tools and fine orange pottery, and scholars have identified numerous workshops and stores where toolmakers

A limestone altar carved in 796 C.E. depicts two Mayan kings playing a ritual ball game to celebrate the negotiation of an agreement.

Pasquale Sorrentino/Science Source

and potters produced and marketed their goods within the city itself. The residents of Teotihuacan also participated in extensive trade and exchange networks. Professional merchants traded their products throughout Mesoamerica. Archaeologists have found numerous samples of the distinctive obsidian tools and orange pottery at sites far distant from Teotihuacan, from the region of modern Guatemala City in the south to Durango and beyond in the north.

Until about 500 C.E. there was little sign of military organization in Teotihuacan. The city did not have defensive walls, and works of art rarely depicted warriors. Yet the influence of Teotihuacan extended to much of modern Mexico and beyond. The Mayan capital of Kaminaljuyú, for example, fell under the influence of Teotihuacan during the fourth century C.E. Although the rulers of Teotihuacan may have established colonies to protect their sources of obsidian and may have undertaken military expeditions to back up their authority throughout central Mexico, the city's influence apparently derived less from military might than from its ability to produce fine manufactured goods that appealed to consumers in distant markets.

Cultural Traditions

Like the Maya, the residents of Teotihuacan built on cultural foundations established by the Olmecs. They played the ball game, adapted the Olmec calendar to their own uses, and expanded the Olmecs' graphic symbols into a complete system of writing. Unfortunately, only a few samples of their writing survive in stone carvings. Because their books have all perished, it is impossible to know exactly how they viewed the world and their place in it. Works of art suggest that they recognized an earth god and a rain god, and it is certain that they carried out human sacrifices during their religious rituals.

Decline of Teotihuacan

Teotihuacan began to experience increasing military pressure from other peoples around 500 C.E. Works of art from this period frequently depicted eagles, jaguars, and coyotes—animals that Mesoamericans associated with fighting and military conquest. After about 650 C.E. Teotihuacan entered a period of decline. About the middle of the eighth century, invaders sacked and burned the city, destroying its books and monuments. After that catastrophe most residents deserted Teotihuacan, and the city slowly fell into ruin.

View of the Pyramid of the Sun and other ceremonial buildings at Teotihuacan from the Pyramid of the Moon.
ibreakstock/Shutterstock

EARLY SOCIETIES OF SOUTH AMERICA

By about 12,000 B.C.E., hunting and gathering peoples had made their way across the narrow isthmus of Central America and into South America. Those who migrated into the region of the northern and central Andes mountains hunted deer, llama, alpaca, and other large animals. Both the mountainous highlands and the coastal regions below benefited from a cool and moist climate that provided natural harvests of squashes, gourds, and wild potatoes. Beginning about 8000 B.C.E., however, the climate of this whole region became increasingly warm and dry, and the changes placed pressure on natural food supplies. To maintain their numbers, the human communities of the region began to experiment with agriculture. Here, as elsewhere, agriculture encouraged population growth, the establishment of villages and cities, the building of states, and the elaboration of organized cultural traditions. During the centuries after 1000 B.C.E., the central Andean region generated complex societies parallel to those of Mesoamerica.

Early Andean Society and the Chavín Culture

Although they were exact contemporaries, early Mesoamerican and Andean societies developed largely independently. The heartland of early Andean society was the region now occupied by the states of Peru and Bolivia. Geography discouraged the establishment of communications between the Andean region and Mesoamerica. Neither the Andes Mountains nor the lowlands of modern Panama and Nicaragua offered an attractive highway linking the two regions. Several agricultural products and technologies diffused slowly from one area to the other: cultivation of maize and squashes spread from its Mesoamerican home to the central Andean region, while Andean gold, silver, and copper metallurgy traveled north to Mesoamerica.

Geography conspired even against the establishment of communications within the central Andean region. Deep valleys crease the western flank of the Andes mountains, as rivers drain waters from the highlands to the Pacific Ocean, so transportation and communication between the valleys has always been difficult. Nevertheless, powerful Andean states sometimes overcame the difficulties and influenced human affairs as far away as modern Ecuador and Colombia to the north and northern Chile to the south.

Early Agriculture in South America

Recent archaeological discoveries suggest that early forms of agriculture may have been practiced in parts of South America by as early as 9000 B.C.E. Certainly by 2000 B.C.E. most of the Andean heartland was under cultivation, and permanent settlements dotted the coastal regions in particular. The earliest cultivators of the region relied on beans, peanuts, and sweet potatoes as their main food crops. Their most important domesticated animals were camel-like llamas and alpacas, which provided them with both meat and wool and which also served as pack animals in some areas of the Andean highlands. They also cultivated cotton, which they used to make fishnets and textiles. The rich marine life of the Pacific Ocean supplemented agricultural harvests, enabling coastal peoples to build an increasingly complex society. Settlements probably appeared later in the Andean highlands than in the coastal regions, but many varieties of potato, which had first been domesticated some time between 8000 and 5000 B.C.E., supported agricultural communities in the highlands after about 2000 B.C.E. By 1800 B.C.E. Andean peoples were constructing canals and irrigation systems to support cultivation on the dry lands at the mouths of the western Andean valleys. They also had begun to fashion distinctive styles of pottery and to build temples and pyramids in large ceremonial centers.

The Chavín Culture

Shortly after the year 1000 B.C.E., a new spiritual belief appeared suddenly in the central Andes. The **Chavín culture** emerged in the northern highlands of Peru around 900 B.C.E. and thrived for some seven hundred years. Scholars have named Chavín culture after the modern town of Chavín de Huántar, which was probably the religious and political center for the Chavín people. The capacity of maize to support large populations might well have served as the stimulus for the emergence of Chavín culture. Archaeologists

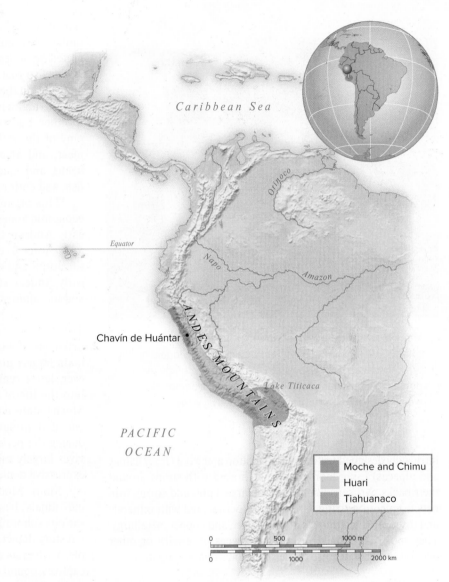

MAP 6.2 Early societies of Andean South America, 1000 B.C.E.–700 C.E.

What geographical factors explain the location and shape of these early South American societies?

working at the site of Chavín de Huantar have uncovered a sophisticated temple built of white granite and black limestone, with several drainage canals constructed underneath to prevent flooding during the rainy season. They have also found intricate stone carvings representing their deities with the features of humans and wild animals such as jaguars, hawks, eagles, and snakes. The extensive distribution of the temples and carvings shows that the Chavín culture was widely influential on agricultural peoples throughout the central Andean region.

During the era of the Chavín culture, Andean society became increasingly complex. Weavers produced elaborate and

Many Mochica pots and jars portray human figures and often depict distinctive characteristics of individuals or typical scenes from daily life. This blackware effigy jar portrays a musician playing a conch shell trumpet.
Werner Forman/Universal Images Group/Getty Images

intricately designed textiles of both cotton and wool (from llamas and alpacas) using looms that they braced with straps around their backs. Artisans manufactured large, light, and strong fishnets from cotton string. Craftsmen experimented with minerals and discovered techniques of gold, silver, and copper metallurgy. They mostly fashioned metals into pieces of jewelry or other decorative items but also made small tools out of copper.

Early Cities Given the scale and complexity of Chavín monumental architecture, which must have required the cooperative labor of many individuals under some form of supervision, it is reasonable to assume that the Chavín culture was organized by some sort of state-like structure, although this remains uncertain. However, complexes such as Chavín de Huantar were more like ritual and cultural centers than actual cities. As the population increased and society became more complex, however, cities began to appear shortly after the disappearance of the Chavín culture. Beginning about 200 B.C.E. large cities emerged at the modern-day sites of Huari, Pucara, and Tiahuanaco. Each of these early Andean cities had a population exceeding ten thousand, and each also featured large public buildings, ceremonial plazas, and extensive residential districts.

Early Andean States: Mochica

Political and Economic Integration of the Andean Valleys Along with cities there appeared regional states. The earliest Andean states arose in the many valleys on the western side of the mountains. These states emerged when conquerors unified the individual valleys and organized them into integrated societies. They coordinated the building of irrigation systems so that the lower valleys could support intensive agriculture, and they established trade and exchange networks that tied the highlands, the central valleys, and the coastal regions together. Each region contributed products to the larger economy of the valley: from the highlands came potatoes, llama meat, and alpaca wool; the central valleys supplied maize, beans, and squashes; and the coasts provided sweet potatoes, fish, and cotton.

This organization of the Andean valleys into integrated economic zones did not come about by accident. Builders of early Andean states worked deliberately and did not hesitate to use force to consolidate their domains. Surviving stone fortifications and warriors depicted in works of art testify that the early Andean states relied heavily on arms to introduce order and maintain stability in their small realms.

The Moche State Because early Andean societies did not make use of writing, their beliefs, values, and ways of life remain largely unknown. One of the early Andean states, however, left a remarkable artistic legacy that allows a glimpse into the life of a society otherwise almost entirely lost. The **Moche** state had its base in the valley of the Moche River, and it dominated the coasts and valleys of northern Peru during the period about 300 to 700 C.E. Moche painting survives largely on pottery vessels, and it offers a detailed and expressive depiction of early Andean society in all its variety.

Many Moche ceramics take the form of portraits of individuals' heads. Others represent the major gods and the various subordinate deities and demons. Some of the most interesting depict scenes in the everyday life of the Moche people: aristocrats embarking on a hunting party, warriors leading captives bound by ropes, women working in a textile factory under the careful eye of a supervisor, rulers receiving messengers or ambassadors from neighboring states, and beggars looking for handouts on a busy street. Even in the absence of writing, Moche artists left abundant evidence of a complex society with considerable specialization of labor.

Moche was only one of several large states that dominated the central Andean region during the first millennium C.E. Although they integrated the regional economies of the various Andean valleys, none of those early states was able to impose order on the entire region or even to dominate a portion of it for very long. The exceedingly difficult geographic barriers posed by the Andes mountains presented challenges that ancient technology and social organization simply could not meet. In addition, during the sixth and seventh centuries C.E., climatic fluctuations brought a long series of severe droughts to the Andean region. As a result, by the end of the first millennium C.E., Moche and several other Andean societies had disappeared, and Andean society exhibited regional differences much sharper than those of Mesoamerica and early complex societies in the eastern hemisphere.

EARLY SOCIETIES OF OCEANIA

Human migrants entered Australia and New Guinea at least by fifty thousand years before the present, and probably earlier than that. They arrived in watercraft—probably rafts, or perhaps canoes fitted with sails—but because of the low sea levels of that era, the migrants did not have to cross large stretches of open ocean. Those earliest inhabitants of **Oceania** also migrated—perhaps over land when sea levels were still low—to the Bismarcks, the Solomons, and other small island groups near New Guinea. Beginning about five thousand years ago, seafaring peoples from southeast Asia visited the northern coast of New Guinea for purposes of trade. Some of them settled there, but many others ventured farther and established communities in the island groups of the western Pacific Ocean. During the centuries that followed, their descendants sailed large, oceangoing canoes throughout the Pacific basin, and by the middle centuries of the first millennium C.E., they had established human communities in all the habitable islands of the Pacific Ocean across an area of some 16 million square miles of ocean.

Windjana figures (cloud and rain spirits) loom from a rock painting produced about twelve thousand years ago by inhabitants of the Chamberlain Gorge region in western Australia.
Christian Heeb/Prisma by Dukas Presseagentur GmbH/
Alamy Stock Photo

Early Societies in Australia and New Guinea

Human migrants reached Australia and New Guinea long before any people had begun to cultivate crops or keep herds of domesticated animals. Inevitably, then, the earliest inhabitants of Australia and New Guinea lived by hunting and gathering their food. For thousands of years, foraging peoples probably traveled back and forth between Australia and New Guinea. Those migrations ceased about ten thousand years ago when rising seas separated the two lands. After that time, human societies in Australia and New Guinea followed radically different paths. The aboriginal peoples of Australia maintained hunting and gathering societies until large numbers of Europeans established settler communities there in the nineteenth and twentieth centuries C.E. New Guinea peoples, however, turned to agriculture: beginning about 3000 B.C.E. the cultivation of root crops such as yams and taro and the keeping of pigs and chickens spread rapidly throughout the island.

Early Hunting and Gathering Societies in Australia
Like hunting and gathering peoples elsewhere, the aboriginal Australians lived in small, mobile communities that undertook seasonal migrations in search of food. Over the centuries, they learned to exploit the resources of the various ecological regions of Australia. Plant foods, including fruits, berries, roots, nuts, seeds, shoots, and green leaves, constituted the bulk of their diet. In the tropical region of Cape York in northern Australia, they consumed hundreds of species of plants. Aboriginal peoples found abundant plant life even in the harsh desert regions of interior Australia. In the vicinity of modern Alice Springs in central Australia, for example, they included about 20 species of greens and 45 kinds of seeds and nuts in their diet. They also

used at least 124 plants as medicines, ointments, and drugs. To supplement their plant-based diet, they used axes, spears, clubs, nets, lassos, snares, and boomerangs to bring down animals ranging in size from rats to giant kangaroos, which grew to a height of 3 meters (almost 10 feet), and to catch fish, waterfowl, and small birds.

Austronesian Peoples
The earliest inhabitants of New Guinea foraged for food, like their neighbors to the south. About five thousand years ago, however, a process of social and economic change began to unfold in New Guinea. The agents of change were seafaring peoples from southeast Asia speaking Austronesian languages, whose modern linguistic relatives include Malayan, Indonesian, Filipino, Polynesian, and other Oceanic languages as well as the Malagasy language of Madagascar and the tongues spoken by the indigenous peoples of Taiwan and southern China. **Austronesian-speaking peoples** possessed remarkable seafaring skills. They sailed the open ocean in large canoes equipped with outriggers, which stabilized their craft and reduced the risks of long voyages. By paying close attention to winds, currents, stars, cloud formations, and other natural indicators, they learned how to find distant lands reliably and return home safely. Beginning about 3000 B.C.E. these mariners visited the northern coast of New Guinea, where they traded with the indigenous peoples and established their own communities.

Early Agriculture in New Guinea
Austronesian seafarers came from societies that depended on the cultivation of root crops and the herding of animals, although there is evidence that some original indigenous peoples had already made the

Austronesian mariners sailed double-hulled voyaging canoes much like those from Ra'iatea in the Society Islands, drawn in 1769 by an artist who accompanied Captain James Cook on his first voyage in the Pacific Ocean. What technological innovations, as depicted by the artist, made it possible for Polynesian migrants to settle such a vast area of the Pacific Ocean?
The Picture Art Collection/Alamy Stock Photo

transition to agriculture by the time Austronesian migrants arrived. When they settled in New Guinea, they introduced yams, taro, pigs, and chickens to the island, and the indigenous peoples themselves soon began to cultivate crops and keep animals. Within a few centuries agriculture and herding had spread to all parts of New Guinea. Here, as in other lands, agriculture brought population growth and specialization of labor: after the change to agriculture, permanent settlements, pottery, and carefully crafted tools appeared throughout the island.

Separated from New Guinea only by the narrow Torres Strait, the aboriginal peoples of northern Australia knew about the cultivation of foodstuffs because they had occasional dealings with traders from New Guinea. Agriculture even spread to the islands of the Torres Strait, but it did not take root in Australia until the arrival of European peoples in the late eighteenth century C.E. Meanwhile, Austronesian-speaking peoples sailed their outrigger canoes farther and established the first human settlements in the islands of the Pacific Ocean.

The Peopling of the Pacific Islands

The hunting and gathering peoples who first inhabited Australia and New Guinea also established a few settlements in the Bismarck and Solomon island groups east of New Guinea. They ventured to those islands during the era when the seas were low and sailing distances from New Guinea were consequently very short. They did not have the maritime technology, however, to sail far beyond the Solomons to the more distant islands in the Pacific Ocean. Even if they had, the small Pacific islands, with limited supplies of edible plants and animals, would not have supported communities of foragers.

Austronesian Migrations to Polynesia Austronesian-speaking peoples possessed a sophisticated maritime technology as well as agricultural expertise, and they established settlements in the islands of the Pacific Ocean. They sailed large, oceangoing canoes with twin hulls joined by a deck on which they carried supplies. When they found uninhabited lands, their food crops and domesticated animals enabled them to establish agricultural societies in the islands. Once they had established coastal settlements in New Guinea, Austronesian seafarers sailed easily to the Bismarck and Solomon islands, perhaps in the interests of trade. From there they undertook exploratory voyages that led them to previously unpopulated islands.

By about 1500 B.C.E. Austronesian mariners had arrived at Vanuatu (formerly called New Hebrides) and New Caledonia, by 1300 B.C.E. at Fiji, and by 1000 B.C.E. at Tonga and Samoa. During the late centuries of the first millennium B.C.E., they established settlements in Tahiti and the Marquesas. From there they launched ventures that took them to the most remote outposts of Polynesia—the territory falling in the triangle with Hawaii, Easter Island, and New Zealand at the points— which required them to sail over thousands of nautical miles of deep ocean water. They reached the islands of Hawaii in the early centuries C.E., Easter Island by 300 C.E., and the large islands of New Zealand by 700 C.E.

A human face stares from these fragments of Lapita pottery, dated 1000 B.C.E. They come from the Santa Cruz group of islands, southeast of the Solomon Islands.
Rogers Fund, 1980/Metropolitan Museum of Art

Austronesian Migrations to Micronesia and Madagascar

While one branch of the Austronesian-speaking peoples populated the islands of Polynesia, other branches sailed in different directions. From the Philippines some ventured to the region of Micronesia, which includes small islands and atolls such as the Mariana, Caroline, and Marshall islands of the western Pacific. Yet others looked west from their homelands in Indonesia, sailed throughout the Indian Ocean, and became the first human settlers of the large island of Madagascar off the east African coast. Malagasy, the principal language of modern-day Madagascar, is clearly identifiable as an Austronesian tongue.

The Lapita Peoples

The earliest Austronesian migrants to sail out into the Pacific Ocean and establish settlements in Pacific islands are known as the **Lapita** peoples. No one knows what they called themselves: the name *Lapita* comes from a beach in New Caledonia where some of the earliest recognizable Lapita artifacts came to the attention of archaeologists. It is clear, however, that between about 1600 and 500 B.C.E., Lapita peoples maintained communication and exchange networks throughout a large region extending about 4,500 kilometers (2,800 miles) from New Guinea and the Bismarck Archipelago to Samoa and Tonga.

Wherever they settled, Lapita peoples established agricultural villages where they raised pigs and chickens and introduced the suite of crops they inherited from their Austronesian ancestors, including yams, taro, breadfruit, and bananas. They supplemented their crops and domesticated animals with fish and seaweed from nearby waters, and they soon killed off most of the large land animals and birds (some of which, in the absence of natural predators, had evolved into flightless species) that were suitable for human consumption. They left abundant evidence of their presence in the form of their distinctive pottery decorated with stamped geometric designs.

For about one thousand years, Lapita peoples maintained extensive networks of trade and communication across vast stretches of open ocean. Their agricultural settlements were largely self-sufficient, but they placed high value on some objects from distant islands. Their pottery was a principal item of long-distance exchange, as was high-quality obsidian, which they sometimes transported over thousands of kilometers because it was available at only a few sites of Lapita settlement. Other trade items brought to light by archaeologists include shell jewelry and stone tools. It is likely that Lapita peoples also traded feathers, foodstuffs, and marriage partners, although evidence for those exchanges does not survive in the archaeological record. In any case, it is clear that, like their counterparts in other regions of the world, the earliest inhabitants of the Pacific islands maintained regular contacts with peoples well beyond their societies.

Chiefly Political Organization

After about 500 B.C.E. Lapita trade networks fell into disuse, probably because the various Lapita settlements had grown large enough that they could supply their own needs and concentrate on the development of their own societies. By the middle part of the first millennium B.C.E., Lapita and other Austronesian peoples had established hierarchical chiefdoms in the Pacific islands. Leadership passed from a chief to his eldest son, and near relatives constituted a local aristocracy. Contests for power and influence between ambitious subordinates frequently caused tension and turmoil, but the possibility of migration offered an alternative to conflict. Dissatisfied or aggrieved parties often built voyaging canoes, recruited followers, and set sail with the intention of establishing new settlements in uninhabited or lightly populated islands. Indeed, the spread of Austronesian peoples throughout the Pacific islands came about partly because of population pressures and conflicts that encouraged small parties to seek fresh opportunities in more hospitable lands.

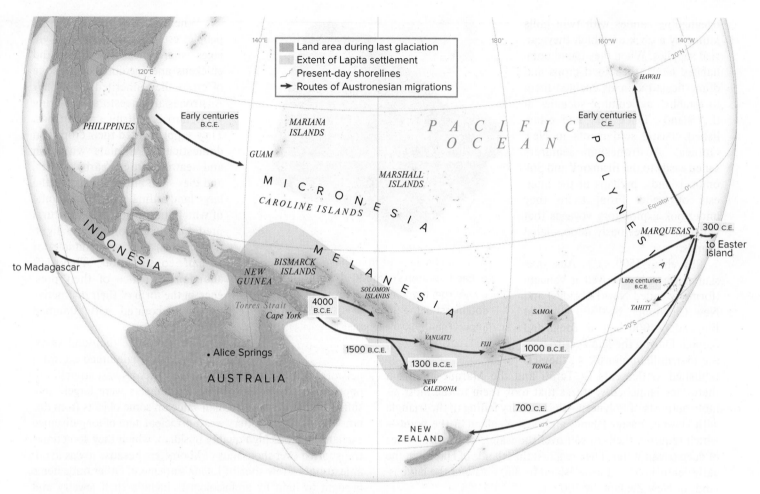

MAP 6.3   Early societies of Oceania, 1500 B.C.E.–700 C.E.

Notice the routes that Austronesian migrants followed.

What technologies and knowledge made it possible for Lapita and other peoples to maintain communication and exchange networks over such a vast area?

What's Left Out?

As we have seen, the migration of Austronesian peoples to Australia beginning as early as sixty thousand years ago, and the voyages of Polynesian peoples to hundreds of island groups across the vast Pacific, are among the most extraordinary migrations in all of world history. It is not surprising, of course, that the arrival of humans in regions that no human had ever seen before had significant environmental impact. This means that, even as we acknowledge the extraordinary ability of aboriginal and Polynesian peoples to adapt and thrive in often very harsh environments, we must also note that the impact of the arrival of these peoples on the plants and animals already living there was profound—and often disastrous. In Australia and New Zealand, for example, the arrival of humans corresponded with high levels of megafaunal extinction, as animals like the giant kangaroo and flightless birds like the Moa succumbed to overhunting and climate change. In Australia, the practice of firestick farming, whereby for tens of thousands of years aboriginal hunters set fire to huge tracts of bushland to aid hunting, led to drastic changes in the types of vegetation that grow across that vast continent even today. And across the Pacific, the inadvertent introduction of the Pacific rat, carried accidentally in the canoes of Polynesian migrants, devastated local bird populations wherever it appeared. Thus, even small groups of humans arriving in previously pristine regions had significant and often negative impacts on the environment.

Source: See David Christian, Cynthia Brown, and Craig Benjamin, *Big History: Between Nothing and Everything.* McGraw-Hill, 2014, Chaps. 9 and 13.

Over the longer term, descendants of Lapita peoples built strong, chiefly societies, particularly on large islands with relatively dense populations like those of the Tongan, Samoan, and Hawaiian groups. In Hawaii, for example, militarily skilled chiefs cooperated closely with priests, administrators, soldiers, and servants in ruling their districts, which might include a portion of an island, an entire island, or even several islands. Chiefs and their retinues claimed a portion of the agricultural surplus produced by their subjects, and they sometimes required subjects to deliver additional products, such as fish, birds, or timber. Apart from organizing public life in their own districts, chiefs and their administrators vied with the ruling classes of neighboring districts, led public ritual observances, and oversaw irrigation systems that watered the taro plants that were crucial to the survival of Hawaiian society. Eventually, the chiefly and aristocratic classes became so entrenched and powerful that they regarded themselves as divine or semidivine, and the law of the land prohibited common subjects from even gazing directly at them.

CONCLUSION

Little writing survives to illuminate the historical development of early societies in the Americas and Oceania. This means it is more difficult to offer the sort of richly detailed account of their political organization, social structures, and cultural traditions that historians commonly provide for societies of Afro-Eurasia. Nevertheless, it is clear that migrations to the Americas and Oceania represented continuations of population movements that began with *Homo erectus* and early *Homo sapiens,* resulting eventually in the establishment of human communities in all habitable parts of the earth. It is also clear that the earliest inhabitants of the Americas and Oceania built productive and vibrant societies whose development roughly paralleled that of their counterparts in the eastern hemisphere. Many communities depended on an agricultural economy, and with their surplus production they supported dense populations, engaged in specialized labor, established formal political authorities, constructed hierarchical social orders, participated in encounters via long-distance trade, and formed distinctive cultural traditions. The early historical development of the Americas and Oceania demonstrates once again the tendency of agriculture to encourage human communities to construct ever more elaborate and complex forms of social organization.

STUDY TERMS

Austronesian-speaking peoples (119)	Maya (110)
bloodletting rituals (114)	Mesoamerica (108)
Chavín culture (117)	Moche (118)
Chichén Itzá (111)	Oceania (119)
colossal human heads (109)	Olmecs (109)
Lapita (121)	Popol Vuh (114)
maize (108)	Teotihuacan (110)
	Tikal (110)

FOR FURTHER READING

Michael Coe. *The Maya.* New York, 2005. Scholarly and readable account of the history and culture of the Maya from one of the world's leading experts on ancient Mesoamerica.

Richard A. Diehl. *The Olmecs: America's First Civilization.* London, 2004. The best brief introduction to Olmec society.

Peter Hiscock. *Archaeology of Ancient Australia.* London, 2008. The most up-to-date account of the key archaeological evidence for Australia's ancient peoples by one of the foremost specialists in the field.

K. R. Howe. *The Quest for Origins: Who First Discovered and Settled the Pacific Islands?* Honolulu, 2003. Reviews the numerous theories advanced to explain the arrival of human populations and the establishment of human societies in the remote islands of the Pacific Ocean.

Kerry Howe and Vaka Moana. *Voyages of the Ancestors.* Auckland, 2006. Fascinating account of Polynesian migrations and particularly the discovery and settlement of New Zealand, published by the Auckland Museum.

Patrick V. Kirch. *On the Road of the Winds: An Archaeological History of the Pacific Islands before European Contact.* Berkeley, 2000. A valuable synthesis of scholarship by the foremost contemporary archaeologist of the Pacific islands.

Charles C. Mann. *1491: New Revelations of the Americas before Columbus.* New York, 2006. Summarizes a great deal of archaeological research on the pre-Columbian Americas.

Simon Martin and Nikolai Grube. *Chronicle of the Maya Kings and Queens: Deciphering the Dynasties of the Ancient Maya.* London, 2000. Offers an important synthesis of Mayan political history on the basis of both inscriptions and archaeological discoveries.

Michael E. Mosley. *The Incas and Their Ancestors: The Archaeology of Peru.* Rev. ed. London, 2001. A comprehensive survey of Andean history through the era of the Incas.

Linda Schele and Mary Ellen Miller. *The Blood of Kings: Dynasty and Ritual in Maya Art.* New York, 1986. A richly illustrated volume that explores Mayan society through works of art and architecture as well as writing.

David Webster. *The Fall of the Ancient Maya: Solving the Mystery of the Maya Collapse.* London, 2002. A careful and readable analysis of the difficulties that confronted Mayan society.

ZOOMING IN ON ENCOUNTERS
King Croesus and the Tricky Business of Predicting the Future

The Greek historian Herodotus told many a tale about the Persian Empire and its conflicts with other peoples, including Greeks. One story had to do with a struggle between **Cyrus,** leader of the expanding Persian realm, and **Croesus,** ruler of the powerful and wealthy kingdom of Lydia in southwestern Anatolia (modern Turkey). Croesus noted the growth of Persian influence with concern and asked the Greek oracle at Delphi whether to go to war against Cyrus. The oracle, which had a reputation for delivering ambiguous predictions, responded that an attack on Cyrus would destroy a great kingdom.

Overjoyed, Croesus lined up his allies and prepared for war. In 546 B.C.E. he launched an invasion, provoking Cyrus to engage the formidable Lydian cavalry. The resulting battle was hard fought but inconclusive. Because winter was approaching, Croesus disbanded his troops and returned to his capital at Sardis, expecting Cyrus to retreat as well. But Cyrus was a brilliant military strategist and he pursued Croesus to Sardis. When he learned of the pursuit, Croesus hastily assembled an army to confront the invaders. Cyrus threw it into disarray, however, by advancing a group of warriors mounted on camels, which

A procession of envoys with offerings for the king makes its way up a ceremonial stairway in the ancient city of Persepolis in modern Iran, one of four capitals of the Achaemenid Persian Empire.
James P. Blair/National Geographic/Getty Images

spooked the Lydian horses and sent them into headlong flight. Cyrus's army then surrounded Sardis and took the city after a siege of only two weeks. Croesus narrowly escaped death in the battle, but he was taken captive and afterward became an adviser to Cyrus. Herodotus could not resist pointing out that events proved the Delphic oracle right: Croesus's attack on Cyrus did indeed lead to the destruction of a great kingdom—his own.

The victory over Lydia was a major turning point in the development of the Persian Empire. Lydia was a fabulously wealthy kingdom partly because it was the first state to use standardized coins guaranteed by the government. Taking advantage of

Cyrus (SIGH-ruhs)
Croesus (CREE-suhs)

its coins and its geographic location on the Mediterranean, Lydia conducted maritime trade with Greece, Egypt, and Phoenicia as well as overland trade with Mesopotamia and Persia. Lydian wealth and resources gave Cyrus tremendous momentum as he extended Persian authority to new lands and a vast imperial state.

CHAPTER OVERVIEW

The first Persian Empire was constructed during the sixth century B.C.E. when warriors conquered the region from the Indus River to Egypt and southeastern Europe. Their conquests created an enormous realm much larger than the earlier Babylonian or Assyrian empires. The very size of the Persian Empire created political and administrative problems for its rulers. Once they solved those problems, however, a series of Persian-based empires governed much of the territory between India and the Mediterranean Sea for more than a millennium—from the mid-sixth century B.C.E. until the early seventh century C.E.—and brought centralized political organization to many different peoples living over vast geographic spaces.

In organizing their realm, Persian rulers relied heavily on Mesopotamian techniques of administration, which they adapted to their own needs. Yet they also created innovative new institutions and administrative practices. In the interest of improved communications and military mobility, they also invested resources in the construction of roads and highways linking the regions of the empire. As a result of those efforts, central administrators were able to send instructions throughout the empire, dispatch armies in times of turmoil, and ensure that local officials would carry out imperial policies.

The organization of the vast territories embraced by the Persian empires had important social, economic, and cultural implications. High agricultural productivity enabled many people to work at tasks other than cultivation: classes of bureaucrats, administrators, priests, craftsmen, and merchants increased in number as the production and distribution of food became more efficient. Meanwhile, social hierarchies became more pronounced: a few individuals and families amassed enormous wealth, many led simple lives, and some fell into slavery. Good roads fostered trade within imperial borders, and Persian society itself served as a commercial and cultural bridge between Indian and Mediterranean societies. As a crossroads, Persia served not only as a link in long-distance trade networks but also as a conduit for the exchange of philosophical and religious ideas. Persian religious traditions did not attract many adherents beyond the imperial boundaries, but they inspired religious thinkers subject to Persian rule and also influenced Judaism, Christianity, and Islam.

CHRONOLOGY

7th–6th centuries B.C.E.(?)	Life of Zarathustra
558–330 B.C.E.	Achaemenid Persian Empire
558–530 B.C.E.	Reign of Cyrus the Achaemenid
521–486 B.C.E.	Reign of Darius
334–330 B.C.E.	Invasion and conquest of the Achaemenid empire by Alexander of Macedon
323–83 B.C.E.	Seleucid Empire
247 B.C.E.–224 C.E.	Parthian Empire
224–651 C.E.	Sasanian Empire

EMPIRES OF PERSIA

The empires of Persia arose in the arid land of Iran. For centuries Iran had developed under the shadow of the wealthier and more productive Mesopotamia to the west while absorbing intermittent migrations and invasions of nomadic peoples coming out of central Asia to the northeast. During the sixth century B.C.E., rulers of the province of Persia in southwestern Iran embarked on a series of conquests that resulted in the formation of an enormous empire. For more than a millennium, four ruling dynasties—the **Achaemenids** (558–330 B.C.E.), the Seleucids (323–83 B.C.E.), the Parthians (247 B.C.E.–224 C.E.), and the Sasanians (224–651 C.E.)—maintained a continuous tradition of imperial rule in much of southwest Asia.

The Achaemenid Empire

The Medes and the Persians The origins of Persian society trace back to the late stages of Mesopotamian society. During the centuries before 1000 B.C.E., two closely related peoples known as the **Medes** and the Persians migrated from central Asia to Persia (the southwestern portion of the modern-day state of Iran), where they lived under the loose control of the Babylonian and Assyrian empires. The Medes and the Persians spoke Indo-European languages, and their movements

Achaemenid (ah-KEE-muh-nid)

Medes (meeds)

125

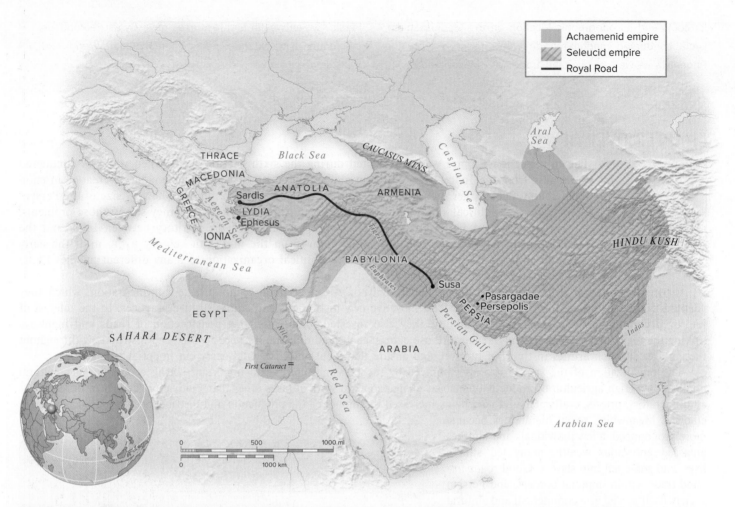

MAP 7.1   The Achaemenid and Seleucid empires, 558–330 B.C.E. and 323–83 B.C.E.

Observe how much larger the Achaemenid and Seleucid empires were compared to the earlier Mesopotamian and Egyptian empires discussed in chapters 2 and 3.

What were some of the techniques Persian rulers used to unify and control their enormous empire?

were part of the larger Indo-European migrations we have discussed in previous chapters. They shared many cultural traits with their distant cousins, the Indo-Aryans, who migrated into South Asia. They were mostly pastoralists, although they also practiced a limited amount of agriculture. They organized themselves by clans rather than by states or formal political institutions, but they recognized leaders who collected taxes and delivered tribute to their Mesopotamian overlords.

Although not tightly organized politically, the Medes and the Persians were peoples of considerable military power. As descendants of nomadic peoples from central Asia, they possessed the equestrian skills common to many steppe peoples. They were expert archers, even when mounted on their horses, and they frequently raided the wealthy lands of Mesopotamia.

When the Assyrian and Babylonian empires weakened in the sixth century B.C.E., the Medes and the Persians embarked on a vastly successful imperial venture of their own.

Cyrus Cyrus, founder of the Achaemenid Empire (reigned 558–530 B.C.E.), launched the Persians' imperial venture. Cyrus proved to be a tough, wily leader and an outstanding military strategist. His conquests laid the foundation of the first Persian Empire, also known as the Achaemenid empire because its rulers claimed descent from Cyrus's Achaemenid clan.

Cyrus's Conquests In 558 B.C.E. Cyrus became king of the Persian tribes, which he ruled from his mountain fortress at **Pasargadae.** In 553 B.C.E. he initiated a rebellion against his Median overlord, whom he defeated within three years. By 548 B.C.E. he had brought all of Iran under his control, and he began to look for opportunities to expand his influence. In 546 B.C.E. he conquered the powerful kingdom of Lydia as

Pasargadae (pah-SAR-gah-dee)

described in the opening of this chapter. Between 545 B.C.E. and 539 B.C.E., he campaigned in central Asia and Bactria (modern Afghanistan). In a swift campaign of 539 B.C.E., he seized Babylonia, whose vassal states immediately recognized him as their lord. Within twenty years Cyrus went from minor regional king to ruler of an empire that stretched from India to the borders of Egypt.

Cyrus no doubt would have mounted a campaign against Egypt, the largest and wealthiest neighboring state outside his control, had he lived long enough. But in 530 B.C.E. he fell, mortally wounded, while protecting his northeastern frontier from nomadic raiders. His troops recovered his body and placed it in a simple tomb, which still stands, that Cyrus had prepared for himself at his palace in Pasargadae.

The tomb of Cyrus at Pasargadae—one of the few Achaemenid monuments that have survived to the present.
Janzig/MiddleEast/Alamy Stock Photo

Successors Cyrus's empire survived and expanded during the reigns of his successors. His son **Cambyses** (reigned 530–522 B.C.E.) conquered Egypt in 525 B.C.E. and brought its wealth into Persian hands. His successor **Darius** (reigned 521–486 B.C.E.), extended the empire both east and west. His armies pushed into northwestern India as far as the Indus River, absorbing parts of northern India, while also capturing lands in southeastern Europe. By the late sixth century, Darius presided over an empire stretching some 3,000 kilometers (1,865 miles) from the Indus River in the east to the **Aegean Sea** in the west and 1,500 kilometers (933 miles) from Armenia in the north to the first cataract of the Nile River in the south. This empire embraced mountains, valleys, plateaus, jungles, deserts, and arable land, and it touched the shores of the Arabian Sea, Aral Sea, Persian Gulf, Caspian Sea, Black Sea, Red Sea, and Mediterranean Sea. With a population of some thirty-five million, Darius's realm was by far the largest empire the world had yet seen.

Darius was just as able an administrator as he was conqueror. Governing a far-flung empire was a much more difficult challenge than conquering it. The Achaemenid rulers presided over more than seventy distinct ethnic groups, including peoples who lived in widely scattered regions, spoke many different languages, and observed a profusion of religious and cultural traditions. To maintain their empire, the Achaemenids needed to establish lines of communication with all parts of their realm and design institutions that would enable them to tax and administer their territories. In doing so, they not only made it possible for the Achaemenid empire to survive but also pioneered administrative techniques that would outlast their dynasty and influence political life in Eurasia for centuries to come.

Persepolis Soon after his rise to power, Darius began to centralize his administration. About 520 B.C.E. he started to build a new capital of astonishing magnificence at **Persepolis,** near Pasargadae. Darius intended Persepolis to serve not only as an administrative center but also as a monument to the Achaemenid dynasty. Structures at Persepolis included vast reception halls, lavish royal residences, and a well-protected treasury. From the time of Darius to the end of the Achaemenid dynasty in 330 B.C.E., Persepolis served as the nerve center of the Persian Empire—a resplendent capital bustling with advisers, ministers, diplomats, scribes, accountants, translators, and bureaucratic officers of all descriptions. Even today, massive columns and other ruins demonstrate the grandeur of Darius's capital.

Achaemenid Administration: The Satrapies The government of the Achaemenid empire depended on a finely tuned balance between central and local administration. The Achaemenid rulers made great claims to authority in their official title—"The Great King, King of Kings, King in Persia, King of Countries." Like their Mesopotamian predecessors, the Achaemenids appointed governors (called *satraps*) to serve as agents of the central administration and oversee affairs in the various regions. Darius divided his realm into twenty-three **satrapies**—administrative and taxation districts governed by satraps. Yet the Achaemenids did not try to push direct rule on their subjects: most of the satraps were Persians, but the Achaemenids occasionally recruited local officials to fill almost all administrative posts below the level of the satrap.

Because the satraps often held posts distant from Persepolis, there was always a possibility that they might ally with local groups and become independent of Achaemenid authority or even threaten the empire itself. The Achaemenid rulers relied on two measures to discourage that possibility. First, each satrapy had a contingent of military officers and tax collectors who served as checks on the satraps' power and independence. Second, the rulers created a new category of officials—essentially imperial spies—known as "the eyes and ears of the king." These agents traveled throughout the empire with their own military forces conducting surprise audits of accounts and procedures in the provinces and collecting intelligence reports. The division of provincial responsibilities and the institution of the eyes and ears of the king helped the Achaemenid rulers maintain control over a vast empire that otherwise might easily have split into a series of independent regional kingdoms.

Cambyses (kam-BIE-sees)
Persepolis (per-SEP-uh-lis)

Ruins of Persepolis, showing the imperial reception hall and palaces. The columns rise about 19 meters (62 feet) and once supported a massive roof.
Fred Maroon/Science Source

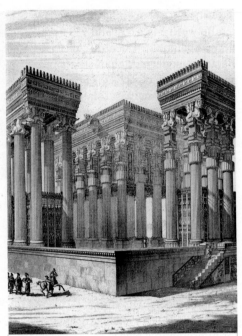

An artist's impression of how the same imperial reception buildings and palaces would have looked when completed during the reign of Darius I in the late sixth century B.C.E. Artist Charles Chipiez, French, 1835–1901
The History Collection/Alamy Stock Photo

Taxes, Coins, and Laws Darius also sought to improve administrative efficiency by regularizing tax levies and standardizing laws. Cyrus and Cambyses had accepted tribute from subject lands and cities. Though often lavish, this tribute did not provide a consistent and reliable source of income for rulers who needed to finance a large bureaucracy and army. Darius replaced irregular tribute payments with formal tax levies. He required each satrapy to pay a set quantity of silver—and in some cases a levy of horses or slaves as well—deliverable annually to the imperial court. Darius followed the example of the Lydian king Croesus and issued standardized coins—a move that fostered trade. In an equally important initiative begun in the year 520 B.C.E., he sought to bring the many legal systems of his empire closer to a single standard. He did not abolish the existing laws of individual lands or peoples, nor did he impose a uniform law code on his entire empire. But he directed legal experts to study and codify the laws of his subject peoples, modifying them when necessary to harmonize them with the legal principles observed in the empire as a whole.

Roads and Communications Alongside their administrative and legal policies, the Achaemenid rulers took other measures to knit their far-flung realm into a coherent whole. They built good roads across their realm, notably the **Persian Royal Road**—parts of it paved with stone—that stretched about 2,575 kilometers (1,600 miles) from the Aegean port of Ephesus to Sardis in Anatolia, through Mesopotamia along the Tigris River, to Susa in Iran, with an extension to Pasargadae and Persepolis. Caravans took some ninety days to travel this road, lodging at inns along the well-policed route.

The imperial government also organized a courier service and built 111 postal stations at intervals of 40 to 50 kilometers (25 to 30 miles) along the Royal Road. Each station kept a supply of fresh horses and food rations for couriers, who sometimes traveled at night as well as during daylight hours. These couriers were able to carry urgent messages from one end of the Royal Road to the other in two weeks' time. The Greek historian Herodotus spoke highly of these imperial servants, and even today the United States Postal Service takes his description of their efforts as a standard for its employees: "Neither snow nor rain nor heat nor gloom of night stays these couriers from the swift completion of their appointed rounds." The Achaemenids also improved existing routes between Mesopotamia and Egypt, and they built new roads linking Persia with northern India, Mesopotamia, Anatolia, Syria, and Egypt. In combination, these imperial highways stretched approximately 13,000 kilometers (8,000 miles). In addition to improving communications, these roads facilitated trade, which helped to integrate the empire's various regions into a larger economy.

Decline of the Achaemenid Empire

The Achaemenid Commonwealth The Achaemenids' roads and administrative machinery enabled them to govern a vast empire and extend Persian influences throughout their territories. Political stability made it possible to undertake extensive public works projects such as the construction of *qanat* (underground canals), which led to enhanced agricultural production and population growth. Iron metallurgy spread to all parts of the empire, and by the end of the Achaemenid dynasty, iron tools were common in Persian agricultural communities. Peoples in the various regions of the Achaemenid empire maintained their ethnic identities, but all participated in a larger Persian commonwealth.

Eventually, however, difficulties between rulers and subject peoples undermined the integrity of the Achaemenid empire. Cyrus and Darius both consciously pursued a policy of toleration in administering their vast multicultural empire: they took care to respect the values and cultural traditions of the peoples they ruled. In Mesopotamia, for example, they did not portray themselves as Persian conquerors but, rather, as legitimate Babylonian rulers and representatives of Marduk, the patron deity of Babylon.

Darius's successor, Xerxes (reigned 486–465 B.C.E.), had more difficult relations with subject peoples. The burden of Persian rule became particularly heavy in Mesopotamia and Egypt—regions with sophisticated cultural traditions and long histories of independence—and subject peoples there frequently rose up in rebellion. Xerxes did not seek to impose specifically Persian values in Mesopotamia and Egypt, but he harshly repressed rebellions and thereby gained a reputation for cruelty and insensitivity to the concerns of subject peoples.

The Persian Wars The Achaemenids had an especially difficult time with their ethnic Greek subjects. Greeks inhabited many of the cities in Anatolia—particularly in the region of Ionia on the Aegean coast of western Anatolia—and they maintained close economic and commercial ties with their cousins in the peninsula of Greece itself. The Ionian Greeks fell under Persian domination during the reign of Cyrus. They became restive under Darius's Persian governors—"tyrants," the Greeks called them—who oversaw their affairs. In 500 B.C.E. the Ionian cities rebelled, expelled or executed their governors, and asserted their independence. Their rebellion launched a series of conflicts that Greeks called the **Persian Wars** (500–479 B.C.E.).

The conflict between the Ionian Greeks and the Persians expanded when the cities of peninsular Greece sent fleets to aid their kinsmen in Ionia. Darius managed to put down the rebellion and reassert Achaemenid authority, but he and his successors became entangled in a difficult and ultimately destructive effort to extend their authority to the Greek peninsula. In 490 B.C.E. Darius attempted to forestall future problems by mounting an expedition to conquer the mainland Greek cities and absorb them into his empire. Though larger and much more powerful than the forces of the disunited Greek city-states, the Persian army had to contend with long and fragile lines of supply as well as a hostile environment. After some initial successes, the Persians suffered a rout at the **battle of Marathon** (490 B.C.E.), and they returned home without achieving their goals. Xerxes sent another expedition ten years later, but within eighteen months, it too had suffered defeat both on land (famously at Thermopylae) and at sea and had returned to Persia. We have more to say about the Persian Wars in chapter 10.

For almost 150 years the Persian Empire sparred intermittently with the Greek cities. The adversaries mounted small expeditions against each other, attacking individual cities or fleets, but they did not engage in large-scale campaigns. The Greek cities were too small and disunited to pose a serious challenge to the enormous Persian Empire. Meanwhile, for

qanat (kah-NAHT)

Stone carving from Persepolis showing an enthroned Darius (with his son Xerxes standing behind him) receiving a high court official, as incense burners perfume the air. In what ways does the official's posture indicate respect for and submission to the emperor?
Smith Archive/Alamy Stock Photo

their part, the later Achaemenids had to concentrate on the other restive and sometimes rebellious regions of their empire and could not embark on new rounds of expansion.

Alexander of Macedon The standoff ended with the rise of **Alexander of Macedon,** often called Alexander the Great (also discussed more fully in chapter 10). In 334 B.C.E. Alexander invaded Persia with an army of some forty-eight thousand tough, battle-hardened Macedonians. Though far smaller than the Persian army in numbers, the well-disciplined Macedonians carried heavier arms and employed more sophisticated military tactics than their opponents. As a result, they sliced through the Persian Empire, advancing almost at will and dealing their adversaries a series of devastating defeats. In 331 B.C.E. Alexander shattered Achaemenid forces at the **battle of Gaugamela,** and within a year the empire founded by Cyrus had dissolved.

Alexander led his forces into Persepolis, confiscated the wealth stored in the imperial treasury there, paid his respects at the tomb of Cyrus in Pasargadae, and proclaimed himself heir to the Achaemenid rulers. After a brief season of celebration, Alexander and his forces ignited a blaze—perhaps intentionally—that destroyed Persepolis. The conflagration was so great that when archaeologists first began to explore the ruins of Persepolis in the eighteenth century, they found layers of ash and charcoal up to 1 meter (3 feet) deep.

The Achaemenid empire had crumbled, but its legacy was by no means exhausted. Alexander portrayed himself in Persia as a legitimate successor of the Achaemenids who observed their precedents and deserved their honors. He retained the Achaemenid administrative structure, and he even confirmed the appointments of many satraps and other officials. As it happened, Alexander had little time to enjoy his conquests because he died in 323 B.C.E. after a brief effort to extend his empire to India. But the states that succeeded him—the Seleucid, Parthian, and Sasanian empires—continued to employ a basically Achaemenid structure of imperial administration. The rulers of these subsequent empires employed Achaemenid methods of government because these provided continuity of administration in the regions under their control and also helped legitimize their claims to power. By linking their imperial names and power to their predecessors, even to those leaders and empires they had just destroyed, new rulers increased their own prestige in the eyes of the peoples who

A gold coin from the early Hellenistic era depicting the Macedonian conqueror, Alexander.
De Agostini Picture Library/Getty Images

were now citizens of a new, replacement empire. This is a mechanism to legitimize claims of usurper rulers and states that has been used throughout history.

The Seleucid, Parthian, and Sasanian Empires

The Seleucids After Alexander died, his chief generals fought among themselves and struggled to take over the conqueror's realms. In Persia the victor was Seleucus, formerly commander of an elite guard corps in Alexander's army, who dominated the territories of the former Achaemenid empire and ruled them from 305 to 281 B.C.E. Like Alexander, Seleucus and his successors retained the Achaemenid systems of administration and taxation as well as the imperial roads and postal service. The **Seleucids** also founded new cities throughout the realm and attracted Greek colonists to occupy them. The migrants, who represented only a small fraction of the whole population of the empire, largely adapted to their new environment. Nonetheless, the establishment of cities greatly stimulated trade and economic development both within the Seleucid empire and beyond.

As foreigners, the Seleucids faced opposition from native peoples and especially their ruling classes. Satraps often revolted against Seleucid rule, or at least worked to build power bases that would enable them to establish their independence. The Seleucids soon lost their holdings in northern India, and the seminomadic Parthians progressively took over Iran during the third century B.C.E. The Seleucids continued to rule a truncated empire until 83 B.C.E., when Roman conquerors put an end to their empire.

The Parthians Meanwhile, the **Parthians** established themselves as rulers of a powerful empire based in Iran that they extended to wealthy Mesopotamia. The Parthians had occupied the region of eastern Iran around Khurasan since Achaemenid times. They retained many of the customs and traditions of nomadic peoples from the steppes of central Asia. They did not have a centralized government, for example, but organized themselves politically through a federation of leaders who met in councils and jointly determined policy for all allied groups. They were skillful warriors, accustomed to defending themselves against constant threats from nomadic peoples farther east.

As they settled and turned increasingly to agriculture, the Parthians also devised an effective means to resist nomadic invasions. Because they had no access to feed grains, nomadic peoples allowed their horses to forage for food on the steppes

Artist's impression of nomadic Parthian horsemen discharging their arrows backwards at a pursuing army.
Chronicle/Alamy Stock Photo

during the winter. The Parthians discovered that if they fed their horses on alfalfa during the winter, their animals would grow much larger and stronger than the small horses and ponies of the steppes. Their larger animals could then support heavily armed warriors outfitted with metal armor, which served as an effective shield against the arrows of the steppe nomads. Well-trained forces of heavily armed cavalry could usually put nomadic raiding parties to flight. Indeed, few existing forces could stand up to Parthian heavy cavalry.

Parthian Conquests As early as the third century B.C.E., the Parthians began to wrest their independence from the Seleucids. The Parthian satrap revolted against his Seleucid overlord in 238 B.C.E., and during the following decades his successors gradually enlarged their holdings. **Mithradates I,** the Parthians' greatest conqueror, came to the throne about 171 B.C.E. and transformed his state into a mighty empire. By about 155 B.C.E. he had consolidated his hold on Iran and had also extended Parthian rule to Mesopotamia.

Parthian Government The Parthians portrayed themselves as enemies of the foreign Seleucids, as restorers of rule in the Persian tradition. To some extent, that characterization was accurate. The Parthians largely followed the example of the Achaemenids in structuring their empire: they governed through satraps, employed Achaemenid techniques of administration and taxation, and built a capital city at **Ctesiphon** on the Euphrates River near modern Baghdad. But the Parthians also retained elements of their steppe traditions. They did not develop nearly so centralized a regime as the Achaemenids or the Seleucids but, rather, vested a great deal of authority and responsibility in their clan leaders. These men often served as satraps, and they regularly worked to build independent bases of power in their regions. They frequently mounted rebellions against

the imperial government, and sometimes two rivals claimed the crown at the same time.

For about three centuries the Parthians presided over a powerful empire between South Asia and the Mediterranean. Beginning in the first century C.E., they faced pressure in the west from the expanding Roman empire. The Parthian empire as a whole never stood in danger of falling to the Romans because the Parthian military was so powerful and the empire so vast, but on three occasions in the second century C.E. Roman armies captured the Parthian capital at Ctesiphon. Combined with internal difficulties caused by the rebellious satraps, Roman pressure contributed to the weakening of the Parthian state. During the early third century C.E., internal rebellion brought it down.

The Sasanians Once again, though, the tradition of imperial rule continued, this time under the **Sasanians,** who came from Persia and claimed direct descent from the Achaemenids. The Sasanians toppled the Parthians in 224 C.E. and ruled until 651 C.E., re-creating much of the splendor of the Achaemenid empire. From their cosmopolitan capital at Ctesiphon, the Sasanian "king of kings" provided strong rule from Parthia to Mesopotamia while also rebuilding an elaborate system of administration and founding or refurbishing numerous cities. Sasanian merchants traded actively with peoples to both east and west, and they introduced into Iran the cultivation of crops such as rice, sugarcane, citrus fruits, eggplant, and cotton that came west over the trade routes from India and China.

During the reign of Shapur I (239–272 C.E.), the Sasanians stabilized their western frontier and created a series of buffer states between themselves and the Roman empire. Shapur even defeated several Roman armies and settled the prisoners in Iran, where they devoted their famous engineering skills to the construction of roads and dams. After Shapur, the Sasanians did not expand militarily but entered into a standoff relationship with remnants of the Kushan empire in the east and the Roman and Byzantine empires in the west. None of those large empires was strong enough to overcome the others, but they contested border areas and buffer states, sometimes engaging in lengthy and bitter disputes that sapped the energies of all involved.

These continual conflicts seriously weakened the Sasanian empire in particular. The empire came to an end in 651 C.E. when Arab warriors killed the last Sasanian ruler, overran his realm, and incorporated it into their rapidly expanding Islamic empire. Yet even conquest by external invaders did not end the legacy of the Persian empires: Persian administrative techniques and cultural traditions were so powerful that the Arab conquerors adopted them to use in building a new Islamic society.

Mithradates (mihth-rah-DAY-teez)
Ctesiphon (TES-uh-phon)
Sasanians (suh-SAHN-iens)

IMPERIAL SOCIETY AND ECONOMY

Throughout Afro-Eurasia during this time, public life and social structure became much more complicated than they had been during the days of the early complex societies. Centralized imperial governments needed large numbers of administrative officials, which led to the emergence of educated classes of bureaucrats. Stable empires enabled many individuals to engage in trade or other specialized labor as artisans, craftsmen, or professionals of various kinds. Some of them accumulated vast wealth, which led to increased distance and tensions between rich and poor. Meanwhile, slavery became more common than in earlier times. The prominence of slavery had to do partly with the expansion of imperial states, which often enslaved conquered foes, but it also reflected the increasing gulf between rich and poor, which placed such great economic pressure on some individuals that they had to give up their freedom in order to survive. All those developments had implications for the social structures of societies in Persia as well as China, India, and the Mediterranean basin.

Social Development in the Persian Empires

During the early days of the Achaemenid empire, Persian society reflected its origins on the steppes of central Asia. When the Medes and the Persians migrated to Iran, their social structure was similar to that of the Aryans in India, consisting primarily of warriors, priests, and peasants. For centuries, when they lived on the periphery and in the shadow of the Mesopotamian empires, the Medes and the Persians maintained steppe traditions. Even after the establishment of the Achaemenid empire, some of them followed a seminomadic lifestyle and maintained ties with their cousins on the steppes. Family and clan relationships were extremely important in the organization of Persian political and social affairs. Male warriors headed the clans, which retained much of their influence long after the establishment of the Achaemenid empire.

Imperial Bureaucrats The development of a cosmopolitan empire, however, brought considerable complexity to Persian society. The requirements of imperial administration, for

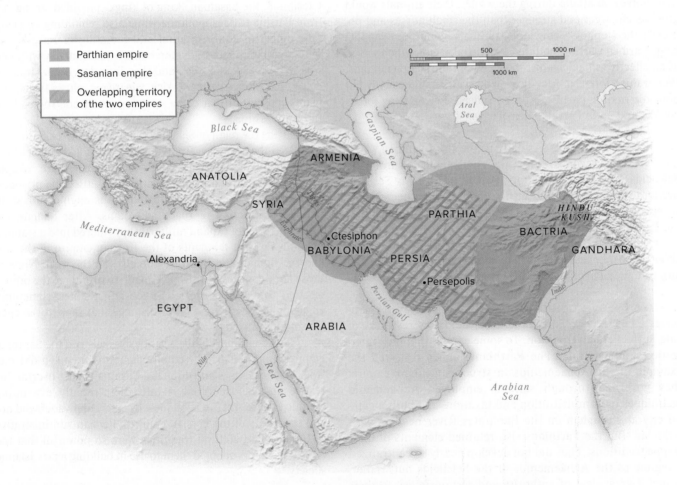

MAP 7.2 The Parthian and Sasanian empires, 247 B.C.E.–651 C.E.

Note the location of the Parthian and Sasanian empires between the Mediterranean Sea and northern India.

How did the Parthian and Sasanian empires serve as bridges between Asia and Europe, both geographically and culturally?

In this sculpture from Persepolis, Persian nobles dressed in fine cloaks and hats ascend the staircase leading to the imperial reception hall.
Fred Maroon/Science Source

example, called for a new class of educated bureaucrats who competed for status with the old warrior elite. The bureaucrats did not directly challenge the patriarchal warriors and certainly did not seek to displace them from their privileged position in society. Nevertheless, the bureaucrats' crucial role in running the day-to-day affairs of the empire guaranteed them a prominent and comfortable place in Persian society. By the time of the later Achaemenids and the Seleucids, Persian cities were home to masses of administrators, tax collectors, and record keepers. The bureaucracy even included a substantial corps of translators, who facilitated communications among the empire's many linguistic groups. Imperial survival depended on these literate professionals, and high-ranking bureaucrats came to share power and influence with warriors and clan leaders.

Free Classes The bulk of the society of the Persian Empire were individuals who were free but did not enjoy the privileges

of warrior elites and bureaucrats. In the cities the free classes included artisans, craftsmen, merchants, and low-ranking civil servants. Priests and priestesses were also prominent urban residents, along with servants who maintained the temple communities in which they lived. In Persian society, as in earlier Mesopotamian societies, members of the free classes participated in religious observances conducted at local temples, and they had the right to share in the income that temples generated from their agricultural operations and from craft industries, such as textile production, that the temples organized. The weaving of textiles was mostly the work of women, who received rations of grain, wine, beer, and sometimes meat from the imperial and temple workshops that employed them.

In the countryside the free classes included peasants who owned land as well as landless cultivators who worked as laborers or tenants on properties owned by the state, temple communities, or other individuals. Free residents of rural areas had the right to marry and move as they wished, and they could seek better opportunities in the cities or in military service. Because the Persian empires embraced a great deal of parched land that received little rainfall, work in the countryside involved not only cultivation but also the building and maintenance of irrigation systems.

The most remarkable of those systems were underground canals known as *qanat,* which allowed cultivators to distribute water to fields without losing large quantities to evaporation through exposure to the sun and open air. Numerous *qanat* crisscrossed the Iranian plateau in the heartland of the Persian Empire, where extreme scarcity of water justified the enormous investment of human labor required to build the canals. Although they had help from slaves, free residents of the countryside contributed much of the labor that went into the excavation and maintenance of the *qanat.*

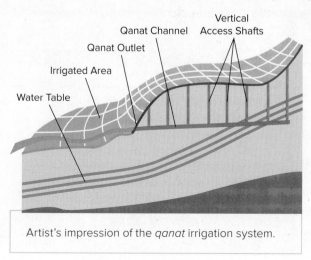

Artist's impression of the *qanat* irrigation system.

Slaves A large class of enslaved people also worked in both the cities and the countryside. Individuals passed into slavery by two main routes. Most were prisoners of war who became slaves as the price of survival. These prisoners usually came from military units, but the Persians also enslaved civilians who resisted their advance or who rebelled against imperial authorities. Other slaves came from the ranks of free subjects who accumulated debts that they could not satisfy.

Slaves became the property of an individual, the state, or an institution such as a temple community: they worked at tasks set by their holders, and they could not move or marry at will, although existing family units usually stayed together. Most slaves probably worked as domestic servants or skilled laborers in the households of the wealthy, but at least some slaves cultivated their owners' fields in the countryside. State-held slaves provided the manual labor for large-scale construction projects such as roads, irrigation systems, city walls, and palaces.

Economic Foundations of the Persian Empires

Agriculture was the economic foundation of Persian society. Like other ancient societies, Persia needed large agricultural surpluses to support military forces and administrative specialists as well as residents of cities who were artisans, craft workers, and merchants rather than cultivators. The Persian empires embraced several regions of exceptional fertility—notably Mesopotamia, Egypt, Anatolia, and northern India—and they prospered by mobilizing the agricultural surpluses of those lands.

Agricultural Production Barley and wheat were the grains cultivated most commonly in the Persian empires. Peas, lentils, mustard, garlic, onions, cucumbers, dates, apples, pomegranates, pears, and apricots supplemented the cereals in diets throughout Persian society, and beer and wine were the most common beverages. In most years agricultural production far exceeded the needs of cultivators, making sizable surpluses available for sale in the cities or for distribution to state servants through the imperial bureaucracy. Vast quantities of produce flowed into the imperial court from state-owned lands cultivated by slaves or leased out to tenants in exchange for a portion of the annual harvest. Even though they are incomplete, surviving records show that, for example, in 500 B.C.E., during the middle period of Darius's reign, the imperial court received almost eight hundred thousand liters of grain, quite apart from vegetables, fruits, meat, poultry, fish, oil, beer, wine, and textiles. Officials distributed some of that produce to the imperial staff as wages in kind, but much of it also found its way into the enormous banquets that Darius organized for as many as ten thousand guests. Satraps and other high officials lived on a less lavish scale than the Persian emperors but also benefited from agricultural surpluses delivered to their courts from their own lands.

Standardized Coins Agriculture was the economic foundation of the Persian empires, but the empires had the effect of encouraging rapid economic development and trade. By ensuring political stability and maintaining an elaborate network of roads, Achaemenid rulers laid solid foundations for economic prosperity and secure transportation of trade goods. Trade benefited also from the invention of standardized coins, which first appeared in the Anatolian kingdom of Lydia. Beginning about 640 B.C.E. the kings of Lydia issued coins of precisely measured metal and guaranteed their value. It was much simpler for merchants to exchange standardized

Tribute bearers from lands subject to Achaemenid rule bring rams, horses, and fabrics to the imperial court at Persepolis. Representatives of twenty-three lands offered tribute at the imperial new year festival.
Janzig/MiddleEast/Alamy Stock Photo

coins than to weigh ingots or bullion when transacting their business. As a result, standardized coins quickly became popular and drew merchants from distant lands to Lydian markets. When Cyrus defeated the forces of King Croesus and absorbed Lydia into his expanding realm, he brought the advantages of standardized coins to the larger Achaemenid empire. Markets opened in all the larger cities of the empire, and the largest cities, such as Babylon, also were home to banks and companies that invested in commercial ventures.

Trade Long-distance trade grew rapidly during the course of the Persian empires and linked lands from India to Egypt in a vast commercial zone. Trade traveled both over land routes, including newly constructed highways such as the Persian Royal Road, and over sea lanes through the Red Sea, the Persian Gulf, and the Arabian Sea. The various regions of the Persian empires all contributed particular products to the larger imperial economy. South Asia supplied gold, ivory, and aromatics. Iran and central Asia provided lapis lazuli, turquoise, and other semiprecious stones. Mesopotamia and Iran were sources of finished products such as textiles, mirrors, and jewelry. Anatolia supplied gold, silver, iron, copper, and tin. Phoenicia contributed glass, cedar, timber, and richly dyed woolen fabrics. Spices and aromatics came from Arabia. Egypt provided grain, linen textiles, and papyrus writing materials as well as gold, ebony, and ivory obtained from Nubia. Greek oil, wine, and ceramics also made their way throughout the empire and even beyond its borders.

Long-distance trade started to intensify after the campaigns of Alexander and the establishment of the Seleucid empire by his successors. The cities they established and the colonists they attracted stimulated trade throughout the whole region, from the Mediterranean to South Asia. Indeed, Greek migrants facilitated cultural as well as commercial exchanges by encouraging the mixing and mingling of religious faiths, art styles, and philosophical speculation throughout the Persian realm. As important as the Greeks and Macedonians were in facilitating commercial and cultural exchange, it was under the Parthians and Sasanians that long-distance trade flourished all across Afro-Eurasia. The Parthians were enthusiastic participants in land and maritime trade during the First Silk Roads Era, while the Sasanians maintained later trade routes that connected East Asia with the Mediterranean. During all these periods, commercial trade played an important role in the spread of religions.

RELIGIONS OF THE PERSIAN EMPIRES

Cross-cultural influences were especially noticeable in the development of Persian religion. Persians came from the family of peoples who spoke Indo-European languages, and their earliest religion closely resembled that of the Aryans of India. After the construction of the Persian empires, however, the new faith of Zoroastrianism emerged and became widely popular in Iran and to a lesser extent also in the larger Persian empires. Zoroastrianism later influenced the beliefs and values of Judaism, Christianity, and Islam. Between about 100 to 500 C.E., three missionary religions—Buddhism, Christianity, and Manichaeism—also found numerous converts in the Persian Empire.

Zarathustra and His Faith

The earliest Persian religion centered on cults that celebrated outstanding natural elements and geographic features such as the sun, the moon, water, and especially fire. Persians recognized many of the same gods as the ancient Aryans, and their priests performed sacrifices similar to those conducted by the brahmins in India. The priests even made ceremonial use of a hallucinogenic agent called *haoma* in the same way that the Indo-Aryans used soma, and indeed the two concoctions were probably the same substance. Like the Aryans, the ancient Persians glorified strength and martial virtues, and the cults of both peoples sought principally to bring about a comfortable material existence for their practitioners.

Zarathustra During the first millennium B.C.E., Persian religion underwent considerable change, as moral and religious thinkers sought to adapt their messages to the circumstances of a complex, cosmopolitan society. One result was the appearance of **Zoroastrianism,** which emerged from the teachings of **Zarathustra.** Though Zarathustra was probably a historical person and the subject of many early stories, little certain information survives about his life and career. It is not even clear exactly when he lived: many scholars date his life to the late seventh and early sixth centuries B.C.E., but others believe he flourished sometime between 1200 and 1000 B.C.E. He came from an aristocratic family, and he probably was a priest who became disenchanted with the traditional religion and its concentration on bloody sacrifices and mechanical rituals. According to the stories, when he was about twenty years old, Zarathustra left his family and home in search of wisdom. After about ten years of travel, he experienced a series of visions and became convinced that the supreme god, whom he called **Ahura Mazda** (the "wise lord"), had chosen him to serve as his prophet and spread his message.

The *Gathas* Like his life, Zarathustra's doctrine has proven to be somewhat elusive for modern analysts. Many of the earliest Zoroastrian teachings have perished because the priests, known as **magi,** at first transmitted them orally. Only during the Seleucid dynasty did magi begin to preserve religious texts in writing, and only under the Sasanians did they compile their scriptures in a holy book known as the *Avesta.* Nevertheless, many of Zarathustra's compositions survive because magi preserved them with special diligence through oral transmission.

Zoroastrianism (zohr-oh-ASS-tree-ahn-iz'm)
Zarathustra (zar-uh-THOO-struh)

How the Past Shapes the Future ▷▷▷ ▷ ▷ ▷ ▷ ▷

Long-Distance Trade Networks

Trans-Eurasian Exchange Networks

Between about 500 B.C.E. and 500 C.E., peoples across Afro-Eurasia established long-distance trade networks on an unprecedented scale. Although we saw in Part I that peoples in the early complex societies had established trade networks in earlier times, the scale of long-distance trade networks in the later societies was far greater and of even more lasting consequence. The vast empires of the Persians, Kushans, Han Chinese, and Romans that arose in this period helped to create the relative political stability that allowed trade to flourish. These large empires also facilitated long-distance trade by issuing standardized coins, by building and maintaining new roads and ports, and by supporting large markets and urban areas. As a result, trade networks in this period extended by land and by sea from Europe to China, from Persia to north Africa and central Asia, and from India to China, southeast Asia, and the Mediterranean basin. Their existence, in turn, had profound long-term consequences because they allowed the diffusion of different foods and the exchange of commodities, and because they laid the foundation for the spread of religions and epidemic disease far from their points of origin.

The Diffusion of Foodstuffs and the Exchange of Commodities

In this chapter, we have already seen that the trade routes of the Persian empires facilitated the diffusion of Egyptian grains and textiles; South Asian gold, ivory, and spices like pepper; and metals from Anatolia to diverse parts of the empire. At roughly the same time, fine Chinese silks were being carried across trade routes from the east and became coveted items in Persia, India, Mesopotamia, and the Roman empire (chapter 8). Pepper, meanwhile, was carried across both land and sea routes from South Asia to China, central Asia, and the Mediterranean (chapter 9), while spices from southeast Asia were carried west from China and India (chapter 12). The spread of such commodities and food products had long-term social and economic consequences in the lands to which they diffused. For example, long-distance trade in coveted luxury items like silk, jewels, gold, and spices became markers of social distinction in the societies where they were traded, meaning that the possession of such items came to symbolize high status and helped to delineate social boundaries. In addition, the numerous markets and ports necessary to maintain such extensive trade networks encouraged urban growth around the hubs of trade networks, allowing for population growth and a new range of urban creature comforts.

Known as the *Gathas,* Zarathustra's works were hymns that he composed in honor of the various deities that he recognized. Apart from the *Gathas,* ancient Zoroastrian literature included a wide variety of hymns, and treatises on moral and theological themes. Though some of these works survive, the arrival of Islam in the seventh century C.E. and the subsequent decline of Zoroastrianism resulted in the loss of most of the *Avesta* and later Zoroastrian works.

Zoroastrian Teachings
Zarathustra and his followers recognized Ahura Mazda as a supreme deity, an eternal and beneficent spirit, and the creator of all good things. But Zarathustra also spoke of six lesser deities, whom he praised in the *Gathas.* Furthermore, he believed that Ahura Mazda engaged in a cosmic conflict with an independent adversary, an evil and malign spirit known as Angra Mainyu (often also referred to as Ahriman, the "destructive spirit" or the "hostile spirit"). Following a struggle

A gold earring depicting Ahura Mazda.
DEA/G. Dagli Orti/De Agostini/Getty Images

of some twelve thousand years, Zarathustra believed, Ahura Mazda and the forces of good would ultimately prevail, and Angra Mainyu and the principle of evil would disappear forever. At that time individual human souls would undergo judgment and would experience rewards or punishments according to the holiness of their thoughts, words, and deeds. Honest and moral individuals would enter into a heavenly paradise, whereas demons would fling their evil brethren into a hellish realm of pain and suffering.

Popularity of Zoroastrianism
Zarathustra did not call for ascetic renunciation of the world in favor of a future heavenly existence. To the contrary, he considered the material world a blessing that reflected the benevolent nature of Ahura Mazda. His moral teachings allowed human beings to enjoy the world and its fruits—including wealth, sexual pleasure, and social prestige—as long as they did so in moderation and behaved honestly toward others. Zoroastrians have often summarized their moral teachings in the simple formula "good words, good thoughts, good deeds."

Gathas (GATH-uhs)

The Spread of Religions

Of course, commodities and agricultural products did not move by themselves: individual people traveled along portions of the trade routes, carrying goods and items back and forth over sizable distances. In the process, individuals from a variety of religious backgrounds and cultural traditions encountered one another and exchanged ideas. Some of the most important ideas people exchanged along these trade networks were about salvation. Along the Silk Roads, which linked vast portions of Eurasia, merchants who had converted to the Indian religion of Buddhism (chapter 9) invited Buddhist monks to establish monasteries across the oasis towns of central Asia (chapter 12). Similarly, adherents of both Christianity and Manichaeism took advantage of stable long-distance trade networks to establish communities of believers in the Mediterranean and southwest Asia (chapter 12). Over the long term, the spread of these religions of salvation had profound effects on the cultures of the regions to which they spread.

Camels laden with goods.
Iberfoto/SuperStock

The Spread of Epidemic Disease

While the establishment of long-distance trade networks in this period allowed unprecedented exchanges of goods and ideas, they also created the conditions that allowed epidemic disease to travel much farther—and much faster—than ever before. During the second and third centuries C.E., epidemics of smallpox, measles, and perhaps bubonic plague tore through both the Roman empire and China, resulting in dramatic population losses and reductions in trade. Over the long term, the epidemic diseases—ironically made possible by long-distance trade routes—contributed to the political instability that destroyed both the western Roman and Han empires (chapter 12).

When reading subsequent chapters, try to keep in mind the often dramatic and long-term social, political, and economic consequences of long-distance trade for all participating societies. In many ways, the great trade networks of the ancient world laid the foundations for globalization in the modern.

Zarathustra's teachings began to attract large numbers of followers during the sixth century B.C.E., particularly among Persian aristocrats and ruling elites. Wealthy patrons donated land and established endowments for the support of Zoroastrian temples. The Achaemenid era saw the emergence of a sizable priesthood, whose members conducted religious rituals, maintained a calendar, taught Zoroastrian values, and preserved Zoroastrian doctrine through oral transmission.

Cyrus and Cambyses probably observed Zoroastrian rites, although little evidence survives to illustrate their religious preferences. Beginning with Darius, however, the Achaemenid emperors closely associated themselves with Ahura Mazda and claimed divine sanction for their rule. Darius ordered stone inscriptions celebrating his achievements, and in those monuments he clearly revealed his devotion to Ahura Mazda and his opposition to the principle of evil. He did not attempt to suppress other gods or religions but tolerated the established faiths of the various peoples in his empire. Yet he personally regarded Ahura Mazda as a deity superior to all others.

In one of his inscriptions, Darius praised Ahura Mazda as the great god who created the earth, the sky, and humanity and who had elevated Darius himself to the imperial honor. With the aid of imperial sponsorship, Zoroastrian temples

cropped up throughout the Achaemenid realm. The faith was most popular in Iran, but it attracted sizable followings also in Mesopotamia, Anatolia, Egypt, and other parts of the Achaemenid empire even though there was no organized effort to spread it beyond its original homeland.

Religions for a Cosmopolitan Society

The arrival of Alexander of Macedon inaugurated a difficult era for the Zoroastrian community. During his Persian campaign, Alexander's forces may have burned many temples and killed magi, although evidence for this is inconclusive. Nonetheless, because at that time the magi still transmitted Zoroastrian doctrines orally, an untold number of hymns and holy verses disappeared. The Zoroastrian faith survived, however, and the Parthians cultivated it to rally support against the Seleucids. Once established in power, the Parthians observed Zoroastrian rituals, though they did not support the faith as enthusiastically as their predecessors had done.

Officially Sponsored Zoroastrianism During the Sasanian dynasty, however, Zoroastrianism experienced a revival. As self-proclaimed heirs to the Achaemenids, the Sasanians identified closely with Zoroastrianism and supported it zealously.

SOURCES FROM THE PAST

Zarathustra on Good and Evil

Like many other ancient religious faiths, Zoroastrianism encouraged the faithful to observe high moral and ethical standards. In this hymn from the Gathas, *Zarathustra relates how Ahura Mazda and Angra Mainyu—representatives of good and evil, might influence the behavior of humans.*

In the beginning, there were two Primal Spirits, Twins spontaneously active;
These are the Good and the Evil, in thought, and in word, and in deed:
Between these two, let the wise choose correctly;
Be good, not bad.

And when these Twin Spirits came together at first,
They established Life and Non-Life,
And so shall it be as long as the world shall last;
The worst existence shall be the lot of the followers of evil,
And the Good Mind shall be the reward of the followers of good.

> According to the source, is it necessary to have both a good and evil spirit in order for the world to function?

Of these Twin Spirits, the Evil One chose to do the worst;
While the bountiful Holy Spirit of Goodness,
Clothing itself with the heavens for a garment, chose the Truth;
And so will those who seek to please Ahura Mazda with
    righteous deeds, performed with faith in Truth.

And when there comes Divine Retribution for the Evil One,
Then at your command shall the Good Mind establish the
    Kingdom of Heaven, O Mazda,
For those who will deliver Untruth into the hands of Righteousness
    and Truth.

> Did each of the spirits make choices regarding their behavior, or was this determined by their essential nature?

Then truly cometh the blow of destruction on Untruth,
And all those of good fame are gathered up in the Fair Abode,
The Fair Abode of the Good Mind, the Wise Lord, and of Truth!

Oh you mortals, mark these commandments—
The commandments which the Wise Lord has given, for Happiness
    and for Pain;
Long punishment for the evil-doer, and bliss for the follower of Truth,
The joy of salvation for the Righteous ever afterwards!

For Further Reflection

▪ According to the source, how did the twin spirits create the world?
▪ What message is the source conveying for the behavior of humans?
▪ What themes and ideas outlined in the source may have been influential on the development of Christianity and Islam?

Source: D. J. Irani. *The Divine Songs of Zarathustra.* London: George Allen & Unwin, 1924.
Updated with modern language by the textbook authors.

Indeed, the Sasanians often persecuted other faiths if they seemed likely to become popular enough to challenge the supremacy of Zoroastrianism. With generous imperial backing, the Zoroastrian faith and the magi flourished as never before. Theologians prepared written versions of the holy texts and collected them in the *Avesta*. They also explored points of doctrine and addressed difficult questions of morality and theology. Most people probably did not understand the theologians' reflections, but they flocked to Zoroastrian temples where they prayed to Ahura Mazda and participated in rituals.

In celebration of his crushing several rebellions throughout the Persian Empire, Darius had this image of himself carved in a rock face at Bisitun, depicting captive rebels bound and brought before him for punishment. Darius even stands on one of the captives, as Ahura Mazda looks down from above.

Babak Tafreshi/Science Source

The Zoroastrian faith faced severe difficulties in the seventh century C.E. when Islamic conquerors toppled the Sasanian empire. The conquerors did not outlaw the religion altogether, but they placed political and financial pressure on the magi and Zoroastrian temples. Some Zoroastrians fled their homeland under persecution and found refuge in India, where their descendants, known as **Parsis** ("Persians"), continue even today to observe Zoroastrian traditions. But most Zoroastrians remained in Iran and eventually converted to Islam. As a result, Zoroastrian numbers progressively dwindled. Only a few thousand faithful maintain a Zoroastrian community in modern-day Iran.

Other Faiths Even though Zoroastrianism ultimately declined in its homeland, the cosmopolitan character of the Persian realm offered it opportunities to influence other religious faiths. Numerous Jewish communities had become established in Mesopotamia, Anatolia, and Persia after the Hebrew kingdom fell in 930 B.C.E. During the Seleucid, Parthian, and Sasanian eras, the Persian Empire attracted merchants, emissaries, and missionaries from the whole region between the Mediterranean and India. Three religions of salvation—Buddhism, Christianity, and **Manichaeism,** all discussed in later chapters—found a footing alongside Judaism and attracted converts. Indeed, Christianity and Manichaeism became extremely popular faiths in spite of intermittent rounds of persecution organized by Sasanian authorities.

Influence of Zoroastrianism While foreign faiths influenced religious developments in Persian society, Zoroastrianism also left its mark on other religions. Jews living in Persia during Achaemenid times adopted several specific teachings of Zoroastrianism, which later found their way into the faiths of Christianity and Islam as well. Those teachings included the notion that an omnipotent and beneficent deity

Manichaeism (man-ih-KEE-iz'm)

was responsible for all creation; the idea that a purely evil being worked against the creator god; the conviction that the forces of good will ultimately prevail over the power of evil after a climactic struggle; the belief that human beings must strive to observe the highest moral standards; and the doctrine that individuals will undergo judgment, after which the morally upright will experience rewards in paradise while evildoers will suffer punishments in hell. Those teachings, which have profoundly influenced Judaism, Christianity, and Islam, all derived ultimately from the faith of Zarathustra and his followers.

What's Left Out?

The most important text of the Zoroastrian religion, the *Avesta,* contains information on the status of women in the Persian empires. References in the *Avesta* suggest that Persian women were treated with more respect than women in many other ancient societies and were fully expected to make important decisions in partnerships with men. Woman were also able to become imperial rulers in certain circumstances; we know the names of female regents who ruled for their infant sons, including Pourandokt, the first Persian regent queen. Indeed, the *Avesta* explicitly sanctions the idea of female rule by stating: "May a good ruler, man or woman, reign in both the material and spiritual existences" (Yasna 41/2).

Greco-Roman authors also noted that the Persian armies (particularly that of the Sasanians) included numerous female fighters and that Persian women had the right to manage their own property, represent themselves and their husbands in court, and perform various religious ceremonies. Treasury texts discovered at Persepolis list professions that were available for men and women, and where either gender could do the same job, their payment in the form of rations was more or less equal. We also know of numerous particularly high-ranking women managers called *arashshara* (great chief) who managed large work groups of women, children, and sometimes men and who were well rewarded for their skills. In every way then, women in the Persian empires participated fully in the commercial, legal, and administrative sectors of society and were valued as equal or near-equal partners in a way that was virtually unheard of in any other ancient society.

Source: Maria Brossius. *Women in Ancient Persia, 539–331 B.C.* Oxford, 1996.

CONCLUSION

The Achaemenid Persian Empire inaugurated a new era of world history. The Achaemenids borrowed military and administrative techniques devised earlier by Babylonian and Assyrian rulers, but they applied those techniques on a much larger scale than did any of their Mesopotamian predecessors. In doing so they constructed a vast empire and then governed its diverse lands and peoples with considerable success for more than two centuries. The Achaemenids demonstrated how it was possible to build and maintain a vast imperial state, and their example inspired later efforts to establish similar large-scale imperial states based in Persia and other Eurasian lands as well. The Achaemenid and later Persian empires integrated much of the territory from the Mediterranean Sea to the Indus River into a commonwealth in which peoples of different regions and ethnic groups participated in a larger economy and society. By sponsoring regular and systematic encounters between peoples of different communities, the Persian empires wielded tremendous cultural as well as political, social, and economic influence. Indeed, Persian religious beliefs helped to shape moral and religious thought throughout much of southwest Asia and the Mediterranean basin. Zoroastrian traditions were particularly influential: although Zoroastrianism declined after the Sasanian dynasty, its doctrines strongly influenced the fundamental teachings of Judaism, Christianity, and Islam.

STUDY TERMS

Achaemenids (125)
Aegean Sea (127)
Ahura Mazda (135)
Alexander of Macedon (130)
Avesta (135)
battle of Gaugamela (130)
battle of Marathon (129)
Cambyses (127)
Croesus (124)
Ctesiphon (131)
Cyrus (124)
Darius (127)
Gathas (136)
magi (135)
Manichaeism (139)

Medes (125)
Mithradates I (131)
Parsis (139)
Parthians (130)
Pasargadae (126)
Persepolis (127)
Persian Royal Road (128)
Persian Wars (129)
qanat (129)
Sasanians (131)
satrapies (127)
Seleucids (130)
Zarathustra (135)
Zoroastrianism (135)

FOR FURTHER READING

Lindsay Allen. *The Persian Empire*. Chicago, 2005. A valuable survey of the Achaemenid empire with special attention to archaeological discoveries.

Mary Boyce, ed. *Textual Sources for the Study of Zoroastrianism*. Totowa, NJ, 1984. Sources in translation with numerous explanatory comments by the author.

Maria Brosius. *The Persians: An Introduction*. London, 2006. Perhaps the best short account of the Persian empires.

————. *Women in Ancient Persia, 559–331 B.C.* Oxford, 1996. Carefully examines both Persian and Greek sources for information about women and their role in Achaemenid society.

J. Curtis and N. Tallis, eds. *Forgotten Empire: The World of Ancient Persia*. Berkeley and Los Angeles, 2005. Excellent collection of essays on the Persians by leading scholars.

Vesta Sarkosh Curtis and Sarah Stewart, eds. *The Age of the Parthians*. London, 2007. Different scholars explore the history and legacy of the Parthians from a range of perspectives in this fascinating new collection.

Touraj Daryaee. *Sasanian Persia: The Rise and Fall of an Empire*. London, 2010. Lucid history of the Sasanian empire by a leading Persian historian.

Richard C. Foltz. *Spirituality in the Land of the Noble: How Iran Shaped the World's Religions*. Oxford, 2004. Includes an accessible discussion of the Zoroastrian faith.

P. Green. *Alexander the Great and the Hellenistic Age*. London 2007. Insightful treatment of the impact of Alexander and the Hellenistic Era by one of the world's leading ancient historians.

The Search for Political and Social Order in
Zhou Dynasty China

    Confucianism

    Daoism

    Legalism

The Unification of China

    The Qin Dynasty

    The Early Han Dynasty

From Economic Prosperity to Social Disorder

    Productivity and Prosperity during the Early Han

    Economic and Social Difficulties

    The Later Han Dynasty

ZOOMING IN ON TRADITIONS

Sima Qian: Speaking Truth to Power in Han China

In about 99 B.C.E., Chinese imperial officials sentenced the historian **Sima Qian** to punishment by castration. Like his father before him, Sima Qian was the official astrologer and historian at the court of the Han dynasty in Chang'an. For more than a decade, he had worked diligently on a project that he had inherited from his father—a history of China from earliest times to his own day. This project brought Sima Qian high prominence at the imperial court. When he spoke in defense of a dishonored general, his views attracted widespread attention. The emperor reacted furiously when he learned that Sima Qian had publicly expressed opinions that contradicted the ruler's judgment and ordered the historian to undergo his humiliating punishment.

Human castration was by no means uncommon in premodern times. Thousands of boys and young men of undistinguished birth underwent voluntary castration in China and many other lands as well in order to pursue careers as **eunuchs.** Ruling elites often appointed eunuchs, rather than nobles, to sensitive posts because eunuchs did not sire families and so could not build power bases to challenge established authorities. As personal servants of ruling elites, eunuchs sometimes

eunuchs (YOO-nihks)

The Great Wall of China, the first version of which was constructed by the first emperor of the Qin, stretches across the mountains of northern China.
axz700/Shutterstock

came to wield enormous power because of their influence with rulers and their families.

But these extreme measures were not appealing to educated elites and other prominent individuals: when sentenced to punitive castration, Chinese men of honor normally avoided the penalty by taking their own lives. Yet Sima Qian chose to endure his punishment. In a letter to a friend, he explained that an early death by suicide would mean that a work that only he was capable of producing would go forever unwritten. To transmit his understanding of the Chinese past, then,

Sima Qian opted to live and work in disgrace until his death about 90 B.C.E.

During his last years Sima Qian completed a massive work consisting of 130 chapters, most of which survive. He consulted court documents and the historical works of his predecessors, and when writing about his own age he supplemented those sources with personal observations and information gleaned from political and military figures who played leading roles in Chinese society. He composed historical accounts of the emperors' reigns and biographical sketches of notable figures, including ministers, statesmen, generals, empresses, aristocrats, scholars, officials, merchants, and rebels. He even described the societies of neighboring peoples with whom Chinese sometimes conducted trade and sometimes made war. The work of the disgraced but conscientious scholar Sima Qian provides the best information available about the development of early imperial China.

CHAPTER OVERVIEW

A rich body of political and social thought prepared the way for the unification of China under the **Qin** and Han dynasties. Confucians, Daoists, Legalists, and others formed schools of thought and worked to bring political and social stability to China during the chaotic years of the late **Zhou** dynasty and the Period of the Warring States. Legalist ideas contributed directly to unification by outlining means by which rulers could strengthen their states and their authority. The works of the Confucians and the Daoists did not lend themselves so readily to the unification process, but both schools of thought survived and profoundly influenced Chinese political and cultural traditions.

Like the rulers of the Persian empires, the Qin and Han emperors built a powerful, centralized state on the foundation of a productive agricultural society. And also like the Persians, the Qin and Han emperors ruled through an elaborate bureaucracy, and built an extensive network of roads that linked the various regions of their empire. The Qin and Han emperors went even further than their Persian counterparts in their efforts to foster cultural unity: they imposed a common written language throughout China and established an educational system based on Confucian thought and values. For almost 450 years the Qin and Han dynasties guided the fortunes of China and established a strong precedent for centralized imperial rule.

Especially during the Early Han dynasty, political stability was the foundation of economic prosperity. High agricultural productivity supported the development of iron and silk industries, and Chinese goods found markets in central Asia, India, the Persian Empire, and even the Mediterranean basin. In spite of economic prosperity, however, later Han society experienced deep divisions between the small class of extremely wealthy landowners and the masses of landless poor. Those divisions eventually led to civil disorder and the emergence of political factions, which ultimately brought the Han dynasty to an end.

THE SEARCH FOR POLITICAL AND SOCIAL ORDER IN ZHOU DYNASTY CHINA

The late centuries of the Zhou dynasty brought political confusion to China and led eventually to the chaos associated with the **Period of the Warring States** (480–221 B.C.E.). During those same centuries, however, there also took place a remarkable cultural flowering that left a permanent mark on Chinese history. In a way, political turmoil helps to explain the cultural creativity of the late Zhou dynasty and the Period of the Warring States because it forced thoughtful people

CHRONOLOGY	
6th century B.C.E.(?)	Laozi
551–479 B.C.E.	Confucius
403–221 B.C.E.	Period of the Warring States
390–338 B.C.E.	Shang Yang
372–289 B.C.E.	Mencius
298–238 B.C.E.	Xunzi
280–233 B.C.E.	Han Feizi
221–207 B.C.E.	Qin dynasty
206 B.C.E.–9 C.E.	Early Han dynasty
141–87 B.C.E.	Reign of Han Wudi
9–23 C.E.	Reign of Wang Mang
25–220 C.E.	Later Han dynasty

Qin (chihn)

Zhou (joh)

to reflect on the nature of society and the proper roles of human beings in society. Some sought to identify principles that would restore political and social order. Others concerned themselves with a search for individual tranquility apart from society. Three schools of thought that emerged during those centuries of confusion and chaos—**Confucianism, Daoism,** and **Legalism**—have gone on to exercise a particularly deep influence on Chinese political and cultural traditions for the past twenty-five hundred years.

Confucianism

Confucius The first Chinese thinker who addressed the problem of political and social order in a straightforward and self-conscious way was **Kong Fuzi** (551–479 B.C.E.)—"Master Philosopher Kong," as his disciples called him, or Confucius, as he is known in English. He came from an aristocratic family in the state of Lu in northern China, and for many years he sought an influential post at the Lu court. But Confucius was a strong-willed man who often did not get along well with others. He could be quite cantankerous: he was known to lodge bitter complaints, for example, if someone undercooked or overcooked his rice. Not surprisingly, then, he refused to compromise his beliefs in the interest of political expediency, and he insisted on observing principles that frequently clashed with state policy. When he realized that he would never obtain anything more than a minor post in Lu, Confucius left in search of a more prestigious appointment elsewhere. For about ten years he traveled to courts throughout northern China, but he found none willing to accept his services. In 484 B.C.E., bitterly disappointed, he returned to Lu, where he died five years later.

Confucian Ideas Confucius never realized his ambition to become a powerful minister. Throughout his career, however,

No contemporary portrait of Confucius survives, but artists have used their imaginations and depicted him in many ways over the years. This portrait from 1735 identifies Confucius as "the Sage and Teacher" and represents him in the distinctive dress of an eighteenth-century Confucian scholar-bureaucrat.
akg-images/Newscom

he served as an educator as well as a political adviser, and in that capacity he left an enduring mark on Chinese society. He attracted numerous disciples who aspired to political careers. Some of his pupils compiled the master's sayings and teachings in a book known as the *Analects,* a work that has profoundly influenced Chinese political and cultural traditions.

Confucius's thought was fundamentally moral, ethical, and political in character. It was also thoroughly practical: Confucius did not address obscure philosophical questions because he thought they would not help to solve the political and social problems of his day. Nor did he deal with religious questions because he thought they went beyond the capacity of mortal human intelligence. He did not even concern himself much with the structure of the state because he thought political and social harmony arose from the proper ordering of human relationships rather than the establishment of state offices. In an age when bureaucratic institutions were not yet well developed, Confucius believed that the best way to promote good government was to fill official positions with individuals who were both well educated and extraordinarily conscientious. Thus Confucius concentrated on the formation of what he called *junzi*—"superior individuals"—who took a broad view of public affairs and did not allow personal interests to influence their judgments.

In the absence of an established educational system and a formal curriculum, Confucius had his disciples study works of poetry and history produced during the Zhou dynasty because he believed that they provided excellent insight into human nature. He carefully examined the *Book of Songs,* the *Book of History,* the *Book of Rites,* and other works with his students, concentrating especially on their practical value for prospective administrators. As a result of Confucius's influence, literary works of the Zhou dynasty became the core texts of the traditional Chinese education. For more than two thousand years, until the early twentieth century C.E., talented Chinese seeking government posts proceeded through a cycle

Confucianism (kuhn-FEW-shuhn-iz'm)
Daoism (DOW-iz'm)

SOURCES FROM THE PAST

Confucius on Government

Confucius never composed formal writings, but his disciples collected his often pithy remarks into a work known as the Analects *("sayings"). In the following excerpts from the* Analects, *Confucius is referred to as "the Master."*

The Master said, "He who exercises government by means of his virtue may be compared to the north polar star, which keeps its place, while all the stars turn toward it. . . ."

The Master said, "If the people are led by laws, and uniformity is imposed on them by punishments, they will try to avoid the punishment, but will have no sense of shame.

"If they are led by virtue, and uniformity is provided for them by the rules of propriety, they will have the sense of shame, and moreover will become good."

Duke Ai asked, saying, "What should be done in order to secure the submission of the people?" Confucius replied, "Advance the upright and set aside the crooked, and then the people will submit. Advance the crooked and set aside the upright, and then the people will not submit."

Ji Kang asked how to cause the people to respect their ruler, to be faithful to him, and to go on to seek virtue. The Master said, "Let him preside over them with gravity; then they will respect him. Let him be filial and kind to all; then they will be faithful to him. Let him advance the good and teach the incompetent; then they will eagerly seek to be virtuous."

Zigong asked about government. The Master said, "The requisites of government are that there be sufficiency of food, sufficiency of military equipment, and the confidence of the people in their ruler."

Zigong said, "If it cannot be helped, and one of these must be dispensed with, which of the three should be foregone first?" "The military equipment," said the Master.

Zigong again asked, "If it cannot be helped, and one of the remaining two must be dispensed with, which of them should be foregone?" The Master answered, "Part with the food. From olden times, death has been the lot of all men; but if the people have no faith in their rulers, there is no standing for the state."

Ji Kang asked Confucius about government, saying, "What do you say to killing the unprincipled for the good of the principled?" Confucius replied, "Sir, in carrying on your government, why should you use killing at all? Let your desire be to do what is good, and the people will be good. The relation between superiors and inferiors is like that between the wind and the grass. The grass must bend when the wind blows across it."

The Master said, "When a prince's personal conduct is correct, his government is effective without the issuing of orders. If his personal conduct is not correct, he may issue orders, but they will not be followed."

> What is Confucius' argument concerning the role of laws in government?

> What is Confucius' advice to political leaders on how to secure the respect of their people?

For Further Reflection

■ In Confucius' opinion, what is the fundamental role of governments?
■ How do these arguments of Confucius reflect and respond to the violence and chaos of the Later Zhou Dynasty?

Source: James Legge, trans. *The Chinese Classics,* 7 vols. Oxford: Clarendon Press, 1893, 1:145, 146, 152, 254, 258–59, 266. Updated with modern language by the textbook authors.

of studies deriving from the one developed by Confucius in the fifth century B.C.E.

For Confucius, though, an advanced education represented only a part of the preparation needed by the ideal government official. More important than formal learning was the possession of a strong sense of moral integrity and a capacity to deliver wise and fair judgments. Thus Confucius encouraged his students to cultivate high ethical standards and to hone their faculties of analysis and judgment.

Confucian Values Confucius emphasized several qualities in particular. One of them he called **ren,** by which he meant an attitude of kindness and benevolence or a sense of humanity. Confucius explained that individuals possessing *ren* were courteous, respectful, diligent, and loyal, and he considered *ren* a characteristic desperately needed in government officials. Another quality of central importance was *li,* a sense of propriety, which called for individuals to behave in conventionally appropriate fashion: they should treat all other humans with courtesy, while showing special respect and deference to elders or superiors. Yet another quality that Confucius emphasized was *xiao,* filial piety, which reflected the high significance of the family in Chinese society. The demands of filial piety obliged children to respect their parents and other family elders, look after their welfare, support them in old age, and remember them along with other ancestors after their deaths.

Confucius emphasized personal qualities such as *ren, li,* and *xiao* because he believed that individuals who possessed those traits would gain influence in the larger society. Those who disciplined themselves and properly molded their characters would not only possess personal self-control but also have the power of leading others by example. Only through enlightened leadership by morally strong individuals, Confucius believed, was there any hope for the restoration of political and social order in China. Thus his goal was not simply the cultivation of personal morality for its own sake but, rather, the creation of *junzi* who could bring order and stability to China.

Because Confucius expressed his thought in general terms, later disciples could adapt it to the particular problems of their times. Indeed, the flexibility of Confucian thought helps to account for its remarkable longevity and influence in China. Two later disciples of Confucius—**Mencius** and **Xunzi**—illustrate especially well the ways in which Confucian thought lent itself to elaboration and adaptation.

Mencius Mencius (372–289 B.C.E.) was the most learned man of his age and the principal spokesman for the Confucian school. During the Period of the Warring States, he traveled widely throughout China, consulting with rulers and offering advice on political issues. Mencius firmly believed that human nature was basically good, and he argued for policies that would allow it to influence society as a whole. Thus he placed special emphasis on the Confucian virtue of *ren* and advocated government by benevolence and humanity. This principle implied that rulers would levy light taxes, avoid wars, support education, and encourage harmony and cooperation. Critics charged that Mencius held a naively optimistic view of human nature, arguing that his policies would rarely succeed in the real world where human interests, wills, and ambitions constantly clash. Indeed, Mencius's advice had little practical effect during his lifetime. Over the long term, however, his ideas deeply influenced the Confucian tradition. Since about

the tenth century C.E., many Chinese scholars have considered Mencius the most authoritative of Confucius's early disciples.

Xunzi Like Confucius and Mencius, Xunzi (298–238 B.C.E.) was a man of immense learning, but unlike his predecessors, he also served for many years as a government administrator. His practical experience encouraged him to develop a view of human nature that was less rosy than Mencius's view. Xunzi believed that human beings selfishly pursued their own interests, no matter what effects their actions had on others, and resisted making any contribution voluntarily to the larger society. He considered strong social discipline the best means to bring order to society. Thus, whereas Mencius emphasized the Confucian quality of *ren,* Xunzi emphasized *li.* He advocated the establishment of clear, well-publicized standards of conduct that would set limits on the pursuit of individual interests and punish those who neglected their obligations to the larger society. Xunzi once likened human beings to pieces of warped lumber: just as it was possible to straighten out bad wood, so too it was possible to turn selfish and recalcitrant individuals into useful, contributing members of society. But the process involved harsh social discipline similar to the steam treatments, heat applications, hammering, bending, and forcible wrenching that turned warped wood into useful lumber.

Like Confucius and Mencius, however, Xunzi also believed that it was possible to improve human beings and restore order to society. This fundamental optimism was a basic characteristic of Confucian thought. It explains the high value that Confucian thinkers placed on education and public behavior, and it accounts also for their activist approach to public affairs. Confucians involved themselves in society: they sought government positions and made conscientious efforts to solve political and social problems and to promote harmony in public life. By no means, however, did the Confucians win universal praise for their efforts: to some of their contemporaries, Confucian activism represented little more than misspent energy.

Daoism

The Daoists were the most prominent critics of Confucian activism. Like Confucianism, Daoist thought developed in response to the turbulence of the late Zhou dynasty and the Period of the Warring States. But unlike the Confucians, the Daoists considered it pointless to waste time and energy on problems that defied solution. Instead of Confucian social activism, the Daoists devoted their energies to reflection and introspection, in hopes that they could understand the natural principles that governed the world and could learn how to live in harmony with them. The Daoists believed that over time, this approach would bring harmony to society as a whole, as people ceased to meddle in affairs that they could not understand or control.

---

xiao (SHAYOH)
Mencius (MEN-shi-us)
Xunzi (SHOON-dzuh)

Laozi and the *Daodejing*

According to Chinese tradition, the founder of Daoism was a sage named **Laozi** who lived during the sixth century B.C.E. Although there might have been a historical Laozi, it is almost certain that several thinkers contributed to the *Daodejing* (*Classic of the Way and of Virtue*), the basic exposition of Daoist beliefs traditionally ascribed to Laozi, and that the book acquired its definitive form over several centuries. After the *Daodejing*, the most important Daoist work was the *Zhuangzi*, named after its author, the philosopher Zhuangzi (369–286 B.C.E.), who provided a well-reasoned summary of Daoist views.

The *Dao* Daoism represents an effort to understand the fundamental character of the world and nature. The central concept of Daoism is *dao*, meaning "the way," more specifically "the way of nature" or "the way of the cosmos." *Dao* is an elusive concept, and the Daoists themselves did not clearly articulate its meaning. In the *Daodejing*, for example, *dao* figures as the original force of the cosmos, an eternal and unchanging principle that governs all the workings of the world. The *Daodejing* envisioned *dao* as a passive force that acted in perfect harmony with the principles of nature. Thus *dao* resembles water, which is soft and yielding yet is also so powerful that it eventually erodes even the hardest rock placed in its path. *Dao* also resembles the cavity of a pot or the hub of a wheel: although they are nothing more than empty spaces, they make the pot and the wheel useful tools.

If the principles of *dao* governed the world, it followed that human beings should tailor their behavior to its passive and yielding nature. To the Daoists, living in harmony with *dao* meant retreating from engagement in the world of politics and administration. Ambition and activism had not

A painting produced during the later Ming Dynasty depicts the sage Laozi on an ox. Legends reported that Laozi rode an ox from China to central Asia when spreading his teachings. Why would simple dress and transport be appropriate for Laozi?
Fine Art Images/Heritage Image Partnership Ltd/Alamy Stock Photo

solved political and social problems. Far from it: human striving had brought the world to a state of chaos. The proper response to that situation was to cease frantic striving and live with a sense of selfless detachment.

The Doctrine of *Wuwei*

Thus early Daoists recognized as the chief moral virtue the trait of *wuwei*—disengagement from the competitive exertions and active involvement in affairs of the world. *Wuwei* required that individuals refrain from advanced education (which concentrated on obscure trivialities) and from personal striving (which indicated excessive concern with the tedious affairs of the world). *Wuwei* called instead for individuals to act selflessly and live simply, unpretentiously, and in harmony with nature.

Wuwei also had implications for state and society: the less government, the better. Instead of expansive kingdoms and empires, the *Daodejing* envisioned a world of tiny, self-sufficient communities where people had no desire to conquer their neighbors or even to trade with them. Indeed, even when people lived so close to the next community that they could hear the dogs barking and cocks crowing, they would be so content with their existence that they would not even have the desire to visit their neighbors!

Daoists subjected their philosophical rivals to ferocious attacks for dwelling on trivial and superficial issues instead of practicing *wuwei* and living in harmony with nature. Zhuangzi in particular possessed a caustic wit that he deployed effectively in mocking the

Daodejing (DOW-DAY-JIHNG)
Zhuangzi (joo-wong-dz)
wuwei (woo-WAY)

SOURCES FROM THE PAST

Laozi on Living in Harmony with *Dao*

Committed Daoists mostly rejected opportunities to play active roles in government. Yet like the Confucians, the Daoists held strong views on virtuous behavior, and their understanding of dao *had deep political implications, as exemplified by the following excerpts from the* Daodejing.

The highest goodness is like water, for water is excellent in benefitting all things, and it does not strive. It occupies the lowest place, which men abhor. And therefore it is near akin to the *dao*.

In governing men and in serving heaven, there is nothing like moderation. For only by moderation can there be an early return to the normal state of humankind. This early return is the same as a great storage of virtue. With a great storage of virtue there is nothing that may not be achieved. If there is nothing that may not be achieved, then no one will know to what extent this power reaches. And if no one knows to what extent a man's power reaches, that man is fit to be the ruler of a state. Having the secret of rule, his rule shall endure. Setting the root deep, and making the spreading roots firm: this is the way to ensure long life to the tree.

Use uprightness in ruling a state; employ indirect methods in waging war; practice non-interference in order to win the empire.

> What, in the opinion of the author, are some of the key virtues of good state governance?

The greater the number of laws and enactments, the more thieves and robbers there will be. Therefore the Sage [Laozi] says: "So long as I do nothing, the people will work out their own reformation. So long as I love calm, the people will right themselves. If only I keep from meddling, the people will grow rich. If only I am free from desire, the people will come naturally back to simplicity."

There is nothing in the world more soft and weak than water, yet for attacking things that are hard and strong, there is nothing that surpasses it, nothing that can take its place.

> What point is the author making by comparing goodness to water?

The soft overcomes the hard; the weak overcomes the strong. There is no one in the world but knows this truth, and no one who can put it into practice.

For Further Reflection

■ How do the author's attitudes toward law differ from those of the Legalists?

■ How practical do the author's suggestions seem to be in constructing a stable political state?

■ What are the political implications of the author's argument that the weak will overcome the strong?

Source: Lionel Giles, trans. *The Sayings of Lao Tzu*. London: John Murray, 1905, pp. 26, 29–30, 41, 50. (Translations slightly modified.)

Confucians and other philosophers for engaging in what he considered meaningless debates.

Political Implications of Daoism By encouraging the development of a reflective and introspective consciousness, Daoism served as a counterbalance to the activism of the Confucian tradition. Indeed, Daoism encouraged the cultivation of self-knowledge in a way that appealed strongly to Confucians as well as to Daoists. Because neither Confucianism nor Daoism was an exclusive faith that precluded observance of the other, it has been possible through the centuries for individuals to study the Confucian curriculum and take administrative posts in the government while devoting their private hours to reflection on human nature and the place of humans

in the larger world—to live as Confucians by day, as it were, and Daoists by night.

Legalism

Ultimately, neither Confucian activism nor Daoist retreat was able to solve the problems that plagued China during the Period of the Warring States. Order returned to China only after the emergence of a third school of thought—that of the Legalists—which promoted a practical and ruthlessly efficient approach to statecraft. Unlike the Confucians, the Legalists did not concern themselves with ethics, morality, or propriety. Unlike the Daoists, the Legalists cared nothing about principles governing the world or the place of human beings in nature. Instead, they devoted their attention exclusively to the state, which they sought to strengthen and expand at all costs.

Shang Yang Legalist doctrine emerged from the insights of men who participated actively in Chinese political affairs during the late fourth century B.C.E. Most notable of them was **Shang Yang** (ca. 390–338 B.C.E.), who served as chief minister to the duke of the Qin state in western China. His policies survive in a work titled *The Book of Lord Shang,* which most likely includes contributions from other ministers as well as from Shang Yang himself. Though a clever and efficient administrator, Shang Yang also was despised and feared because of his power and ruthlessness. Upon the death of his patron, the duke of Qin, Shang Yang quickly fell: his enemies at court executed him, mutilated his body, and annihilated his family.

Han Feizi The most systematic of the Legalist theorists was **Han Feizi** (ca. 280–233 B.C.E.), a student of the Confucian scholar Xunzi. Han Feizi carefully reviewed Legalist ideas from political thinkers in all parts of China and synthesized them in a collection of powerful and well-argued essays on statecraft. Like Shang Yang, Han Feizi served as an adviser at the Qin court, and he too fell afoul of other ambitious men, who forced him to end his life by taking poison. The Legalist state itself thus consumed the two foremost exponents of Legalist doctrine.

Legalist Doctrine Shang Yang, Han Feizi, and other Legalists reasoned that the foundations of a state's strength were agriculture and armed forces. Thus Legalists sought to channel as many individuals as possible into cultivation or military service while discouraging them from pursuing careers as merchants, entrepreneurs, scholars, educators, philosophers, poets, or artists because those lines of work did not directly advance the interests of the state.

The Legalists expected to harness subjects' energy by means of clear and strict laws—hence the name "Legalist." Their faith in laws distinguished the Legalists clearly from the Confucians, who relied on ritual, custom, education, a sense of propriety, and the humane example of benevolent *junzi* administrators to induce individuals to behave appropriately. The Legalists believed that those influences were not powerful enough to persuade subjects to subordinate their self-interest to the needs of the state. They imposed a strict legal code that clearly outlined expectations and provided severe punishment, swiftly administered, for violators. They believed that if people feared to commit small crimes, they would hesitate all the more before committing great crimes. Thus Legalists imposed harsh penalties even for minor infractions: individuals could suffer amputation of their hands or feet, for example, for disposing of ashes or trash in the street. The Legalists also established the principle of collective responsibility before the law. They expected all members of a family or community to observe the others closely, forestall any illegal activity, and report any infractions. Failing those obligations, all members of a family or community were liable to punishment along with the actual violator.

The Legalists' principles of government did not win them much popularity. Over the course of the centuries, Chinese moral and political philosophers have had little praise for the Legalists, and few have openly associated themselves with the Legalist school. Yet Legalist doctrine lent itself readily to practical application, and Legalist principles of government quickly produced remarkable results for rulers who adopted them. In fact, Legalist methods put an end to the Period of the Warring States and brought about the unification of China.

THE UNIFICATION OF CHINA

During the Period of the Warring States, rulers of several regional states adopted elements of the Legalist program. Legalist doctrines met the most enthusiastic response in the state of Qin, in western China, where Shang Yang and Han Feizi oversaw the implementation of Legalist policies. Eventually, the Qin were able to defeat all the rival warring states and impose centralized imperial rule throughout China. Qin rule survived only for a few years, but the succeeding Han dynasty followed the Qin example by governing China through a centralized imperial administration.

The Qin Dynasty

The Kingdom of Qin During the fourth and third centuries B.C.E., the Qin state underwent a remarkable round of economic, political, and military development. Shang Yang encouraged peasant cultivators to migrate to the sparsely populated state. By granting them private plots and allowing them to enjoy generous profits, his policy dramatically boosted agricultural production. By granting land rights to individual cultivators, his policy also weakened the economic position of the hereditary aristocratic classes. That approach allowed Qin rulers to establish centralized, bureaucratic rule throughout their state. Meanwhile, they devoted the newfound wealth of their state to the organization of a powerful army equipped with the most effective iron weapons available. During the third century B.C.E., the kingdom of Qin gradually but consistently grew at the expense of the other Chinese states. Qin rulers attacked one state after another, absorbing each new conquest into their centralized structure, until finally they had brought China for the first time under the sway of a single state.

The First Emperor In the year 221 B.C.E., the king of Qin proclaimed himself the First Emperor and decreed that his descendants would follow him and reign for thousands

Han Feizi (hahn fay-zi)

MAP 8.1 China under the Qin dynasty, 221–207 B.C.E.

Compare the size of Qin territories with those of earlier Chinese kingdoms depicted in Maps 5.1 and 5.2.

What factors contributed to the much greater extent of the territory of the Qin Dynasty compared to previous Chinese dynasties?

of generations. The First Emperor, **Qin Shihuangdi** (reigned 221–210 B.C.E.), could not know that his dynasty would last only fourteen years and in 207 B.C.E. would dissolve because of civil insurrections. Yet the Qin dynasty had a significance out of proportion to its short life. Like the Achaemenid empire in Persia, the Qin dynasty established a tradition of centralized imperial rule that became the template for dynastic government for the next twenty-two hundred years.

Like his ancestors in the kingdom of Qin, the First Emperor of China reduced the influence of nobility and ruled his empire through a centralized bureaucracy. He governed from his capital at **Xianyang,** near the early Zhou capital of Hao and the modern city of Xi'an. The remainder of China he divided into administrative provinces and districts, and he entrusted the communication and implementation of his policies to officers of the central government who served at the pleasure of the emperor himself. He disarmed regional military forces and destroyed fortresses that might serve as points of rebellion or

resistance. He built roads to facilitate communications and the movement of armies: his network of roads extended more than 6,800 kilometers (4,000 miles). He also drafted laborers by the hundreds of thousands to build defensive walls. Regional kings in northern and western regions of China had already constructed many walls in their realms in an effort to discourage raids by nomadic peoples. Qin Shihuangdi ordered workers to link the existing sections into a massive defensive barrier that was effectively the first Great Wall of China.

The Burning of the Books It is likely that many Chinese welcomed the political stability introduced by the Qin dynasty, but by no means did the new regime win universal acceptance. Confucians, Daoists, and others launched a vigorous campaign of criticism. In an effort to reassert his authority, Qin Shihuangdi ordered execution for those who criticized his regime, and he demanded the burning of all books of philosophy, ethics, history, and literature. His decree exempted works on medicine, fortune-telling, and agriculture on the grounds that they had some utilitarian value. The emperor also spared the official history of the Qin state. Other works, however, largely went into the flames during the next few years.

Qin Shihuangdi (chihn she-huang-dee)
Xianyang (SHYAHN-YAHNG)

A life-size model of a general from the tomb complex of Qin Shi Huangdi's. It was the general's job to lead the massive Terracotta Army in battles in the after-world against the enemies of the First Emperor.

Hung Chung Chih/Shutterstock

The First Emperor took his policy seriously and enforced it earnestly. In the year following his decree, Qin Shihuangdi is said to have sentenced some 460 scholars residing in the capital to be buried alive for their criticism of his regime, although no actual evidence of this has ever been discovered. He also forced many other critics from the provinces into the army and dispatched them to dangerous frontier posts. For the better part of a generation, there was no open discussion of classical literary or philosophical works. When it became safe again to speak openly, scholars began a long and painstaking task of reconstructing the suppressed texts. In some cases, scholars had managed, at great personal risk, to hide copies of the forbidden books, which they retrieved and recirculated. In other cases they reassembled texts that they had committed to

memory. In many cases, however, works suppressed by Qin Shihuangdi simply disappeared.

Qin Centralization   The First Emperor launched several initiatives that enhanced the unity of China. In keeping with his policy of centralization, he standardized the laws, currencies, weights, and measures of the various regions of China. Previously, regional states had organized their own legal and economic systems, which often conflicted with one another and hampered commerce and communications across state boundaries. Uniform coinage and legal standards encouraged the integration of China's various regions into a more tightly knit society than had ever been conceivable before. The roads and bridges that Qin Shihuangdi built throughout his realm, like those built in other classical societies, also encouraged economic integration: though constructed largely with military uses in mind, they served as fine highways for interregional commerce.

Standardized Script   Perhaps even more important than his legal and economic policies was the First Emperor's standardization of Chinese script. Before the Qin dynasty, all regions of China used scripts derived from the one employed at the Shang court, but they had developed along different lines and had become mutually unrecognizable. In hopes of ensuring better understanding and uniform application of his policies, Qin Shihuangdi mandated the use of a common script throughout his empire. The regions of China continued to use different spoken languages, as they do even today, but they wrote those languages with a common script—just as if Europeans spoke English, French, German, Italian, Russian, Spanish, and other languages but wrote them all down in Latin. In China, speakers of different languages use the same written symbols but pronounce them and process them mentally in different ways. Nevertheless, the common script enables them to communicate in writing across linguistic boundaries.

In spite of his ruthlessness, Qin Shihuangdi ranks as one of the most effective rulers in Chinese and indeed all of world history. The First Emperor established a precedent for centralized imperial rule, which remained the norm in China until the early twentieth century. He also pointed China in the direction of political and cultural unity, and with some periods of interruption, China has remained politically and culturally unified to the present day.

Tomb of the First Emperor   Qin Shihuangdi died in 210 B.C.E. His final resting place was a lavish tomb constructed by some seven hundred thousand conscripted laborers, effectively people enslaved to the state, as a permanent monument to the First Emperor. Rare and expensive grave goods accompanied the emperor in burial, along with sacrificed slaves, concubines, and many of the craftsmen who designed and built the tomb. According to Sima Qian, Qin Shihuangdi was laid to rest in an elaborate underground palace lined with bronze and protected by traps and crossbows rigged to fire at intruders. The ceiling of the palace featured paintings of the stars and planets, and a vast map of the First Emperor's realm, with flowing mercury representing its rivers and seas, decorated the floor. Buried in the vicinity of the tomb was an entire army of life-size pottery figures to guard the emperor in death. Since 1974, when scholars began to excavate the area around Qin Shihuangdi's tomb, many thousands of terra-cotta sculptures have come to light, including magnificently detailed soldiers, horses, and weapons.

The terra-cotta army of Qin Shihuangdi protected his tomb until recent times, but it could not save his successors or his empire. The First Emperor had conscripted millions of laborers from all parts of China to work on ambitious public works projects such as palaces, roads, bridges, irrigation systems, defensive walls, and his tomb. Although those projects increased productivity and promoted the integration of China's various regions, they also generated tremendous ill will among laborers compelled to leave their families and their lands. Revolts began in the year after Qin Shihuangdi's death,

and in 207 B.C.E. waves of rebels overwhelmed the Qin court, slaughtering government officials and burning state buildings. The Qin dynasty quickly dissolved into chaos.

The Early Han Dynasty

Liu Bang   The bloody end of the Qin dynasty might well have ended the experiment with centralized imperial rule in China. Although ambitious governors and generals could have carved China into regions and contested one another for power in a reprise of the Period of the Warring States, centralized rule returned almost immediately, largely because of a determined commander named **Liu Bang.** Judging from the historian **Sima Qian**'s account, Liu Bang was not a colorful or charismatic figure—indeed, he was a crude and somewhat oafish character with a large appetite for strong drink—but he was also a persistent man and a methodical planner. He surrounded himself with brilliant advisers and enjoyed the unwavering loyalty of his troops. By 206 B.C.E. he had restored order throughout China and established himself at the head of a new dynasty.

Liu Bang called the new dynasty the Han, in honor of his native land. The Han dynasty turned out to be one of the longest and most influential in all of Chinese history. It lasted for more than four hundred years, from 206 B.C.E. to 220 C.E., although for a brief period (9–23 C.E.) a usurper temporarily displaced Han rule. Thus historians conventionally divide the dynasty into the Early Han (206 B.C.E.–9 C.E.) and the Later Han (25–220 C.E.).

The Han dynasty consolidated the tradition of centralized imperial rule that the Qin dynasty had pioneered. During the **Early Han dynasty,** emperors ruled from Chang'an, a cosmopolitan city near modern Xi'an that became the cultural capital of China. They mostly used wood as a building material, and later dynasties built over their city, so nothing of Han-era Chang'an survives. Contemporaries described Chang'an as a thriving metropolis with a fine imperial palace, busy markets, and expansive parks. During the Later Han, the emperors moved their capital east to Luoyang, also a cosmopolitan city second in importance only to Chang'an throughout much of Chinese history.

One detachment of the formidable, life-size terra-cotta army buried in the vicinity of Qin Shihuangdi's tomb to protect the emperor after his death. The army consists of soldiers by the tens of thousands, along with weapons, horses, carts, and equipment. What was the emperor's purpose in having this massive terracotta army constructed? What does the construction of such a tomb suggest about Qin Shihuangdi's power and ability to command resources?

Paul Souders/The Image Bank/Getty Images

Early Han Policies During the early days of the Han dynasty, Liu Bang attempted to follow a middle path between the decentralized network of political alliances of the Zhou dynasty and the tightly centralized state of the Qin. Zhou decentralization encouraged political chaos, he thought, because regional governors were powerful enough to resist the emperor and pursue their own ambitions. Liu Bang thought that Qin centralization created a new set of problems, however, because it provided little incentive for imperial family members to support the dynasty.

Liu Bang tried to save the advantages and avoid the excesses of both Zhou and Qin dynasty policies. On the one hand, he allotted large landholdings to members of the imperial family, in the expectation that they would provide a reliable network of support for his rule. On the other hand, he divided the empire into administrative districts governed by officials who served at the emperor's pleasure in the expectation that he could exercise effective control over the development and implementation of his policies.

Liu Bang learned quickly that reliance on his family did not guarantee support for the emperor. In 200 B.C.E. an army of nomadic **Xiongnu** warriors besieged Liu Bang and almost captured him. He managed to escape—but without receiving the support he had expected from his family members. From that point forward, Liu Bang and his successors followed a policy of centralization. They reclaimed lands from family members, absorbed those lands into the imperial domain, and entrusted political responsibilities to an administrative bureaucracy. Thus, despite a brief flirtation with a decentralized government, the Han dynasty left as its principal political legacy a tradition of centralized imperial rule.

The Martial Emperor, Han Wudi Much of the reason for the Han dynasty's success was the long reign of the dynasty's greatest and most energetic emperor, Han Wudi, the "Martial Emperor," who occupied the imperial throne for fifty-four years, from 141 to 87 B.C.E. **Han Wudi** ruled his empire with vision and vigor. He pursued two policies in particular: administrative centralization and imperial expansion.

Han Centralization Domestically, Han Wudi worked strenuously to increase the authority and the prestige of the central government. He built an enormous bureaucracy to administer his empire, and like Qin Shihuangdi, he sent imperial officers to implement his policies and maintain order in administrative provinces and districts. He also continued the Qin policy of building roads and canals to facilitate trade and communication between China's regions. To finance the vast machinery of his government, he levied taxes on agriculture, trade, and craft industries, and he established imperial monopolies on the production of essential goods such as iron and salt while placing the lucrative liquor industry under state supervision.

In building such an enormous governmental structure, Han Wudi faced a serious problem of recruitment. He needed thousands of reliable, intelligent, educated individuals to run his bureaucracy, but education in China took place largely on an individual, ad hoc basis. Men such as Confucius, Mencius, and Xunzi accepted students and tutored them, but there was no system to provide a continuous supply of educated candidates for office.

The Confucian Educational System Han Wudi addressed that problem in 124 B.C.E. by establishing an imperial institute of higher learning that prepared young men for government service. Han Wudi recognized that the success of his efforts at bureaucratic centralization would depend on creating a corps of educated officials. The imperial institute took Confucianism—the only Chinese cultural tradition developed enough to provide rigorous intellectual discipline—as the basis for its curriculum. Ironically, then, while he partially relied on Legalist principles of government, Han Wudi ensured the long-term survival of the Confucian tradition by establishing it as the official imperial ideology. By the end of the Early Han dynasty, the imperial university was enrolling more than three thousand students, and by the end of the Later Han, the student population had risen to more than thirty thousand.

Han Imperial Expansion While he moved aggressively to centralize power and authority at home, Han Wudi pursued an equally vigorous foreign policy of imperial expansion. He invaded northern Vietnam and Korea, subjected them to Han rule, and brought them into the orbit of Chinese society. He ruled both lands through a Chinese-style government, and Confucian values followed the Han armies into the new colonies. Over the course of the centuries, the educational systems of both northern Vietnam and Korea drew their inspiration almost entirely from Confucianism.

The Xiongnu The greatest foreign challenge that Han Wudi faced came from the Xiongnu, a militarized nomadic people from the steppes of central Asia. Like most of the other nomadic peoples of central Asia, the Xiongnu were superb horsemen. Xiongnu boys learned to ride sheep and shoot rodents at an early age, and as they grew older they graduated to larger animals and aimed their bows and arrows at larger prey. Their weaponry was not as sophisticated as that of the Chinese: in the skilled hands of their warriors, their bows and arrows were nearly as lethal as the ingenious and powerful crossbows wielded by Chinese warriors. In addition, their mobility gave the Xiongnu a distinct advantage. When they could not satisfy their needs and desires through peaceful trade, they mounted sudden raids into villages or trading areas, where they commandeered food supplies or manufactured goods and then rapidly departed. Because they had no cities or settled places to defend, the Xiongnu could quickly disperse when confronted by a superior force.

During the reign of **Modu** (210–174 B.C.E.), their most successful leader, the Xiongnu ruled a vast federation of nomadic

Xiongnu (SHE-OONG-noo)

Model of a luxury chariot of the kind used by high imperial officials in the Qin and Han dynasties. Crafted from bronze with silver inlay, this model is about one-third life size.

DEA/E. Lessing/age fotostock

peoples that stretched from the Aral Sea to the Yellow Sea. Modu brought strict military discipline to the Xiongnu. According to Sima Qian, Modu once instructed his forces to shoot their arrows at whatever target he himself selected. He aimed in succession at his favorite horse, one of his wives, and his father's best horse, and he summarily executed those who failed to discharge their arrows. When his forces reliably followed his orders, Modu targeted his father, who immediately fell under a hail of arrows, leaving Modu as the Xiongnu chief.

With its highly disciplined army, the Xiongnu empire was a source of concern to the Han emperors. During the early days of the dynasty, they attempted to pacify the Xiongnu by paying them tribute—providing them with food and finished goods in hopes that they would refrain from mounting raids in China—or by arranging marriages between the ruling houses of the two peoples in hopes of establishing peaceful diplomatic relations. Neither method succeeded for long.

Han Expansion into Central Asia Ultimately, Han Wudi decided to go on the offensive against the Xiongnu. He invaded central Asia with vast armies—sometimes including as many as one hundred thousand troops—and brought much of the Xiongnu empire under Chinese military control. He pacified a long central Asian corridor extending almost to Bactria (modern Afghanistan), which prevented the Xiongnu from maintaining the integrity of their empire and which served also

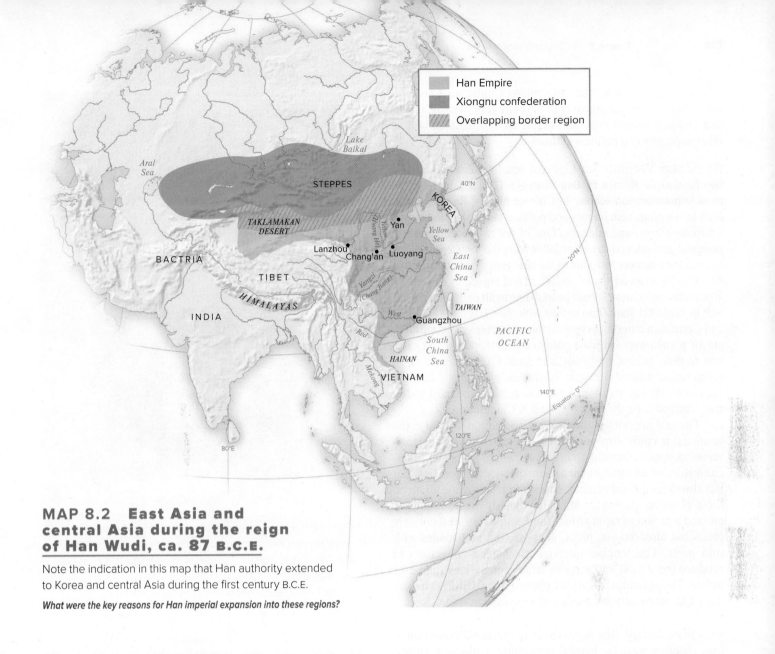

MAP 8.2   East Asia and central Asia during the reign of Han Wudi, ca. 87 B.C.E.

Note the indication in this map that Han authority extended to Korea and central Asia during the first century B.C.E.

What were the key reasons for Han imperial expansion into these regions?

as the lifeline of a trade network that linked much of the Eurasian landmass. He even planted colonies of Chinese cultivators in the oasis communities of central Asia. As a result of those efforts, the Xiongnu empire soon fell into disarray. For the moment, the Han state enjoyed uncontested hegemony in both east Asia and central Asia. Before long, however, economic and social problems within China brought serious problems for the Han dynasty itself.

FROM ECONOMIC PROSPERITY TO SOCIAL DISORDER

Already during the Xia, Shang, and Zhou dynasties, a productive agricultural economy supported the emergence of complex society in China. High agricultural productivity continued during the Qin and Han dynasties, and it supported the development of craft industries such as the forging of iron tools and the weaving of silk textiles. During the Han dynasty, however,

China experienced serious social and economic problems as land became concentrated in the hands of a small, wealthy elite class. Social tensions generated banditry, rebellion, and even the temporary collapse of the Han state itself. Although Han rulers regained the throne, they presided over a much-weakened realm. By the early third century C.E., social and political problems had brought the Han dynasty to an end.

Productivity and Prosperity during the Early Han

Patriarchal Social Order The structure of Chinese society during the Qin and Han dynasties was similar to that of the Zhou era. Patriarchal households averaged five inhabitants, although several generations of aristocratic families sometimes lived together in large compounds. During the Han dynasty, moralists sought to enhance the authority of patriarchal family heads by emphasizing the importance of filial piety and women's subordination to men. The anonymous Confucian *Classic of Filial Piety,* composed probably in the early Han dynasty, taught that children should obey and honor their parents as well as other superiors and political authorities.

Ban Zhao, Woman Scholar An equally influential treatise was *Lessons for Women* by **Ban Zhao** (45–120 C.E.), perhaps the most famous woman scholar in Chinese history. Ban Zhao was born into a prominent literary and political family. Her father was a famous scholar and educator. One of her twin brothers was a powerful general, and the other followed in the footsteps of Sima Qian as the foremost historian of the later Han dynasty. Ban Zhao herself enjoyed an advanced education and argued in *Lessons for Women* that education should be available to all children—girls as well as boys. Yet Ban Zhao agreed with the *Classic of Filial Piety* and Confucian morality in general that the virtues most appropriate for women were humility, obedience, subservience, and devotion to their fathers, husbands, and sons. From the time of its composition around 100 C.E. to the early twentieth century, *Lessons for Women* was one of the most popular and most widely read statements on the role of women in Chinese society.

The vast majority of the Chinese population worked in the countryside cultivating grains and vegetables, which they harvested in larger quantities than ever before. In late Zhou times, cultivators often strengthened their plows with iron tips, but metalworkers did not produce enough iron to provide all-metal tools. However, during the later Han dynasty the iron industry entered a period of rapid growth, and cultivators used not only plows but also shovels, picks, hoes, sickles, and spades with iron parts. The tougher implements enabled cultivators to produce more food and support larger populations than ever before. The agricultural surplus allowed many Chinese to produce fine manufactured goods and to engage in trade.

Iron Metallurgy The significance of this rapid expansion of iron industry went far beyond agriculture. Chinese entrepreneurs had discovered how to make cast iron by the fourth century B.C.E., and production surged during the Han dynasty. The cast-iron industry became so important that Emperor Han Wudi placed it under state control and created forty-six regional offices to supervise iron production. Han artisans experimented with production techniques and learned to craft fine utensils for both domestic and military uses. Iron pots, stoves, knives, needles, axes, hammers, saws, and other tools became standard fixtures in households that could not have afforded more expensive bronze utensils. The ready availability of iron also had important military implications. Craftsmen designed suits of iron armor to protect soldiers against arrows and blows, and the strength and sharpness of Han swords, spears, and arrowheads help to explain the success of Chinese armies against the Xiongnu and other nomadic peoples.

Silk Textiles Textile production—particularly **sericulture,** the manufacture of silk—became an especially important industry. The origins of sericulture date to the fourth millennium B.C.E.,

Ceramic model of a well discovered in a Han dynasty tomb. Such models were placed in tombs so that the dead would have access to useful resources in the afterlife. (Östasiatiska museet, Stockholm-DSC09578.JPG)

Historical Views/age fotostock/Alamy Stock Photo

and possibly even earlier, long before the ancient Xia dynasty, but only in Han times did sericulture expand from its original home in the Yellow River valley to most parts of China. It developed especially rapidly in the southern regions known today as Sichuan and Guangdong provinces, and the industry thrived after the establishment of long-distance trade relations with western Eurasia in the second century B.C.E.

Although silk was made in other regions of Eurasia, Chinese silk was especially fine because of advanced sericulture techniques. Chinese producers bred their silkworms, fed them on finely chopped mulberry leaves, and carefully unraveled their cocoons so as to obtain long fibers of raw silk that they wove into light, strong, lustrous fabrics. (In other lands, producers relied on wild silkworms that ate a variety of leaves and chewed through their cocoons, leaving only short fibers that yielded lower-quality fabrics.) Chinese silk became a prized commodity in India, Persia, Mesopotamia, and even the distant Roman Empire. Commerce in silk and other products led to the establishment of an intricate network of trade routes known collectively as the Silk Roads (discussed in chapter 12).

What's Left Out? ■■■ ■■■■ ■■■ ■■■ ■■■

In this chapter, we discuss some of the major innovations of the Han Dynasty, including its sophisticated production of iron, silk, and military technologies. But perhaps the most remarkable invention of all that appeared during the Han Dynasty was the first paper in world history, made of a composite of natural fibers like hemp and bark, with textile fibers like silk. For the past two thousand years, the Chinese have attributed the invention of paper to an otherwise obscure court eunuch of the Later Han Dynasty named Cai Lun. Western scholars had tended to dismiss him as a legendary figure, but there is plenty of documentary evidence that Cai Lun not only existed but that he indeed greatly pleased the emperor when he presented him with his invention of paper in 105 C.E. The invention can be seen as yet another example of necessity driving innovation. As the bureaucracy reached the height of its size and sophistication in the Later Han, so the volume of official records that needed to be kept grew staggeringly large. We read that transporting even a small number of official documents transcribed on traditional bamboo strips required the use of a wheelbarrow, so the invention of paper must have come as a huge relief to the court and the bureaucrats. We also know that Cai Lun was rewarded by the emperor with a promotion and the title of an aristocrat, but later he got caught up in a deadly palace power struggle and committed suicide by drinking poison while taking a bath!

By the third century, paper was in common use in China, and the invention had made its way into the Arab world by the seventh century. But it was not until the twelfth century that papermaking spread to Europe, making it possible for printers like Johannes Guttenberg to begin to mass-produce printed books. In his 1978 book, *The 100: A Ranking of the Most Influential Persons in History,* historian Michael Hart ranks Cai Lun as number seven, ahead of Guttenberg. Hart argues that the invention of paper allowed Chinese civilization to surge ahead of the West throughout the first millennium of the Common Era. Knowledge was more rapidly disseminated, literacy became more widespread, and government bureaucracy was run much more efficiently because of the invention of paper. Only in the late Middle Ages, and particularly after the Renaissance, would the West begin to close the knowledge gap on the East, a gap that can be attributed directly to the remarkable invention of Cai Lun of the Later Han Dynasty.

Source: Michael Hart, *The 100: A Ranking of the Most Influential Persons in History.*

Han China was thus a major incubator of technological innovation. Quite apart from their production of iron and silk, Chinese artisans found ways to improve on earlier technologies and also to devise entirely new inventions. Shortly before the time of the Qin and Han dynasties, for example, military engineers added to primitive crossbows, which had already been in use for several centuries, a sophisticated trigger mechanism that turned them into powerful weapons. Meanwhile, others invented specially designed horse collars, which enabled cultivators to coax maximum power out of their draft animals. Somewhat later, about the first century C.E., nautical engineers invented the ship's rudder, which greatly simplified the steering of sailing vessels. These and other inventions contributed to high prosperity, especially during the early centuries of the Han dynasty.

Economic and Social Difficulties

In spite of general prosperity, China began to experience economic and social difficulties toward the end of the Early Han period. The military adventures and the central Asian policy of Han Wudi caused severe economic strain. Expeditions against the Xiongnu and the establishment of agricultural colonies in central Asia were extremely expensive undertakings, and they rapidly consumed the empire's surplus wealth. To finance his ventures, Han Wudi raised taxes and confiscated land and personal property from wealthy individuals, sometimes on the pretext that they had violated imperial laws. Those measures did not kill industry and commerce in China, but they discouraged investment in manufacturing and trading enterprises, which in turn had a dampening effect on the larger economy.

How the Past Shapes the Future ▷▷▷ ▷ ▷ ▷ ▷ ▷

Long-Distance Trade Networks

As we saw in chapter 7, the appearance of large empires helped to create the conditions for greatly expanded networks of long-distance trade during the classical period. As you have seen in this chapter, Chinese silk became one of the most highly sought-after items of trade over vast areas of Eurasia in this period. Think about the ways that Han state policies were connected to the enormous popularity of Chinese silk in places as far afield as the Mediterranean basin. How was it that so many people were able to discover the beauty of Chinese silk in this period? How might the demand for Chinese silk have affected regional Chinese economies during the Han dynasty? And what has been the long-term impact of this trade in silk on the eventual emergence of a global system of exchanges in the modern age?

Connecting the Sources

Prescriptive literature and the lives of Chinese women during the Han dynasty

The problem   Writing about culture and social relationships in the distant past poses specific challenges for historians. Even in societies like China, where literary traditions were already highly sophisticated by the time of the Han dynasty (206 B.C.E.–220 C.E.), available sources illuminating particular cultural attitudes or social relations were nevertheless limited. Existing textual sources tended to be written by educated elites rather than by the peasant farmers or laborers who made up the majority of the population. As a result, historians often have to rely on sources that tell us what educated people said about the ways culture and social relationships should be. Historians call these types of texts **prescriptive literature** because they *prescribe* how things should be, at least according to their authors. But what can prescriptive literature tell us about how real people actually interacted? Did prescriptive literature *reflect* what culture and social relationships were like for ordinary people, or did people write prescriptive literature in order to *shape* those aspects of society? These are the sorts of questions historians need to address every day as they seek to understand what peoples lives were really like in the ancient world.

When exploring the effects of Confucianism on women's lives in Han China, for example, historians must rely on a relatively small body of textual sources. Two of the most commonly known of these sources—the *Analects* of Confucius and Ban Zhao's *Lessons for Women*—were written by highly educated elites (one male and one female) centuries apart from one another. Read the following two documents and think about what historians can and cannot understand about the lives of women in Han China by reading prescriptive literature.

The documents   Read the documents below, and consider carefully the questions that follow.

Document 1:

The Analects *of Confucius do not specifically address the subject of women in many places, although women were implicitly included in Confucius's vision of a moral and ethical society. This short selection, titled "On Women and Servants," is one place where women are mentioned explicitly.*

> *The text reads:*

> *17:25 Women and servants are most difficult to nurture. If one is close to them, they lose their reserve, while if one is distant, they feel resentful.*

Document 2:

This is an excerpt from Ban Zhao's Lessons for Women, *written in about 80 C.E.*

> *The text reads:*

> *Being careless, and by nature stupid, I taught and trained my children without system. . . .*
>
> *But I do grieve that you, my daughters, just now at the age for marriage, have not at this time had gradual training and advice; that you still have not learned the proper customs for married women. I fear that by failure in good manners in other families you will humiliate both your ancestors and your clan . . . in order that you may have something wherewith to benefit your persons, I wish every one of you, my daughters each to write out a copy for yourself.*
>
> *From this time on every one of you strive to practice these lessons.*
>
> **HUMILITY**
>
> *On the third day after the birth of a girl the ancients observed three customs: first to place the baby below the bed; second to give her a potsherd [pottery piece] with which to play; and third to announce her birth*

According to this section of the text, what is Ban Zhao's specific purpose in writing *Lessons for Women*?

to her ancestors by an offering. Now to lay the baby below the bed plainly indicated that she is lowly and weak, and should regard it as her primary duty to humble herself before others. To give her potsherds with which to play indubitably signified that she should practice labor and consider it her primary duty to be industrious. To announce her birth before her ancestors clearly meant that she ought to esteem as her primary duty the continuation of the observance of worship in the home.

These three ancient customs epitomize woman's ordinary way of life and the teachings of the traditional ceremonial rites and regulations. Let a woman modestly yield to others; let her respect others; let her put others first, herself last. Should she do something good, let her not mention it; should she do something bad let her not deny it. Let her bear disgrace; let her even endure when others speak or do evil to her. Always let her seem to tremble and to fear. When a woman follows such maxims as these then she may be said to humble herself before others.

. . .

No woman who observes these three fundamentals of life has ever had a bad reputation or has fallen into disgrace. If a woman fails to observe them, how can her name be honored; how can she but bring disgrace upon herself?

. . .

> What might be Ban Zhao's purpose in encouraging women to be humble?

WOMANLY QUALIFICATIONS

A woman ought to have four qualifications: (1) womanly virtue; (2) womanly words; (3) womanly bearing; and (4) womanly work. Now what is called womanly virtue need not be brilliant ability, exceptionally different from others. Womanly words need be neither clever in debate nor keen in conversation. Womanly appearance requires neither a pretty nor a perfect face and form. Womanly work need not be work done more skillfully than that of others.

To guard carefully her chastity; to control circumspectly her behavior; in every motion to exhibit modesty; and to model each act on the best usage, this is womanly virtue.

To choose her words with care; to avoid vulgar language; to speak at appropriate times; and nor to weary others with much conversation, may be called the characteristics of womanly words.

To wash and scrub filth away; to keep clothes and ornaments fresh and clean; to wash the head and bathe the body regularly, and to keep the person free from disgraceful filth, may be called the characteristics of womanly bearing.

With whole-hearted devotion to sew and to weave; to love not gossip and silly laughter; in cleanliness and order to prepare the wine and food for serving guests, may be called the characteristics of womanly work.

These four qualifications characterize the greatest virtue of a woman. No woman can afford to be without them. In fact they are very easy to possess if a woman only treasure them in her heart.

Questions

1. What can these sources definitively tell you about the lives of the people who wrote them? What *facts* can be gleaned from these sources?
2. In Document 1, why did Confucius group women together with servants when describing the difficulty of nurturing both?
3. In Document 2, what is the primary role of women, according to Ban Zhao? What kinds of behaviors should women cultivate if they wish to maintain good virtue and harmonious relationships with others?
4. Taking both documents together, what can they tell us about the effects of Confucianism on the lives of actual women in Han China?
5. Sources such as these can help historians understand attitudes about women in Han China, especially when read in conjunction with other textual and material evidence. But what other forms of evidence would historians need to understand the experiences of the majority of women in China, not just those in the elite classes?

Source Websites: **Document 1:** http://afe.easia.columbia.edu/ps/cup/confucius_women_servants.pdf **Document 2:** http://acc6.its.brooklyn.cuny.edu/~phalsall/texts/banzhao.html

Han gentlemen sport luxurious silk gowns as they engage in sophisticated conversation. Wealthy individuals and ruling elites commonly dressed in silk, but peasants and others of the lower classes rarely if ever donned silk garments.
Art Collection 3/Alamy Stock Photo

Social Tensions Distinctions between rich and poor widened during the course of the Han dynasty. Wealthy individuals wore fine silk garments, leather shoes, and jewelry of jade and gold, whereas the poor classes made do with rough hemp clothing and sandals. Tables in wealthy households held pork, fish, fowl, and fine aged wines, but the diet of the poor consisted mostly of grain or rice supplemented by small quantities of vegetables or meat. By the first century B.C.E., social and economic differences had generated serious tensions, and peasants in hard-pressed regions began to organize rebellions in hopes of gaining a larger share of Han society's resources.

Land Distribution A particularly difficult problem concerned the distribution of land. Individual economic problems brought on by poor harvests, high taxes, or crushing burdens of debt forced many small landowners to sell their property under unfavorable conditions or even to forfeit it in exchange for cancellation of their debts. In extreme cases, individuals had to sell themselves and their families into

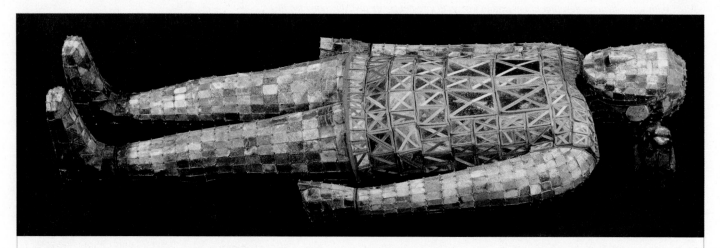

In Han times the wealthiest classes enjoyed the privilege of being buried in suits of jade plaques sewn together with gold threads, like the burial dress of Liu Sheng, who died in 113 B.C.E. at Manzheng in Hebei Province. Legend held that jade prevented decomposition of the deceased's body. Scholars have estimated that a jade burial suit like this one required ten years' labor. What does such a suit tell us about the lives of the Chinese elite during the Han dynasty?
Martha Avery/Asian Art & Archaeology, Inc./Corbis/Getty Images

slavery to satisfy their creditors. Owners of large estates not only increased the size of their holdings by absorbing the property of their less fortunate neighbors but also increased the efficiency of their operations by employing cheap labor. Sometimes cheap laborers came in the form of slaves, other times in the form of tenant farmers who had to deliver as much as half their produce to the landowner for the right to till his property. In either case, the laborers worked on terms that favored the landlords.

By the end of the first century B.C.E., land had been consolidated in the hands of a relatively small number of individuals who owned vast estates, while ever-increasing numbers of peasant cultivators led difficult lives with few prospects for improvement. Landless peasants became increasingly rebellious against this system, and Chinese society faced growing problems of banditry and sporadic rebellion. Because the Han emperors depended heavily on the political cooperation of large landowners, however, they did not attempt any serious reform of the landholding system.

The Reign of Wang Mang Tensions came to a head during the early first century C.E. when a powerful and respected Han minister named **Wang Mang** undertook a comprehensive program of reform. In 6 C.E. a two-year-old boy inherited the Han imperial throne. Because the boy was unable to govern, Wang Mang served as his regent. Many officials regarded Wang as more capable than members of the Han family and urged him to claim the imperial honor for himself. In 9 C.E. he did just that: announcing that the mandate of heaven had passed from the Han to his family, he seized the throne. Wang Mang then introduced a series of wide-ranging reforms that have prompted some historians to refer to him as the "socialist emperor."

The most important reforms concerned landed property: Wang Mang limited the amount of land that a family could hold and ordered officials to break up large estates, redistribute them, and provide landless individuals with property to cultivate. Despite his good intentions, the socialist emperor attempted to impose his policy without adequate preparation and communication. The result was confusion: landlords resisted a policy that threatened their holdings, and even peasants found its application inconsistent and unsatisfactory. After several years of chaos, Wang Mang faced the additional misfortune of poor harvests and famine, which sparked widespread revolts against his rule. In 23 C.E. a coalition of disgruntled landlords and desperate peasants killed Wang Mang and thousands of his supporters.

The Later Han Dynasty

Within two years a recovered Han dynasty returned to power, but it ruled over a weakened realm. The **Later Han dynasty** emperors even decided to abandon Chang'an, which had suffered grave damage during the years of chaos and rebellion,

and establish a new capital at Luoyang. Nevertheless, during the early years of the Later Han, emperors ruled vigorously in the manner of Liu Bang and Han Wudi. They regained control of the centralized administration and reorganized the state bureaucracy. They also maintained the Chinese presence in central Asia, continued to keep the Xiongnu in submission, and exercised firm control over the Silk Roads.

The Yellow Turban Uprising The Later Han emperors did not seriously address the problem of land distribution that had helped to bring down the Early Han dynasty. The wealthy classes still lived in relative luxury while peasants worked under difficult conditions. The empire continued to face theft and rebellions organized by desperate peasants with few opportunities to improve their lot. The **Yellow Turban uprising**—so named because of the distinctive headgear worn by the rebels—was a particularly serious revolt that raged throughout China and tested the resilience of the Han state during the late second century C.E. Although the Later Han dynasty possessed the military power required to keep civil disorder under reasonable control, rebellions by the Yellow Turbans and others weakened the Han state during the second and third centuries C.E.

Collapse of the Han Dynasty The Later Han emperors were unable, however, to prevent the development of factions at court that paralyzed the central government. Factions of imperial family members, Confucian scholar bureaucrats, and

Han Dynasty painting of peasants working in a rice field. The figures above are walking on a path through the flooded rice fields carrying rice sprouts, which the figures in the foreground are planting. Compare this to images of elite life on the previous page. What does this tell us about the strengthening of social hierarchies in the Later Han Dynasty?
The Art Archive/Shutterstock

Though it dates from a somewhat later era, about the sixth century C.E., this cave painting from Dunhuang in Gansu Province (western China) offers some idea of the chaos that engulfed China as the Han dynasty crumbled.

James L. Stanfield/National Geographic Creative

court eunuchs sought to increase their influence, protect their own interests, and destroy their rivals. On several occasions, relations between the various factions became so strained that war broke out. In 189 C.E., for example, a faction led by an imperial relative descended on the Han palace and slaughtered more than two thousand beardless men in an effort to destroy the eunuchs as a political force. In that respect the attack succeeded. From the unmeasured violence of the operation, however, it is clear that the Later Han dynasty had reached a point of internal weakness from which it could not easily recover. Indeed, early in the next century, the central government disintegrated, and for almost four centuries China remained divided into a series of often short-lived regional kingdoms.

CONCLUSION

The Qin state lasted for a short fourteen years, but it opened a new era in Chinese history. Qin conquerors imposed unified rule on a series of politically independent kingdoms and launched an ambitious program to forge culturally distinct regions into a unified Chinese society. The Han dynasty endured for more than four centuries and largely completed the project of unifying China. Using a combination of Legalism and Confucianism, two of the most important philosophies that had emerged during the late Zhou dynasty, Han rulers built a centralized bureaucracy that administered a unified empire. Han emperors worked particularly closely with Confucian moralists who organized a system of advanced education that provided recruits for the imperial bureaucracy. Moreover, on the basis of a highly productive economy stimulated by technological innovations, Han rulers projected Chinese influence abroad to Korea, Vietnam, and central Asia. Thus, like contemporary societies in Persia, India, and the Mediterranean basin, Han China produced a set of distinctive political and cultural traditions that shaped Chinese and neighboring societies over the long term.

STUDY TERMS

Analects (144)	Period of the Warring
Ban Zhao (156)	States (143)
Confucianism (144)	prescriptive literature (158)
Daodejing (147)	Qin (143)
Daoism (144)	Qin Shihuangdi (150)
Early Han dynasty (152)	*ren* (145)
eunuchs (142)	sericulture (156)
Han Feizi (149)	Shang Yang (149)
Han Wudi (153)	Sima Qian (152)
junzi (144)	Wang Mang (161)
Kong Fuzi (144)	*wuwei* (147)
Laozi (147)	Xianyang (150)
Later Han dynasty (161)	*xiao* (146)
Legalism (144)	Xiongnu (153)
li (146)	Xunzi (146)
Liu Bang (152)	Yellow Turban uprising (161)
Mencius (146)	Zhou (143)
Modu (153)	*Zhuangzi* (147)

FOR FURTHER READING

C. Benjamin. *Empires of Ancient Eurasia: The First Silk Roads Era 100 B.C.E.–250 C.E.* Cambridge, 2017. Neat synthesis of the history of ancient China and the other Eurasian empires of the Silk Roads Era, through to the collapse of the Later Han Dynasty.

Nicola Di Cosmo. *Ancient China and Its Enemies: The Rise of Nomad Power in East Asian History.* Cambridge, 2002. Outstanding analysis of the relationship between ancient China and its militarized nomadic neighbors, particularly between the Han dynasty and the Xiongnu.

Ban Gu. *Hou Han Shu, Through the Jade Gate to Rome: A Study of the Silk Roads during the Later Han Dynasty, 1st to 2nd Centuries C.E. An Annotated Translation of the Chronicle on the Western Regions in the Hou Han Shu.* Trans. J. Hill. Charlestown, 2009. Superb and very readable translation of key chapters in the the the annals of the Later Han Dynasty.

Mark Edward Lewis. *The Early Chinese Empires: Qin and Han.* Cambridge, Mass., 2007. Emphasizes the long-term influence of imperial rule established by the Qin and Han dynasties.

Simon Leys, trans. *The Analects of Confucius.* New York, 1997. A modern, fluent, and very readable translation of the classic work of Confucianism.

M. Loewe. *The Government of the Qin and Han Empires 221 B.C.E.–220 C.E.* Indianapolis/Cambridge, 2006. Masterful analysis of the governing techniques of the Qin and Han Dynasties by a leading scholar in the field.

Frederick W. Mote. *Intellectual Foundations of China.* 2nd ed. New York, 1989. A compact and concise introduction to the cultural history of classical China.

Michele Pirazzoli-t'Serstevens. *The Han Dynasty.* Trans. by J. Seligman. New York, 1982. An excellent and well-illustrated survey of Han China that draws on archaeological discoveries.

Benjamin I. Schwartz. *The World of Thought in Ancient China.* Cambridge, Mass., 1985. A synthesis of classical Chinese thought by a leading scholar.

Arthur Waldron. *The Great Wall of China: From History to Myth.* Cambridge, 1989. Places the modern Great Wall in the tradition of Chinese wall building from Qin times forward.

Burton Watson, trans. *Records of the Grand Historian.* Rev. ed. 2 vols. New York, 1993. Excellent translation of Sima Qian's history, the most important narrative source for Han China.

Chapter 6

State, Society, and the Quest for Salvation in South Asia

ZOOMING IN ON TRADITIONS

Megasthenes: A Greek Perspective on Ancient South Asia

The earliest description of South Asia by a foreigner came from the pen of a Greek ambassador named Megasthenes who lived during the late fourth and early third centuries B.C.E. As the diplomatic representative of the Seleucid emperor, Megasthenes traveled throughout much of South Asia. Although his book has long been lost, many quotations from it survive in Greek and Latin literature.

Like travel writers of all times, Megasthenes included a certain amount of exaggerated and untrue information in his account of South Asia. He wrote, for example, of ants the size of foxes that mined gold from the earth and fiercely defended their hoards from any humans who tried to steal them. Only by distracting them with slabs of meat, Megasthenes said, could humans safely make away with their treasure. He also reported races of monstrous humans: some with no mouth who survived by breathing in the odors of fruits, flowers, and roots, others with feet pointing backward and eight toes per

A sculpture of the Buddha in gray schist, from the Gandhara region of modern Pakistan.

World History Archive/Alamy Stock Photo

foot, and yet others with the heads of dogs who communicated by barking.

Beyond the tall tales, Megasthenes offered a great deal of reliable information and expressed respect for the land, peoples, and cultures of South Asia. He portrayed South Asia as a fertile land that supported two harvests of grain per year. He described the city of **Pataliputra** as a rectangle-shaped city situated along the Ganges River and surrounded by a moat and a massive timber wall with 570 towers and sixty-four gates. He mentioned large armies that used elephants as war animals. He pointed out the strongly hierarchical character of South Asian society (although he incorrectly held that there were seven instead of four main castes). He noted that two main schools of "philosophers" (Hindus and Buddhists) enjoyed special prominence as well as exemption from taxes, and he described the ascetic lifestyles and vegetarian diets followed by particularly devout individuals. In short, Megasthenes portrayed South Asia as a wealthy land that supported a distinctive society with well-established cultural traditions.

CHAPTER OVERVIEW

In South Asia as in Persia and China, the centuries after 500 B.C.E. witnessed the development of an ancient society whose influence has persisted over the centuries. Its most prominent features were a well-defined social structure, which left individuals with few doubts about their position and role in society, and several popular religious traditions that helped to shape South Asian beliefs and values. Two religions, Buddhism and Hinduism, also appealed strongly to peoples beyond the subcontinent.

Efforts to maintain an imperial government did not succeed nearly as well in South Asia as they did in Persia and China. For the most part, ancient South Asia was largely ruled by regional kingdoms rather than centralized empires. The two imperial regimes that did emerge were crucial for the consolidation of South Asian cultural traditions, however, because they sponsored cultural leaders and promoted their ideals throughout the subcontinent and beyond. The spread of Buddhism is a case in point: imperial support helped the faith secure its position in South Asia and attract converts in other lands. Thus, even in the absence of a strong and continuing imperial tradition like that of Persia or China, the social and cultural traditions of ancient South Asia not only shaped the lives and experiences of the subcontinent's inhabitants but also influenced peoples in distant lands.

CHRONOLOGY	
563–483 B.C.E.	Life of Siddhartha Gautama, the Buddha
540–468 B.C.E.	Life of Vardhamana Mahavira
520 B.C.E.	Invasion of South Asia by Darius of Persia
327 B.C.E.	Invasion of South Asia by Alexander of Macedon
321–297 B.C.E.	Reign of Chandragupta Maurya
321–185 B.C.E.	Mauryan dynasty
268–232 B.C.E.	Reign of Ashoka Maurya
182 B.C.E.–1 C.E.	Bactrian rule in northern South Asia
1–270 C.E.	Kushan empire in northern South Asia and central Asia
127–153 C.E.	Reign of Kushan emperor Kanishka
320–550 C.E.	Gupta dynasty

THE FORTUNES OF EMPIRE IN ANCIENT SOUTH ASIA

Following their migrations to South Asia after 1500 B.C.E., the Indo-Aryans established a series of small kingdoms throughout the subcontinent. For centuries the rulers of those kingdoms fought constantly among themselves and sought to expand their states by absorbing others. By the sixth century B.C.E., wars of expansion had resulted in the consolidation of several large regional kingdoms that dominated much of the subcontinent. Despite strenuous efforts, none of these kingdoms was able to establish hegemony over the others. During the classical era, the **Mauryan** and the **Gupta dynasties** founded centralized, imperial states that embraced much of South Asia, but neither empire survived long enough to establish centralized rule as a lasting feature of South Asian political life.

Pataliputra (pah-tal-ih-puh-trah)
Gupta (GOOP-tah)

The Mauryan Dynasty and the Temporary Unification of South Asia

The unification of South Asia came about partly as a result of intrusion from beyond the subcontinent. About 520 B.C.E. the Persian emperor Darius I crossed the Hindu Kush mountains, conquered parts of northwestern South Asia, and made the kingdom of **Gandhara** (northern modern-day Pakistan and southern modern-day Afghanistan) a province of the Achaemenid empire. The establishment of Achaemenid authority in South Asia introduced local rulers to Persian techniques of administration. Almost two centuries later, in 327 B.C.E., after overrunning the Persian empire, Alexander of Macedon crossed the Indus River and crushed the states he found there. Alexander remained in South Asia only for a short time, and he did not make a deep impression on the Punjabi people: he departed after his forces mutinied in the year 325 B.C.E., and contemporary South Asian sources did not even mention his name. Yet his campaign had an important effect on South Asian politics and history because he created a political vacuum in northwestern South Asia by destroying the existing states and then withdrawing his forces.

Chandragupta Maurya (chuhn-dra-GOOP-tah MORE-yuh)

Kingdom of Magadha Poised to fill the vacuum was the dynamic kingdom of Magadha, located in the central portion of the Ganges plain. Several regional kingdoms in the valley of the Ganges had become wealthy as workers turned forests into fields and trade became an increasingly prominent feature of the local economy. By about 500 B.C.E. Magadha had emerged as the most important state in northeastern South Asia. During the next two centuries, the kings of Magadha conquered the neighboring states and gained control of South Asian commerce passing through the Ganges Valley as well as overseas trade between South Asia and Burma passing across the Bay of Bengal. The withdrawal of Alexander from the Punjab presented Magadha with a rare opportunity to expand.

Chandragupta Maurya During the late 320s B.C.E., an ambitious regional ruler named **Chandragupta Maurya** exploited that opportunity and laid the foundation for the Mauryan Empire, the first state to bring a centralized and unified government to most of the South Asian subcontinent. Chandragupta began by seizing control of small, remote regions of Magadha and then worked his way gradually toward the center, more or less following the southerly land trade route illustrated in Map 9.2. By 321 B.C.E. he had overthrown the ruling dynasty and consolidated his hold on the kingdom. He then moved into the Punjab and brought northwestern South Asia under

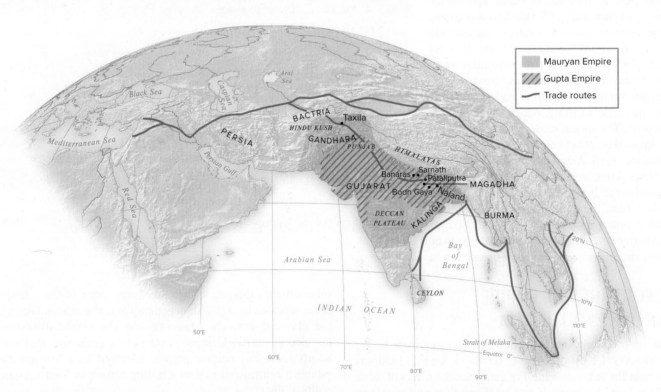

MAP 9.1   The Mauryan and Gupta empires, 321 B.C.E.–550 C.E.

The Mauryan and Gupta dynasties both originated in the kingdom of Magadha.

What geographical and political advantages did Magadha enjoy that gave it advantages over other regions of the subcontinent?

his control. Next he ventured beyond the Indus River and conquered the Greek state in Bactria—a large region shown in Map 9.1 incorporating most of modern Afghanistan and some regions to the north, where Alexander of Macedon's Greek successors maintained a kingdom during the Seleucid era. By the end of the fourth century B.C.E., Chandragupta's empire embraced all of the northern regions of the South Asian subcontinent from the Indus to the Ganges.

Chandragupta's Government A careful and systematic adviser named **Kautalya** devised procedures for the governance of Chandragupta's realm. Some of Kautalya's advice survives in the ancient South Asian political handbook known as the *Arthashastra,* a manual offering detailed instructions on the uses of power and the principles of government. The *Arthashastra* outlined methods of administering the empire, overseeing trade and agriculture, collecting taxes, maintaining order, conducting foreign relations, and waging war. Kautalya also advised Chandragupta to make abundant use of spies. Like the emperors of Persia and China, Chandragupta and Kautalya built a bureaucratic administrative system that enabled them to implement policies throughout the state.

Ashoka Maurya Tradition holds that Chandragupta abdicated his throne to become a Jain monk and led such an ascetic life that he starved himself to death. Whether that account is true or not, it is certain that his son succeeded him in 297 B.C.E. and added much of southern South Asia to the growing empire. The high point of the Mauryan Empire, however, came during the reign of Chandragupta's grandson **Ashoka**.

Ashoka began his reign (268–232 B.C.E.) as a conqueror. When he came to power, the only major region that remained independent of the Mauryan Empire was the kingdom of Kalinga (modern Orissa) in the east-central part of the subcontinent. In fact, Kalinga was not only independent of Mauryan rule but also actively hostile to its spread. The kingdom's resistance created difficulties for Ashoka because Kalinga controlled the principal trade routes, both by land and by sea, between the Ganges plain and southern South Asia. Thus Ashoka's first major undertaking as emperor was to conquer Kalinga and bring it under Mauryan control, which he did in a bloody campaign in 260 B.C.E. By Ashoka's estimate, 100,000 Kalingans died in the fighting, 150,000 were driven from their homes, and untold numbers of others perished in the ruined land.

In spite of that campaign, Ashoka is much better known as an imperial administrator than as a conqueror. With Kalinga subdued, Ashoka ruled almost the entire subcontinent—only the southernmost region escaped his control—and he turned his attention to the responsible government of his realm. As heir to the administrative structure that Chandragupta and Kautalya had instituted, Ashoka ruled through a tightly organized bureaucracy. He established his capital at the fortified city of Pataliputra (near modern Patna), where a central administration developed policies for the whole empire. Pataliputra was a thriving and cosmopolitan city: the Greek ambassador Megasthenes, who we met at the start of this chapter, reported that a local committee looked after the interests of foreigners in the city—and also carefully observed their movements. Ashoka went to great pains to ensure that his local subordinates implemented his policies. A central treasury oversaw the efficient collection of taxes—a hallmark of Kautalya's influence—which supported legions of officials, accountants, clerks, soldiers, and other imperial employees. Ashoka communicated his policies throughout his realm by inscribing edicts in natural stone formations or on pillars that he ordered erected. In these declarations, known as the rock and pillar edicts, Ashoka issued imperial decrees but also encouraged his subjects to observe Buddhist values and expressed his intention to serve as a fair, just, and humane ruler.

As a result of Ashoka's policies, the various regions of South Asia became well integrated, and the subcontinent benefited from both an expanding economy and a stable government. Ashoka encouraged the expansion of agriculture—the foundation of the empire's wealth—by building irrigation systems. He encouraged trade by building roads, most notably a highway of more than 1,600 kilometers (1,000 miles) linking Pataliputra with Taxila, the chief political and commercial center of northern South Asia, which offered access to Bactria, Persia, and other points west. Ashoka also provided comforts for administrators, merchants, and other travelers by planting banyan trees to provide shade, digging wells, and establishing inns along the roads.

Decline of the Mauryan Empire Ashoka's policies did not long survive his rule, nor did his empire. Ashoka died in 232 B.C.E., and decline set in almost immediately. During its later years the Mauryan Empire suffered from acute financial and economic difficulties. The empire depended on a strong army and a large corps of officials to administer imperial policy. Salaries for both soldiers and bureaucrats were expensive: Megasthenes said that in times of peace, military forces spent their time in idleness and drinking bouts while continuing to draw their pay. Eventually, those administrative costs outstripped the revenues that flowed into the central treasury. The later Mauryan emperors often resorted to the tactic of debasing their currency—reducing the amount of precious metal in a coin without reducing its nominal value. Because of their financial difficulties, they were unable to hold the realm together. They maintained control of the Ganges Valley for some fifty years after Ashoka's death, but eventually they lost their grip even on this heartland of the Mauryan Empire. By about 185 B.C.E. the Mauryan Empire had disappeared.

Kautalya (KAHT-ahl-yah)

Arthashastra (UHRR-tha-sha-strah)

Ashoka (ah-SHOW-kuh)

Imperial Fragmentation and Revival

The Greco-Bactrian Kingdom

Although the Mauryan Empire came to an end, the South Asian subcontinent did not crumble into anarchy. Instead, local rulers formed a series of kingdoms that brought order to large regions. Although regional kingdoms emerged throughout the subcontinent, historical records and archaeological excavations have thrown clearest light on developments in the north of the subcontinent. For almost two centuries after the collapse of the Mauryan Empire, much of the north fell under the rule of Greek-speaking conquerors from Bactria—Alexander of Macedon's imperial heirs who had mingled with local populations since establishing an independent Greco-Bactrian kingdom in ca. 250 B.C.E. Indo-Greek forces marched southward as early as 182 B.C.E. and seized a large territory extending as far south as Gujarat. Bactria—essentially the region of modern Afghanistan—was a thriving commercial center linking lands from China in the east to the Mediterranean basin in the west, so Bactrian rule had the effect of promoting cross-cultural interaction and exchange in the northern regions of South Asia. Large volumes of trade provided sources of revenue for the Bactrian rulers, and the city of Taxila flourished because of its strategic location on trade routes leading from northern South Asia to Bactria. The region of Gandhara became a site of intense cultural as well as commercial exchange.

The Kushan Empire

Beginning in the late second century B.C.E., several groups of nomadic conquerors from central Asia attacked Bactria and eventually put an end to the Greco-Bactrian kingdom there. The most successful of those conquerors were the Kushans, who, during the first century B.C.E., created an enormous Inner Asian empire. Under Kanishka, the most prominent of the Kushan kings (reigned 127–153 C.E.), the **Kushan empire** included modern-day Pakistan, Afghanistan, parts of Uzbekistan and Tajikistan, and northern South Asia to the central part of the Ganges Valley.

Like the Greco-Bactrians, the Kushans facilitated commerce throughout Eurasia. Indeed, the Kushan empire played a crucial role in the Silk Roads network (discussed in chapter 12) by pacifying much of the large region between Persia and China, thus making it possible for merchants to travel safely across long distances. Participation in extensive networks

As a symbol of his rule, Ashoka had this sculpture of four lions mounted atop a column about 20 meters (66 feet) tall. The lion capital is the official symbol of the modern Republic of South Asia. Why might modern South Asian peoples still want their nation to be associated with the empire of Ashoka, an empire that disappeared more than twenty-two hundred years ago?

The Art Archive/Shutterstock

enabled Kushan rulers to serve as cultural intermediaries. They generously patronized Bactrian and South Asian artists who employed Greek styles of painting and sculpture. Because many of the Kushan kings were enthusiastic supporters of Buddhism, they commissioned the artists of the so-called Gandharan and Mathuran traditions to create the first-ever depictions of the Buddha, which was a crucial development in facilitating the spread of Buddhism from South Asia into central and east Asia. Following the collapse of the Kushans in the mid-third century C.E., a series of kingdoms appeared in the Indus and Ganges valleys that jostled for local power. It was only with the advent of the Guptas in the mid-fourth century that a genuine and realistic attempt to recreate the empire of the Mauryas emerged.

The Gupta Dynasty

Like the Mauryas, the Guptas based their state in Magadha, a crucial region because of its wealth, its dominance of the Ganges Valley, and its role as intermediary between the various regions of the subcontinent. The new empire arose on foundations laid by Chandra Gupta (not related to Chandragupta Maurya), who forged alliances with powerful families in the Ganges region and established a dynamic kingdom about the year 320 C.E. His successors, Samudra Gupta (reigned 335–375 C.E.) and Chandra Gupta II (reigned 375–415 C.E.), made the Magadhan capital of Pataliputra once again the center of a large empire. Between the two of them, Samudra Gupta and Chandra Gupta II conquered many of the regional kingdoms of South Asia, and they established tributary alliances with others that elected not to fight. Only the Deccan Plateau and the southernmost part of the subcontinent remained outside the orbit of Gupta influence.

As shown in Map 9.1, the Gupta Empire was somewhat smaller in size than the Mauryan, and it also differed considerably in organization. Ashoka had insisted on knowing the details of regional affairs, which he closely monitored from his court at Pataliputra. The Guptas left local government and administration, and even the making of basic regional policy, in the hands of their allies in the various regions of their empire. When nomadic invaders threatened the empire during the later fifth century C.E., it split easily along the fault lines of the administrative regions. During the late fourth and early fifth centuries C.E., however, the Gupta dynasty brought stability and prosperity to the subcontinent.

Ruins of a pillared hall at the archaeological site at Pataliputra.
Historic Collection/Alamy Stock Photo

A Chinese Buddhist monk named Faxian traveled widely in South Asia searching for texts of the Buddhist scriptures during the reign of Chandra Gupta II. In an account of his travels, Faxian reported that South Asia was a prosperous land with little crime. It was possible to travel throughout the country, he said, without fear for one's safety and even without official travel documents.

Science and Mathematics Under conditions of political stability, Gupta prosperity sustained the work of scholars and enabled them to lay the foundations for sophisticated studies in the natural sciences and mathematics. South Asian physicians developed techniques of plastic surgery, and astronomers determined that the earth is a sphere that rotates on its axis. Most influential of the scholars were the mathematicians. Advanced mathematics was possible because South Asian numerals included a symbol for zero, which facilitates adoption of a place-value notation system, which in turn expedites mathematical computations. It is much simpler to multiply 19×84, for example, than XIX × LXXXIV. With their flexible numerals and their system of place-value notation, South Asian mathematicians were able to carry out advanced algebraic calculations and anticipate the invention of calculus. South Asian mathematicians calculated the value of *pi* to 3.1416 and the length of the solar year to 365.3586805 days. In the eighth century, Arab and Persian scholars encountered South Asian mathematics and readily adopted what they called "Hindi numerals (including the concept of zero)," which Europeans later termed "Arabic numberal" because they learned of them through Arab Muslims.

Gupta Decline Gupta administrative talents and cultural creativity were not a match, however, for the invasions of the **White Huns,** a nomadic people from central Asia who occupied Bactria during the fourth century C.E., and then prepared to cross the Hindu Kush mountains into the subcontinent. For the first half of the fifth century, the Guptas repelled the Huns, but the defense cost them dearly in resources and eventually weakened their state. By the end of the fifth century, the Huns moved across the Hindu Kush almost at will and established several kingdoms in the Indus and Ganges valleys.

The Gupta dynasty continued in name only: regional governors progressively usurped imperial rights and powers, and contemporary documents do not even record the names of all the later Gupta emperors. Once again, imperial government survived only for a short term in South Asia. Not until the establishment of the Mughal dynasty in the sixteenth century C.E. did any state rule as much of modern India as the Mauryan and Gupta empires ruled. Memories of empire remained, to be sure, and there were periodic efforts to bring all of the subcontinent again under the control of a unified regime. But for the most part, large regional kingdoms dominated political life in South Asia during the millennium between the Gupta and the Mughal dynasties.

ECONOMIC AND SOCIAL DEVELOPMENTS IN SOUTH ASIA

As we saw in a chapter 4, after migrating from Central Asia into South Asia, Indo-Aryan migrants turned increasingly from herding to agriculture. After about 1000 B.C.E., when they learned the techniques of iron metallurgy, they used iron axes and tools to advance into regions previously inaccessible to them, notably the jungle-covered valley of the Ganges River. The Indo-Aryans dispatched shudras, semifree serfs, to work in recently cleared fields, and from fertile lands they reaped large harvests. Agricultural surpluses supported the large-scale states such as the regional kingdoms and the Mauryan and Gupta empires that organized South Asian public life. Agricultural surpluses also encouraged the emergence of towns, the growth of trade, and further development of the caste system.

Towns and Trade

Towns and Manufacturing After about 600 B.C.E. towns dotted much of the South Asian countryside, especially in the northwestern corner of the subcontinent. These towns served the needs of a productive agricultural society by providing manufactured products for local consumption—pots, textiles, iron tools, and other metal utensils—as well as luxury goods such as jewelry destined for the wealthy and elite classes. Demand for manufactured products was very high, and some entrepreneurs organized businesses on a large scale. During Mauryan times, for example, a pottery manufacturer named Saddalaputta owned about five hundred workshops, whose products he distributed throughout the Ganges Valley in his fleet of boats.

Flourishing towns maintained marketplaces and encouraged the development of trade. Within the subcontinent itself trade was most active along the Ganges River, although trade routes also passed through the Ganges delta east to Burma and down the east coast to the Deccan and southern regions beyond. Roads built by Ashoka also facilitated overland commerce within the subcontinent.

Long-Distance Trade Meanwhile, the volume of long-distance trade also grew as large imperial states in China, southwest Asia, and the Mediterranean basin provided a political foundation enabling merchants to deal with their counterparts in distant lands. Direct political and military links with foreign peoples drew South Asians into long-distance commercial relations. Beginning with Cyrus, the Achaemenid rulers of Persia coveted the wealth of the subcontinent and included the northern kingdom of Gandhara as a province of their empire. The presence of Persian administrators in South Asia and the building of roads between Persia and the subcontinent facilitated commerce between the two lands. Alexander of Macedon's conquests helped to establish even more extensive trade networks by forging links between South Asia and the Mediterranean basin by way of Bactria, Persia, and Anatolia.

Long-distance trade passed overland in two directions: through the Hindu Kush mountains and the Gandharan capital of Taxila to Persia and the Mediterranean basin, and across the Silk Roads of central Asia to markets in China. Cotton, aromatics, black pepper, pearls, and gems were the principal South Asian exports, which were traded for imported horses and bullion from western lands and silk from China.

Trade in the Indian Ocean Basin During the Mauryan era merchants continued to use land routes, but they increasingly turned to the sea to transport their goods. Seaborne trade benefited especially from the rhythms of the monsoon winds that govern weather and the seasons in the Indian Ocean basin. During the spring and summer the winds blow from the southwest, and during the fall and winter they come from the northeast. Once mariners recognized these rhythms, they could sail easily and safely before the wind to any part of the Indian Ocean basin.

As early as the fifth century B.C.E., South Asian merchants had traveled to the islands of Indonesia and the southeast Asian mainland, where they exchanged pearls, cotton, black pepper, and South Asian manufactured goods for spices and exotic local products. Many of those goods did not remain in the subcontinent but, instead, traveled west through the Arabian Sea to the lands bordering the Persian Gulf and the Red Sea. South Asian products also found markets in the Mediterranean basin. Pepper became so popular there that the Romans established direct commercial relations and built several trading settlements along the coasts of the subcontinent. Archaeologists working in southern South Asia have unearthed hoards of Roman coins that testify to the large volume of trade between ancient South Asia and Mediterranean basin.

Family Life and the Caste System

Gender Relations In the midst of urban growth and economic development, South Asian moralists sought to promote stability by encouraging respect for strong patriarchal families and to promote the maintenance of a social order in which all

How the Past Shapes the Future

Long-Distance Trade Networks

The long-distance trade networks of ancient Afro-Eurasia allowed the introduction of foodstuffs and commodities to regional cuisines thousands of miles from their points of origin. South Asian black pepper was one of the most sought-after items in these long-distance networks and was traded over the land routes to central Asia and China as well as over sea routes to the Mediterranean and southeast Asia. At the time, pepper was used for far more than as a condiment to enliven dull food. It was an important preservative for meat and was also used for its medicinal properties to alleviate stomach and other ailments. What might have been the long-term impact of the introduction of pepper as a preservative across Eurasia?

members played well-defined roles. Most people lived with members of their nuclear family. Particularly among higher castes, however, several generations of a family often lived in large compounds ruled by powerful patriarchs.

Literary works offer an ambiguous portrait of prevailing attitudes toward women. In particular the two great South Asian epics, the *Mahabharata* and the *Ramayana,* provide contradictory portrayals of women as sometimes powerful individuals, but other times less independent and solely devoted to their husbands. Historians have sometimes struggled to interpret the depictions of women in these epic texts and, indeed, in references to the status of women more generally in ancient literature. On the one hand, they seem to paint an "idealized" picture of a perfect husband and wife relationship in which each complements the other. On the other hand, these same portraits have often been used by conservative moralists to sanction the subordination of women to male interests. In the *Ramayana,* for example, the beautiful Sita loyally followed her husband Rama into undeserved exile in a wild forest and remained faithful to him even during a long separation.

During the early centuries C.E., patriarchal dominance became more pronounced in South Asian societies. By the Gupta era, child marriage was common: when girls were age eight or nine, their parents betrothed them to men in their twenties. Formal marriage took place just after the girls reached puberty. Wives often came to dominate domestic affairs in their households, but the practice of child marriage placed them under the control of older men and encouraged them to devote themselves to family matters rather than to public affairs in the larger society.

Social Order After their arrival in South Asia, the Indo-Aryans recognized four main castes or classes of people: **brahmins** (priests), **kshatriyas** (warriors and aristocrats), **vaishyas** (peasants and merchants), and **shudras** (serfs). Brahmins in particular endorsed this social order, which brought them honor, prestige, and sometimes considerable wealth as well. The growth of trade and the proliferation of industries, however, had deep implications for the larger structure of South Asian society because they encouraged further development of the caste system.

Buddhist art often depicted individuals as models of proper social relationships. Here a sculpture from a Buddhist temple at Karli, produced about the first century C.E., represents an ideal Buddhist married couple.
Satish Parashar/Shutterstock

Castes and Guilds As trade and industrial activity expanded, new groups of artisans, craftsmen, and merchants appeared, many of whom did not fit easily in the established structure. Individuals working in the same craft or trade usually joined together to form a guild, a corporate body that supervised prices and wages in a given industry and provided for the welfare of members and their families. Guild members lived in the same quarter of town; socialized with one another; intermarried; and cared for the group's widows, orphans, and poor.

In effect, the guilds functioned as subcastes, known as *jati,* based on occupation. In fact, *jati* assumed much of the responsibility for maintaining social order throughout the subcontinent. *Jati* regularly organized courts, through which they disciplined guild members, resolved differences, and regulated community affairs. Individuals who did not abide by group rules were liable to expulsion from the community. These outcastes then had to make their way through life—often by working as butchers, leather tanners, or undertakers or in other occupations deemed low and unclean—without the networks of support provided by *jati.* Thus South Asian guilds and *jati* performed services that central governments provided in other lands. The tendency for individuals and their families to associate closely with others of the same occupation remained a prominent feature of South Asian society well into modern times.

Wealth and the Social Order Beyond encouraging further development of the caste system, economic development in the subcontinent generated tremendous wealth, which posed a serious challenge to the social order that arose in the region following the arrival of the Indo-Aryans. Traditional social theory accorded special honor to the brahmins and the kshatriyas because of the worthy lives they had led during previous incarnations and the heavy responsibilities they

---

Mahabharata (mah-hah-BAH-rah-tah)
Ramayana (rah-mah-yah-nah)
kshatriyas (ke-shat-ri-yas)

Jewel-bedecked flying goddesses drop flowers on the earth from their perch in the heavens. Their gems and personal adornments reflect the tastes of upper-class women during the Gupta dynasty. This painting on a rock wall, produced about the sixth century C.E., survives in modern Sri Lanka.

Pep Roig/Alamy Stock Photo

assumed as priests, warriors, and rulers during their current incarnations. Members of the vaishya and shudra castes, on the other hand, merited no special respect but, rather, had the obligation to work as directed by the higher castes. During the centuries after 600 B.C.E., however, trade and industry brought prosperity to many vaishyas and even shudras, who sometimes became wealthier and more influential in society than their brahmin and kshatriya contemporaries.

Economic development and social change in ancient South Asia had profound implications for the established cultural as well as the social order. The beliefs, values, and rituals that were meaningful in early Indo-Aryan society seemed increasingly irrelevant during the centuries after 600 B.C.E. All these developments—the emergence of towns, the expansion of trade contacts with other regions, and the increasing wealth of a commercial middle class—profoundly influenced spiritual beliefs and practices in South Asia, leading to the emergence of new regions that better addressed the needs of the people in these changing times.

A painting produced in the sixth century C.E. in the Ajanta caves of central South Asia depicts individuals of different castes, *jati,* and ethnic groups in a crowd scene.

PhotosIndia.com/age fotostock

THE EMERGENCE OF RELIGIONS OF SALVATION IN SOUTH ASIA

Ancient South Asian religion revolved around ritual sacrifices offered by brahmin priests in hopes that the gods would reward their loyal human servants with large harvests and abundant herds. Because the brahmins performed services deemed crucial for the survival of society, they enjoyed exemption from taxation. They also received hefty fees and generous gifts in return for their services. As the South Asian economy developed, however, these services seemed less meaningful, especially to the newly wealthy classes of merchants and artisans. Many of these individuals came from the lower castes, and they resented the brahmins' pretensions to superiority.

During the sixth and fifth centuries B.C.E., new religions and philosophies emerged that rejected the brahmins' traditions and appealed to the interests of new social classes. One new philosophy—that of the **Charvaka** sect—argued that the gods were figments of the imagination, that brahmins were charlatans who enriched themselves by fooling others, and that humans came from dust and returned to dust like any other animal in the natural world. The Charvakas' beliefs clearly reflected the increasingly materialistic character of South Asian society and economy. Others, such as the Jains, the Buddhists, and the Hindus, turned to intense spirituality as an alternative to the mechanical rituals of the brahmins.

Jainism and the Challenge to the Established Cultural Order

Vardhamana Mahavira Among the most influential of the new religions was **Jainism.** Although Jainist doctrines first appeared during the seventh century B.C.E., they became popular only when the great teacher **Vardhamana Mahavira** turned to Jainism in the late sixth century B.C.E. Mahavira ("the great hero") was born in about 540 B.C.E. to a prominent kshatriya family. According to the semilegendary accounts of his life, he left home at the age of thirty to seek salvation by escaping from the cycle of incarnation. For twelve years he led an ascetic life wandering throughout the Ganges Valley, after which he gained enlightenment. He abandoned all his worldly goods, even his clothes, and taught an ascetic doctrine of detachment from the world. For the next thirty years, until his death about 468 B.C.E., he expounded his thought to a group of dedicated disciples who formed a monastic order to perpetuate and spread his message. These disciples referred to Mahavira as *Jina* ("the conqueror"), and borrowing from this title his followers referred to themselves as *Jains.*

Much of the inspiration for Jainist doctrine came from the Upanishads. Jains believed that virtually everything in the universe—humans, animals, plants, the air, bodies of water—possessed a soul. As long as they remained trapped in terrestrial bodies, these souls experienced both physical and psychological suffering. Only by purification from selfish behavior could souls gain release from their imprisonment, shed the burdens of karma that they had accumulated during their various incarnations, and attain a state of bliss.

Jainist Ethics Individuals underwent purification by observing the principle of **ahimsa,** or nonviolence to other living things or their souls. Devout Jain monks went to extremes to avoid harming the millions of souls they encountered each day. They swept the ground before them as they walked to avoid causing harm to invisible insects; they strained their drinking water through cloth filters to remove tiny animals they might unwittingly consume; they followed an abstemious and strictly vegetarian diet; they even wore masks and avoided making sudden movements so that they would not bruise or otherwise disturb the tiny souls inhabiting the surrounding air.

Jainist ethics were so demanding that few people other than devout monks could hope to observe them closely. The Jains believed that almost all occupations inevitably entailed violence of some kind: farming involved the killing of pests and the harvesting of living plants, for example, and crafts such as leather tanning depended on the slaughter of animals. Thus for most people Jainism was not a practical alternative to the religion of the brahmins.

Appeal of Jainism For certain groups, however, Jainism represented an attractive alternative to

Vardhamana Mahavira with one of his disciples. Representations of the early Jains often depicted them in the nude because of their rejection of material culture. Eleora Caves, South Asia, tenth century.
Stuart Forster India/Alamy Stock Photo

Charvaka (CHAHR-vah-kuh)
Jainism (JEYEN-iz'm)
Vardhamana Mahavira (vahr-duh-MAH-nuh ma-ha-VIR-uh)
ahimsa (uh-HIM-suh)

the traditional religious beliefs. Jainist values and ethics had significant social implications. If all creatures possessed souls and participated in the ultimate reality of the world, it made little sense to draw sharp distinctions between different classes of human beings. As a result, the Jains did not recognize social hierarchies based on *varna* or *jati*. It is not surprising, then, that their faith became popular especially among members of lower castes who did not command much respect in the traditional social order, including merchants, scholars, and literary figures. In a typical day, individuals in these classes did little overt violence to other creatures or their souls, and they appreciated the spiritual sensitivity and the high moral standards that Jainism encouraged. They provided financial and material support for the Jainist monks and helped to maintain the ideal of ahimsa as a prominent concern of South Asian ethics. Indeed, the doctrine of ahimsa has been an especially influential teaching over the long term, both in India and beyond. Quite apart from some four million South Asian individuals who maintain Jainist traditions in the present day, many Buddhists and Hindus recognize ahimsa as a fundamental element of their beliefs, and prominent reformers of the twentieth century C.E. such as Mohandas K. Gandhi and Martin Luther King Jr., relied on the doctrine of ahimsa when promoting social reform by nonviolent means.

In spite of the moral respect it has commanded and the influence it has wielded through the centuries, however, Jainism has always been the faith of a small minority. It has simply been too difficult—or even impossible—for most people to observe. A more popular and practical alternative to the brahmins' beliefs and rituals came in the form of Buddhism.

Early Buddhism

Siddhartha Gautama Like Mahavira, the founder of Buddhism came from a kshatriya family, but he gave up his position and inheritance in order to seek salvation. His name was **Siddhartha Gautama,** born about 563 B.C.E. in a small tribal state governed by his father in the foothills of the Himalayas. According to early accounts, Gautama lived a pampered and sheltered life in palaces and parks because his father had determined that Gautama would experience only happiness and would never know misery. He married his cousin and excelled in the program of studies that would prepare him to succeed his father as governor.

Eventually, however, Gautama became dissatisfied with his comfortable life. One day, according to legend, while riding toward a park in his chariot, Gautama saw a man made miserable by age and infirmity. When he asked for an explanation of this unsettling sight, Gautama learned from his chariot driver that all humans grow old and weak. On later outings Gautama saw a sick man and a corpse, from whose fates he learned that disease and death were also inevitable

A painting produced in the late fifth century C.E. depicts the Buddha seated under a pavilion as servants attend to his needs and anoint him with holy water.
NiKreative/Alamy Stock Photo

features of the human condition. Finally Gautama noticed a monk traveling by foot in his distinctive dress, and he learned that some individuals withdraw from the active life of the world to lead holy lives and to perfect their spiritual qualities. In light of the misery he had previously witnessed, Gautama considered the monk a noble character and determined to take up an ascetic, wandering life for himself in the hope that it would help him to understand the phenomenon of suffering. Though not a strictly historical account, this story conveys well the Buddhist concern with suffering.

Gautama's Search for Enlightenment About 534 B.C.E. Gautama left his wife, his family, and the comforts of home to lead the existence of a holy man. He wandered throughout the Ganges Valley searching for spiritual enlightenment and an explanation for suffering. He survived for a while by begging for his food but then abandoned society altogether to live as a hermit. He sought enlightenment first by means of intense meditation and later through the rigors of extreme asceticism. None of those tactics satisfied him. Then, according to Buddhist legends, as he sat one day beneath a large bo tree in **Bodh Gaya,** southwest of Pataliputra, Gautama decided that he would remain exactly where he was until he understood the problem of suffering. For forty-nine days he sat in meditation as various demons tempted him with pleasures and threatened him with terrors in efforts to shake his resolution. Eventually the demons withdrew, and Gautama prevailed. After forty-nine days under the bo tree, he received enlightenment: he understood both the problem of suffering and the means by which humans could eliminate it from the world. At that point, Gautama became the Buddha—"the enlightened one."

The Buddha and His Followers The Buddha publicly announced his doctrine for the first time about 528 B.C.E. at the **Deer Park of Sarnath,** near the city of Banaras (modern Varanasi), in a sermon delivered to friends who had formerly been his companions in asceticism. Buddhists refer to this sermon as the "Turning of the Wheel of the Law" because it represented the beginning of the Buddha's quest to promulgate the law of righteousness. His teachings quickly attracted attention, and disciples came from all parts of the Ganges Valley. He organized them into a community of monks who owned only their yellow robes and their begging bowls. They traveled on foot, preaching the Buddha's doctrine and seeking handouts for their meals. For more than forty years, the Buddha led his disciples throughout much of northern South Asia in hopes of bringing spiritual enlightenment to others. About 483 B.C.E., at an age of some eighty years, he died after leaving his companions with a final message: "All component things age and decay. Work hard to gain your own salvation."

Buddhist Doctrine: The Dharma The core of the Buddha's doctrine, known as the **Four Noble Truths,** teaches that all life involves suffering, that desire is the cause of suffering, that elimination of desire brings an end to suffering, and that a disciplined life conducted in accordance with the **Noble Eightfold Path** brings the elimination of desire. The Noble Eightfold Path calls for individuals to lead balanced and moderate lives, rejecting both the devotion to luxury often found in human society and the regimes of extreme asceticism favored by hermits and Jains. Specifically, the Noble Eightfold Path demands right belief, right resolve, right speech, right behavior, right occupation, right effort, right contemplation, and right meditation.

A moderate lifestyle characterized by quiet contemplation, thoughtful reflection, and disciplined self-control would enable Buddhists to reduce their desires for material goods and other worldly attractions, resulting eventually in detachment from the world itself. Ultimately, they believed that this lifestyle would lead them to personal salvation, which for Buddhists meant escape from the cycle of incarnation and attainment of **nirvana,** a state of perfect spiritual independence. Taken together, the teachings of the Four Noble Truths and the Noble Eightfold Path constitute the Buddhist **dharma**—the basic doctrine shared by Buddhists of all sects.

Appeal of Buddhism Like the Jains, the Buddhists sought to escape the cycle of incarnation without depending on the services of the brahmins. Like the Jains, too, they did not recognize social distinctions based on caste or *jati*. As a result, their message also appealed strongly to members of lower castes. Because it was not as demanding as Jainism, Buddhism became far more popular. Merchants were especially prominent in the ranks of the early Buddhists, and they often used Buddhist monasteries as inns when they traveled in the subcontinent.

Apart from the social implications of the doctrine, there were several other reasons for the immense popularity of early Buddhism in South Asia. One has to do with language. Following the example of the Buddha himself, early Buddhist monks and preachers avoided the use of Sanskrit, the literary language of the Vedas that the brahmins employed in their rituals, in favor of local dialects that reached a much larger popular audience. Furthermore, early Buddhists recognized holy sites that served as focal points for devotion. Even in the early days of Buddhism, pilgrims flocked to Bodh Gaya, where Gautama received enlightenment, and the Deer Park of Sarnath, where as the Buddha he preached his first sermon. Also popular with the faithful were **stupas**—shrines housing relics of the Buddha and his first disciples that pilgrims venerated while meditating on Buddhist values.

Yet another reason for the early popularity of Buddhism was the organization of the Buddhist movement. The most enthusiastic and highly motivated converts joined monastic communities where they dedicated their lives to the search for enlightenment and salvation. Later, gifts and grants from supporters provided for the land, buildings, finances, and material needs of the monasteries. The monks themselves spent much of their time preaching, explaining the dharma to audiences, and encouraging their listeners to follow the Noble Eightfold Path in their daily lives. Over time, Buddhist monasteries became important institutions in South Asian society. They served as banks for their communities, and they helped organize life in the South Asian countryside by allocating their lands to individuals or groups of cultivators. Thus, during the centuries following the Buddha's death, monasteries wielded enormous social and economic as well as cultural influence throughout much of the northern subcontinent.

Ashoka's Support The early Buddhist movement also benefited from the official patronage and support of the Mauryan dynasty. The precise reason for Ashoka's conversion to Buddhism is unclear. Early legends held that a devout Buddhist monk brought about Ashoka's conversion by dazzling him with supernatural powers. Ashoka's own account, as

dharma (DHUHR-muh)

preserved in one of his edicts, explains that the emperor adopted Buddhism about 260 B.C.E. after the war against Kalinga, discussed earlier in this chapter. Saddened by the violence of the war and the suffering of the Kalingans, Ashoka said that he decided to pursue his aims henceforth by means of virtue, benevolence, and humanity rather than arms. Quite apart from his sincere religious convictions, it is likely that Ashoka found Buddhism appealing as a faith that could help unify his culturally diverse and far-flung realm. In any case, in honor of ahimsa, the doctrine of nonviolence, Ashoka banned animal sacrifices in Pataliputra, gave up his beloved hunting expeditions, and eliminated most meat dishes from the tables of his court. Ashoka rewarded Buddhists with grants of land, and he encouraged them to spread their faith throughout the empire.

He built monasteries and stupas and made pilgrimages to the holy sites of Buddhism. Ashoka also sent missionaries to Bactria and Ceylon (modern Sri Lanka), thus inaugurating a process by which Buddhism attracted large followings in central Asia, east Asia, and southeast Asia.

Mahayana Buddhism

From its earliest days Buddhism attracted merchants, artisans, and others of low rank in the traditional South Asian social order. Its appeal was due both to its disregard for social classes and to its concern for ethical behavior instead of complicated ceremonies that seemed increasingly irrelevant to the lives and experiences of most people. Even though it vastly

The Buddhist stupa at Sanchi, originally built by Ashoka and enlarged in later times, is a domed shrine—representing the dome of heaven over the earth—intended to contain sacred relics of the Buddha. The shrine is flanked by four entry gateways carved with scenes from the Buddha's life.

Luca Tettoni/robertharding/Getty Images

simplified religious observances, early Buddhism still made heavy demands on individuals seeking to escape from the cycle of incarnation. A truly righteous existence involved considerable sacrifice: giving up personal property and the desire for social standing, and resolutely detaching oneself from the charms of family and the world. The earliest Buddhists thought that numerous physical incarnations, stretching over thousands of years, might be necessary before an individual soul would become pure enough to achieve salvation and pass into nirvana. Though perhaps more attractive than the religion of the brahmins, Buddhism did not promise to make life easy for its adherents.

Development of Buddhism Between the third century B.C.E. and the first century C.E., however, three new developments in Buddhist thought and practice reduced obligations of believers, opened new avenues to salvation, and brought explosive popularity to the faith. In the first place, whereas the Buddha had not considered himself divine, some of his later followers began to worship him as a god. Thus Buddhism acquired a devotional focus that helped converts channel their spiritual energies and identify more closely with their faith. In the second place, theologians articulated the notion of the *bodhisattva* ("an enlightened being"). **Bodhisattvas** were individuals who had reached spiritual perfection and merited the reward of nirvana, but who intentionally delayed their entry into nirvana to help others who were still struggling. Some theologians taught that bodhisattvas could even perform good deeds on behalf of their less spiritually inclined brethren. Like Christian saints, bodhisattvas served as examples of spiritual excellence, and they provided a source of inspiration. Finally, Buddhist monasteries began to accept gifts from wealthy individuals and to regard the bequests as acts of generosity that merited salvation. Thus wealthy individuals could enjoy the comforts of the world, avoid the sacrifices demanded by early Buddhist teachings, and still ensure their salvation.

The Spread of Mahayana Buddhism Because these innovations opened the road to salvation for large numbers of people, their proponents called their faith the **Mahayana** ("the greater vehicle," which could carry more people to salvation), as opposed to the **Hinayana** ("the lesser vehicle"), a pejorative term for the earlier and stricter doctrine known also as Theravada Buddhism. During the early centuries C.E., Mahayana Buddhism spread rapidly throughout the subcontinent and

King Ashoka erected many stone pillars such as this handsome column, which stands 10 meters (32 feet) tall, to promote Buddhist teachings, direct travelers to holy sites, or commemorate significant events of the Buddha's life. Why might Ashoka have chosen the lion to symbolize his leadership and power?
dinodia/123RF

attracted many converts from lay and wealthy classes. In later centuries Mahayana Buddhism became established also in central Asia, China, Japan, and Korea. The stricter Theravada faith did not disappear: it remained the dominant school of Buddhism in Ceylon, and in later centuries it spread also to Burma, Thailand, and other parts of southeast Asia. Since the first century C.E., however, most of the world's Buddhists have sought to ride the greater vehicle to salvation.

Nalanda Mahayana Buddhism flourished partly because of educational institutions that efficiently promoted the faith. During the Vedic era, South Asian education was mostly an informal affair involving a sage and his students. When Jains and Buddhists organized monasteries, however, they began to offer regular instruction and established educational institutions. Most monasteries provided basic education, and larger communities offered advanced instruction as well. Best known of all was the Buddhist monastery at Nalanda, founded during the Gupta dynasty in the Ganges River valley near Pataliputra. At Nalanda it was possible to study not only Buddhism but also the Vedas, Hindu philosophy, logic, mathematics, astronomy, and medicine. Nalanda soon became so famous as an educational center that pilgrims and students from foreign lands traveled there to study with the most renowned masters of Buddhist doctrine. By the end of the Gupta dynasty, several thousand students may have been in residence there.

Popular Hinduism

As Buddhism generated new ideas and attracted widespread popular interest, the traditional Vedic religion of South Asia underwent a similar evolution that transformed it into a popular religion of salvation known as Hinduism. While drawing inspiration from the Vedas and the Upanishads, popular Hinduism increasingly departed from the older traditions of the brahmins. Like Mahayana Buddhism, Hinduism experienced changes in doctrine and observances that resulted in a faith that addressed the interests and met the needs of ordinary people.

The Epics The great epic poems, the *Mahabharata* and the *Ramayana,* illustrate the development of Hindu values. Both works originated as secular tales transmitted orally during the

bodhisattvas (BOH-dih-SAT-vuhs)
Mahayana (mah-huh-YAH-nah)

late years of the Vedic age (1500–500 B.C.E.). Brahmin scholars revised them and committed them to writing probably during the early centuries C.E. The *Mahabharata* dealt with a bloody civil war for the control of northern South Asia between two groups of cousins. Though originally a purely secular work, the brahmins made a prominent place in the poem for the god **Vishnu,** the preserver of the world who intervened frequently on behalf of virtuous individuals.

The *Ramayana* was originally a love and adventure story involving the trials faced by the legendary Prince Rama and his loyal wife, Sita. Rama went to great lengths to rescue Sita after the demon king of Ceylon kidnapped her, and his alliance with Hanuman,

Gold coin of Kanishka I showing on the left the king sacrificing herbs over a small Zoroastrian fire altar, and on the right an image of the Buddha, labeled BODDO.

Heritage Image Partnership Ltd/Alamy Stock Photo

general of the monkeys, led to exciting clashes with his enemies. Later brahmin editors made Rama an incarnation of Vishnu, and they portrayed Rama and Sita as the ideal Hindu husband and wife, devoted and loyal to each other even in times of immense difficulty.

The *Bhagavad Gita* A short poetic work known as the ***Bhagavad Gita*** ("song of the lord") best illustrates both the expectations that Hinduism made of individuals and the promise of salvation that it held out to them. The *Gita* was the work of many hands, and the date of its composition is uncertain. Scholars have placed it at various points between 300 B.C.E. and 300 C.E., and it most likely underwent several rounds of revision before taking on its final form about 400 C.E. Yet it eloquently evokes the cultural climate of South Asia between the Mauryan and the Gupta dynasties.

Vishnu (VISH-noo)
Bhagavad Gita (BUH-guh-vahd GEE-tuh)

What's Left Out?

In the chapter, we discussed how early forms of Buddhism evolved into the more accessible Mahayana (Great Vehicle) school during the second century C.E. It was this version that spread via the Silk Roads out of South Asia through Central Asia and eventually to China, Japan, Korea, and Southeast Asia. One of the most powerful of the Kushan rulers, King Kanishka, who reigned from c. 127–153 C.E., may well have played a significant role in this major diffusion of Buddhism. Although his coins demonstrate that he was personally devoted to Iranian gods, other evidence—including coins, sculpture, and Chinese texts—suggests he was also an important promoter of Buddhism. Prior to the Kushan empire, the Buddha had never been depicted in human form, but during the reign of Kanishka, sculptors in Gandhara and Mathura begin to carve images of the Buddha for the first time. The image used at the start of this chapter is an example of the Buddhist art of Gandhara produced under Kanishka. The Buddha also features on a small selection of Kanishka's coins, including some magnificent gold coins.

The Chinese texts state that Kanishka wished to learn more about the meaning of Buddhism, so he convened a great gathering of Buddhist leaders in Kashmir, deep inside the vast Kushan empire. Following weeks of debate, these leaders apparently agreed on a new and more accurate interpretation of Buddhism, which evolved to become the Mahayana school. Kanishka commissioned poets to compose the new scriptures in flowing verse, which he then had engraved on copper sheets that were housed in a stone container suspended inside a massive new stupa he had constructed. Later Chinese Buddhist pilgrims who passed through former Kushan territory long after the empire had ceased to exist wrote that the ruins of the stupa were still incredibly impressive and that it was the tallest building in Central Asia.

As with Ashoka, if the story is true, Kanishka's reasons for promoting Buddhism in his realm are difficult to determine, although the texts suggest it had a great deal to do with his personal salvation. Like Ashoka, Kanishka had been responsible for the deaths of many people in his lifetime, and he asked his religious advisers whether his adoption of Buddhism could expunge his sins, just like pouring cold water into a hot cauldron. Despite the apparently skeptical response of his advisers, the texts suggest that following his death Kanishka's journey toward Nirvana was indeed able to continue. Whatever his reasons for promoting the faith, the role of Kanishka in helping spread Mahayana Buddhism out of South Asia and on to the east was of enormous significance. It helped ensure that millions of people across vast regions of Eurasia were eventually connected together through their adherence to this single spiritual ideology.

Source: Craig Benjamin, "The Great Deliverer, the Righteous, the Just, the Autocrat, the God, Worthy of Worship: Kanishka I, Kushan Dynastic Religion, and Buddhism," in M. Gervers and G. Long, eds., *Toronto Studies in Central and Inner Asia,* vol. X, Toronto: University of Toronto Press, 2013, pp. 19–45 (peer reviewed).

SOURCES FROM THE PAST

Ashoka Adopts and Promotes Buddhism

Ashoka, grandson of Chandragupta and the greatest of all Mauryan rulers, spent the early part of his reign consolidating and expanding the Mauryan Empire through waging war. After a particularly bloody campaign against the large eastern state of Kalinga, Ashoka, apparently sickened by the violence, adopted Buddhism and promoted it throughout the empire. He then communicated his reasons for adopting Buddhism, and his imperial policies, by having edicts carved in natural stone or on pillars that were erected all over his realm. In the 13th Major Rock Edict below, Ashoka explains the reasons for his renunciation of violence and his adoption of Buddhism (which he calls Dhamma).

13th Major Rock Edict of Ashoka. Beloved-of-the-Gods, King Piyadasi, conquered the Kalingas eight years after his coronation. One hundred and fifty thousand were deported, one hundred thousand were killed and many more died (from other causes). After the Kalingas had been conquered, Beloved-of-the-Gods came to feel a strong inclination towards the *Dhamma*, a love for the *Dhamma* and for instruction in *Dhamma*. Now Beloved-of-the-Gods feels deep remorse for having conquered the Kalingas.

> What is meant by the term *Dhamma* here?

Indeed, Beloved-of-the-Gods is deeply pained by the killing, dying and deportation that take place when an unconquered country is conquered. But Beloved-of-the-Gods is pained even more by this—that Brahmans, ascetics, and householders of different religions who live in those countries, and who are respectful to superiors, to mother and father, to elders, and who behave properly and have strong loyalty towards friends, acquaintances, companions, relatives, servants and employees—that they are injured, killed or separated from their loved ones. Even those who are not affected (by all this) suffer when they see friends, acquaintances, companions and relatives affected. These misfortunes befall all (as a result of war), and this pains Beloved-of-the-Gods.

There is no country, except among the Greeks, where these two groups, Brahmans and ascetics, are not found, and there is no country where people are not devoted to one or another religion. Therefore the killing, death or deportation of a hundredth, or even a thousandth part of those who died during the conquest of Kalinga now pains Beloved-of-the-Gods. Now Beloved-of-the-Gods thinks that even those who do wrong should be forgiven where forgiveness is possible. . . .

I have had this Dhamma edict written so that my sons and great-grandsons may not consider making new conquests, or that if military conquests are made, that they be done with forbearance and light punishment, or better still, that they consider making conquest by Dhamma only, for that bears fruit in this world and the next. May all their intense devotion be given to this, which has a result in this world and the next.

> What advice is Ashoka giving to future rulers and military leaders?

For Further Reflection

■ What are some of the reasons Ashoka feels guilty about his success in this military campaign?
■ Why would Ashoka make his personal feelings so public through having this rock edict erected?
■ What message is he trying to send to his subjects via this edict?

Source: Dhammika Ven. S., trans. *The Wheel Publication,* no. 386/387. Kandy Sri Lanka: Buddhist Publication Society, 1993. Copyright 1993 Ven. S. Dhammika. DharmaNet Edition 1994. Electronic edition offered for free distribution via DharmaNet by arrangement with the publisher. DharmaNet International P.O. Box 4951, Berkeley CA 94704-4951.

The work is a self-contained episode of the *Mahabharata.* It presents a dialogue between Arjuna, a kshatriya warrior about to enter battle, and his charioteer **Krishna,** who was in fact a human incarnation of the god Vishnu. The immediate problem addressed in the work was Arjuna's reluctance to fight: the enemy included many of his friends and relatives, and even though he recognized the justice of his cause, he shrank from the conflict. In an effort to persuade the warrior to fight, Krishna presented Arjuna with several lines of argument. In the first place, he said, Arjuna must not worry

A tenth-century sculptural representation of three of the major Hindu gods, from left to right, Vishnu (preserver), Shiva (destroyer), and Brahma (creator).
Gift of Ramesh and Urmil Kapoor/ Los Angeles County Museum of Art.

about harming his friends and relative because the soul does not die with the human body. Arjuna's weapons did not have the power to touch the soul, so he could never harm or kill another person in any meaningful way.

Krishna also argued that Arjuna's caste imposed specific moral duties and social responsibilities upon him. The duty of shudras was to serve, of vaishyas to work, of brahmins to learn the scriptures and seek wisdom. Similarly, the duty of kshatriyas was to govern and fight. Indeed, Krishna went further and held that an individual's social responsibilities had spiritual significance. He told Arjuna that failure to fulfill caste duties was a grievous sin, whereas their observance brought spiritual rewards.

Finally, Krishna taught that Arjuna would attain everlasting peace and blessedness if he devoted himself to the love, adoration, and service of Krishna himself. Arjuna should abandon his selfish and superficial personal concerns and surrender to the deeper wisdom of the god. As a reward, wholehearted worship would bring Arjuna eternal salvation through unity with his god. Alongside understanding of the soul and caste duties, then, unquestioning faith and devotion would put Arjuna in the proper state of mind for the looming conflict by aligning his actions with divine wisdom and will. Krishna's teaching that faith would bring salvation helped inspire a tradition of ecstatic and unquestioning devotion in popular Hinduism.

Hindu Ethics Hindu ethics thus differed considerably from those of earlier South Asian moralists. The Upanishads had taught that only through renunciation and detachment from the world could individuals escape the cycle of incarnation. As represented in the *Bhagavad Gita,* however, Hindu ethical teachings made life much easier for the embers of the lower castes by holding out the promise of salvation precisely to those who participated actively in the world and met their caste responsibilities. Krishna taught that individuals should not become personally or emotionally involved in their actions, and they especially should not strive for material reward or recognition. Rather, they should perform their duties faithfully, concentrating on their actions alone, with no thought as to their consequences.

Other works by early Hindu moralists acknowledged even more openly than did the *Bhagavad Gita* that individuals could lead honorable lives in the world. Indeed, Hindu ethics commonly recognized four principal aims of human life: *dharma* (obedience to religious and moral laws), **artha** (the pursuit of economic well-being and honest prosperity), **kama** (the enjoyment of social, physical, and sexual pleasure), and **moksha** (the salvation of the soul). According to Hindu morality a proper balance of *dharma, artha,* and *kama* would help an individual to attain *moksha.*

As devotional Hinduism evolved and became increasingly distinct from the teachings of the Upanishads and the older traditions of the brahmins, it also enhanced its appeal to all segments of South Asian society. Hinduism offered salvation to masses of people who, as a matter of practical necessity, had to lead active lives in the world and thus could not even hope to achieve the detachment envisioned in the Upanishads.

Popularity of Hinduism Hinduism gradually displaced Buddhism as the most popular religion in South Asia. Buddhism

SOURCES FROM THE PAST

Caste Duties According to the *Bhagavad Gita*

As we noted earlier in the chapter, the Bhagavad Gita *("song of the lord") is a short poetic work that illustrates the expectations that Hinduism made of individuals and also the promise of salvation that it held out to them. It is presented in the form of a dialogue between Arjuna, a kshatriya warrior who is reluctant to enter battle, and his charioteer Krishna, who was in fact a human incarnation of the god Vishnu. In urging Arjuna to enter battle, Krishna pointed out that Arjuna could not harm the immortal souls of his family and friends on the other side. Beyond that, however, Krishna emphasized the duty to fight that Arjuna inherited as a member of the kshatriya caste.*

As a man, casting off old clothes, puts on others and new ones, so the embodied self, casting off old bodies, goes to others and new ones. Weapons do not divide the self into pieces; fire does not burn it; waters do not moisten it; the wind does not dry it up. It is not divisible; it is not combustible; it is not to be moistened; it is not to be dried up. It is everlasting, all-pervading, stable, firm, and eternal. It is said to be unperceived, to be unthinkable, to be unchangeable. Therefore knowing it to be such, you ought not to grieve. But even if you think that the self is constantly born, and constantly dies, still, O you of mighty arms, you ought not to grieve thus. For to one that is born, death is certain; and to one that dies, birth is certain. Therefore about this unavoidable thing, you ought not to grieve. . . .

> According to Krishna, why is it pointless to grieve for the dead?

Having regard to your own duty, you ought not to falter, for there is nothing better for a kshatriya than a righteous battle. Happy those kshatriyas who can find such a battle—an open door to heaven! But if you will not fight this righteous battle, then you will have abandoned your own duty and your fame, and you will incur sin. All beings, too, will tell of your everlasting infamy; and to one who has been honored, infamy is a greater evil than death. Warriors who are masters of great chariots will think that you have abstained from the battle through fear, and having been highly thought of by them, you will fall down to littleness. Your enemies, too, decrying your power, will speak much about you that should not be spoken. And what, indeed, could be more lamentable than that? Killed, you will obtain heaven; victorious, you will enjoy the earth. Therefore arise, resolved to engage in battle. Looking on pleasure and pain, on gain and loss, on victory and defeat as the same, prepare for battle, and thus you will not incur sin. . . .

> What arguments is Krishna making to urge Arjuna not to shirk his duties in battle?

The state of mind that consists in firm understanding regarding steady contemplation does not belong to those who are strongly attached to worldly pleasures and power, and whose minds are drawn away by that flowery talk that is full of specific acts for the attainment of pleasures and power, and that promises birth as the fruit of actions—that flowery talk uttered by unwise ones who are enamored of Vedic words, who say there is nothing else, who are full of desires, and whose goal is heaven. . . .

Your business is with action alone, not by any means with the fruit of the action. Let not the fruit of action be your motive to action. Let not your attachment be fixed on inaction. Having recourse to devotion, perform actions, casting off all attachment, and being equable in success or ill success.

For Further Reflection

■ What attitude does Krishna urge Arjuna to adopt when performing his caste duties?

■ How does the approach of Krishna to warfare and battle compare to that of Ashoka in his 13th Rock Edict?

■ How do these reflections on caste duty compare to the arguments made by Confucius about the behavior of leaders, as discussed in chapter 5?

Source: The Bhagavad Gita. Trans. by Kashinath Trimbak Telang. In F. Max Müller, ed., *The Sacred Books of the East,* vol. 8. Oxford: Clarendon Press, 1908, pp. 45–48. (Translation slightly modified.)

remained strong through much of the first millennium C.E., and until about the eleventh century pilgrims traveled to South Asia from as far away as China to visit the holy sites of Buddhism and learn about the faith in its original homeland. Within South Asia, however, Buddhism grew remote from the popular masses. Later Buddhist monks did not seek to communicate their message to the larger society in the zealous way of their predecessors but increasingly confined themselves to the comforts of monasteries richly endowed by wealthy patrons.

Meanwhile, devotional Hinduism also attracted political support and patronage, particularly from the Gupta emperors.

The Guptas and their successors bestowed grants of land on Hindu brahmins and supported an educational system that promoted Hindu values. Just as Ashoka Maurya had advanced the cause of Buddhism, the Guptas and their successors later helped Hinduism become the dominant religious and cultural tradition in the subcontinent. By about 1000 C.E., Buddhism had entered a noticeable decline in South Asia while Hinduism grew in popularity. Within a few centuries devotional Hinduism and the more recently introduced faith of Islam almost completely eclipsed Buddhism in its homeland.

CONCLUSION

In South Asia, as in ancient Persia and China, a successful agricultural economy supported the creation of large-scale states and interregional trade. Although an imperial state did not become a permanent feature of South Asian political life, the peoples of the subcontinent maintained an orderly society based on the caste system and regional states. South Asian cultural and religious traditions reflected the conditions of the larger society in which they developed. Mahayana Buddhism and devotional Hinduism in particular addressed the needs of the increasingly prominent lay classes, and the two faiths profoundly influenced the religious life of Asian peoples over the long term of history.

STUDY TERMS

ahimsa (173)	Kautalya (167)
artha (180)	Krishna (179)
Arthashastra (167)	kshatriyas (171)
Ashoka (167)	Kushan empire (168)
Bhagavad Gita (178)	*Mahabharata* (171)
Bodh Gaya (175)	Mahayana Buddhism (177)
bodhisattva (177)	Mauryan dynasty (165)
brahmins (171)	*moksha* (180)
Chandragupta Maurya (166)	nirvana (175)
Charvaka (173)	Noble Eightfold Path (175)
Deer Park of Sarnath (175)	Pataliputra (165)
dharma (175)	*Ramayana* (171)
Four Noble Truths (175)	shudras (171)
Gandhara (166)	Siddhartha Gautama (174)
Gupta dynasty (165)	stupas (175)
Hinayana Buddhism (177)	vaishyas (171)
Jainism (173)	Vardhamana Mahavira (173)
jati (171)	Vishnu (178)
kama (180)	White Huns (169)

FOR FURTHER READING

Karen Armstrong. *Buddha*. New York, 2001. An accessible introduction to the Buddha by a prominent scholar of South Asian religions.

Jeannine Auboyer. *Daily Life in Ancient South Asia*. Trans. by S. W. Taylor. London, 2002. An excellent introduction to South Asian social history during the classical era.

A. L. Basham. *The Origins and Development of Classical Hinduism*. *Oxford,* 1989. Classic account of the origins and development of classical Hinduism by one of the world's leading ancient South Asian scholars.

William Theodore De Bary, ed. *Sources of South Asian Tradition*. 2 vols. 2nd ed. New York, 1988. Important collection of sources in translation.

Xinru Liu. *Ancient South Asia and Ancient China: Trade and Religious Exchanges, A.D. 1–600*. Delhi, 1988. Important study exploring the early spread of Buddhism from South Asia to central Asia and China.

Juan Mascaró, trans. *The Bhagavad Gita*. Harmondsworth, 1962. Brilliant and evocative English version by a gifted translator.

Upinder Singh and Nayanjot Lahiri. *Ancient India: New Research*. Oxford University Press, 2010. Important collection of new interpretations of aspects of ancient South Asian history—including gender, archaeology, religion, landscapes, and literature—by modern South Asian scholars.

John S. Strong. *The Legend of King Ashoka: A Study and Translation of the* Ashokavadana. Princeton, 1983. Valuable translation of an important early Buddhist account of King Ashoka's life and reign.

Romila Thapar. *Early South Asia: From the Origins to A.D. 1300*. Berkeley, 2003. A fresh view by one of the leading scholars of early South Asian history.

Stanley Wolpert. *A New History of South Asia*. 7th ed. New York, 2004. A concise and readable survey of South Asian history.

ZOOMING IN ON ENCOUNTERS

Homer: A Poet and the Sea

For a man who perhaps never existed, Homer has been a profoundly influential figure. According to tradition, Homer composed the two great epic poems of ancient Greece, the *Iliad* and the *Odyssey*. In fact, scholars now know that bards recited both poems for generations before Homer lived—the mid-eighth century B.C.E., if he was indeed a historical figure. Some experts believe that Homer was not a real man so much as a convenient name for several otherwise anonymous scribes who committed the *Iliad* and the *Odyssey* to writing. Others believe that a man named Homer had a part in preparing a written version of the epics but that others also contributed significantly to his work.

Whether Homer ever really lived or not, the epics attributed to him deeply influenced the development of ancient Greek thought and literature. The *Iliad* offered a Greek perspective on a campaign waged by a band of Greek warriors against the city of Troy in Anatolia (modern Turkey) during the twelfth century B.C.E. The *Odyssey* recounted the experiences of the Greek hero Odysseus as he sailed home after the Trojan war. The two works described scores of difficulties faced by Greek warriors—not only battles with Trojans but also challenges posed by deities and monsters, conflicts among themselves, and even psychological barriers that individuals had to surmount. Between them, the two epics preserved a rich collection of stories

An Athenian vase produced in the late fifth century B.C.E. depicts Odysseus and the sirens, in an episode from Homer's epic poem *The Odyssey*. Note the superbly constructed Greek ship powered by both sails and oars.
Universal Images Group/SuperStock

that literary figures have mined ever since, reworking Homer's material and exploring his themes from fresh perspectives.

Quite apart from their significance as literary masterpieces, the *Iliad* and the *Odyssey* testify to the frequency and normality of travel, communication, and interaction in the Mediterranean basin during the second and first millennia B.C.E. Both works portray Greeks as expert and fearless seamen, almost as comfortable aboard their ships as on land, who did not hesitate to venture into the waters of what Homer called the "wine-dark sea" in pursuit of their goals. Homer lovingly described the sleek galleys in which Greek warriors raced across the waters, sometimes to plunder the slower but heavily laden cargo vessels that plied the Mediterranean sea lanes, more often to launch strikes at enemy targets. He even had Odysseus construct a sailing ship single-handedly when he was shipwrecked on an island inhabited only by a goddess. The *Iliad* and the *Odyssey* make it clear that maritime links touched peoples throughout the Mediterranean basin in Homer's time and, further, that Greeks were among the most prominent seafarers of the age.

Already during the second millennium B.C.E., Phoenician merchants had established links between lands and peoples at the far ends of the Mediterranean Sea. During the first millennium B.C.E., however, the Mediterranean basin became much more tightly integrated as Greeks, and later Romans as well, organized commercial exchange and sponsored interaction throughout the region. Under Greek and Roman supervision, the Mediterranean served not as a barrier but, rather, as a highway linking Anatolia, Egypt, Greece, Italy, France, Spain, north Africa, and even southern Russia (by way of routes through the Black Sea).

CHAPTER OVERVIEW

Unlike other ancient cultures, throughout most of the first millennium B.C.E. the Greeks lived in autonomous city-states. Only after the late third century B.C.E. did they play prominent roles in the large, centralized empire established by their neighbors to the north in Macedon. Yet from the seventh through the second centuries B.C.E., the Greeks integrated the societies and economies of distant lands through energetic commercial activity over the Mediterranean sea lanes. They also generated a remarkable body of moral thought and philosophical reflection. Just as the traditions of ancient Persia, China, and South Asia shaped the cultural experiences of those lands, the traditions of the Greeks profoundly influenced the long-term cultural development of the Mediterranean basin, Europe, and southwest Asia as well.

BEFORE THE GREEKS

Humans inhabited the Balkan region and the Greek peninsula from an early but indeterminate date. During the third millennium B.C.E., they increasingly encountered and mingled with peoples from different societies who traveled and traded in the Mediterranean basin. As a result, early inhabitants of the Greek peninsula built their societies under the influence of Mesopotamians, Egyptians, Phoenicians, and others active in the region. Beginning in the ninth century B.C.E., the Greeks organized a series of city-states, which served as the political context for the development of ancient Greek society.

Minoan and Mycenaean Societies

Knossos During the late third millennium B.C.E., a sophisticated society arose on the island of Crete. Scholars refer to it as

CHRONOLOGY	
2200–1100 B.C.E.	Minoan society
1600–1100 B.C.E.	Mycenaean society
800–338 B.C.E.	Era of the classical Greek polis
ca. 600 B.C.E.	Life of Sappho
500–479 B.C.E.	Persian Wars
490 B.C.E.	Darius's invasion of Greece; Battle of Marathon
480 B.C.E.	Xerxes' invasion of Greece; Battle of Salamis
479 B.C.E.	Battle of Plataea
470–399 B.C.E.	Life of Socrates
443–429 B.C.E.	Pericles' leadership in Athens
431–404 B.C.E.	Peloponnesian War
430–347 B.C.E.	Life of Plato
384–322 B.C.E.	Life of Aristotle
359–336 B.C.E.	Reign of Philip II of Macedon
336–323 B.C.E.	Reign of Alexander of Macedon

"Priest-king Relief," plaster relief at the end of the Corridor of Processions in the Place at Knossos. Archaeologist Arthur Evans believed this depicted a Minoan ruler, who may have functioned as both high priest and king, wearing a crown with peacock feathers and leading an unseen animal to sacrifice.
Heritage Image Partnership Ltd/Alamy Stock Photo

Minoan society, after Minos, a legendary king of ancient Crete. Between 2000 and 1700 B.C.E., the inhabitants of Crete built a series of lavish palaces throughout the island, most notably the enormous complex at **Knossos** decorated with vivid frescoes depicting Minoans at work and play. These palaces were the nerve centers of Minoan society: they were residences of rulers, and they also served as storehouses where officials collected taxes in kind from local cultivators.

Minoan (mih-NOH-uhn)
Peloponnesus (pell-uh-puh-NEE-suhs)
Mycenaean (meye-seh-NEE-uhn)

Palace officials devised a script known as Linear A, in which written symbols stood for syllables rather than words, ideas, vowels, or consonants. Although linguists have not yet been able to decipher Linear A, it is clear that Minoan administrators used the script to keep detailed records of economic and commercial matters.

Between 2200 and 1450 B.C.E., Crete was a principal center of Mediterranean commerce. Because of its geographic location in the east-central Mediterranean, Crete received early influences from Phoenicia and Egypt. By 2200 B.C.E. Cretans were traveling aboard advanced sailing craft of Phoenician design. Minoan ships sailed to Greece, Anatolia, Phoenicia, and Egypt, where Cretan wine, olive oil, and wool were exchanged for grains, textiles, and manufactured goods. Archaeologists have discovered pottery vessels used as storage containers for Minoan wine and olive oil as far away as Sicily. After 1600 B.C.E. Minoans established colonies on Cyprus and many islands in the Aegean Sea, probably to mine local copper ores and gain better access to markets where tin was available.

Decline of Minoan Society After 1700 B.C.E. the Minoans experienced a series of earthquakes, volcanic eruptions, and tidal waves. Most destructive was a devastating volcanic eruption about 1628 B.C.E. on the island of Thera (Santorini) north of Crete. Between 1600 and 1450 B.C.E., Minoans embarked on a new round of palace building to replace structures destroyed by those natural catastrophes: they built luxurious complexes with indoor plumbing and drainage systems and even furnished some of them with flush toilets. After 1450 B.C.E., however, the wealth of Minoan society attracted a series of invaders, and Crete fell under foreign domination. Yet the Minoan traditions of maritime trade, writing, and construction deeply influenced the inhabitants of nearby Greece.

Mycenaean Society Beginning about 2200 B.C.E., migratory Indo-European peoples filtered through the Balkans and into the Greek peninsula. By 1600 B.C.E. they had begun to trade with Minoan merchants and visit Crete, where they learned about writing and large-scale construction. They adapted Minoan Linear A to their language, which was an early form of Greek, and devised a syllabic script known as Linear B. After 1450 B.C.E. they also built massive stone fortresses and palaces throughout the southern part of the Greek peninsula, known as the Peloponnesus. Because the fortified sites offered protection, they soon attracted settlers who built small agricultural communities. Their society is known as **Mycenaean,** after Mycenae, one of their most important settlements.

From 1500 to 1100 B.C.E., the Mycenaeans expanded their influence beyond peninsular Greece. They largely overpowered Minoan society, and they took over the Cretan palaces, where they established craft workshops. Archaeologists have unearthed thousands of clay tablets in Linear B that came from the archives of Mycenaean rulers in Crete as well as peninsular Greece. The Mycenaeans also established settlements in Anatolia, Sicily, and southern Italy.

Chaos in the Eastern Mediterranean
About 1200 B.C.E. the Mycenaeans engaged in a conflict with the city of Troy in Anatolia. This Trojan war, which the poet **Homer** recalled from a Greek perspective in his *Iliad,* coincided with invasions of foreign mariners—sometimes called the "Sea Peoples"—in the Mycenaean homeland. Indeed, from 1100 to 800 B.C.E. chaos reigned throughout the eastern Mediterranean region. Invasions and civil disturbances made it impossible to maintain stable governments or even productive agricultural societies. Mycenaean palaces fell into ruin, the population sharply declined, and people abandoned most settlements. Many inhabitants of the Greek peninsula fled to the islands of the Aegean Sea, Anatolia, or Cyprus. Writing in both Linear A and Linear B disappeared. The violent character of the era comes across clearly in Homer's works. Although set in an earlier era, both the *Iliad* and the *Odyssey* reflect the tumultuous centuries after 1100 B.C.E. They portray a society riven with conflict, and they recount innumerable episodes of aggression, treachery, and violence alongside heroic bravery and courage.

The Lion Gate at Mycenae illustrates the heavy fortifications built by Mycenaeans to protect their settlements.
Walter Clark/Science Source

The World of the Polis

The Polis
In the absence of a centralized state or empire, local institutions took the lead in restoring political order in Greece. The most important institution was the city-state, or **polis.** The term *polis* originally referred to a citadel or fortified site that offered refuge for local communities during times of war or other emergencies. These sites attracted increasing populations, and many of them gradually became lively commercial centers. They took on an increasingly urban character and extended their authority over surrounding regions. They levied taxes on their hinterlands and appropriated a portion of the agricultural surplus to support the urban population. By about 800 B.C.E. many *poleis* (the plural of polis) had become bustling city-states that functioned as the principal centers of Greek society.

The poleis took various political forms. Some differences reflected the fact that poleis emerged independently and elaborated their traditions with little outside influence. Others arose from different rates of economic development. A few poleis developed as small monarchies, but most were under the collective rule of local notables who ruled as oligarchs. Some poleis fell into the hands of generals or ambitious politicians—called "tyrants" by the Greeks—who gained power by irregular means. (The tyrants were not necessarily oppressive despots: indeed, many of them were extremely popular leaders. The term *tyrant* referred to their routes to power rather than their policies.) The most important of the poleis were Sparta and Athens, whose contrasting constitutions illustrate the variety of political structures in classical Greece.

Sparta
Sparta was situated in a fertile region of the Peloponnesus. As their population and economy expanded during the eighth and seventh centuries B.C.E., the Spartans progressively extended their control over the Peloponnesus. In doing so, they reduced neighboring peoples to the status of **helots,** effectively slaves of the Spartan state. The helots could form families, but they could not leave the land. Their role in society was to provide agricultural labor and keep Sparta supplied with food. By the sixth century B.C.E., the helots probably outnumbered the Spartan citizens by more than ten to one. With their large subject population, the Spartans were able to cultivate the Peloponnesus efficiently, but they also faced the constant threat of rebellion. As a result, the Spartans devoted most of their resources to maintaining a powerful and disciplined military machine.

Spartan Society
In theory, Spartan citizens were equal in status. To discourage the development of economic and social distinctions, Spartans observed an extraordinarily austere

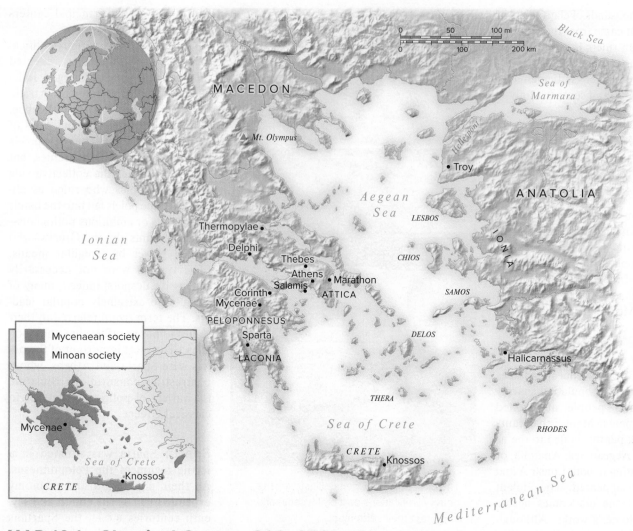

MAP 10.1 Classical Greece, 800–350 B.C.E.

Note the mountainous topography of the Greek peninsula and western Anatolia.

What role did geography play in encouraging the Greeks to become mariners?

lifestyle as a matter of policy. They did not wear jewelry or elaborate clothes, nor did they pamper themselves with luxuries or accumulate private wealth on a large scale. They generally did not even circulate coins made of precious metals but, instead, used iron bars for money. It is for good reason, then, that the adjective *spartan* refers to a lifestyle characterized by simplicity, frugality, and austerity.

Distinction among the ancient Spartans came not by wealth or social status but by prowess, discipline, and military talent, which the Spartan educational system cultivated from an early age. All boys

Sixth century terracotta drinking cup depicting a Spartan warrior and his horse.

Artokoloro Quint Lox Limited/Alamy Stock Photo

from families of Spartan citizens left their homes at age seven and went to live in military barracks, where they underwent a rigorous regime of physical training. At age twenty they began active military service, which they continued until retirement. Spartan authorities also prescribed vigorous physical exercise for girls in hopes that they would bear strong children. When they reached age eighteen to twenty, young women married and had occasional sexual relations, but did not live with their husbands. Only at about age thirty did men leave the barracks and set up households with their wives and children.

By the fourth century B.C.E., Spartan society had lost much of its egalitarian and austere nature. Aristocratic families had accumulated great wealth, and Spartans had developed a taste for luxury in food and dress. Nevertheless, Spartan society stood basically on the foundation of military discipline, and its institutions both reflected and reinforced the larger society's commitment to military values. In effect, Sparta sought to maintain public order—and discourage rebellion by the helots—by creating a military state that could crush any threat.

Athens In **Athens** as in Sparta, population growth and economic development caused political and social strain, but the Athenians relieved tensions by establishing a government based on democratic principles. Whereas Sparta sought to impose order by military means, Athens sought to negotiate order by considering the interests of the polis's various constituencies. Official positions were by no means open to all residents: only free adult males from Athens played a role in public affairs, leaving foreigners, slaves, and women with no direct voice in government. In seeking to resolve social problems, Athenians opened government offices to all male citizens and broadened the base of political participation in classical Greece.

Athenian Society During the seventh century B.C.E., an increasing volume of maritime trade brought prosperity to **Attica,** the region around Athens. The principal beneficiaries of that prosperity were aristocratic landowners, who also controlled the Athenian government. As their wealth grew, the aristocrats increased their landholdings and cultivated them with greater efficiency. Owners of small plots could not compete and fell heavily into debt. Competitive pressures often forced them to sell their holdings to aristocrats, and debt burdens sometimes overwhelmed them and pushed them into slavery.

By the early sixth century B.C.E., Attica had a large and growing class of people extremely unhappy with the structure of their society and poised to engage in war against their wealthy neighbors. Many poleis that experienced similar economic conditions suffered decades of brutal civil war between aristocrats and less privileged classes. In Athens, however, an aristocrat named **Solon** served as a mediator between classes, and he devised a solution to class conflict in Attica.

Solon and Athenian Democracy Solon forged a compromise between the classes. He allowed aristocrats to keep their lands—rather than confiscate them and redistribute them to landless individuals, as many of the less privileged preferred—but he cancelled debts, forbade debt slavery, and liberated those already enslaved for debt. To ensure that aristocrats would not undermine his reforms, Solon also provided representation for the common classes in the Athenian government by opening the councils of the polis to any citizen wealthy enough to devote time to public

affairs, regardless of his lineage. Later reformers went even further. During the late sixth and fifth centuries B.C.E., Athenian leaders increased opportunities for commoners to participate in government, and they paid salaries to officeholders so that financial hardship would not exclude anyone from service.

Pericles Those reforms gradually transformed Athens into a more democratic state. The high tide of Athenian power and prosperity came under the leadership of the statesman **Pericles.** Though he was of aristocratic birth, Pericles was the most popular Athenian leader from 461 B.C.E. until his death in 429 B.C.E. He wielded enormous personal influence in a government with hundreds of officeholders from the common classes, and he supported building programs that provided employment for thousands of construction workers

Pericles (PEH-rih-kleez)

The image of Pericles, wearing a helmet that symbolizes his post as Athenian leader, survives in a Roman copy of a Greek statue.

DEA/G. NIMATALLAH/De Agostini Picture Library/Getty Images

and laborers. Under the leadership of Pericles, Athens became the most sophisticated of the poleis, with a vibrant community of scientists, philosophers, poets, dramatists, artists, and architects. Little wonder, then, that in a moment of civic pride, Pericles boasted that Athens was "the education of Greece."

GREECE AND THE LARGER WORLD

As the poleis prospered, Greeks became increasingly prominent in the larger world of the Mediterranean basin. They established colonies along the shores of the Mediterranean and the Black Sea, and they traded throughout the region. Eventually, their political and economic interests brought them into conflict with the expanding Persian Empire. During the fifth century B.C.E., a round of intermittent war between the Greeks and the Persians ended in stalemate, but in the next century **Alexander of Macedon** toppled the Achaemenid empire. Indeed, Alexander built an empire stretching from India to Egypt and Greece. His conquests created a vast zone of trade and communication that encouraged commercial and cultural exchange on an unprecedented scale.

Greek Colonization

By about 800 B.C.E. the poleis were emerging as centers of political organization in Greece. During the next century increasing population strained the resources available in the rocky and mountainous Greek peninsula. To relieve population pressures, the Greeks began to establish colonies in other parts of the Mediterranean basin. Between the mid-eighth and the late sixth centuries B.C.E., they founded more than four hundred colonies along the shores of the Mediterranean Sea and the Black Sea.

The Greeks established their first colonies in the central Mediterranean during the early eighth century B.C.E. The most popular sites were Sicily and southern Italy, particularly the region around modern Naples, which was itself originally a Greek colony called Neapolis ("new polis"). These colonies provided merchants not only with fertile fields that yielded large agricultural surpluses but also with convenient access to the copper, zinc, tin, and iron ores of central Italy. By the sixth century B.C.E., Greek colonies dotted the shores of Sicily and southern Italy, and more Greeks lived in these colonies than in the Greek peninsula itself. By 600 B.C.E. the Greeks had

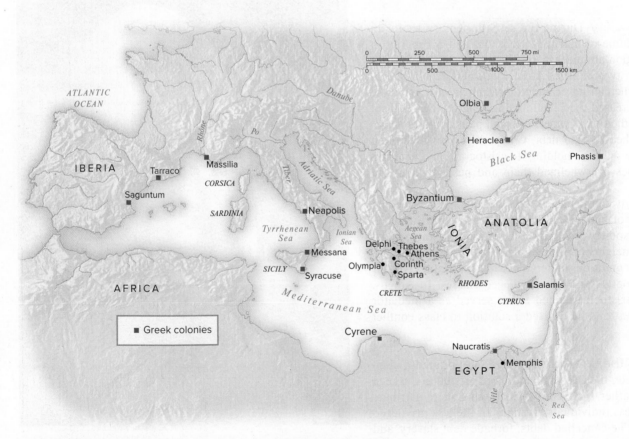

MAP 10.2   Classical Greece and the Mediterranean basin, 800–500 B.C.E.

All the Greek colonies were located on the coastlines of the Mediterranean Sea and the Black Sea.

What impacts did Greek colonization have on the peoples already living along the shores of the Mediterranean and Black seas?

ventured even farther west and established the important colony of Massilia (modern Marseilles) in what is now southern France.

Greek Colonies Greek colonies arose also in the eastern Mediterranean and the Black Sea. Hundreds of islands in the Aegean Sea beckoned to a maritime people such as the Greeks. Colonists also settled in Anatolia, where their Greek cousins had established communities during the centuries of political turmoil after 1100 B.C.E. During the eighth and seventh centuries B.C.E., Greeks ventured into the Black Sea in large numbers and established colonies all along its shores. These settlements offered merchants access to rich supplies of grain, fish, furs, timber, honey, wax, gold, and amber as well as slaves captured in southern Russia and transported to markets in the Mediterranean.

Two Greek ships under sail and powered by sails and oars, painted on a Greek Kylix cup.
CM Dixon/agefotostock

Unlike their counterparts in Persia, China, and South Asia, the Greeks did not build a centralized imperial state. Greek colonization was not a process controlled by a central government so much as an ad hoc response of individual poleis to population pressures. Colonies often did not take guidance from the poleis from which their settlers came but, rather, relied on their own resources and charted their own courses.

Effects of Greek Colonization Nevertheless, Greek colonization sponsored more communication, interaction, and exchange than ever before among Mediterranean lands and peoples. From the early eighth century B.C.E., colonies facilitated trade between their regions and the poleis in peninsular Greece and Anatolia. At the same time, colonization spread Greek language and cultural traditions throughout the Mediterranean basin. Moreover, the Greek presence quickened the tempo of social life, especially in the western Mediterranean and the Black Sea. Except for a few urban districts surrounding Phoenician colonies in the western Mediterranean, these regions were home mostly to small-scale agricultural societies organized by clans. As Greek merchants brought wealth into these societies, local clan leaders built small states in areas such as Sicily, southern Italy, southern France, the Crimean peninsula, and southern Russia where trade was especially strong. Thus Greek colonization had important political and social effects throughout the Mediterranean basin.

Conflict with Persia

During the fifth century B.C.E., their links abroad brought the poleis of the Greek peninsula into direct conflict with the Persian

empire in a long struggle known as the **Persian Wars** (500–479 B.C.E.). As the Persian emperors Cyrus and **Darius I** tightened their grip on Anatolia, the Greek cities on the Ionian coast became increasingly restless. In 500 B.C.E. they revolted against Persian rule and expelled the Achaemenid administrators. In support of their fellow Greeks and commercial partners, the Athenians sent a fleet of ships to aid the Ionian effort. Despite that gesture, Darius repressed the Ionian rebellion by 493 B.C.E.

The Persian Wars To punish the Athenians and forestall future interference in Persian affairs, Darius then mounted a campaign against peninsular Greece. In 490 B.C.E. he sent an army and a fleet of ships to attack Athens. Although greatly outnumbered, the Athenians routed the Persian army at the battle of Marathon and then marched back to Athens in time to fight off the Persian fleet.

Ten years later Darius's successor, Xerxes, decided to avenge the Persian losses. In 480 B.C.E. he dispatched a force consisting of perhaps one hundred thousand troops and a fleet of one thousand ships to subdue the Greeks. After being famously delayed by Spartan troops at Thermopylae, the Persian army succeeded in capturing and burning Athens, but a Greek fleet led by Athenians shattered the Persian navy at the battle of Salamis. Xerxes himself viewed the conflict from a temporary throne set up on a hillside overlooking the narrow strait of water between Athens and the island of Salamis. The following year a Greek force at Plataea routed the Persian army, whose survivors retreated to Anatolia.

Greeks and Persians continued to skirmish intermittently for more than a century, although their conflict did not expand into full-scale war. The Persian rulers were unwilling to invest resources in the effort to conquer small and distant Greece, and after Xerxes' reign they faced domestic problems that prevented them from undertaking foreign adventures. For their part, the Greeks had neither the resources nor the desire to challenge the Persian Empire, and they remained content with maintaining their independence.

The Delian League Once the Persian threat subsided, however, serious conflict arose among the Greek poleis themselves. After the Persian Wars, the poleis created an alliance known as the **Delian League** to discourage further Persian actions in Greece. Because of its superior fleet, Athens became the leader of the alliance. In effect, Athens supplied the league's

Thermopylae (ther-MOP-ih-lee)

military force, and the other poleis contributed financial support, which went largely to the Athenian treasury. Indeed, those contributions financed much of the Athenian bureaucracy and the vast construction projects that employed Athenian workers during the era of Pericles' leadership. In the absence of a continuing Persian threat, however, the other poleis resented having to make contributions that seemed to benefit only the Athenians.

The Peloponnesian War Ultimately, the tensions resulted in a bitter and destructive civil conflict known as the **Peloponnesian War** (431–404 B.C.E.). Both in peninsular Greece and throughout the larger Greek world, poleis divided into two armed camps under the leadership of Athens and Sparta, the most powerful of the poleis and the principal contenders for hegemony in the Greek world. The fortunes of war favored first one side, then the other, but by 404 B.C.E. the Spartans and their allies had forced the Athenians to unconditional surrender. Sparta's victory soon generated new jealousies, however, and conflicts broke out again. During the decades following Athenian surrender, control of the Greek world passed to Sparta, Thebes, Corinth, and other poleis.

Thucydides (thoo-SID-ih-deez)

The Peloponnesian War was both a debilitating and a demoralizing conflict. The historian **Thucydides** wrote a detailed history of the war, and even though he was himself a loyal native of Athens, he did not hide the fact that Athenians as well as other parties to the conflict adopted brutal tactics. Athenians bullied smaller communities, disregarded the interests and concerns of other poleis, insisted that allies resolutely toe the Athenian line, and subjected insubordinate communities to severe punishments. When the small island of Melos refused to acknowledge the authority of Athens, for example, Thucydides reported that Athenian forces conquered the island, massacred all the men of military age, and sold the women and children into slavery. As a result of that and other atrocities, Athens lost its reputation as the moral and intellectual leader of the Greek people and gained notoriety as an arrogant, insensitive imperialist power. Meanwhile, as the Peloponnesian War divided and weakened the world of the Greek poleis, a formidable power took shape to the north.

The Macedonians and the Origins of Empire

The Kingdom of Macedon Until the fourth century B.C.E., the kingdom of Macedon was a frontier state north of peninsular

Pericles organized the construction of numerous marble buildings, partly with funds collected from poleis belonging to the Delian League. Most notable of his projects was the Parthenon, located at the top of the Acropolis (the elevated fortress overlooking Athens). A temple dedicated to the goddess Athena, the Parthenon symbolizes the prosperity and grandeur of classical Athens.
Scott E Barbour/Getty Images

What's Left Out?

As we have seen elsewhere in the chapter, although the Persians had been driven out of Greece, the Greeks established a defensive alliance known as the Delian League. From the beginning, Athens dominated the league, insisting that the allied states pay large amounts of cash to Athens so that it could maintain its navy and thus protect members of the league in case of renewed conflict with the Persians. But what many allies resented as the years went by, with no further outbreak of hostilities, was that the coins they were paying to Athens were really being used to finance massive Athenian building projects.

Resentment grew stronger during the thirty-two-year reign of Pericles, when Delian League contributions were used—some would say stolen—to partly finance the massive and very expensive construction projects that still astonish visitors to Athens even today, twenty-five hundred years later. Pericles justified Athenian imperialism by arguing that having a strong Athens meant that all of Greece was free from fear of outside invasion. And he justified his building projects by arguing that the construction of an assembly of buildings like the Acropolis would leave a legacy of magnificent architectural brilliance that would forever glorify the city *and* its allies. As Pericles put it: "All kinds of enterprises should be created which will provide an inspiration for every art . . . we must devote ourselves to acquiring things that will be the source of everlasting fame."

The construction of the centerpiece of the project, the temple knows as the Parthenon, was personally supervised by Pericles, and he spared no expense; records indicate an enormous cost of 5000 talents (close to U.S. $7 billion today) just in the first year, and the building took fifteen years to complete! Pericles undoubtedly succeeded in creating magnificent architecture that has indeed been a source of everlasting fame for Athenian brilliance ever since. But other Greek city-states that were not in the Delian League were unimpressed and began to ally themselves with Sparta in a new power block that came to be known as the Spartan League. They argued that Athens was acting like a tyrant city, a charge that soon led to a declaration of war and the outbreak of the bloody Peloponnesian War, which effectively brought an end to Greek civilization.

Greece. The Macedonian population consisted partly of farmers and partly of sheepherders who migrated seasonally between the mountains and the valleys. Although the Macedonians recognized a king, semiautonomous clans controlled political affairs.

Proximity to the wealthy poleis of Greece brought change to Macedon. From the seventh century B.C.E., the Greek cities traded with Macedon. They imported grain, timber, and other natural resources in exchange for olive oil, wine, and finished products. Macedonian political and social elites, who controlled trade from their side of the border, became well acquainted with Greek merchants and their society.

Philip of Macedon During the reign of King Philip II (359–336 B.C.E.), Macedon underwent a thorough transformation. Philip built a powerful military that enabled him to overcome the traditional clans and make himself the ruler of Macedon. His military force featured an infantry composed of small landowners and a cavalry staffed by aristocrats holding large estates. During the fourth century B.C.E., both elements

Marble bust of a young Alexander of Macedon, produced during the subsequent Hellenistic era. After Alexander's death his vast empire was divided into three separate states during the Hellenstic (or "Greek like") era that followed.
Spiroview Inc/Shutterstock

proved to be hardy, well trained, and nearly invincible.

When Philip had consolidated his hold on Macedon, he turned his attention to two larger prizes: Greece and the Persian Empire. During the years following 350 B.C.E., Philip moved into northern Greece, annexing poleis and their surrounding territories. The poleis recognized the Macedonian threat, but the Peloponnesian War had poisoned the atmosphere so much that the poleis could not agree to form an alliance against Philip. Thus, as he moved into Greece, Philip faced nothing more than small forces patched together by shifting and temporary alliances. By 338 B.C.E. he had overcome all organized resistance and brought Greece under his control.

Alexander of Macedon Philip intended to use his conquest of Greece as a launching pad for an invasion of Persia. He did not have the opportunity to carry out his plans, however, because he was assassinated by one of his bodyguards in 336 B.C.E. The invasion of Persia thus fell to his son, the young Alexander of Macedon, often called Alexander the Great.

Alexander's Conquests At the age of twenty, Alexander succeeded Philip as ruler of an expanding empire. He soon began to assemble an army of about forty-eight thousand men to invade the Persian Empire. Alexander was a brilliant strategist and an inspired leader, and he inherited a well-equipped, well-disciplined, highly spirited veteran force from his father. By 333 B.C.E. Alexander had gained control over Ionia and Anatolia; within another year he held Syria, Palestine, and Egypt; by 331 B.C.E. he was in control of Mesopotamia and preparing to invade the Persian homeland. Next Alexander captured the Persian capitals of Pasargadae and Persepolis, where in 331 B.C.E. he burned the royal palace to the ground. He pursued the dispirited Persian army for another year until the last Achaemenid ruler fell to an assassin. Alexander established himself as the new emperor of Persia in 330 B.C.E.

But Alexander had larger ambitions, and in 327 he took his army into South Asia and crossed the Indus River, entering the Punjab. He subjected local rulers and probably would have continued to campaign in India except that his troops refused to proceed any farther from home. By 324 B.C.E. Alexander and his army had returned to Susa in Mesopotamia, where they celebrated their exploits in almost continuous feasting. Alexander busied himself with plans for governing his empire and for conducting further explorations. In June of 323 B.C.E., however, after an extended round of feasting and drinking, he suddenly fell ill and died at age thirty-three.

During the course of a meteoric career, Alexander proved to be a brilliant conqueror, but he did not live long enough to construct a genuine state for his vast realm or to develop a system of administration. He established cities throughout the lands he conquered and reportedly named about seventy of

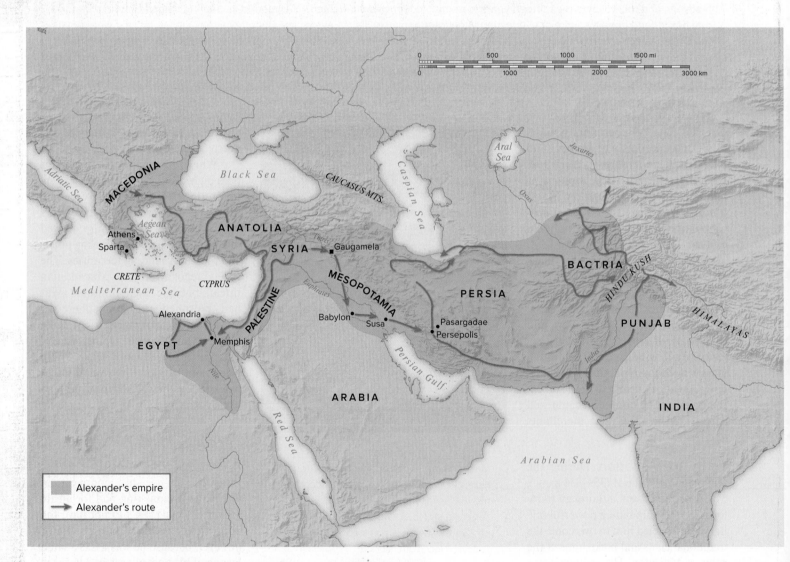

MAP 10.3   Alexander's empire, ca. 323 B.C.E.

Compare the boundaries of Alexander's empire with those of the Achaemenid empire as depicted in Map 7.1.

Alexander was a brilliant conqueror, but what mechanisms did he leave in place to administer the vast realm he had created?

SOURCES FROM THE PAST

Arrian on the Character of Alexander of Macedon

One of the earliest surviving accounts of Alexander's life and career is that of Flavius Arrianus Xenophon, better known as Arrian. Although Greek, Arrian served in the armies of the early Roman empire and developed a strong interest in military history. About the middle of the second century C.E., he composed his work on Alexander, drawing on contemporary accounts that no longer survive. Here he assesses Alexander's character:

He was very handsome in person, and much devoted to exercise, very active in mind, very heroic in courage, very tenacious of honor, exceedingly fond of incurring danger, and strictly observant of his duty to the gods. In regard to the pleasures of the body, he had perfect self-control; and of those of the mind, praise was the only one of which he was insatiable. He was very clever in recognizing what was necessary to be done, even when it was still a matter unnoticed by others; and very successful in deducing from the observation of facts what was likely to occur. In marshalling, arming, and ruling an army, he was exceedingly skillful; and very renowned for rousing the courage of his soldiers, filling them with hopes of success, and dispelling their fear in the midst of danger by his own courage. Therefore, even what he had to do in secret he did with the greatest boldness. He was also very clever in getting a head start on his enemies, and snatching from them their advantages by secretly forestalling them, before any one even knew what was about to happen. He was likewise very steadfast in keeping the agreements and settlements which he made, as well as very secure from being entrapped by liars. Finally, he was very sparing in the expenditure of money for the gratification of his own pleasures; but he was exceedingly bountiful in spending it for the benefit of his friends.

That Alexander should have committed errors in his conduct from quickness of temper or from anger, and that he should have been induced to comport himself like the Persian monarchs to an immoderate degree, I do not think remarkable if we consider both his youth and his uninterrupted career of good fortune. And like all kings he was surrounded by associates who aimed at their best interests . . . However, I am certain that Alexander was the only one of the ancient kings who, from nobility of character, repented of the errors which he had committed . . .

Aristobulus (one of Alexander's generals who composed an account of the conqueror that was available to Arrian but that does not survive today) asserts that Alexander used to have long drinking parties, not for the purpose of enjoying the wine, as he was not a great wine-drinker, but in order to exhibit his sociality and friendly feeling to his Companions.

Whoever therefore reproaches Alexander as a bad man, let him do so; but let him first not only bring before his mind all his actions deserving reproach, but also gather into one view all his deeds of every kind. Then, indeed, let him reflect who he is himself, and what kind of fortune he has experienced; and then consider who that man was whom he reproaches as bad, and to what a height of human success he attained, becoming without any dispute king of two continents, and reaching every place by his fame; while he himself who reproaches him is of smaller account, spending his labor on petty objects, which, however, he does not succeed in effecting, petty as they are. For my own part, I think there was at that time no race of men, no city, nor even a single individual to whom Alexander's name and fame had not penetrated. For this reason it seems to me that a hero totally unlike any other human was conceived as something more than human. And this is said to have been revealed after Alexander's death by the oracles, by visions which presented themselves to various people, and by the dreams which were seen by different individuals. It is also shown by the honor paid to him by men up to the present time, and by the recollection which is still held of him as more than human. Even at the present time, after so long an interval, other oracle responses in his honor have still been received by the Macedonians.

> What two continents is Arrian referring to here?

> What is Arrian implying when he says Alexander had some power more than god?

For Further Reflection

■ What factors might have influenced Arrian to shower so much praise upon Alexander?

■ What allowances is Arrian asking people to make because of Alexander's youth?

■ On the basis of Arrian's characterization, do you think Alexander had strong potential to become an effective governor as well as a talented conqueror?

Source: The Anabasis of Alexander, by Arrian of Nocomedia, Trans. E.J. Chinnock, originally pub. 1893. Project Gutenberg (some minor changes to update text).

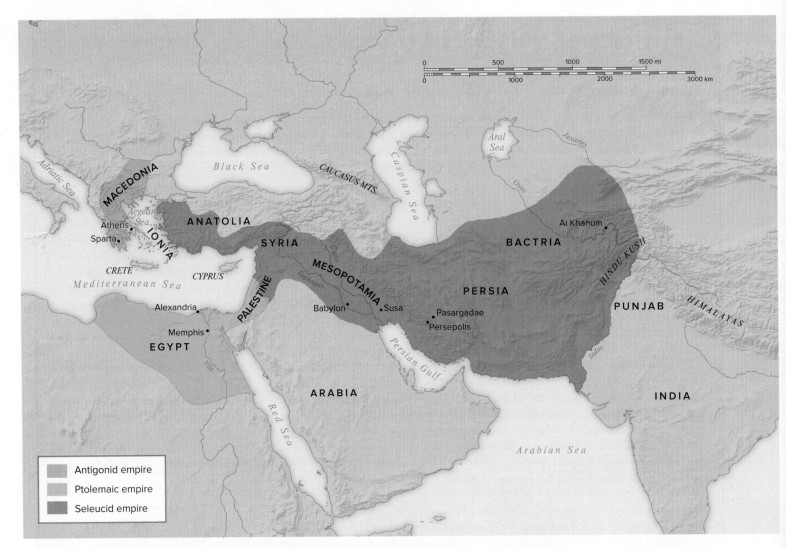

MAP 10.4 The Hellenistic empires, ca. 275 B.C.E.

Note the differences in size between the three Hellenistic empires.

Consider the geographic conditions, political challenges, and economic potential of the three empires.

them Alexandria in his own honor. Alexander also toyed with some intriguing ideas about governing his empire, notably a scheme to marry his officers to Persian women and create a new ruling class of Greek, Macedonian, and Persian ancestry, but his early death prevented him from turning that plan into a coherent policy. So long as he lived, he relied on established institutions such as the Persian satrapies (imperial provinces) to administer the lands he conquered.

The Hellenistic Empires

Following Alexander's death, his generals jockeyed for position in hopes of taking over choice parts of his realm, and by 275 B.C.E. they had divided the empire into three large states. Antigonus took Greece and Macedon, which his Antigonid successors ruled until the Romans took control of the eastern

Mediterranean during the second century B.C.E. Ptolemy took Egypt, which the Ptolemaic dynasty ruled until the Roman conquest of Egypt in 31 B.C.E. Seleucus took the largest portion, the former Achaemenid empire stretching from Bactria to Anatolia, which his Seleucid successors ruled until the Parthians displaced them during the second century B.C.E.

The Hellenistic Era Historians refer to the age following the death of Alexander as the **Hellenistic era**—an age when Greek cultural traditions expanded their influence beyond Greece (*Hellas*) to a much larger world. During the centuries between Alexander's death and the expansion of the Roman empire in the eastern Mediterranean, the Hellenistic empires governed cosmopolitan societies and facilitated encounters between peoples from Greece to the subcontinent. Like imperial states in Persia, China, and South Asia, the Hellenistic empires helped to integrate the economies and societies of distant regions. They facilitated trade, and they made it possible for beliefs, values, and religions to spread over greater distances than ever before.

The Antigonid Empire

Although the Antigonid realm of Greece and Macedon was the smallest of the Hellenistic empires, it benefited handsomely from the new order. There was continual tension between the Antigonid rulers and the Greek cities, which sought to retain their independence by forming defensive leagues that stoutly resisted Antigonid efforts to control the Greek peninsula. The poleis often struck bargains with the Antigonids, offering to recognize their rule in exchange for tax relief and local autonomy. Internal social tensions also flared because Greeks wrestled with the perennial problem of land and its equitable distribution. Yet cities such as Athens and Corinth flourished during the Hellenistic era as enormous volumes of trade passed through their ports. Moreover, the overpopulated Greek peninsula sent large numbers of colonists to newly founded cities, especially in the Seleucid empire.

The Ptolemaic Empire

Perhaps the wealthiest of the Hellenistic empires was **Ptolemaic Egypt.** Greek and Macedonian overlords did not interfere in Egyptian society but contented themselves with the efficient organization of agriculture, industry, and tax collection. They maintained the irrigation networks and monitored the cultivation of crops and the payment of taxes. They also established royal monopolies over the most lucrative industries, such as textiles, salt making, and the brewing of beer.

Alexandria

Much of Egypt's wealth flowed to the Ptolemaic capital of **Alexandria.** Founded by Alexander at the mouth of the Nile, Alexandria served as the Ptolemies' administrative headquarters, but it became much more than a bureaucratic center. Alexandria's enormous harbor was able to accommodate 1,200 ships simultaneously, and the city soon became the most important port in the Mediterranean. Its wealth attracted migrants from all parts of the Mediterranean basin and beyond. Alongside Greeks, Macedonians, and Egyptians lived sizable communities of Phoenicians, Jews, Arabs, and Babylonians. The city was indeed an early megalopolis, where peoples of different ethnic, religious, and cultural traditions conducted their affairs. Under the Ptolemies, Alexandria also became the cultural capital of the Hellenistic world. It was the site of the famous Alexandrian Museum—a state-financed institute of higher learning where philosophical, literary, and scientific scholars carried on advanced research—and of the equally famous Alexandrian Library, which supported the scholarship sponsored by the museum and which, by the first century B.C.E., boasted a collection of more than seven hundred thousand works.

The Seleucid Empire

It was in the Seleucid realm, however, that Greek influence reached its greatest extent. The principal channels of that influence were the numerous cities that Alexander and his successors founded in the former Persian Empire. Most of them were small settlements intended to serve as fortified sites or administrative centers, though some developed into thriving commercial centers. Greek and Macedonian colonists flocked to these cities, where they joined the ranks of imperial bureaucrats and administrators. Though few in number compared with the native populations, the colonists created a Mediterranean-style urban society that left its mark on lands as distant as Bactria and South Asia. So widely was the Greek language being used that the Mauryan dynasty ruler Ashoka had his edicts promulgated in Greek and Aramaic, the two most commonly used languages of the Hellenistic empires.

Greeks in Bactria

Archaeological excavations have thrown considerable light on one of those Greek settlements—the Hellenistic colony at Ai Khanum on the Oxus River in ancient Bactria (modern-day Afghanistan). The colony at Ai Khanum was founded either by Alexander of Macedon or by Seleucus shortly after Alexander's death. As an important part of the Seleucid empire, Bactria was in constant communication with Greece and the Mediterranean world. After about 250 B.C.E. the governors of Bactria withdrew from the Seleucid empire and established an independent Greek kingdom. Excavations at Ai Khanum show that the colony's inhabitants spoke the Greek language, dressed according to Greek fashions, read Greek literature and philosophy, and constructed buildings and produced works of art in Greek styles. At the same time, while honoring Greek gods at Greek shrines, residents of Ai Khanum also welcomed Persian and central Asian deities into their midst. Indeed, some Greeks even converted to Buddhism. Most prominent of the converts was King Menander, who ruled in Bactria approximately 155 to 130 B.C.E. In many ways, like the Achaemenids before them, the Hellenistic ruling classes constituted a thin, supervisory veneer over long-established societies that largely continued to observe inherited traditions. Nevertheless, like states in Persia, China, and South Asia, the Hellenistic empires brought distant lands into interaction by way of trade and cultural exchange.

GREEK ECONOMY AND SOCIETY

The geography of the Greek peninsula posed difficult challenges for its inhabitants: its mountainous terrain and rocky soil yielded only small harvests of grain, and the southern Balkan mountains hindered travel and communication. Indeed, until the construction of modern roads, much of Greece was more accessible by sea than by land. As a result, early Greek society depended heavily on maritime trade.

Ptolemaic (TAWL-oh-may-ihk)

Trade and the Integration of the Mediterranean Basin

Trade Although it produced little grain, much of Greece is ideally suited to the cultivation of olives and grapes. After the establishment of the poleis, the Greeks discovered that they could profitably concentrate their efforts on the production of olive oil and wine. Greek merchants traded these products around the Mediterranean, returning with abundant supplies of grain and other items as well.

By the early eighth century B.C.E., trade had generated considerable prosperity in the Greek world. Merchants and mariners linked Greek communities throughout the Mediterranean world—not only those in the Greek peninsula but also those in Anatolia, the Mediterranean islands, and the Black Sea. The populations of all these communities grew dramatically, encouraging further colonization. In the colonies, merchants offered Greek olive oil and wine for local products. Grain came from Egypt, Sicily, and southern Russia; salted fish from Spain and Black Sea lands; timber from Macedon; tin from Anatolia; and slaves from Egypt and Russia. Merchant ships with a capacity of four hundred tons were common in the ancient Mediterranean, and a few vessels had a capacity of one thousand tons. Some cities, such as Athens and Corinth, relied more on commerce than on agriculture for their livelihood and prosperity.

The Diskobolos, or discus thrower, attributed to Myron (c. 450 B.C.E.) captures the athlete's powerful muscular motion and illustrates the Greeks' appreciation for the human body and athletic endeavor.
Gianni Dagli Orti/Shutterstock

partnerships to spread the risks of commercial ventures. Usually, a merchant borrowed money from a banker or an individual to purchase cargo and rented space from a shipowner, who transported the goods and returned the profits to the merchant. In the event of a shipwreck, the contract became void, leaving both the merchant and the lender to absorb their losses.

The production of cultivators and manufacturers filled the holds of Mediterranean merchant vessels. Manufacturers usually operated on a small scale, but there are records of pottery workshops with upwards of sixty employees. One factory in fourth-century Athens used 120 enslaved people in the manufacture of shields. Throughout the trading world of the Mediterranean basin, entrepreneurs established small businesses and offered their wares in the larger market.

Panhellenic Festivals Trade links between the Greek cities and their colonies contributed to a sense of a larger Greek community. Colonists recognized the same gods as their cousins in the Greek peninsula. They spoke Greek dialects, and they maintained commercial relationships with their native communities. Greeks from all parts gathered periodically to participate in panhellenic festivals that reinforced their common bonds. Many of those festivals featured athletic, literary, or musical contests in which individuals sought to win glory for their polis.

Commercial and Economic Organization Large volumes of trade promoted commercial and economic organization in the Mediterranean basin. In Greece, for example, shipowners, merchants, and moneylenders routinely formed

How the Past Shapes the Future ▶ ▶ ▶ ▶

Long-Distance Trade Networks

Greeks traveled long distances, both by land and by sea, to trade during the Hellenistic era. As trade circulated between Greece and the many and growing Greek colonies, Greek language, cultural traditions, and political structures accompanied material items such as wine, slaves, and timber. Long-distance trade thus had the effect of more closely unifying the Greek cultural world and of spreading Greek ideas about the world more widely through the Mediterranean and Black Sea basins.

The Olympic Games Best known of the panhellenic festivals were the **Olympic Games.** According to tradition, in 776 B.C.E. Greek communities from all parts of the Mediterranean sent their best athletes to the polis of Olympia to engage in contests of speed, strength, and skill. Events included footracing, long jump, boxing, wrestling, javelin tossing, and discus throwing. Winners of events received olive wreaths, and they became celebrated heroes in their home poleis. The ancient Olympic Games took place every four years for more than a millennium before quietly disappearing from Greek life. So, although they were not united politically, by the sixth century B.C.E. Greek communities had nevertheless established a sense of collective identity.

During the Hellenistic era, trade drew the Greeks into an even larger world of commerce and communication as colonists and traders expanded the range of their operations throughout

Alexander's empire and the realms that succeeded him. Caravan trade linked Persia and Bactria to the western regions of the Hellenistic world. Dependent on horses and donkeys, caravans could not transport heavy or bulky goods but, rather, carried luxury products such as gems and jewelry, perfumes and aromatic oils. These goods all had high value relative to weight so that merchants could feed themselves and their animals, pay the high costs of overland transport, and still turn a profit. Traffic in bulkier goods traveled the sea lanes of the Mediterranean, the Red Sea, the Persian Gulf, and the Arabian Sea.

Family and Society

Homer's works portrayed a society composed of heroic warriors and their outspoken wives. Strong-willed human beings clashed constantly with one another and sometimes even defied the gods in pursuing their interests. These aggressive and assertive characters depended on everyday individuals to provide them with food and other necessities, but Homer had no interest in discussing the ordinary lives of farmers and their families.

Patriarchal Society With the establishment of poleis in the eighth century B.C.E., the nature of Greek family and society came into clearer focus. Like urban societies in southwest Asia and Anatolia, the Greek poleis adopted strictly patriarchal family structures. Male family heads ruled their households, and fathers even had the right to decide whether to keep infants born to their wives. They could not legally kill infants, but they could abandon newborns in the mountains or the countryside where they would soon die of exposure unless found and rescued by others.

Greek women fell under the authority of their fathers, husbands, or sons. Upper-class women living in poleis spent most of their time in the family home, and they ventured outside in the company of servants or chaperones and often wore veils to discourage the attention of men from other families. In most of the poleis, women could not own landed property, but they sometimes operated small businesses such as shops and food stalls. The only public position open to Greek women was that of priestess of a religious cult. Sparta was something of a special case when it came to gender relations: there women participated in athletic contests, went about town by

One of the earliest surviving images of Sappho, from c. 470 B.C. She is shown holding a lyre and plectrum, and turning to listen to another musician.
Chronicle/Alamy Stock Photo

themselves, joined in public festivals, and sometimes even took up arms to defend the polis. Even in Sparta, however, men were family authorities, and men alone determined state policies.

Sappho Literacy was common among upper-class Greek women, and a few women earned reputations for literary talent. Most famous of them was the poet **Sappho,** who composed nine volumes of poetry around 600 B.C.E. Sappho, probably a widow from an aristocratic family, invited young women into her home for instruction in music and literature. Critics charged her with homosexual activity, and her surviving verse speaks of her strong physical attraction to young women. Greek society readily tolerated sexual relationships between men but frowned on female homosexuality. As a result, Sappho fell under a cloud of moral suspicion, and only fragments of her poetry survive.

Aristocratic families with extensive landholdings could afford to provide girls with a formal education, but in less privileged families all hands contributed to the welfare of the household. In rural families, men performed most of the outside work and women took care of domestic chores and wove wool textiles. In artisan families living in the poleis, both men and women often participated in businesses and maintained stands or booths in the marketplace.

Slavery Throughout the Greek world, as in other classical societies, slavery was a prominent means of mobilizing labor. Slaves came from differing backgrounds. Some were formerly free Greeks who entered slavery because they could not pay their debts. Many came from the ranks of soldiers captured in war. A large number came from the peoples with whom the Greeks traded: slave markets at Black Sea ports sold seminomadic Scythians captured in Russia, and Egyptians provided African slaves from Nubia and other southern regions.

Greek law regarded all slaves as the private chattel of their owners, and the conditions of slaves' lives depended on the needs and the temperament of their owner. Physically powerful slaves with no special skills most often provided heavy labor in mines or on the estates of large landholders. Other unskilled slaves worked at lighter tasks as domestic servants or caretakers of their owners' children. Educated slaves and those skilled at some craft or trade had different circumstances. Their slaveholders often regarded them as economic investments, provided them with shops, and allowed them to keep a portion of their earnings as an incentive and a reward for efficient work.

In some cases, enslaved people with entrepreneurial talent succeeded well enough in their businesses to win their freedom. A enslaved man named **Pasion,** for example, worked first as a porter and then as a clerk at a prominent Athenian bank during the late fifth and early fourth centuries B.C.E. Pasion developed into a shrewd businessman who worked efficiently and turned considerable profits for his slaveholders, who in turn entrusted him with greater responsibilities and rewarded him for successful efforts. Ultimately, Pasion gained his freedom, took over management of the bank, outfitted five warships from his own pocket, and won a grant of Athenian citizenship.

CULTURAL LIFE IN ANCIENT GREECE

During the eighth and seventh centuries B.C.E., as Greek merchants ventured throughout the Mediterranean basin, they became acquainted with the sophisticated cultural traditions of Mesopotamia and Egypt. They learned astronomy, science, mathematics, medicine, and magic from the Babylonians as well as geometry, medicine, and divination from the Egyptians. They also drew inspiration from the myths, religious beliefs, art motifs, and architectural styles of Mesopotamia and Egypt. About 800 B.C.E. they adapted the Phoenician alphabet to their language: to the Phoenicians' consonants they added symbols for vowels and thus created an exceptionally flexible system for representing speech in written form.

Rational Thought and Philosophy

Greek Science and Mathematics

As early as the seventh century B.C.E., Greek thinkers in the cosmopolitan cities of the Ionian coast were working with scientific and mathematical knowledge that reached them from Mesopotamia and Egypt. They did not fully accept the fanciful stories of the Greek myths, which attributed creation of the world to the gods. Rather, they inaugurated a tradition by which Greek scientists relied on observable evidence, rational thought, and human reason to explain the world as the result of natural processes. Thus, for example, the Ionian scientist Thales accurately predicted an eclipse of the sun that took place 28 May 585 B.C.E., and the Greek theorist Democritus suggested that all physical

matter was composed of indivisible particles that he called *atoms* (a word that means indivisible). The Ionian mathematician Pythagoras drew upon Babylonian ideas in developing a systematic approach to mathematics, and the Athenian physician Hippocrates worked to base medical practice on the understanding of human anatomy and physiology. Greek science was remarkable for its reliance on human reason to understand the world, and it served as a rich foundation for later scientific developments throughout the Mediterranean basin and beyond in both Christian Europe and the Muslim world.

Greek Philosophy

Perhaps the most distinctive expression of classical Greek thought was philosophy, which brought the power of reason to bear on human issues as well as the natural world.

Socrates

The pivotal figure in the development of philosophy was **Socrates** (470–399 B.C.E.), a thoughtful and reflective Athenian driven by a powerful urge to understand human beings and human affairs in all their complexity. During his youth, Socrates studied the ideas of the Greek scientists, but he ultimately decided to focus his attention on human affairs rather than the natural world.

Socrates did not commit his thought to writing, but his disciple Plato later composed dialogues that represented Socrates' views. Nor did Socrates expound his views assertively: rather, he posed questions that encouraged reflection on human issues, particularly on matters of ethics and morality. He suggested that human beings could lead ethical lives and that honor and integrity were far more important than wealth, fame, or other superficial attributes. He scorned those who preferred public accolades to personal integrity, and he insisted on the need to reflect on the purposes and goals of life. "The unexamined life is not worth living," he held, implying that human beings had an obligation to strive for personal integrity, behave honorably toward others, and work toward the construction of a just society.

In elaborating those views, Socrates often played the role of a gadfly who subjected traditional ethical teachings to critical scrutiny. This tactic outraged some of his fellow citizens, who brought him to trial on charges that he encouraged immorality and corrupted the Athenian youths who joined him in the marketplace to discuss moral and ethical issues. A jury of Athenian citizens decided that Socrates had indeed passed the bounds of propriety and condemned him to death. In 399 B.C.E. Socrates drank a potion of hemlock sap and died in the company of his friends.

Tradition holds that Socrates was not a physically attractive man, but this statue emphasizes his sincerity and simplicity. Judging from his clothing and posture, what message was the sculptor trying to convey about Socrates' character?
Nils Jorgensen/
Shutterstock

Pasion (pahs-ee-on)
Socrates (SAHK-rah-teez)

SOURCES FROM THE PAST

Socrates' View of Death

In one of his earliest dialogues, the Apology, *Plato offered an account of Socrates' defense of himself during his trial before a jury of Athenian citizens. After the jury had convicted him and condemned him to death, Socrates reflected on the nature of death and reemphasized his commitment to virtue rather than to wealth or fame.*

And if we reflect in another way we shall see that we may well hope that death is a good thing. For the state of death is one of two things: either the dead man wholly ceases to be and loses all sensation; or, according to the common belief, it is a change and a migration of the soul unto another place. And if death is the absence of all sensation, like the sleep of one whose slumbers are unbroken by any dreams, it will be a wonderful gain. For if a man had to select that night in which he slept so soundly that he did not even see any dreams, and had to compare with it all the other nights and days of his life, and then had to say how many days and nights in his life he had slept better and more pleasantly than this night, I think that a private person, nay, even the great king of Persia himself, would find them easy to count, compared with the others. If that is the nature of death, I for one count it a gain. For then it appears that eternity is nothing more than a single night.

But if death is a journey to another place, and the common belief be true, that all who have died dwell there, what good could be greater than this, my judges? Would a journey not be worth taking if at the end of it, in the other world, we should be released from the self-styled judges of this world, and should find the true judges who are said to sit in judgment below? . . . It would be an infinite happiness to converse with them, and to live with them, and to examine them. Assuredly there they do not put men to death for doing that. For besides the other ways in which they are happier than we are, they are immortal, at least if the common belief be true.

And you too, judges, must face death with a good courage, and believe this as a truth, that no evil can happen to a good man, either in life, or after death. His fortunes are not neglected by the gods, and what has come to me today has not come by chance. I am persuaded that it is better for me to die now, and to be released from trouble. . . . And so I am hardly angry with my accusers, or with those who have condemned me to die. Yet it was not with this mind that they accused me and condemned me, but rather they meant to do me an injury. Only to that extent do I find fault with them.

Yet I have one request to make of them. When my sons grow up, visit them with punishment, my friends, and vex them in the same way that I have vexed you if they seem to you to care for riches or for anything other than virtue: and if they think that they are something when they are nothing at all, reproach them as I have reproached you for not caring for what they should and for thinking that they are great men when in fact they are worthless. And if you will do this, I myself and my sons will have received our deserts at your hands.

But now the time has come, and we must go hence: I to die, and you to live. Whether life or death is better is known to God, and to God only.

> How do you understand Socrates' characterization of the two possible outcomes of death?

> How would you describe the fault Socrates finds with his judges?

For Further Reflection

■ What is Socrates' greatest hope for his sons, and, indeed, for all men?
■ How do Socrates' ideas about virtue and morality compare to the views of Buddhists and Hindus we discussed in the previous chapter?

Source: F. J. Church, trans. *The Trial and Death of Socrates,* 2nd ed. London: Macmillan, 1886, pp. 76–78. (Translation slightly modified.)

Plato Socrates' influence survived in the work of his most important disciple, **Plato** (430–347 B.C.E.), and in Plato's disciple Aristotle (384–322 B.C.E.). Inspired by his mentor's reflections, Plato elaborated a systematic philosophy of great subtlety. He presented his thought in a series of dialogues in which Socrates figured as the principal speaker. In the earliest dialogues, written shortly after Socrates' death, Plato largely represented his mentor's views. As time passed, Plato gradually formulated his thought into a systematic vision of the world and human society.

The cornerstone of Plato's thought was his theory of Forms or Ideas. Plato developed his belief that the world in which we live was not the only world—indeed, it was not the world of genuine reality but only a pale and imperfect reflection of the world of Forms or Ideas. Displays of virtue or other qualities in the world imperfectly reflected the ideal qualities. Only by entering the world of Forms or Ideas was it possible to understand the true nature of virtue and other qualities. The secrets of that world were available only to philosophers—those who applied their rational faculties to the pursuit of wisdom.

Though abstract, Plato's thought had important political and social implications. In his dialogue *Republic,* for example, Plato sketched an ideal state that reflected his philosophical views. Because philosophers were in the best position to understand ultimate reality, and hence to design policies in accordance with the Form or Idea of justice, he held that the best state was one where either philosophers ruled as kings or kings were themselves philosophers. In effect, then, Plato advocated an intellectual aristocracy: the philosophical elite would rule, and other, less educated, classes would work at functions for which their talents best suited them.

Aristotle During the generation after Plato, **Aristotle** elaborated a systematic philosophy that equaled Plato's work in its long-term influence. Though originally a disciple of Plato, Aristotle came to distrust the theory of Forms or Ideas, which he considered artificial intellectual constructs unnecessary for understanding the world. Unlike Plato, Aristotle believed that philosophers could rely on their senses to provide accurate information about the world and then depend on reason to sort out its mysteries. Like Plato, Aristotle explored the nature of reality in subtle metaphysical works, and he devised rigorous rules of logic in an effort to construct powerful and compelling arguments. But he also wrote on biology, physics, astronomy, psychology, politics, ethics, and literature. His work provided such a coherent and comprehensive vision of the world that his later disciples, the Christian scholastic philosophers of medieval Europe, called him "the master of those who know."

The Greek philosophers deeply influenced the development of European and Islamic cultural traditions. Until the seventeenth century C.E., most European philosophers regarded the Greeks as intellectual authorities. Christian and Muslim theologians alike went to great lengths to harmonize their religious convictions with the philosophical views of Plato and Aristotle. Thus, like philosophical and religious figures in other ancient societies, Plato and Aristotle provided a powerful intellectual framework that shaped thought about the world and human affairs for two millennia and more.

Popular Religion

Because most Greeks of the classical era did not have an advanced education and did not chat with the philosophers on a regular basis, they did not rely on systems

Aristotle (AHR-ih-stot-uhl)

A mosaic from the Italian town of Pompeii, near Naples, depicts Plato (standing at left) discussing philosophical issues with students. Produced in the early first century C.E., this illustration testifies to the popularity of Greek philosophy in classical Roman society.
Bettmann/Getty Images

of formal logic when seeking to understand their place in the larger world. Instead, they turned to traditions of popular culture and popular religion that shed light on human nature and offered guidance for human behavior.

Greek Deities

The Greeks did not recognize a single, exclusive, all-powerful god. Their Indo-European ancestors had attributed supernatural powers to natural elements such as the sun, wind, and rain. Over the course of the centuries, the Greeks personified these powers and came to think of them as gods. They constructed myths that related the stories of the gods, their relations with one another, and their roles in bringing the world to its present state.

In the beginning, they believed, there was the formless void of chaos out of which emerged the earth, the mother and creator of all things. The earth then generated the sky, and together they produced night, day, sun, moon, and other natural phenomena. Struggles between the deities led to bitter heavenly battles, and ultimately Zeus, grandson of the earth and sky gods, emerged as paramount ruler of the divine realm. Zeus's heavenly court included scores of subordinate deities who had various responsibilities: the god Apollo promoted wisdom and justice, for example; the goddess Fortune brought unexpected opportunities and difficulties; and the Furies wreaked vengeance on those who violated divine law.

Religious Cults

Like religious traditions in other lands, Greek myths sought to explain the world and the forces that shape it. They served also as foundations for religious cults that contributed to a powerful sense of community in classical Greece. Many of the cults conducted ritual observances that were open only to initiates. One especially popular cult known as the **Eleusinian mysteries,** for example, sponsored a ritual community meal and encouraged initiates to observe high moral standards.

Women's Cults

Some cults admitted only women. Because women could not participate in legal and political life, the cults provided opportunities for them to play roles in society outside the home. The fertility cult of Demeter, goddess of grain, excluded men. In honor of Demeter, women gathered on a hill for three days, offered sacrifices to the goddess, and took part in a celebratory feast. This event occurred in October or November before the planting of grain and sought to ensure bountiful harvests.

The Cult of Dionysus

Women were also the most prominent devotees of Dionysus, the god of wine, also known as Bacchus, although men sometimes joined in his celebration. During the spring of the year, when the vines produced their fruit, devotees, called Bacchae, retreated into the hills to celebrate Dionysus with song and dance. The dramatist Euripides offered an account of one such Dionysian season in his play *The Bacchae.* Euripides described the preparations for the festival and the celebrants' joyful march to the mountains. Spirited music and dance brought the devotees to such a state of frenzy that they fell on a sacrificial goat—and also a man hiding in the brush in an unwise effort to observe the proceedings—ripped the victims apart, and presented them as offerings to Dionysus. Though he was a skeptic who regarded much of Greek religion as sham and hypocrisy, Euripides nonetheless recognized that powerful emotional bonds held the Dionysian community together.

During the fifth century B.C.E., as the poleis strengthened their grip on public and political life, the religious cults became progressively more tame. The **cult of Dionysus,** originally one of the most unrestrained, became one of the most thoroughly domesticated. The venue of the rituals shifted from the mountains to the polis, and the nature of the observances changed dramatically. Instead of emotional festivals, the Dionysian season saw the presentation of plays that honored the traditions of the polis, examined relations between humans and the gods, or reflected on problems of ethics and morality.

Tragic Drama

This transformation of Dionysus's cult set the stage for the emergence of Greek dramatic literature as dramatists composed plays for presentation at annual theatrical festivals. Of the thousands of plays written in classical Greece, only a few survive: thirty-two tragedies and a dozen comedies have come down to the present in substantially complete form. Yet this small sample shows that the dramatists engaged audiences in subtle reflection on complicated themes. The great tragedians—Aeschylus, Sophocles, and Euripides—whose lives spanned the fifth century B.C.E., explored the possibilities and limitations of human action. To what extent could human beings act as responsible agents in society? What was their proper role when they confronted the limits that the gods or other humans placed on their activity? How should they proceed when the gods and human authorities presented them with conflicting demands?

Comic dramatists such as Aristophanes also dealt with serious issues of human striving and responsible behavior. They took savage delight in lampooning the public and political figures of their time. The comedians aimed to influence popular attitudes by ridiculing the foibles of prominent public figures and calling attention to the absurd consequences of ill-considered action.

Hellenistic Philosophy and Religion

As the Hellenistic empires seized the political initiative in the Mediterranean basin and eclipsed the poleis, Greek philosophy and religion lost their civic character. Because the poleis no longer controlled their destinies but, rather, figured as small elements in a large political structure, residents ceased

---

Bacchae (bahk-ee)

Aeschylus (ES-kuh-luhs)

to regard their polis as the focus of individual loyalties. Instead, they inclined toward cultural and religious alternatives that ministered to the needs and interests of individuals living in a large, cosmopolitan society.

The Hellenistic Philosophers The most popular Hellenistic philosophers—the Epicureans, the Skeptics, and the Stoics—addressed individual needs by searching for personal tranquility and serenity. **Epicureans,** for example, identified pleasure as the greatest good. By *pleasure* they meant a state of quiet satisfaction that would shield them from the pressures of the Hellenistic world. **Skeptics** refused to take strong positions on political, moral, and social issues because they doubted the possibility of certain knowledge. Rather than engage in fruitless disputes, they sought equanimity and left contentious issues to others.

The most respected and influential of the Hellenistic philosophers were the **Stoics,** who considered all human beings members of a universal family. Unlike the Epicureans and the Skeptics, the Stoics did not seek to withdraw from the pressures of the world. Rather, they taught that individuals had the duty to aid others and lead virtuous lives. The Stoics believed that individuals could avoid anxieties caused by the

---

Epicureans (ehp-ih-KYOOR-ee-uhns)
Stoics (STOH-ihks)

pressures of Hellenistic society by concentrating their attention strictly on the duties that reason and nature demanded of them. Thus, like the Epicureans and the Skeptics, the Stoics sought ways to bring individuals to a state of inner peace and tranquility.

Religions of Salvation Although the philosophers' doctrines appealed to educated elites, religions of salvation enjoyed surging popularity in Hellenistic society. Mystery religions promised eternal bliss for initiates who observed their rites and lived in accordance with their doctrines. Some faiths spread across the trade routes and found followers far from their homelands. The Egyptian cult of Osiris, for example, became popular because it promised salvation for those who led honorable lives. Cults from Persia, Mesopotamia, Anatolia, and Greece also attracted disciples throughout the Hellenistic world.

Many of the mystery religions involved the worship of a savior whose death and resurrection would lead the way to eternal salvation for devoted followers. Some philosophers and religious thinkers speculated that a single god might rule the entire universe—just as Alexander and his successors governed enormous empires on earth—and that this god had a plan for the salvation of all humankind. Like the Hellenistic philosophies, then, religions of salvation addressed the interests of individuals searching for security in a complex world.

CONCLUSION

Greek travelers linked the regions of the Mediterranean basin in classical times. Although they did not build a centralized empire, the Greeks dotted the Mediterranean and Black Sea shorelines with their colonies, and their merchant fleets stimulated both commercial and cultural interactions between peoples of distant lands. Greek merchants, soldiers, and administrators also played prominent roles in the vast empires of Alexander and the Hellenistic rulers. Quite apart from their political and economic significance, the Greeks also left a remarkably rich cultural legacy. Greek philosophy, literature, and science profoundly influenced the intellectual and cultural development of peoples from southwest Asia to western Europe. The Greek poleis and the Hellenistic cities provided nurturing environments for rational thought and academic pursuits, and the frequent travels of the Greeks promoted the spread of popular religious faiths throughout the Mediterranean basin and beyond. Like the regions of Persia, China, and South Asia, the Mediterranean basin became an integrated world.

STUDY TERMS

Alexander of Macedon (190)	Olympic Games (198)
Alexandria (197)	Pasion (200)
Aristotle (202)	Peloponnesian War (192)
Athens (189)	Pericles (189)
Attica (189)	Persian Wars (191)
cult of Dionysus (203)	Plato (202)
Darius I (191)	polis (187)
Delian League (191)	Ptolemaic Egypt (197)
Eleusinian mysteries (203)	Sappho (199)
Epicureans (204)	Skeptics (204)
Hellenistic era (196)	Socrates (200)
helots (187)	Solon (189)
Homer (187)	Sparta (187)
Knossos (186)	Stoics (204)
Minoan (186)	Thucydides (192)
Mycenaean (186)	

FOR FURTHER READING

Walter Burkert. *Babylon, Memphis, Persepolis: Eastern Contexts of Greek Culture.* Cambridge, Mass., 2004. Explores Mesopotamian, Egyptian, and Persian influences on Greek literature, philosophy, and science.

Lionel Casson. *The Ancient Mariners: Seafarers and Sea Fighters of the Mediterranean in Ancient Times.* 2nd ed. Princeton, 1991. Draws on discoveries of underwater archaeologists in reconstructing the maritime history of the ancient Mediterranean.

M. I. Finley. *Ancient Slavery and Modern Ideology.* Expanded ed. Princeton, 1998. Presents a thoughtful analysis of Greek and Roman slavery in light of modern slavery and contemporary debates.

Frederick C. Grant, ed. *Hellenistic Religions: The Age of Syncretism.* Indianapolis, 1953. Fascinating collection of translated documents and texts that throw light on religious and philosophical beliefs of the Hellenistic era.

N. G. L. Hammond. *The Genius of Alexander the Great.* Chapel Hill, N.C., 1997. A scholarly and reliable study of Alexander of Macedon.

W. V. Harris, ed. *Rethinking the Mediterranean.* New York, 2005. A collection of scholarly essays exploring issues that linked the various lands bordering the Mediterranean in premodern times.

Donald Kagan. *The Peloponnesian War.* New York, 2003. Synopsis of the debilitating conflict by the foremost contemporary scholar of the Peloponnesian War.

Josiah Ober. *The Rise and Fall of Classical Greece.* Princeton, 2015. Thoughtful analysis that links new evidence on the economic activity of ancient Greece to the democratic principles that underlined the political structures of many of the poleis.

Susan Sherwin-White and Amélie Kuhrt. *From Samarkhand to Sardis: A New Approach to the Seleucid Empire.* Berkeley, 1993. Detailed scholarly analysis of the Seleucid empire concentrating on political and economic matters.

ZOOMING IN ON ENCOUNTERS

Paul of Tarsus and the Long Arm of Roman Law

About 55 C.E. Roman guards transported a prisoner named Paul of Tarsus from the port of Caesarea in Palestine to the city of Rome. The journey turned out to be more eventful than the travelers had planned. The party boarded a sailing ship loaded with grain and carrying 276 passengers as well. The ship departed in the fall—after the main sailing season, which ran from May through September—and soon encountered a violent storm. For two frightening weeks crew and passengers alike worked furiously to keep the ship afloat, jettisoning baggage, tackle, and cargo to lighten the load as wind and rain battered the vessel. Eventually, the ship ran aground on the island of Malta, where storm-driven waves destroyed it. Yet most of the passengers and crew survived, including Paul and his guards, who spent three months on Malta before catching another ship to Rome.

Paul had become embroiled in a dispute between Jews and early proponents of the fledgling Christian religion. Christianity first emerged as a sect of Judaism accepted by only a small number of individuals who regarded Jesus of Nazareth as a savior for the Jewish community. By the mid-first century C.E., Christianity was attracting numerous converts throughout the Mediterranean basin. Paul himself was a devout Jew from Anatolia who eventually accepted Christian teachings and

A marble relief sculpture of about 100 C.E. depicts a crew of men working in a treadmill that powers a crane used in construction of a Roman temple, demonstrating the extraordinary technological and engineering skills of the Romans.
DEA/G. NIMATALLAH/De Agostini/Getty Images

became a zealous missionary seeking converts from outside as well as within the Jewish community. Indeed, he was the principal figure in the development of Christianity from a Jewish sect to an independent religious faith. When a crowd of Paul's enemies attacked him in Jerusalem, where he was promoting his recently adopted faith, the resulting disturbance became so severe that authorities of the Roman imperial government intervened to restore order. Under normal circumstances Roman authorities would deliver an individual like Paul to the leaders of his ethnic community, and the laws and customs of that community would determine the person's fate.

Paul's case, however, was different. Knowing that Jewish leaders would condemn him and probably execute him, Paul asserted his rights as a Roman citizen. Although he had never traveled west of Greece, Paul had inherited Roman citizenship from his father. As a result, he had the right to appeal his case to Rome, and he did so. His appeal did not succeed. No record of his case survives, but tradition holds that imperial authorities executed him out of concern that Christianity threatened the peace and stability of the Roman state.

Paul's experience reflects the cosmopolitan character of the early Roman Empire, which by the first century C.E. dominated the entire Mediterranean basin. Roman administrators oversaw affairs from Anatolia and Palestine in the east to Spain and Morocco in the west. Roman military forces maintained order in an empire with scores of different and sometimes conflicting ethnic and religious groups. Like many others, Paul of Tarsus traveled freely through much of the Roman Empire in an effort to attract converts to Christianity. Indeed, except for the integration of the Mediterranean basin by the Roman Empire, Paul's message and his faith might never have expanded beyond the small community of early Christians in Jerusalem.

CHAPTER OVERVIEW

Like the Phoenicians and the Greeks before them, the Romans established close links between the various Mediterranean regions. As they conquered new lands, pacified them, and brought them into their empire, the Romans enabled merchants, missionaries, and others to travel readily throughout the Mediterranean basin. The Romans differed from their Phoenician and Greek predecessors, however, by building an extensive land empire and centralizing the administration of their realm. At its high point the Roman Empire dominated the entire Mediterranean basin and parts of southwest Asia, including Anatolia, Mesopotamia, Syria, Egypt, and north Africa, besides much of continental Europe, and even much of Britain.

The Roman Empire also served as a forum for the communication of philosophical ideas and religious beliefs. Educated elites often embraced sophisticated Hellenistic philosophies, particularly Stoicism, which found adherents throughout the Roman Empire. The larger population took comfort in popular religious beliefs, many of which promised personal salvation to devout followers. Over the long term, Christianity was the most successful of the popular religions of salvation. The early Christians encountered harsh opposition and persecution from Roman officials. Yet the new faith took advantage of the Romans' well-organized imperial provinces and spread rapidly throughout the Mediterranean basin and beyond. Eventually, Christianity became the official religion of the Roman Empire, and imperial sponsorship enabled Christianity to spread more effectively than before.

FROM KINGDOM TO REPUBLIC

Founded in the eighth century B.C.E., the city of Rome was originally a small city-state ruled by a single king. Late in the sixth century B.C.E., the city's aristocrats deposed the king, ended the monarchy, and instituted a republic—a form of government in which delegates represented the interests of various constituencies. The **Roman Republic** survived for more than five hundred years, and it was under the republican constitution that Rome established itself as the dominant power in the Mediterranean basin.

CHRONOLOGY	
753 B.C.E.	Founding of Rome, according to tradition
509 B.C.E.	Establishment of the Roman Republic
264–146 B.C.E.	Roman expansion in the Mediterranean basin
106–43 B.C.E.	Life of Marcus Tullius Cicero
1st century B.C.E.	Civil war in Rome
46–44 B.C.E.	Rule of Gaius Julius Caesar as dictator
31 B.C.E.–14 C.E.	Rule of Augustus
4 B.C.E.–early 30s C.E.	Life of Jesus of Nazareth
1st century C.E.	Life of Paul of Tarsus
66–70 C.E.	Jewish War

The Etruscans and Rome

Romulus and Remus The city of Rome arose from origins both obscure and humble. According to the ancient legends, the city owed its existence to the flight of Aeneas, a refugee from Troy who migrated to Italy when Greek invaders destroyed his native land. Two of his descendants, the twins **Romulus** and **Remus,** almost did not survive infancy because an evil uncle abandoned them by the flooded Tiber River, fully expecting them to drown or die of exposure. But a kindly she-wolf found them and nursed them to health. The boys grew strong and courageous, and in 753 B.C.E. Romulus founded the city of Rome and established himself as its first king.

Modern scholars do not tell so colorful a tale, but they agree that Rome grew from humble beginnings. Beginning about 2000 B.C.E., bands of Indo-European migrants crossed the Alps and settled throughout the Italian peninsula. Like their distant cousins in South Asia, Greece, and northern Europe, these migrants blended with the neolithic inhabitants of the region, adopted agriculture, and established tribal federations. Sheepherders and small farmers occupied much of the Italian peninsula, including the future site of Rome itself. Bronze metallurgy appeared about 1800 B.C.E. and iron about 900 B.C.E.

The Etruscans During the middle centuries of the first millennium B.C.E., all the communities dwelling in the Italian peninsula underwent rapid political and economic development. The agents of that development were the **Etruscans,** a dynamic people who dominated much of Italy between the eighth and the fifth centuries B.C.E. The Etruscans probably migrated to Italy from Anatolia. They settled first in Tuscany, the region around modern Florence, but they soon controlled much of the territory from the Po River valley in northern Italy to the region around modern Naples in the south. They built thriving cities and established political and economic alliances between their settlements. They manufactured high-quality bronze and iron goods, and they worked gold and silver into jewelry. They built a fleet and traded actively in the western Mediterranean. During the late sixth century B.C.E., however, the Etruscans encountered a series of challenges from other peoples, and their society began to decline. Greek fleets defeated the Etruscans at sea while Celtic peoples attacked them from **Gaul** (modern France).

The Kingdom of Rome The Etruscans deeply influenced the early development of Rome. Like the Etruscan cities, Rome was a monarchy during the early days after its foundation, and several Roman kings were Etruscans. The kings ruled Rome through the seventh and sixth centuries B.C.E., and they provided the city with paved streets, public buildings, defensive walls, and large temples.

Etruscan merchants drew a large volume of traffic to Rome, thanks partly to the city's geographic advantages. Rome enjoyed easy access to the Mediterranean by way of the Tiber River, but since it was not on the coast, it did not run the risk of invasion or attack from the sea. Already during the period of Etruscan dominance, trade routes from all parts of Italy converged on Rome. When Etruscan

Etruscan riders, silver panel 540–520 B.C., discovered by archaeologists at Castel San Marino, near Perugia, in the heartland of the Etruscan realm. Like all advanced ancient cultures, the Etruscans produced superb artists.
The Picture Art Collection/
Alamy Stock Photo

Ruins of the Roman forum, where political leaders conducted public affairs during the era of the republic, still stand today.
Robert Harding/Alamy Stock Photo

society declined, Rome was in a strong position to play a more prominent role both in Italy and in the larger Mediterranean world.

The Roman Republic and Its Constitution

Establishment of the Republic In 509 B.C.E. the Roman nobility deposed the last Etruscan king and replaced the monarchy with an aristocratic republic. At the heart of the city, they built the Roman forum, a political and civic center filled with temples and public buildings where leading citizens tended to government business. They also instituted a republican constitution that entrusted executive responsibilities to two consuls who wielded civil and military power. Consuls were elected by members of an elite class determined by birth known as the **patricians,** and they served one-year terms. The powerful Senate, whose members were patricians with extensive political experience, advised the consuls and ratified all major decisions. Later the election of consuls was transferred to the Senate, but because the consuls and Senate both represented the interests of the patricians, there was constant tension between the elites and the common people, known as the **plebeians.**

Conflicts between Patricians and Plebeians During the early fifth century B.C.E., relations between the classes became so strained that the plebeians threatened to secede from Rome and establish a rival settlement. To maintain the integrity of the Roman state, the patricians granted plebeians the right to elect officials, known as **tribunes,** who represented their interests in the Roman government. Originally, plebeians chose two tribunes, but the number eventually rose to ten.

Tribunes had the power to intervene in all political matters, and they possessed the right to veto measures that they judged unfair. In 449 B.C.E. patricians made a further concession to plebeians by promulgating Rome's first set of laws, known as the **Twelve Tables,** which drew upon Greek laws in establishing a framework for the social organization of the Roman state. The Twelve Tables served as the foundation for a long tradition of Roman law making.

Although the tribunes provided a voice in government for the plebeians, the patricians continued to dominate Rome. Tensions between the classes persisted for as long as the republic survived. During the fourth century B.C.E., plebeians became eligible to hold almost all state offices and gained the right to have one of the consuls come from their ranks. By the early third century, plebeian-dominated assemblies won the power to make decisions binding on all of Rome. Thus, like fifth-century Athens, republican Rome gradually broadened the base of political participation.

Constitutional compromises eased class tensions, but they did not solve all political problems confronted by the republic. When faced with civil or military crises, the Roman Senate appointed an official, known as a dictator, who wielded absolute power for a term of six months. By providing for strong leadership during times of extraordinary difficulty, the republican constitution enabled Rome to maintain a reasonably stable society throughout most of the republic's history. Meanwhile, by allowing various constituencies a voice in government, the constitution also helped to prevent the emergence of crippling class tensions.

plebeians (plih-BEE-uhns)

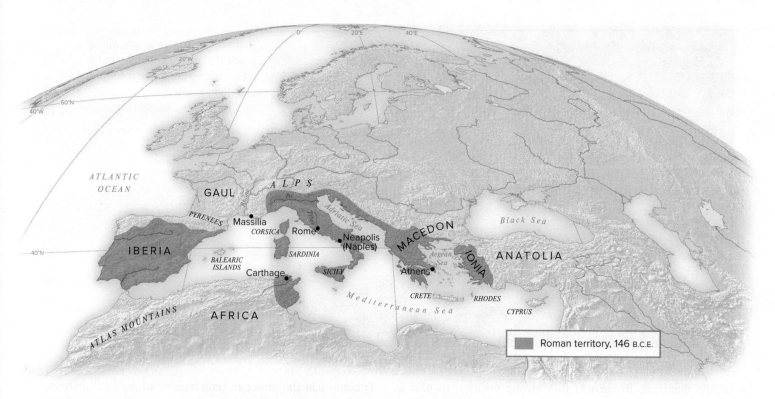

MAP 11.1   **Expansion of the Roman Republic to 146 B.C.E.**

By the mid-second century B.C.E., the Roman Republic controlled extensive territories outside Italy.

How did Roman control of these regions facilitate economic and cultural unification across the Mediterranean Basin?

The Expansion of the Republic

While the Romans dealt constructively with internal problems, external challenges mounted. During the fifth century B.C.E., for example, Rome faced threats not only from peoples living in the neighboring hills but also from the Etruscans. Beyond Italy were the Gauls, a powerful Celtic people who on several occasions invaded Italy. Between the fourth and second centuries B.C.E., however, a remarkable expansion of power and influence transformed Rome from a small and vulnerable city-state to the center of an enormous empire.

First the Romans consolidated their position in central Italy. During the fifth and early fourth centuries B.C.E., the Romans founded a large regional state in central Italy at the expense of the declining Etruscans and other neighboring peoples. Their conquests gave them access to the iron industry built by the Etruscans and greatly expanded the amount of land under Roman control.

During the later fourth century, the Romans built on their early conquests and emerged as the predominant power in the Italian peninsula. The Romans secured control of the peninsula partly because they established military colonies in regions they overcame and partly because of a generous policy toward the peoples they conquered. Instead of ruling them as vanquished

subjects, the Romans often exempted them from taxation and allowed them to govern their internal affairs. Conquered peoples in Italy enjoyed the right to trade in Rome and take Roman spouses. Some gained Roman citizenship and rose to high positions in Roman society. The Romans forbade conquered peoples from making military or political alliances, except with Rome, and required them to provide soldiers and military support. Those policies provided the political, military, and diplomatic support Rome needed to put down occasional rebellions and to dominate affairs throughout the Italian peninsula.

Expansion in the Mediterranean

With Italy under its control, Rome began to play a major role in the affairs of the larger Mediterranean basin and to experience conflicts with other Mediterranean powers. The principal power in the western Mediterranean during the fourth and third centuries B.C.E. was **Carthage**, located near modern Tunis. Originally established as a Phoenician colony, Carthage enjoyed a strategic location that enabled it to trade actively and build a strong regional empire in the western Mediterranean region. From the wealth generated by that commerce, Carthage became the dominant political power in north Africa (excluding Egypt), the southern part of the Iberian peninsula, and the western region of grain-rich Sicily as well. Meanwhile, the three Hellenistic empires that succeeded Alexander of Macedon continued to dominate the eastern Mediterranean: the Antigonids

Carthage (KAHR-thihj)

ruled Macedon, the Ptolemies ruled Egypt, and the Seleucids included wealthy Syria and Anatolia among their many possessions. The prosperity of the Hellenistic realms supported a thriving network of maritime commerce in the eastern Mediterranean, and as in the case of Carthage, commercial wealth enabled rulers to maintain powerful states and armies.

The Punic Wars The Romans clashed first with Carthage. Between 264 and 146 B.C.E., they fought three devastating conflicts known as the **Punic Wars,** in which Rome and Carthage struggled for regional supremacy. Friction first arose from economic competition, particularly over Sicily, the most important source of grain in the western Mediterranean. In the Second Punic War the very survival of Rome was at stake after Carthaginian general **Hannibal Barca** devastated the Italian peninsula for fifteen years. The rivalry ended after Roman forces subjected Carthage to a long siege, conquered the city, burned much of it to the ground, and forced some fifty thousand survivors into slavery. With their victory over Carthage, Romans became the dominant power brokers in the western Mediterranean region. They also annexed Carthaginian possessions in north Africa and Iberia—rich in grain, oil, wine, silver, and gold—and used those resources to finance continued imperial expansion.

Shortly after the beginning of the Carthaginian conflict, Rome became embroiled in disputes in the eastern Mediterranean. Conflict arose partly because pirates and ambitious local lords ignored the weakening Hellenistic rulers and threatened regional stability. On several occasions Roman leaders dispatched armies to protect the interests of Roman citizens and merchants, and those expeditions brought them into conflict with the Antigonids and the Seleucids. Between 215 and 148 B.C.E., Rome fought five major wars, mostly in Macedon and Anatolia, against Antigonid and Seleucid opponents. The Romans did not immediately annex lands in the eastern Mediterranean but, rather, entrusted them to allies in the region. Nevertheless, by the middle of the second century B.C.E., Rome clearly ranked as the preeminent power in the eastern as well as the western Mediterranean.

FROM REPUBLIC TO EMPIRE

Imperial expansion brought wealth and power to Rome, but wealth and power brought problems as well as benefits. Unequal distribution of wealth aggravated class tensions and gave rise to conflict over political and social policies. Meanwhile, the need to administer conquered lands efficiently strained the capacities of the republican constitution. During the first century B.C.E. and the first century C.E., Roman civil and military leaders gradually dismantled the republican constitution and imposed a centralized imperial form of government on the city of Rome and its empire.

Imperial Expansion and Domestic Problems

In Rome, as in ancient China and Greece, patterns of land distribution caused serious political and social tensions.

Roman expansion depended on well-equipped and highly disciplined military forces. In this detail from the third-century Ludovisi sarcophagus, Roman soldiers can be seen battling "barbarian" troops.

Vladimir Korostyshevskiy/Shutterstock

Conquered lands were largely confiscated by wealthy elites, who organized enormous plantations known as *latifundia.* Because they enjoyed economies of scale and often employed slave labor, owners of latifundia operated at lower costs than did owners of smaller holdings, who often had to mortgage their lands or sell out to their wealthier neighbors.

The Gracchi Brothers During the second and first centuries B.C.E., relations between the classes became so strained that they led to violent social conflict and civil war. The chief proponents of social reform in the Roman republic were the brothers Tiberius and Gaius Gracchus. Just as Wang Mang, the imperial usurper of the Han dynasty, tried to bring about a redistribution of land resources in classical China, the **Gracchi brothers** worked to limit the amount of conquered land that any individual could hold. Those whose lands exceeded the limit would lose some of their property, which officials would then allocate to small farmers. Again, as in the case of Wang Mang, the Gracchi had little success because most members of the wealthy and ruling classes considered them dangerous radicals and found ways to undermine their efforts. Indeed, fearing that the brothers might gain influence over Roman affairs, their enemies assassinated Tiberius in 132 B.C.E. and executed Gaius on trumped-up charges in 121 B.C.E.

The experiences of the Gracchi brothers clearly showed that the constitution of the Roman republic, originally designed for a small city-state, might not be suitable for a large and growing empire. Formal political power remained in the hands of a small, privileged class of people in Rome, and their policies often reflected the interests of their class rather than the concerns of the empire as a whole. For the century following the assassinations of the Gracchi brothers, Roman politicians

latifundia (lah-tee-FOON-dya)

and generals jockeyed for power and position as they sought to mobilize support. Several military commanders began to recruit personal armies not from the ranks of small farmers—traditionally the core of the Roman army—but from landless rural residents and urban workers. Because these troops had no economic cushion to fall back on, they were intensely loyal to their generals and placed the interests of the army before those of the state. Most important of these generals were Gaius Marius, who sided with social reformers who advocated redistribution of land, and Lucius Cornelius Sulla, a veteran of several foreign campaigns who allied with the conservative and aristocratic classes.

Civil War During the early first century B.C.E., Rome fell into civil war. In 87 B.C.E. Marius marched on Rome, placed the city under military occupation, and hunted down his political enemies. After Marius died the following year, Sulla made plans to take his place. In 83 B.C.E. he seized Rome and initiated a grisly slaughter of his enemies. Sulla posted lists naming proscribed individuals whom he labeled enemies of the state, and he encouraged the Roman populace to kill those individuals on sight and confiscate their properties. During a reign of terror that lasted almost five years, Sulla brought about the murder or execution of perhaps ten thousand individuals. By the time Sulla died in 78 B.C.E., he had imposed an extremely conservative legislative program that weakened the influence of the lower classes and strengthened the hand of the wealthy in Roman politics.

Because Sulla's program did not address Rome's most serious social problems, however, it had no chance to succeed over the long term. Latifundia continued to pressure small farmers, who increasingly left the countryside and swelled the ranks of the urban lower classes. Poverty in the cities, especially Rome, led to periodic social eruptions when the price of grain rose or the supply fell. Meanwhile, the urban poor increasingly joined the personal armies of ambitious generals, who themselves posed threats to social and political stability. In this chaotic context, Gaius **Julius Caesar** inaugurated the process by which Rome replaced its republican constitution with a centralized imperial form of government.

The Foundation of Empire

A nephew of the general Marius, Julius Caesar favored liberal policies and social reform. In spite of these well-known political sympathies, he escaped danger during the reign of Sulla and the conservatives who followed him. Caesar's survival was due in some measure to his youth, but partly also to a well-timed excursion to

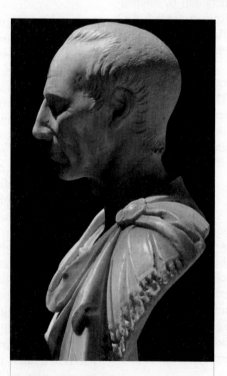

A bust of Julius Caesar depicts a seasoned conqueror and a canny political leader.
John Ross/Robert Harding/Alamy Stock Photo

Greece and the eastern Mediterranean. During the decade of the 60s B.C.E., Caesar played an active role in Roman politics, as a member of an unofficial but powerful alliance known as the First Triumvirate. He spent enormous sums of money sponsoring public spectacles—such as battles between gladiators and wild animals—which helped him build a reputation and win election to posts in the republican government. This activity kept him in the public eye and helped to publicize his interest in social reform. During the next decade Caesar led a Roman army to Gaul, which he conquered and brought into the still-growing Roman Empire.

The conquest of Gaul led directly to a political crisis. As a result of his military victories, Caesar had become extremely popular in Rome. Conservative leaders sought to maneuver him out of power and regain the initiative for their own programs. Caesar refused to stand aside, and in 49 B.C.E. he turned his army toward Rome. By early 46 B.C.E. he had made himself master of the Roman state and named himself dictator—an office that he claimed for life rather than for the constitutional six-month term. Caesar then centralized military and political functions and brought them under his control. He confiscated property from conservatives and distributed it to veterans of his armies and other supporters. He launched large-scale building projects in Rome as a way to provide employment for the urban poor. He also extended Roman citizenship to peoples in the imperial provinces, and he even appointed Gauls to the Roman Senate.

Caesar's policies pointed the way toward a centralized, imperial form of government for Rome and its possessions, but the consolidation of that government had to wait for a new generation of leaders. Caesar's rule alienated many members of the Roman elite classes, who considered him a tyrant. In 44 B.C.E. they organized a plot to assassinate Caesar and restore the republic. They attacked Caesar and stabbed him to death in the Roman forum, but the restoration of an outmoded form of government was beyond their powers. Instead, they plunged Rome into a fresh round of civil conflict that persisted for thirteen more years.

Augustus When the struggles ended, power belonged to Octavian, a grandnephew and protégé of Julius Caesar and the dictator's adopted son. In a naval battle at Actium in Greece (31 B.C.E.), Octavian defeated his principal rival, Mark Antony, who had joined forces with Cleopatra, last of the Ptolemaic rulers of Egypt. He then moved quickly and efficiently to consolidate his rule. In 27 B.C.E. the Senate bestowed on him the title **Augustus,** a term with strong religious connotations suggesting the divine

In this statue, Augustus wears the uniform of a Roman general. What impression of Augustus's qualities is the sculptor attempting to project in his portrayal?

adam eastland/Alamy Stock Photo

or semidivine nature of its holder. During his forty-five years of virtually unopposed rule, Augustus fashioned an imperial government that guided Roman affairs for the next three centuries.

Augustus's Administration Augustus's government was a monarchy disguised as a republic. Like Julius Caesar, Augustus ruled by centralizing political and military power. Yet he proceeded more cautiously than had his patron: Augustus preserved traditional republican offices and forms of government and included members of the Roman elite in his government. At the same time, though, he fundamentally altered the nature of that government. He accumulated vast powers for himself and ultimately took responsibility for all important governmental functions. He reorganized the military system, creating a new standing army with commanders who owed allegiance directly to the emperor—a reform that eliminated problems caused during the late republic by generals with personal armies. He also was careful to place individuals loyal to him in all important

positions. Augustus served as emperor until his death in 14 C.E. During his long reign he stabilized a land racked by civil war and enabled the institutions of empire to take root.

Continuing Expansion and Integration of the Empire

During the two centuries following Augustus's rule, Roman armies conquered distant lands and integrated them into a larger economy and society. By the end of the republic, Rome already held Italy, Greece, Syria, Gaul, and most of the Iberian peninsula, with small outposts in north Africa and Anatolia. By Augustus's reign imperial holdings included much of southeastern Europe; most of north Africa, including Egypt; and sizable territories in Anatolia and southwest Asia. At its high point, during the early second century C.E., the **Roman Empire** embraced much of Britain as well as a continuous belt of possessions surrounding the Mediterranean and extending to rich agricultural regions inland, including Mesopotamia. After Octavian's conquest of Egypt in 30 B.C.E., Roman forces even made forays deep into the kingdom of Kush, and for more than three centuries they occupied a stretch of the Nile Valley about 110 kilometers (70 miles) south of the river's first cataract near Aswan.

Roman expansion had especially dramatic effects in European regions now incorporated into the empire. Egypt, Anatolia, Syria, and Mesopotamia had long been sites of complex city-based societies, but Gaul, Germany, Britain, and Spain were sparsely populated lands occupied by cultivators who lived in small villages. When Roman soldiers, diplomats, governors, and merchants began to arrive in large numbers, they stimulated the development of local economies and states. They sought access to resources such as tin, and they encouraged local inhabitants to cultivate wheat, olives, and grapes. Local ruling elites allied with Roman representatives and used the wealth that came into their communities to control natural resources and build states on a much larger scale than ever before. Cities emerged where administrators and merchants conducted their business, and the tempo of European society noticeably quickened: Paris, Lyons, Cologne, Mainz, London, Toledo, and Segovia all trace their origins to Roman times.

The *Pax Romana* Within the boundaries of the Roman Empire itself, a long era of peace facilitated economic and political integration from the first to the middle of the third century C.E. Augustus brought peace not only to Rome, by ending the civil disturbances that had plagued the city for more than a century, but also to the empire. His reign inaugurated the era known as the ***pax romana*** ("Roman peace") that persisted for two and a half centuries. In spite of occasional flare-ups, especially among conquered peoples who resented Roman rule, the *pax romana* facilitated trade and communication throughout the region from Mesopotamia to the Atlantic Ocean.

Roman Roads Like their Persian, Chinese, Indian, and Hellenistic counterparts, the Romans integrated their empire

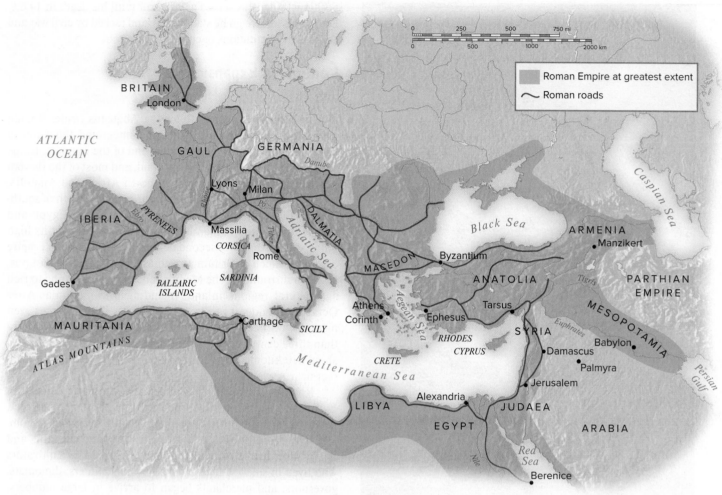

MAP 11.2 The Roman Empire, ca. 117 C.E.

Compare this map of the Roman Empire at its height with Map 11.1 showing territories controlled by the Roman Republic almost two centuries earlier.

What impact would these roads have had on the maintenance of empire, transregional trade, and cultural integration throughout the Mediterranean Basin and adjacent lands?

by building networks of transportation and communication. Since ancient times, Roman engineers have enjoyed a reputation as outstanding road builders. Roman engineers prepared a deep bed for their roads, edged them with curbs, provided for drainage, and then topped them off with large, flat paving stones. Their main roads were 6 to 8 meters (20 to 26 feet) wide—large enough to accommodate two-way traffic—and even roads winding through mountains were 2 to 3 meters (6 to 10 feet) wide. Builders placed milestones along the roads, and the imperial postal system maintained stations for couriers. The roads and postal system permitted urgent travel and messages to proceed with remarkable speed: Tiberius, successor of Augustus as Roman emperor, once traveled 290 kilometers (180 miles) in a single day over Roman roads.

Roads linked all parts of the Roman Empire. One notable highway of more than 2,500 kilometers (1,554 miles) stretched along the northeast imperial frontier from the Black Sea to the North Sea, parallel to the Danube and Rhine Rivers. Another road linked Rome to the city of Gades (modern Cadiz) in southern Spain. A road of 4,800 kilometers (2,983 miles) ran parallel to the coast of north Africa, and numerous spurs reached south, enabling merchants and soldiers to range deep into the Sahara desert. Romans also built new roads that facilitated travel and trade in the eastern Mediterranean region. One route linked the port of Berenice on the Red Sea to Alexandria, and others linked the towns and ports of the eastern Mediterranean seaboard to Palmyra, a principal way station of caravan traffic coming west from central Asia. Scholars estimate the combined length of the Roman roads was greater than 80,000 kilometers (50,000 miles).

Sea Lanes Where roads came to the water's edge, Romans made use of sea lanes throughout the Mediterranean Sea

SOURCES FROM THE PAST

Tacitus on the Abuse of Power in the Early Roman Empire

Augustus's imperial regime and the pax romana brought peace and stability to the Roman Empire, but some contemporaries thought there was a darker side to the new imperial order. Cornelius Tacitus (56–120 C.E.) was a prominent aristocrat and the most important historian of the early Roman Empire. Written in the early second century, The Annals *by Tacitus is one of the most important sources we have on the reigns of Augustus and his successors.*

Both the successes and reverses of the old Roman people have been recorded by famous historians; and fine intellects were not wanting to describe the time of Augustus, until growing sycophancy scared them away. The histories of Tiberius, Gaius, Claudius and Nero, while they were in power, were falsified through terror, and after their death were written under the influence of recent hatred. Hence my purpose is to relate a few facts about Augustus—more particularly his last acts, then the reign of Tiberius, and all which follows—without either bitterness or partiality, from the motives to which I am far removed . . .

Augustus won over the soldiers with gifts, the people with cheap corn, and all men with the sweet gift of peace. And so his power grew greater by degrees, while he concentrated on the functions of the senate, the magistrates, and the law. There was no opposition. Civil war or political murders had eliminated all spirited men. Elite men found that servile obedience was how to get ahead politically and financially. These men had enjoyed the fruits of the revolution, and now preferred their secure position under the new regime compared with the uncertainties they experienced under the old. The new regime was also popular in the provinces, where the Senate and magistrates had been viewed with suspicion as extortionists. There had been no laws to protect them, because the system was blighted by violence, cronyism and corruption . . .

No one had any fear while Augustus remained in good health, and kept his life and that of his house going, and also maintained peace throughout the Empire. But as Augustus became more incapacitated, some people began to think of change. Some people even started thinking of freedom. Most feared a return to civil war; but some welcomed the idea. Yet the majority of the populace focused more on possible candidates for succession . . .

Then two announcements were made at the same time: Augustus was dead, and his successor was Tiberius who had taken control of the state . . .

The new reign commenced with the assassination of Agrippa Postumus. He was murdered by a centurion. Tiberius gave no explanation of the matter to the Senate; he pretended that there were directions from his father ordering the tribune in charge of the prisoner not to delay the slaughter of Agrippa, whenever he should himself have breathed his last. Beyond a doubt, Augustus had often complained of the young man's character, and had succeeded in obtaining the sanction of a decree of the Senate for his banishment. But he never was hard-hearted enough to destroy any of his kinsfolk, nor was it creditable that death was to be the sentence of the grandson in order that the stepson might feel secure. It was more probable that Tiberius and Livia, the one from fear, the other from a stepmother's enmity, hurried on the destruction of a youth whom they suspected and hated . . .

Meanwhile at Rome people plunged into slavery—consuls, senators, knights. The higher a man's rank, the more eager his hypocrisy, and his looks the more carefully studied, so as neither to betray joy at the death of one emperor nor sorrow at the rise of another, while he mingled delight and lamentation with his flattery.

> What does the author mean by stating that the accounts written by historians of these emperors "while they were in power, were falsified through terror, and after their death were written under the influence of recent hatred"?

> What motives might Tiberius and his mother Livia have had that made them so determined to murder Agrippa Postumus?

For Further Reflection

■ What aspects of political life under Augustus and Tiberius is the author most concerned about?

■ How did different groups within the recently created empire respond to this new political reality?

■ How might a representative of the emperors have responded to the author's criticisms?

Source: Annals of Tacitus, *translated by Alfred John Church and William Jackson Broadribb, London: Macmillan and Co, 1876.*

and the Black Sea. Established sea lanes linked ports from Syria and Palestine to Spain and north Africa. Indeed, the Mediterranean became essentially a Roman lake, which the Romans themselves called ***mare nostrum*** ("our sea"). Thus, by sea as well as by land, Romans found ways to maintain communications with all regions of their empire.

Roman Law   Under conditions of political stability and the *pax romana,* jurists constructed an elaborate system of law. As we saw earlier in the chapter, Romans began a tradition of written law in 449 B.C.E., when they promulgated the Twelve Tables as a basic law code for citizens of the early republic. As armies spread Roman influence throughout the Mediterranean, jurists worked to construct a rational body of law that would apply to all peoples under Roman rule. During the late republic and especially during the empire, the jurists articulated standards of justice and gradually applied them throughout Roman territory. They established the principle that defendants were innocent until proven guilty, and they ensured that defendants had a right to challenge their accusers before a judge in a court of law. They also permitted judges to set aside laws that were unfair. Like transportation and communication networks, Roman law helped to integrate the diverse lands that made up the empire, and the principles of Roman law continued to shape Mediterranean and European society long after the empire had disappeared.

ECONOMY AND SOCIETY IN THE ROMAN MEDITERRANEAN

The rapid expansion of Roman influence and the imposition of Roman imperial rule brought economic and social changes to peoples throughout the Mediterranean basin. Good roads and the *pax romana* encouraged trade between regions. Existing cities benefited handsomely from the wealth generated by trade, and in the lands they conquered, the Romans founded new cities to serve as links between local regions and the larger Mediterranean economy. Meanwhile, like most other peoples of ancient times, the Romans built a strictly patriarchal society and made extensive use of slave labor.

Trade and Urbanization

Commercial Agriculture   Like other ancient societies, the Roman Mediterranean experienced economic development and social change as the state expanded and brought new regions into its network of trade and communication. Agricultural production, the economic foundation of the Roman and indeed all ancient empires, also underwent transformation with the expansion of empire and the growth of trade. Instead of planting crops for immediate local use, owners of latifundia concentrated on production for export. Grain from latifundia in north Africa, Egypt, and Sicily routinely found its way over the Roman roads and the Mediterranean sea lanes to the large cities of the empire. The ship that Paul of Tarsus boarded at Caesarea, which we discussed at the beginning of the chapter, for example, carried several hundred tons of wheat destined for consumers in Rome.

Commercial agriculture played an important role in the economic specialization and integration of the empire. Because it was possible to import grain at favorable prices

Roman engineers built paved roads far from home. This road served as the main street through the bustling city of Ephesus in Anatolia (modern-day Turkey).
De Agostini Picture Library/Getty Images

mare nostrum (MA-reh NAHS-truhm)

from lands that routinely produced large surpluses, other regions could concentrate on the cultivation of fruits and vegetables or on the production of manufactured items. Greece, for example, concentrated on olives and grapevines. Syria and Palestine produced fruits, nuts, and wool fabrics. Gaul produced grain, supplied copper, and began to experiment with the cultivation of grapevines. Spain produced high-quality olive oil as well as wine, horses, and most of the precious metal used in the Roman Empire. Italy became a center for the production of pottery, glassware, and bronze goods. Archaeologists have uncovered one pottery factory north of Rome that may have employed hundreds of workers and that had a mixing vat capable of holding more than 40,000 liters (10,568 gallons) of clay.

How the Past Shapes the Future

Long-Distance Trade Networks

The long-distance trade networks in which the Romans took part facilitated the movement of people and products around a vast area of Eurasia. But long-distance trade also encouraged the transformation of fixed locations, like capital cities and ports, as a result of the money such networks could bring in from profits and taxes. Consider carefully the ways long-distance trade networks of the ancient world were linked to architectural innovation, artistic expression, and the development of new cultural forms in the Roman Empire and all the other imperial states of ancient Eurasia. To what extent does trade and cultural exchange in today's globalized world continue to influence the development of new architectural and cultural innovations?

Mediterranean Trade Specialized production of agricultural commodities and manufactured goods set the stage for vigorous trade over the Mediterranean sea lanes. Roman military and naval power kept the seas largely free of pirates so that sizable cargoes could move safely over long distances, barring foul weather. As Roman military forces, administrators, tax collectors, and other officials traveled throughout the empire carrying out their duties, they joined the merchants in linking the Mediterranean's regions into a well-integrated network of communication and exchange. Archaeologists have discovered that even in remote rural areas, peasants routinely used high-quality pottery, ate food off fine tableware, consumed wines and oils imported from afar, and slept under tiled roofs. Beyond the Mediterranean, the port of Berenice on the Red Sea coast of Egypt offered access to the Indian Ocean and distant markets. Sometime in the mid-first century C.E., an anonymous Greek merchant captain composed a remarkable work called the *Periplus maris erythraei* (meaning a "sailing itinerary of the Red Sea"), which provided a description of the ports on the Red Sea itself as well as east African and Indian ports that Roman merchants commonly visited.

The City of Rome Cities benefited handsomely from Mediterranean integration and played a prominent role in promoting economic and social change. Along with taxes, tributes, booty, and other wealth generated by military expansion, much of the profit from Mediterranean trade flowed to Rome, where it fueled remarkable urban development. In the first century C.E., some ten thousand statues decorated the city, along with seven hundred pools, five hundred fountains, and thirty-six monumental marble arches celebrating military victories and other achievements. The Roman state financed the construction of temples; bathhouses; public buildings; stadiums; and, most important of all, aqueducts

that brought freshwater into the city from the neighboring mountains. Construction projects benefited from the use of concrete, invented by Roman engineers during the republican era, which strengthened structures and allowed builders to meet high standards of precision required for plumbing and water control.

Construction provided employment for hundreds of thousands of workers. As a result, the population of Rome surged, and the city's economy experienced rapid growth. Shopkeepers, artisans, merchants, and bankers proliferated in the imperial capital. Economic development attracted large numbers of migrants from the countryside and from foreign lands. Most received low wages as laborers, construction workers, or servants, but those with skills sometimes found good employment as craftsmen. Some who went to Rome with a bit of money established successful businesses, and by hard work or good fortune, a few entrepreneurs became wealthy and respected businessmen.

Urban growth and development also took place beyond the capital. Some parts of the empire, such as Greece and Syria, had long-standing urban traditions. There trade and economic development brought additional prosperity. Elsewhere the Romans founded cities at strategic sites for purposes of government and administration, especially in Spain, Gaul, and Britain, which encouraged economic and social development at the far reaches of the empire.

Roman Cities and Their Attractions As wealth concentrated in the cities, urban residents came to expect a variety of comforts not available in rural areas. Merchants traveling the roads and sea lanes brought delicacies and luxury items from all parts of the Roman Empire: Spanish hams; oysters from British waters; fine wool cloaks from Gaul; and Syrian nuts, dates, and figs all made their way to consumers in Rome and other prosperous cities. Roman cities enjoyed abundant supplies of freshwater, sometimes brought from

A wall painting from Stabiae (a small community near Pompeii destroyed by the eruption of Vesuvius in 79 C.E.) depicts an Italian harbor with ships, wharves, warehouses, markets, and decorative columns topped by statues. DEA PICTURE LIBRARY/De Agostini/ Getty Images

distant mountains by aqueducts, and elaborate sewage and plumbing systems. All sizable cities and even many smaller towns had public baths featuring hot and cold rooms, and often swimming pools and gymnasia as well. Underground sewers carried away wastewater.

Enormous circuses, stadiums, and theaters provided sites for the entertainment of the urban masses. Circuses were oval structures with tracks for chariot races, which were wildly popular in the Roman Empire. The Circus Maximus at Rome accommodated about 250,000 spectators. Entertainment in stadiums often took forms now considered coarse and cruel—battles to the death between gladiators or between humans and wild animals—but urban populations flocked to such events, which they looked on as exciting diversions from daily routine. The Roman Colosseum, a magnificent marble stadium and sports arena opened in 80 C.E., provided seating for about 50,000 spectators. The structure had a multicolored awning that protected viewers from sun and rain, and its construction was so precise that it was possible to flood the arena with water and stage mock naval battles within its walls.

Family and Society in Roman Times

The *Paterfamilias* Roman law vested immense authority in male heads of families. The Roman family consisted of an entire household, including slaves, free servants, and close relatives who lived together. Usually the eldest male ruled the household as ***paterfamilias*** ("father of the family"). Roman law gave the *paterfamilias* the authority to arrange marriages for his children, determine the work or duties they

This huge gladiator mosaic, dated to the first half of the fourth century, was discovered in a villa outside Rome in the early nineteenth century. The name of each gladiator depicted is given in inscription next to the figure, with a Ø-shaped symbol marking the names of gladiators who died in combat. The History Collection/Alamy Stock Photo

paterfamilias (PAH-tehr-fah-MEE-lyas)

What's Left Out? ▀▄▄ ▀▀▀▀ ▀▀▀ ▀▀ ▀▀▀▀

Roman authors have left us with vivid insights into daily life in Rome, including the spectacular public entertainment we discuss in the chapter, such as chariot races at the Circus Maximus and gladiatorial combat. By the Age of Empire, the Roman calendar contained about one hundred public holidays a year, and on most of these days, some sort of public entertainment was provided by the wealthy elite and by ambitious politicians. There was always plenty of variety in the extraordinary events staged at the Colosseum in Rome. Sometimes it would be animal hunts, or it might be African wild cats fighting each other, men fighting bears, or naval battles in the flooded arena. But the most popular "entertainment" of all was gladiators fighting gladiators in one-on-one combat that cost the lives of roughly 50 percent of the fighters each show. As we note in the text, the philosopher Seneca bitterly noted that, for a gladiator, "the only exit is death," although some gladiators managed to survive long enough to become superstars in the city!

Historians are divided on the question of the origin of gladiatorial combat. Some suggest that the practice first emerged as part of a funeral rite, while others argue the idea was of Etruscan origin. The oldest pictorial evidence indicates that gladiator schools and combat first emerged in the Campanian city of Paestum in the fourth century B.C.E., but other images might suggest the practice was inherited from Greek colonists who settled on the Italian peninsula as early as the eighth century B.C.E. Roman historian Livy writes that gladiatorial spectacles first emerged during punitive military campaigns the Romans launched against the Samnites, a group of Italic peoples who went over to the side of Hannibal in the Second Punic War. That is, gladiators were always cast in the role of "enemies of Rome," which helped justify their slaughter in pubic spectacles.

Rome's extraordinary entertainment events were regarded as cathartic and, when combined with free bread that the governments regularly doled out to the people, as a way of keeping the commoners of Rome content. Of course, the astute literary observers of Roman life understood exactly what was going on, particularly the satirist Juvenal, who famously wrote: "Long ago the people shed their anxieties; ever since we do not sell our votes to anyone. For the people—who once conferred imperium, symbols of office, legions, everything—now hold themselves in check and anxiously desire only two things, the grain dole and chariot races in the Circus."

How accurately Juvenal's famous phrase, *panem et circenses* ("bread and circuses"), captures the trade-off humans often make between political rights and distracting entertainment. Imagine how the history of the world might have turned out differently if elites had not proven so good at diverting the energies of the populace as a way of heading off political unrest.

Source: See Donald Kyle. *Sport and Spectacle in the Ancient World.* Blackwell, 2007.

---

would perform, and punish them for offenses as he saw fit. He had rights also to sell them into slavery and even to execute them.

Although legally endowed with extraordinary powers, the Roman *paterfamilias* rarely ruled tyranically over his charges. In fact, women usually supervised domestic affairs in Roman households, and by the time they reached middle age, women generally wielded considerable influence within their families. They helped select marriage partners for their offspring, and they sometimes played large roles in managing their families' financial affairs. Although Roman law placed strict limits on the ability of women to receive inheritances, enforcement was inconsistent, and clever individuals found ways to evade the law or take advantage of its loopholes. During the third and second centuries B.C.E., as Roman expansion in the Mediterranean brought wealth to the capital, women came to possess a great deal of property. By the first century B.C.E., in spite of the authority legally vested in the *paterfamilias,* many elite women supervised the financial affairs of family businesses and wealthy estates.

The closest thing to a gender war that occurred in the long history of Rome erupted in 195 B.C.E., when women objected publicly to attempts in the Senate to retain the *Lex Oppia*. This law, which had been passed in 215 B.C.E. in the aftermath of the disastrous loss to Hannibal at the Battle of Cannae, barred women from wearing gold or silver jewelry or expensive clothing and from driving about in public in chariots or expensive litters. Two decades later, with the Punic Wars having been won, elite women revolted against those politicians who were attempting to retain the law; they poured into the Forum and surrounding streets and blocked all access to the city. Although conservative senators like Cato the Elder were outraged that women should be congregating in public and insisted that it was men who should be deciding such matters, the law was abolished and the women were triumphant.

Women in Rome made further gains in the early empire, notably under Augustus, whose own formidable wife, Livia Drusilla Augusta (58 B.C.E.–29 C.E.), was the most powerful Roman woman of her time. Augustus came under heavy criticism from conservatives because, probably under the influence of his wife, he proposed new laws to strengthen the rights of women within the family. However, Rome was facing a demographic crisis at the time, with serious population decline among the patricians. The cause of this decline was the century-long civil wars that had preceded the Augustan Age, but women were being blamed by conservative politicians because of their fixation on pleasure, silk, and adultery and their unwillingness to bear children. In this atmosphere of "women out of control," Augustus attempted to placate the conservatives who had opposed his policy of strengthening women's private rights by also proposing a series of moral laws to regulate the sexual lives of elite women. This led to a series of adultery court cases that resulted in several women from within his own family being exiled.

Roman women made further legal gains in the first two centuries of the Common Era, including gaining the right to own and inherit property, which had been legally denied to them by the *Lex Voconia* in 169 B.C.E. It wasn't until 178 C.E., however, that women were given the legal right to inherit from their children. As the empire expanded, women of many regions and ethnicities came to settle in Rome, where their often more liberated lifestyles influenced gender attitudes. By the Late Roman Empire, women had won the right to institute divorce proceedings against their husbands, but only if "she should prove that her husband is a homicide, a sorcerer, or a destroyer of tombs" (Theodosian Code 331 C.E.). If the woman were to send notice of a divorce to her husband for any other than these three reasons, she would forfeit her dowry and possessions "even to the last hairpin"! On the other hand, if a man were to cast off an innocent wife to marry another, the first wife would have the right to enter her former home by force and "transfer to herself the entire dowry of his later wife in recompense for the outrage inflicted upon her" (Theodosian Code).

From the earliest days of the republic until the late empire then, patriarchy dominated Roman society; men possessed all public and private power, and the state generally enshrined these "rights" in law. As was the case within many ancient civilizations, although women were denied a public role, they were often able to influence the society around them in subtle ways, and the state was eventually forced to pass laws that at least offered them basic rights and some level of protection, even if they never resembled equality.

Wealth and Social Change

Increasing wealth had important consequences for Roman society. New classes of merchants, landowners, and construction contractors accumulated enormous private wealth and rivaled the old nobility for prominence. The newly rich classes built palatial houses with formal gardens and threw lavish banquets with rare and exotic foods such as boiled ostrich, parrot-tongue pie, and tree fungus served in a sauce of fish fat, jellyfish, and eggs. While wealthy classes probed culinary frontiers, cultivators and urban masses subsisted largely on porridge and vegetables occasionally supplemented by eggs, fish, sausage, or meat.

By the first century B.C.E., poverty had become a considerable problem in Rome and other large cities of the empire. Often unemployed, the urban masses sometimes rioted to express their dissatisfaction and seek improved conditions, and they readily provided recruits for private armies of ambitious generals such as Marius and Sulla. Imperial authorities never developed a true urban policy but, rather, sought to keep the masses contented with what the Roman poet Juvenal cynically described as "bread and circuses"—subsidized grain and spectacular public entertainments.

Slavery

Roman society made extensive use of slave labor: by the second century C.E., enslaved people may have represented as much as one-third of the population of the Roman Empire. In the countryside they worked mostly on latifundia, though many labored in state quarries and mines. Enslaved people in rurual areas worked under extremely harsh conditions, often chained together in teams. Discontent led to several large-scale revolts, especially during the second and first centuries B.C.E. During the most serious uprising, in 73 B.C.E., **Spartacus** (a man who had escaped slavery) assembled an army of seventy thousand rebellious slaves. The Roman army dispatched eight legions, comprising

From the days of the republic, residents of Rome consumed subsidized grain imported from distant territories. In this painting from a tomb, workers load grain onto a boat at the port of Ostia, at the mouth of the Tiber River, for transport upriver to the city of Rome.

Peter Horree/Alamy Stock Photo

Spartacus (SPAHR-tah-cus)

This delicate painting of the Queen of Lydia, Omphale, was discovered in the house of the prince of Montenegro in the city of Pompeii. The queen holds a fan in her right hand and is flanked by two young servant women dressed in flowing silk robes. What does this painting suggest about the lives of elite women in the early Roman Empire?

Sites & Photos/Shmuel Magal/Alamy Stock Photo

more than forty thousand well-equipped, veteran troops, to quell the revolt.

In the cities, conditions were much less difficult than in the countryside. Enslaved women commonly worked as domestic servants while males worked as servants, laborers, craftsmen, shopkeepers, or business agents for their owners. Enslaved people who had an education or possessed some particular talent had the potential to lead comfortable lives. The first-century enslaved Anatolian Epictetus even became a prominent Stoic philosopher. He spent much of his life studying with Rome's leading intellectuals, and he lectured to large audiences that included high Roman officials and perhaps even emperors.

More than their counterparts in rural areas, enslaved people in urban areas could hope for manumission as a reward for a long term of loyal service: it was common, though not mandatory, for slaveholders to free urban slaves about the time they reached age thirty. Until freed, however, enslaved people remained under the strict authority of their slaveholders who, by law, could sell them, arrange their family affairs, punish them, and even execute them for serious offenses.

THE COSMOPOLITAN MEDITERRANEAN

The integration of the Mediterranean basin had important effects not only for the trade and economy of the Roman Empire but also for its cultural and religious traditions. As travelers ventured throughout the Mediterranean basin, they encountered other cultural and religious traditions. When migrants moved to Rome and other large cities, they often continued to observe their inherited traditions and thus contributed to the cosmopolitan cultural atmosphere of the empire. Roads and communication networks helped to spread new popular religions. Most important of these over time was Christianity, which originated as a small and persecuted Jewish sect. Within three centuries, however, Christianity had become the official religion of the Roman Empire and the predominant faith of the Mediterranean basin.

A wall painting of the fourth century C.E. from a Christian catacomb depicts a group of pagan students gathered around their teacher, who presents a lesson in anatomy with the aid of a cadaver. This scene reflects the influence of Greek scientific and medical studies in the Roman Empire.

Sonia Halliday Photo Library/Alamy Stock Photo

Greek Philosophy and Religions of Salvation

Roman Deities During the early days of their history, the Romans recognized many gods and goddesses, who they believed intervened directly in human affairs. Jupiter was the principal god, lord of the heavens. Mars was the god of war, Ceres the goddess of grain, Janus the god who watched the threshold of individual houses, and Vesta the goddess of the hearth. In addition to these major deities, most Roman households also honored lesser gods who looked after the welfare of individual families.

As the Romans expanded their political influence and built an empire, they encountered the religious and cultural traditions of other peoples. Often, they adopted the deities of other peoples and used them for their own purposes. From the Etruscans, for example, they learned of Juno, a goddess associated with women and marriage, and Minerva, the goddess of wisdom, as well as certain religious practices, such as divination of the future through examination of the internal organs of ritually sacrificed animals.

Cicero (SIHS-er-oh)
Mithraism (MITH-rah-iz'm)

Greek Influence The Romans also drew inspiration from the Greek tradition of rational thought and philosophy. When the Romans established political control of the eastern Mediterranean in the third and second centuries B.C.E., the most prominent school of thought in Hellenistic Greece was **Stoicism.** Recognizing that they lived in a large and interdependent world, the Stoics sought to identify a set of universal moral standards based on nature and reason that would transcend local ethical codes.

Cicero and Stoicism That approach to moral thought appealed strongly to Roman intellectuals, and thinkers such as Marcus Tullius **Cicero** (106–43 B.C.E.) readily adopted Stoic values. Cicero studied in Greece and became thoroughly acquainted with both classical and Hellenistic schools of thought. He was a persuasive orator, and he wrote clear, elegant, polished Latin prose. In adapting Hellenistic thought to Roman needs, Cicero drew heavily from the Stoics' moral and ethical teachings. His letters and treatises emphasized the individual's duty to live in accordance with nature and reason. He argued that the pursuit of justice was the individual's highest public duty, and he scorned those who sought to accumulate wealth or to become powerful through immoral, illegal, or unjust means. Through his speeches and especially his writings, Cicero helped to establish Stoicism as the most prominent school of moral philosophy in Rome.

Religions of Salvation Both educated elites and unschooled masses found comfort in religions of salvation that established their presence throughout the Mediterranean basin and beyond. Like Stoicism, these religions clearly reflected the political and social conditions of the Hellenistic period: in an imperial era, when close-knit city-states no longer served as a focus for individual loyalties, religions of salvation appealed to the popular masses by providing a sense of purpose and the promise of a glorious future existence.

These religions became prominent features of Mediterranean society during Hellenistic times and became increasingly noticeable in Rome during the late republic as migrants settled in the capital and brought their faiths with them. Under the Roman Empire, religions of salvation flourished both in Rome and throughout the Mediterranean basin. Merchants, soldiers, and administrators carried their cults as they conducted their business, and missionaries traveled alongside them in search of converts. The roads of the empire and the sea lanes of the Mediterranean thus served not only as trade routes and lines of official communication but also as highways for religions of salvation, which traveled to all the ports and large cities of the empire.

Mithraism Among the most popular of these religions of salvation was **Mithraism,** a faith dedicated to the Persian deity Mithras. In Zoroastrian mythology, Mithras was a god closely identified with the sun and light. Roman soldiers serving in the Hellenistic world, particularly Anatolia,

A Mithraeum—shrine to the god Mithrus—found in the ruins of Ostia, Italy. Ostia was the port of the city of Rome The sculpture on the altar depicts Mithras sacrificing a bull to the god Apollo. Worshippers sat on the benches on either side of the shrine.

Oreste C./Alamy Stock Photo

Judaism and Early Christianity

The Jews and the Empire After the dissolution of the Jewish kingdom of David and Solomon in the tenth century B.C.E., the Jewish people maintained their faith and their communities under various imperial regimes: Babylonian, Achaemenid, Alexandrian, Seleucid, and Roman. All these empires embraced many different ethnic and religious groups and mostly tolerated the cultural preferences of their subjects, providing that communities paid their taxes and refrained from rebellious activities. In an effort to encourage political loyalty, these empires often created state-sponsored spiritual ideologies that honored their emperors as gods and encouraged participation in rituals to revere the emperor-gods.

That requirement created a serious problem for the strictly monotheistic Jews, who recognized only their god, Yahweh, as divine. Jews considered the state-sponsored faiths to be blasphemous, and many of them refused to pay homage to a mortal being who laid claim to divinity. Sometimes they even declined to pay taxes to regimes that required subjects to revere their emperors. Relations between Jews and imperial authorities became especially tense as the Romans extended their empire in the eastern Mediterranean region. Between the third century B.C.E. and the first century C.E., Jews in Palestine mounted several rebellions against their Seleucid and Roman overlords. Ultimately the resistance failed, and Roman forces decisively defeated the rebels during the Jewish War of 66 to 70 C.E.

The Essenes While some Jews actively fought the Romans, others founded new sects that looked for saviors to deliver them from subjection. The **Essenes** formed one such sect. In 1947 shepherds accidentally discovered some Essene writings known as the Dead Sea scrolls, which have shed fascinating light on the sect and its beliefs. The Essenes formed their community in Palestine during the first century B.C.E. They observed a strict moral code and participated in rituals designed to reinforce a sense of community: they admitted new members after a rite of baptism in water, and they took part in ritual community meals. They also looked for a savior who would deliver them from Roman rule and lead them in the establishment of a community in which they could practice their faith without interference.

encountered the cult of Mithras and adapted it to their interests. They associated Mithras less with the sun than with military virtues such as strength, courage, and discipline, and Mithraism quickly became exceptionally popular among the Roman armed forces. During the late republic, Mithraic altars and temples appeared in military garrisons throughout the empire. During the early centuries C.E., administrators and merchants also became enchanted with Mithras, and his faith attracted followers among the male populations of all sizable communities and commercial centers in the Roman Empire.

Worship of Isis Mithraic religion did not allow women to participate in rituals, but other spiritual ideologies dedicated to the Anatolian mother goddess Cybele, the Egyptian goddess Isis, and other deities made a place for both men and women. Indeed, the **worship of Isis** may have been the most popular of all the Mediterranean religions of salvation before the rise of Christianity. Devotees built temples to Isis throughout the Roman Empire, and they adored the Egyptian goddess as a benevolent and protective deity who nurtured her worshipers and helped them cope with the stresses of life in cosmopolitan society. The immense popularity of these religions of salvation provides a context that helps to explain the remarkable success of Christianity in the Roman Empire.

Essenes (ih-SEENS)

Jesus of Nazareth The early Christians probably had little contact with the Essenes, but they shared many of the same concerns. The Christians formed their community around **Jesus of Nazareth,** a charismatic Jewish teacher whom they recognized as their savior. Born about the year 4 B.C.E., Jesus grew up at a time of high tension between Roman overlords and their Jewish subjects. He was a peaceful man who taught devotion to God and love for fellow humans. He attracted large crowds because of a reputation for wisdom and miraculous powers, especially the ability to heal the sick.

Yet Jesus alarmed the Romans because he also taught that "the kingdom of God is at hand." To Jesus, the kingdom of God may well have referred to a spiritual realm in which God would gather those faithful to him. To Roman administrators, however, his message carried political overtones: an impending kingdom of God sounded like a threat to Roman rule in Palestine, especially since enthusiastic crowds routinely accompanied Jesus. In an effort to forestall a new round of rebellion, Roman administrators executed Jesus by fixing him to a cross in the early 30s C.E.

Jesus' Early Followers Jesus' crucifixion did not put an end to his movement. Even after his execution, Jesus' close followers strongly felt his presence and proclaimed that he had triumphed over death by rising from his grave. They called him "Christ," meaning "the anointed one," the savior who would bring individuals into the kingdom of God. They taught that he was the son of God and that his sacrifice served to offset the sins of those who had faith in him. They taught further that like Jesus, the faithful would survive death and would experience eternal life in the spiritual kingdom of God. Following Jesus' teachings, the early Christians observed a demanding moral code and devoted themselves uncompromisingly to God. They also compiled a body of writings—accounts of Jesus' life, reports of his followers' works, and letters outlining Christian teachings—that gained recognition as the New Testament. Together with the Jews' Hebrew scriptures, which Christians referred to as the Old Testament, the New Testament became the holy book of Christianity.

Paul of Tarsus Jesus and his earliest followers were all Jews. Beginning about the middle of the first century C.E., however, some Christians avidly sought converts from non-Jewish communities in the Hellenistic world and the Roman Empire. The principal figure in the expansion of Christianity beyond Judaism was **Paul of Tarsus,** who we first encountered at the beginning of this chapter. Paul was a Jew from Anatolia who zealously preached his faith, especially in the Greek-speaking eastern region of the Roman Empire. Paul taught a Christianity that attracted the urban masses in the same way as other religions of salvation that spread widely in the Roman Empire. His doctrine called for individuals to observe high moral standards and to place their faith ahead of personal and family interests. His teaching also explained the world and human history as the results of God's purposeful activity and so provided a framework of meaning for individuals' lives. Furthermore,

Paul's doctrine promised a glorious future existence for those who conscientiously observed the faith.

Like missionaries of other faiths, Paul was no stranger to Roman roads and Mediterranean sea lanes. As we saw earlier, he traveled widely in search of converts and made several journeys through Greece, Anatolia, Syria, and Palestine to visit fledgling Christian communities and offer them guidance. His last journey took him by ship from Palestine to Rome, where he took the opportunity to promote Christianity and seek converts for about two years before losing his appeal to the emperor and suffering execution.

Early Christian Communities For two centuries after the crucifixion of Jesus, there was no central authority for the fledgling church. Rather, individual communities selected supervisors, known as bishops, who oversaw priests and governed their jurisdictions according to their best understanding of Christian doctrine. As a result, until the emergence of Rome as the principal seat of church authority in the third century C.E., Christians held doctrinal views and followed practices that varied considerably from one community to the next: as different groups of people adopted Christianity, they interpreted Christian teachings in very different ways, just as different communities had earlier understood the spiritual ideologies of Mithras, Isis, and other deities in their own ways.

Early Christians generated a large number of writings to express their various understandings of Christianity and its implications. After the third century C.E., church authorities suppressed many of those writings and declared them heretical. Yet dozens of letters, gospels, and interpretative historical accounts survive to document the complexity and diversity of early Christian teachings. Some early Christians maintained that the faithful must accept specific doctrines, whereas others encouraged believers to find truth within themselves and express it in their own ways. Some religious leaders taught that Jesus had literally risen from the dead and come back to life, whereas others held that his resurrection was spiritual rather than physical. Some communities forbade women to play active public roles in the church, but others allowed women to serve as priests. Some congregations permitted individuals to seek their own understanding of spiritual matters, but others insisted that access to spiritual truth was available only through properly ordained priests and bishops. Only gradually did believers agree to recognize certain texts—the New Testament—as authoritative scripture and adopt them as fundamental guides for Christian doctrine and practice.

The Growth of Early Christianity Like the Jews from whose ranks they had sprung, the early Christians refused to honor the Roman state religions or revere the emperor as a god. As a result, Roman imperial authorities launched sporadic campaigns of persecution designed to eliminate Christianity as a threat to the empire. In spite of that repression, Christian numbers grew rapidly. During the first three centuries of the faith's existence, Christianity found its way to almost all parts of the Roman Empire, and Christians established thriving

SOURCES FROM THE PAST

Jesus' Moral and Ethical Teachings

Several accounts of Jesus' life record the Sermon on the Mount in which Jesus challenged his followers to honor God and observe a demanding code of ethics. In this sermon, Jesus is asking his followers to refrain from revenge against those who had caused them harm, for example, and instead to repay harm with kindness.

Blessed are the poor in spirit: for theirs is the kingdom of heaven. Blessed are they that mourn: for they shall be comforted. Blessed are the meek: for they shall inherit the earth. Blessed are they which do hunger and thirst after righteousness: for they shall be filled. Blessed are the merciful: for they shall obtain mercy. Blessed are the pure in heart: for they shall see God. Blessed are the peacemakers: for they shall be called the children of God. Blessed are they which are persecuted for righteousness's sake: for theirs is the kingdom of heaven. Blessed are ye when men shall revile you and persecute you and shall say all manner of evil against you falsely for my sake. Rejoice, and be exceeding glad: for great is your reward in heaven. . . .

Ye have heard that it hath been said, "An eye for an eye, and a tooth for a tooth." But I say unto you that ye resist not evil: but whosoever shall smite thee on thy right cheek, turn to him the other also. And if any man will sue thee at the law, and take away thy coat, let him have thy cloak also. And whosoever shall compel thee to go a mile, go with him two. Give to him that asketh thee, and from him that would borrow of thee turn not thou away.

> What ancient law code does Jesus seem to be referring to with his comment about "an eye for an eye, and a tooth for a tooth"?

Ye have heard that it hath been said, "Thou shalt love thy neighbour, and hate thine enemy." But I say unto you, love your enemies, bless them that curse you, do good to them that hate you, and pray for them which despitefully use you and persecute you, that ye may be the children of your Father which is in heaven: for he maketh his sun to rise on the evil and on the good, and sendeth rain on the just and on the unjust. . . .

Ask, and it shall be given you; seek, and ye shall find; knock, and it shall be opened unto you. For every one that asketh receiveth; and he that seeketh findeth; and to him that knocketh it shall be opened. What man is there of you, whom if his son ask bread, will he give him a stone? Or if he ask a fish, will he give him a serpent? If ye then, being evil, know how to give good gifts unto your children, how much more shall your Father which is in heaven give good things to them that ask him? Therefore all things whatsoever ye would that men should do to you, do ye even so to them.

> What is it Jesus is referring to when he says knock and it shall be opened, or seek and you will find?

For Further Reflection

- What aspects of Jesus' sermon might the Roman government and Roman military have been most concerned with?
- How do the arguments of Jesus concerning those who will be most rewarded in the afterlife compare to the approach of other law codes we have considered in previous chapters?
- What similarities and differences do you see between the teachings of Jesus and those of other spiritual leaders we have discussed, including Zoroaster and the Buddha?

Source: Matthew 5:3–13, 5:38–45, 7:7–12 (Authorized Version). (Translation slightly modified.)

communities throughout the Mediterranean basin and farther east in Mesopotamia and Iran. Rome itself had a sizable Christian population by 300 C.E.

The remarkable growth of Christianity reflected the new faith's appeal particularly to the lower classes, urban populations, and women. Christianity accorded honor and dignity to individuals who did not enjoy high standing in Roman society, and it endowed them with a sense of spiritual freedom more meaningful than wealth, power, or social prominence. Unlike the popular religion of Mithraism, which admitted only men, Christianity taught the spiritual equality of the sexes and welcomed the contributions of both men and women. Like Mithraism and other religions of salvation, Christianity provided a sense of purpose and a promise of future glory for those who placed their faith in Jesus. Thus, although Christianity originated as a minor sect of Judaism, urban populations in the Roman Empire embraced the new faith with such enthusiasm that by the third century C.E. it had become the most dynamic and influential religious faith in the Mediterranean basin.

CONCLUSION

Under Roman influence, the Mediterranean region became a tightly integrated society. The Roman Empire provided a political structure that administered lands as distant as Mesopotamia and Britain. Highly organized trade networks enabled peoples throughout the empire to concentrate on specialized agricultural or industrial production and to import foods and other goods that they did not produce themselves. Popular religions spread widely and attracted enthusiastic converts. Like Confucianism and Buddhism in ancient China and India, rational philosophy and Christianity became prominent sources of intellectual and religious authority in the Roman Empire and continued to influence cultural traditions in the Mediterranean, Europe, and southwest Asia over the centuries that followed.

STUDY TERMS

Augustus (212)	patricians (209)
Carthage (210)	Paul of Tarsus (224)
Cicero (222)	*pax romana* (213)
Essenes (223)	plebeians (209)
Etruscans (208)	Punic Wars (211)
Gaul (208)	Remus (208)
Gracchi brothers (211)	Roman Empire (213)
Hannibal Barca (211)	Roman Republic (207)
Jesus of Nazareth (224)	Romulus (208)
Julius Caesar (212)	Spartacus (220)
latifundia (211)	Stoicism (222)
mare nostrum (216)	tribunes (209)
Mithraism (222)	Twelve Tables (209)
paterfamilias (218)	worship of Isis (223)

FOR FURTHER READING

Mary T. Boatwright. *The Romans: From Village to Empire: A History of Rome from Earliest Times to the End of the Western Empire.* Oxford, 2013. Vividly written and accessible, *The Romans* traces Rome's remarkable evolution from village to monarchy, to republic, to one-man rule by an emperor.

Keith R. Bradley. *Discovering the Roman Family: Studies in Roman Social History.* New York, 1991. A provocative analysis of Roman family life with illustrations from individual experiences.

Peter Brown. *The Rise of Western Christendom: Triumph and Diversity, A.D. 200–1000.* 2nd ed. Oxford, 2003. A landmark analysis of early Christian history by an unusually perceptive scholar.

Barry Cunliffe. *Greeks, Romans, and Barbarians: Spheres of Interaction.* New York, 1988. Draws on archaeological evidence in assessing the effects of the Roman presence in Gaul, Britain, and Germany.

Sandra Joshel. *Slavery in the Roman World.* Cambridge, 2010. Detailed account of the lives of slaves in the Roman world and the wide range of tasks they were expected to do.

Ramsay MacMullen. *Romanization in the Time of Augustus.* New Haven, 2000. Charts the diffusion of a Roman way of life throughout the empire.

Elaine Pagels. *Beyond Belief: The Secret Gospel of Thomas.* New York, 2003. Explores some of the many diverse understandings of Christianity in the early years of the faith.

Sarah B. Pomeroy. *Goddesses, Whores, Wives, and Slaves: Women in Classical Antiquity.* New York, 1975. Outstanding study analyzing the status and role of women in classical Greece and Rome.

Romolo Augusto Staccioli. *The Roads of the Romans.* Los Angeles, 2003. A well-illustrated volume that surveys the entire Roman road system.

Geza Vermes. *The Dead Sea Scrolls: Qumran in Perspective.* Rev. ed. London, 1994. A reliable introduction to scholarship on the Dead Sea scrolls and the community that produced them.

Chapter 12

Cross-Cultural Exchanges on the Silk Roads

ZOOMING IN ON ENCOUNTERS

Zhang Qian: An Early Traveler on the Silk Roads

In about 139 B.C.E., the Chinese emperor **Han Wudi** sent an envoy named **Zhang Qian** on a mission to lands west of China. The emperor's purpose was to find allies who could help combat the nomadic Xiongnu, who menaced the northern and western borders of the Han empire. From captives he had learned that other nomadic peoples in far western lands bore grudges against the Xiongnu, and he reasoned that they might ally with Han forces to pressure their common enemy.

The problem for Zhang Qian was that to communicate with potential allies against the Xiongnu, he had to pass directly through lands they controlled. Soon after Zhang Qian left Han territory, Xiongnu forces captured him. For ten years the Xiongnu held him in comfortable captivity: they allowed him to keep his personal servant, and he was able

to marry a Xiongnu wife, with whom he had a son. When suspicions about him subsided, however, Zhang Qian escaped with his family and servant. He even had the presence of mind to keep with him the emblem that Han Wudi had given him as a sign of his ambassadorial status. He fled to the west and traveled as far as Bactria, but he did not succeed in lining up allies against the

A cave painting from the late seventh century C.E. depicts the Chinese emperor Han Wudi (seated on horse) as he dispatches Zhang Qian (kneeling at left) on his mission to western lands in search of an alliance against the Xiongnu. Why did Zhang Qian's mission hold such great interest for the emperor?
Art Collection 3/Alamy Stock Photo

Han Wudi (hahn woo-dee)
Zhang Qian (jung-chen)

Xiongnu. While returning to China, Zhang Qian again fell into Xiongnu hands but managed to escape after one year's detention when the death of the Xiongnu leader led to a period of turmoil. In about 126 B.C.E. Zhang Qian and his party returned to China and a warm welcome from Han Wudi.

Although his diplomatic efforts did not succeed, Zhang Qian's mission had far-reaching consequences. Apart from political and military intelligence about western lands and their peoples, Zhang Qian brought back information of immense commercial value. While in Bactria in about 128 B.C.E., he noticed Chinese goods—textiles and bamboo articles—offered for sale in local markets. Upon inquiry he learned that they had come from southwest China by way of Bengal. From that information he deduced the possibility of establishing trade relations between China and Bactria through India.

Han Wudi responded enthusiastically to that idea and dreamed of trading with people inhabiting lands west of China. From 102 to 98 B.C.E., he mounted an ambitious campaign that broke the power of the Xiongnu and pacified parts of central Asia. His conquests simplified trade relations because it became unnecessary to route commerce through India. The intelligence that Zhang Qian gathered during his travels thus contributed to the opening of the Silk Roads—the network of trade routes that linked lands as distant as China and the Roman Empire—and more generally to the establishment of relations between China and lands to the west.

CHAPTER OVERVIEW

China and other ancient societies, including the Parthian and Kushan empires, imposed political and military control over vast territories. They promoted trade and communication within their own empires, bringing regions that had previously been self-sufficient into a larger economy and society. They also fostered the spread of cultural and religious traditions to distant regions, and they encouraged the construction of institutional frameworks that promoted the long-term survival of those traditions.

The influence of imperial states did not stop at their borders. Nearby peoples regarded their powerful neighbors with a mixture of envy and suspicion, and they sought to share the wealth that those neighbors generated. They pursued that goal by various means, both peaceful and violent, and relations with neighboring peoples, particularly nomadic groups, became a major preoccupation of all the imperial societies.

Beyond their encounters with neighboring peoples, these imperial societies established a broad zone of communication and exchange throughout much of the earth's eastern hemisphere. Trade networks crossed the deserts of central Asia and the breadth of the Indian Ocean. Long-distance trade passed through much of Eurasia and north Africa, from China to the Mediterranean basin, and to parts of sub-Saharan Africa as well.

This long-distance trade profoundly influenced the experiences of peoples and the development of societies throughout the eastern hemisphere. It brought wealth and access to foreign products, and it enabled peoples to concentrate their efforts on economic activities best suited to their regions. It facilitated the spread of religious traditions beyond their original homelands because merchants carried their beliefs and sometimes attracted converts in the lands they visited. It also facilitated the transmission of disease: pathogens traveled the trade routes alongside commercial wares and religious faiths. Indeed, the transmission of disease over the Silk Roads helped bring an end to these Eurasian states because infectious and contagious diseases sparked devastating epidemics that caused political, social, and economic havoc. Long-distance trade thus had deep political, social, and cultural as well as economic and commercial implications for classical societies during the First Silk Roads Era.

CHRONOLOGY	
3rd century B.C.E.	Spread of Buddhism and Hinduism to southeast Asia
2nd century B.C.E.	Introduction of Buddhism to central Asia
139–126 B.C.E.	Travels of Zhang Qian in central Asia
1st century B.C.E.	Introduction of Buddhism to China
2nd century C.E.	Spread of Christianity in the Mediterranean basin and southwest Asia
184 C.E.	Yellow Turban rebellion
216–272 C.E.	Life of Mani
220 C.E.	Collapse of the Han dynasty
284–305 C.E.	Reign of Diocletian
313 C.E.	Edict of Milan and the legalization of Christianity in the Roman Empire
313–337 C.E.	Reign of Constantine
325 C.E.	Council at Nicaea
451 C.E.	Council at Chalcedon
476 C.E.	Collapse of the western Roman Empire

LONG-DISTANCE TRADE AND THE SILK ROADS NETWORK

In ancient Afro-Eurasia, two developments occurred that reduced the risks associated with travel and stimulated long-distance trade. First, rulers invested heavily in the construction of roads and bridges. They undertook those expensive projects primarily for military and administrative reasons, but roads also had the effect of encouraging trade within individual societies and facilitating exchanges between different societies. And second, some ancient societies built large imperial states that sometimes expanded to the point that they bordered on one another: the campaigns of Alexander of Macedon, for example, brought Hellenistic and South Asian societies into direct contact, and only small buffer states separated the Roman and Parthian empires. Even when they did not encounter each other so directly, these powerful empires pacified large stretches of Eurasia and north Africa. As a result, merchants did not face such great risk as in previous eras, the costs of long-distance trade dropped, and its volume rose dramatically.

Trade Networks of the Hellenistic Era

The tempo of long-distance trade increased noticeably during the Hellenistic era, partly because of the many colonies established by Alexander of Macedon and the Seleucid rulers in Persia and Bactria. Though originally populated by military forces and administrators, these settlements soon attracted Greek merchants who linked the recently conquered lands to the Mediterranean basin. The Seleucid rulers worked diligently to promote trade. They controlled land routes linking Bactria, which offered access to South Asian markets, to Mediterranean ports in Syria and Palestine. Archaeologists have unearthed hundreds of coins, pieces of jewelry, and other physical remains, including Greek-style sculptures and buildings, that testify to the presence of Greek communities in Persia and Bactria during the Hellenistic era.

Like the Seleucids, the Ptolemies maintained land routes—in their case, routes going south from Egypt to the kingdom of Nubia and Meroë in east Africa—but they also paid close attention to sea lanes and maritime trade. They ousted pirates from sea lanes linking the Red Sea to the Arabian Sea and the Indian Ocean. They also built several new ports, the most important being Berenice on the Red Sea, and Alexandria served as their principal window on the Mediterranean.

The Monsoon System Even more important, perhaps, mariners from Ptolemaic Egypt learned about the **monsoon** winds that governed sailing and shipping in the Indian Ocean. During the summer the winds blow regularly from the southwest, whereas in the winter they blow from the northeast. Knowledge of these winds enabled mariners to sail safely and reliably to all parts of the Indian Ocean basin. During the second century B.C.E., Hellenistic mariners learned the rhythm of these winds from Arab and South Asian mariners whose ancestors had sailed before the monsoons for centuries. Merchant sailors then established regular links by way of the Red Sea between the Indian subcontinent and Arabia in the east and Egypt and the Mediterranean basin in the west. The anonymous Greek-speaking merchant captain who composed the *Periplus maris erythraei*—the sailing itinerary of the Red Sea mentioned in chapter 11—understood the wind system of the Indian Ocean and described ports as far distant as east Africa and South Asia that sailors could reach with the aid of the monsoons.

Establishment and maintenance of these trade routes was an expensive affair calling for substantial investment in military forces, construction, and bureaucracies to administer the commerce that passed over the routes. But the investment paid handsome dividends. Long-distance trade stimulated economic development within the Hellenistic realms themselves, bringing benefits to local economies throughout the empires. Moreover, Hellenistic rulers closely supervised foreign trade and levied taxes on it, thereby deriving income from even foreign products.

Trade in the Hellenistic World With official encouragement, a substantial trade developed throughout the Hellenistic world, from the Indian subcontinent in the east to the Mediterranean basin in the west. Spices, pepper, cosmetics, gems, and pearls from South Asia traveled by caravan and ship to Hellenistic cities and ports. Grain from Persia and Egypt fed urban populations in distant lands. Mediterranean wine, olive oil, jewelry, and works of art made their way to Persia and Bactria. And throughout the region, from the subcontinent to the Mediterranean, merchants conducted a brisk trade in enslaved people, largely kidnapping victims or prisoners of war.

Indeed, maritime trade networks through the Indian Ocean linked not only the large states of Eurasia and north Africa but also smaller societies in east Africa. During the late centuries B.C.E., the port of **Rhapta** emerged as the principal commercial center on the east African coast. Archaeologists have not discovered the precise location of Rhapta, but it probably was located near modern Dar es Salaam in Tanzania. With increasing trade, groups of professional merchants and entrepreneurs emerged at Rhapta, and coins came into general use on the east African coast. Merchants of Rhapta imported iron goods such as spears, axes, and knives from southern Arabia and the eastern Mediterranean region in

Tomb figure of a camel and a foreign rider. The majority of the Silk Road trade was handled by the nomadic peoples of central and west Africa.

Werner Forman/Universal Images Group/Getty Images

exchange for ivory, rhinoceros horn, tortoise shell, and enslaved people obtained from interior regions. Just as trade in the Mediterranean basin encouraged economic and political development in regions such as western Europe, far-flung commercial networks of the Hellenistic era fostered economic organization and the emergence of states in the distant lands that they brought into interaction.

The First Silk Roads Era

The establishment of classical empires greatly expanded the scope of long-distance trade, as large portions of Eurasia and north Africa fell under the sway of one powerful imperial state

or another. The **Han dynasty** empire maintained order in China and pacified much of central Asia, including a sizable corridor offering access to Bactria and western markets. The Parthian empire displaced the Seleucids in Persia and extended its authority to Mesopotamia. The Roman Empire brought order to the Mediterranean basin. With the decline of the Mauryan dynasty, the Indian subcontinent lacked a strong imperial state, but the Kushan empire and other regional states provided stability and security, particularly in northern India, that favored long-distance trade.

Overland Trade Routes As the classical empires expanded, merchants and travelers created an extensive network of trade routes that linked much of Eurasia and north Africa. Historians refer to these routes collectively as the **Silk Roads** because high-quality silk from China was one of the principal commodities exchanged over the roads. The overland Silk Roads took caravan trade from China to the Roman Empire, thus linking the extreme ends of the Eurasian landmass. From the Han capital of **Chang'an,** the main Silk Road went west until it arrived at the Taklamakan desert, located in the Tarim Basin. This desert is one of the most dangerous and inhospitable regions of the earth: one interpretation of its name, Taklamakan, warns that "he who enters does not come back out." The Silk Road then split into two main branches that skirted the desert proper and passed through oasis towns that ringed it to the north and south. The branches came together at Kashgar (now known as Kashi, located in the westernmost corner of modern China). From Kashgar, one branch went south, more or less following the route of the modern Karakorum Highway through modern Pakistan, then down the Indus River Valley to ports along the west coast of the Indian subcontinent. Another route continued west, passing through Bactria and across the Iranian Plateau before reaching the valleys of the Tigris and Euphrates rivers. There it joined with roads to ports on the Persian Gulf and proceeded to Palmyra (in modern Syria), where it met roads coming from Arabia and ports on the Red Sea. Continuing west, it terminated at the Mediterranean ports of Antioch (in modern Turkey) and Tyre (in modern Lebanon).

Sea Lanes and Maritime Trade The Silk Roads also included a network of sea lanes that sustained maritime commerce throughout much of the eastern hemisphere. From Guangzhou in southern China, sea lanes through the South

Chang'an (chahng-ahn)
Tyre (tah-yer)

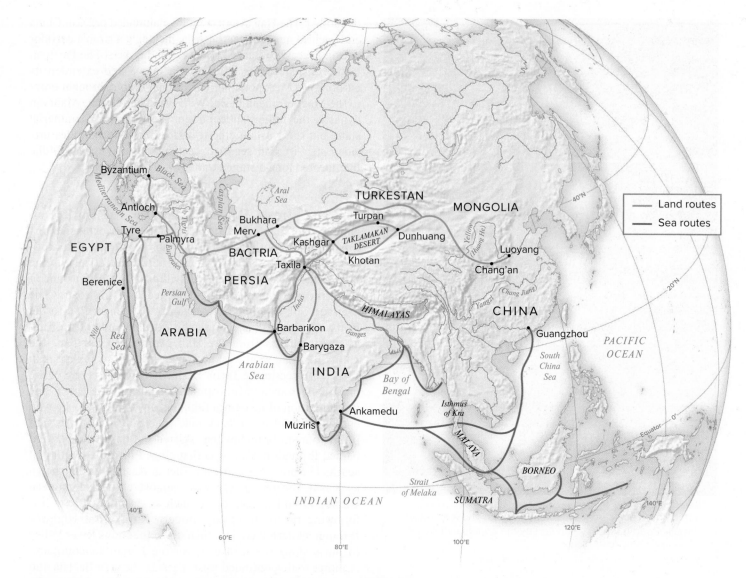

MAP 12.1   The Silk Roads, 100 B.C.E.–250 C.E.

Note the extent of the land and sea routes known collectively as the Silk Roads.

Consider the political, economic, and geographic conditions that would be necessary for regular travel and trade across the Silk Roads.

China Sea linked the east Asian seaboard to the mainland and the islands of southeast Asia. Routes linking southeast Asia with Ceylon (modern Sri Lanka) and the Indian subcontinent became increasingly important in later Silk Roads periods. From a handful of major ports along the west coast of the subcontinent sea lanes passed through the Arabian Sea to Persia and Arabia, and through the Persian Gulf and the Red Sea they offered access to land routes and the Mediterranean basin, which already possessed a well-developed network of trade routes.

Trade Goods A wide variety of manufactured products and agricultural commodities traveled over the Silk Roads. Generally speaking, silk and spices traveled west from producers in southeast Asia, China, and South Asia to consumers in central Asia, Iran, Arabia, and the Roman Empire (including Egypt and north Africa as well as the European regions of the empire). Silk came

mostly from China, the only land in ancient times where cultivators and weavers had developed techniques for producing high-quality silk fabrics. The fine spices—cloves, nutmeg, mace, and cardamom—all came from southeast Asia. Ginger came from China, cinnamon from China and south-east Asia, pepper and sesame oil from Arabia and south and southwest Asia. Spices were extremely important commodities during the First Silk Roads Era because they had many more uses than they do in the modern world. They served not only as condiments and flavoring agents but also as drugs, anesthetics, aphrodisiacs, perfumes, aromatics, and magical potions. Apart from spices, India exported cotton textiles and valuable items such as pearls, coral, and ivory.

Central Asian and Mediterranean lands exchanged a variety of manufactured goods and other commodities for the silks and spices that they imported. Central Asia produced large, strong horses and high-quality jade, much prized in

China by stone carvers. From the Roman Empire came glassware, jewelry, works of art, decorative items, perfumes, bronze goods, wool and linen textiles, pottery, iron tools, olive oil, wine, and gold and silver bullion. Mediterranean merchants and manufacturers often imported raw materials such as uncut gemstones, which they exported as finished products in the form of expensive jewelry and decorative items.

Some individuals made very long journeys during the First Silk Roads Era. Zhang Qian ventured from China as far west as Bactria, Chinese merchants traveled regularly to central Asia and Persia, several South Asian embassies called on Roman emperors, Roman merchants traveled by sea at least as far east as the southern tip of the Indian subcontinent, and Malay merchant mariners sailed from the islands of southeast Asia as far as east Africa. On a few occasions individuals even traveled across much or all of the eastern hemisphere between China and the Roman Empire. A Chinese ambassador named Gang Ying embarked on a mission to distant western lands in 97 C.E. and proceeded as far as Mesopotamia before reports of the long and dangerous journey ahead persuaded him to return home. And Chinese sources reported the arrival in 166 C.E. of a delegation claiming to represent the Roman emperor Marcus Aurelius. No information survives to throw light on the experiences of this party—or even to confirm its identity—but Roman subjects from Egypt or Syria might well have traveled as far as China in search of trading opportunities.

An enameled glass goblet produced about the second century C.E. in Begram (modern-day Afghanistan) depicts a party harvesting dates in a grove of palms. The production technique is Roman, testifying to Mediterranean influence in central Asia.
Thierry Ollivier/Getty Images

The Organization of Long-Distance Trade

Individual merchants did not usually travel from one end of Eurasia to the other. Instead, they handled long-distance trade in stages. On the caravan routes between China and Bactria, for example, Chinese and central Asian peoples such as the Kushans dominated trade. Rarely if ever did they go farther west, however, because the Parthians took advantage of their power and geographic position to control overland trade within their boundaries and to reserve it for their subjects. Once it reached Palmyra, merchandise passed mostly into the hands of Roman subjects such as Greeks, Jews, and Armenians, who were especially active in the commercial life of the Mediterranean basin.

Meanwhile, on the seas, other peoples became involved in long-distance trade.

Roman coin depicting the great lighthouse at Alexandria, regarded as one of the seven wonders of the ancient world. Minted at Alexandria during the second century C.E.
The Art Archive/Shutterstock

From southern China through southeast Asia, Ceylon and the Indian subcontinent, the principal figures were Malay and South Asian mariners. In the Arabian Sea, Persians joined Egyptian and Greek subjects of the Roman Empire as the most prominent trading peoples. The Parthian empire largely controlled trade in the Persian Gulf, whereas the Ptolemaic dynasty and later the Roman Empire dominated affairs in the Red Sea. After Roman emperors absorbed Egypt in the first century C.E., their subjects carried on an especially brisk trade between the Indian subcontinent and the Mediterranean. The Greek geographer Strabo reported in the early first century C.E. that as many as 120 ships departed annually from the Red Sea for India. Most of those ships left from the bustling port of Berenice, which Roman authorities considered so important that they maintained ten forts to guard its approaches. Archaeologists have unearthed the remains of a Roman trading outpost at Arikamedu, near modern Pondicherry in southern India, and literary sources report that merchants subject to Roman rule established colonies also at Muziris (near modern Cranganore), Barygaza (near modern Broach), Barbarikon (near modern Karachi), and other sites as well. Meanwhile, since the mid-first century C.E., the Romans also had dominated both the eastern and the western regions of *mare nostrum,* the Mediterranean.

It is impossible to determine the quantity or value of trade that passed over the Silk Roads in classical times, but it clearly made a deep impression on contemporaries. By the first century C.E., pepper, cinnamon, and other spices graced the tables of the wealthy classes in the Roman Empire, where silk garments had become items of high fashion. Indeed, silk was in such demand that Roman merchants often stretched their supplies by unraveling the densely woven fabrics that came from China and then reweaving them into larger numbers of sheer garments that were sometimes so light as to be transparent. Some Romans fretted that see-through silk attire would lead to moral decay, and others worried that hefty expenditures for luxury items would ruin the imperial economy. In both cases, their anxieties testified to the powerful attraction of imported silks and spices for Roman consumers.

As it happened, long-distance trade did not cause moral or economic problems for the Roman Empire or any other state during the First Silk Roads Era.

What's Left Out?

Striking evidence of some of the high-value luxury goods that were being transported from the Mediterranean basin and Han China through Central Asia comes in the form of a major discovery made by French archaeologists in the 1930s, near the modern town of Begram, about 80 kilometers north of Kabul, the capital of Afghanistan. Inside two storage rooms that were discovered in the remains of a royal Kushan city, the archaeologists discovered an extraordinary array of artistic luxury goods from all over Eurasia. The goods appear to have been deliberately cached, and the thick walls and blocked entrances of the storerooms suggest that these goods were stashed away for safe keeping during a period of political unrest. Dating the discovery has been difficult, but most specialists now agree that these goods were probably stashed away in these secure rooms sometime in the late first or early second centuries of the Common Era.

The initial conclusion of archaeologists was that, if the goods had been stored late in the Kushan period (say, in the early third century C.E.), the collection must have been some sort of royal treasure, hidden away for safekeeping during the latter stages of the fragmenting Kushan Empire. However, the now more widely accepted dates of the late first or early second centuries C.E. place this cache at the height of Kushan stability and prosperity, which means it is far more likely that these treasures were part of the commercial stock of merchants stored temporarily in a warehouse before being shipped in various directions along the Silk Roads.

If this interpretation is correct, the collection provides striking evidence of the extraordinary value and diversity of the trade in valuable luxury goods that characterize trans-Eurasian commerce during the First Silk Roads Era. Among the treasures were magnificent carved ivories from India; molded stucco ornaments of Greek origin; superb glassware from Syria and Roman Egypt, such as the goblet illustrated on page 233, bronze art objects from Egypt and elsewhere in the Roman Empire; and lacquer objects from Han China. Along with bales of Chinese silk, these are examples of the sort of high-value trade goods that were passing back and forth along the Silk Roads during the height of their operation, through major commercial hubs like the Kushan Empire. Although we lack many details about how that trade was actually conducted, the astonishing diversity and value of that trade as represented by the Begram Hoard, along with the critical role played by Kushan political stability in making such high-value trade possible, is indisputable.

Source: D. Whitehouse, "Begram, the *Periplus* and Gandharan Art," *Journal of Roman Archaeology* 2 (1989), 93–100; S. Mehendale, "Begram: Along Ancient Central Asian and Indian Trade Routes," *Cahiers d'Asia centrale,* 1 (1996), pp. 47–64.

Indeed, it more likely stimulated rather than threatened local economies. Yet long-distance trade did not occur in a vacuum. Commercial exchanges encouraged cultural and biological exchanges, some of which had large implications for ancient societies.

A mosaic of the second century C.E. depicts a musician playing flutes and a dancer wearing a thin and revealing silk garment.
Brenda Kean/Alamy Stock Photo

CULTURAL AND BIOLOGICAL EXCHANGES ALONG THE SILK ROADS

The Silk Roads served as magnificent highways for merchants and their commodities, but others also took advantage of the opportunities they offered to travel in relative safety over long distances. Merchants, missionaries, and other travelers carried their beliefs, values, and religious convictions to distant lands: Buddhism, Hinduism, and Christianity all traveled the Silk Roads and attracted converts far from their original homelands. Meanwhile, invisible travelers such as disease pathogens also crossed the Silk Roads and touched off devastating epidemics when they found fresh populations to infect. Toward the end of the First Silk Roads Era, epidemic disease that was spread over the trade network caused dramatic demographic decline, especially in China and the Mediterranean basin and to a lesser extent in other parts of Eurasia as well.

The Spread of Buddhism and Hinduism

By the third century B.C.E., **Buddhism** had become well established in northern regions of the Indian subcontinent, and with the sponsorship of the emperor Ashoka it spread to Bactria and Ceylon. Buddhism was particularly successful in attracting merchants as converts. When they traveled, Buddhist merchants practiced their religion among themselves and explained it to others. Gradually, Buddhism made its way along the Silk Roads to Iran, central Asia, China, and southeast Asia.

Buddhism in Central Asia

Buddhism first established a presence in the oasis towns along the Silk Roads—notably Merv, Bukhara, Samarkand, Kashgar, Khotan, Kuqa, Turpan, and Dunhuang—where merchants and their caravans found food, rest, lodging, and markets. The oases depended heavily on trade for their prosperity, and they allowed merchants to build monasteries and invite monks and scribes into their communities. Because they hosted travelers who came from different lands, spoke different languages, and observed different religious practices, the oasis towns became cosmopolitan centers. By the late second century B.C.E., many residents of the oases themselves adopted Buddhism, which was the most prominent religion of Silk Roads merchants for almost a millennium, from about 100 B.C.E. to 800 C.E.

From the oasis communities Buddhism spread to the steppe lands of central Asia and to China. Nomadic peoples from the steppes visited the oases regularly to trade animal products from their herds for grains and manufactured items. They often found Buddhism intriguing, and in the early centuries C.E. they increasingly responded to its appeal. By the fourth century C.E., they had sponsored the spread of Buddhism throughout much of central Asia.

Buddhism in China

By the first century C.E. Buddhism had also established a foothold in China. The earliest Buddhists in China were probably foreign merchants from other regions of Eurasia who practiced their religion in the enclaves that Han dynasty officials allowed them to inhabit in Chang'an and other major cities. For several centuries Buddhism did not appeal very strongly to native Chinese. Yet the presence of monasteries and missionaries offered Buddhism the potential to attract Chinese converts. Beginning about the third century C.E., Chinese began to respond enthusiastically to Buddhism, which during the first millennium of the Common Era became the most popular religion throughout all of east Asia, including Japan and Korea as well as China.

Buddhism and Hinduism in Southeast Asia

As Buddhism spread north from South Asia into central Asia and China, both Buddhism and Hinduism also began to attract a following in southeast Asia. Once again, merchants traveling the Silk Roads—in this case, the sea lanes through the Indian Ocean—played prominent roles in spreading these religious traditions. Merchant mariners regularly plied the waters between the Indian subcontinent and southeast Asia, and by the first century C.E., clear signs of Indian cultural influence had appeared in southeast Asia. In Java, Sumatra, and other islands, as well as in the Malay peninsula and territories in modern Vietnam and Cambodia, rulers of southeast Asian states called themselves *rajas* ("kings"), in the manner of South Asian rulers, and they adopted Sanskrit as a means of written communication. Many rulers converted to Buddhism, and others promoted the Hindu sects of Shiva and Vishnu. They built walled cities around lavish temples constructed in the South Asian style. They appointed Buddhist or Hindu advisers, and they sought to enhance their authority by associating themselves with honored religious traditions.

The Spread of Christianity

Early Christians faced intermittent persecution from Roman officials. During the early centuries C.E., Roman authorities launched a series of campaigns to stamp out Christianity because most Christians refused to observe the state cults that honored emperors as divine beings. Imperial officials considered Christianity a menace to society because zealous missionaries attacked other religions and generated sometimes violent conflict. Nevertheless, Christian missionaries took full advantage of the Romans' magnificent network of roads and sea lanes, which enabled them to carry their message throughout the Roman Empire and the Mediterranean basin.

Early Buddhist sculpture in Bactria reflected the influence of Mediterranean and Greek artistic styles. This seated Buddha from the first or second century C.E. was clearly influenced by Mediterranean cultural styles.
akg-images/Newscom

Christianity in the Mediterranean Basin

During the second and third centuries C.E., countless missionaries took Paul of Tarsus as their example and worked zealously to attract converts. One of the more famous was Gregory the Wonderworker, a tireless missionary with a reputation for performing miracles, who popularized Christianity in central Anatolia during the mid-third century C.E. Contemporaries reported that Gregory not only preached Christian doctrine but also expelled demons, moved boulders, diverted a river in flood, and persuaded observers that he had access to impressive supernatural powers. Gregory and his fellow missionaries helped to make Christianity an enormously popular religion of salvation in the Roman Empire. By the late third century C.E., in spite of continuing imperial opposition, devout Christian communities flourished throughout the Mediterranean basin in Anatolia, Syria, Palestine, Egypt, and north Africa as well as in Greece, Italy, Spain, and Gaul.

Christianity in Southwest Asia

As Christianity became a prominent source of religious inspiration within the Roman Empire, its missionaries also traveled the trade routes and found followers beyond the Mediterranean basin. By the second century C.E., sizable Christian communities flourished throughout Mesopotamia and Iran, and a few Christian churches had appeared as far away as Central and South Asia and China. Christians did not dominate eastern lands as they did the Roman Empire, but they attracted large numbers of converts in southwest Asia. Indeed, beside Jews and Zoroastrians, Christians constituted one of the major religious communities in the region, and they remained so even after the seventh century C.E., when the Islamic religion favored by Arab Muslim conquerors began to displace the older religious communities.

Christian communities in Mesopotamia and Iran deeply influenced Christian practices in the Roman Empire. To

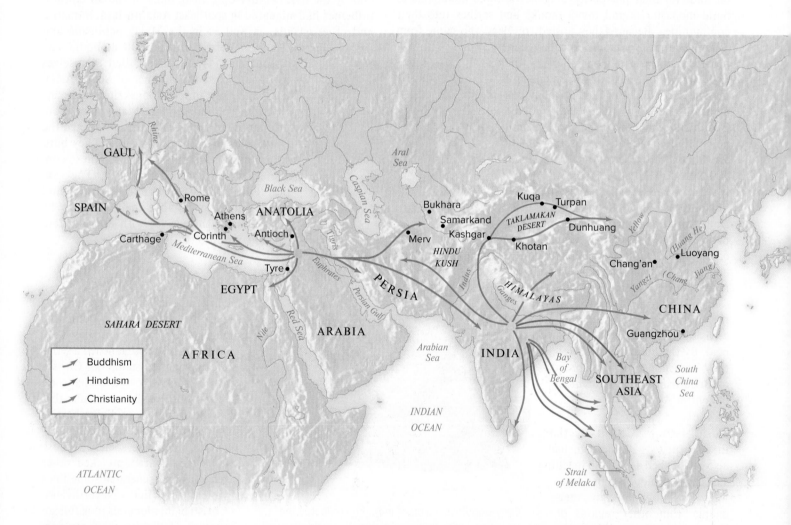

MAP 12.2   The spread of Buddhism, Hinduism, and Christianity, 200 B.C.E.– 400 C.E.

Compare the routes taken by Buddhism, Hinduism, and Christianity with the routes followed by merchants on Silk Roads depicted on Map 12.1.

What role did Silk Roads trade play in the diffusion of these religions?

demonstrate utter loyalty to their faith, Christians in southwest Asia often followed strict ascetic regimes: inspired by South Asian traditions, they abstained from sexual contact, refused fine foods and other comforts, and sometimes even withdrew from family life and society. These practices impressed devout Christians in the Roman Empire. By the third century C.E., some Mediterranean Christians had begun to abandon society altogether and live as hermits in the deserts of Egypt, the mountains of Greece, and other isolated locations. Others withdrew from lay society but lived in communities of like-minded individuals who devoted their efforts to prayer and praise of God. Thus ascetic practices of Christians living in lands east of the Roman Empire helped to inspire the formation of Christian monastic communities in the Mediterranean basin.

After the fifth century C.E., Christian communities in southwest Asia and the Mediterranean basin increasingly went separate ways. Most of the faithful in southwest Asia became **Nestorians**—followers of the Greek theologian Nestorius, who lived during the early fifth century and emphasized the human as opposed to the divine nature of Jesus. Mediterranean church authorities rejected Nestorius's views, and many of his disciples departed for Mesopotamia and Iran. They soon became prominent in local Christian communities, and they introduced a strong organizational framework to the church in southwest Asia. Although they had limited dealings with Mediterranean Christians, the Nestorians spread their beliefs east across the Silk Roads. Nestorian merchants took their version of Christianity with them on trade missions and established communities in Central and South Asia and China.

The Spread of Manichaeism

Mani and Manichaeism The explosive spread of **Manichaeism** dramatically illustrated how missionary religions made

effective use of the Silk Roads trading network. Manichaeism derived from the prophet **Mani** (circa 216–272 C.E.), a devout Zoroastrian from Babylon in Mesopotamia. Apart from Zoroastrianism, Mani drew deep influence from Christianity and Buddhism. He regarded Zarathustra as the prophet of Persia, Buddha as the prophet of South Asia, and Jesus as the prophet of the Mediterranean world. Because of the intense interaction between peoples of different societies, Mani saw a need for a prophet for all humanity, and he promoted a blend of Zoroastrian, Christian, and Buddhist elements as a syncretic religion that would serve the needs of a cosmopolitan world.

Mani was a dualist: he viewed the world as the site of a cosmic struggle between the forces of light and darkness, good and evil. He associated light with spiritual awareness and darkness with the material world. He urged his followers to reject worldly pleasures, which entangled the spirit in matter, and rise toward the light. His doctrine had strong appeal because it offered a rational explanation for the presence of good and evil in the world while also providing a means for individuals to achieve personal salvation and contribute to the triumph of good over evil.

Manichaean Ethics Mani promoted an ascetic lifestyle and insisted that disciples observe high ethical standards. Devout Manichaeans, known as "the elect," abstained from marriage, sexual relations, fine clothing, meat, rich foods, and other personal comforts, dedicating themselves instead to prayer, fasting, and ritual observances. Less zealous Manichaeans, known as "hearers," led more conventional lives, but they followed a strict moral code and provided food and gifts to sustain the elect. All Manichaeans looked forward to individual salvation and eternal association with the forces of light and good.

Mani was a fervent missionary: he traveled widely to promote his beliefs, corresponded tirelessly with Manichaean adherents, and dispatched disciples to lands that he could

A cave painting from about the seventh century C.E. depicts a group of devout Manichaean faithful, whose austere regimen called for them to dress in plain white garments and keep their hair uncut.
Chronicle/Alamy Stock Photo

Manichaeism (man-ih-KEE-iz'm)

not visit himself. He also created a Manichaean church with its own services, rituals, hymns, and liturgies. His doctrine attracted converts first in Mesopotamia, and before Mani's death it had spread throughout the Sasanid empire and into the eastern Mediterranean region. In spite of its asceticism, Manichaeism appealed especially strongly to merchants, who accepted the religion as hearers and supported the Manichaean church. By the end of the third century C.E., Manichaean communities had appeared in all the large cities and trading centers of the Roman Empire.

Decline of Manichaeism Manichaeism soon came under tremendous pressure. Zoroastrian leaders urged the Sasanid rulers to suppress Mani's movement as a threat to public order. Mani himself died in chains as a prisoner of the Sasanid emperor, who sought to use Zoroastrianism as a cultural foundation for the unification of his realm. Authorities in the Roman Empire also persecuted Manichaeans, whom they distrusted because of the religion's origins in the rival Sasanid empire. Indeed, during the fifth and sixth centuries, political authorities largely exterminated Manichaeism in the Mediterranean basin. Yet Manichaeism survived in central Asia, where it attracted converts among nomadic Turkish peoples who traded with merchants from China, India, and southwest Asia. Thus like Buddhism, Hinduism, and Christianity, Manichaeism relied on the trade routes of the Silk Roads to extend its influence to new lands and peoples.

The Spread of Epidemic Disease

While serving as routes for the distribution of trade goods and highways for the spread of religious beliefs, the roads and the sea lanes of the classical world also facilitated the movement of biological agents. The Silk Roads were the routes by which grapes, camels, and donkeys made their way from the Mediterranean region to China, while cherries, apricots, peaches, and walnuts traveled in the other direction, from central Asia and China to the Mediterranean. Alongside the fruits and nuts were some less welcome traveling companions—infectious and contagious diseases that sparked ferocious epidemics when they found their way to previously unexposed populations.

Information about human populations in classical times is scanty and full of gaps. Scholars often do not have records to work with and must draw inferences about population size from the area enclosed by city walls, the number of houses discovered in a settlement, the agricultural potential of a region, and similar considerations. As a result, population estimates for premodern societies are rough approximations rather than precise figures. Moreover, within a single society, individual regions often had very different demographic experiences. Nevertheless, even for ancient Eurasia the general outlines of population history are reasonably clear.

Epidemic Diseases During the second and third centuries C.E., the Han and Roman empires suffered large-scale outbreaks of **epidemic disease**. The most destructive diseases were probably smallpox and measles, and epidemics of bubonic plague may also have erupted. All three diseases are devastating when they break out in populations without resistance, immunity, or medicines to combat them. As disease ravaged the two empires, Chinese and Roman populations declined sharply.

During the reign of Augustus, the population of the Roman Empire stood at about sixty million people. During the second century C.E., epidemics reduced Roman population by about one-quarter, to forty-five million. Most devastating was an outbreak of smallpox that spread throughout the Mediterranean basin during the years 165 to 180 C.E. The epidemic was especially virulent in cities, and it even claimed the life of the Roman emperor Marcus Aurelius (180 C.E.). In combination with war and invasions, continuing outbreaks caused a significant population decline during the third and fourth centuries: by 400 C.E. the number of Romans had fallen to perhaps forty million. During the fifth and early sixth centuries, the Roman population stabilized, but an epidemic of bubonic plague broke out in the mid-sixth century and caused a general population decline throughout the Mediterranean region.

Epidemics appeared slightly later in China than in the Mediterranean region. From fifty million people at the beginning of the millennium, Chinese population rose to sixty million in 200 C.E. As diseases found their way east, however, Chinese numbers fell back to fifty million by 400 C.E. and to forty-five million by 600 C.E. Thus by 600 C.E. both Mediterranean and Chinese populations had fallen by a quarter to a third from their high points during classical times.

How the Past Shapes the Future ▷ ▷ ▷ ▷

Long-Distance Trade Networks

The long-distance trade networks of the First Silk Roads Era introduced people across Eurasia and North Africa to diverse foods, commodities, ideas, and religions for many centuries. Yet the same networks that allowed for the diffusion of things and people also allowed for the rapid diffusion of microbes. Is it possible to argue that by creating the conditions in which disease could ravage huge areas with greater speed than ever before, the very success and stability of these networks paved the way for the eventual collapse of ancient Eurasian states? But this spread of diseases had consequences beyond even the end of the ancient world. Survivors of these epidemics acquired immunities that other peoples of the world did not have. When Europeans began to colonize much of the world in the sixteenth century, they carried with them these same diseases, which had a disastrous impact on peoples in the Americas and other previously isolated regions of the planet.

SOURCES FROM THE PAST

St. Cyprian on Epidemic Disease in the Roman Empire

St. Cyprian, bishop of Carthage, was an outspoken proponent of Christianity during the early and middle decades of the third century C.E. When epidemic disease struck the Roman Empire in 251 C.E., imperial authorities blamed the outbreak on Christians who refused to honor pagan gods. In this extract from Cyprian's On Mortality, *the bishop attempts to refute that charge.*

It serves as validation of the [Christian] faith when the bowels loosen and drain the body's strength, when fever generated in bone marrow causes sores to break out in the throat, when continuous vomiting roils the intestines, when blood-shot eyes burn, when the feet or other bodily parts are amputated because of infection by putrefying disease, when through weakness caused by injuries to the body either mobility is impeded, or hearing is impaired, or sight is obscured. It requires enormous greatness of heart to struggle with resolute mind against so many onslaughts of destruction and death. It requires great loftiness to stand firm amidst the ruins of the human race, not to concede defeat with those who have no hope in God, but rather to rejoice and embrace the gift of the times. With Christ as our judge, we should receive this gift as the reward of his faith, as we vigorously affirm our faith and, having suffered, advance toward Christ by Christ's narrow path. . . .

> Why does the author see the onset of fatal disease as a validation of the Christian faith?

Many of us [Christians] are dying in this epidemic—that is, many of us are being liberated from the world. The epidemic is a pestilence for the Jews and the pagans and the enemies of Christ, but for the servants of God it is a welcome event. True, without any discrimination, the just are dying alongside the unjust, but you should not imagine that the evil and the good face a common destruction. The just are called to refreshment, while the unjust are herded off to punishment: the faithful receive protection, while the faithless receive retribution. We are unseeing and ungrateful for divine favors, beloved brethren, and we do not recognize what is granted to us. . . .

> What divine favors does the author imagine the faithful are receiving through their suffering from this disease?

How suitable and essential it is that this plague and pestilence, which seems so terrible and ferocious, probes the justice of every individual and examines the minds of the human race to determine whether the healthy care for the ill, whether relatives diligently love their kin, whether masters show mercy to their languishing slaves, whether physicians do not abandon those seeking their aid, whether the ferocious diminish their violence, whether the greedy in the fear of death extinguish the raging flames of their insatiable avarice, whether the proud bend their necks, whether the shameless mitigate their audacity, whether the rich will loosen their purse strings and give something to others as their loved ones perish all around them and as they are about to die without heirs.

For Further Reflection

■ Why does the author argue the plague is essential in probing the justice of every individual?

■ What behaviors, in the author's opinion, separate the faithful from the unfaithful in terms of how they respond to the plague?

■ How successful is the author in defending Christianity from the charge that the plague was a result of Christians refusing to worship the traditional Roman gods?

Source: Wilhelm von Hartel, ed. *S. Thasci Caecili Cypriani opera omnia* in *Corpus scriptorum ecclesiasticorum latinorum.* Vienna: 1868, vol. 3, pp. 305–6. (Translation by Jerry H. Bentley.)

Effects of Epidemic Diseases Demographic decline in turn brought economic and social change. Trade within the empires declined, and both the Chinese and the Roman economies contracted. Both economies also moved toward regional self-sufficiency: whereas previously the Chinese and Roman states had integrated the various regions of their empires into a larger network of trade and exchange, after about 200 C.E. they increasingly established several smaller regional economies that concentrated on their own needs instead of the larger imperial market. In the Roman Empire, for example, the eastern Mediterranean regions of Anatolia, Egypt, and Greece continued to form a larger, integrated society, but regional economies increasingly emerged in western Mediterranean lands, including Italy, Gaul, Spain, and northwest Africa.

The demographic histories of classical Persia, South Asia and other lands are not as clear as they are for China and the Roman Empire. Persia most likely experienced demographic, economic, and social problems similar to those that afflicted China and the Mediterranean basin. Peoples in South Asia may well have suffered from epidemic disease and population losses, although there is limited evidence. In east Asia and the Mediterranean basin, however, it is clear that epidemic disease seriously weakened Chinese and Roman societies. Indeed, epidemic disease contributed to serious instability in China after the collapse of the Han dynasty, and in weakening Mediterranean society, it helped bring about the collapse of the western Roman Empire.

CHINA AFTER THE HAN DYNASTY

By the time epidemic diseases struck China, internal political problems had already begun to weaken the Han dynasty. By the late second century C.E., Han authorities had largely lost their ability to maintain order. Early in the third century C.E., the central government dissolved, and a series of

autonomous regional kingdoms took the place of the Han state. With the disappearance of the Han dynasty, China experienced significant cultural change, most notably an increasing interest in Buddhism.

Internal Decay of the Han State

The Han dynasty collapsed largely because of internal problems that its rulers could not solve. One problem involved the development of factions within the ranks of the ruling elites. Marriage alliances between imperial and aristocratic families led to the formation of many factions whose members sought to advance their prospects in the imperial government and exclude others from important positions. That atmosphere led

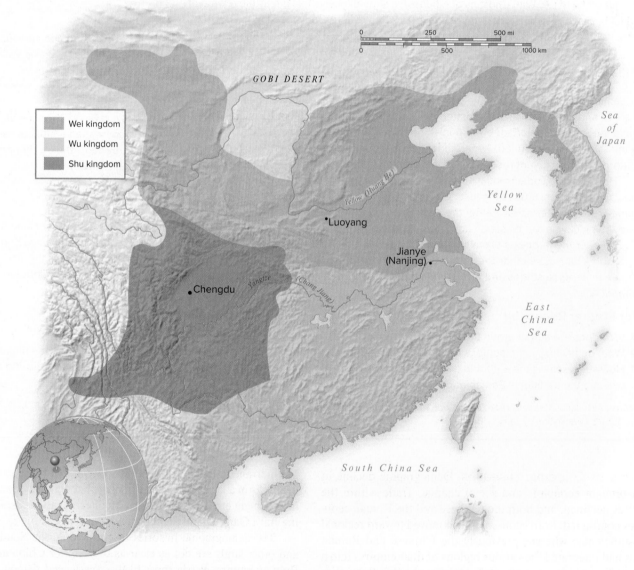

MAP 12.3   China after the Han dynasty, 220 C.E.

Compare this map with Map 8.2 showing the Han empire at its height.

Why did the powerful Han dynasty fragment into a series of smaller kingdoms under the control of warlords?

to constant infighting and backstabbing among the ruling elites, which in turn reduced the effectiveness of the central government.

An even more difficult problem had to do with the perennial issue of land and its equitable distribution. At the turn of the millennium, the usurper Wang Mang had attempted to redistribute land in China, but his program did not survive his brief reign (9–23 C.E.). During the last two centuries of the Han dynasty, large landowners gained new influence in the government. They managed to reduce their share of taxes and shift the burden onto peasants. They even formed private armies to advance their class interests.

Peasant Rebellion Those developments provoked widespread unrest, particularly among peasants, who found themselves under increasing economic pressure with no means to influence the government. Pressures became particularly acute during the late second and third centuries when epidemics began to take their toll. In 184 C.E. peasant discontent fueled an immense uprising known as the Yellow Turban rebellion, so called because the rebels wore yellow headbands that represented the color of the Chinese earth and symbolized their peasant origins. Although authorities suppressed it after five years of fighting, the rebellion proved to be only the first in a series of insurrections that plagued the late Han dynasty.

Collapse of the Han Dynasty Meanwhile, Han generals increasingly usurped political authority. By 190 C.E. the Han emperor had become a mere puppet, and the generals effectively ruled the regions controlled by their armies. They allied with wealthy landowners of their regions and established themselves as warlords who maintained a kind of rough order based on force of arms. The generals continued to recognize an emperor for a short time, but in 220 C.E. they formally abolished the Han dynasty and divided the empire into three large kingdoms.

Once the dynasty had disappeared, large numbers of nomadic peoples, including Xiongnu, migrated into China, especially the northern regions, and they helped to keep China disunited for more than 350 years. Between the fourth and sixth centuries C.E., nomadic peoples established large kingdoms that dominated much of northern China as well as the steppe lands.

Cultural Change in Post-Han China

In some ways, the centuries following the fall of the Han dynasty present a spectacle of chaos and disorder. One kingdom toppled another, only to fall in its turn to a temporary successor. War and nomadic invasions led to population decline in much of northern China. By the mid-fifth century, the region around Chang'an and Luoyang—the heartland of classical China—had experienced almost complete devastation because of armies that ravaged the region in search of food and plunder. Contemporaries reported that the Former Han

After the collapse of the Han dynasty, China experienced social and economic difficulty. Wealthy classes often traveled in ox carts instead of more expensive, horse-drawn carriages. Archaeologists found these ceramic models of ox carts in tombs. They were produced during different dynasties that ruled parts of China from the third to the seventh centuries.
DEA Picture Library/age fotostock

capital of Chang'an had no more than one hundred households and that the Later Han capital of Luoyang resembled a trash heap more than a city.

Sinicization of Nomadic Peoples Beneath the disorderly surface of political events, however, several important social and cultural changes were taking place. First, nomadic peoples increasingly adapted to the Chinese environment. They took up agriculture and built permanent settlements. They married Chinese spouses and took Chinese names. They wore the clothes, ate the food, and adopted the customs of China. Some sought a formal Chinese education and became well versed in Chinese philosophy and literature. In short, nomadic peoples became increasingly influenced by the process of **sinicization**, and as the generations passed, distinctions between peoples of nomadic and Chinese ancestry became less and less obvious. Partly because of that development, a new imperial dynasty was eventually able to reconstitute a centralized imperial state in north China.

Second, with the disintegration of political order, the Confucian tradition lost much of its credibility. The original goal of Confucius and his early followers was to find some means to move from chaos to stability during the Period of the Warring States. As long as Confucian methods and principles helped to maintain order, ruling elites and intellectual classes honored the Confucian tradition. When the Han dynasty collapsed, **Confucianism** seemed irrelevant to many people.

Individuals who in earlier centuries might have committed themselves to Confucian values turned instead to Daoism and Buddhism. As in the Period of the Warring States, **Daoism** once again offered a way to find peace in a turbulent world. Originally, Daoism was a school of speculative philosophical thought that appealed mostly to an educated elite. After the fall of the Han, however, it became more a religious than a philosophical doctrine. Daoist sages not only promised salvation to those who observed their doctrines and rituals but also experimented with spices, herbs, and drugs to concoct elixirs or potions that they claimed would confer health and immortality. Daoism attracted widespread interest among a population afflicted by war and disease and became much more popular than before, especially because it faced less competition from the Confucian tradition.

Popularity of Buddhism Even more important than Daoism for Chinese cultural history was Buddhism. Until about the fourth century C.E., Buddhism was largely the faith of foreign merchants in China and attracted little interest on the part of native Chinese. After the fall of the Han Empire, however, Buddhism received strong support from nomadic peoples who migrated into northern China and who in many cases had long been familiar with Buddhism in central Asia. Meanwhile, as a result of missionary efforts, the faith began to attract a following among native Chinese as well. Indeed, between the fourth and sixth centuries C.E., Buddhism became well established in China. When a centralized imperial state took shape in the late sixth century C.E., Buddhism provided an important cultural foundation for the restoration of a unified political order.

THE COLLAPSE OF THE WESTERN ROMAN EMPIRE

Moralists have often interpreted the disintegration of the Roman Empire as a symbol of the transitory nature of human political structures. Fascination with imperial Rome has encouraged the proliferation of theories—many of them untenable—seeking to explain the collapse of the empire as the result of some single, simple cause. By various accounts, the Roman Empire disintegrated because of lead poisoning, radiation given off by bricks, immorality, or the rise of Christianity. Notwithstanding the zeal with which proponents have promoted pet theories, there was no single cause for the disintegration of the Roman Empire. Instead, a combination of internal problems and external pressures weakened the empire and brought an end to Roman authority in the western portion of the empire, although imperial rule continued until the fifteenth century C.E. in the eastern Mediterranean. In the Mediterranean basin as in China, imperial weakness and collapse coincided with significant cultural change, notably the increasing popularity of Christianity.

Sculpture of the tetrarchs, or four corulers of the Roman Empire, during the late third century C.E.; from left, Galerius, Constantius, Diocletian, and Maximian. What message is the apparent closeness of the tetrarchs intended to convey?
Leemage/Universal Images Group/Getty Images

Internal Decay in the Roman Empire

The Barracks Emperors As in the case of the Han dynasty, internal political problems go a long way toward explaining the fragmentation of the Roman Empire. Like their Han counterparts, the Roman emperors faced internal opposition. During the half century from 235 to 284 C.E., there were twenty-six recognized emperors (and many others who staked temporary claims to the imperial office). Known as the "barracks emperors," most of them were generals who seized power, held it briefly, and then suddenly lost it when they were displaced by rivals or by their mutinous troops. Not surprisingly, most of the barracks emperors died violently: only one is known for sure to have succumbed to natural causes.

Apart from divisions and factions, the Roman Empire faced problems because of its sheer size. Even during the best of times, when the emperors could count on abundant revenues and disciplined armed forces, the sprawling empire posed a challenge for central government. After the third century, as epidemics spread throughout the empire and its various regions moved toward local, self-sufficient economies, the empire as a whole became increasingly unmanageable.

Diocletian The emperor **Diocletian** (reigned 284–305 C.E.) attempted to deal with this problem by dividing the empire into two administrative districts. The eastern district included the wealthy lands of Anatolia, Syria, Egypt, and Greece, and the western district embraced Italy, Gaul, Spain, Britain, and north Africa. A coemperor ruled each district with the aid of a powerful lieutenant, and Diocletian hoped the four officials, known as the *tetrarchs,* would be able to administer the vast empire more effectively than an individual emperor could. Diocletian was a skillful administrator. He managed to bring Rome's many armies, including unpredictable maverick forces, under firm imperial control. He also tried to deal with a crumbling economy by strengthening the imperial currency, forcing the government to adjust its expenditures to its income, and imposing

Diocletian (dah-yuh-KLEE-shuhn)

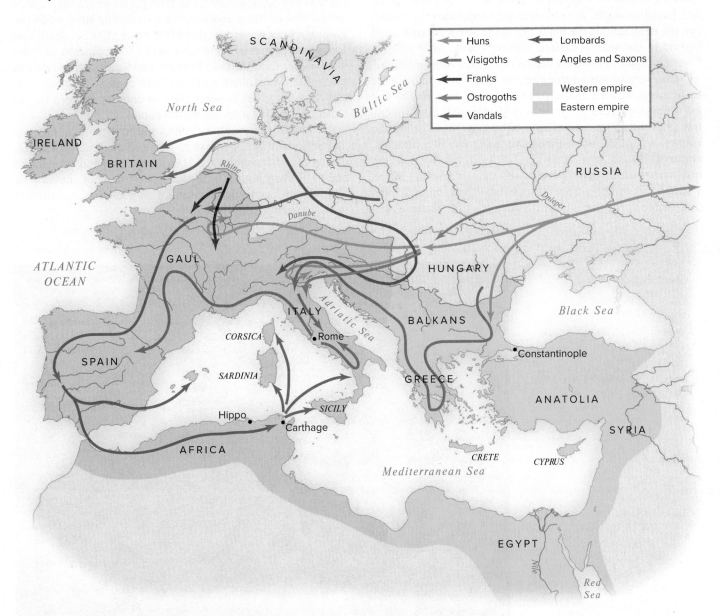

MAP 12.4 Germanic invasions and the collapse of the Western Roman Empire, 450–476 C.E.

Many different groups invaded the Roman Empire following many different routes.

What has been the long-term impact on Europe and the Mediterranean basin of the invasions of the Roman Empire by Germanic peoples?

price caps to dampen inflation. His economic measures were less successful than his administrative reforms, but they helped stabilize an economy ravaged by half a century of civil unrest.

Constantine   Yet Diocletian's reforms also encouraged ambition among the four top corulers and their generals, and his retirement from the imperial office in 305 C.E. set off a round of internal struggles and bitter civil war. Already in 306 C.E. **Constantine,** son of Diocletian's coruler Constantius, moved to stake his claim as sole emperor. By 313 C.E. he had defeated most of his enemies, although he overcame his last rivals only in 324 C.E. Once he had consolidated his grip on power, Constantine ordered the construction of a new capital city, Constantinople, at a strategic site overlooking the Bosporus, the strait linking the Black Sea to the Sea of Marmara and beyond to the wealthy eastern Mediterranean. After 330 C.E. Constantinople became the capital of a united Roman Empire.

Constantine was an able emperor. With the reunion of the eastern and western districts of the empire, however, he and his successors faced the same sort of administrative difficulties that Diocletian had attempted to solve by dividing the empire. As population declined and the economy contracted, emperors found it increasingly difficult to marshal the resources needed to govern and protect the vast Roman Empire. The need for protection against external threats became especially acute during the late fourth and early fifth centuries C.E.

Conflict with Sasanians and Germanic Invasions

Apart from internal problems, the Roman Empire faced several formidable military threats. One arose on the empire's southeastern frontiers when the Sasanian dynasty toppled the Parthians in 224 C.E. and established a powerful state in Iran. Sasanian and Roman forces clashed repeatedly in Anatolia, Syria, and Mesopotamia as each side sought to consolidate its authority in border regions. Some of the conflicts dealt devastating blows. In the year 260 C.E., the Roman emperor Valerian fell captive to Sasanian forces. He spent his last few years at the Sasanian court in Ctesiphon, where his captors forced him to stoop and serve as a mounting stool when the Sasanian king wanted to ride his horse. (After his death, the Sasanians preserved Valerian's skin as a memento of their victory over the Romans.) Romans and Sasanians engaged in intermittent hostilities until the sixth century C.E., but a series of buffer states between the two empires reduced the intensity of conflict after the third century.

Migratory Germanic peoples posed a more immediate and serious military threat to the Roman Empire. Indeed, during the fifth century C.E., Germanic invasions brought an end to Roman authority in the western half of the empire, although imperial rule survived for an additional millennium in the eastern Mediterranean.

In this relief sculpture carved into a sarcophagus in the second century C.E., a clean-shaven Roman soldier battles bearded Germanic forces along the Danube River.
Deco Images/Alamy DEA/G. DAGLI ORTI/Getty Images

Germanic Migrations Germanic peoples had migrated from their homelands in northern Europe and lived on the eastern and northern borders of the Roman Empire since the second century C.E. Most notable were the Visigoths, who came originally from Scandinavia and Russia. Like the nomadic peoples who moved into northern China after the fall of the Han dynasty, the Visigoths settled, adopted agriculture, and drew deep inspiration from Roman society. They adapted Roman law to the needs of their society, for example, converted to Christianity, and translated the Bible into the Visigothic language. They also contributed large numbers of soldiers to the Roman armies. In the interests of social order, however, the Romans discouraged settlement of the Visigoths and other Germanic peoples within the empire, preferring that they constitute buffer societies outside imperial borders.

The Huns During the late fourth century, the relationship between Visigoths and Romans changed dramatically when the nomadic **Huns** began an aggressive westward migration from their homeland in central Asia. The Huns spoke a Turkic language, and they may have been related to the nomadic Xiongnu who inhabited the central Asian steppe lands west of China. During the mid-fifth century C.E., the warrior-king **Attila** organized the Huns into a virtually unstoppable military juggernaut. Under Attila, the Huns invaded Hungary, probed Roman frontiers in the Balkan region, menaced Gaul and northern Italy, and attacked Germanic peoples living on the borders of the Roman Empire.

Collapse of the Western Roman Empire Attila did not create a set of political institutions or a state structure, and the Huns disappeared as a political and military force soon after his death in 453 C.E. By that time, however, the Huns had placed such pressure on Visigoths, Ostrogoths, Vandals, Franks, and other Germanic peoples that they streamed en masse into the Roman Empire in search of refuge. Once inside imperial boundaries, they encountered little effective resistance and moved around almost at will. They established settlements throughout the western half of the empire—Italy, Gaul, Spain, Britain, and north Africa—where populations were less dense than in the eastern Mediterranean. Under the command of Alaric, the Visigoths even stormed and sacked Rome in 410 C.E. By the middle of the fifth century, the western part of the Roman Empire was in shambles. In 476 C.E. imperial

The colossal head of Constantine is one of the few remaining fragments from a marble statue that originally stood about 14 meters (46 feet) tall.

Deco Images/Alamy Stock Photo

authority came to an ignominious end when the Germanic general **Odoacer** deposed Romulus Augustulus, the last of the Roman emperors in the western half of the empire.

Unlike the Han dynasty, the Roman Empire did not entirely disintegrate: imperial authority survived for another millennium in the eastern half of the empire, known after the fifth century C.E. as the **Byzantine Empire.** In the western half, however, Roman authority gradually dissolved, and nomadic peoples built successor states in regions formerly subject to Rome. Vandals and then Visigoths governed Spain, Franks ruled Gaul, Angles and Saxons invaded Britain, and Italy fell under the sway of a variety of peoples, including Visigoths, Vandals, and Lombards.

Cultural Change in the Late Roman Empire

In the Roman Empire, as in China, the collapse of the imperial state coincided with important social and cultural changes. The Germanic peoples who toppled the empire looked to their own traditions for purposes of organizing society and government. When they settled in the regions of the former empire, however, they absorbed a good deal of Roman influence. They adapted Roman law to their needs, for example, thus preserving one of the most important features of Roman society. Over time, the mingling of Roman and Germanic traditions led to the emergence of an altogether new society—medieval Europe.

Prominence of Christianity **Christianity** was perhaps the most prominent survivor of the western Roman Empire. During the fourth century C.E., several developments enhanced its influence throughout the Mediterranean basin. In the first place, Christianity won recognition as a legitimate religion in the Roman Empire. In 312 C.E., while seeking to establish himself as sole Roman emperor, Constantine experienced a vision that impressed on him the power of the Christian God. He believed that the Christian God helped him to prevail over his rivals, and in 313 he promulgated the Edict of Milan, which allowed Christians to practice their faith openly in the Roman Empire. At some point during his reign, perhaps after his edict, Constantine converted to Christianity, and in the late fourth century the emperor Theodosius made

Odoacer (AHD-oh-vah-ser)

Byzantine (BIHZ-uhn-teen)

Theodosius (thee-hu-DOH-see-uhs)

Christianity the official religion of the Roman Empire. By the mid-fourth century, Christians held important political and military positions, and imperial sponsorship helped their proponents attract more converts than ever before.

Christianity also began to attract thoughtful and talented converts who articulated a Christian message for the intellectual elites of the Roman Empire. The earliest Christians had come largely from the ranks of ordinary working people, and their doctrine struck philosophers and the educated elites as both unsophisticated and unbelievable. During its first three centuries, Christianity grew as a popular religion of salvation favored by the masses rather than as a reasoned doctrine of intellectual substance. During the fourth century, however, intellectual elites began to take more interest in Christianity.

St. Augustine The most important and influential of these figures was **St. Augustine** (354–430 C.E.), bishop of the north African city of Hippo (modern-day Annaba in Algeria). Augustine was well educated and conversant with the leading intellectual currents of the day. During his youth he drew great inspiration from Stoicism and Platonism, and for nine years he belonged to a community of Manichaeans. Eventually, he became disillusioned with both Hellenistic philosophy and Manichaeism, and in 387 C.E., while studying in Italy, he converted to Christianity. For the remainder of his life, he worked to reconcile Christianity with Greek and Roman philosophical traditions, especially Platonism, and to articulate Christianity in terms that were familiar and persuasive to the educated classes. More than any others, Augustine's writings made Christianity an intellectually respectable alternative to Hellenistic philosophy and popular religions of salvation.

Besides winning the right to practice their religion openly and attracting intellectual talent, Christian leaders constructed an institutional apparatus that transformed a popular religion of salvation into a powerful church. In the absence of recognized leadership, the earliest Christians generated a range of conflicting and sometimes contradictory doctrines. Some taught that Jesus was a mortal human being, others that he was a god, and yet others that he was both human and divine. Some allowed women to serve as priests and attributed great powers to Jesus' mother, Mary, and others restricted church offices to men and conceived of Christian deities as males.

The New Testament and the Emergence of Orthodox Christianity Early Christians might well have continued to express their understandings of their faith in individual ways. During the third and fourth centuries, however, as the Roman Empire experienced political turmoil and underwent administrative changes, some church leaders sought doctrinal stability and worked to define essential tenets that all Christians must accept. As Christians became more prominent in the Roman Empire, state authorities also promoted efforts to standardize teachings. Emperor Constantine himself pushed for a clear statement of Christian doctrine that he hoped would create a foundation for cultural unity in the Roman Empire.

This fifteenth century painting by Sandro Botticelli depicts St. Augustine in his study. In his voluminous writings, Augustine sought to explain the meaning of history from a Christian perspective.

Leemage/Corbis Historical/Getty Images

In search of clearly defined doctrine, church leaders conducted intense debates about the quality and authority of the numerous writings that the earliest Christians had generated. Those writings, which numbered in the scores or perhaps even hundreds, included gospels that told the story of Jesus' life, epistles that outlined the authors' views of moral and religious issues, and historical accounts that offered interpretations of early Christian experiences from different perspectives. By the late fourth century, church leaders were reaching consensus that twenty-seven short writings were more authoritative than the others, and they recognized these writings as canonical scriptures known later as the New Testament. By adopting a small number of writings as canonical, church leaders rejected many others as misguided, untruthful, or even heretical. As a result, they profoundly influenced the development of doctrine that most Christian authorities eventually came to recognize as the orthodox or correct teaching.

The Institutional Church To standardize their faith, Christian leaders also instituted a hierarchy of church officials. At the top were five religious authorities—the bishop of Rome and the patriarchs of Jerusalem, Antioch, Alexandria, and Constantinople—who resided in the most important spiritual and political centers of the Roman Empire. These five authorities wielded roughly equal influence in the larger Christian community, although the bishop of Rome enjoyed somewhat greater prestige than the others. (His enhanced status derived both from his claim to be the spiritual descendant of Jesus' chief disciple, St. Peter, and from the fact that he had his seat at Rome, the original imperial capital.)

Subordinate to the five principal authorities were bishops, who presided over religious affairs in their districts, known as dioceses, which included all the prominent cities of the Roman Empire. When theological disputes arose, the **patriarchs** and bishops assembled in church councils to determine which views would prevail as official doctrine. The **councils at Nicaea** (325 C.E.) and Chalcedon (451 C.E.), for example, took up the difficult and contentious issue of Jesus' nature. Delegates at the councils proclaimed that Jesus was both fully human and fully divine at the same time, in contrast to Nestorians, Arians, and other Christian groups who held that Jesus was either primarily human or primarily divine. The decisions and decrees of the church councils did not put an end to all debate, nor did they prevent new divisions and new grounds of contention from arising. Nevertheless, by defining the doctrines that most church authorities regarded as orthodox, council delegates left enduring influences on the beliefs and values of Christianity.

As Roman imperial authority crumbled, the bishop of Rome, known as the pope (from the Latin *papa,* meaning "father"), emerged as spiritual leader of Christian communities in the western regions of the empire. As the only sources of established and recognized authority, the popes and the bishops of other important cities organized local government and defensive measures for their communities. They also mounted missionary campaigns to convert Germanic peoples to Christianity. Although Roman imperial authority disappeared, Roman Christianity survived and served as a foundation for cultural unity in lands that had formerly made up the western half of the Roman Empire.

patriarch (PAY-tree-ahrk)
Nicaea (nahy-SEE-uh)
Chalcedon (KAL-suh-dawn)

CONCLUSION

By 500 C.E. ancient societies in Persia, China, South Asia and the Mediterranean basin had either collapsed or fallen into decline. Yet all the societies that had flourished throughout the previous millennium left rich legacies that shaped political institutions, social orders, and cultural traditions for centuries to come. Moreover, by sponsoring commercial and cultural relations between different peoples, these ancient states laid a foundation for intensive and systematic cross-cultural encounters in later times. After the third century C.E., the decline of the Han, Kushan, Parthian, and Roman empires resulted in significantly less activity over the Silk Roads than in the preceding three hundred years. But the trade routes survived, and when a new series of imperial states reestablished order throughout much of Eurasia and north Africa in the sixth century C.E., the peoples of the eastern hemisphere avidly resumed their crossing of cultural boundary lines in the interests of trade and communication.

STUDY TERMS

Attila (245)	Han Wudi (228)
Buddhism (235)	Huns (245)
Byzantine Empire (245)	Mani (237)
Chang'an (231)	Manichaeism (237)
Christianity (245)	monsoon (230)
Confucianism (241)	Nestorians (237)
Constantine (244)	Odoacer (245)
council at Nicaea (247)	Rhapta (230)
Daoism (242)	Silk Roads (231)
Diocletian (243)	sinicization (241)
epidemic disease (238)	St. Augustine (246)
Han dynasty (231)	Zhang Qian (228)

FOR FURTHER READING

Thomas J. Barfield. *The Perilous Frontier: Nomadic Empires and China.* Cambridge, Mass., 1989. Provocative study of the Xiongnu and other central Asian peoples.

Craig Benjamin. *Empires of Ancient Eurasia. The First Silk Roads Era 100 B.C.E.-250 C.E.* Cambridge, UK, 2018. Focused entirely on the First Silk Roads Era, the author explores the political, economic, social, and cultural developments that characterize this important period in world history.

Jerry H. Bentley. *Old World Encounters: Cross-Cultural Contacts and Exchanges in Pre-Modern Times.* New York, 1993. Studies the spread of cultural and religious traditions before 1500 C.E.

Peter Brown. *The Making of Late Antiquity.* Cambridge, Mass., 1978. Brilliant and evocative analysis of the cultural and religious history of the late Roman Empire.

Peter Frankopan. *The Silk Roads. A New History of the World.* London, 2015. A fascinating recent book that places Silk Roads exchanges at the very heart of world history.

C. D. Gordon, ed. *The Age of Attila: Fifth-Century Byzantium and the Barbarians.* Ann Arbor, 1972. Translations of primary sources on the society and history of nomadic and migratory peoples.

Mark Edward Lewis. *China between Empires: The Northern and Southern Dynasties.* Cambridge, Mass., 2009. Discusses social and cultural change in China after the collapse of the Han dynasty.

Samuel Hugh Moffett. *A History of Christianity in Asia,* vol. 1. San Francisco, 1992. An important volume that surveys the spread of early Christianity east of the Roman Empire.

Elaine Pagels. *Beyond Belief: The Secret Gospel of Thomas.* New York, 2003. Discusses the emergence of orthodox Christianity and the recognition of the New Testament as a body of canonical writings.

Jonathan Tucker. *The Silk Road: Art and History.* London, 2003. Lavishly illustrated volume exploring Silk Roads history and geography.

Susan Whitfied. *Silk, Slaves and Stupas. Material Culture of the Silk Roads.* Berkeley and Los Angeles, 2018. Uses ten case studies of different artifacts discovered along the Silk Roads to offer a deep investigation of what material remains can tell us about the Silk Roads and their historical ramification.

Chapter 13

The Resurgence of Empire in East Asia

ZOOMING IN ON ENCOUNTERS

Xuanzang: A Young Monk Hits the Road

Early in the seventh century C.E., the emperor of China issued an order forbidding his subjects to travel beyond Chinese borders into central Asia. In 629, however, in defiance of the emperor, a young Buddhist monk slipped past imperial watchtowers under cover of darkness and made his way west. His name was **Xuanzang,** and his destination was South Asia, homeland of Buddhism. Although educated in Confucian texts as a youth, Xuanzang had followed his older brother into a monastery where he became devoted to Buddhism. While studying the Sanskrit language, Xuanzang noticed that Chinese writings on Buddhism contained many teachings that were

Panels from the twelfth-century Qingming scroll, depicting cosmopolitan life in the city of Kaifeng during the Northern Song dynasty.
Werner Forman Archive/Palace Museum, Beijing/Heritage Image Partnership Ltd/Alamy Stock Photo
Heritage Image Partnership Ltd/Alamy Stock Photo

Xuanzang (SHWEN-ZAHNG)

confusing or even contradictory to those in the original Buddhist texts. He decided to travel to the Indian subcontinent, visit the holy sites of Buddhism, and study with the most knowledgeable Buddhist teachers and sages to learn about Buddhism from the purest sources.

Xuanzang could not have imagined the difficulties he would face. Immediately after his departure from China, his guide abandoned him in the Gobi desert. After losing his water bag and collapsing in the heat, Xuanzang made his way to the oasis town of Gaochang in the Turpan Depression, a key town on the Silk Roads. The Buddhist ruler of Gaochang provided the devout pilgrim with travel supplies and rich gifts to support his mission. Among the presents were twenty-four letters of introduction to rulers of lands on the way to India, each one attached to a bolt of silk, five hundred additional bolts of silk and two carts of fruit for the most important ruler, thirty horses, twenty-five laborers, and yet another five hundred bolts of silk along with gold, silver, and silk clothes for Xuanzang to use as travel funds. After departing from Turpan, Xuanzang crossed three of the world's highest mountain ranges—the Tian Shan, Hindu Kush, and Pamir ranges—and lost one-third of his party to exposure and starvation in the Tian Shan. He crossed yawning gorges thousands of meters deep on footbridges fashioned from rope or chains, and he faced numerous attacks by bandits.

Yet Xuanzang persisted and arrived in the northern region of the Indian subcontinent in 630. He lived there for more than twelve years, visiting the holy sites of Buddhism and devoting himself to the study of languages and Buddhist doctrine, especially at Nalanda, the center of advanced Buddhist education in the Ganges Valley. He also amassed a huge collection of relics and images as well as 657 books, all of which he packed into 527 crates and transported back to China to advance the understanding of Buddhism in his native land.

By the time of his return in 645, Xuanzang had logged more than 16,000 kilometers (10,000 miles) on the road. News of the holy monk's efforts had reached the imperial court, and even though Xuanzang had violated the ban on travel, he received a hero's welcome and an audience with the emperor. Until his death in 664, Xuanzang spent his remaining years translating Buddhist treatises into Chinese and clarifying their doctrines. His efforts helped to popularize Buddhism throughout China.

CHAPTER OVERVIEW

Xuanzang undertook his journey at a fortunate time. For more than 350 years after the fall of the Han dynasty, war, invasion, conquest, and foreign rule disrupted Chinese society. Toward the end of the sixth century, however, centralized imperial rule returned to China. The Sui and Tang dynasties restored order and presided over an era of rapid economic growth in China. Agricultural yields rose dramatically, and technological innovations boosted the production of manufactured goods. China ranked with the Abbasid and Byzantine empires as a political and economic anchor of the Afro-Eurasian world zone.

For China the later first and early second millennia CE was an age of intense interaction with other peoples. Chinese merchants participated in trade networks that linked most regions of the eastern hemisphere. Buddhism spread beyond its homeland of India, attracted a large popular following in China, and even influenced the thought of Confucian scholars. A resurgent China made its influence felt throughout east Asia: diplomats and armed forces introduced Chinese ways into Korea and Vietnam, and rulers of the Japanese islands looked to China for guidance in matters of political organization. Korea, Vietnam, and Japan retained their distinctiveness, but all three lands drew deep inspiration from China and participated in a larger east Asian society centered on China.

CHRONOLOGY

589–618	Sui dynasty (China)
602–664	Life of Xuanzang
604–618	Reign of Sui Yangdi
618–907	Tang dynasty (China)
627–649	Reign of Tang Taizong
669–935	Silla dynasty (Korea)
710–794	Nara period (Japan)
755–757	An Lushan's rebellion
794–1185	Heian period (Japan)
875–884	Huang Chao's rebellion
960–976	Reign of Song Taizu
960–1279	Song dynasty (China)
1024	First issuance of government-sponsored paper money
1130–1200	Life of Zhu Xi
1185–1333	Kamakura period (Japan)
1336–1573	Muromachi period (Japan)

THE RESTORATION OF CENTRALIZED IMPERIAL RULE IN CHINA

During the centuries following the Han dynasty, several regional kingdoms made bids to assert their authority over all of China, but none possessed the resources to dominate its rivals over the long term. In the late sixth century, however, **Yang Jian,** an ambitious ruler in northern China, embarked on a series of military campaigns that brought all of China once again under centralized imperial rule. Yang Jian's Sui dynasty survived less than thirty years, but the tradition of centralized rule outlived his house. The Tang dynasty replaced the Sui, and the Song succeeded the Tang. The Tang and Song dynasties organized Chinese society so efficiently that China became a center of exceptional agricultural and industrial production. Indeed, much of the eastern hemisphere felt the effects of the powerful Chinese economy of the Tang and Song dynasties.

The Sui Dynasty

Establishment of the Dynasty Like Qin Shihuangdi some eight hundred years earlier, Yang Jian imposed tight political discipline on his state and then extended his rule to the rest of China. Yang Jian began his rise to power when a Turkish ruler appointed him duke of Sui in northern China. In 580 Yang Jian's patron died, leaving a seven-year-old son as his heir. Yang Jian installed the boy as ruler but forced his abdication one year later, claiming the throne and the "mandate of heaven" (chapter 5) for himself. During the next decade Yang Jian sent military expeditions into central Asia and southern China. By 589 the house of Sui ruled all of China.

Like the rulers of the Qin dynasty, the emperors of the **Sui dynasty** (589–618 C.E.) placed enormous demands on their subjects in the course of building a strong, centralized government. The Sui emperors ordered the construction of palaces and granaries, carried out extensive repairs on defensive walls, dispatched military forces to central Asia and Korea, levied high taxes, and demanded compulsory labor services.

The Grand Canal The most elaborate project undertaken during the Sui dynasty was the construction of the **Grand Canal,** which was one of the world's largest waterworks projects before modern times. The second emperor, **Sui Yangdi** (reigned 604–618 C.E.), completed work on the canal to facilitate trade between northern and southern China, particularly to make the abundant supplies of rice and other food crops from the Yangzi River valley available to residents of northern regions. The only practical and economical way to transport food crops in large quantities was by water. But since Chinese rivers generally flow from west to east, only an artificial waterway could support a large volume of trade between north and south.

Yang Jian (yahng jyahn)
Sui Yangdi (sway yahng-dee)
Tang Taizong (TAHNG TEYE-zohng)

The Grand Canal was really a series of artificial waterways that ultimately reached from Hangzhou in the south to the imperial capital of Chang'an in the west to a terminus near modern Beijing in the north. Sui Yangdi used canals dug as early as the Zhou dynasty, but he linked them into a network that served much of China. When completed, the Grand Canal extended almost 2,000 kilometers (1,240 miles) and reportedly was forty paces wide, with roads running parallel to the waterway on either side.

Though expensive to construct, Sui Yangdi's investment in the Grand Canal paid enormous dividends for the future. It integrated the economies of northern and southern China, thereby establishing an economic foundation for political and cultural unity. Until the arrival of railroads in the twentieth century, the Grand Canal served as the principal conduit for internal trade. Indeed, the canal continues to function even today, although modern forms of transport have diminished its significance as a trade route.

Sui Yangdi's construction projects served China well over the long term, but their dependence on high taxes and forced labor generated hostility toward his rule. The Grand Canal alone required the services of conscripted laborers by the millions. But it was disastrous military expeditions into Korea that ultimately prompted discontented subjects to revolt against Sui rule. During the late 610s, rebellions broke out in northern China when Sui Yangdi sought additional resources for his Korean campaign. In 618 a disgruntled minister assassinated the emperor and brought the dynasty to an end.

The Tang Dynasty

Soon after Sui Yangdi's death, a rebel leader seized Chang'an and proclaimed himself emperor of a new dynasty that he named the **Tang dynasty** after his hereditary title. The dynasty survived for almost three hundred years (618–907 C.E.), and Tang rulers organized China into a powerful, productive, and prosperous society.

Tang Taizong Much of the Tang's success was due to the energy, ability, and policies of the dynasty's second emperor, **Tang Taizong** (reigned 627–649 C.E.). Taizong was both ambitious and ruthless: in making his way to the imperial throne, he murdered two of his brothers and pushed his father aside. Once on the throne, however, he displayed a high sense of duty and strove conscientiously to provide an effective, stable government. He built a splendid capital at Chang'an, and he saw himself as a Confucian ruler who heeded the interests of his subjects. Contemporaries reported that banditry ended during his reign, that the price of rice remained low, and that taxes levied on peasants amounted to only one-fortieth of the annual harvest—a 2.5 percent tax rate—although required rent payments and compulsory labor services meant that the effective rate of taxation was somewhat higher. These reports suggest that China enjoyed an era of unusual stability and prosperity during the reign of Tang Taizong.

Three policies in particular help to explain the success of the early Tang dynasty: maintenance of a well-articulated

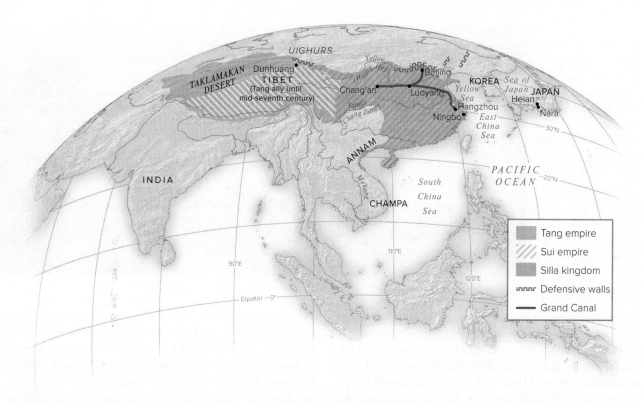

MAP 13.1   The Sui and Tang dynasties, 589–907 C.E.

Compare the size of the Sui and Tang empires.

What impact did the Grand Canal have on helping reunify China after 350 years of disunity?

What techniques did the Tang Dynasty use that allowed it to create such a vast tributary empire in East and Central Asia?

transportation and communications network, distribution of land according to the principles of the equal-field system, and reliance on a bureaucracy based on merit. All three policies originated in the Sui dynasty, but Tang rulers applied them more systematically and effectively than their predecessors had.

Transportation and Communications Apart from the Grand Canal, which served as the principal route for long-distance transportation within China, Tang rulers maintained an extensive communications network based on roads, horses, and sometimes human runners. Along the main routes, Tang officials maintained inns, postal stations, and stables, which provided rest and refreshment for travelers, couriers, and their mounts. Using couriers traveling by horse, the Tang court could communicate with the most distant cities in the empire in about eight days. Even human runners provided impressively speedy services: relay teams of some 9,600 runners supplied the Tang court at Chang'an with seafood delivered fresh from Ningbo, more than 1,000 kilometers (620 miles) away.

The Equal-Field System The **equal-field system** governed the allocation of agricultural land. Its purposes were to ensure an equitable distribution of land and to avoid the concentration of landed property that had caused social problems during the Han dynasty. The system allotted land to individuals and their

families according to the land's fertility and the recipients' needs. About one-fifth of the land became the hereditary possession of the recipients, and the rest remained available for redistribution when the original recipients' needs and circumstances changed.

For about a century, administrators were able to apply the principles of the equal-field system relatively consistently. By the early eighth century, however, the system showed signs of strain. A rapidly rising population placed pressure on the land available for distribution. Meanwhile, through favors, bribery, or intimidation of administrators, influential families found ways to retain land scheduled for redistribution. Furthermore, large parcels of land fell out of the system altogether when Buddhist monasteries acquired them. Nevertheless, during the first half of the Tang dynasty, the system provided a foundation for stability and prosperity in the Chinese countryside.

Bureaucracy of Merit The Tang dynasty also relied heavily on a bureaucracy based on merit, as reflected by performance on imperial civil service examinations. Following the example of the Han dynasty, Sui and Tang rulers recruited government officials from the ranks of candidates who had progressed through the Confucian educational system and had mastered a sophisticated curriculum concentrating on the classic works of Chinese literature and philosophy. During the early Tang dynasty, most officeholders were

Barges make their way through a portion of the Grand Canal near the city of Wuxi in southern China. Built during the Sui dynasty, the waterways of the Grand Canal fostered the economic integration of northern and southern China.
Dean Conger/Corbis Documentary/Getty Images

aristocrats. By the late Tang era, however, when educational opportunities were more widely available, officeholders came largely from the ranks of common families. The Confucian educational system and the related civil service served Chinese governments so well that, with modifications and an occasional interruption, they survived for thirteen centuries, disappearing only after the collapse of the Qing dynasty in the early twentieth century.

Military Expansion   Soon after its foundation, the powerful and dynamic Tang state began to flex its military muscles. In the north, Tang forces brought Manchuria under imperial authority and forced the Silla kingdom in Korea to acknowledge the Tang emperor as overlord. To the south, Tang armies conquered the northern part of Vietnam. To the west they extended Tang authority almost as far as the Aral Sea and brought a portion of the high plateau of Tibet under Tang control. Territorially, the Tang empire ranks among the largest in Chinese history.

Tang Foreign Relations   In an effort to fashion a stable diplomatic order, the Tang emperors revived the Han dynasty's practice of maintaining tributary relationships between China and neighboring lands. According to Chinese political theory, China was the Middle Kingdom, a powerful realm with the responsibility to bring order to subordinate lands through a system of tributary relationships. Neighboring lands and peoples would recognize Chinese emperors as their overlords. As tokens of their subordinate status, envoys from those states would regularly deliver gifts to the court of the Middle Kingdom and would perform the kowtow—a ritual prostration in which subordinates knelt before the emperor and touched their foreheads to the ground. In return, tributary states received confirmation of their authority as well as lavish gifts.

Because Chinese authorities often had little real influence in these supposedly subordinate lands, there was always something of a fictional quality to the system. Nevertheless, it was extremely important throughout east Asia and central Asia because it institutionalized relations between China and neighboring lands, fostering trade and cultural exchanges as well as diplomatic contacts.

Tang Decline   Under able rulers such as Taizong, the Tang dynasty flourished. During the mid-eighth century, however, casual and careless leadership brought the dynasty to a crisis from which it never fully recovered. In 755, while the emperor neglected public affairs in favor of music and his favorite concubine, one of the dynasty's foremost military commanders, An Lushan, mounted a rebellion and captured the capital at Chang'an, as well as the secondary capital at Luoyang. His revolt was short-lived: in 757 a soldier murdered An Lushan, and by 763 Tang forces had suppressed his army and recovered their capitals. But the rebellion left the dynasty in a gravely weakened state. Tang commanders were unable to defeat rebellious forces by themselves, so they invited a nomadic Turkic people, the **Uighurs,** to bring an army into China. In return for their services, the Uighurs demanded the right to sack Chang'an and Luoyang after the expulsion of the rebels.

The Tang imperial house never regained control of affairs after this crisis. The equal-field system deteriorated, and dwindling tax receipts failed to meet dynastic needs. Imperial armies were unable to resist the encroachments of Turkic peoples in the late eighth century. During the ninth century a series of rebellions devastated the Chinese countryside. One uprising, led by the military commander Huang Chao, embroiled much of eastern China for almost a decade, from 875 to 884. Huang Chao's revolt reflected and fueled popular discontent: he routinely pillaged the wealthy and distributed a portion of his plunder among the poor. In an effort to control the rebels, the Tang emperors granted progressively greater power and authority to regional military commanders, who gradually

Uighurs (WEE-goors)

In this wall painting from the tomb of a Tang prince, three Chinese officials (at left) receive envoys from foreign lands who pay their respects to representatives of the Middle Kingdom. The envoys probably come from the Byzantine empire and Korea. What features of their personal appearance and dress provide clues to the envoys' lands of origin?
Henry Westheim Photography/Alamy Stock Photo

became the effective rulers of China. In 907 the last Tang emperor abdicated his throne, and the dynasty came to an end.

The Song Dynasty

Following the Tang collapse, warlords ruled China until the Song dynasty reimposed centralized imperial rule in the late tenth century. Though it survived for more than three centuries, the **Song dynasty** (960–1279 C.E.) never built a very powerful state. Song rulers mistrusted military leaders, and they placed much more emphasis on civil administration, industry, education, and the arts than on military affairs.

Song Taizu The first Song emperor, **Song Taizu** (reigned 960–976 C.E.), inaugurated this policy. Song Taizu began his career as a junior military officer serving one of the most powerful warlords in northern China. He had a reputation for honesty and effectiveness, and in 960 his troops proclaimed him emperor. During the next several years, he and his army subjected the warlords to their authority and consolidated Song control throughout China. He then persuaded his generals to retire honorably to a life of leisure so that they would not seek to displace him, and he set about organizing a centralized administration that placed military forces under tight supervision.

Song Taizu regarded all state officials, even minor functionaries in distant provinces, as servants of the imperial government. In exchange for their loyalty, Song rulers rewarded these officials handsomely. They vastly expanded the bureaucracy based on merit by creating more opportunities for individuals to seek a Confucian education and take civil service examinations. They accepted many more candidates into the bureaucracy than their Sui and Tang predecessors, and they provided generous salaries for those who qualified for government appointments. They even placed civil bureaucrats in charge of military forces.

Song Weaknesses The Song approach to administration resulted in a more centralized imperial government than earlier Chinese dynasties had enjoyed. But it caused two big problems that weakened the dynasty and eventually brought about its fall. The first problem was financial: the enormous Song bureaucracy devoured China's surplus production. As the number of bureaucrats and the size of their rewards grew, the imperial treasury came under tremendous pressure. Efforts to raise taxes aggravated the peasants, who mounted two major rebellions in the early twelfth century. By that time, however, bureaucrats dominated the Song administration to the point that it was impossible to reform the system.

The second problem was military. Scholar-bureaucrats generally had little military education and little talent for military affairs, yet they led Song armies in the field and made military decisions. It was no coincidence that nomadic peoples flourished along China's northern border throughout the Song dynasty. From the early tenth through the early twelfth century, the Khitan, a seminomadic people from Manchuria, ruled a vast empire stretching from northern Korea to Mongolia. During the first half of the Song dynasty, the Khitan

Song Taizu (sawng tahy-zoo)

SOURCES FROM THE PAST

The Poet Du Fu on Tang Dynasty Wars

The eighth century was a golden age of Chinese poetry. Among the foremost writers of the era was Du Fu (712–770 C.E.), often considered one of China's two greatest poets. Born into a prominent Confucian family, Du Fu wrote in his early years about the beauty of the natural world. After the rebellion of An Lushan, however, he fell into poverty and experienced difficulties. Not surprisingly, poetry of his later years lamented the chaos of the late eighth century. In the three following poems, Du Fu offered a bitter perspective on the wars that plagued China in the 750s and 760s.

The Recruiting Officers at the Village of the Stone Moat

I sought a lodging for the night, at sunset, in the Stone Moat village.
Recruiting officers, who seize people by night, were there.
A venerable old man climbed over the wall and fled.
An old woman came out of the door and peered.
What rage in the shouts of the Recruiting Officers.
What bitterness in the weeping of the old woman.
I heard the words of the woman as she pled her cause before them:

'My three sons are with the frontier guard at Yeh Cheng,
From one son I have received a letter.
A little while ago two sons died in battle.
He who remains has stolen a temporary lease of life;
The dead are finished forever.
In the house there is still no grown man;
Only my grandson at the breast.
The mother of my grandson has not gone;
Going out, coming in, she has not a single whole skirt.
I am an old, old woman, and my strength is failing,
But I beg to go with the Recruiting Officers when they return this night.
I will eagerly agree to act as a servant at Ho Yang;——
I am still able to prepare the early morning meal.'
The sound of words ceased in the long night,
It was as though I heard the darkness choke with tears.
At daybreak I went on my way.
Only the venerable old man was left.

> Why is the old woman offering to go with the recruiting officers as a servant?

Crossing the Frontier I

When bows are bent, they should be bent strongly;
When arrows are used, they should be long.
The bowmen should first shoot the horses.
In taking the enemy prisoner, the leader should be taken first.
There should be no limit to the killing of men.
In making a country, there should naturally be a border.
If it were possible to regulate rebellion,——
Would so many be killed and wounded?

> What does the author mean by "regulate rebellion"?

Crossing the Frontier II

At dawn, the conscripted soldiers enter the camp outside the Eastern Gate.
At sunset they cross the bridge at Ho Yang.
The setting sunlight is reflected on the great flags.
Horses neigh. The wind whines—whines

Ten thousand tents are spread across the level sand.

Officers instruct their companies.

The bright moon hangs in the middle of the sky.

The written orders are strict that the night shall be still and empty.

Sadness everywhere. A few sounds from the nomad flute fill the air.

The strong soldiers are no longer proud, they quiver with sadness.

May one ask who is their general?

Perhaps it is Ho Piao Yao.

For Further Reflection

▪ In Poem 1, what has been the impact of ongoing wars on the family of the old woman and the village in general?

▪ In Poem 2, is the poet offering military strategic advice or making some larger point about warfare?

▪ In Poem 3, why are the newly conscripted soldiers so sad?

▪ From your reading of these poems, what was the impact of the Tang wars on the poet Du Fu personally, and on Chinese society in general?

Source: Lowell, Amy. Fir-flower Tablets: Poems Translated from the Chinese. Massachusetts: Houghton Mifflin Harcourt, 1921, 109.

demanded and received large tribute payments of silk and silver from the Song state to the south. In the early twelfth century, the nomadic Jurchen conquered the Khitan, overran northern China, captured the Song capital at Kaifeng, and proclaimed establishment of the Jin empire. Thereafter the Song dynasty moved its capital to the prosperous port city of **Hangzhou** and survived only in southern China, so that the latter part of the dynasty is commonly known as the Southern Song. This truncated Southern Song shared a border with the Jin empire about midway between the Yellow River and the Yangzi River until 1279, when Mongol forces ended the dynasty and incorporated southern China into their empire.

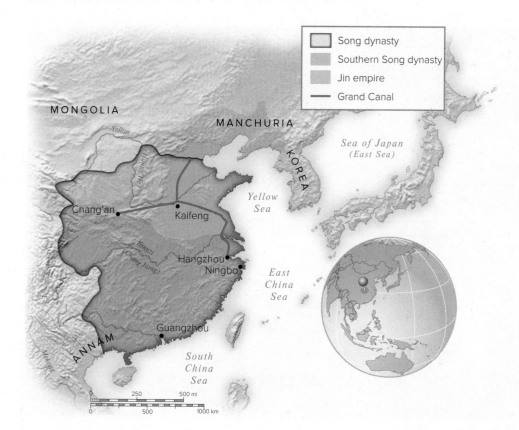

MAP 13.2   The Song dynasty, 960–1279 C.E.

After the establishment of the Jin empire, the Song dynasty moved its capital from Kaifeng to Hangzhou.

Why would Song rulers have chosen Hangzhou as their new capital? What advantages did it offer?

THE ECONOMIC DEVELOPMENT OF TANG AND SONG CHINA

Although the Song dynasty did not develop a particularly strong military capacity, it benefited from a remarkable series of agricultural, technological, industrial, and commercial developments that transformed China into the economic powerhouse of Eurasia. This economic development originated in the Tang dynasty, but its results became most clear during the Song, which presided over a land of enormous prosperity. The economic surge of Tang and Song times had implications that went well beyond China because it stimulated trade and production throughout much of the eastern hemisphere for more than half a millennium, from about 600 to 1300 C.E.

Agricultural Development

Fast-Ripening Rice The foundation of economic development in Tang and Song China was a surge in agricultural production. Sui and Tang armies prepared the way for increased agricultural productivity when they imposed their control over southern China and ventured into Vietnam. In Vietnam they encountered strains of fast-ripening rice that enabled cultivators to harvest two crops per year. When introduced to the fertile fields of southern China, fast-ripening rice quickly resulted in an expanded supply of food. Like the *dar al-Islam*, Tang and Song China benefited enormously from the introduction of new food crops.

New Agricultural Techniques Chinese cultivators also increased their productivity by adopting improved agricultural techniques. They made increased use of heavy iron plows, and they harnessed oxen (in the north) and water buffaloes (in the south) to help prepare land for cultivation. They enriched the soil with manure and composted organic matter. They also organized extensive irrigation systems. These included not only reservoirs, dikes, dams, and canals but also pumps and waterwheels, powered by both animals and humans, that moved water into irrigation systems. Artificial irrigation made it possible to extend cultivation to difficult terrain, including terraced mountainsides—a development that vastly expanded China's agricultural potential.

Population Growth Increased agricultural production had dramatic results. One was a rapid expansion of the Chinese population. After the fall of the Han dynasty, the population of China probably reached a low point, about 45 million in 600 C.E. By 800 it had rebounded to 50 million, and two centuries later to 60 million. By 1127, when the Jurchen conquered the northern half of the Song state, the Chinese population had passed 100 million, and by 1200 it stood at about 115 million. This rapid population growth reflected both the productivity of the agricultural economy and the well-organized distribution of food through transportation networks built during Sui and Tang times.

Urbanization Increased food supplies encouraged the growth of cities. During the Tang dynasty the imperial capital

A Northern Song Dynasty (960–1127) era Chinese painting of a water-powered mill for grain, with surrounding river transport.
The Picture Art Collection/ Alamy Stock Photo

of Chang'an was the world's most populous city, with perhaps as many as two million residents. During the Song dynasty, China was the most urbanized land in the world. In the late thirteenth century, Hangzhou, capital of the Southern Song dynasty, had more than one million residents. These cities supported hundreds of restaurants; noodle shops; taverns; teahouses; brothels; music halls; theaters; clubhouses; gardens; markets; craft shops; and specialty stores dealing in silk, gems, porcelain, lacquerware, and other goods. Hangzhou residents, like those in most cities, observed peculiar local customs. Taverns often had several stories, for example, and patrons gravitated to higher or lower stories according to their plans: those desiring only a cup or two of wine sat at street level, whereas those planning an extended evening of revelry sought tables on the higher stories, much like the situation in restaurants in Chinese cities today.

Although the capital Hangzhou was an exceptionally large city, it wasn't the only one with a large number of people. During the Tang and Song eras, scores of Chinese cities boasted populations of one hundred thousand or more. **Li Bai** (701–761 C.E.), who was perhaps the most popular poet of the Tang era, took the social life of these Chinese cities as one of his principal themes. Li Bai mostly wrote light, pleasing verse celebrating life, friendship, and especially wine. (Tradition holds that the drunken poet died by drowning when he fell out of a boat while attempting to embrace the moon's reflection in the water.) The annual spring festival was an occasion dear to the heart of urban residents, who flocked to the streets to shop for new products, have their fortunes told, and eat tasty snacks from food vendors.

Another result of increased food production was the emergence of a commercialized agricultural economy. Because fast-ripening rice yielded bountiful harvests, many cultivators could purchase inexpensive rice and raise vegetables and fruits for sale on the commercial market. Cultivators specialized in crops that grew well in their regions, and they often exported their harvests to distant regions. By the twelfth century, for example, the wealthy southern province of Fujian imported rice and devoted its land to the production of lychees, oranges, and sugarcane, which fetched high prices in northern markets. Indeed, market-oriented cultivation went so far that authorities tried—with only limited success—to require Fujianese to grow rice so as to avoid excessive dependence on imports.

Patriarchal Social Structures

With increasing wealth and agricultural productivity, Tang and especially Song China experienced a tightening of patriarchal social structures,

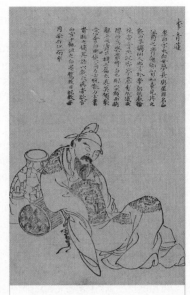

The great Tang dynasty poet Li Bai by Ming dynasty artist Jin Guilang.

The Picture Art Collection/Alamy Stock Photo

which perhaps reflected a concern to preserve family fortunes through enhanced family solidarity. During the Song dynasty the veneration of family ancestors became much more elaborate. Instead of simply remembering ancestors and invoking their aid in rituals performed at home, descendants diligently sought the graves of their earliest traceable forefathers and then arranged elaborate graveside rituals in their honor. Whole extended families often traveled great distances to attend annual rituals venerating their ancestors—a practice that strengthened the sense of family identity and cohesiveness.

Foot Binding Strengthened patriarchal authority also helps to explain the popularity of foot binding, which spread widely during the Song era. **Foot binding** involved the tight wrapping of young girls' feet with strips of cloth that prevented natural growth of the bones and resulted in tiny, malformed, curved feet. Women with bound feet could not walk easily or naturally. Usually, they needed canes to walk by themselves, and sometimes they depended on servants to carry them around in litters. Foot binding never became universal in China, but many wealthy families and sometimes also peasant families bound the feet of their daughters to enhance their attractiveness and gain increased control over the girls' behavior. Foot binding thus placed women under tight supervision of their husbands or other male guardians, who then managed the women's affairs in the interests of the larger family.

Wu Zhao: The Lady Emperor Ironically, this era of strong patriarchal authority produced a rare female ruler. **Wu Zhao** (626–706 C.E.), also known as Wu Zetian, was the daughter of a scholar-official. At the age of thirteen, she became a concubine at the court of Tang Taizong, where she attracted notice because of her intelligence, wit, and beauty. After Taizong's death, Wu Zhao became the concubine and later the wife of his successor. In 660 the emperor suffered a debilitating stroke, and Wu Zhao seized the opportunity to direct affairs as administrator of the court. In 690 she went further and claimed the imperial title for herself.

Confucian principles held that political leadership was a man's duty and that women should obey their fathers, husbands, and sons. Thus it was not surprising that factions emerged to oppose Wu Zhao's rule. The emperor, however, was resourceful in garnering support. She organized a secret police force to monitor dissident factions, and she ordered brutal punishment for those who stood in her way. She strengthened the civil service system as a way of undercutting aristocratic families that might attempt to displace her. She also generously patronized

What's Left Out? ▮▮▮ ▮▮▮ ▮▮▮ ▮▮ ▮▮

At several places in this chapter we refer to concubines, who were personal and often sexual partners of powerful men, including many Chinese emperors. The practice continued for thousands of years in China, from the most ancient dynasties through to the twentieth century, when it was banned by the Communist government. Historians have tried to understand the practice of concubinage through various lenses—in particular, those of gender and family relations, legal and social status, filial piety, and political influence. The practice seems to have emerged as a result of early social norms in China that made it illegal and socially disreputable for a man to have more than one wife. As a way of getting around this, however, these same norms determined that it was perfectly fine for a man to have as many concubines as he could afford. During the Later Han Dynasty, the number of concubines was restricted by law, although men of high rank could still possess as many as they could afford.

The manner in which a concubine was treated in society varied enormously and was influenced by the social status of the men involved. Yet the situation of concubines was always very different to that of legal wives, who had brought a dowry to the relationship. Once a concubine had entered a relationship with a man—and even if the concubine later ended the relationship—it was impossible for her to marry or even to return to her parents' home. The position of a concubine was thus always inferior to that of a wife, and this affected even the rules of filial piety. For example, although children and grandchildren would continue to offer rites to deceased legal mothers for generations, after the death of a concubine, only her sons were expected to make an offering—but not her grandsons nor any other descendants.

By the era of Qing Dynasty (1644–1911), the laws had changed, and it became easier for a man to marry a concubine, but only if his legitimate wife had died. During both the Ming and Qing Dynasties, imperial concubines were housed in luxury in the Forbidden City in Beijing, usually guarded by eunuchs to make sure no other man could have sexual relations with the concubines, ensuring that the only offspring they would produce would be those of the emperor. The Ming introduced an official selection system. Potential concubines had to be aged between fourteen and sixteen, and the criteria for selection included virtue, behavior, and facial and body appearance.

Concubines have been treated sympathetically in many works of Chinese literature, including the classic novel *Dream of the Red Chamber,* and also in many modern novels and television dramas. These tend to focus on the lives of those extraordinary women who rose out of concubinage to become politically powerful, including Empress Dowager Cixi of the Qing Dynasty—arguably the most powerful member of the imperial family in the last decade of the Qing—and, of course, Empress Wu Zhao (Zetian), who rose from her early status as teenage concubine of Tang Emperor Taizong to become the only empress ever to rule China!

Buddhists, who returned the favor by composing treatises seeking to legitimize her rule. Although Confucian scholars reviled her, Wu Zhao was an energetic and effective ruler. She quashed rebellions, organized military campaigns, and opened the imperial administration to talented commoners who rose through the civil service system. She held on to her rule until age eighty, when opponents were finally able to force an ailing Wu Zhao to abdicate in favor of her son. She was unique as a woman who publicly and officially wielded power in a rigidly patriarchal society. Other women exercised influence indirectly or even "ruled from behind a screen," but Wu Zhao was the only woman in Chinese history to claim the imperial title and rule as emperor.

Technological and Industrial Development

Porcelain Abundant supplies of food enabled many people to pursue technological and industrial interests. During the Tang and Song dynasties, Chinese crafts workers generated a remarkable range of technological innovations. During Tang times they discovered techniques of producing high-quality **porcelain,** which was lighter, thinner, and adaptable to more uses than earlier pottery. When fired with glazes, porcelain could also become an aesthetically appealing utensil and even a work of art. Porcelain technology gradually diffused to

other societies, and Abbasid crafts workers in particular produced porcelain in large quantities. Yet demand for Chinese porcelain remained strong, and the Chinese exported vast quantities of porcelain during the Tang and Song dynasties. Archaeologists have turned up Tang and Song porcelain at sites all along the trade networks of the later first millennium. Chinese porcelain graced the tables of wealthy and refined households in southeast Asia, India, Persia, and the port cities of east Africa. Tang and Song products gained such a reputation that fine porcelain has come to be known generally as *chinaware.*

Metallurgy Tang and Song craftsmen also improved metallurgical technologies. Production of iron and steel surged during this era, partly because of techniques that resulted in stronger and more useful metals. Chinese craftsmen discovered that they could use coke instead of coal in their furnaces and produce superior grades of metal. Between the early ninth and the early twelfth centuries, iron production increased almost tenfold according to official records, which understate total production. Most of the increased supply of iron and steel went into weaponry and agricultural tools: during the early Song dynasty, imperial armaments manufacturers produced 16.5 million iron arrowheads per year. Iron and steel also went into construction projects involving large structures such as bridges and pagodas. As in the case of porcelain technology, metallurgical techniques soon diffused to lands beyond China. Indeed, Song military difficulties stemmed partly from the fact that nomadic peoples quickly learned Chinese techniques and fashioned their own iron weapons for use in campaigns against China.

Gunpowder Quite apart from improving existing technologies, Tang and Song craftsmen invented entirely new products, tools, and techniques, most notably **gunpowder,** printing, and naval technologies. Daoist alchemists discovered how to make gunpowder during the Tang dynasty, as they tested the properties of various experimental concoctions while seeking elixirs to prolong life. They soon learned that it was unwise to mix charcoal, saltpeter, sulphur, and arsenic because the volatile compound often resulted in singed beards and even destroyed buildings. Military officials, however, recognized opportunity in the explosive mixture. By the mid-tenth century, they were using gunpowder in bamboo "fire lances," a kind of flamethrower, and by the eleventh century they had fashioned primitive bombs.

The earliest gunpowder weapons had limited military effectiveness: they probably caused more confusion because of noise and smoke than damage because of their destructive potential. Over time, however, refinements enhanced their effectiveness. Knowledge of gunpowder chemistry quickly diffused through Eurasia, and by the late thirteenth century peoples of southwest Asia and Europe were experimenting with metal-barreled cannons.

Printing The precise origins of printing lie obscured in the mists of time. Although some form of printing may have predated the Sui dynasty, only during the Tang era did printing become common. The earliest printers employed block-printing techniques: they carved a reverse image of an entire page into a wooden block, inked the block, and then pressed a sheet of paper on top. By the mid-eleventh century, printers had begun to experiment with reusable, movable type: instead of carving images into blocks, they fashioned dies in the shape of ideographs, arranged them in a frame, inked them, and pressed the frame over paper sheets. Because formal writing in the Chinese language involved as many as forty thousand characters, printers often found movable type to be unwieldy and inconvenient, so they continued to print from wooden blocks long after movable type became available.

Printing made it possible to produce texts quickly, cheaply, and in huge quantities. By the late ninth century, printed copies of Buddhist texts, Confucian works, calendars, agricultural treatises, and popular works appeared in large quantities, particularly in southwestern China (modern Sichuan province). Song dynasty officials broadly disseminated printed works by visiting the countryside with pamphlets that outlined effective agricultural techniques.

Naval Technology Chinese inventiveness extended also to naval technology. Before Tang times, Chinese mariners did not venture far from land. They traveled the sea lanes to Korea, Japan, and the Ryukyu Islands but relied on Persian, Arab, Indian, and Malay mariners for long-distance maritime trade. During the Tang dynasty, however, Chinese consumers developed a taste for the spices and exotic products of southeast Asian islands, and Chinese mariners increasingly visited those lands in their own ships. By the time of the Song dynasty, Chinese seafarers sailed ships fastened with iron nails, waterproofed with oils, furnished with watertight bulkheads, driven by canvas and bamboo sails, steered by rudders, and navigated with the aid of the "south-pointing needle"—the magnetic

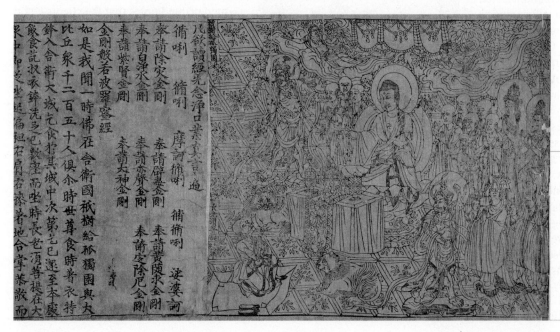

A printed book from the twelfth century presents a Chinese translation of a Buddhist text along with a block-printed illustration of the Buddha addressing his followers.
PBL Collection/Alamy Stock Photo

A detail from a Song-era painting on silk depicts two sturdy, broad-bottomed junks, the workhorses of the Chinese merchant fleet.
Werner Forman Archive/Shutterstock

compass. Larger ships sometimes even had small rockets powered by gunpowder. Chinese ships mostly plied the waters between Japan and the Malay peninsula, but some ventured into the Indian Ocean and called at ports in India, Ceylon, Persia, and east Africa. Those long-distance travels helped to diffuse elements of Chinese naval technology, particularly the compass, which soon became the common property of mariners throughout the Indian Ocean basin.

The Emergence of a Market Economy

Increased agricultural production, improved transportation systems, population growth, urbanization, and industrial production combined to stimulate the Chinese economy. China's various regions increasingly specialized in the cultivation of particular food crops or the production of particular manufactured goods, trading their products for imports from other regions. The market was not the only influence on the Chinese economy: government bureaucracies played a large role in the distribution of staple foods such as rice, wheat, and millet, and dynastic authorities closely watched militarily sensitive enterprises such as the iron industry. Nevertheless, millions of cultivators produced fruits and vegetables for sale on the open market, and manufacturers of silk, porcelain, and other goods supplied both domestic and foreign markets. The Chinese economy became more tightly integrated than ever before, and foreign demand for Chinese products fueled rapid economic expansion.

Financial Instruments Indeed, trade grew so rapidly during Tang and Song

An example of the world's oldest paper money, known as Jiaozi, first printed during the Southern Song dynasty. What economic conditions during the Southern Song demanded the introduction of paper money?
The Picture Art Collection/Alamy Stock Photo

times that China experienced a shortage of the copper coins that served as money for most transactions. To alleviate the shortage, Chinese merchants developed alternatives to cash that resulted in even more economic growth. Letters of credit came into common use during the early Tang dynasty. Known as "flying cash," they enabled merchants to deposit goods or cash at one location and draw the equivalent in cash or goods elsewhere in China. Later developments included the use of promissory notes, which pledged payment of a given sum of money at a later date, and checks, which entitled the bearer to draw funds against cash deposited with bankers.

Paper Money The search for alternatives to cash eventually led to the invention of paper money. Wealthy merchants pioneered the use of printed paper money during the late ninth century. In return for cash deposits from their clients, they issued printed notes that the clients could redeem for merchandise. In a society short of cash, these notes greatly facilitated commercial transactions. Occasionally, however, because of temporary economic reverses or poor management, merchants were not able to honor their notes. The resulting discontent among creditors often led to disorder and sometimes even to riots.

By the eleventh century, however, the Chinese economy had become so dependent on alternatives to cash that it was impractical to banish paper money altogether. To preserve its convenience while forestalling public disorder, government authorities forbade private parties to issue paper money and reserved that right for the state. The first paper money printed under government auspices appeared in

SOURCES FROM THE PAST

The Arab Merchant Suleiman on Business Practices in Tang China

The Arab merchant Suleiman made several commercial ventures by ship to South Asia and China during the early ninth century C.E. In 851 an Arab geographer wrote an account of Suleiman's travels, describing the lands he visited for Muslim readers in southwest Asia. His report throws particularly interesting light on the economic conditions and business practices of Tang China.

The Chinese are dressed in silk both winter and summer; and this kind of dress is common to the prince, the soldier, and to every other person, though of the lowest degree. In winter they wear drawers of a particular make, which fall down to their feet. Of these they put on two, three, four, five or more if they can, one over another, and are very careful to be covered quite down to their feet, because of the damp which is very great and much dreaded by them. In summer they only wear a single garment of silk or some such dress, but have no turbans . . . (p. 13)

In China commerce is carried out with the assistance of copper coins. They coin a great deal of copper money, like what the Arabs know by the name of Falus. They have treasuries like other kings, but no others have this sort of small money, and no other is current all over the country. For though they have gold, silver, pearls, silk, and rich stuffs in great abundance, they consider these only as merchandise, and copper pieces are the only current coin. From foreign parts [the Chinese] import ivory, incense, copper, the shells of turtles, and the horn of rhinoceros, from which they make ornaments . . . (p. 62)

> Why would the Tang government so strictly regulate commerce in their ports?

When merchants enter China by sea the government agents seize on their cargo and convey it to warehouses, and so put a stop to their business for six months, and till the last merchantman has arrived. Then they take three in ten, or thirty percent of each commodity, and return the rest to the merchant. If the emperor wants any particular thing, his officers have a right to take it preferable to any other persons whatsoever; and paying for it at the utmost penny it is valued at, they dispatch this business immediately and without the least injustice. (p. 63)

[The Chinese] administer justice with great strictness and equity in all their tribunals. When any person enters into a business transaction with another, he (the lender) sets down his claim in writing and the defendant (the borrower) writes down his understanding, which he signs and affixes the imprint of two of his fingers. These two writings are delivered together, and after being examined . . . the parties each have his paper returned to him.

When one party denies what the other affirms, he is ordered to return his writing. And if the defendant thinks he may do it safely, he accordingly delivers in his paper again. They also call for that of the plaintif, and then they say to him who denies what the other seems to have reason to maintain, exhibit a writing whereby they make it appear that your antagonist has no right to demand of you what is in debate. But if it clearly betrays the truth of what you deny, you shall undergo twenty strokes of the bamboo upon the back side, and pay a fine of 20 Fakuges, which is about two hundred dinars [Arab currency of the time]. Now this punishment is such that the criminal could not survive. It is so grievous that no person in all of China may, of his own authority, inflict it upon another upon pain of death and confiscation of goods. And so . . . justice is well administered and very exactly distributed to everyone. (pp. 67–68)

For Further Reflection

- Given the Chinese clothing the author describes, what class of Chinese did Suleiman most likely deal with?
- What is the economic value to the Chinese of treating gold and silver as commodities and only minting coins from copper?
- What affect would the various business practices the author describes have on the conduct of trade among Chinese merchants during the Tang Dynasty?

Source: Sirafi, Abu Zayd Hasan ibn Yazid, and Sulayman al-Tajir. Ancient accounts of India and China. Trans. by Eusebius Renaudot. London: Boston Public Library, 1733.

1024 in Sichuan province, the most active center of early printing. By the end of the century, government authorities throughout most of China issued printed paper money—complete with serial numbers and dire warnings against the printing of counterfeit notes. Rulers of nomadic peoples in central Asia soon began to adopt the practice in their states.

Printed paper money caused serious problems for several centuries after its appearance. Quite apart from contamination of the money supply by counterfeit notes, government authorities frequently printed currency representing more value than they actually possessed in cash reserves—a practice not unknown in more recent times. The result was a partial loss of public confidence in paper money. By the late eleventh century, some notes of paper money would fetch only 95 percent of their face value in cash. Not until the **Qing dynasty** (1644–1911 C.E.) did Chinese authorities place the issuance of printed money under tight fiscal controls. In spite of abuses, however, printed paper money provided a powerful stimulus to the Chinese economy.

A Cosmopolitan Society Trade and urbanization transformed Tang and Song China into a prosperous, cosmopolitan society. Trade came to China both by land and by sea. Muslim merchants from the Abbasid empire and central Asia helped to revive the Silk Roads network and flocked to large Chinese trading centers. Even subjects of the Byzantine empire made their way across the Silk Roads to China. Residents of large Chinese cities such as Chang'an and Luoyang became quite accustomed to merchants from foreign lands. Indeed, musicians and dancers from Persia became popular entertainers in the vibrant cities of the Tang dynasty. Meanwhile, Arab, Persian, Indian, and Malay mariners arriving by way of the Indian Ocean and South China Sea established sizable merchant communities in the bustling southern Chinese port cities of Guangzhou and Quanzhou. Contemporary reports said that the rebel general Huang Chao massacred 120,000 foreigners when he sacked Guangzhou and subjected it to a reign of terror in 879.

China and the Hemispheric Economy Indeed, high productivity and trade brought the Tang and Song economy a dynamism that China's borders could not restrain. Chinese consumers developed a taste for foreign goods that stimulated trade throughout much of the eastern hemisphere. Spices from the islands of southeast Asia made their way to China, along with products as diverse as kingfisher feathers and tortoise shell from Vietnam, pearls and incense from South Asia, and horses and melons from central Asia. Those items became symbols of a refined, elegant lifestyle—in many cases because of attractive qualities inherent in the commodities themselves but sometimes simply because of their scarcity and distant provenance. In exchange for such coveted items, Chinese sent abroad vast quantities of silk, porcelain, and lacquerware. In central Asia, southeast Asia, India, Persia, and the port cities of east Africa, wealthy merchants and rulers wore Chinese silk and set their tables with Chinese porcelain. China's economic surge during the Tang and Song dynasties thus promoted trade and economic growth throughout much of the eastern hemisphere.

CULTURAL CHANGE IN TANG AND SONG CHINA

Interactions with peoples of other societies encouraged cultural change in China during the Tang and Song Dynasties. The Confucian and Daoist traditions did not disappear. But

they made way for a foreign religion—**Mahayana Buddhism**—and they developed along new lines that reflected the conditions of Tang and Song society.

The Establishment of Buddhism

Buddhist merchants traveling the ancient Silk Roads visited China as early as the second century B.C.E. During the Han dynasty their faith attracted little interest there: Confucianism, Daoism, and faiths that honored family ancestors were the most popular cultural alternatives. After the fall of the Han, however, the Confucian tradition suffered a loss of credibility. The purpose and rationale of **Confucianism** was to maintain public order and provide honest, effective government. But in an age of warlords and nomadic invasions, it seemed that the Confucian tradition had simply failed. Confucian educational and civil service systems went into decline, and rulers sometimes openly scorned Confucian values.

Foreign Religions in China During the unsettled centuries following the fall of the Han dynasty, several foreign religions established communities in China. Nestorian Christians and Manichaeans settled in China, followed later by Zoroastrians fleeing the Islamic conquerors of Persia. When the Nestorian Christians established communities in China by the late sixth century, the emperor Tang Taizong issued a proclamation praising their doctrine, and he allowed them to open monasteries in Chang'an and other cities. By the mid-seventh century, Arab and Persian merchants had also established Muslim communities in the port cities of south China. Indeed, legend holds that an uncle of Muhammad built a small red mosque in the port city of Guangzhou. These religions of salvation mostly served the needs of foreign merchants trading in China and converts from nomadic societies. Sophisticated residents of Chinese cities appreciated foreign music and dance as well as foreign foods and trade goods, but most foreign religious traditions attracted little interest.

Dunhuang Yet Mahayana Buddhism gradually found a popular following in Tang and Song China. **Buddhism** came to China over the Silk Roads. Residents of oasis cities in central Asia had converted to Buddhism during the last two centuries before the Common Era, and the oases became sites of Buddhist missionary efforts. By the fourth century C.E., a sizable Buddhist community had emerged at **Dunhuang** in western China (modern Gansu province). Between about 600 and 1000 C.E., Buddhists built hundreds of cave temples in the vicinity of Dunhuang and decorated them with murals depicting events in the lives of the Buddha and the bodhisattvas who played prominent roles in Mahayana Buddhism. They also assembled libraries of religious literature and operated scriptoria (a room in a monastery where manuscripts were stored and copied) to produce Buddhist texts. Missions supported by establishments such as those at Dunhuang helped Buddhism to establish a foothold in China.

How the Past Shapes the Future ▷ ▷ ▷ ▷ ▷ ▷ ▷

The Spread of Religious Traditions

One of the defining characteristics of the late first and early second millennia C.E. was that the religions of Buddhism, Islam, Hinduism, and Christianity each won large numbers of converts far beyond their regions of origin. As a result, the values and doctrines of each religion profoundly shaped the societies where it won converts. At the same time, individual societies also shaped the beliefs and practices of each religion, so that Buddhism, Islam, Hinduism, and Christianity were all at least partially modified in the image of the new societies that adopted them. The consequences of these processes—which in most cases occurred gradually as a result of revived trade networks and the work of missionaries—had deep and long-lasting consequences that can still be seen in the religious distribution of the world's peoples today.

New Homes for Religious Traditions

In this chapter we have already seen how Buddhism—which originated in South Asia but had already spread along the Silk Roads in Central Asia—began to attract large numbers of converts in China from the seventh to the tenth centuries. Chinese influence, in turn, encouraged the spread of Buddhism to Korea, Vietnam, and Japan. By 1000 C.E., in fact, Buddhism had become a minority religion in its region of origin but continues to thrive in its adopted region of east Asia up to the present. But Buddhism was only one of several religious traditions to win converts in distant lands in this period. Indeed, from the seventh to the sixteenth centuries, Islam spread far from its origins in the Arabian peninsula, attracting converts in central and southwest Asia, north Africa, Iberia, India, and southeast Asia (chapters 14 and 15). Even as Islam was attracting converts in parts of the Indian subcontinent, traders and religious figures from the subcontinent encouraged a variety of states and kingdoms in southeast Asia to adopt either Buddhism or Hinduism between the sixth and fifteenth centuries (chapter 15). Orthodox Christianity, meanwhile, was adopted by Slavic peoples in eastern Europe on a massive scale during the ninth and tenth centuries, largely due to the political influence of Byzantium and the self-conscious efforts of Byzantine missionaries to proselytize among the Slavs (chapter 16). Over the course of the postclassical period, then, the spread of Buddhism, Islam, Hinduism, and Christianity from their regions of origin resulted in dramatic changes in the religious faith of millions of people.

The Influence of Religious Traditions on Culture and Society

The spread of these religious traditions deeply influenced social, cultural, and political developments in the lands where they were adopted. For example, in China the concerns of Mahayana Buddhism with logical thought and the nature of the soul were so influential on Confucian thought that the two blended to become a new tradition known as neo-Confucianism—which itself influenced societies in east Asia for more than a millennium. In lands where Islam was widely adopted, shared beliefs in the values expressed by the Quran, the system of Islamic law (*sharia*), and the circulation of judges (*quadis*) and legal scholars (*ulama*) qualified to interpret such law contributed to a shared sense of cultural unity across many parts of Eurasia (chapter 14). In southeast Asia, rulers of a variety of states borrowed Hindu notions of political authority by assuming the title of *raja*, adopted the South Asian epic story of the *Ramayana* as their own, and built monumental architecture closely modeled on South Asian styles (chapter 15). And in eastern Europe, the Cyrillic alphabet devised by Byzantine monks in the ninth century to represent the Slavic language in translations of Christian literature became the primary vehicle for printed works and continues to be used in Russia and other states of the former Soviet Union in the present (chapter 16).

The Influence of Societies on Religious Traditions

At the same time, the societies into which new religious traditions spread also had an impact on the beliefs and practices of the religions themselves. For example, as Islam spread, it was also deeply influenced by Persian literary traditions, South Asian scientific and mathematic traditions, Greek philosophy, and patriarchal traditions from the eastern Mediterranean (chapter 14). When Islam spread to southeast Asia, its expression was modified both by Hindu elements that had already shaped the region and by indigenous mystical traditions (chapter 15). Additionally, when Buddhism was adopted on a large scale by Chinese adherents, it was modified in ways that appealed to Chinese Daoist beliefs about spiritual life and in ways that complemented the primacy of the family in Chinese tradition. As a result of their adoption in lands far from their regions of origin, then, each of these major religions took on new forms of expression that remained influential for many centuries and, in some cases, to the present day.

These are only a small sampling of the historical reverberations of the spread of religious traditions in the late first and early second millennia. When reading subsequent chapters, try to identify additional short- and long-term consequences that resulted from these momentous processes.

Buddhism in China Buddhism attracted Chinese interest partly because of its high standards of morality, its intellectual sophistication, and its promise of salvation. Practical concerns also help to account for its appeal. Buddhists established monastic communities in China and accumulated sizable estates donated by wealthy converts. They cultivated those lands intensively and stored a portion of their harvests for distribution among local residents during times of drought, famine, or other hardship. Some monasteries engaged in banking or money-lending activities, and many others maintained schools that provided a basic education for local populations. Buddhist monasteries thus became important elements in the local economies of Chinese communities. Buddhism even had implications for everyday life in China. Buddhist monks introduced chairs into China: originally a piece of monastic furniture, the chair quickly became popular in secular society and found a place in domestic interiors throughout the land. Buddhist monks also introduced refined sugar into China and thus influenced both diet and cuisine.

In some ways, Buddhism posed a challenge to Chinese cultural and social traditions. Buddhist theologians typically took written texts as points of departure for elaborate, speculative investigations into metaphysical themes such as the nature of the soul. Among Chinese intellectuals, however, only the Confucians placed great emphasis on written texts, and they devoted their energies mostly to practical rather than metaphysical issues. Meanwhile, Daoists had limited interest in written texts of any kind. Buddhist morality called for individuals to strive for perfection by observing an ascetic ideal, and it encouraged serious Buddhists to follow a celibate, monastic lifestyle. In contrast, traditional Chinese morality centered on the family unit and the obligations of filial piety, and it strongly encouraged procreation so that generations of offspring would be available to venerate family ancestors. Some Chinese held that Buddhist monasteries were economically harmful because they paid no taxes, whereas others scorned Buddhism as an inferior creed because of its foreign origins.

Buddhism and Daoism Because of those differences and concerns, Buddhist missionaries sought to tailor their message to Chinese audiences. They explained Buddhist concepts in vocabulary borrowed from Chinese cultural traditions, particularly **Daoism**. They translated the Indian term *dharma* (the basic Buddhist doctrine) as *dao* ("the way" in the Daoist sense of the term), and they translated the Indian term **nirvana** (personal salvation that comes after an individual soul escapes from the cycle of incarnation) as **wuwei** (the Daoist ethic of noncompetition). While encouraging the establishment of monasteries and the observance of celibacy, they also recognized the validity of family life and offered Buddhism as a religion that would benefit the extended Chinese family: one son in the monastery, they taught, would bring salvation for ten generations of his kin.

Mural commemorating the victory of General Zhang Yichai and Chinese military forces over the forces of the Tibetan Empire. Mogao Caves 156, near Dunhuang, Late Tang Dynasty.
The History Collection/Alamy Stock Photo

Pilgrimage to South Asia Monks and pilgrims helped popularize Buddhism in China. The monk Xuanzang (602–664 C.E.), who we first met at the start of this chapter, was only one among hundreds of Chinese pilgrims who made the dangerous and difficult journey to the Indian subcontinent to visit holy sites and learn about Buddhism in its homeland. Xuanzang and other pilgrims returned to China with copies of treatises that deepened the understanding of Buddhism, and they were able to relate the teachings of South Asian Buddhist masters to Chinese disciples.

Schools of Buddhism Over the years, monks and scholars organized several distinctive schools of Buddhism that appealed to Chinese tastes and interests. Buddhists of the Chan school (also known by its Japanese name, Zen) placed little emphasis on written texts but held intuition and sudden flashes of insight in high regard. Thus Chan Buddhists made a place for Daoist values in Chinese Buddhism. Even more popular than **Chan Buddhism** was the Pure Land school, which held out the prospect of personal salvation for those who devoted themselves to the Buddha. The emperor Wu Zhao herself followed Pure Land teachings, and she enthusiastically promoted the school—especially after friendly monks circulated a treatise predicting reincarnation of the Buddha as a female ruler. Wu Zhao eventually proclaimed herself the universal ruler and protector of Buddhism, and she sponsored the construction of monasteries and stupas (a domed building constructed to house relics of the Buddha) throughout China.

This scroll painting depicts the return of the monk Xuanzang to China. His baggage included 657 books, mostly Buddhist treatises but also a few works on grammar and logic, as well as hundreds of relics and images.

Ivy Close Images/Age Fotostock

largely by a desire to seize property belonging to foreign religious establishments, the Tang rulers did not implement their policy in a thorough way. Although it discouraged further expansion, Tang policy did not eradicate foreign faiths from China. Buddhism in particular enjoyed popular support that enabled it to survive. Indeed, it even influenced the development of the Confucian tradition during the Song dynasty.

Neo-Confucianism

The Song emperors did not persecute Buddhists, but they actively supported traditional Chinese cultural traditions in hopes of limiting the influence of foreign religions. They contributed particularly generously to the Confucian tradition. They sponsored the studies of Confucian scholars, for example, and subsidized the printing and dissemination of Confucian writings.

Confucians and Buddhism Yet the Confucian tradition of the Song dynasty differed from that of earlier times. The earliest Confucians had concentrated resolutely on practical issues of politics and morality because they took the organization of a stable social order as their principal concern. Confucians of the Song dynasty studied the classic works of their tradition, but they also became familiar with the writings of Buddhists. They found much to admire in Buddhist thought. Buddhism not only offered a tradition of logical thought and argumentation but also dealt with issues, such as the nature of the soul and the individual's relationship with the cosmos, not systematically explored by Confucian thinkers. Thus Confucians of the Song dynasty drew a great deal of inspiration from Buddhism. Because their thought reflected the influence of Buddhism as well as original Confucian values, it has come to be known as **neo-Confucianism.**

Zhu Xi The most important representative of Song neo-Confucianism was the philosopher **Zhu Xi** (1130–1200 C.E.). A prolific writer, Zhu Xi maintained a deep commitment to Confucian values emphasizing proper personal behavior and social harmony. Among his writings was an influential treatise titled *Family Rituals* that provided detailed instructions for weddings, funerals, veneration of ancestors, and

Hostility to Buddhism In spite of its popularity, Buddhism met determined resistance from Daoists and Confucians. Daoists resented the popular following that Buddhists attracted, which resulted in diminished resources available for their tradition. Confucians despised Buddhists' exaltation of celibacy, and they denounced its teachings as alien superstition. They also condemned Buddhist monasteries as wasteful, unproductive burdens on society.

Persecution During the late Tang dynasty, Daoist and Confucian critics of Buddhism found allies in the imperial court. Beginning in the 840s the Tang emperors ordered the closure of monasteries and the expulsion of Buddhists as well as Zoroastrians, Nestorian Christians, and Manichaeans. Motivated

Zhu Xi (ZHOO SHEE)

Artist's impression of Japanese Buddhist monk Ippen Shonen arriving at a town in rural Japan. Ippen Shonen popularized a Buddhist ceremonial practice that combined prayer with dance. Burstein Collection/Getty Images

other family ceremonies. As a good Confucian, Zhu Xi considered it a matter of the highest importance that individuals play their proper roles both in their family and in the larger society.

Yet Zhu Xi became fascinated with the philosophical and speculative features of Buddhist thought. He argued in good Confucian fashion for the observance of high moral standards, and he believed that academic and philosophical investigations were important for practical affairs. But he concentrated his efforts on abstract and abstruse issues of more theoretical than practical significance. He wrote extensively on metaphysical themes such as the nature of reality. He argued in a manner reminiscent of Plato that two elements accounted for all physical being: *li,* a principle somewhat similar to Plato's Forms or Ideas that defines the essence of the being, and *qi,* its material form.

Neo-Confucian Influence Neo-Confucianism ranks as an important cultural development for two reasons. First, it illustrates the deep influence of Buddhism in Chinese society. Even though the neo-Confucians rejected Buddhist religious teachings, their writings adapted Buddhist themes and reasoning to Confucian interests and values. Second, neo-Confucianism influenced east Asian thought over a very long term. In China, neo-Confucianism enjoyed the status of an officially recognized creed from the Song dynasty until the early twentieth century, and in lands that fell within China's cultural orbit—particularly Korea, Vietnam, and Japan—neo-Confucianism shaped philosophical, political, and moral thought for half a millennium and more.

DEVELOPMENT OF COMPLEX SOCIETIES IN KOREA, VIETNAM, AND JAPAN

Like the *dar al-Islam,* Chinese society influenced the development of neighboring lands during the Tang and Song dynasties. Chinese armies periodically invaded Korea and Vietnam, and Chinese merchants established commercial relations with Japan as well as with Korea and Vietnam. Chinese techniques of government and administration helped shape public life in Korea, Vietnam, and Japan, and Chinese values and cultural traditions won a prominent place alongside native traditions. By no means did those lands become absorbed into China: all maintained distinctive identities and cultural traditions. Yet they also drew deep inspiration from Chinese examples and built societies that reflected their participation in a larger east Asian society revolving around China.

Korea and Vietnam

Chinese armies ventured into Korea and Vietnam on campaigns of imperial expansion as early as the Qin and Han dynasties. As the Han dynasty weakened, however, local aristocrats organized movements that ousted Chinese forces from both lands. Only during the powerful Tang dynasty did Chinese resources once again enable military authorities to mount large-scale campaigns. Although the two lands responded differently to Chinese imperial expansion, both borrowed Chinese political and cultural traditions and used them in their societies.

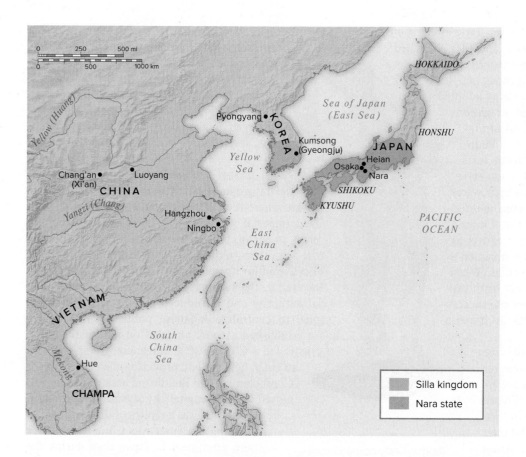

MAP 13.3
Borderlands of China in the first millennium C.E.: Korea, Vietnam, and Japan.

Note the geographic relationship of Korea, Vietnam, and Japan to China.

What geographic conditions help to account for the varying degrees of Chinese influence in Korea, Vietnam, and Japan?

The Silla Dynasty During the seventh century, Tang armies conquered much of Korea before the native **Silla dynasty** rallied to prevent Chinese domination of the peninsula. Both Tang and Silla authorities preferred to avoid a long and costly conflict, so they agreed to a political compromise: Chinese forces withdrew from Korea, and the Silla rulers recognized the Tang emperor as their overlord. In theory, Korea was a vassal state in a vast Chinese empire. In practice, however, Korea was in most respects an independent kingdom, although the ruling dynasty prudently maintained cordial relations with its powerful neighbor.

Thus Korea entered into a tributary relationship with China. Envoys of the Silla rulers regularly delivered gifts to Chinese emperors, but those concessions brought considerable benefits to the Koreans. Moreover, the tributary relationship opened the doors for Korean merchants to trade, and students to study, in China.

Chinese Influence in Korea
Meanwhile, the tributary relationship facilitated the spread of Chinese political and cultural influences to Korea. Embassies delivering tribute to China included Korean royal officials who observed the workings of the Chinese court and bureaucracy and then organized the Korean court on similar lines. The Silla monarchs (one of the most important of whom was a woman, Queen Seondeok) built a lavish new capital at their ancestral town of Kumsong (modern-day Kyongju in southeastern Korea), taking the Tang

capital at Chang'an as their model. Silla rulers developed Kumsong from a small walled town with a few hundred families into a major capital with 179,000 households and nearly one million people. Their embassies to China included not only royal officials but also scholars who studied Chinese thought and literature and who took copies of Chinese writings back to Korea. Their efforts helped to build Korean interest in the Confucian tradition, particularly among educated aristocrats. While Korean elite classes turned to Confucius, Chinese schools of Buddhism attracted widespread popular interest. Chan Buddhism, which promised individual salvation, won the allegiance of peasants and commoners.

China and Korea differed in many respects. Most notably, perhaps, aristocrats and royal houses dominated Korean society much more than was the case in China. Although the Korean monarchy sponsored Chinese schools and a Confucian examination system, Korea never established a bureaucracy based on merit such as that of Tang and Song China. Political initiative remained firmly in the hands of the ruling classes. Nevertheless, extensive dealings with its powerful neighbor ensured that Korea reflected the influence of Chinese political and cultural traditions.

China and Vietnam
Chinese relations with Vietnam were far more tense than with Korea. When Tang armies ventured into the land that Chinese called **Nam Viet,** they encountered spirited resistance on the part of the Viet people, who had

settled in the region around the Red River. Tang forces soon won control of Viet towns and cities, and they launched efforts to absorb the Viets into Chinese society, just as their predecessors had absorbed the indigenous peoples of the Yangzi River valley. The Viets readily adopted Chinese agricultural methods and irrigation systems as well as Chinese schools and administrative techniques. Like their Korean counterparts, Viet elites studied Confucian texts and took examinations based on a Chinese-style education, and Viet traders marketed their wares in China. Vietnamese authorities even entered into tributary relationships with the Chinese court. Yet the Viets resented Chinese efforts to dominate the southern land, and they mounted a series of revolts against Tang authorities. When the Tang dynasty fell during the early tenth century, the Viets won their independence and successfully resisted later Chinese efforts at imperial expansion to the south.

Like Korea, Vietnam differed from China in many ways. Many Vietnamese retained their indigenous religions in preference to Chinese cultural traditions. Women played a much more prominent role in Vietnamese society and economy than did their counterparts in China. Southeast Asian women had dominated local and regional markets for centuries, and they participated actively in business ventures closed to women in the more rigidly patriarchal society of China.

Chinese Influence in Vietnam Nevertheless, Chinese traditions found a place in the southern land. Vietnamese authorities established an administrative system and bureaucracy modeled on that of China, and Viet ruling classes prepared for their careers by pursuing a Confucian education. Furthermore, Buddhism mostly came to Vietnam from China and won a large popular following. Thus, like Korea, Vietnam absorbed political and cultural influence from China and reflected the development of a larger east Asian society centered on China.

Early Japan

Chinese armies never invaded Japan, but Chinese traditions deeply influenced early Japanese political and cultural development. The earliest inhabitants of Japan were nomadic peoples from northeast Asia who migrated to Japan about thirty-five thousand years ago. Their language, material culture, and religion derived from their parent society in northeast Asia. Later

Tang dynasty pottery figure of a Vietnamese dancer. Commercial and tributary relationships introduced southeast Asian performers to China, where sophisticated urban communities appreciated their exotic entertainment.
Heritage Image Partnership Ltd/ Alamy Stock Photo

migrants, who arrived in several waves from the Korean peninsula, introduced cultivation of rice, bronze and iron metallurgy, and horses into Japan. As the population of the Japanese islands grew and built a settled agricultural society, small states dominated by aristocratic clans emerged. By the middle of the first millennium C.E., several dozen states ruled small regions.

Nara Japan The establishment of the powerful Sui and Tang dynasties in China had repercussions in Japan, where they demonstrated the value of centralized imperial government. One of the aristocratic clans in Japan, the Soga, insisted on its precedence over the others, although in fact it had never wielded effective authority outside its territory in central Japan. Inspired by the Tang example, this clan claimed imperial authority and introduced a series of reforms designed to centralize Japanese politics. The imperial house established a court modeled on that of the Tang, instituted a Chinese-style bureaucracy, implemented an equal-field system, provided official support for Confucianism and Buddhism, and in the year 710 moved to a new capital city at Nara (near modern Kyoto) that was a replica of the Tang capital at Chang'an. Never was Chinese influence more prominent in Japan than during the **Nara** period (710–794 C.E.).

Yet Japan did not lose its distinctive characteristics or become simply a smaller model of Chinese society. While adopting Confucian and Buddhist traditions from China, for example, the Japanese continued to observe the rites of **Shinto,** their indigenous religion, which revolved around the veneration of ancestors and a host of nature spirits and deities. Japanese society reflected the influence of Chinese traditions but still developed along its own lines.

The experiences of the Heian, Kamakura, and Muromachi periods clearly illustrate this point. In 794 the emperor of Japan transferred his court from Nara to a newly constructed capital at nearby Heian (modern Kyoto). During the next four centuries, Heian became the seat of a refined and sophisticated society that drew inspiration from China but also developed distinctively Japanese political and cultural traditions.

Heian Japan During the **Heian** period (794–1185 C.E.), local rulers on the island of Honshu mostly recognized the emperor as Japan's supreme political authority. Unlike their Chinese counterparts, however, Japanese emperors rarely ruled but, rather, served as ceremonial figureheads and symbols of authority. Effective power lay in the hands of the Fujiwara family, an aristocratic clan that controlled affairs

Heian (HAY-ahn)

from behind the throne through its influence over the imperial house and manipulation of its members.

After the ninth century the Japanese political order almost continuously featured a split between a publicly recognized imperial authority and a separate agent of effective rule. This pattern helps to account for the remarkable longevity of the Japanese imperial house. Because emperors have not ruled, they have not been subject to deposition during times of turmoil: ruling parties and factions have come and gone, but the imperial house has survived.

The cultural development of Heian Japan also reflected both the influence of Chinese traditions and the elaboration of peculiarly Japanese ways. Most literature imitated Chinese models and indeed was written in the Chinese language. Boys and young men who received a formal education in Heian Japan learned Chinese, read the classic works of China, and wrote in the foreign tongue. Officials at court conducted business and kept records in Chinese, and literary figures wrote histories and treatises in the style popular in China. Even Japanese writing reflected Chinese influence because scholars borrowed many Chinese characters and used them to represent Japanese words. They also adapted some Chinese characters into a Japanese syllabic script, in which symbols represent whole syllables rather than a single sound, as in an alphabetic script.

The Tale of Genji Because Japanese women rarely received a formal Chinese-style education, in Heian times aristocratic women made the most notable contributions to literature in the Japanese language. Of the many literary works that have survived from that era, none reflects Heian court life better than **The Tale of Genji.** Composed by Murasaki Shikibu, a lady-in-waiting at the Heian court who wrote in Japanese syllabic script rather than Chinese characters, this sophisticated work relates the experiences of a fictitious imperial prince named Genji. Living amid gardens and palaces, Genji and his friends devoted themselves to the cultivation of an ultrarefined lifestyle, and they became adept at mixing subtle perfumes, composing splendid verses in fine calligraphic hand, and wooing elegant women.

The Tale of Genji also offers a meditation on the passing of time and the sorrows that time brings to sensitive humans. As Genji and his friends age, they reflect on past joys and relationships no longer recoverable. Their thoughts suffuse *The Tale of Genji* with a melancholy spirit that presents a subtle contrast to the elegant atmosphere of their surroundings at the Heian court. Because of her limited command of Chinese, Lady Murasaki created one of the most remarkable literary works in the Japanese language.

Decline of Heian Japan As the charmed circle of aristocrats and courtiers led elegant lives at the imperial capital, the Japanese countryside underwent fundamental changes that brought an end to the Heian court and its refined society. The equal-field system gradually fell into disuse in Japan as it had in

China, and aristocratic clans accumulated most of the islands' lands into vast estates. By the late eleventh century, two clans in particular—the Taira and the Minamoto—overshadowed the others. During the mid-twelfth century the two engaged in outright war, and in 1185 the Minamoto emerged victorious. The Minamoto did not seek to abolish imperial authority in Japan but, rather, claimed to rule the land in the name of the emperor. They installed the clan leader as *shogun*—a military governor who ruled in place of the emperor—and established the seat of their government at Kamakura, near modern Tokyo, while the imperial court remained at Kyoto. For most of the next four centuries, one branch or another of the Minamoto clan dominated political life in Japan.

The armor and weaponry of the samurai bespeak the militarism of the Kamakura era.
Library of Congress, Prints & Photographs Division
[LC-DIG-jpd-01046]

Medieval Japan

Historians refer to the Kamakura and Muromachi periods as Japan's medieval period—a middle era falling between the age of Chinese influence and court domination of political life in Japan, as represented by the Nara and Heian periods, and the modern age, inaugurated by the Tokugawa dynasty in the sixteenth century, when a centralized government unified and ruled all of Japan. During this middle era, Japanese society and culture took on increasingly distinctive characteristics.

Political Decentralization In the Kamakura (1185–1333 C.E.) and Muromachi (1336–1573 C.E.) periods, Japan developed a decentralized political order in which provincial lords wielded effective power and authority in local regions where they controlled land and economic affairs. As these lords and their clans vied for power and authority in the countryside, they found little use for the Chinese-style bureaucracy that Nara and Heian rulers had instituted in Japan and still less use for the elaborate protocol and refined conduct that prevailed at the courts. In place of etiquette and courtesy, they valued military talent and discipline. The mounted warrior, the *samurai,* thus played the most distinctive role in Japanese political and military affairs.

The Samurai The **samurai** were professional warriors, specialists in the use of force and the arts of fighting. They served the provincial lords of Japan, who relied on the samurai both to enforce their authority in their own territories and to extend their claims to other lands. In return for those police and military services, the lords supported the samurai from the agricultural surplus and labor services of peasants working under their jurisdiction. Freed of obligations to feed, clothe, and house themselves and their families, samurai devoted themselves to hunting, riding, archery, and martial arts.

Japan and East Asia Thus, although it had taken its original inspiration from the Tang empire in China, the Japanese political order developed along lines different from those of the Middle Kingdom. Yet Japan clearly had a place in the larger east Asian society centered on China. Japan borrowed from China, among other things, Confucian values, Buddhist religion, a system of writing, and the ideal of centralized imperial rule. Though somewhat suppressed during the Kamakura and Muromachi periods, those elements of Chinese society not only survived in Japan but also decisively influenced Japanese development during later periods.

CONCLUSION

The revival of centralized imperial rule in China had profound implications for all of east Asia and indeed for most of the eastern hemisphere. When the Sui and Tang dynasties imposed their authority throughout China, they established a powerful state that guided political affairs throughout east Asia. Tang armies extended Chinese influence to Korea, Vietnam, and central Asia. They did not invade Japan, but the impressive political organization of China prompted the islands' rulers to imitate Tang examples. Moreover, the Sui and Tang dynasties laid a strong political foundation for rapid economic development. Chinese society prospered throughout the later first and early second millenia C.E., partly because of technological and industrial innovation. Tang and Song prosperity touched all of China's neighbors because it encouraged surging commerce in east Asia. Chinese silk, porcelain, and lacquerware were prized commodities among trading peoples from southeast Asia to east Africa. Chinese inventions such as paper, printing, gunpowder, and the magnetic compass found a place in societies throughout the eastern hemisphere as they diffused across the Silk Roads and the sea lanes. It was also an age of religious as well as commercial and technological exchanges: Nestorian Christians, Zoroastrians, Manichaeans, and Muslims all maintained communities in Tang China, and Buddhism became the most popular religious tradition in all of east Asia. Finally, Chinese traditions of social organization and economic dynamism helped to sustain encounters between the peoples of the eastern hemisphere on an unprecedented scale.

STUDY TERMS

Buddhism (262)	Qing dynasty (262)
Chan Buddhism (265)	samurai (270)
Confucianism (262)	Shinto (268)
Daoism (264)	*shogun* (269)
Dunhuang (262)	Silla dynasty (267)
equal-field system (251)	Song dynasty (253)
foot binding (257)	Song Taizu (253)
Grand Canal (250)	Sui dynasty (250)
gunpowder (259)	Sui Yangdi (250)
Hangzhou (255)	*The Tale of Genji* (269)
Heian (268)	Tang dynasty (250)
Li Bai (257)	Tang Taizong (250)
Mahayana Buddhism (262)	Uighurs (252)
Nam Viet (267)	*wuwei* (264)
Nara (268)	Wu Zhao (257)
neo-Confucianism (265)	Xuanzang (248)
nirvana (264)	Yang Jian (250)
porcelain (258)	Zhu Xi (265)

FOR FURTHER READING

Robert Finlay. *The Pilgrim Art: The Culture of Porcelain in World History.* Berkeley, 2010. Brilliant study outlining the Chinese invention of porcelain and the product's appeal in the larger world.

Karl Friday. *Samurai, Warfare and the State in Early Medieval Japan.* New York, 2004. A lively analysis with apt comparisons to medieval Europe.

John Kieschnick. *The Impact of Buddhism on Chinese Material Culture.* Princeton, 2003. Fascinating scholarly study exploring the social effects of Buddhism in China.

Dieter Kuhn. *The Age of Confucian Rule: The Song Transformation of China.* Cambridge, Mass., 2009. Emphasizes social and economic developments.

Mark Edward Lewis. *China's Cosmopolitan Empire: The Tang Dynasty.* Cambridge, Mass., 2009. Perhaps the best single volume on Tang China.

Victor Mair, ed. *The Columbia Anthology of Traditional Chinese Literature.* New York, 1994. A comprehensive collection of the classics of Chinese literature, including the superb poetry of the Tang dynasty.

Murasaki Shikibu. *The Tale of Genji.* New York, 2019. trans. by Dennis Washburn. Fresh translation of Genji that communicates with the modern author with immediacy and energy.

H. Paul Varley. *Japanese Culture.* 4th ed. Honolulu, 2000. An authoritative analysis of Japanese cultural development from early times to the present.

Roderick Whitfield, Susan Whitfield, and Neville Agnew. *Mogao: Art and History on the Silk Road.* Los Angeles, 2000. Excellent brief discussion of the cave temples and archaeological remains from Dunhuang.

Sally Hovey Wriggins. *The Silk Road Journey with Xuanzang.* Boulder, 2004. A fascinating and well-illustrated account of Xuanzang's journey to India and his influence on the development of Buddhism in China.

ZOOMING IN ON TRADITIONS
Season of the Mecca Pilgrimage

In 632 C.E. the prophet Muhammad visited his native city of Mecca from his home in exile at Medina, and in doing so he set an example that devout Muslims have sought to emulate ever since. Today the *hajj*—the holy pilgrimage to Mecca—draws Muslims by the hundreds of thousands from all parts of the world to Saudi Arabia. Each year Muslims travel to Mecca by land, sea, and air to make the pilgrimage and visit the holy sites of Islam.

In centuries past the numbers of pilgrims were smaller, but their observance of the hajj was no less conscientious. By the ninth century, pilgrimage had become so popular that Muslim rulers went to some lengths to meet the needs of travelers passing through their lands. With the approach of the pilgrimage season—the last month of the Islamic lunar calendar—crowds gathered at major trading centers such as Baghdad, Damascus, and Cairo. There they lived in tent cities, surviving on food and water provided by government officials, until they could join caravans bound for Mecca. Muslim rulers invested considerable sums in the mainte-nance of roads, wells, cisterns, and lodgings that accommo-dated pilgrims—as well as castles and police forces that protected travelers—on their journeys to Mecca and back.

The hajj was not only solemn observance but also an occasion for joy and celebration. Muslim rulers and wealthy pilgrims often made lavish gifts to caravan companions and

A sixteenth-century Turkish manuscript depicts pilgrims praying at Mecca in the mosque surrounding the Ka'ba.
Leemage/Getty Images

others they met en route to Mecca. During her famous hajj of 976–977, for example, the Mesopotamian princess Jamila bint Nasir al-Dawla provided food and fresh green vegetables for her fellow pilgrims and furnished five hundred camels for handicapped travelers. She also purchased freedom for five hundred slaves and distributed fifty thousand fine robes among the common people of Mecca.

Most pilgrims did not have the resources to match Jamila's generosity, but for common travelers, too, the hajj became a special occasion. Merchants and craftsmen made acquaintances and arranged business deals with pilgrims from other lands. Students and scholars exchanged ideas during their weeks of traveling together. For all pilgrims, participation in ritual activities lent new meaning and significance to their faith.

CHAPTER OVERVIEW

The word *Islam* means "submission," signifying obedience to the rule and will of Allah, the only deity recognized in the strictly monotheistic Islamic religion. An individual who accepts the Islamic faith is a *Muslim,* meaning "one who has submitted." Though it began as one man's expression of unqualified faith in Allah, Islam quickly attracted followers and took on political and social as well as religious significance. During its first century, Islam reached far beyond its Arabian homeland, bringing Sasanian Persia and parts of the Byzantine Empire into its orbit. By the eighth century the realm of Islam and the Byzantine Empire stood as political and economic anchors of much of western and central Afro-Eurasia.

Early Islamic religious beliefs reflected the deep influence of Jewish and Christian traditions, while early Muslim society reflected the nomadic and mercantile Arabian society from which Islam arose. Over time, Muslims also drew inspiration from other societies and other cultural traditions. After toppling the Sasanians, Muslim conquerors adopted Persian techniques of government and finance to administer their lands. Persian literature, science, and religious values also found a place in Islamic society. During later centuries Muslims drew inspiration from Greek and Indian traditions as well.

Thus Muslims did not invent a new Islamic society but, rather, fashioned it by blending elements from Arab, Persian, Greek, and Indian societies.

While drawing influence from other societies, however, Islam thoroughly transformed the cultural traditions that it absorbed. The expansive realm of Islam eventually provided a political framework for trade and diplomacy over a vast portion of the eastern hemisphere, from west Africa to the islands of southeast Asia. Many lands of varied cultural background thus became part of a larger society often called the *dar al-Islam*—an Arabic term that means the "house of Islam" and that refers to lands under Islamic rule.

CHRONOLOGY	
570–632	Life of Muhammad
622	The *hijra*
632	Muhammad's hajj
650s	Compilation of the Quran
661–750	Umayyad dynasty
750–1258	Abbasid dynasty
786–809	Reign of Harun al-Rashid
1050s	Establishment of Seljuq control over the Abbasid dynasty
1058–1111	Life of al-Ghazali
1126–1198	Life of Ibn Rushd

A PROPHET AND HIS WORLD

Islam arose in the Arabian peninsula, and the new religion faithfully reflected the social and cultural conditions of its homeland. Desert covers most of the peninsula, and agriculture is possible only in the well-watered area of Yemen in the south and in a few other places, such as the city of Medina, where oases provide water. Yet human communities have occupied Arabia for millennia. Nomadic peoples known as **bedouin** kept herds of sheep, goats, and camels, migrating through the deserts to find grass and water for their animals. The bedouin organized themselves in family and clan groups. Individuals and their immediate families depended heavily on

their larger kinship networks for support in times of need. In an environment as harsh and unforgiving as the Arabian desert, cooperation with kin often made the difference between death and survival. Bedouin peoples developed a strong sense of loyalty to their clans and guarded their common interests with determination. Clan identities and loyalties survived for centuries after the appearance of Islam.

Arabia also figured prominently in the long-distance trade networks of the first millennium of the Common Era. Commodities arrived at ports on the Persian Gulf (near modern Bahrain),

---

bedouin (BEHD-oh-ihn)

Some northern Arabs went to great lengths to demonstrate their devotion to Christianity. This structure, carved out of sheer rock along the wall of a ravine at Petra in modern-day Jordan, served as a monastery.

Salail Wadhavkar/National Geographic Stock

the Arabian Sea (near modern Aden), and the Red Sea (near Mecca) and then traveled overland by camel caravan to Palmyra or Damascus, which offered access to the Mediterranean basin. After the third century C.E., Arabia became an increasingly important link in trade between China and India in the east and Persia and Byzantium in the west. With the weakening of classical empires, trade routes across central Asia had become insecure. Merchants abandoned the overland routes in favor of sea lanes connecting with land routes in the Arabian peninsula. Trade passing across the peninsula was especially important for the city of Mecca, which became an important site of fairs and a stopping point for caravan traffic.

Muhammad and His Message

Muhammad's Early Life The prophet **Muhammad** came into this world of bedouin herders and worldly merchants. Born about 570 C.E. into a reputable family of merchants in Mecca, Muhammad ibn (a term than means son of) Abdullah lost both of his parents by the time he was six years old. His grandfather and uncle cared for him and provided him with an education, but Muhammad's early life was difficult. As a young man, he worked for a woman named Khadija, a wealthy widow whom he married about 595 C.E. Through this marriage he gained a position of some prominence in Meccan society, although he did not by any means enter the ranks of the elite.

By age thirty Muhammad had established himself as a merchant. He made a comfortable life for himself in Arabian society, where peoples of different religious and cultural traditions regularly dealt with one another. Most Arabs recognized many gods, goddesses, demons, and nature spirits whose favor they sought through prayers and sacrifices. Large communities of Jewish merchants also worked throughout Arabia, and, especially in the north, many Arabs had converted to Christianity by Muhammad's time. Although he was not deeply knowledgeable about Judaism or Christianity, Muhammad

had a basic understanding of both traditions. He may even have traveled by caravan to Syria, where he would certainly have dealt with Jewish and Christian merchants.

Muhammad's Spiritual Transformation About 610 C.E., as he approached age forty, Muhammad underwent a profound spiritual experience that transformed his life and left a deep mark on world history. His experience left him with the convictions that in all the world there was only one true deity; **Allah** ("God"); that he ruled the universe; that idolatry and the recognition of other gods amounted to wickedness; and that Allah would soon bring his judgment on the world, rewarding the righteous and punishing the wicked. Muhammad experienced visions, which he understood as messages or revelations from Allah, delivered through the archangel Gabriel (also recognized by Jews and Christians as a special messenger of God), instructing him to explain his views to others. He did not set out to construct a new religion by combining elements of Arab, Jewish, and Christian beliefs. In light of his cultural context, however, it is not surprising that he shared numerous specific beliefs with Jews and Christians—and indeed also with Zoroastrians, whose views had profoundly influenced the development of both Judaism and Christianity. In any case, in accordance with instructions transmitted to him by Gabriel, Muhammad began to expound his beliefs to his family and close friends. Gradually, others showed interest in his message, and by about 620 C.E. an enthusiastic and expanding minority of Mecca's citizenry had joined his circle.

The Quran Muhammad originally presented oral recitations of the revelations he received during his visions. As the Islamic community grew, his followers prepared written texts of his teachings. During the early 650s devout Muslims

Muhammad (muh-HAHM-mahd)

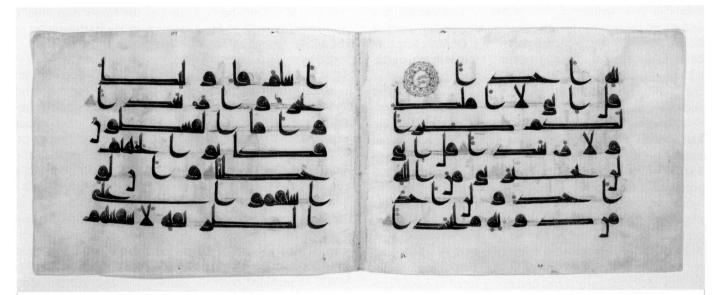

Current Islamic doctrine forbids artistic representations of Muhammad and Allah to prevent the worship of their images as idols. Although artists of previous centuries occasionally produced paintings of Muhammad, Islamic art has emphasized geometric design and calligraphy. This handsome page from a Quran written on vellum dates from the ninth or early tenth century.
Purchase, Friends of Islamic Art Gifts, 2004/Metropolitan Museum of Art

What's Left Out?

Before the advent of Muhammad and Islam, the Ka'ba in the city of Mecca was just one of many religious sanctuaries recognized by the Arabs. As pilgrims traveled to these sacred sites, they naturally engaged in trade in the towns that surrounded them, and commercial fairs were established that coincided with the season of the pilgrimage. However, the question of just how extensive trade in Mecca was has led to considerable disagreement among historians. The standard argument has been that Mecca was the hub of extensive transregional trade routes that connected the ports of Yemen with the Byzantine and Sasanian empires, facilitating commerce in gold, silver, and spices in particular. But, more recently, scholars have pushed back against this theory, pointing out that the only sources that make this claim are Arabic and that not a single non-Arabic source has yet been discovered that supports this idea of Mecca as a hub of extensive transregional trade. They also point out that Mecca is not actually located on any trade routes and visiting it would have required a considerable and costly detour away from the main trading routes of the Arabian Peninsula. Some of these scholars go so far as to reject these Arabic source depictions of pre-Islamic Mecca as propaganda and myth.

There is no doubt that Mecca was out of the way, located in a barren valley and with nothing in particular to encourage a merchant caravan to visit. But Mecca did have one undeniable attraction—and that was the Ka'ba itself. There were many other sanctuaries in Arabia that were important to pilgrims, but none was as important as the Ka'ba. All the other sanctuaries were dedicated to a specific local deity, but the Ka'ba was a universal shrine that was believed to house all the deities of pre-Islamic Arabia. This undoubtedly meant that despite the long detour it required, all the merchants of Arabia would have felt a serious spiritual obligation to visit Mecca. This probably also means that even if the Arabic sources exaggerate the level of *transregional* trade that was being carried on in Mecca, considerable *regional* trade was undoubtedly occurring, and all of it was wholly dependent on the Ka'ba. This helps explain why Muhammad, on his triumphal return to Mecca from Medina in 630, retained the pre-Islamic sanctuary of the Ka'ba for both spiritual and commercial reasons and established the hajj as one of the Five Pillars of Islam. This decision has ensured Mecca's centrality to the Islamic faith ever since and also meant that the city has continued to depend on economic activity that is, still to this day, almost totally generated by the annual pilgrimage of the hajj.

Source: Reza Aslan. *No God but God.* New York, 2005.

compiled these written versions of Muhammad's revelations and issued them as the **Quran** ("recitation"), the holy book of Islam. A work of magnificent poetry, the Quran communicates in powerful and moving terms Muhammad's understanding of Allah and his relation to the world, and it serves as the definitive authority for Islamic religious doctrine and social organization.

Apart from the Quran, several other sources have provided moral and religious guidance for the Islamic community. Most important after the Quran are traditions known as *hadith,* which include sayings attributed to Muhammad and accounts of the prophet's deeds. Several collections of *hadith* written by leading Islamic intellectuals appeared between the ninth and eleventh centuries C.E., and Muslim scholars have often taken them as guides for interpretation of the Quran. Regarded as less authoritative than the Quran and the *hadith,* but still important as inspirations for Islamic thought, were various additional early works describing social and legal customs, biographies of Muhammad, and pious commentaries on the Quran.

Muhammad's Migration to Medina

Conflict at Mecca The growing popularity of Muhammad's preaching brought him into conflict with the ruling elites at **Mecca.** Conflict centered on religious issues. Muhammad's insistence that Allah was the only divine power in the universe struck many polytheistic Arabs as offensive and dangerous as well because it disparaged long-recognized deities and spirits thought to wield influence over human affairs. The tensions also had a personal dimension. Mecca's ruling elites, who were also the city's wealthiest merchants, took it as a personal affront and a threat to their position when Muhammad denounced greed as moral wickedness that Allah would punish.

Muhammad's attack on idolatry also represented an economic threat to those who owned and profited from the many shrines to deities that attracted merchants and pilgrims to Mecca. The best known of those shrines was a large black rock long considered to be the dwelling of a powerful deity. Housed in a cube-shaped building known as the **Ka'ba,** it drew worshipers from all over Arabia and brought considerable wealth to Mecca. As Muhammad relentlessly condemned the idolatry officially promoted at the Ka'ba and other shrines, the ruling elites of Mecca began to persecute the prophet and his followers.

The *Hijra* The pressure became so great that some of Muhammad's followers fled to Abyssinia (modern Ethiopia). Muhammad himself remained in Mecca until 622 C.E., when he too fled and joined a group of his followers in Yathrib, a rival trading city 345 kilometers (214 miles) north of Mecca. Muslims called their new home **Medina** ("the city," meaning

"the city of the prophet"). Known as the *hijra* ("migration"), Muhammad's move to Medina serves as the starting point of the official Islamic calendar.

The *Umma* In Mecca, Muhammad had lived within the established political framework and concentrated on the moral and religious dimensions of his faith. In Medina he found himself at the head of a small but growing society in exile that needed guidance in practical as well as spiritual affairs. He organized his followers into a cohesive community called the *umma* ("community of the faithful") and provided it with a comprehensive legal and social code. He led this community both in daily prayers to Allah and in battle with enemies at Medina, Mecca, and other places. He looked after the economic welfare of the *umma*—sometimes by organizing commercial ventures and sometimes by launching raids against caravans from Mecca. Remembering the difficult days of his youth, he provided relief for widows, orphans, and the poor, and he made almsgiving a prime moral virtue.

The "Seal of the Prophets" Muhammad's understanding of his religious mission expanded during his years at Medina. He began to refer to himself as a prophet, indeed as the "seal of the prophets"—the final prophet through whom Allah would reveal his message to humankind. Muhammad accepted the authority of earlier Jewish and Christian prophets, including Abraham, Moses, and Jesus, and he held the Hebrew scriptures and the Christian New Testament in high esteem. He also accepted his predecessors' monotheism: Allah was the same omnipotent, omniscient, omnipresent, and exclusive deity as the Jews' Yahweh and the Christians' God. Muhammad taught, however, that the message entrusted to him offered a more complete revelation of Allah and his will than Judaism and Christianity had made available. Thus, while at Medina, Muhammad came to see himself consciously as Allah's final prophet: not simply as a devout man who explained his spiritual insights to a small circle of family and friends, but as the messenger who communicated Allah's wishes and his plan for the world to all humankind.

The Establishment of Islam in Arabia

Muhammad's Return to Mecca Throughout their sojourn at Medina, Muhammad and his followers planned ultimately to return to Mecca, which was both their home and the leading city of Arabia. In 629 C.E. they arranged with the authorities to participate in the annual pilgrimage to the Ka'ba, but they were not content with a short visit. In 630 they attacked Mecca and conquered the city. They forced the elites to adopt Muhammad's faith, and they imposed a government dedicated to Allah. They also destroyed the pagan shrines and replaced them with mosques, buildings that sought to instill a sense of sacredness and community where Muslims gathered for prayers. Only the Ka'ba escaped their efforts to cleanse Mecca of pagan monuments.

Quran (koo-RAHN)
Ka'ba (KAH-buh)

SOURCES FROM THE PAST

The Quran on Allah and His Expectations of Humankind

The foundation of the Islamic faith is the understanding of Allah, his nature, and his plan for the world as outlined in the Quran. Through his visions Muhammad came to understand Allah as the one and only god, the creator and sustainer of the world in the manner of the Jews' Yahweh and the Christians' God. Those who rejected Allah and his message would suffer eternal punishment, but those who recognized and obeyed him would receive his mercy and secure his blessings.

In the name of Allah, most benevolent, ever-merciful.
All praise be to Allah,
Lord of all the worlds,
Most beneficent, ever-merciful,
King of the Day of Judgement.
You alone we worship, and to You
alone turn for help.
Guide us (O Lord) to the path that is straight,
The path of those You have blessed,
Not of those who have earned Your anger,
nor those who have gone astray. . . .

Verily men and women who have come to submission,
men and women who are believers,
men and women who are devout,
truthful men and women,
men and women with endurance,
men and women who are modest,
men and women who give alms,
men and women who observe fasting,
men and women who guard their private parts,
and those men and women who remember God a great deal,
for them God has forgiveness and a great reward.
No believing men and women have any choice in a matter
after God and His Apostle [i.e., Muhammad] have decided it.
Whoever disobeys God and His Apostle
has clearly lost the way and gone astray. . . .
O you who believe, remember God a great deal,
And sing His praises morning and evening.
It is He who sends His blessings on you,
as (do) His angels, that He may lead you out of darkness into light,
for He is benevolent to the believers. . . .

> How many of the Five Pillars of Islam do you see references to up to this point in the passage?

I call to witness
the early hours of the morning,
And the night when dark and still,
Your Lord has neither left you,
nor despises you.
What is to come is better for you
than what has gone before;
For your Lord will certainly give you,
and you will be content.
Did He not find you an orphan

(Continued)

and take care of you?
Did He not find you poor
and enrich you?
So do not oppress the orphan,
And do not drive
the beggar away,
And keep recounting the favours of your Lord. . . .

Say: "He is God
the one the most unique,
God the immanently indispensable.
He has begotten no one,
and is begotten of none.
There is no one comparable to Him."

For Further Reflection

■ What similarities and differences do you see between the teachings contained in the Quran and those of other leaders we have considered in previous chapters including Zoroaster, the Buddha and Jesus?

■ Do you see any gender distinctions in these passages? That is, does Allah seem to have different expectations for men and women, or similar?

■ Based on these passages, what kind of god is Allah for his believers? Is he an angry or a caring god?

Source: Al-Qur'an: A Contemporary Translation. Trans. by Ahmed Ali. Princeton: Princeton University Press, 1984, pp. 11, 358, 359, 540, 559.

Muhammad and his followers denied that the Ka'ba was the home of a deity, but they preserved the black rock and its housing as a symbol of Mecca's greatness. They allowed only the faithful to approach the shrine, and in 632 Muhammad himself led the first Islamic pilgrimage to the Ka'ba, thus establishing the hajj as an example for all devout Muslims. Building on the conquest of Mecca, Muhammad and his followers launched campaigns against other towns and bedouin clans, and by the time of the prophet's death in 632, shortly after his hajj, they had brought most of Arabia under their control.

The Five Pillars of Islam Muhammad's personal leadership decisively shaped the values and the development of the Islamic community. The foundation of Islam as elaborated by Muhammad consists of obligations known as the **Five Pillars of Islam:** (1) Muslims must acknowledge Allah as the only god and Muhammad as his prophet. (2) They must pray to Allah daily while facing Mecca. (3) They must observe a fast during the daylight hours of the month of Ramadan. (4) They must contribute alms for the relief of the weak and poor. (5) And, in honor of Muhammad's visits to Mecca in 629 and 632, those who are physically and financially able must undertake the hajj and make at least one pilgrimage to Mecca. During the centuries since its appearance, Islam has generated many schools and sects, each with its own particular legal, social, and doctrinal features. The Five Pillars of Islam, however,

constitute a simple but powerful framework that has bound the *umma* into a cohesive community.

Jihad Some Muslims, though by no means all, have taken jihad as an additional obligation. The term *jihad* literally means "struggle," and Muslims have understood its imperatives in various ways. In one sense, jihad imposes spiritual and moral obligations on Muslims by requiring them to combat vice and evil. In another sense, jihad calls on Muslims to struggle against ignorance and unbelief by spreading the word of Islam and seeking converts to the faith. In some circumstances, jihad also involves physical struggle, obliging Muslims to take up the sword and wage war against unbelievers who threaten Islam.

Islamic Law: The *Sharia* Beyond the general obligations prescribed by the Five Pillars, Islamic holy law, known as the *sharia,* emerged during the centuries after Muhammad and offered detailed guidance on proper behavior in almost every aspect of life. Elaborated by jurists and legal scholars, the sharia drew its inspiration especially from the Quran and the early historical accounts of Muhammad's life and teachings. It offered precise guidance on matters as diverse as marriage and family life, inheritance, slavery, business and commercial relationships, political authority in the *dar al-Islam,* and crime. Like many law codes in history, the sharia tended to be interpreted differently by different Islamic societies, but in all cases, the sharia evolved to become something more than a religious doctrine: it developed into a way of life complete with social and ethical values derived from Islamic religious principles.

sharia (shah-REE-ah)

A watercolor painting from sixteenth-century Iran depicts a caravan of pilgrims traveling to Mecca while making the hajj. In what ways did the hajj facilitate social and business relationships?

Album/Alamy Stock Photo

THE EXPANSION OF ISLAM

After Muhammad's death the Islamic community might well have unraveled and disappeared. Muhammad had made no provision for a successor, and there was serious division within the *umma* concerning the selection of a new leader. Many of the towns and bedouin clans that had recently accepted Islam took the opportunity of Muhammad's death to renounce the fledgling religion, reassert their independence, and break free from Mecca's control. Within a short time, however, the many different cultural and political groups that came to constitute the Islamic community throughout Afro-Eurasia had embarked on a stunningly successful round of military expansion

that extended its political and cultural influence far beyond the boundaries of Arabia. Those conquests laid the foundation for the rapid growth of Islamic society.

The Early Caliphs and the Umayyad Dynasty

The Caliph Because Muhammad was the "seal of the prophets," it was inconceivable that another prophet should succeed him. Shortly after Muhammad's death his advisers selected **Abu Bakr,** a genial man who was one of the prophet's closest friends and most devoted disciples, to serve as *caliph* ("deputy"). Thus Abu Bakr and later caliphs led the *umma* not as prophets but as lieutenants or substitutes for Muhammad. Abu Bakr became head of state for the Islamic community as well as chief judge, religious leader, and military commander. Under the caliph's leadership, the *umma* went on the offensive against the towns and bedouin clans that had renounced Islam after Muhammad's death, and within a year it had compelled them to recognize Islam and the rule of the caliph.

The Shia Immediately after the death of Muhammad the umma faced a crisis over who would succeed the prophet. These disagreements led to the emergence of the **Shia** sect, the most important and enduring of all the alternatives to the form of Islam observed by the majority of Muslims, known as **Sunni** Islam. The Shia sect originated as a party supporting the appointment of Ali and his descendants as caliphs. A cousin and son-in-law of Muhammad, Ali was a candidate for caliph when the prophet died, but support for Abu Bakr was stronger. Ali served briefly as the fourth caliph (656–661 C.E.), but his enemies assassinated him while he was praying in a mosque, killed many of his relatives, and imposed their own candidate as caliph. Partisans of Ali then organized the Shia ("party"), furiously resisted the victorious faction, and struggled to return the caliphate to the line of Ali. Although persecuted, the Shia survived and strengthened its identity by adopting doctrines and rituals distinct from those of the Sunnis ("traditionalists"), who accepted the legitimacy of the early caliphs. Shia partisans, for example, observed holy days in honor of their leaders and martyrs to their cause, and they taught that descendants of Ali were infallible, sinless, and divinely appointed to rule the Islamic community. Shia Muslims also advanced interpretations of the Quran that support the party's views, and the Shia itself has often served as a source of support for those who oppose the policies of Sunni leaders.

The Expansion of Islam During the century after Muhammad's death, Islamic armies ranged well beyond the boundaries of Arabia, carrying their religion and their authority

Abu Bakr (ah-BOO BAHK-uhr)
caliph (KHA-leef)
Shia (SHEE-ah)
Sunni (SOON-nee)

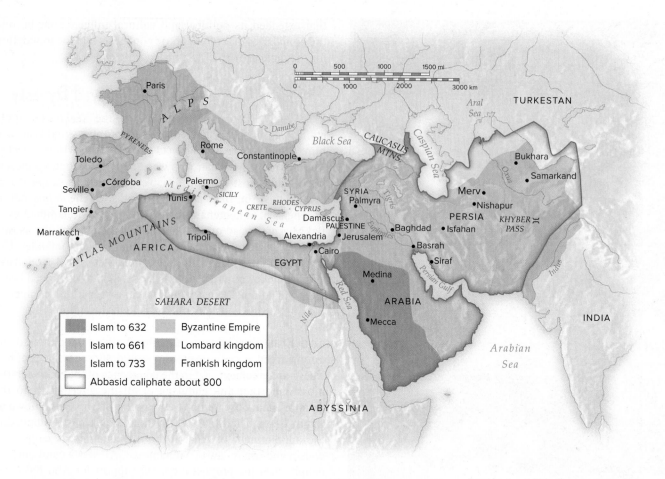

MAP 14.1   The expansion of Islam, 632–733 C.E.

During the seventh and eighth centuries, the new faith of Islam expanded rapidly and dramatically beyond its Arabian homeland.

What environmental, political, and social circumstances facilitated the rapid spread of the new faith? What were the cultural and political effects of the expansion of Islam?

to Byzantine and Sasanian territories and beyond. Although much less powerful than either the Byzantine Empire or the Sasanian empire, Muslim armies fought with particular effectiveness because their leaders had forged previously competing tribal groups into a powerful state unified by their allegiance to Islam. Moreover, the well-organized and superbly led Muslim armies attacked at a moment when the Byzantine and Sasanian empires were exhausted from perennial conflicts with each other and when they also faced internal uprisings by overtaxed peasants and oppressed ethnic or religious minorities. Between 633 and 637 C.E., taking advantage of those difficulties, Muslim forces seized Byzantine Syria and Palestine and took most of Mesopotamia from the Sasanians. During the 640s they conquered Byzantine Egypt and north Africa. In 651 they toppled the Sasanian dynasty and incorporated Persia into their expanding empire. In 711 they conquered the Hindu kingdom of Sind in northwestern India. Between

711 and 718 they extended their authority to northwest Africa and crossed the Strait of Gibraltar, conquering most of the Iberian peninsula and threatening the Frankish kingdom in Gaul. By the mid-eighth century an immense Islamic Empire ruled lands from India and the central Asian steppe lands in the east to northwest Africa and Iberia in the west.

During this rapid expansion the empire's rulers encountered difficult problems of governance and administration. One problem had to do with the selection of caliphs. During the early decades after Muhammad's death, leaders of the most powerful Arab clans negotiated among themselves and appointed the first four caliphs. Political ambitions, personal differences, and clan loyalties complicated their deliberations, however, and disputes soon led to the rise of factions and parties within the Islamic community.

The Umayyad Dynasty After the assassination of Ali, the establishment of the **Umayyad dynasty** (661–750 C.E.) solved the problem of succession, at least temporarily. The Umayyads ranked among the most prominent of the Meccan

Umayyad (oo-MEYE-ahd)

The early expansion of Islam was achieved largely through warfare. This illustration from an Arabic manuscript of the thirteenth century depicts a battle between Muhammad's cousin Ali and his adversaries.

Iberfoto/SuperStock

merchant clans, and their reputation and network of alliances helped them bring stability to the Islamic community. Despite their association with Mecca, the Umayyads established their capital at Damascus, a thriving commercial city in Syria, whose central location enabled them to maintain better communication with the vast and still-expanding Islamic Empire.

Although the Umayyads' dynasty solved the problem of succession, their tightly centralized rule and the favor they showed to their fellow Arabs generated an administrative problem. The Umayyads ruled the *dar al-Islam* as conquerors, and

their policies reflected the interests of the Arab military aristocracy. The Umayyads appointed members of this elite as governors and administrators of conquered lands, and they distributed the wealth that they extracted among this privileged class.

Policy toward Conquered Peoples This policy contributed to high morale among Arab conquerors, but it caused severe discontent among the scores of ethnic and religious groups conquered by the Umayyad empire. Apart from Muslims, the empire included Christians, Jews, Zoroastrians, and Buddhists. In addition to Arabs and bedouin, it included Indians, Persians, Mesopotamians, Greeks, Egyptians, and nomadic Berbers in north Africa. The Arabs mostly allowed conquered peoples to observe their own religions—particularly Christians and Jews—but they levied a special head tax, called the *jizya,* on those who did not convert to Islam. Even those who converted did not enjoy access to wealth and positions of authority, which the Umayyads reserved almost exclusively for members of the Arab military aristocracy. This caused deep resentment among conquered peoples and led to restiveness against Umayyad rule.

Umayyad Decline Beginning in the early eighth century, the Umayyad caliphs became alienated even from other Arabs. They devoted themselves increasingly to luxurious living rather than to competent leadership of the *umma,* and they scandalized devout Muslims by their casual attitudes toward Islamic doctrine and morality. By midcentury the Umayyad caliphs faced not only the resistance of the Shia, whose members continued to promote descendants of Ali for caliph, but also the discontent of conquered peoples throughout their empire and even the disillusionment of Muslim Arab military leaders.

The Abbasid Dynasty

Abu al-Abbas Rebellion in Persia brought the Umayyad dynasty to an end. The chief leader of the rebellion was Abu al-Abbas, a descendant of Muhammad's uncle. Although he was a Sunni Arab, Abu al-Abbas allied readily with Shias and with Muslims who were not Arabs, such as converts to Islam from southwest Asia. Particularly prominent among his supporters were Persian converts who resented the preference shown by the Umayyads to Arab Muslims. During the 740s Abu al-Abbas's party rejected Umayyad authority and seized control of Persia and Mesopotamia. In 750 his army shattered Umayyad forces in a huge battle. Afterward, Abu al-Abbas invited the remaining members of the Umayyad clan to a banquet under the pretext of reconciling their differences. During the festivities his troops arrested the Umayyads and slaughtered them, effectively bringing to an end the caliphate. Abu al-Abbas then founded the **Abbasid dynasty**, which was the principal source of authority in the *dar al-Islam* until the Mongols toppled it in 1258 C.E.

***

Abbasid (ah-BAH-sihd)

The Abbasid Dynasty The Abbasid dynasty differed considerably from the Umayyad. For one thing, the Abbasid state was far more cosmopolitan than its predecessor. Even though they sprang from the ranks of conquering Arabs, Abbasid rulers did not show special favor to the Arab military aristocracy. Arabs continued to play a large role in government, but Persians, Egyptians, Mesopotamians, and others also rose to positions of wealth and power.

The Abbasid dynasty differed from the Umayyad also in that it was not a conquering dynasty. The Abbasids sparred intermittently with the Byzantine Empire, they clashed frequently with nomadic peoples from central Asia, and in 751 they defeated a Chinese army at Talas River near Samarkand. The battle of Talas River was exceptionally important: it ended the expansion of China's Tang dynasty into central Asia (discussed in chapter 13), and it opened the door for the spread of Islam among Turkish peoples. Only marginally, however, did the Abbasids expand their empire by conquest. The *dar al-Islam* as a whole continued to grow during the Abbasid era, but the caliphs had little to do with the expansion. During the ninth and early tenth centuries, for example, largely autonomous Islamic forces from distant Tunisia mounted naval expeditions throughout the Mediterranean, conquering Crete, Sicily, and the Balearic Islands while seizing territories also in Cyprus, Rhodes, Sardinia, Corsica, southern Italy, and southern France. Meanwhile, Muslim merchants introduced Islam to southern India and sub-Saharan Africa (see chapter 18).

Abbasid Administration Instead of conquering new lands, the Abbasids largely contented themselves with administering the empire they inherited. Fashioning a government that could administer a sprawling realm with scores of linguistic, ethnic, and cultural groups was a considerable challenge. Before Muhammad, Arabs had no governments larger than city-states, nor did the Quran offer guidance for the administration of a huge empire. The Umayyad practice of allowing the Arab aristocracy to exploit subject lands and peoples had proven to be a failure. Thus Abu al-Abbas and his successors turned to long-standing Mesopotamian and Persian techniques of administration whereby rulers devised policies, built capital cities to oversee affairs, and organized their territories through regional governors and bureaucracies.

Baghdad Central authority emanated from the Abbasid court at Baghdad (capital of modern Iraq), a magnificent new city that the early Abbasid caliphs constructed near the Sasanid capital of Ctesiphon. By building this new center of government to replace the Umayyad capital at Damascus, the Abbasids associated themselves with the cosmopolitan environment of Mesopotamia. Baghdad was a round city protected by three round walls. At the heart of the city was the caliph's green-domed palace, from which instructions flowed to the distant reaches of the Abbasid realm. In the provinces, governors represented the caliph and implemented his political and financial policies.

Learned officials known as *ulama* ("people with religious knowledge") and *qadis* ("judges") set moral standards in local communities and resolved disputes. *Ulama* and *qadis* were not priests—Islam does not recognize priests as a distinct class of religious specialists—but they had a formal education that emphasized study of the Quran and the sharia. *Ulama* were pious scholars who sought to develop public policy in accordance with the Quran and sharia. *Qadis* heard cases at law and rendered decisions based on the Quran and sharia. Because of their moral authority, *ulama* and *qadis* became extremely influential officials who helped to ensure widespread observance of Islamic values. Apart from provincial governors, *ulama,* and *qadis,* the Abbasid caliphs kept a standing army, and they established bureaucratic ministries in charge of taxation, finance, coinage, and postal services. They also maintained the magnificent network of roads that the Islamic Empire inherited from the Sasanids.

Harun al-Rashid The high point of the Abbasid dynasty came during the reign of the caliph **Harun al-Rashid** (786–809 C.E.). By the late eighth century, Abbasid authority had lost some of its force in provinces distant from Baghdad, but it remained strong enough to bring reliable tax revenues from most parts of the empire. Flush with wealth, Baghdad became a center of banking, commerce, crafts, and industrial production, a metropolis with a population of several hundred thousand people. According to stories from his time, Harun al-Rashid provided liberal support for artists and writers, bestowed lavish and luxurious gifts on his favorites, and distributed money to the poor and the common classes by tossing coins into the streets of Baghdad. Once, he sent an elephant and a collection of rich presents as gifts to his contemporary Charlemagne, who ruled the Carolingian empire of western Europe.

Harun al-Rashid receiving a delegation sent by Charlemagne at his court in Baghdad. 1864 painting by Julius Köckert.
Historic Collection/Alamy Stock Photo

Abbasid Decline Soon after Harun al-Rashid's reign, the Abbasid empire entered a period of decline. Civil war between Harun's sons seriously damaged Abbasid authority, and disputes over succession rights became a recurring problem for the dynasty. Provincial governors took advantage of disorder in the ruling house by acting independently of the caliphs: instead of implementing imperial policies and delivering taxes to Baghdad, they built up local bases of power and in some cases actually seceded from the Abbasid empire. Meanwhile, popular uprisings and peasant rebellions, which often enjoyed the support of dissenting sects and heretical movements, further weakened the empire.

As a result of those difficulties, the Abbasid caliphs became mere figureheads long before the Mongols extinguished the dynasty in 1258. In 945, members of a Persian noble family seized control of Baghdad and established their clan as the power behind the Abbasid throne. Later, imperial authorities in Baghdad fell under the control of the Seljuq Turks, a nomadic people from central Asia who also invaded the Byzantine Empire. In response to rebellions mounted by peasants and provincial governors, authorities in Baghdad allied with the Seljuqs, who began to enter the Abbasid realm and convert to Islam about the mid-tenth century. By the mideleventh century the Seljuqs effectively controlled the Abbasid empire. During the 1050s they took possession of Baghdad, and during the following decades they extended their authority to Syria, Palestine, and Anatolia. They retained Abbasid caliphs as nominal sovereigns, but for two centuries, until the arrival of the Mongols, the Seljuq *sultan* ("chieftain" or "ruler") was the true source of power in the Abbasid empire.

ECONOMY AND SOCIETY OF THE EARLY ISLAMIC WORLD

In the *dar al-Islam,* as in other agricultural societies, peasants tilled the land as their ancestors had done for centuries before them, while manufacturers and merchants supported a thriving urban economy. Here, as in other lands, the creation of large empires had dramatic economic implications. The Umayyad and Abbasid empires created a zone of trade, exchange, and communication stretching from India to Iberia. Commerce throughout this zone served as a vigorous economic stimulus for both the countryside and the cities of the early Islamic world.

New Crops, Agricultural Experimentation, and Urban Growth

The Spread of Food and Industrial Crops As soldiers, administrators, diplomats, and merchants traveled throughout the *dar al-Islam,* they encountered plants, animals, and agricultural techniques peculiar to the empire's various regions. They often introduced particularly useful crops to other regions. The most important of the transplants traveled west from

In a thirteenth-century manuscript illustration, a fictional Muslim traveler passes a lively agricultural village. Sheep, goats, chickens, and date palms figure prominently in the local economy.
DEA/J.E. Bulloz/Getty Images

India to Persia; southwest Asia; Arabia; Egypt; north Africa; Spain; and the Mediterranean islands of Cyprus, Crete, Sicily, and Sardinia. They included staple crops such as sugarcane, rice, and new varieties of sorghum and wheat; vegetables such as spinach, artichokes, and eggplants; fruits such as oranges, lemons, limes, bananas, coconuts, watermelons, and mangoes; and industrial crops such as cotton, indigo, and henna.

Effects of New Crops The introduction of these crops into the western regions of the Islamic world had wide-ranging effects. New food crops led to a richer and more varied diet. They also increased quantities of food available because they enabled cultivators to extend the growing season. In much of the Islamic world, summers are so hot and dry that cultivators traditionally left their fields fallow during that season. Most of the transplanted crops grew well in high heat, however, so cultivators in southwest Asia, north Africa, and other hot zones could till their lands year-round. The result was a dramatic increase in food supplies.

Some new crops had industrial uses. The most important of these was cotton, which became the basis for a thriving textile industry throughout much of the Islamic world. Indigo and henna yielded dyes that textile manufacturers used in large quantities.

Agricultural Experimentation Travel and communication in the *dar al-Islam* also encouraged experimentation with agricultural methods. Cultivators paid close attention to methods of irrigation, fertilization, crop rotation, and the like, and they outlined their findings in hundreds of agricultural manuals. Copies of these works survive in numerous manuscripts that circulated widely throughout the Islamic world. The combined effect of new crops and improved techniques was a far more productive agricultural economy, which in turn supported vigorous economic growth throughout the *dar al-Islam.*

Urban Growth Increased agricultural production contributed to the rapid growth of cities in all parts of the Islamic world from India to Spain. Delhi, Samarkand, Bukhara, Merv, Nishapur, Isfahan, Basra, Baghdad, Damascus, Jerusalem, Cairo, Alexandria, Palermo, Tunis, Tangier, Córdoba, and Toledo were all bustling cities, some with populations of several hundred thousand people. All these cities had flourishing markets supporting thousands of artisans, craftsmen, and merchants. Most of them were also important centers of

industrial production, particularly of textiles, pottery, glassware, leather, iron, and steel.

One new industry appeared in Islamic cities during the Abbasid era: paper manufacture. Chinese craftsmen had made paper since the first century C.E., but their technology did not spread far beyond China until the eighth century. Paper was cheaper and easier to use than writing materials such as vellum sheets made from calfskin, and it soon became popular throughout the Islamic world. Paper facilitated the keeping of administrative and commercial records, and it made possible the dissemination of books and treatises in larger quantities than ever before. By the tenth century, mills produced paper in Persia, Mesopotamia, Arabia, Egypt, and Spain, and the industry soon spread to western Europe.

The Formation of a Hemispheric Trading Zone

From its earliest days Islamic society drew much of its prosperity from commerce. Muhammad himself was a merchant, and he held merchants in high esteem. According to early accounts of his life, Muhammad once said that honest merchants would stand alongside martyrs to the faith on the day of judgment. By the time of the Abbasid caliphate, elaborate trade networks linked all the regions of the Islamic world and joined it to a larger, hemispheric economy.

Overland Trade When they overran the Sasanian empire, Muslim conquerors brought the prosperous trading cities of central Asia under control of the expanding *dar al-Islam.* Merv, Nishapur, Bukhara, and Samarkand were long-established

An artist's impression of a caravanserai, which is a Persian compound word meaning a place of shelter for travelers. Caravanserais were large, single-building structures, generally without roofs but with many places to house and feed merchants and their animals. What would the atmosphere have been like inside these caravanserais, where so many intense conversations took place between merchants and pilgrims of so many cultures and faiths?
DEA/G. Dagli Orti/Age Fotostock

commercial centers, and they made it possible for Muslim merchants to trade over a revived Silk Roads network extending from China in the east to the Mediterranean in the west. Thus Muslim merchants were able to take advantage of the extensive road networks originally built during the ancient era by imperial authorities in India, Persia, and the Mediterranean basin. Umayyad and Abbasid rulers maintained the roads that they inherited because they provided splendid routes for military forces and administrative officials traveling through the *dar al-Islam*. But those same roads also made excellent highways for merchants as well as missionaries and pilgrims. Travel along the roads could be remarkably speedy and efficient. After the tenth century, for example, the Muslim rulers of Egypt regularly imported ice from the mountains of Syria to their palace in Cairo. Even during the summer months, they received five camel loads of ice weekly to cool their food and drink.

Camels and Caravans Overland trade traveled mostly by camel caravan. Although they can be difficult to manage, camels endure the rigors of desert travel much better than oxen, horses, or donkeys. Moreover, when fitted with a well-designed saddle, camels can carry heavy loads. During the early centuries C.E., the manufacture of camel saddles spread throughout Arabia, north Africa, southwest Asia, and central Asia, and camels became the favored beasts of burden in deserts and other dry regions. As camel transport became more common, the major cities of the Islamic world and central Asia built and maintained caravanserais—inns offering lodging for caravan merchants as well as food, water, and care for their animals.

Maritime Trade Meanwhile, innovations in nautical technology contributed to a steadily increasing volume of maritime trade in the Red Sea, Persian Gulf, Arabian Sea, and Indian Ocean. Arab and Persian mariners borrowed the compass from its Chinese inventors and used it to guide them on the high seas. From southeast Asian and Indian mariners, they borrowed the lateen sail, a triangular sail that increased a ship's maneuverability. From the Hellenistic Mediterranean they borrowed the astrolabe, an instrument that enabled them to calculate latitude.

Thus equipped, Arab and Persian mariners ventured throughout the Indian Ocean basin, calling at ports from southern China to southeast Asia, Ceylon, India, Persia, Arabia, and the eastern coast of Africa. The twelfth-century Persian merchant Ramisht of Siraf (a flourishing port city on the Persian Gulf) amassed a huge fortune from long-distance trading ventures. One of Ramisht's clerks once returned to Siraf from a commercial voyage to China with a cargo worth half a million dinars—gold coins that were the standard currency in the Islamic world. Ramisht himself was one of the wealthiest men of his age, and he spent much of his fortune on pious causes. He outfitted the Ka'ba with a Chinese silk cover that reportedly cost him eighteen thousand dinars, and he also founded a hospital and a religious sanctuary in Mecca.

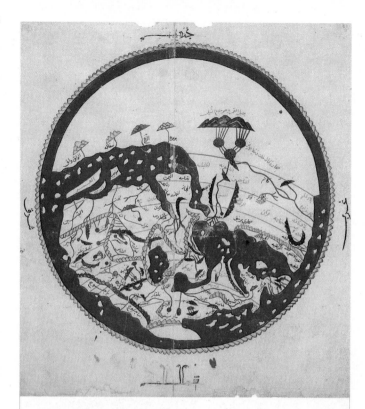

A map produced in the eleventh century by the Arab geographer al-Idrisi shows the lands known and reported by Muslim merchants and travelers. Note that, in accordance with Muslim cartographic convention, this map places south at the top and north at the bottom.
World History Archive/Alamy Stock Photo

Banks Banking also stimulated the commercial economy of the Islamic world. Banks had operated since antiquity, but Islamic banks of the Abbasid period conducted business on a much larger scale and provided a more extensive range of services than did their predecessors. They not only lent money to entrepreneurs but also served as brokers for investments and exchanged different currencies. They established multiple branches that honored letters of credit known as *sakk*—the root of the modern word *check*—drawn on the parent bank. Thus merchants could draw letters of credit in one city and cash them in another, and they could settle accounts with distant business partners without having to deal in cash.

The Organization of Trade Trade benefited also from techniques of business organization. Like banking, these techniques had precedents in ancient Mediterranean society, but increasing volumes of trade enabled entrepreneurs to refine their methods of organization. Furthermore, Islamic law provided security for entrepreneurs by explicitly recognizing certain forms of business organization. Usually, Islamic businessmen preferred not to embark on solo ventures because

١٠٩

In this thirteenth-century manuscript illustration, merchants at a slave market in southern Arabia deal in black slaves captured in sub-Saharan Africa. Slaves traded in Islamic markets also came from Russia and eastern Europe.
akg-images/Newscom

an individual could face financial ruin if an entire cargo of commodities fell prey to pirates or went down with a ship that sank in a storm. Instead, like their counterparts in other contemporary societies, Abbasid entrepreneurs often pooled their resources in group investments. If several individuals invested in several cargoes, they could distribute their risks and more easily absorb losses. Furthermore, if several groups of investors rented cargo space on several different ships, they spread their risks even more. Entrepreneurs entered into a variety of legally recognized joint endeavors during the Abbasid caliphate. Some involved simply the investment of money in an enterprise, whereas others called for some or all of the partners to play active roles in their business ventures.

As a result of improved transportation, expanded banking services, and refined techniques of business organization, long-distance trade surged in the early Islamic world. Muslim merchants dealt in silk and ceramics from China, spices and aromatics from India and southeast Asia, and jewelry and fine textiles from the Byzantine Empire. Merchants also ventured beyond settled societies in China, India, and the Mediterranean basin to distant lands that previously had not engaged systematically in long-distance trade. They crossed the Sahara desert by camel caravan to trade salt, steel, copper, and glass for gold and slaves from the kingdoms of west Africa. They visited the coastal regions of east Africa, where they obtained slaves and exotic local commodities such as animal skins. They engaged in trade with Russia and Scandinavia by way of the Dnieper and Volga rivers and obtained high-value commodities such as animal skins, furs, honey, amber, and slaves as well as bulk goods such as timber and livestock. The vigorous economy of the Abbasid empire thus helped to establish networks of communication and exchange throughout much of the eastern hemisphere.

Al-Andalus The prosperity of Islamic Spain, known as **al-Andalus,** illustrates the far-reaching effects of long-distance trade during the Abbasid era. Most of the Iberian peninsula had fallen into the hands of Muslim Berber conquerors from north Africa during the early eighth century. The governors of al-Andalus were Umayyads who refused to recognize the Abbasid dynasty, and beginning in the tenth century they styled themselves caliphs in their own right rather than governors subject to Abbasid authority. Despite political and diplomatic tensions, al-Andalus participated actively in the commercial life of the larger Islamic world. The merchant-scholar al-Marwani of Córdoba, for example, made his hajj in 908 and then traveled to Iraq and India on commercial ventures. His profits amounted to thirty thousand dinars—all of which he lost in a shipwreck during his return home.

Imported crops increased the supply of food and enriched the diet of al-Andalus, enabling merchants and manufacturers to conduct thriving businesses in cities such as Córdoba, Toledo, and Seville. Ceramics, painted tiles, lead crystal, and gold jewelry from al-Andalus enjoyed a reputation for excellence and helped pay for imported goods and the building of a magnificent capital city at Córdoba. During the tenth century, Córdoba had more than 16 kilometers (10 miles) of lighted public roads as well as free Islamic schools, a gargantuan mosque, and a splendid library with four hundred thousand volumes.

The Changing Status of Women

A patriarchal society had emerged in Arabia long before Muhammad's time, but Arab women enjoyed rights not accorded to women in many other lands. They could legally inherit property, divorce husbands on their own initiative, and engage in business ventures. Khadija, the first of Muhammad's wives, managed a successful commercial business.

In some respects the Quran enhanced the security of women in Arabian society. It outlawed female infanticide, and it provided that dowries went directly to brides rather

al-Andalus (ahl ahn-duh-LUHS)

Interior of the mosque at Córdoba, originally built in the late eighth century and enlarged during the ninth and tenth centuries. One of the largest structures in the *dar al-Islam,* the mosque rests on 850 columns and features nineteen aisles.

Fernando Fernandez/age fotostock

than to their husbands and male guardians. It portrayed women not as the property of male guardians but as honorable individuals, equal to men before Allah, with their own rights and needs. Muhammad's kindness and generosity toward his wives, as related in early accounts of the prophet's life, also served as an example that may have improved the lives of Muslim women.

The Quran and Women For the most part, however, the Quran—and later the sharia as well—reinforced male dominance. The Quran and Islamic holy law recognized descent through the male line, and to guarantee proper inheritance, they placed a high premium on genealogical purity. To ensure the legitimacy of heirs, they subjected the social and sexual

lives of women to the strict control of male guardians—fathers, brothers, and husbands. Though teaching that men should treat women with sensitivity and respect, the Quran and the sharia permitted men to take up to four wives, whereas women could have only one husband. The Quran and the sharia thus provided a religious and legal foundation for a decisively patriarchal society.

Veiling of Women When Islam expanded into the Byzantine and Sasanian empires, it encountered strong patriarchal traditions, and Muslims readily adopted long-standing customs such as the veiling of women. Social and family pressures had induced upper-class urban women to veil themselves in Mesopotamia as early as the thirteenth century B.C.E., and long before Muhammad the practice of veiling had spread to Persia and the eastern Mediterranean. As a sign of modesty, upper-class urban women covered their faces and ventured outside their homes only in the company of servants or chaperones so as to discourage the attention of men. When Muslim Arabs conquered Mesopotamia, Persia, and eastern Mediterranean lands, they adopted the veiling of women.

The Quran served as the preeminent source of authority in the world of Islam, and it provided specific rights for Muslim women. Over the centuries, however, jurists and legal scholars interpreted the Quran in ways that progressively limited those rights and placed women increasingly under the control of male guardians. To a large extent the increased emphasis on male authority in Islamic law reflected the influence of the strongly hierarchical and patriarchal societies of Mesopotamia, Persia, and eastern Mediterranean lands as Islam developed from a local faith to a large-scale complex society.

ISLAMIC VALUES AND CULTURAL EXCHANGES

Since the seventh century C.E., the Quran has served as the cornerstone of Islamic society. Arising from a rich tradition of bedouin poetry and song, the Quran established Arabic as a flexible and powerful medium of communication. Even today Muslims regard the Arabic text of the Quran as the only definitive and reliable scripture: translations do not possess the power and authority of the original. When carrying their faith to new lands during the era of Islamic expansion, Muslim missionaries spread the message of Allah and provided instruction in the Quran's teachings, although usually they also permitted continued observance of pre-Islamic traditions. Muslim intellectuals drew freely from the long-established cultural traditions of Persia, India, and Greece, which they became acquainted with during the Umayyad and Abbasid eras.

The Formation of an Islamic Cultural Tradition

Muslim theologians and jurists looked to the Quran, stories about Muhammad's life, and other sources of Islamic doctrine in their efforts to formulate moral guidelines appropriate for

In this manuscript illustration a Muslim teacher (the figure with the open book) instructs students in a library near Baghdad in the fine points of Islamic law.
DEA Picture Library/Getty Images

of the Quran and the sharia into the lives of peoples living far from the birthplace of Islam.

Formal educational institutions also promoted Islamic values. Many mosques maintained schools that provided an elementary education and religious instruction, for both girls and boys, and wealthy Muslims sometimes established schools and provided endowments for their support. By the tenth century institutions of higher education known as **madrasas** had begun to appear, and by the twelfth century they had become established in the major cities of the Islamic world. Muslim rulers often supported the madrasas in the interests of recruiting literate and learned students with an advanced education in Islamic theology and law for administrative positions. Inexpensive paper enhanced scholars' ability to instruct students and disseminate their views.

Sufis Among the most effective Islamic missionaries were mystics known as Sufis, a community that included both men and women. The term *Sufi* probably came from the patched woolen garments favored by the mystics. Sufis did not deny Islamic doctrine, and indeed many of them had an advanced education in Islamic theology and law. But they also did not find formal religious teachings to be especially meaningful. Thus, instead of concerning themselves with fine points of doctrine, Sufis worked to deepen their spiritual awareness. Most Sufis led pious and ascetic lives. Some devoted themselves to helping the poor. A few gave up their possessions and lived as mendicant beggars. Many sought a mystical, ecstatic union with Allah, relying on rousing sermons, passionate singing, or spirited dancing to bring them to a state of high emotion. Muslim theologians sometimes mistrusted Sufis, fearing that in their lack of concern for doctrine they would adopt erroneous beliefs. Nevertheless, after the ninth century Sufis became increasingly popular in Muslim societies because of their piety, devotion, and eagerness to minister to the needs of their fellow human beings.

Al-Ghazali Most important of the early Sufis was the Persian theologian al-Ghazali (1058–1111), who argued that human reason was too frail to understand the nature of Allah and hence could not explain the mysteries of the world. Only through devotion and guidance from the Quran could human beings begin to appreciate the uniqueness and power of Allah. Indeed, al-Ghazali held that philosophy and human reasoning were vain pursuits that would inevitably lead to confusion rather than understanding.

Sufi Missionaries Sufis were especially effective as missionaries because they emphasized devotion to Allah above mastery of doctrine. They sometimes encouraged individuals to revere Allah in their own ways, even if those ways did not have a basis in the Quran. They tolerated the continued observance of pre-Islamic customs, for example, as well as the association of Allah with deities recognized and revered in other faiths. The Sufis themselves led ascetic and holy

their society. The body of civil and criminal law embodied in the sharia provided a measure of cultural unity for the vastly different lands of the Islamic world. Islamic law did not by any means erase the differences, but it established a common cultural foundation that facilitated dealings between peoples of various Islamic lands and that lent substance to the concept of the *dar al-Islam.*

Promotion of Islamic Values On a more popular level, *ulama, qadis,* missionaries, and Muslim traders helped to bridge differences in cultural traditions and to spread Islamic values throughout the *dar al-Islam. Ulama* and *qadis* held positions at all Islamic courts, and they were prominent in the public life of all cities in the Islamic world. By resolving disputes according to Islamic law and ordering public observance of Islamic social and moral standards, they brought the values

madrasas (MAH-drahs-uhs)
Sufi (SOO-fee)

lives, which won them the respect of the peoples to whom they preached. Because of their kindness, holiness, tolerance, and charismatic appeal, Sufis attracted numerous converts particularly in lands such as Persia and India, where long-established religious faiths such as Zoroastrianism, Christianity, Buddhism, and Hinduism had enjoyed a mass following for centuries.

Hajj The symbol of Islamic cultural unity was the Ka'ba at Mecca, which from an early date attracted pilgrims from all parts of the Islamic world. The Abbasid caliphs especially encouraged observance of the hajj: they saw themselves as supreme leaders of a cohesive Islamic community, and as a matter of policy they sought to enhance the cultural unity of their realm. They built inns along the main roads to Mecca for the convenience of travelers, policed the routes to ensure the safety of pilgrims, and made lavish gifts to shrines and sites of pilgrimage. Individuals from far-flung regions of the

How the Past Shapes the Future

The Spread of Religious Traditions

As we saw in chapter 13, the first millennium of the Common Era was marked by the spread of religious traditions—including Islam—well beyond their regions of origin. In the case of Islam, people (including *qadis* and *ulama* who were trained in interpreting sharia law), institutions (including madrasas and mosques), and the Arabic languages (as expressed in the Quran) provided multiple avenues for the diffusion of Islamic values to areas distant from its birthplace in the Arabian peninsula. Consider the long-term legacies of this common religious foundation— even in the absence of a unified Islamic state—across the *dar al-Islam*. How might this common religious foundation have affected political relationships, cultural developments, or the movement of products and people within the *dar al-Islam* over the long term? How might it have affected relationships between Islamic regions and non-Islamic regions? And to what extent does the early expansion of Islam throughout large regions of Afro-Eurasia continue to affect politics and culture in the world of the twenty-first century?

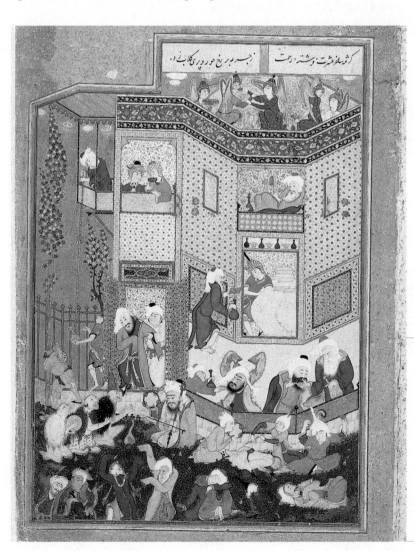

Through song, dance, and ecstatic experiences, sometimes enhanced by wine, Persian Sufis expressed their devotion to Allah, as in this sixteenth-century painting. How did Sufis facilitate the spread of Islam beyond Arabia?

Harvard Art Museums promised Gift of Mr. and Mrs. Stuart Cary Welch, Jr. Partially owned by the Metropolitan Museum of Art and the Harvard University, 1998. In honor of the students of Harvard University and Radcliffe college, 1988.460.3. Photo: Allan Macintyre. ©President and Fellows of Harvard College

Abbasid empire made their way to Mecca, visited the holy sites, and learned firsthand the traditions of Islam. Over the centuries those pilgrims spread Islamic beliefs and values to all parts of the Islamic world, and with the work of *ulama, qadis,* and Sufi missionaries, their efforts helped to make the *dar al-Islam* not just a name but also a reality.

Islam and the Cultural Traditions of Persia, India, and Greece

As the Islamic community expanded, Muslims of Arab ancestry interacted regularly with peoples from other cultural traditions, especially those of Persia, India, and Greece. In some cases, particularly in lands ruled by the Umayyad and Abbasid dynasties, large numbers of conquered peoples

Connecting the Sources

Sufi mysticism and the appeal of Islam

The problem   Although Muslim armies conquered vast territories in central and southwest Asia, north Africa, and Iberia in the century after Muhammad's death in 632 C.E., conquest alone cannot explain why so many people in the *dar al-Islam* made sincere and lasting conversions to Islam. Many individuals converted to Islam because of its profound spiritual appeal, made especially popular by Sufi mystics who often served as missionaries. While all Muslims believed that individuals would become close to God in the afterlife, Sufi mystics preached that it was possible to grow close to God while one was still alive if only individuals would surrender themselves, in love, to God. For Sufis, the key to surrendering to and loving God was learning to gain control over one's own ego, which they termed the "greater jihad," or *al-jihad al-akbar* (as opposed to the "lesser jihad," or *al-jihad al-asghar,* of fighting oppressors or injustice). Sufis taught, in short, that the path to God was a path of love, and that this path was open to all who wished to follow.

Below are two excerpts from texts written by well-known and influential Sufi mystics: Rabi'a al-'Addawiyya, a woman from Basra (modern Iraq) who lived from about 717 to 801 C.E., and Abu Hamid al-Ghazali, a man from Khorasan (modern Iran) who lived from 1058 to 1128 C.E. As you read the documents, think about the reasons their writings might have appealed to contemporaries and to generations who came after them.

The documents   Read the documents below, and consider carefully the questions that follow.

Document 1:

Rabi'a al-'Adawiyya was an early Sufi saint and is the best-known woman Sufi mystic in Islamic history. She was sold into slavery as a child, but was reportedly freed later in life because of her religious devotion. She was known for her celibate and ascetic lifestyle and for her passionate devotion to the love of God. Rabi'a herself did not publish any of her poetry or writings, but they were later collected and printed by Faridu d'Din Attar in the thirteenth century. The following is one of the poems attributed to her.

O Lord,

    If tomorrow on Judgment Day
    You send me to Hell,
    I will tell such a secret
    That Hell will race from me
    Until it is a thousand years away.

O Lord,

    Whatever share of this world
    You could give to me,
    Give it to Your enemies;
    Whatever share of the next world
    You want to give to me,
    Give it to Your friends.
    You are enough for me.

O Lord,

    If I worship You
    From fear of Hell, burn me in Hell.

Depiction of Rabi'a grinding grain.
The History Collection/Alamy Stock Photo

O Lord,

　If I worship You

　From hope of Paradise, bar me from its gates.

But if I worship You for Yourself alone

　Then grace me forever the splendor of Your Face. ————————————

> How does Rabi'ai's understanding of Allah compare to Christian conceptions of their God?

Document 2:

Abu Hamid al-Ghazali was one of the most important Sufi philosophers and Muslim theologians. As a young man he became a professor at Nizamiyah University in Baghdad, but spiritual transformation caused him to give up the academic life for a life of asceticism, reflection, and writing. He wrote numerous important works seeking to balance the rationalism of Greek philosophy with spiritualism derived from Sufi mysticism. The following selection is taken from his Alchemy of Happiness, *originally published in the early twelfth century.*

On the Love of God

O traveller on the way and seeker after the love of God! know that the love of God is a sure and perfect method for the believer to attain the object of his desires. It is a highly exalted station of rest, during the journey of the celestial traveler. It is the consummation of the desires and longings of those who seek divine truth. It is the foundation of the vision of the beauty of the Lord.

The love of God is of the most binding obligation upon every one. It is indeed the spirit of the body, and the light of the eye.

The prophet of God declares that the faith of the believer is not complete, unless he loves God and his prophet more than all the world besides. The prophet was once asked, what is faith? He replied, "It is to love God and his prophet more than wife, children and property." And the prophet was continually in the habit of praying, "O my God! I ask for thy love, I ask that I may love whomsoever loves thee, and that I may perform whatsoever thy love makes incumbent upon me."

On the resurrection day all sects will be addressed by the name of the prophet whom each followed, "O people of Moses! O people of Jesus! O people of Mohammed!" even to all the beloved servants of God, and it will be proclaimed to them, "O Friends and beloved of God, come to the blessed union and society of God! Come to Paradise and partake of the grace of your beloved!" When they hear this proclamation, their hearts will leap out of their places, and they will almost lose their reason. Yahya ben Moa'z says, "It is better to have as much love of God, even if only as much as a grain of mustard seed, than seventy years of devotion and obedience without love." Hassan of Basra says, "Whoever knows God, will certainly love him, and whoever knows the world, will shun it." ————————————

> What does the author mean by stating that whoever knows the world will shun it?

. . .

O! seeker of divine love, that which renders man favorably inclined to persons of virtuous character, is the fact that God has created man after his own character; as it has come to us in the tradition that, "verily God created man after his own image." Hence whenever man sees or hears of a quality belonging to his own race and kind, as justice, generosity, forgiveness or patience, he will certainly have a sympathy with that quality and exercise love to its possessor. If we hear for instance that in a certain country there is a just sovereign or a just vizier, we heartily love that king or vizier, and we are always praising his excellence and worth, although there is not the least probability of any advantage accruing to us from his justice. If we hear of a generous man, although he may be in a foreign country, and we have no hope of any advantage from him or of any token of his generosity to ourselves, yet still from necessity we will love him, and whenever his name is mentioned we will invoke blessings upon him and praise him. It is thus with Hatem Tai whose name, though he was an infidel, is upon every tongue, because he was a generous and benevolent man, and all hearts are irresistibly led to love him. . . .

We see then that the love we bear to persons endowed with the virtuous qualities of man, is not bestowed by us for the sake of any fancied advantage from them or any hope of gain, but that on the contrary it is because the spirits of men are created in correspondence with the character of God, and when we see a trace or mark of a quality or affection of a kind like our own, we cannot help being attracted towards it, and must necessarily love it.

Questions

1. What can these sources definitively tell you about the lives of the people who produced them? Are there any actual biographical details contained in these sources?
2. In Document 1, how does the fact that Rabi'a was a woman complicate our understanding of the role of women in Islam in the century after Muhammad's death?
3. In Document 2, how does al-Ghazali's view of loving other people, even non-Moslems (or infidels), compare with common contemporary visions of Islam as a "religion of the sword"?
4. For both documents, how might these exhortations about loving God have appealed to individuals coming into contact with them for the first time?
5. To what extent can sources such as these help historians understand the spiritual dimensions of conversion to Islam, especially when read in conjunction with other textual and material evidence?

Source Websites: **Document 1:** Perfume of the Desert: Inspirations from Sufi Wisdom. Translated by Andrew Harvey and Eryk Hanut. Illinois: Quest Books, 1999. This material was reproduced by permission of Quest Books, the imprint of the Theosophical Publishing House(www.questbook.net). **Document 2:** Ghazali, Al. The Alchemy of Happiness. Translated by Henry Augustus Homes. New York: J. Munsell, 1873.

converted to Islam, and they brought elements of their inherited cultural traditions into Islamic society. In other cases, particularly in lands beyond the authority of Islamic rulers, Muslims became acquainted with the literary, artistic, philosophical, and scientific traditions of peoples who chose not to convert. Nevertheless, their traditions often held considerable interest for Muslims, who adapted them for their own purposes.

Translators and Travelers Muslims learned about different cultural traditions in several ways. The Abbasid dynasty officially supported the effort to acquire knowledge from other societies by inviting foreign scholars to the court at Baghdad and sponsoring translations of literary and scientific works from Greek, Latin, and Sanskrit into Arabic and Persian languages. By the tenth century Muslim as well as Jewish, Christian, and Zoroastrian translators had made a massive library of foreign knowledge available to Muslims. Meanwhile, Muslim merchants, missionaries, and other travelers compiled the most comprehensive body of geographic information ever assembled before European mariners made their way to all parts of the world after 1492. Drawing on Greek and Roman geographic knowledge as well as contemporary travelers' reports, Muslim geographers and cartographers produced maps, atlases, sea charts, and general descriptions of the world known to them, which included much of the eastern hemisphere. Particularly during its early centuries, the world of Islam was remarkably open to knowledge and ideas from other societies.

Persian Influences on Islam Persian traditions quickly found a place in Islamic society because the culturally rich land of Persia fell under Islamic rule at an early date. Especially after the establishment of the Abbasid dynasty and the founding of its capital at Baghdad, Persian traditions deeply influenced Islamic political and cultural leaders. Persian administrative

Arab physicians made note of medicines used in Persian, Indian, and Greek societies and added more of their own. In this manuscript illustration, a physician instructs a pharmacist in the preparation of medicines.
myLAM/Alamy Stock Photo

An illustration from a thirteenth-century Arabic-language manuscript depicts the Greek philosopher Aristotle teaching three students about the astrolabe, an instrument that enabled the user to determine latitude.
DEA/G. Dagli Orti/Getty Images

techniques, which Muslim conquerors borrowed from the Sasanid empire, were crucial for the organization of the imperial structure through which Umayyad and Abbasid rulers governed their vast empire. Meanwhile, Persian ideas of kingship profoundly influenced Islamic political thought. Muslim caliphs and regional governors drew readily on Persian views of kings as wise and benevolent but nonetheless absolute rulers.

Persian influence was also noticeable in literary works from the Abbasid dynasty. Although Arabic served as the language of religion, theology, philosophy, and law, Persian was the principal language of literature, poetry, history, and political reflection. The verses of Omar Khayyam titled the **Rubaiyat** ("quatrains") are widely known to western audiences because of a popular English translation by the Victorian poet Edward Fitzgerald, but many other writers composed works that in Persian display even greater literary elegance and originality. The marvelous collection of stories known as *The Arabian Nights,* or *The Thousand and One Nights,* for example, presented popular tales of adventure and romance set in the Abbasid empire and the court of Harun al-Rashid.

Indian Influences on Islam

Indian mathematics, science, and medicine captured the attention of Arab and Persian Muslims who established Islamic states in northern India. The sophisticated mathematical tradition of Gupta India was attractive to Muslims both as a field of scholarship and for the practical purposes of reckoning and keeping accounts. Muslims readily adopted what they called "Hindi" numerals, which European peoples later called "Arabic" numerals, because they learned about them through Arab Muslims. Hindi numerals enabled Muslim scholars to develop an impressive tradition of advanced mathematics, concentrating on algebra (an Arabic word) as well as trigonometry and geometry. From a more practical point of view, Indian numerals vastly simplified bookkeeping for Muslim merchants working in the lively commercial economy of the Abbasid dynasty.

Muslims also found much to appreciate in the scientific and medical thought they encountered in India. With the aid of their powerful and flexible mathematics, Indian scholars were able to carry out precise astronomical calculations, which helped inspire the development of Muslim astronomy. Similarly, Indian medicine appealed to Muslims because of its treatments for specific ailments and its use of antidotes for poisons. Muslim visitors often railed against Indian religious beliefs—both Hindu and Buddhist—but they uniformly praised Indian mathematical, scientific, and medical thought, which they avidly adopted for their own uses and purposes.

Greek Influences on Islam

Muslims also admired the philosophical, scientific, and medical writings of classical Greece. They became especially interested in Plato and Aristotle, whose works they translated and interpreted in commentaries. During the tenth and eleventh centuries, some Muslim philosophers sought to synthesize Greek and Muslim thought by harmonizing Plato with the teachings of Islam. They encountered resistance among conservative theologians such as the Sufi al-Ghazali, who considered Greek philosophy a completely unreliable guide to ultimate truth because it relied on frail human reason rather than on the revelation of the Quran.

Partly in response to al-Ghazali's attacks, twelfth-century Muslim philosophers turned their attention more to Aristotle than to Plato. The most notable figure in this development was **Ibn Rushd** (1126–1198), *qadi* of Seville in the caliphate of Córdoba, who followed Aristotle in seeking to articulate a

Ibn Rushd (IB-uhn RUSHED)

Fourteenth-century illustration of an imaginary debate between Averroes and third-century philosopher Porphyry, by Monfredo de Monte Imperiali *Liber de herbis,* 14th century FLHC 90/Alamy Stock Photo

purely rational understanding of the world. Ibn Rushd's work not only helped to shape Islamic philosophy but also found its way to the schools and universities of western Europe, where Christian scholars knew Ibn Rushd as Averroes. During the thirteenth century his work profoundly influenced the development of scholasticism, the effort of medieval European philosophers to harmonize Christianity with Aristotelian thought.

Ibn Rushd's reliance on natural reason went too far for many Muslims, who placed more value on the revelations of the Quran than on the fruits of human logic. After the thirteenth century, Muslim philosophers and theologians who dominated the madrasas drew inspiration more from Islamic sources than from Greek philosophy. Platonic and Aristotelian influences did not disappear, but they lost favor in official seats of learning and fell increasingly under the shadow of teachings from the Quran and Sufi mystics. As they did with political and cultural traditions from Persia and India, Muslim thinkers absorbed Greek philosophy, reconsidered it, and used it to advance the interests of their society.

Quite apart from philosophy, Greek mathematics, science, and medicine appealed strongly to Muslims. Like their Indian counterparts, scholars in classical Greek and Hellenistic societies had developed elaborate traditions of scientific thought. Greek mathematics did not make use of Indian numerals, but it offered a solid body of powerful reasoning, particularly when dealing with calculations in algebra and geometry. Greek mathematics supported the development of astronomical and geographical scholarship, and studies of anatomy and physiology served as foundations for medical thought. Muslim scholars quickly absorbed those Greek traditions, combined them with influences from India, and used them all as points of departure for their studies. The result was a brilliant flowering of mathematical, scientific, and medical scholarship that provided Muslim societies with powerful tools for understanding the natural world.

CONCLUSION

The prophet Muhammad did not intend to found a new religion. Instead, his intention was to express his convictions about Allah and perfect the teachings of earlier Jewish and Christian prophets by announcing a revelation more comprehensive than those Allah had entrusted to his predecessors. His message soon attracted a circle of devout and committed disciples, and by the time of his death most of Arabia had accepted Islam. During the two centuries following the prophet's death, Arab conquerors and missionaries spread Islam throughout southwest Asia and north Africa and introduced their faith to central Asia, India, the Mediterranean islands, and Iberia. This rapid expansion of Islam encouraged the development of an extensive trade and communication network: merchants, diplomats, and other travelers moved easily throughout the Islamic world exchanging goods and introducing agricultural crops to new lands. Rapid expansion also led to encounters between Islam and long-established religious and cultural traditions such as Hinduism, Judaism, Zoroastrianism, Christianity, Persian literature and political thought, and classical Greek philosophy and science. Muslim thinkers readily adapted those earlier traditions to their needs. As a result of its expansion, its extensive trade and communication networks, and its engagement with other religious and cultural traditions, the *dar al-Islam* became one of the most prosperous and cosmopolitan societies of Afro-Eurasia during the first millennium and a half of the common era.

STUDY TERMS

Abbasid dynasty (281)	Islam (273)
Abu Bakr (279)	jihad (278)
al-Andalus (286)	*jizya* (281)
Allah (274)	Ka'ba (276)
bedouin (273)	*madrasas* (288)
caliph (279)	Mecca (276)
dar al-Islam (273)	Medina (276)
Five Pillars of Islam (278)	Muhammad (274)
hadith (276)	Muslim (273)
hajj (272)	*qadis* (282)
Harun al-Rashid (282)	Quran (276)
hijra (276)	*Rubaiyat* (283)
Ibn Rushd (293)	*sakk* (285)

sharia (278)

Shia (279)

Sufi (288)

Sunni (279)

ulama (282)

umma (276)

Umayyad dynasty (280)

FOR FURTHER READING

Muhammad Manazir Ahsan. *Social Life under the Abbasids.* New York, 1979. Draws on a wide range of sources in discussing dress, food, drink, housing, and daily life during the Abbasid era.

Reza Aslan. *No God but God. The Origins, Evolution and Future of Islam.* New York, 2005. Offers a vivid and realistic account of the social and religious environment in which the Prophet Muhammad forged his message.

Jonathan P. Berkey. *The Formation of Islam: Religion and Society in the Near East, 600-1800.* Cambridge, 2003. Views the development of Islamic society in the context of relations among Muslims, Jews, and Christians.

John Esposito. *Islam: The Straight Path.* 3rd ed. New York, 2005. The best brief introduction to Islam.

Richard C. Foltz. *Spirituality in the Land of the Noble: How Iran Shaped the World's Religions.* Oxford, 2004. Includes an accessible discussion of Persian influences on the Islamic faith.

Ira M. Lapidus. *A History of Islamic Societies.* Cambridge, 1988. Authoritative survey of Islamic history, concentrating on social and cultural issues.

Ilse Lichtenstadter. *Introduction to Classical Arabic Literature.* New York, 1974. A brief overview, accompanied by an extensive selection of texts in English translation.

M. Lombard. *The Golden Age of Islam.* Princeton, 2004. Concentrates on the social and economic history of the Abbasid period.

Al Qur'an: A Contemporary Translation. Trans. by Ahmed Ali. Princeton, 1984. A sensitive translation of the holy book of Islam.

Francis Robinson, ed. *The Cambridge Illustrated History of the Islamic World.* Cambridge, 1996. An excellent and lavishly illustrated introduction to Islam and the Muslim world.

Michael Wolfe, ed. *One Thousand Roads to Mecca: Ten Centuries of Travelers Writing about the Muslim Pilgrimage.* New York, 1997. Presents selections from twenty-three accounts describing travelers' hajj experiences.

ZOOMING IN ON ENCOUNTERS

Buzurg Sets His Sights on the Seven Seas

Buzurg ibn Shahriyar was a tenth-century shipmaster from Siraf, a prosperous and bustling port city on the Persian Gulf coast. He probably sailed frequently to Arabia and India, and he may have ventured also to Malaya, the islands of southeast Asia, China, and east Africa. Like all sailors, he heard stories about the distant lands that mariners had visited, the different customs they observed, and the adventures that befell them during their travels. About 953 C.E. he compiled 136 such stories in his *Book of the Wonders of India.*

Buzurg's collection included a generous proportion of tall tales. He told of a giant lobster that seized a ship's anchor and dragged the vessel through the water, of mermaids and sea dragons, of creatures born from human fathers and fish mothers who lived in human society but had flippers that enabled them to swim through the water like fish, of serpents that ate cattle and elephants, of birds so large that they crushed houses, of a monkey that seduced a sailor, and of a talking lizard. Yet alongside the tall tales, many of Buzurg's stories accurately reflected the conditions of his time. One recounted the story of a king from northern India who converted to Islam and requested translations of Islamic law.

Others reported on Hindu customs, shipwrecks, encounters with pirates, and slave trading.

Several of Buzurg's stories tempted readers with visions of vast wealth attainable through maritime trade. Buzurg mentioned fine diamonds from Kashmir, pearls from Ceylon, and a merchant

An oceangoing dhow (commercial ship favored by Indian, Persian, and Arab sailors) off the coast of Zanzibar, Indian Ocean. Although this is a modern photograph, the design and sailing technique of dhows have changed little over the centuries.

Charles O. Cecil/Alamy Stock Photo

who left Persia penniless and returned from India and China with a shipload of priceless merchandise. Despite their embellishments and exaggerations, his stories faithfully reflected the trade networks that linked the lands surrounding the Indian Ocean in the tenth century. Although Buzurg clearly thought of India as a distinct land with its own customs, he also recognized a larger world of trade and communication that extended from east Africa to southeast Asia and beyond to China.

CHAPTER OVERVIEW

Just as China served as the principal inspiration of a larger east Asian society in the first millennium of the Common Era, India influenced the development of a larger cultural zone in south and southeast Asia. Yet China and India played different roles in their respective spheres of influence. In east Asia, China was the dominant power, even if it did not always exercise authority directly over its neighbors. In south and southeast Asia, however, there emerged no centralized imperial authority like the Tang dynasty in China. Indeed, although several states organized large regional kingdoms, no single state was able to extend its authority to all parts of the Indian subcontinent, much less to the mainland and islands of southeast Asia.

Though politically disunited, India remained a coherent and distinct society as a result of powerful social and cultural traditions: the caste system and the Hindu religion shaped human experiences and values throughout the subcontinent during the first millennium C.E. Beginning in the seventh century Islam also began to attract a popular following in India, and by the eleventh century, had also become a powerful influence on Indian culture and society.

Beyond the subcontinent, Indian traditions helped to shape a larger cultural zone extending to the mainland and islands of southeast Asia. Throughout most of the region, ruling classes adopted Indian forms of political organization and Indian techniques of statecraft. Indian merchants took their Hindu and Buddhist faiths to southeast Asia, where they attracted the interest first of political elites and then of the popular masses. Somewhat later, Indian merchants also helped to introduce Islam to southeast Asia.

While Indian traditions influenced the political and cultural development of southeast Asia, the entire Indian Ocean basin began to move toward economic integration during this era, as Buzurg ibn Shahriyar's stories suggest. Lands on the rim of the Indian Ocean retained distinctive political and cultural traditions inherited from times past. Yet innovations in maritime technology, development of a well-articulated network of sea lanes, and the building of port cities enabled peoples living around the Indian Ocean to trade and communicate more actively than ever before. As a result, peoples from east Africa to southeast Asia and China increasingly participated in the larger economic, commercial, and cultural life of the Indian Ocean basin.

CHRONOLOGY	
1st to 6th century	Kingdom of Funan
606–648	Reign of Harsha
670–1025	Kingdom of Srivijaya
711	Conquest of Sind by Umayyad forces
early 9th century	Life of Shankara
850–1267	Chola kingdom
889–1431	Kingdom of Angkor
1001–1027	Raids on India by Mahmud of Ghazni
11th to 12th century	Life of Ramanuja
12th century	Beginning of the bhakti movement
1206–1526	Sultanate of Delhi
1336–1565	Kingdom of Vijayanagar
1440–1518	Life of guru Kabir

ISLAMIC AND HINDU KINGDOMS

Like the Han and Roman empires, the Gupta dynasty came under severe threat from nomadic invaders. From the mid-fourth to the mid-fifth century C.E., Gupta rulers resisted the pressures and preserved order throughout much of the Indian subcontinent. Beginning in 451 C.E., however, White Huns from central Asia also known as Hephthalites, invaded India and disrupted the Gupta administration. By the mid-sixth century, the Gupta state had collapsed, and effective political authority quickly devolved to invaders, local allies of the Guptas, and independent regional power brokers. From the end of the Gupta dynasty until the sixteenth century, when a Turkic-Mongol people known as the Mughals extended their authority and their empire to most of the subcontinent, India remained a politically divided land.

The Quest for Centralized Imperial Rule

Northern and southern India followed different political trajectories after the fall of the Gupta empire. In the north, politics became turbulent and almost chaotic. Local states contested for power and territory, and northern India became a region of continuous tension and intermittent war. Nomadic Turkish-speaking peoples from central Asia frequently took advantage of that unsettled state of affairs to cross the Khyber Pass and force their way into India. They eventually found niches for themselves in the **caste system** and became completely absorbed into Indian society. However, this process of social absorption took a long time and came only after the arrival of nomadic peoples caused a long period of disruption in northern India.

Harsha Even after the collapse of the Gupta dynasty, the ideal of centralized imperial rule did not entirely disappear. During the first half of the seventh century, King **Harsha** (reigned 606–648 C.E.) temporarily restored unified rule in most of northern India and sought to revive imperial authority. Harsha came to the throne of his kingdom in the lower Ganges valley at the age of sixteen. Full of energy and ambition, he led his army throughout northern India. His forces included twenty thousand cavalry, fifty thousand infantry, and five thousand war elephants, and by about 612 he had subdued those who refused to recognize his authority. He also made his presence felt beyond India. He extended his influence to several Himalayan states, and he exchanged a series of embassies with his contemporary, Emperor Tang Taizong of China.

Harsha enjoyed a reputation for piety, tolerance, and scholarship. He was a Buddhist, but he looked kindly on other faiths. He built hospitals and provided free medical care for his subjects. The Chinese pilgrim Xuanzang visited northern India during his reign and reported that Harsha liberally distributed wealth to his subjects. On one occasion, Xuanzang said, the king and his aides doled out resources continuously for seventy-five days, making gifts to half a million people. Harsha also generously patronized scholars and reportedly even wrote three plays himself.

Collapse of Harsha's Kingdom Despite his energy and his favorable reputation, Harsha was unable to restore permanent centralized rule. Since the fall of the Gupta dynasty, local rulers had established their authority too securely in India's regions for Harsha to overcome them. Harsha spent much of his reign on horseback traveling throughout his realm to solidify alliances with local rulers, who were virtually kings in their own lands. He managed to hold his loose empire together mainly by the force of his personality and his constant attention to political affairs. Ultimately, however, he fell victim to an assassin and left no heir to maintain his realm. His Empire immediately disintegrated, and local rulers once again turned northern India into a contested region as they sought to enlarge their realms at the expense of their neighbors.

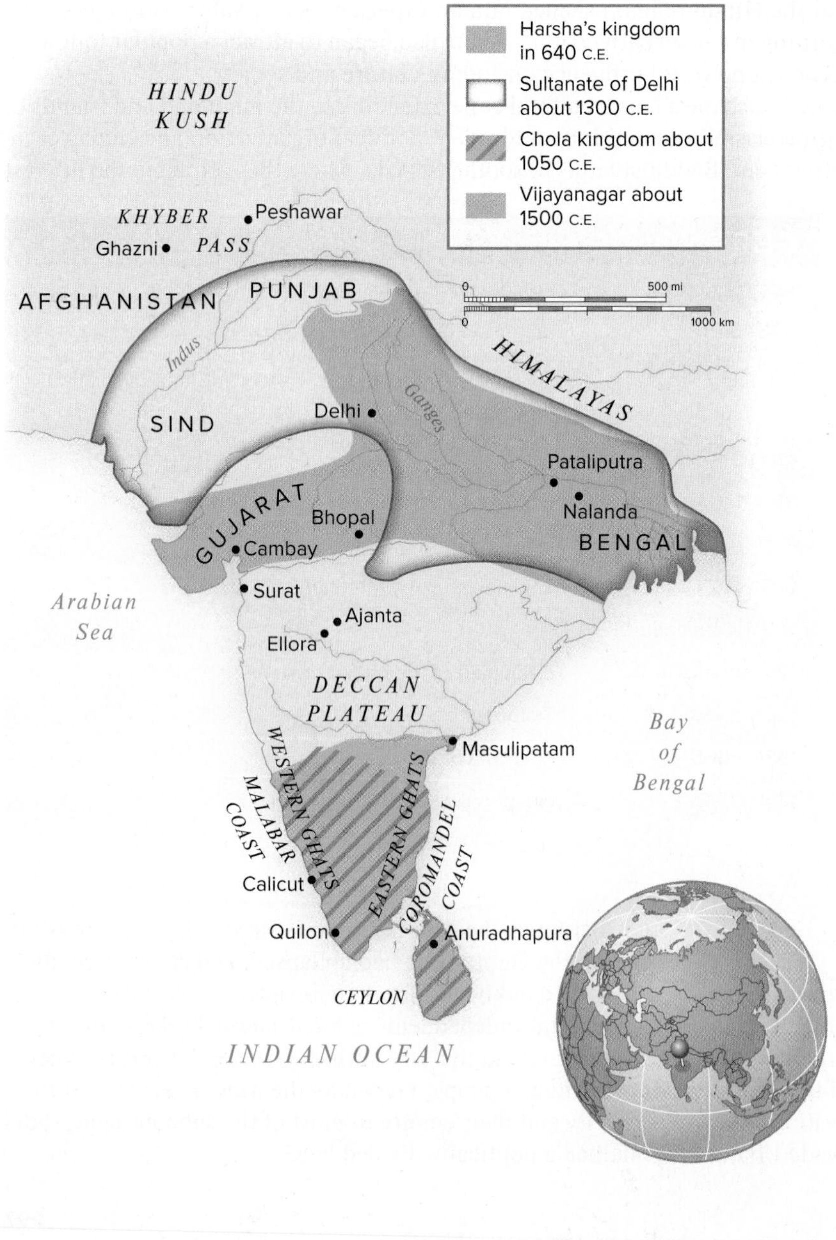

Map legend:
- Harsha's kingdom in 640 C.E.
- Sultanate of Delhi about 1300 C.E.
- Chola kingdom about 1050 C.E.
- Vijayanagar about 1500 C.E.

MAP 15.1   Major states of India, 600–1600 C.E.

Several large rivers and river valleys offered opportunities for inhabitants of northern India.

What geographical and economic factors helped the peoples of southern India organize themselvs into flourishing states?

Painting by an unknown
Medieval artist depicting
Mahmud of Ghazni and his
court.
UtCon Collection/Alamy Stock
Photo

The Introduction of Islam to Northern India

The Conquest of Sind Amid nomadic incursions and contests for power, northern India also experienced the arrival of Islam and the establishment of Islamic states. Islam reached India by several routes. One was military: Arab forces entered India as early as the mid-seventh century, even before the establishment of the Umayyad caliphate, although their first expeditions were exploratory ventures rather than campaigns of conquest. In 711, however, a well-organized expedition conquered Sind, the Indus River valley in northwestern India, and incorporated it as a province of the expanding Umayyad empire. At mid-century, along with most of the rest of the *dar al-Islam,* Sind passed into the hands of the Abbasid caliphs.

Sind stood on the fringe of the Islamic world, well beyond the effective authority of the Abbasid caliphs. Much of its population remained Hindu, Buddhist, or Parsee, and it also sheltered a series of unorthodox Islamic movements. Infighting between Arab administrators eventually offered opportunities for local political elites to reassert Hindu authority over much of Sind. Yet the region remained nominally under the jurisdiction of the caliphs until the collapse of the Abbasid dynasty in 1258.

Merchants and Islam While conquerors brought Islam to Sind, Muslim merchants took their faith to coastal regions in both northern and southern India. Arab and Persian mariners had visited Indian ports for centuries before Muhammad, and their Muslim descendants dominated trade and transportation networks between India and western lands from the seventh through the fifteenth century. Muslim merchants formed small communities in all the major cities of coastal India, where they played a prominent role in Indian business and

commercial life. They frequently married local women, and in many cases they also found places for themselves in Indian society. Thus Islam entered India's port cities in a more gradual but no less effective way than was the case in Sind. Well before the year 1000, for example, the Gujarat region housed a large Muslim population. Muslim merchants congregated there because of the port city of Cambay, the most important trading center in India throughout the millennium from 500 to 1500 C.E.

Migrants and Islam Islam also entered India by a third route: the migrations and invasions of Turkic-speaking peoples from central Asia. During the tenth century, several Turkish groups had become acquainted with Islam through their dealings with the Abbasid caliphate and had converted to the faith. Some of these Muslim Turks entered the Abbasid realm as mercenary soldiers or migrated into Byzantine Anatolia, and others moved into Afghanistan, where they established an Islamic state.

Mahmud of Ghazni **Mahmud of Ghazni,** leader of a Turkic-Iranian state in Afghanistan, soon turned his attention to the rich land to the south. Mahmud was a complex figure. He was a patron of the arts who built Ghazni (near Kabul in modern-day Afghanistan) into a refined capital, where he supported historians, mathematicians, and literary figures at his court. At the same time, Mahmud was a determined and ruthless warrior who spent much of his time in the field with his armies. Between 1001 and 1027 he mounted seventeen raiding expeditions into India. Taking advantage of infighting between local rulers, he annexed several states

Mahmud of Ghazni (mah-muhd of gahz-nee)

in northwestern India and the Punjab. For the most part, however, Mahmud had less interest in conquering and ruling India than in plundering the wealth stored in its many well-endowed temples. Mahmud and his forces demolished hundreds of sites associated with Hindu or Buddhist faiths, and their campaigns hastened the decline of Buddhism in the land of its birth. In 1025 Mahmud infamously destroyed the great Somnath Hindu Temple of Gujarat, killing more than fifty thousand people who tried to defend it, and taking away a booty of some 20 million dinars. Not surprisingly, Mahmud's raids did not encourage Indians to turn to Islam.

The Sultanate of Delhi During the late twelfth century, Mahmud's successors mounted a more systematic campaign to conquer northern India and place it under Islamic rule. By the early thirteenth century, they had conquered most of the

Hindu kingdoms in northern India and established an Islamic state known as the **sultanate of Delhi.** The sultans established their capital at Delhi, a strategic site controlling access from the Punjab to the Ganges valley, and they ruled northern India, at least in name, for more than three centuries, from 1206 to 1526.

During the fourteenth century the sultans of Delhi commanded an army of three hundred thousand, and their state ranked among the most prominent in the Islamic world. They built mosques, shrines, and fortresses throughout their realm, and, like Mahmud of Ghazni, they were generous patrons of the arts and literature. Yet for the most part, the authority of the sultans did not extend far beyond Delhi. They often conducted raids in the Deccan region of southern India, but they never overcame Hindu resistance there. They had no permanent bureaucracy or administrative

Lodi Gardens near Delhi is the cemetery of the Lodi sultans, the last dynasty to rule the sultanate of Delhi. Here a tomb reflects the introduction of Islamic architecture into India.
GeoMuse/Alamy Stock Photo

apparatus. Even in northern India, they imposed a thin veneer of Islamic political and military authority on a land populated mostly by Hindus, and they depended on the goodwill of Hindu kings to carry out their policies and advance their interests in local regions. Indeed, they did not even enjoy comfortable control of their own court: of the thirty-five sultans of Delhi, nineteen perished at the hands of assassins. Nevertheless, the sultans prominently sponsored Islam and played a large role especially in the establishment of Islam in the Bengal region.

The Hindu Kingdoms of Southern India

Although it too remained politically divided, the southern part of the Indian subcontinent largely escaped the invasions, chronic war, and turmoil that troubled the north. Most Hindu rulers in the south presided over small, loosely administered states. Competition between states sometimes resulted in regional wars, but southern conflicts were less

frequent, less intense, and less damaging than those that plagued the north.

The Chola Kingdom Although many regional states organized affairs in local jurisdictions, two kingdoms expanded enough to exercise at least nominal rule over much of southern India. The first was the **Chola kingdom,** situated in the deep south, which ruled the Coromandel coast for more than four centuries, from 850 to 1267 C.E. At its high point, during the eleventh century, Chola forces conquered Ceylon and parts of southeast Asia. Financed by the profits of trade, the Chola navy dominated the waters from the South China Sea to the Arabian Sea.

Chola rulers did not build a tightly centralized state: they allowed considerable autonomy for local and village institutions as long as they maintained order and delivered tax revenues on time. Chola rulers had less interest in building a powerful

Coromandel (kawr-uh-MAN-dul)

The Virupaksha Temple complex was built by Vijayanagar rulers in the capital of their empire, Hampi, located today in the modern state of Karnataka, India.

Dinodia Photos/Alamy Stock Photo

state than in realizing profits that came from their domination of trade in the Indian Ocean basin. Indeed, partly because of its loose institutional structure, the Chola state was in decline by the twelfth century. Native Sinhalese forces expelled Chola officials from Ceylon, and revolts erupted within southern India. The Chola realm did not entirely collapse, but by the early thirteenth century, much reduced in size and power, it had reverted to the status of one regional kingdom among many in southern India.

The Kingdom of Vijayanagar The second state that dominated much of southern India was the **Vijayanagar kingdom,** based in the northern Deccan. The kingdom owed its origin to efforts by the sultans of Delhi to extend their authority to southern India. Exploratory forays by Turkish forces provoked a defensive reaction in the south. Officials in Delhi dispatched two brothers, Harihara and Bukka, to represent the sultan and implement court policies in the south. Although they had converted from their native Hinduism to Islam, Harihara and Bukka recognized an opportunity to establish themselves as independent rulers. In 1336 they renounced Islam, returned to their original Hindu faith, and proclaimed the establishment of an independent empire of Vijayanagar (meaning "city of victory"). Their unusual coup did not lead to hostilities between Muslims and Hindus: Muslim merchants continued to trade unmolested in the ports of southern India, as they had for more than half a millennium. But the Hindu kingdom of Vijayanagar was the dominant state in southern India from the mid-fourteenth century until 1565, when it fell to an alliance of Muslim kingdoms.

As in northern India, then, political division and conflict between states characterized southern India's political history in postclassical times. India did not generate the sort of large-scale, centralized, imperial state that guided the fortunes of complex societies in the eastern Mediterranean, southwest Asia, or China. States such as the sultanate of Delhi in northern India and the kingdoms of Chola and Vijayanagar in the south were not powerful enough to organize political life throughout the subcontinent. Nevertheless, on the basis of trade, common social structures, and inherited cultural traditions, a coherent and distinctive society flourished in India during the first millennium and a half of the Common Era.

PRODUCTION AND TRADE IN THE INDIAN OCEAN BASIN

As in the Mediterranean, southwest Asia, and China, agricultural yields increased significantly in postclassical India, enabling large numbers of people to devote themselves to trade

Vijayanagar (vee-juh-yah-NAH-gahr)

and manufacturing rather than the production of food. Trade forged links between the various regions of the subcontinent and fostered economic development in southern India. Trade also created links between India and distant lands, as merchants and manufacturers transformed the Indian Ocean basin into a vast zone of communication and exchange. The increasing prominence of trade and industry brought change to Indian society, as merchant and artisan guilds became stronger and more influential than before. Yet caste identities and loyalties also remained strong, and the caste system continued to serve as the most powerful organizing feature of Indian society.

Agriculture in the Monsoon World

The Monsoons Because of the rhythms of the **monsoons,** irrigation was essential for the maintenance of a large, densely populated, agricultural society. Because of cyclical changes in atmospheric pressure, during the spring and summer, warm, moisture-laden winds from the southwest bring most of India's rainfall. During the autumn and winter, cool and very dry winds blow from the northeast. To achieve their agricultural potential, Indian lands required a good watering by the southern monsoon, supplemented by irrigation during the dry months. Light rain during the spring and summer months or short supplies of water for irrigation commonly led to drought, reduced harvests, and widespread famine.

Irrigation Systems In northern India, irrigation had been a fixture of the countryside since the era of the Indus Civilization, when cultivators tapped the waters of the Indus River. Later, as Indo-Aryans migrated into the Ganges River valley, they found plentiful surface water and abundant opportunities to build irrigation systems. For the most part, however, southern India is an arid land without rivers like the Indus or the Ganges that can serve as sources for large-scale irrigation. Thus, as southern India became more densely populated, irrigation systems became crucial, and a great deal of energy and effort went into the construction of waterworks. Dams, reservoirs, canals, wells, and tunnels appeared in large numbers. Particularly impressive were monumental reservoirs lined with brick or stone that captured the rains of the spring and summer months and held them until the dry season, when canals carried them to thirsty fields. One such reservoir—actually an artificial lake constructed near Bhopal during the eleventh century—covered some 650 square kilometers (250 square miles). Projects of that size required enormous investments of human energy, both for their original construction and for continuing maintenance, but they led to significant increases in agricultural productivity.

Population Growth As a result of that increased productivity, India's population grew steadily throughout the first millennium and a half of the Common Era. In 600 C.E., shortly after the fall of the Gupta dynasty, the subcontinent's population stood at about 53 million. By 800 it had increased almost

20 percent to 64 million, and by 1000 it had grown by almost an additional 25 percent to 79 million. During the following centuries the rate of growth slowed, as Indian numbers increased by 4 to 5 million individuals per century. Toward 1500, however, the rate of growth increased again, and by 1500 the subcontinent's population had reached 105 million.

Urbanization This demographic surge encouraged the concentration of people in cities. During the fourteenth century, the high point of the sultanate of Delhi, the capital city had a population of about four hundred thousand, which made it second only to Cairo among Muslim cities. Many other cities—particularly ports and trading centers, such as Cambay, Surat, Calicut, Quilon, and Masulipatam—had populations well over one hundred thousand. Cities in southern India grew especially fast, partly as a result of increasing agricultural productivity in the region.

Trade and the Economic Development of Southern India

Political fragmentation of the subcontinent did not prevent robust trade between the different states and regions of India. As the population grew, opportunities for specialized work became more numerous. Increased trade was a natural result of that process.

Internal Trade Most regions of the Indian subcontinent were self-sufficient in staple foods such as rice, wheat, barley, and millet. The case was different, however, with iron, copper, salt, pepper, spices, condiments, and specialized crops that grew well only in certain regions. Iron came mostly from the Ganges River valley near Bengal, copper mostly from the Deccan Plateau, salt mostly from coastal regions, and pepper from southern India. Those and other commodities sometimes traveled long distances to consumers in remote parts of the subcontinent. Pepper, saffron, and sugar were popular commodities in subcontinental trade, and even rice sometimes traveled as a trade item to northern and mountainous regions where it did not grow well.

Southern India and Ceylon benefited especially well from this trade. As invasions and conflicts disrupted northern India, southern regions experienced rapid economic development. The Chola kingdom provided relative stability in the south, and Chola expansion in southeast Asia opened markets for Indian merchants and producers. Coastal towns such as Calicut and Quilon flourished, and they attracted increasing numbers of residents.

Temples and Society The Chola rulers allowed considerable autonomy to their subjects, and the towns and villages of southern India largely organized their own affairs. Public life revolved around Hindu temples that served as economic and social centers. Southern Indians used their growing wealth to build hundreds of elaborate Hindu temples, which organized agricultural activities, coordinated work on irrigation systems, and maintained reserves of surplus production for use in times of need. These temples also provided basic schooling for boys in the community, and larger temples offered advanced instruction as well. Temples often possessed large tracts of agricultural land, and they sometimes employed hundreds of people, including brahmins, attendants, musicians, servants, and slaves. To meet their financial obligations to employees, temple administrators collected a portion of the agricultural yield from lands subject to temple authority. Administrators were also responsible for keeping order in their communities and delivering tax receipts to the Cholas and other political authorities.

Temple authorities also served as bankers, made loans, and invested in commercial and business ventures. As a result, temples promoted the economic development of southern India by encouraging production and trade. Temple authorities cooperated closely with the leaders of merchant guilds in seeking commercial opportunities to exploit. The guilds often made gifts of land or money to temples by way of consolidating their relationship with the powerful economic institutions. Temples thus grew prosperous and became crucial to the economic health of southern India.

Cross-Cultural Trade in the Indian Ocean Basin

Indian prosperity sprang partly from the productivity of Indian society, but it depended also on the vast wealth that circulated in the commercial world of the Indian Ocean basin. Trade in the Indian Ocean Basin was not new in the first millennium of the Common Era. Indian merchants had been engaged in trans-regional maritime trade since the First Silk Roads Era, when they had regularly engaged with Roman merchants in search of pepper and other South Asian spices. During the first millennium c.e., however, larger ships and improved commercial organization supported a dramatic surge in the volume and value of trade in the Indian Ocean basin.

Dhows and Junks The earliest voyaging in the Indian Ocean followed the coastlines, but during the First Silk Roads Era mariners had recognized the rhythms of the monsoons. Over time they built larger ships, which enabled them to leave the coasts behind and ply the blue waters of the Indian Ocean: the **dhows** favored by Indian, Persian, and Arab sailors averaged about one hundred tons burden in 1000 and four hundred tons in 1500. After the naval and commercial expansion of the Song dynasty, large Chinese and southeast Asian **junks** also sailed the Indian Ocean: some of them could carry one thousand tons of cargo.

As large, stable ships came into use, mariners increasingly entrusted their crafts and cargoes to the reasonably predictable monsoons and sailed directly across the Arabian Sea and the

During the eighth century C.E., workers carved a massive temple out of sheer rock at Ellora in central India. Temple communities such as the one that grew up at Ellora controlled enormous resources in India during the first millennium C.E. How did temple communities become such wealthy institutions?

Mazur Travel/Shutterstock

Bay of Bengal. In the age of sail, it was impossible to make a round trip across the entire Indian Ocean without spending months at distant ports waiting for the winds to change, so merchants usually conducted their trade in stages.

Emporia Because India stood in the middle of the Indian Ocean basin, it was a natural site for **emporia** (commercial centers) and warehouses. Merchants coming from east Africa or Persia exchanged their cargoes at Cambay, Calicut, or Quilon for goods to take back west with the winter monsoon. Mariners from China or southeast Asia called at Indian ports and traded their cargoes for goods to ship east with the summer monsoon. Merchants also built emporia outside India: the storytelling mariner Buzurg ibn Shahriyar, who we met at the start of this chapter, came from the emporium of Siraf on the Persian Gulf, a port city surrounded by desert that nevertheless enjoyed fabulous wealth because of its trade with China, India, and east Africa. Because of their central location,

however, Indian ports became the principal clearinghouses of trade in the Indian Ocean basin, and they became remarkably cosmopolitan centers. Hindus, Buddhists, Muslims, Jews, and others who inhabited the Indian port cities did business with counterparts from all over the eastern hemisphere and swapped stories like those recounted by Buzurg ibn Shahriyar. In combination, the sea lanes and emporia of the Indian Ocean basin made up a network of maritime Silk Roads—a web of transportation, communication, and exchange that complemented the land-based Silk Roads and promoted interaction between peoples throughout much of Afro-Eurasia.

Particularly after the establishment of the Umayyad and Abbasid dynasties in southwest Asia and the Tang and Song dynasties in China, trade in the Indian Ocean surged. Indian merchants and mariners sometimes traveled to distant lands in search of marketable goods, but the carrying trade between India and points west fell mostly into Arab and Persian hands. During the Tang and Song dynasties, Chinese vessels also

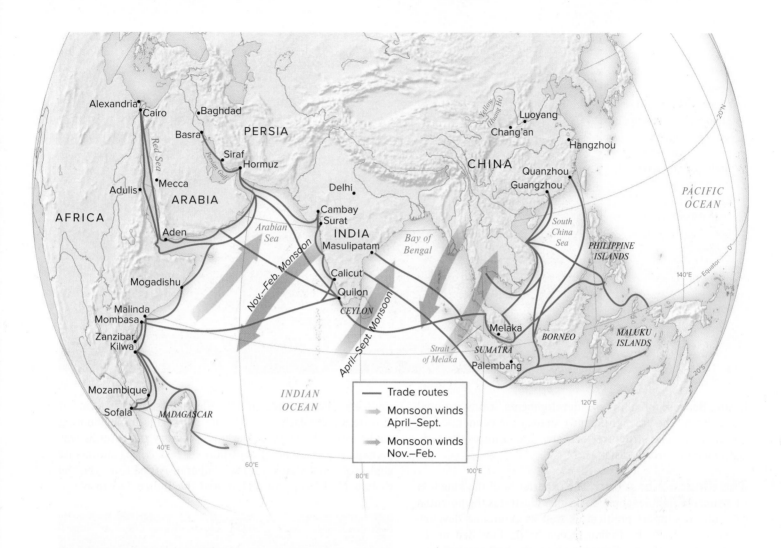

MAP 15.2 The trading world of the Indian Ocean basin, 600–1600 C.E.

Note the directions of seasonal winds in the Indian Ocean basin.

What impact would the monsoon winds have had on the direction and schedule of maritime trade during the era?

ventured into the western Indian Ocean and called at ports as far away as east Africa. In the Bay of Bengal and the China seas, Malay and Chinese vessels were most prominent.

Specialized Production

As the volume of trade in the Indian Ocean basin increased, lands around the ocean began to engage in specialized production of commodities for the commercial market. For centuries Indian artisans had enjoyed a reputation for the manufacture of fine cotton textiles, which they produced in small quantities for wealthy consumers. During the first millennium their wares came into high demand throughout the trading world of the Indian Ocean basin. In response to that demand, Indian artisans built thriving local industries around the production of high-quality cotton textiles. These industries influenced the structure of the Indian economy: they created a demand for specific agricultural products, provided a livelihood for thousands of artisans,

and enabled consumers to import goods from regions that specialized in the production of other commodities.

Alongside textiles, other specialized industries that emerged in postclassical India included sugar refining, leather tanning, stone carving, and carpet weaving. Iron and steel production also emerged as prominent industries. Indian artisans became well known especially for the production of high-carbon steel, which held a lethal cutting edge and consequently came into high demand for use in knives and swords. Other lands concentrated on the production of different manufactured goods and agricultural commodities: China produced silk, porcelain, and lacquerware; southeast Asian lands provided fine spices; incense, horses, and dates came from southwest Asia; and east Africa contributed gold, ivory, and slaves. Thus trade encouraged specialized production and economic development in all lands participating in the trade networks of the Indian Ocean

One of many stelae (elaborately carved obelisks) in the city of Axum in modern-day Ethiopia. The stelae were royal grave markers that were probably erected during the fourth century C.E.
Dave Bartruff/Corbis Documentary/Getty Images

basin: Because of all these developments, trans-regional trade during the era significantly shaped the economic, political, and social structures of states and cultures throughout much of Afro-Eurasia.

The Kingdom of Axum

The experience of the kingdom of **Axum** (sometimes spelled Aksum) illustrates the potential of trade to support political as well as economic development throughout the Indian Ocean basin. Founded in the highlands of northern Ethiopia about the first century C.E., Axum was originally a small kingdom whose merchants traded from the port of Adulis on the Red Sea. Axum soon displaced Kush as Egypt's principal link to southern lands and sent the Nubian kingdom into economic and political decline: about 360 C.E. Axumite forces even invaded Kush and destroyed the capital city of Meroë. During the fourth and fifth centuries, Axumites adopted Christianity and established a distinctive church that maintained relations with Christian communities in Egypt and the Mediterranean basin. During the sixth century Axum embarked on a round of territorial expansion, building an empire that included most of modern-day Ethiopia as well as Yemen in southern Arabia. Indeed, an Axumite army and elephant corps campaigned as far north as Mecca in the year 571 C.E., birth year of the prophet Muhammad.

During the seventh and eighth centuries, Arab conquerors sought to bring Axum into the expanding realm of Islam, but the kingdom maintained its independence and its Christian religion. Because neighboring lands mostly adopted Islam, Axum fell out of communication with other Christian societies. Nevertheless, Axumite merchants not only maintained commercial ties with distant lands, as ships from Adulis

routinely sailed for India and the islands of southeast Asia, but also traded regularly with Muslim merchants in neighboring lands. From the sixth to the ninth century C.E., Adulis was perhaps the most prominent port in east Africa, funneling gold, ivory, and slaves from sub-Saharan Africa to Egypt, the eastern Mediterranean region, and the Indian Ocean basin.

Mealtime for a Persian merchant and his two companions served by three women attendants in this ceiling decoration from the Ajanta caves in central India.
Shreekant Jadhav/ephotocorp/Alamy Stock Photo

Thus, even though challenged by Muslim forces, Axum was able to maintain its independence and prosperity, largely because of its participation in trading networks of the Indian Ocean and Mediterranean Sea.

Caste and Society

The political, economic, and social changes of the postclassical era brought a series of challenges for India's caste system. Migrations, the growing prominence of Islam, economic development, and urbanization all placed pressures on the caste system as it had developed during the Vedic and classical eras. But the caste system has never been a rigid, unchanging structure. Rather, individuals and groups have continuously adjusted it and adapted it to new circumstances. Adjustments and adaptations of the postclassical era resulted in a caste system that was more complex than in earlier ages and that also extended its geographic reach deeper into southern India than ever before. In the absence of strong central governments, the caste system helped to maintain order in local communities by providing guidance on individuals' roles in society and their relationships with others.

Caste and Migration The caste system closely reflected changes in Indian society. It adapted to the arrival of migrants, for example, and helped to integrate them into Indian society. As Turkish peoples or Muslim merchants pursued opportunities in India, they gained recognition as distinct groups under the umbrella of the caste system. They established codes of conduct both for the regulation of behavior within their own groups and for guidance in dealing with members of other castes. Within a few generations their descendants had become absorbed into Indian society.

Caste and Social Change The caste system also accommodated the social changes brought about by trade and economic development. Indeed, the caste system influenced the lives of most people by helping to order their work and their relationships with other workers. The castes that individuals most closely identified with were the subcastes (*jati*), which often took the form of workers' guilds. As merchants and manufacturers became increasingly important in the larger economy, they organized powerful guilds to represent their interests. Merchant guilds in particular wielded political and economic influence because their members enjoyed access to considerable wealth and contributed in large measure to the economic health of their states. Guild members forged group identities by working within the caste system. Merchants specializing in particular types of commerce, such as the silk, cotton, or spice trade, established themselves as distinct subcastes, as did artisans working in particular industries, such as the iron, steel, or leather business.

Expansion of the Caste System Besides becoming more complex, the caste system also extended its geographic reach. Caste distinctions first became prominent in northern India following Aryan migrations into the subcontinent. During the postclassical era, the caste system became securely established in southern India as well. Economic development aided that process by encouraging commercial relationships between southern merchants and their caste-conscious counterparts in the north. The emergence of merchant and craft guilds in southern regions strengthened the caste system because guild members usually organized as a subcaste. Powerful temples also fostered caste distinctions. Caste-conscious brahmins who supervised the temples were particularly effective promoters of the system because temples provided the only formal education available in most regions and also served as centers of local social life. By about the eleventh century C.E., caste had become the principal basis of social organization in southern India.

SOURCES FROM THE PAST

Three Sources on Chinese Trade with Ports and Regions of the Indian Ocean Basin

China was located at the eastern edge of the Indian Ocean Basin trading network, but it was absolutely fundamental to the vigor and success of that vast commercial enterprise for most of the first and early second millennia of the Common Era. The following three sources provide eyewitness accounts of the wealth being generated in China and elsewhere between the eighth and thirteenth centuries.

Source 1: The Superintendent of the Shipping Trade Trade between various Southeast Asian ports and Tang China was so intense by the early eighth century that the government created a new official position to help regulate it: the Superintendent of the Shipping Trade. An official Chinese report created a century later comments on the regulation of trade between Southeast Asian countries and ports along the southern Chinese coast and the work of the Superintendent. During the Tang Dynasty, the Chinese referred to this as the *Nanhai* trade:

(Continued)

When [the laden Nanhai ships] arrive, a report is sent to the Court and announcements are made to the cities. The [chief merchants] who commanded them are made to register with Superintendent of the Shipping Trade their names and their cargo [or submit their manifest]. [The Superintendent collects the duties on the goods and sees that there are no prohibited precious and rare goods [of which the government had a monopoly]. There were some foreign merchants who were imprisoned for trying to deceive him.

> What crime had the foreign merchants been imprisoned for?

Source: Wang Gungwu, *The Nanhai Trade: Early Chinese Trade in the South Chinese Sea* (Singapore: Eastern Universities Press, 2003), p. 94.

Source 2: Chinese Report on the Wealth of a Javanese Commercial Kingdom By the thirteenth century trade between China and other regions of the Indian Ocean Basin had generated enormous wealth for the various Southeast Asian states that functioned as commercial intermediaries. In this report a Chinese official, who is probably basing his information on reports received from Chinese merchants who regularly traveled to the Indonesian island of Java, comments on the political and commercial status of a wealthy West Javan kingdom:

The king wears his hair in a knot, on his head is a golden bell; he wears a silken robe and leather shoes. His throne is a square seat and his officers at their daily audience bow three times when withdrawing. When he goes forth he rides an elephant, or is carried in a chair followed by a company of some 500 to 700 armed soldiers. When any one of the people see the king, he squats down until [the king] has passed by . . . The [government does] not inflict corporal punishment and imprisonment on criminals; they are fined an amount in gold varying according to the gravity of the crime . . . [The country] produces rice, hemp, millet, beans, but no wheat. Ploughing is done with buffaloes. They also pay attention to the raising of silkworms and the weaving of the silk; they have various colored brocaded silks, cotton, and damasked cotton gauzes. They cast coins in an alloy of copper, silver, white copper and tin. Foreign merchants use gold and silver in trading. There is a vast store of pepper and the [Chinese] merchant ships, in view of the profit they derive from that trade, are in the habit of smuggling out of China copper cash for bartering purposes.

> Why would the government fine criminals rather than physically punish or imprison them? Which would be the greater deterrent in a wealthy commercial state?

Source: Frederick Hurth and W. W. Rockhill, *Chau Ju-kua: His Work on the Chinese and Arab Trade in the Twelfth and Thirteenth Centuries, entitled Chu-fan-chi,* reprint edition (Taipei: Literature House, 1965), pp. 76–78.

Source 3: Marco Polo of the Wealth of the Chinese Port City of Quanzhou Venetian merchant Marco Polo visited China when it was under the control of the Mongol Yuan Dynasty (1271–1368), events discussed in chapter 17. From the account he later compiled, it appears as though the Yuan had further strengthened commercial connections between the southern Chinese ports and the thriving Indian Ocean commercial network. Marco Polo vividly describes the port city of Quanzhou, which he refers to as Zaiton, located in modern Fujian Province:

The splendid city of Zaiton . . . is the port for all the ships that arrive from India laden with costly wares and precious stones of great price and pearls of great quality . . . It is also the port for the merchandise of Manzi [Fujian], that is of all the surrounding territory, so that the total amount of traffic in gems and other merchandise entering and leaving the port is a marvel to behold. From this city and its port goods are exported to the whole province of Manzi. And I assure you that for one spice ship that goes to Alexandria or elsewhere to pick up pepper for export to Christendom, Zaiton is visited by a hundred. For you must know that it is one of the two ports in the world with the biggest flow of commerce.

> Which other global ports in the fourteenth century might Marco Polo have been thinking of as candidates for having a flow of commerce equal to that of Zaiton?

Source: Ronald Latham, trans. and ed., *The Travels of Marco Polo* (London: Penguin, 1958), p. 237.

For Further Reflection

- Collectively, what do these sources tell us about the evolution of Indian Ocean Basin trade between the eighth and fourteenth centuries?
- What role were governments playing in the regulation of transregional trade across the Indian Ocean?
- What financial and cultural impact was extensive trade having not only on the key commercial ports involved but on wider society?

RELIGIOUS DEVELOPMENTS IN SOUTH ASIA

The Indian cultural landscape underwent a thorough transformation during the first millennium and a half of the Common Era. Jainism and Buddhism lost much of their popular following. Neither belief completely disappeared from India, and indeed, a small community continues to observe each faith there even today. After 1000 C.E., however, Hindu and Islamic traditions increasingly dominated the cultural and religious life of India.

Hinduism and Islam differed profoundly as religious traditions. The Hindu pantheon made places for numerous gods and spirits, for example, whereas Islamic theology stood on a firm foundation of monotheism. Yet both religions attracted large popular followings throughout the subcontinent, with Hinduism predominating in southern India and Islam in the north.

The Increasing Popularity of Hinduism

Toward the end of the first millennium C.E., Buddhism flourished in east Asia, central Asia, and parts of southeast Asia but came under great pressure in India. Like Mahayana Buddhism, both Hinduism and Islam promised salvation to devout individuals, and they gradually attracted Buddhists to their own communities. Invasions of India by Turkish peoples hastened the decline of Buddhism because the invaders looted and destroyed Buddhist stupas and shrines. In 1196 Muslim forces overran the city of Nalanda and ravaged the schools where centuries earlier, Xuanzang and other foreign pilgrims had studied with the world's leading Buddhist philosophers and theologians. The conquerors torched Buddhist libraries and either killed or exiled thousands of monks living at Nalanda. Buddhism soon became a minor faith in the land of its birth.

Vishnu and Shiva Hinduism benefited from the decline of Buddhism. One reason for the increasing popularity of Hinduism was the remarkable growth of devotional communities, particularly those dedicated to **Vishnu** and **Shiva**, two of the most important deities in the Hindu pantheon. Vishnu was the preserver of the world, a god who observed the universe from the heavens and who occasionally entered the world in human form to resist evil or communicate his teachings. In contrast, Shiva was both a god of fertility and a destructive deity: he brought life but also took it away when its season had passed. Hindus recognized many other gods and goddesses associated with Vishnu and Shiva, but these two powerful deities were by far the most popular and important deities of veneration.

Devotional Cults The veneration of Vishnu and Shiva became especially popular in southern India, where individuals or family groups went to great lengths to honor their chosen deities. Often, new avenues of worship opened up when

Southern Indian artists often portrayed Shiva in bronze sculptures as a four-armed lord of dancers. In this figure from the Chola dynasty, Shiva crushes with his foot a dwarf demon symbolizing ignorance. One hand holds a bell to awaken his devotees, another bears the fire used by Shiva as creator and destroyer of the world, and a third gestures Shiva's benevolence toward his followers.
Kate S. Buckingham Fund/Art Institute of Chicago

individuals identified Vishnu or Shiva with a local spirit or deity associated with a particular region or a prominent geographic feature. The worship of Shiva as lord of the dancers arose, for example, about the fifth or sixth century C.E. when devotees identified a stone long venerated locally in a southern Indian village as a symbol of Shiva. In the tenth century Chola kings took the dancing Shiva as their family god and spread the idea throughout southern India. By venerating images of Vishnu or Shiva, offering them food and drink, and meditating on the deities and their qualities, Hindus hoped to achieve a mystic union with the gods that would bring grace and salvation. As these spiritual approaches proliferated, temples and shrines dotted the landscape of southern India. Veneration of Vishnu and Shiva gradually became popular among Hindus in northern as well as southern India.

Shankara The significance of Hinduism extended well beyond popular religion: it also influenced philosophy. Just as Buddhism, Christianity, and Islam influenced moral thought and philosophy in other lands, devotional Hinduism guided the efforts of the most prominent philosophers in postclassical India. Brahmin philosophers such as Shankara and Ramanuja took the Upanishads as a point of departure for subtle reasoning and sophisticated metaphysics. **Shankara,** a southern Indian devotee of Shiva who was active during the early ninth century C.E., took it upon himself to digest all sacred Hindu writings and harmonize their sometimes contradictory teachings into a single, consistent system of thought. In a manner reminiscent of Plato, Shankara held that the physical world was illusion—a figment of the imagination—and that ultimate reality lay beyond the physical senses. Although he was a worshiper of Shiva, Shankara mistrusted emotional services and ceremonies, insisting that only by disciplined logical reasoning could human beings understand the ultimate reality of Brahman, the impersonal world-soul of the Upanishads. Only then could they appreciate the fundamental unity of the world, which Shankara considered a perfectly understandable expression of ultimate reality, even though to human physical senses that same world appears chaotic and incomprehensible.

Ramanuja Ramanuja, a devotee of Vishnu who was active during the eleventh and early twelfth centuries C.E., challenged Shankara's uncompromising insistence on logic. Also a brahmin philosopher from southern India, Ramanuja's thought reflected the deep influence of devotional cults. According to Ramanuja, intellectual understanding of ultimate reality was less important than personal union with the deity. Ramanuja granted that intellectual efforts could lead to comprehension of reality, but he held that genuine bliss came from salvation and identification of individuals with their gods. He followed the *Bhagavad Gita* in recommending intense devotion to Vishnu, and he taught that by placing themselves in the hands of Vishnu, devotees would win the god's grace and live forever in his presence. Thus, in contrast to Shankara's consistent, intellectual system of thought, Ramanuja's philosophy pointed toward a Hindu theology of salvation. Indeed, his thought

An elaborate open-air rock carving at Mamallapuram, south of modern Madras, celebrates the Ganges River as a gift from Shiva and other gods.
Maciej Dakowicz/Alamy Stock Photo

inspired the development of new avenues of devotion throughout India, and it serves even today as a philosophical foundation for Hindu popular religion.

Islam and Its Appeal

The Islamic faith did not attract much immediate interest among Indians when it arrived in the subcontinent. It won gradual acceptance in merchant communities where foreign Muslim traders took local spouses and found a place in Indian society. Elsewhere, however, circumstances did not favor its adoption because it was often brought to the region by conquering peoples. Muslim conquerors generally reserved important political and military positions for their Arab, Persian, and Turkish companions. Only rarely did they allow Indians—even those who had converted to Islam—to hold sensitive posts. Thus, quite apart from the fact that they introduced a foreign religion radically different from those of the subcontinent, conquerors offered little incentive for Indians to convert to Islam.

Conversion to Islam Gradually, however, many Indians did convert to Islam. By 1500 C.E. Indian Muslims numbered perhaps twenty-five million—about one-quarter of the subcontinent's population. Some Indians adopted Islam in hopes of improving their positions in society: Hindus of lower castes, for example, hoped to escape discrimination by converting to a faith that recognized the equality of all believers. In fact, Hindus rarely improved their social standing by conversion. Often, members of an entire

How the Past Shapes the Future ▶ ▶ ▶ ▶

The Spread of Religious Traditions

As religious traditions spread from their regions of origin during the first millennium C.E., the Indian subcontinent became a region to which Islam spread from central Asia and also a region that exported its own religion of Hinduism to many parts of southeast Asia. By the tenth century, Indian merchants were also bringing knowledge of Islam to southeast Asia. Consider the long-term effects of the meeting of Islam and Hinduism in India. What were the effects of the popularity of these two religions on Jainism and Buddhism, which had also developed in India? Consider also the long-term effects of the Indianization of southeast Asia through the spread of both Hinduism and Islam. How did Indianization influence social organization, cultural expression, and political life in southeast Asia? And to what extent are these religious developments still affecting South and Southeast Asia today?

caste or subcaste adopted Islam en masse, and after conversion they continued to play the same social and economic roles that they had before.

Sufis In India as elsewhere, the most effective agents of conversion to Islam were Sufi mystics. **Sufis** encouraged a personal, emotional, devotional approach to Islam. They did not insist on fine points of doctrine, and they sometimes even permitted their followers to observe rituals or venerate spirits not recognized by the Islamic faith. Because of their piety and sincerity, however, Sufi missionaries attracted individuals searching for a faith that could provide comfort and meaning for their personal lives. Thus, like Hinduism, Indian Islam emphasized piety and devotion. Even though Hinduism and Islam were profoundly different religions, they encouraged the cultivation of similar spiritual values that transcended the social and cultural boundary lines of postclassical India.

The Bhakti Movement In some ways, the gap between Hinduism and Islam narrowed in India during the early second millennium because both religions drew on long-established and long-observed cultural traditions. Sufis, for example, often attracted schools of followers in the manner of Indian gurus, spiritual leaders who taught Hindu values to disciples who congregated around them. Even more important was the development of the ***bhakti* movement,** a spiritual movement of love and devotion that ultimately sought to erase the distinction between Hinduism and Islam. The bhakti movement emerged in southern India during the twelfth century, and it originally encouraged a traditional piety and devotion to Hindu values. As the movement spread to the north, bhakti leaders increasingly encountered Muslims and became deeply attracted to certain Islamic values, especially monotheism and the notion of spiritual equality of all believers.

Guru Kabir The bhakti movement gradually rejected the exclusive features of both Hinduism and Islam. Thus **guru Kabir** (1440–1518), a blind weaver who was one of the most famous bhakti teachers, went so far as to teach that Shiva, Vishnu, and Allah were all manifestations of a single, universal deity, whom all devout believers could find within their own hearts. The bhakti movement did not succeed in harmonizing Hinduism and Islam. Nevertheless, like the Sufis, bhakti teachers promoted values that helped to build bridges between India's social and cultural communities.

INDIAN SOCIAL AND POLITICAL INFLUENCE IN SOUTHEAST ASIA

Just as China stood at the center of a larger east Asian society, India served as the principal source of political and cultural traditions widely observed throughout south and southeast Asia. For a millennium and more, southeast Asian peoples

In India as in other lands, Sufi mystics were the most effective Muslim missionaries. This seventeenth-century painting depicts the legendary Sufi master Khwaja Khidr, beloved in Muslim communities throughout northern India as one associated with springtime, fertility, water, and happiness. Why would Sufis believe that showing respect for more traditional beliefs and spirits was the best way to encourage their followers to develop a personal relationship with the Islamic faith?
The History Collection/Alamy Stock Photo

adapted Indian political structures and religions to local needs and interests. Although Indian armed forces rarely ventured into the region, southeast Asian lands reflected the influence of Indian society, as merchants introduced Hinduism, Buddhism, Sanskrit writings, and Indian forms of political organization. Beginning about the twelfth century, Islam also found solid footing in southeast Asia, as Muslim merchants, many of them Indians, established trading communities in the important

MAP 15.3 Early states of southeast Asia: Funan and Srivijaya, 100–1025 C.E.

Both Funan and Srivijaya relied heavily on maritime trade.

What impact did the trans-regional maritime trade illustrated in Map 15.2 have on the development of states in Southeast Asia?

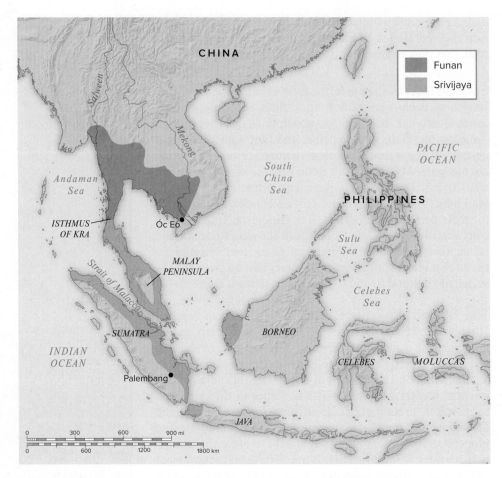

port cities of the region. During the next five hundred years, Islam attracted a sizable following and became a permanent feature in much of southeast Asia.

The States of Southeast Asia

Indian Influence in Southeast Asia Indian merchants visited the islands and mainland of southeast Asia from an early date, perhaps as early as 500 B.C.E. By the early centuries C.E., they had become familiar figures throughout southeast Asia, and their presence brought opportunities for the native ruling elites of the region. In exchange for spices and exotic products such as pearls, aromatics, and animal skins, Indian merchants brought textiles, beads, gold, silver, manufactured metal goods, and objects used in political or religious rituals. Southeast Asian rulers used the profits from that trade to consolidate their political control.

Meanwhile, southeast Asian ruling elites became acquainted with Indian political and cultural traditions. Without necessarily giving up their own traditions, they borrowed Indian forms of political organization and accepted Indian religious faiths. On the model of Indian states, for example, they adopted kingship as the principal form of political authority. Regional kings in southeast Asia surrounded

themselves with courts featuring administrators and rituals similar to those found in India.

Ruling elites also sponsored the introduction of Hinduism or Buddhism—sometimes both—into their courts. They embraced Indian literature such as the *Ramayana* and the *Mahabharata,* which promoted Hindu values, as well as treatises that explained Buddhist views on the world. They did not adopt the Indian caste system and continued to acknowledge the deities and nature spirits that southeast Asian peoples had venerated for centuries. But ruling elites readily adopted Hinduism and Buddhism, which they found attractive because the Indian faiths reinforced the principle of monarchical rule.

Funan The first state known to have reflected Indian influence in this fashion was **Funan,** which dominated the lower reaches of the Mekong River (including parts of modern Cambodia and Vietnam) between the first and the sixth centuries C.E. The rulers of Funan consolidated their grip on the Mekong Valley and built a capital city at the port of Oc Eo. Funan grew wealthy because it dominated the Isthmus of Kra, the narrow portion of the Malay peninsula across which merchants transported trade goods between China and India. (Directly crossing this small width of land enabled them to avoid a long voyage around the Malay peninsula.) The rulers of Funan drew enormous wealth by controlling trade between

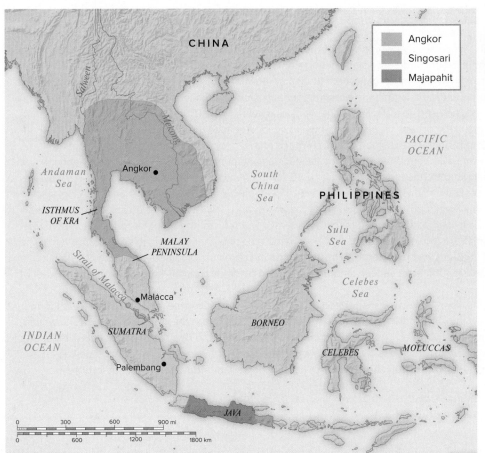

MAP 15.4 Later states of southeast Asia: Angkor, Singosari, and Majapahit, 889–1520 C.E.

Angkor was a largely agricultural society, whereas Singosari and Majapahit were more active in maritime trade.

To what extent did these three states owe their success to continuing trans-regional trade between East and South Asia?

East and South Asia. They used their profits to construct an elaborate system of water storage and irrigation—so extensive that aerial photography still reveals its lines—that served a productive agricultural economy in the Mekong delta.

As trade with India became an increasingly important part of Funan's economy, the ruling classes adopted Indian political, cultural, and religious traditions. They took the Sanskrit term *raja* ("king") for themselves and claimed divine sanction for their rule in the manner of Hindu rulers in India. They established positions for administrators and bureaucrats such as those found at Indian courts and conducted official business in Sanskrit. They introduced Indian ceremonies and rituals and worshiped Vishnu, Shiva, and other Hindu deities. They continued to honor local deities, particularly water spirits venerated widely throughout southeast Asia, but they eagerly welcomed Hinduism, which offered additional recognition and divine legitimacy for their rule. At first, Indian cultural and religious traditions were most prominent and most often observed at ruling courts. Over the longer term, however, those traditions extended well beyond ruling elites and won a secure place in southeast Asian society.

During the sixth century C.E., a bitter power struggle weakened Funan internally. Peoples from the north took advantage of that weakness, migrated to the lower Mekong Valley in large numbers, and overwhelmed Funan. Chams settled in the southern portion of modern Vietnam, and Khmers dominated in the region occupied by modern Cambodia. By the late sixth century, Funan's intricate irrigation system had fallen into ruin, and Funan itself soon passed into oblivion.

Srivijaya After the fall of Funan, political leadership in southeast Asia passed to the kingdom of **Srivijaya** (670–1025 C.E.) based on the island of Sumatra. The kings of Srivijaya built a powerful navy and controlled commerce in southeast Asian waters. They compelled port cities in southeast Asia to recognize their authority, and they financed their navy and bureaucracy from taxes levied on ships passing through the region. They maintained an all-sea trade route between China and India, eliminating the need for the portage of trade goods across the Isthmus of Kra. As the volume of shipping increased in the second half of the first millennium, the Srivijaya kingdom prospered until the expansive Chola kingdom of southern India eclipsed it in the eleventh century.

With the decline of Srivijaya, the kingdoms of **Angkor** (889–1431 C.E.), **Singosari** (1222–1292 C.E.), and **Majapahit** (1293–1520 C.E.) dominated affairs in southeast Asia. Many

Srivijaya (sree-vih-JUH-yuh)

Angkor (AHN-kor)

What's Left Out?

To the extent that we can generalize, it is fair to say that women in Southeast Asian societies enjoyed greater equality and a more prominent public role than women in other South and East Asian societies at this time. This is demonstrated by the life of Queen Pwa Saw of the wealthy state of Pagan, which ruled much of modern Myanmar (Burma) at the same time the Khmer people were ruling the kingdom of Angkor in modern Cambodia. Women in both kingdoms played significant public roles as village leaders, merchants, scribes, bankers, scholars, and advisers to the ruling kings. According to a chronicle that was written in the nineteenth century, one of the most influential rulers of Pagan was Queen Pwa Saw. However, because the chronicle was produced six hundred years after the events it discusses, historians are divided over how much of the story is fact and how much is myth.

According to the chronicle, young Pwa Saw entered the Pagan royal palace as one of many wives of King Uzana, although she quickly became the most powerful. Following the death of the king in 1256 from a hunting accident, Pwa Saw and her advisers influenced the succession so that one of Uzana's sons, Narathihapade, was crowned king, and Pwa Saw became his chief queen. As Narathihapade's reign progressed, however, he became increasingly paranoid, and only Pwa Saw was able to moderate his destructive behaviors. The king eventually went mad, executed many of his rivals, and refused the Mongols' offer of a tribute relationship to avoid an invasion, which led to the Mongol devastation of Pagan and a decline in the kingdom's fortunes. Even in the midst of this chaos, Pwa Saw arranged for Buddhist monasteries to be supported by her estate, and after mad King Narathihapade was murdered in 1287, the queen was able to facilitate a second smooth succession of the throne, this time to Kyawswar, another of the slain king's sons.

However, according to the chronicles, Pwa Saw was disappointed in Kyawswar's ineffective rule, and she plotted with former Pagan military commanders to overthrow the king and appoint a fourteen-year-old prince to the throne. Somehow Pwa Saw managed to survive decades of court intrigue, Mongol invasions, and royal madness, and live to the ripe old age of seventy-three. She was posthumously given the name Pwa Saw, which means "Queen Grandmother," and is remembered in Burma today as a wise, funny, beautiful, and powerful woman who was effectively the real power behind the Pagan throne for more than forty years.

Source: Craig A. Lockard, *Southeast Asia in World History* (Oxford: Oxford University Press, 2009), chap. 3.

differences characterized these states. Funan had its base of operations in the Mekong Valley, Srivijaya at Palembang in southern Sumatra, Angkor in Cambodia, and Singosari and Majapahit on the island of Java. Funan and Angkor were land-based states that derived most of their wealth from productive agricultural economies, whereas Srivijaya, Singosari, and Majapahit were island-based states that prospered because they controlled maritime trade. Funan and Majapahit were largely Hindu states, but the kings of Srivijaya and Angkor made deep commitments to Buddhism. Native southeast Asian traditions survived in all these states, and at the court of Singosari, religious authorities fashioned a cultural blend of Hindu, Buddhist, and indigenous values. Sculptures at the Singosari court depicted Hindu and Buddhist personalities, for example, but used them to honor local deities and natural spirits rather than Indian deities.

Angkor The magnificent monuments of Angkor testify eloquently to the influence of Indian traditions in southeast Asia. Beginning in the ninth century, the kings of the Khmers began to build a capital city at Angkor Thom. With the aid of brahmin advisers from India, the kings designed the city as a microcosmic reflection of the Hindu world order. At the center, they built a temple representing the Himalayan Mount Meru, the sacred abode of Shiva, and surrounded it with numerous smaller temples representing other parts of the Hindu universe.

As the Khmers turned to Buddhism during the twelfth and thirteenth centuries, they added Buddhist temples to the complex, though without removing the earlier structures inspired by Hinduism. The entire complex formed a square with sides of about three kilometers (two miles), surrounded by a moat filled from the nearby Tonle Sap River. During the twelfth century the Khmer kings constructed a smaller but even more elaborate temple center at Angkor Wat, about one kilometer (just over half a mile) from Angkor Thom.

The Khmers abandoned Angkor in 1431 after Thai peoples invaded the capital and left much of it in ruins. Soon the jungle reclaimed both Angkor Thom and Angkor Wat, which remained largely forgotten until French missionaries and explorers rediscovered the sites in the mid-nineteenth century. Rescued from the jungle, the temple complexes of Angkor stand today as vivid reminders of the influence of Indian political, cultural, and religious traditions in southeast Asia and of the wealth generated in the region by trade between East and South Asia.

The Arrival of Islam

Muslim merchants had ventured into southeast Asia by the eighth century, but only during the tenth century did they become prominent in the region. Some came from southern Arabia or Persia, but many were Indians from Gujarat or the port cities of southern India. Thus Indian influence helped to establish Islam as well as Hinduism and Buddhism in southeast Asia.

Maritime trade flourished in southeast Asia during postclassical times. This ninth-century relief carving from the Buddhist temple at Borobodur in Java depicts a typical southeast Asian merchant's ship.
Werner Forman/Universal Images Group/Getty Images

Conversion to Islam For several centuries Islam maintained a quiet presence in southeast Asia. Small communities of foreign merchants observed their faith in the port cities of the region but attracted little interest on the part of the native inhabitants. Gradually, however, ruling elites, traders, and others who had regular dealings with foreign Muslims became interested in the faith. During the late thirteenth century, the Venetian traveler Marco Polo visited the island of Sumatra and noted that many residents of the towns and cities had converted to Islam, whereas those living in the countryside and the hills retained their inherited traditions.

Like Hinduism and Buddhism, Islam did not enter southeast Asia as an exclusive faith. Ruling elites who converted to Islam often continued to honor Hindu, Buddhist, or native southeast Asian traditions. They adopted Islam less as an exclusive and absolute creed than as a faith that facilitated their dealings with foreign Muslims and provided additional divine sanction for their rule. Rarely did they push their subjects to convert to Islam, although they allowed Sufi mystics to preach their faith before popular audiences. As in India, Sufis in southeast Asia appealed to a large public because of their reputation for sincerity and holiness. They allowed converts to retain inherited customs while adapting the message of Islam to local needs and interests.

Melaka During the fifteenth century the spread of Islam gained momentum in southeast Asia, largely because the powerful state of **Melaka** sponsored the faith throughout the region. Founded during the late fourteenth century by Paramesvara, a rebellious prince from Sumatra, Melaka took advantage of its strategic location in the Strait of Melaka, near modern Singapore, and soon became prominent in the trading world of southeast Asia. During its earliest days Melaka was more a lair of pirates than a legitimate state. By the mid-fifteenth century, however, Melaka had built a substantial navy that patrolled the waters of southeast Asia and protected the region's sea lanes. Melakan fleets compelled ships to call at the port of Melaka, where ruling authorities levied taxes on the value of their cargoes. Thus, like southeast Asian states of earlier centuries, Melaka became a powerful state through the control of maritime trade.

In one respect, though, Melaka differed significantly from the earlier states. Although it began as a Hindu state, Melaka soon became predominantly Islamic. About the mid-fifteenth century the Melakan ruling class converted to Islam. It welcomed theologians, Sufis, and other Islamic authorities to

Melaka (muh-LAHK-kah)

General view of the temple complex dedicated to Vishnu at Angkor Wat. These temples reflect the deep influence of Indian political, cultural, and religious traditions in southeast Asia.

Alain Evrard/Science Source

Melaka and sponsored missionary campaigns to spread Islam throughout southeast Asia. By the end of the fifteenth century, mosques had begun to define the urban landscapes of Java, Sumatra, and the Malay peninsula, and Islam had made its first appearance in the spice-bearing islands of Maluku and in the southern islands of the Philippine archipelago.

Thus, within several centuries of its arrival, Islam was a prominent feature in the cultural landscape of southeast Asia. Along with Hinduism and Buddhism, Islam helped link southeast Asian lands to the larger cultural world of India and to the larger commercial world of the Indian Ocean basin.

CONCLUSION

Unlike the political situation in China, southwest and central Asia, and the eastern Mediterranean during the first millennium C.E., India did not experience a return of centralized imperial rule such as that provided by the Tang and Song dynasties, the Umayyad and Abbasid dynasties, and the Byzantine Empire. In other respects, however, India's development was similar to that experienced in these other regions. Increased agricultural production fueled population growth and urbanization, and trade encouraged specialized industrial production and rapid economic growth. The vigorous and voluminous commerce of the Indian Ocean basin influenced the

structure of economies and societies from east Asia to east Africa. It brought prosperity especially to India, which not only contributed cotton, pepper, sugar, iron, steel, and other products to the larger hemispheric economy but also served as a major clearinghouse of trade. Like contemporary societies, India also experienced cultural change, and Indian traditions deeply influenced the cultural development of other lands. Hinduism and Islam emerged as the two most popular religious faiths within the subcontinent, and Indian merchants helped to establish Hinduism, Buddhism, and Islam in southeast Asian lands. Throughout the first and early second millennia C.E., India participated fully in the larger hemispheric zone of cross-cultural communication and exchange.

STUDY TERMS

Angkor (313)	Majapahit (313)
Axum (306)	Melaka (315)
bhakti movement (311)	monsoons (302)
caste system (298)	Ramanuja (310)
Chola kingdom (301)	Shankara (310)
dhows (303)	Shiva (309)
emporia (304)	Singosari (313)
Funan (312)	Srivijaya (313)
guru Kabir (311)	Sufis (311)
Harsha (298)	sultanate of Delhi (300)
junks (303)	Vijayanagar kingdom (302)
Mahmud of Ghazni (299)	Vishnu (309)

FOR FURTHER READING

Al-Biruni. *Alberuni's India.* 2 vols. Trans. by E. Sachau. London, 1910. English translation of al-Biruni's eleventh-century description of Indian customs, religion, philosophy, geography, and astronomy.

Edward Alpers. *The Indian Ocean in World History.* Oxford, 2014. A sweeping overview of the relationship between trade, politics and culture in the Indian Ocean world zone from ancient to modern times.

K. N. Chaudhuri. *Asia before Europe: Economy and Civilisation of the Indian Ocean from the Rise of Islam to 1750.* Cambridge, 1990. Controversial and penetrating analysis of economic, social, and cultural structures shaping societies of the Indian Ocean basin.

Ainslie T. Embree and Stephen Hay, eds. *Sources of Indian Tradition.* 2 vols. 2nd ed. New York, 1988. An important collection of primary sources in English translation.

Charles Higham. *The Civilization of Angkor.* London, 2001. Draws usefully on archaeological research in placing Angkor in historical context.

Michel Jacq-Hergoualc'h. *The Malay Peninsula: Crossroads of the Maritime Silk Road (100 B.C.–1300 A.D.).* Leiden, 2002. Scholarly study emphasizing the significance of maritime trade for southeast Asian societies.

Craig Lockard. *Southeast Asia in World History.* Oxford, 2009. Explores the history of Southeast Asia from ancient times to the present, with a strong focus on what the author terms the Golden Age between 800 and 1400 C.E.

Patricia Risso. *Merchants and Faith: Muslim Commerce and Culture in the Indian Ocean.* Boulder, 1995. Surveys the activities of Muslim merchants in the Indian Ocean basin from the seventh to the nineteenth century.

Tansen Sen. *Buddhism, Diplomacy, and Trade: The Realignment of Sino-Indian Relations, 600–1400.* Honolulu, 2003. A pathbreaking study exploring trade, diplomacy, and cultural exchanges between postclassical India and China.

Burton Stein. *Vijayanagara.* Cambridge, 1989. A study of the southern Hindu kingdom concentrating on political and economic history.

Romila Thapar. *Early India: From the Origins to A.D. 1300.* Berkeley, 2003. A scholarly analysis by one of the leading scholars of early Indian history.

The Quest for Political Order

The Early Byzantine Empire

Muslim Conquests and Byzantine Revival

The Rise of the Franks

The End of the Carolingian Empire

The Age of the Vikings

Economy and Society in Early Medieval Europe

The Two Economies of Early Medieval Europe

Social Development in Early Medieval Europe

Religious Developments in Byzantium and Western Europe

Popes and Patriarchs

Monks and Missionaries

Two Churches

ZOOMING IN ON ENCOUNTERS

Emperor Charlemagne and His Elephant

In the year 802 C.E., an unusual traveler arrived at Aachen (in modern Germany), capital of the western European empire ruled by Charlemagne. The traveler was a rare albino elephant, a diplomatic gift from the Abbasid caliph Harun al-Rashid to Charlemagne. The elephant—whom Harun named Abu al-Abbas, in honor of the Abbasid dynasty's founder—was born in India and went to Baghdad with his trainer in about 798. From Baghdad the animal accompanied an embassy overland through Syria and Egypt to a port on the Tunisian coast, then sailed across the Mediterranean to Portovenere (near Genoa in northern Italy), and finally trekked across the Alps and overland to Charlemagne's court. Abu al-Abbas must have shivered through the cold, damp winters of Europe. Yet he enjoyed swimming in the Rhine River, and until his death in 810, he amazed and delighted all who beheld him.

The church of Hagia Sophia ("Holy Wisdom") rises above the modern city of Istanbul. Originally a Christian church, the building then became an Islamic mosque, and finally a museum.

Catherine Leblanc/Corbis Documentary/Getty Images

Despite his enjoyment in receiving such an unusual gift from the Muslim court of Harun al-Rashid, Charlemagne was not a friend of Islam. At the battle of Tours (732 C.E.), his grandfather, Charles Martel, had defeated a Muslim army that ventured into Frankish territory after Muslim forces had conquered most of the Iberian peninsula. Charlemagne himself fought Muslims in an unsuccessful effort to restore Christian rule in northern Spain. One of the battles from his campaign provided the raw material for a popular poetic work called the *Song of Roland*. Nevertheless, in spite of his personal religious preferences, Charlemagne found it both necessary and convenient to have diplomatic dealings with Harun al-Rashid.

Charlemagne dispatched at least three embassies to Baghdad and received three in return. The embassies dealt with several issues: the safety of Christian pilgrims and merchants traveling in Abbasid-controlled Syria and Palestine, Charlemagne's relations with Muslim neighbors, and policy toward the Byzantine Empire, which stood between western Europe and the Abbasid caliphate. Charlemagne's realm was weak and poor compared with the Abbasid empire, but for about half a century, it seemed that Charlemagne and his successors might be able to reestablish a centralized imperial state in western Europe. His dealings with Harun al-Rashid—and the unusual odyssey of the elephant Abu al-Abbas—reflected a general recognition that Charlemagne had the potential to establish a western European empire similar to the Byzantine and Abbasid realms.

CHAPTER OVERVIEW

Some historians refer to the period from about 500 to 1500 C.E. as the medieval period of European history—the "middle ages" falling between ancient and modern times. During the early medieval period, from about 500 to 1000 C.E., European peoples recovered from the many problems that plagued the later Roman Empire—epidemic disease, declining population, economic contraction, political turmoil, social unrest, and invasions by Germanic peoples. In doing so, they laid the foundations of subsequent European civilization.

The two very different halves of medieval Europe were the **Byzantine Empire** in the eastern half of the Mediterranean basin and the Germanic states that succeeded the Western Roman Empire after its collapse in the fifth century C.E. The Byzantine Empire was in fact a direct continuation of the Roman Empire in the east. It did not extend its authority to the entire Mediterranean basin, but it inherited the most prosperous and productive regions of the Roman Empire. Even after Muslim conquerors seized the wealthy provinces of Egypt and Syria in the seventh century, the Byzantine Empire remained a political and economic powerhouse throughout the first millennium of the Common Era. As a centralized imperial state like the Abbasid empire in southwest Asia or the Tang and Song dynasties in China, the Byzantine Empire dominated the eastern Mediterranean and Black Sea regions. As an urbanized center of manufacturing, the Byzantine Empire was also a highly productive society that both supported and benefited from trade throughout the eastern hemisphere.

Meanwhile, lands to the west of the Byzantine Empire fell under the sway of invading peoples who dismantled the western part of the Roman Empire and established a series of Germanic successor states. Charlemagne made extraordinary efforts to unify much of western Europe and establish a western counterpart to the Byzantine Empire, but internal tensions and new rounds of invasions brought an early end to his own imperial creation. Thus, during the era 500 to 1000 C.E., western Europe resembled the political situation in India at this time, where a restoration of imperial unity also turned out to be a fleeting experience. When Charlemagne's empire dissolved, western European peoples fashioned alternatives to imperial rule by creating new decentralized forms of government

CHRONOLOGY	
313–337	Reign of Constantine
329–379	Life of St. Basil of Caesarea
476	Collapse of the Western Roman Empire
480–547	Life of St. Benedict of Nursia
482–543	Life of St. Scholastica
527–565	Reign of Justinian
590–604	Reign of Pope Gregory I
717–741	Reign of Leo III
726–843	Iconoclastic controversy
732	Battle of Tours
751–843	Carolingian kingdom
768–814	Reign of Charlemagne
800	Coronation of Charlemagne as emperor
9th century	Missions of St. Cyril and St. Methodius to the Slavs
989	Conversion of Prince Vladimir of Kiev to Christianity
1054	Schism between Eastern Orthodox and Roman Catholic churches

Byzantine (BIHZ-uhn-teen)

that vested public authority mostly in local or regional rulers. At the same time, they also began a process of economic recovery by dramatically boosting agricultural production.

Both the Byzantine Empire and the European states to the west inherited Christianity from the Roman Empire, and rulers in both regions promoted Christianity as a cultural and moral foundation for their rule. After the eighth century C.E., however, political and religious tensions increasingly complicated relations between the two halves of the former Roman Empire. Byzantine rulers bristled at the claims to empire made by Charlemagne and other western Christian rulers, and theologians in the two regions developed differing views on proper religious doctrine and practice. By the mid-eleventh century, the Byzantine and Roman churches had publicly and formally condemned each other. Byzantine missionaries promoted their brand of Christianity in Russia and other Slavic lands, while western Christians following the leadership of the popes in Rome spread their own views from the British Isles to Scandinavia and eastern Europe. Just as Abbasid leaders helped consolidate Islam as the principal cultural influence in the Muslim world, Byzantine and western Christians expanded the religious and moral authority of Christianity throughout Europe. In doing so, they created two culturally distinctive regions of Europe, a situation that to a certain extent has continued through to today.

THE QUEST FOR POLITICAL ORDER

During the fourth and fifth centuries, the eastern half of the Roman Empire suffered from invasions by Germanic peoples, but it did not collapse. The political challenge for rulers in this region—direct successors of the Roman emperors—was to restore order following the invasions. In the sixth century Byzantine rulers even tried to reestablish Roman authority throughout the Mediterranean basin. Their efforts fell short of that goal, and they soon lost considerable territories to expansive Muslim forces, but they nevertheless presided over a powerful society in the eastern Mediterranean region.

Political challenges were greater in lands to the west. Germanic invaders mostly passed through the Eastern Roman Empire, but they mostly settled in western regions. Throughout Roman Europe and north Africa, Germanic invaders disrupted Roman authority, deposed Roman officials, and imposed new states of their own making. After two centuries of fighting, it looked as though one group of Germanic invaders, the Franks, might reestablish imperial authority in much of Roman Europe. If they had succeeded, they might have played a role similar to that of the Sui and Tang dynasties in China by reviving centralized imperial rule after a hiatus of several centuries. By the late ninth century, however, the Frankish empire had fallen victim to internal power struggles and a fresh series of devastating invasions. Political authority in western Europe then devolved to local and regional jurisdictions, whose leaders fashioned a decentralized political order.

The Early Byzantine Empire

The Byzantine Empire takes its name from Byzantion—latinized as Byzantium—a modest market town and fishing village that occupied a site of enormous strategic significance. Situated on a defensible peninsula and blessed with a magnificent natural harbor known as the Golden Horn, Byzantion had the potential to control the Bosporus, the strait of water leading from the Black Sea to the Sea of Marmara and beyond

to the Dardanelles, the **Aegean Sea,** and the Mediterranean. Apart from its maritime significance, Byzantion offered convenient access to the rich lands of Anatolia, southwestern Asia, and southeastern Europe. Sea lanes linked the city to ports throughout the Mediterranean basin.

The City of Constantine Recognizing its strategic value, the Roman emperor Constantine designated Byzantion the site of a new imperial capital, which he named **Constantinople** ("city of Constantine"). He built the new capital partly because the eastern Mediterranean was the wealthiest and most productive region of the Roman Empire and partly because relocation enabled him to maintain close watch over both the Sasanian empire in Persia and the Germanic peoples who lived along the lower stretches of the Danube River. The imperial government moved to Constantinople after 330 C.E., and the new capital rapidly reached metropolitan dimensions. Constantine filled the city with libraries, museums, and artistic treasures, and he constructed magnificent marble palaces, churches, baths, and public buildings—all in an effort to create a new Rome fit for the ruler of a mighty empire. The city kept the name Constantinople until it fell to the Ottoman Turks (1453 C.E.), who renamed it Istanbul. By convention, however, historians refer to the realm governed from Constantinople between the fifth and fifteenth centuries C.E. as the Byzantine Empire, or simply Byzantium, in honor of the original settlement.

Caesaropapism Constantine and his successors reinforced their rule with the aura of divinity and awesome splendor. As a Christian, Constantine could not claim the divine status that some of the earlier Roman emperors had appropriated for themselves. As the first Christian emperor, however, he claimed divine favor and sanction for his rule. He intervened in theological disputes and used his political position to support the views he considered orthodox while condemning those he deemed heretical. He initiated the policy of **"caesaropapism,"** whereby the emperor not only ruled as secular lord but also played an active and prominent role in ecclesiastical affairs.

Aegean (ih-JEE-uhn)

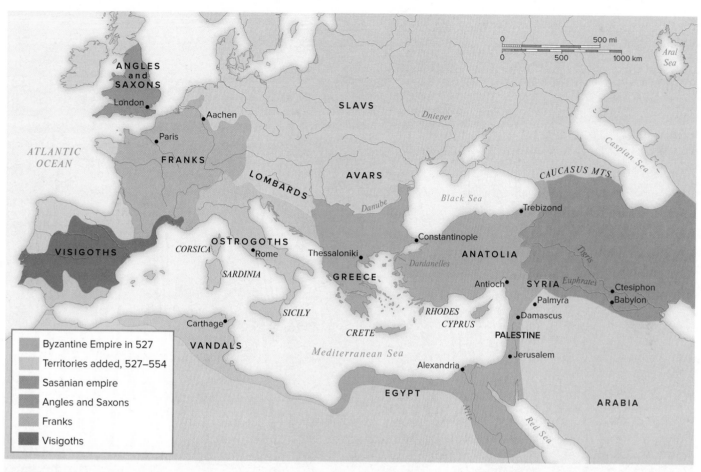

MAP 16.1   Successor states to the Roman Empire, ca. 600 C.E.

Compare this map with Map 11.2 showing the Roman Empire at its height.

What political, cultural, and environmental factors might explain the different outcomes in eastern and western Europe following the fragmentation of the Roman Empire?

Following Constantine's example, Byzantine emperors presented themselves as exalted, absolute rulers. Even dress and court etiquette testified to their lofty status. The emperors wore bejeweled crowns and dressed in magnificent silk robes dyed a dark, rich purple—a color reserved for imperial use and strictly forbidden to those not associated with the ruling house. High officials presented themselves to the emperor as slaves. When approaching the imperial majesty, they prostrated themselves three times and then ceremoniously kissed the imperial hands and feet before raising matters of business. By the tenth century, engineers had contrived a series of mechanical devices that worked dazzling effects and impressed foreign envoys at the Byzantine court: imitation birds sang as ambassadors approached the emperor while mechanical lions roared and swished their tails. During an audience the imperial throne itself sometimes moved up and down to emphasize the awesome splendor of the emperor.

Justinian and Theodora   The most important of the early Byzantine emperors was **Justinian** (reigned 527–565 C.E.), an energetic worker known to his subjects as "the sleepless

emperor," who ruled with the aid of his wife, **Theodora.** The couple came from obscure origins: Justinian was born into a Macedonian peasant family, and Theodora, the daughter of a bear keeper in the circus, worked as a striptease artist before meeting the future emperor. Yet both Justinian and Theodora were smart, strong-willed, and disciplined. Thanks to those qualities, Justinian received an education, found a position in the imperial bureaucracy, and mastered the intricacies of Byzantine finance. Theodora proved to be a sagacious adviser and a determined supporter of her emperor husband.

Like Constantine, Justinian lavished resources on the imperial capital. His most notable construction project was the church of **Hagia Sophia** ("Holy Wisdom"), a magnificent domed structure—later turned into a mosque by Ottoman conquerors—that ranks as one of the world's most important examples of Christian architecture. Visitors marveled at the church's enormous dome, which they likened to the heavens encircling the earth, and at the gold, silver, gems, and thousands of lamps that decorated and illuminated Hagia Sophia.

Hagia Sofia (HAH-yah soh-FEE-uh)

MAXIMIANVS

Byzantine emperor Justinian wears imperial purple robes (which have faded to brown over the centuries) in this mosaic, from the church of San Vitale in Ravenna, which depicts him in the company of ecclesiastical, military, and court officials.

Leemage/Universal Images Group/Getty Images

Justinian's Code Justinian's most significant political contribution was his codification of Roman law. The origins of Roman law went back more than a thousand years to the times of the kings of Rome, and even though earlier scholars worked to codify the law, it had become a confusing mass of sometimes conflicting injunctions. Justinian ordered a systematic review of Roman law and issued the ***Corpus iuris civilis*** (*Body of the Civil Law*), which immediately won recognition as the definitive codification of Roman law. Updated by later emperors, Justinian's code has influenced civil law codes in most of Europe, in Japan, and in parts of the United States.

Byzantine Conquests Justinian's most ambitious venture was his effort to reconquer the Western Roman Empire from Germanic peoples and reestablish Roman authority throughout the Mediterranean basin. Between 533 and 565, Byzantine forces under General Belisarius gained control over Italy, Sicily, much of northwestern Africa, and southern Spain. Yet Byzantium did not possess the resources to sustain a long-term occupation and consolidate those conquests. Shortly after Justinian's death, Byzantine forces abandoned Rome, leaving the city of Ravenna on Italy's Adriatic coast as the headquarters of Byzantine authority in the western Mediterranean. As a result, Ravenna possesses magnificent examples of Byzantine art and architecture, but Justinian's dream of reconstituting the old Roman Empire soon faded into oblivion.

Corpus iuris civilis (KOR-poos EW-rees sih-VEE-lees)

The interior of the church of Hagia Sophia ("Holy Wisdom"), built by Justinian and transformed into a mosque in the fifteenth century. The dome rises almost 60 meters (197 feet) above the floor, and its windows allow abundant light to enter the massive structure.
mediacolor's/Alamy Stock Photo

Muslim Conquests and Byzantine Revival

Justinian's efforts showed that the ancient Roman Empire was beyond recovery. While the emperor devoted his efforts to the western Mediterranean, the Sasanians threatened Byzantium from the east and Slavic peoples approached from the north. Later Byzantine emperors had no choice but to redeploy their resources to meet other threats.

Muslim Conquests After the seventh century C.E., the expansion of Islam (discussed in chapter 14) posed even more serious challenges to Byzantium. Shortly after Muhammad's death, Arab warriors conquered the Sasanian empire in Persia and overran large portions of the Byzantine Empire as well. By the mid-seventh century, Byzantine Syria, Palestine, Egypt, and north Africa had fallen under Muslim rule. Muslim forces later subjected Constantinople itself to two prolonged sieges (in 674–678 and again in 717–718).

Byzantium resisted this northward thrust of Islam partly because of advanced military technology. Byzantine forces used a weapon known as **"Greek fire"**—a highly effective incendiary weapon whose ingredients were a state secret that has since been lost—which they launched at both the fleets and the ground forces of the invaders. Greek fire burned even when floating on water and thus created a hazard when deployed around wooden ships. On land it caused panic among enemy forces because it was extremely difficult to extinguish and often burned troops to death. As a result of this defensive effort, the Byzantine Empire retained its hold on Anatolia, Greece, and the Balkan region.

The *Theme* System Although diminished by Muslim conquests, the Byzantine Empire was more manageable after the eighth century than was the far-flung realm of Justinian. Byzantine rulers responded to the threat of Islam with political and social adjustments that strengthened their reduced empire. Their most important innovation was the reorganization of Byzantine society under the **theme system.** They placed an imperial province called a *theme* under the authority of a general, who assumed responsibility for both its military defense and its civil administration. Generals received their appointments from the emperor, who closely monitored their activities to prevent decentralization of power and authority. Generals recruited armies from the ranks of free peasants, who received allotments of land for their military service.

Armies raised under the *theme* system were effective fighting forces, and they enabled Byzantium to expand its influence between the ninth and the twelfth centuries. During the tenth century Byzantine forces reconquered Syria and pushed their authority west into the Balkan region. By the mid-eleventh century, the Byzantine Empire encompassed lands from Syria and Armenia in the east to southern Italy in the west, from the Danube River in the north to the islands of Cyprus and Crete in the south. Once again, Byzantium dominated the eastern Mediterranean region.

The Rise of the Franks

In the year 476 C.E., the Germanic general **Odoacer** deposed the last of the western Roman emperors. He did not claim the imperial title for himself, however, nor did he appoint anyone

A manuscript illustration depicts Byzantine naval forces using Greek fire on their Arab enemies. Photo Researchers/ Science History Images/ Alamy Stock Photo

else as a replacement. The emperor's post simply remained vacant. Roman administrators and armies continued to function, temporarily, but urban populations declined as continuing invasions and power struggles disrupted trade and manufacturing. Deprived of legitimacy and resources supplied from Rome and other major cities, imperial institutions progressively weakened.

Germanic Kingdoms Gradually, a series of Germanic kingdoms emerged as successor states to the Roman empire. Visigoths, Ostrogoths, Lombards, Franks, and other Germanic peoples occupied imperial provinces, displacing Roman authorities and institutions. As they built successor states, Germanic peoples absorbed a great deal of Roman influence. Many of them converted to Christianity, for example, and others adapted Roman law to the needs of their own societies.

The Franks Most successful and most influential of the Germanic peoples were the **Franks.** By the early sixth century, the Franks had conquered most of Roman Gaul and emerged as the preeminent military and political power in western Europe. They also gained popular support when they abandoned their inherited polytheistic religion and converted to Christianity—a move that brought them the allegiance of the Christian population of the former Roman Empire as well as support from the pope and the western Christian church.

In the eighth century the aristocratic clan of the Carolingians dramatically extended Frankish power. The **Carolingian dynasty** takes its name from its founder, Charles (*Carolus* in Latin)—known as Charles Martel ("Charles the Hammer") because of his military prowess. In 732 at the battle of Tours

(in central France), he turned back a Muslim army that had ventured north from recently conquered Spain. His victory helped persuade Muslim rulers of Spain that it was not worthwhile for them to seek further conquests in western Europe.

Charlemagne The Frankish realm reached its high point under Charles Martel's grandson **Charlemagne** ("Charles the Great"), who reigned from 768 to 814. Like King Harsha in India, Charlemagne temporarily reestablished centralized imperial rule in a society disrupted by invasion and contests for power between ambitious local rulers. Like Harsha again, Charlemagne possessed enormous energy, and the building of the Carolingian Empire was in large measure his personal accomplishment. Although barely literate, Charlemagne was intelligent. He spoke Latin, understood some Greek, and regularly conversed with learned men. He maintained diplomatic relations with the Byzantine Empire and the Abbasid caliphate. The gift of the albino elephant Abu al-Abbas, discussed earlier in the chapter, symbolized relations between the Carolingian and Abbasid empires, and until its death in 810, the animal accompanied Charlemagne on many of his travels.

When Charlemagne inherited the Frankish throne, his realm included most of modern France as well as the lands that now form Belgium, the Netherlands, and southwestern Germany. By the time of his death in 814, Charlemagne had extended his authority to northeastern Spain, Bavaria, and Italy as far south as Rome. He campaigned for thirty-two years to impose his rule on the Saxons of northern Germany and to repress their rebellions. Beyond the Carolingian Empire proper, rulers in eastern Europe and southern Italy paid tribute to Charlemagne as imperial overlord.

Pope Leo III, crowning Charlemagne from *Chroniques de France ou de Saint Denis,* vol. 1; France, second quarter of 14th century.
Historic Images/Alamy Stock Photo

Charlemagne's Administration Charlemagne built a court and capital at Aachen (in modern Germany), but like Harsha in India, he spent most of his reign on horseback, traveling throughout his realm to maintain authority. Constant travel was necessary because Charlemagne did not have the financial resources to maintain an elaborate bureaucracy or an administrative apparatus that could enforce his policies. Instead, he relied on aristocratic deputies, known as counts, who held political, military, and legal authority in local jurisdictions. In an effort to keep the counts under control, Charlemagne instituted a group of imperial officials called the ***missi dominici*** ("envoys of the lord ruler"), who traveled annually to all jurisdictions and reviewed the accounts of local authorities.

Thus Charlemagne built the Frankish kingdom into an empire on the basis of military expeditions, and he began to outfit it with some centralized institutions. Yet he hesitated to call himself emperor because an imperial claim would constitute a direct challenge to the authority of the Byzantine emperors, who regarded themselves as the only legitimate successors of the Roman emperors.

Charlemagne as Emperor Only in the year 800 did Charlemagne accept the title of emperor. While campaigning in Italy, Charlemagne attended religious services conducted by Pope Leo III on Christmas Day. During the services, the pope proclaimed Charlemagne emperor and placed an imperial crown on his head. It is not certain, but it is possible that Charlemagne did not know of the pope's plan and that Leo surprised him with an impromptu coronation. Charlemagne had no desire for strained relations with the Byzantine emperors, who deeply resented his imperial title, which they saw as a

pretentious affront to their own dignity. In any case, Charlemagne had already built an imperial state, and his coronation constituted public recognition of his accomplishments.

The End of the Carolingian Empire

If Charlemagne's empire had endured, Carolingian rulers might well have built a bureaucracy, used the *missi dominici* to enhance the authority of the central government, and reestablished imperial rule in western Europe. As it happened, however, internal disunity and external invasions brought the Carolingian Empire to an early end.

Charlemagne's only surviving son, **Louis the Pious** (reigned 814–840), succeeded his father and attempted to hold the empire together. Lacking Charlemagne's strong will and military skills, however, Louis lost control of local authorities, who increasingly pursued their own interests. Moreover, Louis's three sons disputed the inheritance of the empire and waged bitter wars against one another. In 843 they divided the empire into three roughly equal portions and ruled as three kings. Thus, less than a century after its creation, the Carolingian Empire dissolved.

The Age of the Vikings

Even if internal divisions had not dismembered the Carolingian Empire, external pressures might well have brought it down. Beginning in the late eighth century, three groups of invaders pillaged the Frankish realm in search of wealth stored in towns

missi dominici (MISS-ee doh-MIN-ih-chee)

MAP 16.2 The Carolingian Empire, 814 C.E.

Notice the location of Charlemagne's capital at Aachen and also the extent of his empire.

What geographic and political challenges did he face in his efforts to hold his empire together?

and monasteries. From the south came Muslims, sometimes called Saracens by medieval historians, who raided towns, villages, churches, and monasteries in Mediterranean Europe. Muslim invaders also conquered the island of Sicily and seized territories in southern Italy and southern France. From the east came the **Magyars,** descendants of nomadic peoples who had settled in Hungary. Expert horsemen, the Magyars raided settlements in Germany, Italy, and southern France. From the north came the Vikings, most feared of all the invaders, who began mounting raids in northern France even during Charlemagne's lifetime.

The Viking invasions were part of a much larger process of expansion by the Nordic peoples of Scandinavia. One cause of Norse expansion was probably population growth fueled by increased agricultural production in Scandinavia. The main cause, however, was the quest for wealth through trading and raiding in European lands to the south of Scandinavia.

Norse expansion depended on a remarkable set of shipbuilding techniques and seafaring skills that Scandinavian mariners developed during the seventh and eighth centuries. They built rugged, shallow-draft boats outfitted both with sails, which enabled them to travel through the open ocean, and with oars, which enabled them to navigate rivers.

Vikings Many Norse seafarers were merchants seeking commercial opportunities or migrants seeking lands to settle and cultivate. However, some of them, known as the **Vikings,** turned their maritime skills more toward raiding and plundering than trading or raising crops. The term *Viking* originally referred to a group that raided the British Isles from their home at Vik in southern Norway. Over time, however, the term came to refer more generally to Norse mariners who mounted invasions and plundered settlements from Russia and eastern Europe to Mediterranean lands. With their shallow-draft boats, the Vikings were able to make their way up the many rivers offering access to interior regions of

Magyars (MAH-jahrs)

Europe. Vikings coordinated their ships' movements and timed their attacks to take advantage of the tides. Fleets of Viking boats with ferocious dragon heads mounted on their prows could sail up a river, surprise a village or a monastery far from the sea, and spill out crews of warriors who conducted lightning raids on unprepared victims.

The first Viking invaders began to attack unprotected monasteries in the 790s. Learning from experience, Viking forces mounted increasingly daring raids. In 844 C.E., more than 150 Viking ships sailed up the Garonne River in southern France, plundering settlements along the way. Sometimes Viking fleets attacked sizable cities: in 845, some 800 vessels appeared without warning before the city of Hamburg in northern Germany; in 885, a Viking force consisting

The Osenberg ship, the best-preserved Viking vessel from the early middle ages, was built in about 800 C.E. Using ships like these, the Vikings undertook extraordinary voyages across a vast region stretching from North America to central Asia.

World History Archive/Alamy Stock Photo

Danish Vikings prepare to invade England in this manuscript illustration produced at an English monastery from about 1130. Although renowned for their raiding, many Vikings later turned to trade and used their maritime skills to help connect western Europe, the Byzantine Empire, and the Islamic caliphate in a vigorous transregional trading network.

Album/Alamy Stock Photo

of at least 700 ships sailed up the Seine River and besieged Paris; and in 994, an armada of about 100 ships sailed swiftly up the Thames River and raided London. Some Vikings bypassed relatively close targets and ventured into the Mediterranean, where they plundered sites in the Balearic Islands, Sicily, and southern Italy. By following the Russian rivers to the Black Sea, other Vikings made their way to Constantinople, which they raided at least three times during the ninth and tenth centuries.

Devolution of Political Authority The Carolingians had no navy, no means to protect vulnerable sites, and no way to predict the movements of Viking raiders. Defense against the Magyars and the Muslims as well as the Vikings rested principally with local forces that could respond rapidly to invasions. Because imperial authorities were unable to defend their territories, the Carolingian Empire became the chief casualty of the invasions. After the ninth century, political and military initiative in western Europe increasingly devolved to regional and local authorities.

The devolution of political authority took different forms in different lands. In England and Germany, regional kingdoms emerged and successfully defended territories more compact than the sprawling Carolingian Empire. In France, the counts and other Carolingian subordinates usurped royal rights and prerogatives for themselves. The Vikings themselves established settlements in northern France and southern Italy, where they carved out small, independent states.

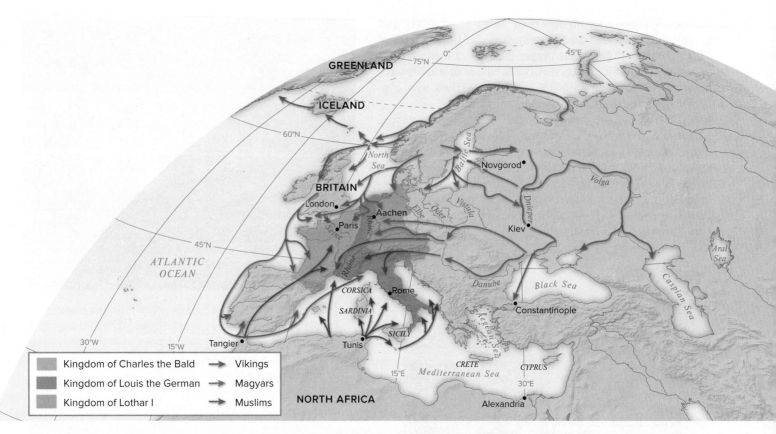

MAP 16.3   The dissolution of the Carolingian Empire (843 c.e.) and the invasions of early medieval Europe in the ninth and tenth centuries.

The various invaders of early medieval Europe took many routes and attacked both coastal and interior regions.

What were some of the political, economic, and cultural effects of the Viking invasions?

Following a century of internal conflict and external invasion, the emergence of regional kingdoms and local authorities made it increasingly unlikely that imperial rule would return to western Europe. Like India in the first millennium c.e., but unlike the situation in China, southwest Asia, and the eastern Mediterranean region, western Europe became a society of competing regional states. By putting an end to the ninth-century invasions and establishing a stable political order, these states laid a foundation for social, economic, and cultural development in later centuries.

ECONOMY AND SOCIETY IN EARLY MEDIEVAL EUROPE

Economic and social development in eastern and western Europe reflected the different political structures that emerged in each region. Byzantium was an economic power-house in the eastern Mediterranean region. The Byzantine countryside produced abundant agricultural surpluses, which supported large urban populations and fueled the work of manufacturers. Byzantine merchants participated in long-distance commercial networks that linked lands throughout the eastern hemisphere. The small states and kingdoms of western Europe, by contrast, experienced both a decline of agricultural production and a weakening of cities as repeated invasions disrupted economic and social as well as political affairs. By the tenth century, however, a measure of political stability had been restored that served as a foundation for economic recovery, and western European peoples began to participate more actively in the larger trading world of the eastern hemisphere.

The Two Economies of Early Medieval Europe

Economy of the Byzantine Empire Byzantium was strongest when its large class of free peasants had the freedom to cultivate land to the extent of their abilities as farmers. This was enhanced after the adoption of the *theme* system in the eighth century, which meant that soldiers received allotments of land when they mustered out of the army. This arrangement supported a large and prosperous class of free peasants, who cultivated their land intensively in hopes of improving their families' fortunes. The free peasantry entered an era of gradual decline after the eleventh century as wealthy cultivators managed to accumulate large estates. For as long as it flourished, however, the free peasantry provided agricultural surpluses that served as the foundation for general prosperity in the Byzantine Empire.

Manufacturing Agricultural surpluses supported manufacturing in Byzantium's cities, especially Constantinople, which was already a manufacturing megalopolis during Roman imperial times. The city was home to throngs of artisans and crafts workers, not to mention thousands of imperial officials and bureaucrats. Byzantine crafts workers enjoyed a reputation especially for their glassware, linen and woolen textiles, gems, jewelry, and fine work in gold and silver.

Silk In the sixth century, crafts workers added high-quality silk textiles to the list of products manufactured in the Byzantine Empire. The Byzantine historian Procopius reported that two Christian monks from Persia traveled to China, where they observed the techniques of silk production, which at that time were unknown outside China. According to Procopius, the monks hollowed out their walking staffs and filled them with silkworm eggs, which they smuggled out of China, through their native land of Persia, and into the Byzantine Empire. It is likely that Procopius simplified a more complex story by focusing attention on the monks, who by themselves could hardly have introduced a full-blown silk industry to Byzantium. The production of fine, Chinese-style silks required more than a few silkworm eggs. It called also for the mastery of sophisticated technologies and elaborate procedures that probably reached Byzantium by several routes.

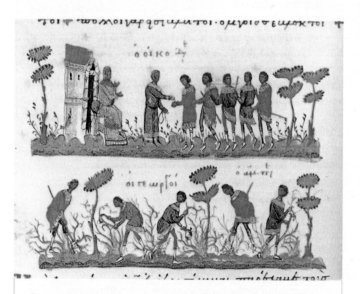

Peasants—probably sharecroppers—receive seeds and tend to vineyards in this painting from a Byzantine manuscript. What does this illustration suggest about the relationship between the two landowners or overseers (left, in the top register) and the five laborers?

The History Collection/Alamy Stock Photo

In any case, silk textiles soon made major contributions to the Byzantine economy. By the late sixth century, Byzantine silks matched the quality of Chinese textiles, and Byzantium had become the principal supplier of the fashionable fabric to lands in the Mediterranean basin. The silk industry was so important to the Byzantine economy that the government closely supervised every step in its production and sale. Regulations allowed individuals to participate in only one activity—such as weaving, dyeing, or sales—to prevent the creation of a monopoly by a few wealthy or powerful entrepreneurs.

Byzantine Trade The Byzantine economy also benefited from trade. Sitting astride routes going east and west as well as north and south, Constantinople served as the main clearinghouse for trade in the western part of Eurasia. The merchants of Constantinople maintained commercial links with manufacturers and merchants in central Asia, Russia, Scandinavia, northern Europe, and the lands of the Black Sea and the Mediterranean basin. Even after the early Islamic conquests, Byzantine merchants traded regularly with their Muslim counterparts in Persia, Syria, Palestine, and Egypt except during periods of outright war between Byzantium and Muslim states. Indeed, Byzantium was so dominant in trade that the Byzantine gold coin, the *bezant,* served as the standard currency of the Mediterranean basin for more than half a millennium, from the sixth through the twelfth century.

Byzantium drew enormous wealth simply by controlling trade and levying customs duties on merchandise that passed through its lands. Moreover, Byzantium served as the western anchor of the Eurasian trading network during revivals of the ancient Silk Roads network. Silk and porcelain came to Constantinople from China, spices from India and southeast Asia. Carpets arrived from Persia and woolen textiles from western Europe, while timber, furs, honey, amber, and slaves came from Russia and Scandinavia. Byzantine subjects consumed some commodities from distant lands, but they redistributed most products, often after adding to their value by further processing—by fashioning jewelry out of gems imported from India, for example, or by dyeing raw woolen cloth imported from western Europe.

Economy of Western Europe As Byzantium prospered, western Europe struggled to find its economic footing in an era of intermittent invasion and political turmoil, which disrupted both agricultural production and large-scale manufacturing. While dealing with political and military challenges, though, western Europeans also adopted a series of innovations that yielded increased agricultural production.

Heavy Plows One innovation was a new kind of heavy plow that gradually replaced the light Mediterranean plows that had made their way north at the time of the Roman Empire. In light, well-drained Mediterranean soils, cultivators used small wooden plows that broke the surface of the soil, created a

SOURCES FROM THE PAST

The Wealth and Commerce of Constantinople

The Spanish rabbi Benjamin of Tudela traveled throughout Europe, north Africa, and southwest Asia between 1165 and 1173 C.E. He may have ventured as far as India, and he mentioned both India and China in his travel account. His main purpose was to record the conditions of Jewish communities, but he also described the many lands and about three hundred cities that he visited. His travels took place during an era of political decline for the Byzantine Empire, yet he still found Constantinople a flourishing and prosperous city.

The circumference of the city of Constantinople is eighteen miles; half of it is surrounded by the sea, and half by land, and it is situated upon two arms of the sea, one coming from the sea of Russia [the Black Sea], and one from the sea of Sepharad [the Mediterranean].

All sorts of merchants come here from the land of Babylon, from the land of Shinar [Mesopotamia], from Persia, Media [western Iran], and all the sovereignty of the land of Egypt, from the land of Canaan [Palestine], and the empire of Russia, from Hungary, Patzinakia [Ukraine], Khazaria [southern Russia], and the land of Lombardy [northern Italy] and Sepharad [Spain].

Constantinople is a busy city, and merchants come to it from every country by sea or land, and there is none like it in the world except Baghdad, the great city of Islam. In Constantinople is the church of Hagia Sophia, and the seat of the pope of the Greeks, since Greeks do not obey the pope of Rome. There are also as many churches as there are days of the year. . . . And in this church [Hagia Sophia] there are pillars of gold and silver, and lamps of silver and gold more than a man can count.

> Why is it that the Greeks do not obey the pope of Rome?

Close to the walls of the palace is also a place of amusement belonging to the emperor, which is called the Hippodrome, and every year on the anniversary of the birth of Jesus the emperor gives a great entertainment there. And in that place men from all the races of the world come before the emperor and empress with jugglery and without jugglery, and they introduce lions, leopards, bears, and wild asses, and they engage them in combat with one another; and the same thing is done with birds. No entertainment like this is to be found in any other land. . . .

> What Roman imperial form of entertainment does this description remind you of?

From every part of the Byzantine empire tribute is brought here every year, and they fill strongholds with garments of silk, purple, and gold. Like unto these storehouses and this wealth there is nothing in the whole world to be found. It is said that the tribute of the city amounts every year to 20,000 gold pieces, derived both from the rents of shops and markets and from the tribute of merchants who enter by sea or land.

The Greek inhabitants are very rich in gold and precious stones, and they go clothed in garments of silk and gold embroidery, and they ride horses and look like princes. Indeed, the land is very rich in all cloth stuffs and in bread, meat, and wine.

Wealth like that of Constantinople is not to be found in the whole world. Here also are men learned in all the books of the Greeks, and they eat and drink, every man under his vine and his fig-tree.

For Further Reflection

■ What role did the geographical location of Constantinople play in making it such a successful commercial center?
■ In what ways does this passage support the idea that the Byzantine Empire was an extension of the Roman Empire?
■ As well as information about the economy, what does the passage tell us about political organization in the Byzantine Empire?

Source: Benjamin of Tudela. *The Itinerary of Benjamin of Tudela.* Trans. by M. N. Adler. London: H. Frowde, 1907. (Translation slightly modified.)

In this twelfth-century manuscript illustration, a peasant guides a heavy, wheeled plow while his wife prods the oxen that pull the plow.
Album/Oronoz/Newscom

furrow, and uprooted weeds. This type of plow made little headway in the dense, moist soils of the north. After the eighth century a more serviceable plow came into use: a heavy tool equipped with iron tips and a mould-board that turned the soil so as to aerate it thoroughly and break up the root networks of weeds. The heavy plow was a more expensive piece of equipment than the light Mediterranean plow, and it required cultivators to harness more energy to pull it through damp northern soils. Once hitched to oxen or draft horses, however, the heavy plow contributed to greater agricultural production.

As the heavy plow spread throughout western Europe, cultivators took several additional steps that increased agricultural production. They cleared new lands for cultivation and built ponds for fish. They constructed water mills, which enabled them to take advantage of a ready and renewable source of inanimate energy, thus freeing human and animal energy for other work. They employed a special horse collar, which allowed them to rely less on slow-moving oxen and more on speedier horses to pull their heavy plows. They increased cultivation of beans and other legumes, which enriched diets throughout western Europe. Thus western Europeans made numerous small adaptations that created a foundation for rural prosperity after 1000 C.E.

Trade in Western Europe By no means did trade disappear from western Europe. Local markets and fairs offered opportunities for small-scale exchange, and itinerant peddlers shopped their wares from one settlement to another. Maritime trade flourished in the Mediterranean despite Muslim conquests in the region. Christian merchants from Italy and Spain regularly traded across religious boundary lines with Muslims of Sicily, Spain, and north Africa, who linked Europe indirectly with a larger world of communication and exchange.

Norse Merchant-Mariners Maritime trade flourished also in the North Sea and the Baltic Sea. Most active among the early medieval merchants in the northern seas were Norse seafarers, kinsmen of the Vikings. Norse traders followed the same routes as Viking raiders, and many individual mariners no doubt turned from commerce to plunder and back again as opportunities arose. Norse merchants called at ports from Russia to Ireland, carrying cargoes of fish and furs from Scandinavia, honey from Poland, wheat from England, wine from France, beer from the Low Countries, and swords from Germany. By traveling down the Russian rivers to the Black Sea, they were able to trade actively in both the Byzantine and the Abbasid empires. Thus, like Mediterranean merchants, but by different routes, Norse mariners linked western Europe with the world of Islam. Indeed, the Carolingian Empire depended heavily on this connection: Norse merchants took Scandinavian products to the Abbasid empire and exchanged them for silver, which they traded at Carolingian ports for wine, jugs, glassware, and other products. The silver transported from the Abbasid empire by Norse merchants was a principal source of bullion used for minting coins in early medieval Europe and hence a crucially important element of the western European economy. Thus, even if western European merchants were not as numerous or prominent as their Byzantine counterparts, they nevertheless participated in the trading networks of the larger Afro-Eurasian region.

Social Development in Early Medieval Europe

Byzantium: An Urban Society The Byzantine Empire was rich in large, prosperous, cosmopolitan cities, including Alexandria, Antioch, and Damascus, to mention only a few. Indeed, until the Muslim conquests of the late seventh and eighth centuries, Byzantium was probably the world's most urbanized society, and residents of its cities enjoyed the

What's Left Out? ◼◼ ◼◼ ◼◼ ◼◼ ◼◼

This chapter offers several comparisons between the political, economic, social and religious structures of Eastern and Western Europe during the millennium following the fragmentation of the Roman Empire. In keeping with the theme of many of the What's Left Out features in other chapters, another way of comparing these two European regions is by looking at their attitudes towards women. We have seen that in the Byzantine Empire some women did rise to positions of power, notably the Empress Theodora. In fact, several Byzantine empresses are known to history, most of whom managed to play significant political and social roles by exerting influence on their imperial husbands. Yet these women were the exceptions; in general elite Byzantine women played virtually no part in their husband's public lives. Women lived in separate sections of the residences, were forbidden from receiving male visitors, and were not allowed to attend parties or banquets. The only public role acceptable for most elite women in Byzantium was to visit relatives, and even this had to be done in the company of male chaperones. Girls were married in their early teens, through contracts arranged by parents to improve a family's social standing. Education was limited to reading and writing, although some Byzantine women did excel as physicians, composers, and historians.

An exception to the norm was the Byzantine historian Anna Comnena (1083–1153). She was born into one of the most powerful families in Constantinople, and as the daughter of Emperor Alexis I received an excellent education; indeed she may have been one of the most educated European women who had lived to that point in history. She was groomed for leadership and had strong claims upon the throne, but in the end she was bypassed in succession by her younger brother John II. Bitterly disappointed and still with a burning ambition for power, she became involved in a plot against John which, when discovered, resulted in her forfeiting her property and status as a member of the imperial family. Sent in exile to a monastery, Anna dedicated herself to learning instead, particularly to the study of history and philosophy. She wrote her own study of the history of her time, the *Alexiad*, and because of this many regard Anna Comnena as the first female historian of Europe.

The *Alexiad*, which is focused on the reign of her father, was actually started by her husband, but upon his death Anna took up her pen at the age of 55. Using the works of Thucydides and Polybius as her model, Anna produced an insightful analysis of the political and military affairs of the Byzantines, particularly their conflicts with Western European states. Much of her analysis of the First Crusade was based on eye-witness accounts, and her description of the erratic often brutal behavior of the Crusaders, and the alarm this caused in Constantinople, provides a very different perspective on these 'Christian soldiers' to that offered by contemporary western historians. Although the *Alexiad* is somewhat biased because of Anna's attempts to praise her father and ridicule his successors, it is chronologically sound, highly analytical, and still useful to historians today.

Another exceptional woman emerges from the pages of Western European history at more or less the same time, Hildegard of Bingen (1098-1179), a near contemporary of Anna Comnena. She came from a long line of distinguished members of religious orders, and took her vows to become a Nun in her teens. Entering a nunnery was one of the few avenues available to elite western European women who wanted to receive a decent education. Hildegard rose to the position of abbess at Disibodenberg, but at age 49 after experiencing a number of visions, she left the abbey to found her own convent near Bingen. Here she worked with her nuns to explain her visions in a series of illuminated books, beginning with *Know the Ways of the Lord*, followed by *Book of Divine Works*. In the latter she articulated a unified vision of the history of humanity from Adam to the Apocalypse, and argued for the harmonious interaction of humans with the cosmos. Hildegard also wrote books on natural science and medicine. In the *Book of Medicine Carefully Arranged* she discussed dozens of different diseases, their causes and possible herbal and other cures, and also described the development of the human female reproductive system. Hildegard was highly regarded and even sought out by powerful men of both the secular and religious worlds, but this did not stop here from condemning rulers and Church authorities for corruption.

As remarkable as the lives of these two women were, most historians agree that they are the exceptions who very much prove the rule. Because we can find very few such examples of women who managed to rise to positions of influence and prestige in their male-dominated societies, it is clear that for most women in both Eastern and Western Europe during the Early Medieval Period, avenues to power, or even to anything approaching equality of opportunity, were so limited as to be almost non-existent.

See Bonnie Anderson and Judith Zinsser point out in their important 1988 book *A History of their Own: Women in Europe from Prehistory to the Present*, 1988, Vol 1, 190.

Women workers were prominent in Byzantine textile production. A manuscript illustration depicts one Byzantine woman weaving cloth (left) while another spins thread (right). Both women veil their hair for modesty.
The Picture Art Collection/Alamy Stock Photo

benefits and observed urban traditions inherited from the classical Mediterranean world. Yet Constantinople had no rival among Byzantine cities. Subjects of the Byzantine Empire referred to it simply as "the City." The heart of the City was the imperial palace, which employed twenty thousand workers as palace staff. Peacocks strutted through gardens filled with sculptures and fountains. Most famous of them was a gold fountain that spouted wine for imperial guests.

City Life Aristocrats maintained enormous palaces that included courtyards, reception halls, libraries, chapels, and quarters for members of the extended family as well as servants and enslaved people. In the fifth century Constantinople boasted 4,388 mansions, as well as fourteen imperial and princely palaces. Women lived in separate apartments and did not receive male visitors from outside the household. Nor did they participate in banquets and parties, especially when wine flowed freely or when the affairs were likely to become so boisterous that they could compromise a woman's reputation. In Constantinople as well as other cities, upper-class women generally wore veils, like their Mediterranean ancestors from centuries past, to discourage the attention of men outside their own families.

Dwellings of less privileged classes were not so splendid. Artisans and crafts workers commonly lived in rooms above their shops, while clerks and government officials occupied multistory apartment buildings. Workers and the poor lived in rickety tenements where they shared kitchens and sanitary facilities with their neighbors.

Attractions of Constantinople Even for the poor, however, the City had its attractions. As the heir of Rome, Constantinople was a city of baths, which were sites of relaxation and exercise as well as hygienic bathing. Taverns and restaurants offered settings for social gatherings—checkers, chess, and dice games were especially popular activities at taverns—and theaters provided entertainment in the form of song, dance, and striptease. Mass entertainment took place in the Hippodrome, a large stadium adjacent to the imperial palace, where Byzantine subjects watched chariot races; athletic matches; contests between wild animals; and circuses featuring acts by clowns, jugglers, acrobats, and dwarfs.

Western Europe: A Rural Society Cities to the west had once offered similar pleasures, but they largely disappeared in the wake of Germanic invasions and the collapse of the Western Roman Empire in the late fifth century. The agricultural surplus of western Europe was sufficient to sustain local political elites but not substantial enough to support large, urban populations of artisans, crafts workers, merchants, and professionals. Towns survived, but they served more as economic hubs of surrounding regions than as vibrant centers integrating the economic activities of distant lands.

The Question of Feudalism How did the peoples of western Christendom reorganize their society after the collapse of the Western Roman Empire? Historians once routinely used

SOURCES FROM THE PAST

Pope Gregory the Great on Peasant Taxation on the Papal Estates, ca. 600

Some useful insights into the lives and experiences of peasants can be found in this letter written by Pope Gregory I in about 600 C.E. The pope demonstrates concern for the excessive tax burden tenant farmers working in papal estates are being forced to pay. Despite papal concern, the document reminds us just how harsh the lives of peasant farmers in early medieval Europe were.

We have also learned that in some of the holdings of the Church a most unjust exaction is made, so that three half measures out of seventy—it is shameful to say it—are solicited from the tenants; and furthermore, even this does not suffice, but they are said to be asked for something more, over and above this, by reason of a long-standing custom. This practice we absolutely detest, and we wish it to be absolutely eradicated from our patrimony. But let your experience guide you, whether it be a case of receiving a pound more, or whether it be a case of taking more than rightful measure from the serfs; and let everything count towards the sum total of the rent; and insofar as the serfs can bear it, let them pay full rent reckoned at two parts out of seventy by weight. Nor should the market tax be collected at more than a just pound weight, neither an excessive pound weight, nor other burdens greater than a pound; but by your calculation, so far as you are able to do it, let it be reckoned against the sum total of the rent, and so let filthy exaction never occur.

> What problems with the pound weight is the pope concerned with here?

But in order that these very burdens, imposed unjustly, which we have caused to be reckoned as part of the rent, may not in some way be increased after our death, and the rent be thus increased, and the serfs again be compelled to pay the burdens of superadding, we desire you to make out schedules of security about the rents, inscribing therein the amount of rent which each ought to pay, including the market tax, the grain tax, and other payments. But as for what has been taken for the use of the overseer from these little excrescences, we desire this to be taken from the sum total of the rent and applied to your own use.

Above all we wish you to attend to this carefully, that unjust weights be not used in collecting the rents. If you should find such, destroy them, and introduce new and just ones. For my son, the servant of God, the Deacon, has already found such as displeased him, but he did not have the authority to change them. Except in the case of inferior and cheap provisions, we want nothing over and above just weights to be demanded of the coloni of the Church.

We have further learned that if any one of the serfs has done wrong, punishment is not inflicted upon the man himself, but payment is levied on his property. Concerning this we ordain that whoever commits wrong shall, as is fitting, be punished; but let there be no acceptance of any payment whatever from him, except, perchance, a small sum which may defray the expenses of the bailiff sent to him.

> Why would punishments have evolved so that they were inflicted on the property of the perpetrator rather than on the person?

We have further learned that as often as a tenant has taken anything from a colonus it has not been returned, though repayment was demanded of the tenant; therefore we order that whatever has been taken with violence from any of the serfs be restored to him from whom it was taken and not put to our use, lest we ourselves seem to be the authors of violence. Further, we wish, that when you send outside the patrimony, those who are engaged in your service, small payments be received from them. Yet so that it turn out to their advantage, because we do not desire that the purse of the Church be disgraced by filthy lucre. We also order you carefully to prevent the placing of tenants on the holdings of the Church for payments, lest, through payments being sought, tenants be frequently changed, from which changing what else takes place but that the estates of the Church are never cultivated? Even the payments from charter lands should be reduced according to the sum total of the rent. On the score of filling the barns and collecting their contents we desire you to receive from the holdings of the Church only what is customary; what we have ordered you to buy should be bought from strangers.

Have that part of my letter which relates to the serfs read throughout all our holdings, that they may know wherein they might protect themselves from violence with our authority, and let there be given to them either an authentic document or a copy of the same.

For Further Reflection

■ On the basis of the letter from Pope Gregory I, what were some of the ways in which peasants and their labor were being exploited on papal estates at the end of the fifth century?

■ What are the major practices in the relationship between the Church and the tenant farmers that the pope is concerned with in this letter?

■ What might the pope's intentions be in demanding an end to some of these exploitative practices?

■ To what extent could historians use this letter as evidence of the lives of feudal tenant farmers more generally in Early Medieval western Europe?

Source: J. P. Migne, *Patrologiae Cursus Completus*, Vol. LXXVII p. 498 (Paris, 1849), reprinted in Roy C. Cave and Herbert H. Coulson, eds., *A Source Book for Medieval Economic History* (Milwaukee: The Bruce Publishing Co., 1936; reprint ed., New York: Biblo & Tannen, 1965), pp. 41–43. (Translation slightly modified.)

the term *feudalism* to characterize the political and social order of medieval Europe. They spoke of a "feudal system" involving a hierarchy of lords and vassals, who collectively took charge of political and military affairs on the basis of personal relationships. Lords supposedly provided grants of land to their retainers in exchange for loyalty and military service. Over the years, scholarship has somewhat undermined that view of medieval society, and some historians have abandoned the concept of feudalism as a model that tends to oversimplify a more complex society. They argue that it is more accurate to view early medieval Europe as a society in which local political and military elites worked in various ad hoc ways to organize their territories and maintain social order. The arrangements they adopted had deep implications for the lives of political and military elites themselves and also for their relationships with commoners.

In the absence of an effective central authority such as an emperor, local notables or lords mobilized small private armies composed of armed supporters and mercenaries. Some of these lords were descendants of Carolingian or other ruling houses, and others were ambitious strongmen—essentially local warlords. Both the lords and their retainers were warriors with horses, weapons, and military expertise. Lords sometimes rewarded their retainers with grants of land or some other valuable, such as the right to income generated by a mill, the right to receive rents or payments from a village, or even a payment of money. In other cases, lords supported their retainers by maintaining them in their own households, where they provided equipment and training in military affairs. After the year 1000, lords increasingly hired their retainers, paying them for services on the basis of need. By one mechanism or another, lords and retainers constituted themselves as privileged political and military elites who dominated local regions.

Peasants Lords and retainers supported themselves and their families principally on the basis of the surplus agricultural production that they commandeered from a subject peasantry. Political and military elites obliged local peasants to provide labor services and payments of rents in kind, such as a portion of the harvest, a chicken, or a dozen eggs. Male peasants typically worked three days a week for their lords while also providing additional labor services during planting and harvesting season. Women peasants churned butter, made cheese, brewed beer, spun thread, wove cloth, or sewed clothes for their lords as well as for their own families. Some peasants also kept sheep or cattle, and their obligations to lords included products from their herds. Because lords provided peasants with land to cultivate and often with tools and animals as well, peasants had little opportunity to move to different lands. Indeed, they were commonly able to do so only with permission from their lords. They even had to pay fees for the right to marry a peasant who worked for a different lord.

Population During the fifth and sixth centuries, epidemic disease and political turmoil took a demographic toll in both Byzantium and western Europe. From a high point of about thirty-six million at the time of the Roman Empire in 200 C.E., population fell to about twenty-six million in the year 600—nineteen million in Byzantium and seven million in western Europe. Population fluctuated dramatically over the next two centuries, as Byzantium lost territories to Muslims, and western Europeans suffered repeated invasions. After the eighth century, however, both Byzantium and western Europe entered an era of demographic recovery. Political stability created a foundation for a more productive agricultural economy just as new food crops made their way from the Muslim world to Byzantium and Mediterranean Europe. Hard durum wheat, rice, spinach, artichokes, eggplant, lemons, limes, oranges, and melons brought increased calories and dietetic variety that supported increasing populations. By the year 800 eastern and western Europe had a combined population of about twenty-nine million, which rose to about thirty-two million in 900 and thirty-six million in 1000—the level of the Roman Empire's population some eight centuries earlier. Thus by the year 1000, both Byzantium and western Europe had built productive agricultural economies that sustained sizable and increasing populations.

RELIGIOUS DEVELOPMENTS IN BYZANTIUM AND WESTERN EUROPE

As heirs of the Roman Empire, Byzantium and western Europe were both Christian societies. In the cases of political, social, and economic affairs, though, the two regions created distinctive and ultimately competing forms of their common religious inheritance. In both Byzantium and western Europe, Christianity served as the principal source of religious, moral, and cultural authority. Both lands supported ecclesiastical hierarchies with networks of monasteries. Both societies also worked to extend the reach of Christianity by sending missionaries to seek converts in northerly territories from Russia and Slavic lands to Scandinavia and the British Isles. By the year 1000 the twin heirs of Roman Christianity had laid the foundations for a large Christian cultural zone in the western part of the Eurasian continent that paralleled the Buddhist and Islamic cultural zones farther east. Yet even as they were promoting Christianity in their own societies and beyond, church authorities in Byzantium and western Europe fell into deep disagreement on matters of doctrine, ritual, and church authority. By the mid-eleventh century, their differences had become so great that church leaders formally denounced one another and established two rival communities: the Eastern Orthodox church in Byzantium and the Roman Catholic church in western Europe.

Popes and Patriarchs

Christianity had a more hierarchical organizational structure than any other major religious tradition. For example, there was no pope of Buddhism, no patriarch in the Islamic world. Christianity inherited its strong organizational structure from the time of the late Roman Empire. In the early middle ages, the two most important Christian authorities were the bishop of Rome, known as the pope, and the patriarch of Constantinople.

A twelfth century illustration depicting Pope Gregory I.
Bettmann/Getty Images

The Papacy

The Papacy When the Western Roman Empire collapsed, the **papacy** survived and claimed continuing spiritual authority over all the lands formerly embraced by the Roman Empire. At first the popes cooperated closely with the Byzantine emperors, who seemed to be the natural heirs of the emperors of Rome. Beginning in the late sixth century, however, the popes acted more independently and devoted their efforts to strengthening the western Christian church based at Rome and clearly distinguishing it from the eastern Christian church based at Constantinople.

Pope Gregory I The individual most responsible for charting an independent course for the Roman church was **Pope Gregory I** (590–604 C.E.). As pope, Gregory faced an array of challenges. During the late sixth century, the Germanic

Lombards campaigned in Italy, menacing Rome and the church in the process. Gregory mobilized local resources and organized the defense of Rome, thus saving both the city and the church. He also faced difficulties within the church because bishops frequently acted as though they were supreme ecclesiastical authorities within their own dioceses. To regain the initiative, Gregory reasserted claims to papal primacy—the notion that the bishop of Rome was the ultimate authority for all the Christian church. Gregory also made contributions as a theologian. He emphasized the sacrament of penance, which required individuals to confess their sins to their priests and atone for them by penitential acts—a practice that enhanced the influence of the Roman church in the lives of individuals.

The Patriarchs The **patriarchs** of Constantinople were powerful officials, but they did not enjoy the independence of their brethren to the west. Following the tradition of caesaropapism inaugurated by the emperor Constantine in the fourth century, Byzantine emperors treated the church as a department of state. They appointed the patriarchs, and they instructed patriarchs, bishops, and priests to deliver sermons that supported imperial policy and encouraged obedience to imperial authorities. This caesaropapism was a source of tension between imperial and ecclesiastical authorities, and it also had the potential to provoke popular dissent when imperial views clashed with those of the larger society.

Iconoclasm The most divisive ecclesiastical policy implemented by Byzantine emperors was **iconoclasm,** inaugurated by Emperor Leo III (reigned 717–741 C.E.). Byzantium had a long tradition of producing icons—paintings of Jesus, saints, and other religious figures—many of which were splendid works of art. Most theologians took these icons as visual stimulations that inspired reverence for holy personages. Leo, however, became convinced that the veneration of images was sinful, tantamount to the worship of idols. In 726 C.E., he embarked on a policy of iconoclasm (which literally means "breaking of icons"), destroying religious images and prohibiting their use in churches. The policy immediately sparked protests and even riots throughout the empire because icons were extremely popular among the people. Debates about iconoclasm raged for more than a century. Only in 843 did Leo's followers abandon the policy of iconoclasm.

Monks and Missionaries

Consumed with matters of theology, ritual, and church politics, popes and patriarchs rarely dealt directly with the lay population of their churches. For personal religious instruction and inspiration, lay Christians looked less to the church hierarchy than to local monasteries.

Asceticism Christian **monasticism** grew out of the efforts of devout individuals to lead especially holy lives. Early Christian ascetics in Egypt, Mesopotamia, and Persia adopted

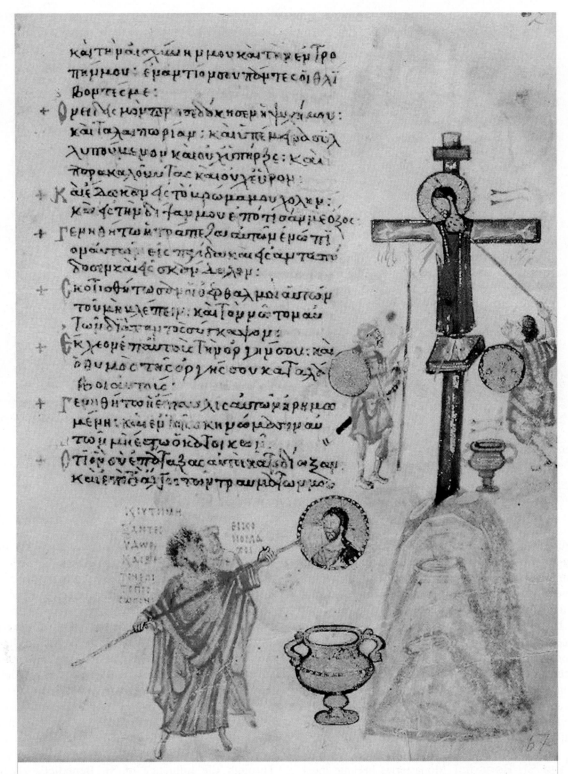

This illustration from a psalter prepared about 900 C.E. depicts an iconoclast whitewashing an image of Jesus painted on a wall.

Art Collection 3/Alamy Stock Photo

A fourteenth-century manuscript illustration shows St. Benedict with his crosier, the staff carried by abbots to symbolize their position (left), and meeting with two monks beside a fishpond at their monastery (right). What does the fishpond suggest about the economic significance of monasteries?

Darling Archive/Alamy Stock Photo; Ann Ronan Pictures/Print Collector/Getty Images

extreme regimes of self-denial in order to focus all their attention on religious matters. Some lived alone as hermits. Others formed communes where they devoted themselves to the pursuit of holiness rather than worldly success. Many dedicated themselves to celibacy, fasting, and prayer.

Drawn by their reputation for piety, disciples gathered around these ascetics and established communities of men and women determined to follow their example. These communities became the earliest monasteries. During the early days of monasticism, each community developed its own rules, procedures, and priorities. The result was wild inconsistency: some monasteries imposed harsh and austere regimes of self-denial, and others offered little or no guidance.

St. Basil and St. Benedict Monasteries became much more influential when reformers provided them with discipline and a sense of purpose. The two most important reformers were the patriarch **St. Basil** of Caesarea (329–379 C.E.) in Byzantium and **St. Benedict** of Nursia (480–547 C.E.) in Italy. Both

men prepared regulations for monasteries that provided for mild but not debilitating **asceticism** combined with meditation and work on behalf of the church. In both Basilian and Benedictine monasteries, individuals gave up their personal possessions and lived communal, celibate lives under the direction of the abbots who supervised the communities. Poverty, chastity, and obedience became the prime virtues for Basilian and Benedictine monks. At certain hours monks came together for religious services and prayers, dividing the remainder of the day into periods for study, reflection, and labor.

St. Scholastica Monasteries throughout Byzantium adopted the Basilian rule for their own use, while their counterparts in western Europe largely followed the rule of St. Benedict. Through the influence of St. Benedict's sister, the nun **St. Scholastica** (482–543 C.E.), an adaptation of the Benedictine rule soon provided guidance for the religious life of women living in convents.

Monasticism and Society Like Buddhist monasteries in Asian lands and charitable religious foundations in Muslim lands, Christian monasteries provided a variety of social

asceticism (uh-SET-uh-siz-uhm)

services that enabled them to build close relations with local communities. Monks and nuns offered spiritual counsel to local laity, and they organized relief efforts by supplying food and medical attention at times of natural or other calamities. Monasteries and convents served both as orphanages and as inns for travelers. Sometimes they also provided rudimentary educational services for local communities.

Because of the various roles they played in the larger society, monasteries were particularly effective agents in the spread of Christianity. While providing social services, monks also preached Christianity and tended to the spiritual needs of rural populations. For many people, a local neighboring monastery was the only source of instruction in Christian doctrine, and a local monastic church offered the only practical opportunity for them to take part in religious services. Thus, over decades and centuries, monks and nuns helped spread Christian teachings to countless generations of European peasants.

Missionaries Some monks went beyond the bounds of their own society and sought to spread Christianity in the larger world. Indeed, one of the remarkable developments of the early middle ages was the creation of a large Christian cultural zone in the western part of the Eurasian continent.

Christianity was already well established in the Mediterranean region, but pagan Germanic and Slavic peoples occupied the more northerly parts of Europe. In the late sixth century, Pope Gregory I sent **missionaries** to England and targeted the pagan Germanic kings who ruled various parts of the island, hoping that their conversion would induce their subjects to adopt Christianity. This tactic largely succeeded: by the early seventh century Christianity enjoyed a stable foothold, and by 800 England was securely within the fold of the Roman church. The Franks and Charlemagne later sponsored efforts to extend Christianity to northern Germany and Scandinavia. They met spirited resistance from Germanic peoples, who had no desire to abandon their inherited gods or pagan beliefs, but by the year 1000 Christianity had won a sizable and growing following.

Meanwhile, Byzantine authorities sent missionaries to Balkan and Slavic lands. The most famous of the missionaries to the Slavs were Saints Cyril and Methodius, two brothers from Thessaloniki in Greece. During the mid-ninth century, Cyril and Methodius conducted missions in Bulgaria and Moravia (which included much of the modern Czech, Slovakian, and Hungarian territories). There they devised an alphabet, known as the Cyrillic alphabet, for the previously illiterate Slavic peoples. Although adapted from written Greek, the Cyrillic alphabet represented the sounds of Slavic languages more precisely than did the Greek, and it remained in use in much of eastern Europe until supplanted by the Roman alphabet in the twentieth century. In Russia and many other parts of the former Soviet Union, the Cyrillic alphabet survives to the present day.

North of Bulgaria another Slavic people began to organize large states: the Russians. About 989, at the urging of

Monasteries were the principal centers of literacy in western Europe during the early middle ages. In this manuscript illustration, one monk copies a manuscript, another makes geometric calculations, a third cuts parchment, two work on the building, and one more rings the bells that call monks and members of the surrounding community to religious services.
Album/Alamy Stock Photo

Byzantine missionaries, Prince Vladimir of Kiev converted to Christianity and ordered his subjects to follow his example. Vladimir was no paragon of virtue: he lauded drunkenness and reportedly maintained a harem of eight hundred young women. After his conversion, however, Byzantine influences flowed rapidly into Russia. Cyrillic writing, literacy, and Christian missions all spread quickly throughout Russia. Byzantine teachers traveled north to establish schools, and Byzantine priests conducted services for Russian converts. Thus Kiev served as a conduit for the spread of Byzantine cultural and religious influence in Russia.

Two Churches

Although they professed the same basic Christian doctrine, the churches of Constantinople and Rome experienced increasing friction after the sixth century. Tensions mirrored political strains, such as deep resentment in Byzantium after Charlemagne accepted the title of emperor from the pope in Rome. Yet church authorities in Constantinople and Rome also harbored different views on religious and theological issues. The iconoclastic movement of the eighth and ninth centuries was one focus of difference. Western theologians regarded religious images as perfectly appropriate aids to devotion and resented Byzantine claims to the contrary, whereas the iconoclasts took offense at the efforts of their Roman counterparts to have images restored in Byzantium.

Religious Rivalry Over time the Christian churches based in Constantinople and Rome disagreed on many other points. Some ritual and doctrinal differences concerned forms of worship and the precise wording of theological teachings—relatively minor issues that in and of themselves need not have caused deep division in the larger Christian community. Byzantine theologians objected, for example, to the fact that western priests shaved their beards and used unleavened rather than leavened bread when saying Mass. Other differences concerned more substantive theological matters, such as the precise relationship between God, Jesus, and the Holy Spirit—all regarded as manifestations of God by most Christian theologians of the day.

How the Past Shapes the Future

The Spread of Religious Traditions

Between the late sixth century and 1000 C.E., missionaries from both the Roman and Byzantine churches moved north and west in quests to bring Christianity to nonbelievers. While the Roman missionaries were successful in the British Isles, in Scandinavia, and among Germanic peoples, the Byzantine missionaries had their greatest successes in the Balkans and in Slavic lands. Consider the long-term impact that the spread of these different traditions had in the lands where they won converts in terms of art, literature, and culture. In what ways are these legacies still visible in western and eastern Europe today?

Schism Alongside ritual and doctrinal differences, the Byzantine patriarchs and the Roman popes disputed their respective rights and powers. Patriarchs argued for the autonomy of all major Christian jurisdictions, including that of Constantinople, whereas popes asserted the primacy of Rome as the sole seat of authority for all Christendom. Ultimately, relations became so strained that the eastern and western churches went separate ways. In 1054 the patriarch and pope mutually excommunicated each other, each refusing to recognize the other's church as properly Christian. This decision had profound historical consequences because, despite efforts at reconciliation, the **schism** between eastern and western churches has persisted to the present day. In light of the schism, historians refer to the eastern Christian church after 1054 as the Eastern Orthodox church and its western counterpart as the Roman Catholic church.

CONCLUSION

After the collapse of the Western Roman Empire, the two halves of Europe followed very different historical paths. Byzantium inherited a thriving economy, a set of governing institutions, an imperial bureaucracy, an established church, and a rich cultural tradition from ancient Mediterranean society and the Roman Empire. Even after the loss of territories to Muslim conquerors, Byzantium remained a powerful and productive society in the eastern Mediterranean region. By contrast, western Europe experienced turmoil in the face of repeated invasion, which thoroughly disrupted social and economic as well as political affairs. Only after the ninth century did western Europeans gradually manage to achieve political stability and lay the foundations for a more predictable and prosperous society. For all their differences, though, the eastern and western European states both advanced the construction of a large Christian cultural zone that paralleled the lands of Islamic and Buddhist influence to the east. This Christian cultural zone harbored different and competing versions of a common religion—like the Islamic cultural zone with both Sunni and Shia advocates or the Buddhist cultural zone with Mahayana as well as Theravada adherents—but Byzantium and western Europe both relied on religion as a foundation for cultural unity and made Christianity the most important source of cultural and moral authority throughout Europe.

STUDY TERMS

Aegean Sea (320)	Charlemagne (324)
asceticism (338)	Constantinople (320)
Byzantine Empire (319)	*Corpus iuris civilis* (322)
Carolingian dynasty (324)	Franks (324)
caesaropapism (320)	Greek fire (323)

Hagia Sofia (321)
iconoclasm (336)
Justinian (321)
Louis the Pious (325)
Magyars (326)
missi dominici (325)
missionaries (339)
monasticism (336)
Odoacer (323)
papacy (336)

patriarchs (336)
Pope Gregory I (336)
schism (340)
St. Basil (338)
St. Benedict (338)
St. Scholastica (338)
theme system (323)
Theodora (321)
Vikings (326)

FOR FURTHER READING

Peter Brown. *The Rise of Western Christendom: Triumph and Diversity, A.D. 200–1000.* 2nd ed. Oxford, 2003. A landmark analysis of early Christian history.

Einhard and Notker the Stammerer. *Two Lives of Charlemagne.* Trans. by Lewis Thorpe. New York, 1969. Translations of two early biographies of Charlemagne.

Patrick J. Geary. *Before France and Germany: The Creation and Transformation of the Merovingian World.* 2nd ed. New York, 1997. Insightful study of Germanic societies in early medieval Europe.

Judith Herrin. *Byzantium: The Surprising Life of a Medieval Empire.* Princeton, 2009. A judicious survey of Byzantine history.

Anthony Kaldellis. *The Byzantine Empire. People and Power in New Rome.* Cambridge, Mass., 2015. Connects Byzantine politics and social structures with their Roman roots and argues that during its early centuries at least, the Byzantine Empire functioned similarly to the Roman republic.

Michael McCormick. *Origins of the European Economy: Communications and Commerce, A.D. 300–900.* Cambridge, Mass., 2001. A comprehensive analysis that emphasizes the participation of early medieval Europe in a larger Mediterranean economy.

Procopius. *History of the Wars, Secret History, and Buildings.* Trans. by A. Cameron. New York, 1967. Translations of writings by the most important historian in the time of Justinian.

Susan Reynolds. *Fiefs and Vassals: The Medieval Evidence Reinterpreted.* Oxford, 1994. A densely written but important book offering a powerful scholarly critique of the concept of feudalism.

Julian D. Richards. *The Vikings. A Very Short Introduction.* Oxford, 2005. A brief but surprisingly detailed and up-to-date survey of the significance of the Vikings.

John M. Riddle. *A History of the Middle Ages 300–1500.* Lanham, Md., 2008. A comprehensive and lively account of the history and culture of western Europe and the Byzantine Empire from the late classical era to the late medieval period.

ZOOMING IN ON ENCOUNTERS

The Goldsmith of the Mongolian Steppe

Guillaume Boucher was a goldsmith who lived during the early and middle decades of the thirteenth century. In the 1230s, he left his native Paris and went to Budapest. His new city, then part of the kingdom of Hungary, was in the midst of invasion by Mongol warriors. Mongols were known for their fearsome and destructive skills in battle, and we can only imagine the chaos that Boucher must have witnessed or the fear he may have felt. Yet Boucher survived and went on to become a valuable part of the Mongol enterprise. Noticing Boucher's metalworking skills, the Mongols took him captive. When they left Hungary in 1242, they took him back to their Central Asian homeland.

For at least the next fifteen years, Boucher lived at the Mongol capital at **Karakorum.** Though technically a slave, he enjoyed some prestige and the freedom to marry a fellow Frenchwoman. He supervised fifty assistants in a workshop that produced decorative objects of gold and silver for the Mongol court. Boucher also produced gold and silver statues in built carriages, designed buildings, and even sewed ritual garments for Roman Catholic priests conducting services for Christians living at Karakorum.

Karakorum (kahr-uh-KOR-uhm)

A thirteenth-century painting from an illustrated Persian history text depicts Mongol mounted warriors pursuing their fleeing enemies. Note the superb discipline and coordination of the Mongols, who used their superior military skills and organization to regularly defeat armies from a wide range of cultures and states.
DEA/A.DAGLI ORTI/De Agostini/Getty Images

Boucher was by no means the only European living at the Mongol court. In fact, the Mongols had a deliberate policy of resettling people who were skilled in specialized crafts and occupations. When they conquered an area, Mongols separated out those they considered "useful"—including soldiers, textile workers, secretaries, carpenters, and jewelsmiths like Boucher himself—and then sent them to areas where their talents were needed. Indeed, visitors to the Mongol court at Karakorum around the time Boucher lived encountered Germans, Slavs, and Hungarians as well as Chinese, Koreans, Turks, Persians, and Armenians, among others. This policy of resettlement encouraged Eurasian integration by fostering, often forcibly, increased exchanges between peoples of very different traditions.

CHAPTER OVERVIEW

Between the eleventh and the fifteenth centuries, nomadic peoples became more prominent than ever before in Eurasian affairs. Turkish groups migrated to Persia, Anatolia, and India, where they overcame existing authorities and established new states. During the thirteenth and fourteenth centuries, the Mongols established themselves as the most powerful people of the central Asian steppes and then turned on settled societies in China, Persia, Russia, and eastern Europe. By the early fourteenth century, the Mongols had built the largest empire the world has ever seen, stretching from Korea and China in the east to Russia and Hungary in the west.

Most of the Mongol states collapsed during the late fourteenth and fifteenth centuries, but the decline of the Mongols did not signal the end of nomadic peoples' influence on Eurasian affairs. Although a native Chinese dynasty replaced the Mongol state in China, the possibility of a Mongol revival forced the new dynasty to focus attention and resources on its central Asian frontier. Moreover, from the fourteenth through the seventeenth century, Turkish peoples embarked on new campaigns of expansion that eventually brought most of India, much of central Asia, all of Anatolia, and a good portion of eastern Europe under their domination.

The military campaigns of nomadic peoples were exceedingly destructive. Nomadic warriors often demolished cities, slaughtered urban populations, and ravaged surrounding agricultural lands. Yet those same forces also encouraged systematic peaceful interaction between peoples of different societies. Between the eleventh and the fifteenth centuries, Turkish and Mongol peoples forged closer links than ever before between peoples of neighboring lands. By fostering cross-cultural communication and exchange on an unprecedented scale, the nomadic empires encouraged encounters between peoples from many different traditions. In so doing, they helped to integrate societies throughout much of the eastern hemisphere.

CHRONOLOGY	
1055	Tughril Beg named sultan
1071	Battle of Manzikert
1206–1227	Reign of Chinggis Khan
1211–1234	Mongol conquest of northern China
1219–1221	Mongol conquest of Persia
1237–1241	Mongol conquest of Russia
1258	Mongol capture of Baghdad
1264–1279	Mongol conquest of southern China
1264–1294	Reign of Khubilai Khan
1279–1368	Yuan dynasty
1295	Conversion of Ilkhan Ghazan to Islam
1336–1405	Life of Tamerlane
1453	Ottoman capture of Constantinople

TURKISH MIGRATIONS AND IMPERIAL EXPANSION

Turkish peoples never formed a single, homogeneous group but instead organized themselves into clans and tribes that often fought bitterly with one another. All Turkish peoples spoke related languages, and all were nomads or descendants of nomads. From modest beginnings they expanded their influence until they dominated not only the steppes of central Asia but also settled societies in Persia, Anatolia, and India.

Economy and Society of Nomadic Pastoralism

Nomadic Pastoralists and Their Animals Nomadic peoples of central Asia built societies by adapting to the ecological conditions of the arid lands they lived on. They were pastoralists who kept herds of animals—horses, sheep, goats, cattle, and camels. Central Asia does not receive enough rain to support large-scale agriculture, but grasses and shrubs flourish on the steppe lands. Maintenance of flocks required pastoral peoples of central Asia to move frequently. They

A painting from the late fourteenth century by the central Asian artist Mehmed Siyah Qalem suggests the physical hardships of nomadic life. In this scene from a nomadic camp, two men wash clothes (upper left), while another blows on a fire, and a companion tends to a saddle. Bows, arrows, and other weapons are readily available (top right).
The Picture Art Collection/Alamy Stock Photo

drove their animals to lands with abundant grass and then moved them along as the animals thinned the vegetation. They did not wander aimlessly through the steppes but, rather, followed migratory cycles that accounted for the seasons and local climatic conditions. They lived mostly off the meat, milk, and hides of their animals. They used animal bones for tools and animal dung as fuel for fires. They made shoes and clothes out of wool from their sheep and skins from their other animals. Wool was also the source of the felt that they used to fashion large tents called **yurts** in which they lived. They even prepared an alcoholic drink from animal products by fermenting mare's milk into a potent concoction known as *kumiss.*

The arid climate and the nomadic lifestyle limited the size of human societies in central Asia. Agriculture is necessary for dense populations to congregate, and that was only possible at oases, which were few and far between. Most settlements were few and small—and often temporary as well because nomads carried their collapsible felt yurts with them as they drove their herds. Nomads often engaged in small-scale cultivation of millet or vegetables when they found sources of water, but the harvests were sufficient only to supplement animal products, not to sustain whole societies. Nomads also produced limited amounts of pottery, leather goods, iron weapons, and tools. However, given their migratory habits, intensive agriculture and large-scale craft production were not possible.

Nomadic and Settled Peoples As a result, nomads avidly sought opportunities to trade with settled peoples, and as early as the classical era brisk trade linked nomadic and settled societies. Much of that commerce took place on a small scale as nomads sought agricultural products and manufactured goods to satisfy their immediate needs. But nomads also did participate in long-distance trade networks. Because of their mobility and their familiarity with large regions of central Asia, nomadic peoples were ideally suited to organize and lead the caravans that crossed central Asia and linked settled societies from China to the Mediterranean basin. During the postclassical era and later, Turkish peoples were especially prominent on the caravan routes of central Asia.

Nomadic Society Nomadic society typically had two social classes: elites and commoners. Elite charismatic leaders acquired the prestige needed to organize clans and tribes into alliances. Normally, these elite leaders did little governing

SOURCES FROM THE PAST

William of Rubruck on Gender Roles among the Mongols

Mongol attacks on Hungary and Poland in 1241 deeply alarmed the pope in Rome. In 1245 he called a council to determine how best to respond to the threat Mongols seemed to pose for Europe. The council decided to send two Franciscan missionaries to the Mongol court as emissaries. William of Rubruck was the second missionary to make the journey, and from 1253 to 1255 he traveled extensively in the recently established Mongol Empire. During his travels he met all the leading Mongol figures of the day, including the Great Khan Möngke. After his return to France, William composed a long account of his journey with descriptions of life on the steppes. One of the things that intrigued him greatly about the Mongols was their gender roles.

A matron makes for themselves the most beautiful wagons. A single rich Tartar has quite one hundred or two hundred such wagons. Baatu [a prominent Mongol general and grandson of Chinggis Khan] has twenty-six wives, each of which has a dwelling, exclusive of the other little ones which they set up after the big one, and which are like closets, in which the sewing girls live, and to each of these large dwellings are attached quite two hundred wagons. And when they set up their houses, the first wife places her dwelling on the extreme west side. and after her the others according to their rank, so that the last wife will be in the extreme east; and there will be the distance of a stone's throw between the yurt of one wife and that of another . . .

> Why do you think William of Rubruck thought this was worth mentioning to his European readers?

It is the duty of the women to drive the wagons, get the dwellings on and off them, milk the cows, make butter and *grut* [a kind of cheese], and to dress and sew skins, which they do with a thread made of tendons. They divide the tendons into fine shreds, and then twist them into one long thread. They also sew the boots, the socks, and the clothing. They never wash clothes, for they say that God would be angered thereat, and that it would thunder if they hung them up to dry. Thunder they fear extraordinarily; and when it thunders they will turn out of their dwellings all strangers, wrap themselves in black felt, and thus hide themselves till it has passed away. Furthermore, they never wash their bowls, but when the meat is cooked they rinse out the dish in which they are about to put it with some of the boiling broth from the kettle, which they pour back into it. They also make the felt and cover the houses.

> How might the practices described here have been different in a settled society?

The men make bows and arrows, manufacture stirrups and bits, make saddles, do the carpentering on their dwellings and the carts; they take care of the horses, milk the mares, churn the *cosmos* or mare's milk, make the skins in which it is put; they also look after the camels and load them. Both sexes look after the sheep and goats, sometimes the men, other times the women, milking them.

For Further Reflection

■ Why did women play such prominent social and economic roles in nomadic pastoral societies?

Source: The Journey of William of Rubruck to the Eastern Parts of the World, 1253–55, as Narrated by Himself. Trans. William Woodville Rockhill. London: The Haklyut Society, 1800.

because clans and tribes looked after their own affairs and resented interference. During times of war, however, elite rulers wielded absolute authority over their forces, and they immediately executed those who did not obey orders.

This nomadic "nobility" was a fluid class. Leaders passed elite status along to their heirs, but the heirs could lose their status if they did not continue to provide appropriate leadership for their clans and tribes. Over the course of a few generations, elites could return to the status of commoners who tended their own herds and followed new leaders. Meanwhile, commoners could become elites by their conduct, particularly by courageous behavior during war. Then, if they were clever diplomats, they could arrange alliances between clans and tribes and gain enough support to displace established leaders.

Gender Relations Adult males dominated nomadic pastoral societies, but women enjoyed much higher status than women in settled agricultural societies. In most nomadic pastoral societies, able-bodied men were frequently away from their herds on hunting expeditions or military campaigns. Thus women were primarily responsible for tending to the animals. Nomadic women were skilled horse riders and archers, and they sometimes fought alongside men in war. Because of their crucial economic roles, women wielded considerable influence—sometimes as advisers with strong voices in family or clan matters and occasionally as regents or rulers in their own right.

Nomadic Religion The earliest religion of the Turkish peoples revolved around **shamans**—religious specialists believed to be able to communicate with the gods and nature spirits, ask for divine help on behalf of their communities, and inform their companions of their gods' will. Yet many Turkish peoples became attracted to the religious and cultural traditions they encountered when trading with peoples of settled societies. They did not abandon their inherited beliefs or their shamans, but by the sixth century C.E. many Turks had converted to Buddhism, Nestorian Christianity, or **Manichaeism.** Partly because of their newly adopted religious and cultural traditions and partly because of their prominence in Eurasian trade networks, Turkish peoples also developed a written script.

Turkish Conversion to Islam Over the longer term, most Turks converted to Islam as a result of their continual encounters with Muslim peoples. The earliest converts were Turkish nomads captured in border raids by forces of the **Abbasid** caliphate in the early ninth century and integrated into the caliphate's armies as slave soldiers. The first large-scale conversion came in the late tenth century, when a Turkish ruling clan known as the Seljuqs converted to Islam. Although historians cannot be sure of the motivation behind this conversion, the fact that the Seljuqs then migrated to Persia suggests it may have been an attempt to improve their fortunes through alliance with Abbasid authorities. Between the tenth and the fourteenth centuries, most Turkish clans on the steppes of central Asia also adopted Islam, and they carried the new religion with them when they expanded their political and military influence to new regions.

Military Organization That expansion took place when nomadic leaders organized vast confederations of peoples all subject, at least nominally, to a **khan** ("ruler"). In fact, khans rarely ruled directly but, rather, through the leaders of allied tribes. Yet when organized on a large scale, nomadic peoples wielded enormous military power, mostly because of their outstanding cavalry forces. Nomadic warriors learned to ride

horses as children, and they had excellent equestrian skills. Their arrows flew with deadly accuracy even when launched from the backs of galloping horses. Moreover, units of warriors coordinated their movements to outmaneuver and overwhelm their opponents.

Few armies were able to resist the mobility and discipline of well-organized nomadic warriors. When they found themselves at a disadvantage, they often were able to beat a hasty retreat and escape from their less speedy adversaries. Because of their military skills, several groups of Turkish nomads began in the tenth century C.E. to seize the wealth of settled societies and build imperial states in the regions surrounding central Asia.

Turkish Empires in Persia, Anatolia, and India

Seljuq Turks and the Abbasid Empire Turkish peoples entered Persia, Anatolia, and India at different times and for different purposes. They approached Abbasid Persia much as Germanic peoples had earlier approached the Roman Empire. From about the mid-eighth to the mid-tenth century, Turkish peoples lived mostly on the borders of the Abbasid realm, which offered abundant opportunities for trade. By the mid- to late tenth century, large numbers of **Seljuq Turks** served in Abbasid armies and lived in the Abbasid realm itself. By the mid-eleventh century the Seljuqs overshadowed the Abbasid caliphs. Indeed, in 1055 the caliph recognized the Seljuq leader Tughril Beg as **sultan** ("chieftain" or "ruler"). Tughril first consolidated his hold on the Abbasid capital at Baghdad, then he and his successors extended Turkish rule to Syria, Palestine, and other parts of the realm. For the last two centuries of the Abbasid state, the caliphs served as figureheads of authority while actual governance lay in the hands of the Turkish sultans.

Seljuq Turks and the Byzantine Empire While some Turkish peoples established themselves in Abbasid Persia, others turned their attention to the rich land of Anatolia, breadbasket of the Byzantine Empire. Led by the Seljuqs, Turkish peoples began migrating into Anatolia in large numbers in the early eleventh century. In 1071, Seljuq forces inflicted a devastating defeat on the Byzantine army at Manzikert in eastern Anatolia and even took the Byzantine emperor captive. Following that victory, Seljuqs and other Turkish groups entered Anatolia almost at will. The peasants of Anatolia, who mostly resented their Byzantine overlords, often looked upon the Seljuqs as liberators rather than conquerors.

The migrants thoroughly transformed Anatolia. Turkish groups displaced Byzantine authorities and set up their own political and social institutions. They levied taxes on the Byzantine church, restricted its activities, and sometimes confiscated church property. Meanwhile, they welcomed converts to Islam and made political, social, and economic

---

Manichaeism (MAN-ih-kee-izm)
Seljuq (sahl-JYOOK)

opportunities available to them. By 1453, when Ottoman Turks captured the Byzantine capital at Constantinople, Byzantine and Christian Anatolia had become largely a Turkish and Islamic land.

Ghaznavid Turks and the Sultanate of Delhi

While the Seljuqs spearheaded Turkish migrations in Abbasid Persia and Byzantine Anatolia, Mahmud of Ghazni led the **Ghaznavid Turks** of Afghanistan in raids on lucrative sites in northern India. When the Ghaznavids began their campaigns in the early eleventh century, their principal goal was plunder. Gradually, though, they became more interested in permanent rule. They asserted their authority first over the Punjab and then over Gujarat and Bengal. By the thirteenth century, the Turkish **sultanate of Delhi** claimed authority over all of northern India. Several of the Delhi sultans conceived plans to conquer southern India and extend Muslim rule there, but none was able to realize those ambitions. The sultans faced constant challenges from Hindu princes in neighboring lands, and they periodically

Mahmud of Ghazni on his throne.
Album/Alamy Stock Photo

had to defend their northern frontiers from new Turkish or Mongol invaders. They maintained an enormous army with a large elephant corps, but those forces only enabled them to hold on to their territories rather than to expand their empire.

Turkish rule had great social and cultural implications in India, as it did in Anatolia. Mahmud of Ghazni was a zealous foe of Buddhism and Hinduism alike, and he launched frequent raids on shrines, temples, and monasteries. His forces stripped Buddhist and Hindu establishments of their wealth, destroyed their buildings, and often slaughtered their residents and attendants as well. As Turkish invaders repressed Buddhism and Hinduism, they encouraged conversion to Islam and enabled their faith to establish a secure presence in northern India.

Though undertaken by different groups, for different reasons, and by different means, the Turkish conquests of Persia, Anatolia, and India represented part of a larger expansive movement by nomadic peoples. In all three cases, the formidable military prowess of Turkish peoples enabled them to move beyond the steppe lands of central Asia and dominate settled societies. By the thirteenth century, the influence of nomadic peoples was greater than ever before in Eurasian history. Yet the Turkish conquests represented only a prelude to an astonishing round of empire building launched by the Mongols during the thirteenth and fourteenth centuries.

THE MONGOL EMPIRES

For most of their history the nomadic **Mongols** lived on the high steppe lands of eastern central Asia. Like other nomadic peoples, they displayed deep loyalty to kin groups organized into families, clans, and tribes. They frequently allied with Turkish peoples who built empires on the steppes, but they rarely played a leading role in the organization of states before the thirteenth century. Strong loyalties to kinship groups made it difficult for the Mongols to organize a stable society on a large scale. During the early thirteenth century, however, **Chinggis Khan** (sometimes spelled "Genghis Khan") forged the various Mongol tribes into a powerful alliance that built the largest empire the world has ever seen. Although the vast Mongol realm soon dissolved into a series of smaller empires—most of which disappeared within a century—the Mongols' imperial venture brought the societies of Eurasia into closer contact than ever before.

Chinggis Khan and the Making of the Mongol Empire

The unifier of the Mongols was **Temüjin,** born about 1167 into a noble family. His father was a prominent warrior who

Chinggis Khan (CHIHN-gihs Kahn)

Temüjin (TEM-oo-chin)

This painting by a Chinese artist depicts Chinggis Khan at about age sixty. Though most of his conquests were behind him, Chinggis Khan's focus and determination are readily apparent in this portrait.

GL Archive/Alamy

forged an alliance between several Mongol clans and seemed likely to become a powerful leader. When Temüjin was about ten years old, however, rivals poisoned his father and destroyed the alliance. Abandoned by his father's allies, Temüjin led a precarious existence for some years. He lived in poverty because rivals seized the family's animals, and several times he eluded enemies seeking to eliminate him as a potential threat to their own ambitions. A rival once captured him and imprisoned him in a wooden cage, but Temüjin made a daring midnight escape and regained his freedom.

Chinggis Khan's Rise to Power

During the late twelfth century, Temüjin made an alliance with a prominent Mongol clan leader. He also mastered the art of steppe diplomacy, which called for displays of personal courage in battle, combined with intense loyalty to allies—as well as a willingness to betray allies or superiors to improve one's position—and the ability to entice previously unaffiliated tribes into cooperative relationships. Temüjin gradually strengthened his position, sometimes by forging useful alliances, often by conquering rival contenders for power, and occasionally by

turning suddenly against a troublesome ally. He eventually brought all the Mongol tribes into a single confederation, and in 1206 an assembly of Mongol leaders recognized Temüjin's supremacy by proclaiming him Chinggis Khan ("universal ruler").

Mongol Political Organization Chinggis Khan's policies greatly strengthened the Mongol people. Earlier nomadic state builders had ruled largely through the leaders of allied tribes. Because of his personal experiences, however, Chinggis Khan mistrusted the Mongols' tribal organization. He broke up the tribes and forced men of fighting age to join new military units with no tribal affiliations. He chose high military and political officials not on the basis of kinship or tribal status but, rather, because of their talents or their loyalty to him. Chinggis Khan spent most of his life on horseback and did not establish a proper capital, but his successors built a sumptuous capital at Karakorum—present-day Har Horin, located about 300 kilometers (186 miles) west of the modern Mongolian capital of Ulaanbaatar. As command center of a growing empire, Karakorum symbolized a source of Mongol authority superior to the clan or the tribe.

The most important institution of the Mongol state was the army, which magnified the power of the small population. In the thirteenth century the Mongol population stood at about one million people—less than 1 percent of China's numbers. During Chinggis Khan's life, his army numbered only 100,000 to 125,000 Mongols, although allied peoples also contributed forces. How was it possible for so few people to conquer the better part of Eurasia?

Mongol Arms Like earlier nomadic armies, Mongol forces relied on outstanding equestrian skills. Mongols grew up riding horses, and they honed their skills by hunting and playing competitive games on horseback. Their bows, short enough for archers to use while riding, were also stiff, firing arrows that could fell enemies at 200 meters (656 feet). Mongol horsemen were among the most mobile forces of the premodern world, sometimes traveling more than 100 kilometers (62 miles) per day to surprise an enemy. Furthermore, the Mongols understood the psychological dimensions of warfare and used them to their advantage. If enemies surrendered without resistance, the Mongols usually spared their lives, and they provided generous treatment for artisans, crafts workers, and those with military skills. In the event of resistance, however, the Mongols ruthlessly slaughtered whole populations, sparing only a few, whom they sometimes drove before their armies as human shields during future conflicts.

Once he had united the Mongols, Chinggis Khan turned his army and his attention to other parts of central Asia and particularly to nearby settled societies. He attacked the various Turkish peoples ruling in Tibet, northern China, Persia, and the central Asian steppes. His conquests in central Asia were important because they protected him against the

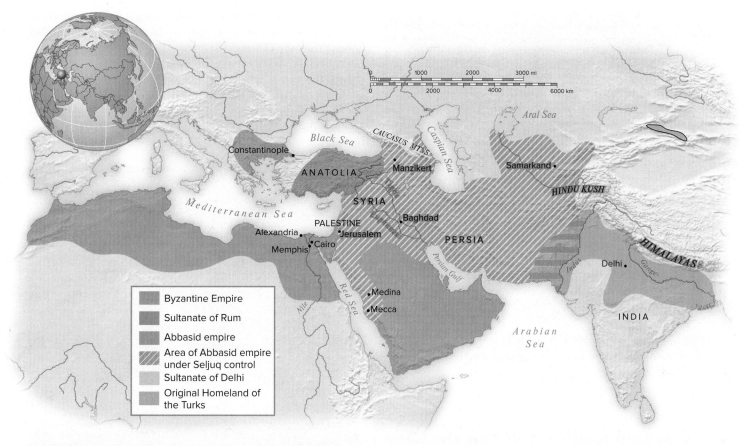

Byzantine Empire

Sultanate of Rum

Abbasid empire

Area of Abbasid empire under Seljuq control

Sultanate of Delhi

Original Homeland of the Turks

MAP 17.1   Turkish empires and their neighbors, ca. 1210

After about 1000 C.E., nomadic Turkish peoples conquered and ruled settled agricultural societies in several regions of Eurasia and north Africa.

What motivated Turkish people to expand so far from their original homeland, and why were they so successful in creating new states?

possibility that other nomadic leaders might challenge his rule. But the Mongol campaigns in China and Persia had especially far-reaching consequences.

Mongol Conquest of Northern China   Chinggis Khan himself extended Mongol rule to northern China, dominated since 1127 C.E. by the nomadic **Jurchen** people, while the Song dynasty continued to rule in southern China. The conquest of China began in 1211 C.E. when Mongol raiding parties invaded the Jurchen realm. Raids quickly became more frequent and intense, and soon they developed into a campaign of conquest. By 1215 the Mongols had captured the Jurchen capital near modern Beijing, which under the new name of **Khanbaliq** ("city of the khan") served also as the Mongol capital in China. Fighting between Mongols and Jurchen continued until 1234, but by 1220 the Mongols had largely established control over northern China.

Mongol Conquest of Persia   While part of his army consolidated the Mongol hold on northern China, Chinggis Khan

led another force to Afghanistan and Persia, ruled at that time by a successor to the Seljuqs known as the **Khwarazm shah.** In 1218 Chinggis Khan sought to open trade and diplomatic relations with the Khwarazm shah. The shah despised the Mongols, however, and he ordered his officials to murder Chinggis Khan's envoys and the merchants accompanying them. The following year Chinggis Khan took his army west to seek revenge. Mongol forces pursued the Khwarazm shah to an island in the Caspian Sea where he died. Meanwhile, they shattered the shah's army and seized control of his realm.

To forestall any possibility that the shah's state might survive and constitute a challenge to his own empire, Chinggis Khan wreaked utter destruction on the conquered land. The Mongols ravaged one city after another, demolishing buildings and massacring hundreds of thousands of people. Some cities never recovered. The Mongols also destroyed the delicate *qanat* irrigation systems that sustained agriculture in the arid region, resulting in severely reduced agricultural production. For centuries after the Mongol conquest, Persian chroniclers cursed the invaders and the devastation they visited upon the land.

Mongol soldiers firing their arrows from horseback, from a thirteenth-century illustrated history produced by Persian historian Rashid al-Din.
akg-images/Newscom

By the time of his death in 1227, Chinggis Khan had laid the foundation of a vast and mighty empire. He had united the Mongols, established Mongol supremacy in central Asia, and extended Mongol control to northern China in the east and Persia in the west. Chinggis Khan was a conqueror, however, not an administrator. He ruled the Mongols themselves through his control over the army, but he did not establish a central government for the lands that he conquered. Instead, he assigned Mongol overlords to supervise local administrators and to extract a generous tribute for the Mongols' own uses. Chinggis Khan's heirs continued his conquests, but they also undertook the task of designing a more permanent administration to guide the fortunes of the Mongol Empire.

The Mongol Empires after Chinggis Khan

Chinggis Khan's death touched off a struggle for power among his sons and grandsons, several of whom had ambitions to succeed the great khan. Eventually, his heirs divided Chinggis Khan's vast realm into four regional empires. The great khans ruled China, the wealthiest of Mongol lands. Descendants of Chaghatai, one of Chinggis Khan's sons, ruled the **khanate of Chaghatai** in central Asia. Persia fell under the authority of rulers known as the ilkhans, and the **khans of the Golden Horde** dominated Russia. The great khans were nominally superior to the others, but they were rarely able to enforce their claims

Khubilai (KOO-bih-lie)

to authority. In fact, for as long as the Mongol Empires survived, ambition fueled constant tension and occasional conflict among the four khans.

Khubilai Khan The consolidation of Mongol rule in China came during the reign of **Khubilai Khan** (sometimes spelled Qubilai), one of Chinggis Khan's grandsons. Khubilai was perhaps the most talented of the great conqueror's descendants.

Depiction of Khubilai Khan on the hunt. Khubilai sits on the dark horse near the center.
Attributed to Liu Kuan-tao/Getty Images

SOURCES FROM THE PAST

Marco Polo on Mongol Military Tactics

The Venetian Marco Polo is one of the best-known Europeans who traveled through Mongol territories in the late thirteenth century. His book of travel writings is an especially valuable source of information about the Mongol age because the Mongols left very little in the way of a written record. Among other things, he described the Mongol way of making war.

Their arms are bows and arrows, sword and mace; but above all the bow, for they are capital archers, indeed the best that are known. . . .

When a Mongol prince goes forth to war, he takes with him, say, 100,000 men. Well, he appoints an officer to every ten men, one to every hundred, one to every thousand, and one to every ten thousand, so that his own orders have to be given to ten persons only, and each of these ten persons has to pass the orders only to another ten, and so on, no one having to give orders to more than ten. And every one in turn is responsible only to the officer immediately over him; and the discipline and order that comes of this method is marvellous, for they are a people very obedient to their chiefs. . . .

When they are going on a distant expedition they take no gear with them except two leather bottles for milk, a little earthenware pot to cook their meat in, and a little tent to shelter them from rain. And in case of great urgency they will ride ten days on end without lighting a fire or taking a meal. On such an occasion they will sustain themselves on the blood of their horses, opening a vein and letting the blood jet into their mouths, drinking till they have had enough, and then staunching it. . . .

When they come to an engagement with the enemy, they will gain the victory in this fashion. They never let themselves get into a regular medley, but keep perpetually riding round and shooting into the enemy. And as they do not count it any shame to run away in battle, they will sometimes pretend to do so, and in running away they turn in the saddle and shoot hard and strong at the foe, and in this way make great havoc. Their horses are trained so perfectly that they will double hither and thither, just like a dog, in a way that is quite astonishing. Thus they fight to as good purpose in running away as if they stood and faced the enemy because of the vast volleys of arrows that they shoot in this way, turning round upon their pursuers, who are fancying that they have won the battle. But when the Mongols see that they have killed and wounded a good many horses and men, they wheel round bodily and return to the charge in perfect order and with loud cries, and in a very short time the enemy are routed. In truth they are stout and valiant soldiers, and inured to war. And you perceive that it is just when the enemy sees them run, and imagines that he has gained the battle, that he has in reality lost it, for the Mongols wheel round in a moment when they judge the right time has come. And after this fashion they have won many a fight.

> What kind of reaction might this detail have produced among Marco Polo's European audience?

> Does it seem that Marco Polo admires the Mongol warriors? What language indicates how he feels about their tactics?

For Further Reflection

■ In what ways do the military practices described by Marco Polo reflect the influence of the steppe environment on the Mongols?

Source: Marco Polo. *The Book of Ser Marco Polo,* 3rd ed. Trans. and ed. by Henry Yule and Henri Cordier. London: John Murray, 1921, pp. 260–63. (Translation slightly modified.)

He unleashed ruthless attacks against his enemies, but he also took an interest in cultural matters and worked to improve the welfare of his subjects. He actively promoted Buddhism, and he provided support also for Daoists, Muslims, and Christians in his realm. The famous Venetian traveler Marco Polo, who lived almost two decades at Khubilai's court, praised him for his generosity toward the poor and his efforts to build roads. Though named great khan in 1260, Khubilai spent four years fighting off contenders. From 1264 until his death in 1294, Khubilai Khan presided over the Mongol Empire at its height.

Mongol Conquest of Southern China Khubilai extended Mongol rule to all of China. From his base at Khanbaliq, he

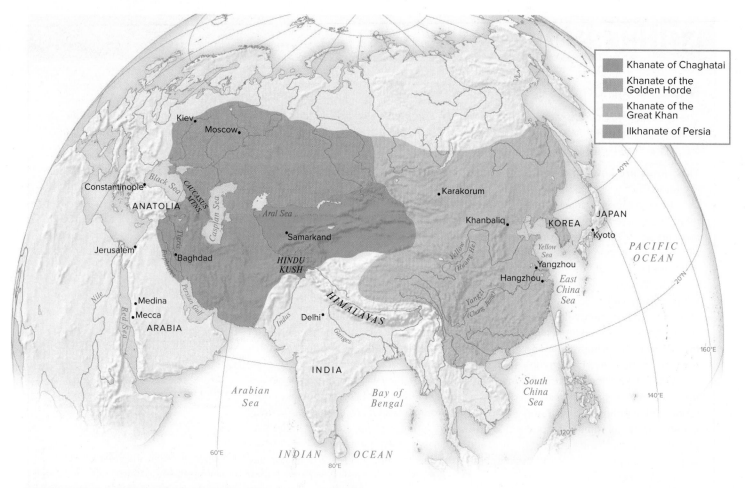

MAP 17.2   The Mongol Empires, ca. 1300

The Mongol Empires stretched from Manchuria and China to Russia and eastern Europe.

In what ways did Mongol Empires and Mongol policies facilitate trade, travel, and communication throughout Eurasia?

relentlessly attacked the Song dynasty in southern China. The Song capital at Hangzhou fell to Mongol forces in 1276, and within three years Khubilai had eliminated resistance throughout China. In 1279 he proclaimed himself emperor and established the **Yuan dynasty,** which ruled China until its collapse in 1368.

Beyond China, Khubilai had little success as a conqueror. During the 1270s and 1280s, he launched several invasions of Vietnam, Cambodia, and Burma as well as a naval expedition against Java involving between five hundred to one thousand ships and twenty thousand troops. But Mongol forces did not adapt well to the humid, tropical jungles of southeast Asia. Pasturelands were inadequate for their horses, and the fearsome Mongol horsemen were unable to cope with the guerrilla tactics employed by the defenders. In 1274 and again in 1281, Khubilai also attempted seaborne invasions of Japan, but on both occasions typhoons thwarted his plans. The storm of 1281 was especially vicious: it destroyed about 4,500 Mongol vessels carrying more than one hundred thousand armed troops—the largest seaborne expedition before World War II. Japanese defenders attributed their continued independence to the *kamikaze* ("divine winds").

The Golden Horde As Khubilai consolidated his hold on east Asia, his cousins and brothers tightened Mongol control on lands to the west. Mongols of the group known as the Golden Horde overran Russia between 1237 and 1241 and then mounted exploratory expeditions into Poland, Hungary, and eastern Germany in 1241 and 1242. Mongols of the Golden Horde prized the steppes north of the Black Sea as prime pastureland for their horses. They maintained a large army on the steppes from which they mounted raids into Russia. They did not occupy Russia, which they regarded as an unattractive land of forests, but they extracted tribute from the Russian cities and agricultural provinces. The Golden Horde maintained its hegemony in Russia until the mid-fifteenth century, when the princes of Moscow rejected

Yuan (yoo-AHN)

The siege of Baghdad in 1258: a Persian manuscript illustration depicts Mongol forces camped outside the city walls while residents huddle within. What role did catapults (at bottom left and center right) play in sieges like this? DEA/J. E. BULLOZ/De Agostini/Getty Images

its authority while building a powerful Russian state. By the mid-sixteenth century, Russian conquerors had extended their control to the steppes, but Mongol khans descended from the Golden Horde continued to rule the Crimea until the late eighteenth century.

The Ilkhanate of Persia While the Golden Horde established its authority in Russia, Khubilai's brother Hülegü toppled the Abbasid empire and established the Mongol **ilkhanate of Persia.** In 1258 he captured the Abbasid capital of Baghdad after a brief siege. His troops looted the city, executed the caliph, and massacred more than two hundred thousand residents by Hülegü's own estimate. From Persia, Hülegü's army ventured into Syria, but Muslim forces from Egypt soon expelled them and placed a limit on Mongol expansion to the southwest.

When the Mongols crushed ruling regimes in large settled societies, particularly in China and Persia, they discovered that they needed to become governors as well as conquerors. The Mongols had no experience administering complex societies, where successful governance required talents beyond the equestrian and military skills esteemed on the steppes. They had a difficult time adjusting to their role as administrators. Indeed, they never became entirely comfortable in the role, and most of their conquests fell out of their hands within a century.

Mongol Rule in Persia The Mongols adopted different tactics in the different lands that they ruled. In Persia they

made important concessions to local interests. Although Mongols and their allies occupied the highest administrative positions, Persians served as ministers, provincial governors, and state officials at all lower levels. The Mongols basically allowed the Persians to administer the ilkhanate as long as they delivered tax receipts and maintained order.

Over time, the Mongols even assimilated to Persian cultural traditions. The early Mongol rulers of Persia mostly observed their native shamanism, but they tolerated all religions—including Islam, Nestorian Christianity, Buddhism, and Judaism—and they ended the privileges given Muslims during the Abbasid caliphate. Gradually, however, the Mongols themselves gravitated toward Islam. In 1295 Ilkhan Ghazan publicly converted to Islam, and most of the Mongols in Persia followed his example. Ghazan's conversion sparked large-scale massacres of Christians and Jews, and it signaled the return of Islam to a privileged position in Persian society. It also indicated the absorption of the Mongols into Muslim Persian society.

Mongol Rule in China In China, by contrast, the Mongol overlords stood aloof from their subjects, whom they scorned as mere cultivators. They outlawed intermarriage between Mongols and Chinese and forbade the Chinese from learning the Mongol language. Soon after their conquest some of the victors went so far as to suggest that the Mongols exterminate

ilkhanate (EEL-kahn-ate)

the Chinese people and convert China itself into pastureland for their horses. Cooler heads eventually prevailed, and the Mongols decided simply to extract as much revenue as possible from their Chinese subjects. In doing so, however, they did not make as much use of native administrative talent as did their counterparts in Persia. Instead, they brought foreign administrators into China and placed them in charge. Along with their nomadic allies, the Mongols' administrative staff included Arabs, Persians, and perhaps even Europeans: Marco Polo may have served as an administrator in the city of Yangzhou during the reign of Khubilai Khan.

The Mongols also resisted assimilation to Chinese cultural traditions. They ended the privileges enjoyed by the Confucian scholars, and they dismantled the Confucian educational and examination system, which had produced untold generations of civil servants for the Chinese bureaucracy. They did not persecute Confucians, but they allowed the Confucian tradition to wither in the absence of official support. Meanwhile, to remain on good terms with subjects of different faiths, the Mongols allowed the construction of churches, temples, and shrines, and they even subsidized some religious establishments. They tolerated all cultural and religious traditions in China, including Confucianism, Daoism, Buddhism, and Christianity. Of Khubilai Khan's four wives, his favorite was Chabi, a Nestorian Christian.

The Mongols and Buddhism For their part the Mongols mostly continued to follow their native shamanist traditions, although many of the ruling elite became enchanted with the Lamaist school of Buddhism that developed in Tibet. Lamaist Buddhism held several attractions for the Mongols. It made a prominent place for magic and supernatural powers, and in that respect it resembled the Mongols' shamanism. Moreover, Lamaist Buddhist leaders officially recognized the Mongols as legitimate rulers and went out of their way to court the Mongols' favor. They numbered the Mongols in the ranks of universal Buddhist rulers and even recognized the Mongol khans as incarnations of the Buddha. It is therefore not surprising that the Mongol ruling elites would find Lamaist Buddhism attractive.

Chabi, a Nestorian Christian and the favorite wife of Khubilai Khan, wearing the distinctive headgear reserved for Mongol women of the ruling class.
History and Art Collection/Alamy Stock Photo

The Mongols and Eurasian Integration

In building their vast empire, the Mongols brought tremendous destruction to lands throughout much of the Eurasian landmass. While the human cost of such destruction should not be

What's Left Out?

The Mongols ruled such a vast array of territories that major textual sources documenting their rule exist in at least twelve languages. Many of these sources have not been translated from their original languages, which means that our historical knowledge of Mongol rule has tended to be partial and regional. Additionally, some khanates—such as those in China and Persia—produced many more contemporary sources than the khanates of Chagatai or the Golden Horde. Complicating the matter is that the Mongols left very few written sources of their own, which means that most of the sources we have were written by contemporary observers rather than by Mongols themselves. Given the fragmented nature of the sources, both by language and region, the ability of historians to tell a comprehensive and balanced story of the Mongols has been limited. How might the unbalanced nature of these sources affect the story of the Mongols presented in this chapter?

Source: There are few general surveys of the Mongols, but David Morgan, *The Mongols,* 2nd edition (2007), serves as one of the most respected.

minimized, the Mongols also sponsored interaction and encounters among peoples of different societies and linked Eurasian lands more directly than ever before. Indeed, Mongol rulers positively encouraged travel and communication over long distances. Recognizing the value of regular communications for their vast empire, Chinggis Khan and his successors maintained a courier network that rapidly relayed news, information, and government orders. The network included relay stations with fresh horses and riders so that messages could travel almost nonstop throughout Mongol territories. The Mongols' encouragement of travel and communication facilitated trade, diplomatic travel, missionary efforts, and movements of peoples to new lands.

The Mongols and Trade As a nomadic people dependent on commerce with settled agricultural societies, the Mongols worked to secure trade routes and ensure the safety of merchants passing through their territories. The Mongol khans frequently fought among themselves, but they maintained reasonably good order within their realms and allowed merchants to travel unmolested through their empires. As a result, long-distance travel and trade became much less risky than in earlier times. Merchants increased their commercial investments, and the volume of long-distance trade across central Asia dwarfed that of earlier eras. Lands as distant as China and western Europe became directly linked for the first time because of the ability of individuals to travel across the entire Eurasian landmass.

Diplomatic Missions Like trade, diplomatic communication was essential to the Mongols, and their protection of roads and travelers benefited ambassadors as well as merchants. Chinggis Khan destroyed the Khwarazm shah in Persia because the shah unwisely murdered the Mongol envoys Chinggis Khan dispatched in hopes of opening diplomatic and commercial relations. Throughout the Mongol era the great khans in China, the ilkhans in Persia, and the other khans maintained close communications by means of diplomatic embassies. They also had diplomatic dealings with rulers in Korea, Vietnam, India, western Europe, and other lands as well. Some diplomatic travelers crossed the entire Eurasian landmass. Several European ambassadors traveled to Mongolia and China to deliver messages from authorities seeking to ally with the Mongols against Muslim states in southwest Asia. Diplomats also traveled west: Rabban Sauma, a Nestorian Christian monk born in Khanbaliq, visited Italy and France as a representative of the Persian ilkhan.

Missionary Efforts Like the Silk Roads in earlier times, Eurasian routes during the era of the Mongol Empires served as highways for missionaries as well as merchants and diplomats. Sufi missionaries helped popularize Islam among Turkish peoples in central Asia, while Lamaist Buddhism from Tibet attracted considerable interest among the Mongols. Nestorian Christians, who had long been prominent in oasis communities throughout central Asia, found new opportunities to win converts when they went to China to serve as administrators for Mongol rulers there. Roman Catholic Christians also mounted missionary campaigns in China. (See chapter 21 for further discussion of travel during the Mongol era.)

Resettlement Another Mongol policy that encouraged Eurasian integration was the practice of resettling peoples in new lands. As a nomadic people, the Mongols had limited numbers of skilled artisans and educated individuals, but the more their empire expanded, the more they needed the services of specialized crafts workers and literate administrators. Mongol overlords recruited the talent they needed largely from the ranks of their allies and the peoples they conquered, and they often moved people far from their homelands to sites where they could best make use of their services. Among the most important of the Mongols' allies were the Uighur Turks, who lived mostly in oasis cities along the Silk Roads. The **Uighurs** were literate and often highly educated, and they provided not only many of the clerks, secretaries, and administrators who ran the Mongol Empires but also units of soldiers who bolstered Mongol garrisons. Arab and Persian Muslims were also prominent among those who administered the Mongols' affairs far from their homelands.

Conquered peoples also supplied the Mongols with talent. When they overcame a city, Mongol forces routinely surveyed the captured population, separated out those with specialized skills, and sent them to the capital at Karakorum or some other place where there was demand for their services. From the ranks of conquered peoples came soldiers, bodyguards, administrators, secretaries, translators, physicians, armor makers, metalsmiths, miners, carpenters, masons, textile workers, musicians, and jewelers. After the 1230s the Mongols often took censuses of lands they conquered, partly to levy taxes and conscript military forces and partly to locate talented individuals. The Parisian goldsmith Guillaume Boucher, who we met at the beginning of this chapter, was only one among thousands of foreign-born individuals who became permanent residents of the Mongol capital at Karakorum because of their special talents. Like their protection of trade and diplomacy, the Mongols' policy of resettling allies and conquered peoples promoted Eurasian integration by increasing communication and exchange between peoples of different societies and traditions.

Decline of the Mongols in Persia and China

Collapse of the Ilkhanate Soon after the long and prosperous reign of Khubilai Khan, the Mongols encountered

How the Past Shapes the Future ▶ ▷ ▶ ▷ ▶ ▷ ▶ ▷

The Diffusion of Technologies

Between about 1000 and 1500 C.E., increased intercultural encounters—especially across and between Eurasia and Africa—led to a spectacular diffusion of technologies that would have an impact on the world's history for centuries to come. Technologies include tools and techniques that humans use to adapt the natural environment to their needs, and thus can range from items like plows and horseshoes to irrigation systems or ideas about which crops to plant. Of course, both the existence of technologies and their diffusion were hardly unique to the period between 1000 and 1500 C.E.—indeed, we have already seen numerous examples of technological diffusion (such as the spread of horse-drawn chariots and iron smelting, among many others) in chapters 1–16. But one of the reasons for the increased pace of interactions across Eurasia and Africa was because of the spread of the *dar-al-Islam* after the eighth century, which we read about in chapter 14, and especially because of the Muslim merchants who established stable trade routes within and beyond its bounds. Another reason was the huge conquests made by nomadic Turkic and Mongolian peoples from the eleventh to the thirteenth centuries. In the thirteenth century, Mongol conquests alone provided stable trade routes that connected Eurasia all the way from China to eastern Europe. Each of these developments provided the pathways not only for the introduction of new trade items and spiritual beliefs but also for the diffusion of technologies from distant regions. Here, we discuss two types of technologies that were widely diffused in this period: technologies of warfare and technologies of transportation.

Technologies of Warfare

When the Mongols were trying to conquer China, they learned about gunpowder for the first time. Gunpowder, of course, was not new to the Chinese: as we saw in chapter 13, Chinese alchemists discovered the compound during the Han dynasty, and by the eighth century Chinese strategists were using it for military purposes. But when Mongol invaders were introduced to gunpowder, they quickly incorporated its destructive powers into their arsenal of weapons: as early as 1214, for example, Chinggis Khan's armies included an artillery unit. Faced with the power of gunpowder—especially its usefulness in breaking sieges—societies all over Eurasia quickly sought to acquire the technology. Since the Mongols used gunpowder weapons to conquer Persia and other parts of southwest Asia in the mid-thirteenth century, Muslim armies were inspired to incorporate the technology quickly in order to defend themselves. By the mid-thirteenth century gunpowder technology had also reached Europe, and by the early fourteenth century armies across Eurasia possessed cannons. Although early cannons were not particularly accurate, the diffusion of gunpowder technologies permanently altered the nature of warfare. Indeed, over the eight centuries since Mongol armies began to use it, the use of gunpowder technologies has affected every part of the globe in profound ways.

Technologies of Transportation

The period from around 1000 to 1500 C.E. also witnessed the widespread diffusion of technologies that improved both animal and maritime transportation—technologies that, in turn, allowed for both greater economic integration across long distances as well as greater economic growth. For example, Islamic merchants from north Africa utilized camels to cross the Sahara by the late eighth century C.E. (chapter 18). The diffusion of camels across the Sahara led to significant and long-term changes in a variety of sub-Saharan African societies, which included both the introduction of Islam as well as growing wealth resulting from being incorporated into much larger Eurasian markets. In Europe, meanwhile, the diffusion of the horse collar—most likely from both central Asia and north Africa—during the High Middle Ages helped to fuel European economic growth by allowing horses to pull much heavier loads without choking (chapter 19). The result was that Europeans could use horses for plowing and for transporting heavy loads rather than much slower oxen, which increased the amount of land that could be plowed as well as the rapidity with which goods could be brought to market.

Maritime technologies also diffused widely in this period. For example, the magnetic compass was invented by the Chinese during the Tang or Song dynasty, but by the mid-eleventh century it was being used by mariners throughout the Indian Ocean basin. By the mid-twelfth century, Europeans were also using compasses in the Mediterranean and Atlantic—devices that helped Portuguese mariners find their way into the Indian Ocean in the fifteenth century (chapter 21). In subsequent centuries, European mariners adopted many other maritime technologies from distant cultures—including the astrolabe—which were eventually used to cross the Atlantic to the Americas. Maritime technologies were not only important in Eurasia, however: during the twelfth and thirteenth centuries, voyages using sophisticated maritime techniques between the Hawaiian Islands and Tahiti allowed for the transfer of improved fishhook technologies to Hawaii (chapter 20).

When reading subsequent chapters, consider the effects that the diffusion of technologies have had on societies around the world over the very long term.

Siege of a north African town, fourteenth century.
Album/Alamy Stock Photo

serious difficulties governing Persia and China. In Persia excessive spending strained the treasury, and overexploitation of the peasantry led to reduced revenues. In the early 1290s the ilkhan tried to resolve his financial difficulties by introducing paper money and ordering all subjects to accept it for payment of all debts. The purpose of that measure was to drive precious metals into the hands of the government, but the policy was a miserable failure: rather than accept paper that they regarded as worthless, merchants simply closed their shops. Commerce ground to a halt until the ilkhan rescinded his order. Meanwhile, factional struggles plagued the Mongol leadership. The regime went into steep decline after the death of Ilkhan Ghazan in 1304. When the last of the Mongol rulers died without an heir in 1335, the ilkhanate itself simply collapsed. Government in Persia devolved to local levels until late in the fourteenth century when Turkish peoples reintroduced effective central government.

Decline of the Yuan Dynasty Mongol decline in China was a more complicated affair. As in Persia, it had an economic dimension. The Mongols continued to use the paper money that the Chinese had introduced during the Tang and Song dynasties, but they did not maintain adequate reserves of the bullion that backed up paper notes. The general population soon lost confidence in paper money, and prices rose sharply as a reflection of its diminished value. As in Persia, too, factions and infighting hastened Mongol decline in China. As the richest of the Mongol Empires, China attracted the attention of ambitious warriors. Beginning in the 1320s power struggles, imperial assassinations, and civil war convulsed the Mongol regime in China.

Bubonic Plague Apart from financial difficulties and factional divisions, the Mongol rulers of China also faced an onslaught of epidemic disease. By facilitating trade and communications throughout Eurasia, the Mongols unwittingly expedited the spread of bubonic plague (discussed in chapter 21). During the 1330s plague erupted in southwestern China. From there it spread throughout China and central Asia, and by the late 1340s it had reached southwest Asia and Europe, where it became known as the Black Death. Bubonic plague sometimes killed half or more of an exposed population, particularly during the furious initial years of the epidemic, and it seriously disrupted economies and societies throughout much of Eurasia. In China depopulation and labor shortages that followed on the heels of epidemic plague weakened the Mongol regime. (Plague would also have caused serious problems for the Mongol rulers of Persia had the ilkhanate not collapsed before its arrival.)

The Mongols also faced a rebellious subject population in China. The Mongols stood apart from their Chinese subjects, who returned the contempt of their conquerors. Beginning in the 1340s southern China became a hotbed of peasant rebellion and banditry, which the Mongols could not control. In 1368 rebel forces captured Khanbaliq, and the Mongols departed China en masse and returned to the steppes.

Surviving Mongol Khanates Despite the collapse of the Mongol regimes in Persia and China, Mongol states did not completely disappear. The khanate of Chaghatai continued to prevail in central Asia, and Mongols posed a threat to the northwestern borders of China until the eighteenth century. Meanwhile, the khanate of the Golden Horde continued to dominate the Caucasus and the steppe lands north of the Black Sea and the Caspian Sea until the mid-sixteenth century when a resurgent Russian state brought the Golden Horde down. Like Mongols in China, however, Mongols in Russia continued to threaten until the eighteenth century, and Mongols who had settled in the Crimean peninsula retained their identity until Josef Stalin forcibly moved them to other parts of the Soviet Union in the mid-twentieth century.

AFTER THE MONGOLS

By no means did the decline of the Mongols signal the end of nomadic peoples' influence in Eurasia. As Mongol strength waned, Turkish peoples resumed the expansive campaigns that the Mongols had interrupted. During the late fourteenth and early fifteenth centuries, the Turkic-Mongol conqueror **Tamerlane** built a central Asian empire rivaling that of Chinggis Khan himself. Although Tamerlane's empire foundered soon after his death, it deeply influenced three surviving Turkish Muslim states—the Mughal empire in India, the Safavid empire in Persia, and the **Ottoman Empire** based in Anatolia—and also embraced much of southwest Asia, southeastern Europe, and north Africa.

Tamerlane (TAM-er-lane)

Tamerlane and the Timurids

The Lame Conqueror The rapid collapse of the Mongol states left gaping power vacuums in China and Persia. While the native Ming dynasty filled the vacuum in China, a self-made Turkic-Mongol conqueror named Timur moved on Persia. Because he walked with a limp, contemporaries referred to him as Timur-i lang—"Timur the Lame," an appellation that made its way into English as **Tamerlane.**

Born about 1336 near Samarkand, Tamerlane took Chinggis Khan as his model. Like Chinggis Khan, Tamerlane came from a family of minor Mongol and Turkish elites, and had to make his own way to power. Like Chinggis Khan, too, he was a charismatic leader and a courageous warrior, and he attracted a band of loyal followers. During the 1360s he eliminated rivals to power, either by persuading them to join him as allies or by defeating their armies on the battlefield, and he won recognition as leader of his own tribe. By 1370 he had extended his authority throughout the khanate of Chaghatai and begun to build a magnificent imperial capital in Samarkand.

Tamerlane's Conquests For the rest of his life, Tamerlane led his armies on campaigns of conquest. He turned first to the region between Persia and Afghanistan, and he took special care to establish his authority in the rich cities of the region so that he could levy taxes on trade and agricultural production. Next he attacked the Golden Horde in the Caucasus region and Russia, and by the mid-1390s he had severely weakened it. During the last years of the century, he invaded India and brutally conquered Delhi: contemporary chroniclers reported, with some exaggeration, that for a period of two months after the attack not even birds visited the devastated city. Later, Tamerlane campaigned along the Ganges, although he never attempted to incorporate India into his empire. He opened the new century with campaigns in southwest Asia and Anatolia. In 1404 he began preparations for an invasion of China, and he was leading his army east when he fell ill and died in 1405.

Like his model Chinggis Khan, Tamerlane was a conqueror, not a governor. He spent almost his entire adult life planning and fighting military campaigns: he even had himself carried around on a litter during his final illness, as he prepared to invade China. He did not create an imperial administration but, rather, ruled through tribal leaders who were his allies. He appointed overlords in the territories he conquered, but they relied on existing bureaucratic structures and simply received taxes and tributes on his behalf.

Tamerlane's Heirs Given its loose organization, it is not surprising that Tamerlane's Timurid empire experienced stresses and strains after the conqueror's death. Tamerlane's sons and grandsons engaged in a long series of bitter conflicts that resulted in the contraction of the Timurid empire and its division into four main regions. For a century after Tamerlane's death,

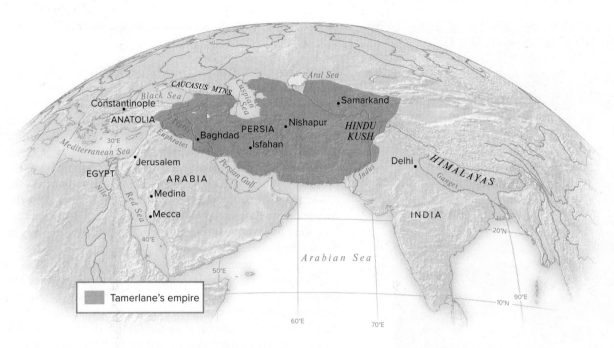

MAP 17.3   Tamerlane's empire, ca. 1405

Notice the similarity between Tamerlane's empire and the ilkhanate of Persia outlined in Map 17.2.

To what extent do you think the cities and the administrative infrastructure of the region both helped and hindered Tamerlane's efforts to control his empire?

Spoils from Tamerlane's campaigns and raids enriched the conqueror's capital at Samarkand. They financed, among other buildings, the magnificent tomb where Tamerlane's remains still rest.

silverfox999/Shutterstock

however, they maintained control over the region from Persia to Afghanistan. When the last vestiges of Tamerlane's imperial creation disappeared, in the early sixteenth century, the Mughal, Safavid, and Ottoman empires that replaced it all clearly reflected the Turkish, Mongol, and Muslim legacy of the lame conqueror.

The Foundation of the Ottoman Empire

Chapter 27 will discuss the Mughal empire in India and the Safavid empire in Persia, both of which emerged during the early sixteenth century as Tamerlane's empire finally dissolved. The early stages of Ottoman expansion predated Tamerlane, however, and the foundation of the influential Ottoman Empire throws additional light on the influence of nomadic peoples during the period 1000 to 1500 C.E.

Osman After the Mongol conquest of Persia, large numbers of nomadic Turks migrated from central Asia to the ilkhanate and beyond to the territories in Anatolia that the Seljuq Turks had seized from the Byzantine Empire. There they followed charismatic leaders who organized further campaigns of conquest. Among those leaders was **Osman,** who

Safavid (SAH-fah-vihd)

Osman (os-MAHN)

Although besieged by Ottoman forces, Constantinople received supplies from the sea for almost two months before Ottomans destroyed the city walls and completed their conquest of the Byzantine Empire.

Christophel Fine Art/Universal Images Group/Getty Images

attracted more and more followers, who came to be known as Osmanlis or Ottomans.

Ottoman Conquests During the 1350s the Ottomans gained a considerable advantage over their Turkish rivals when they established a foothold across the Dardanelles at Gallipoli on the Balkan peninsula. The Ottomans quickly moved to expand the boundaries of their Balkan holdings. Byzantine forces resisted Ottoman incursions, but because of political fragmentation, ineffective government, and exploitation of the peasantry, the Ottomans found abundant local support. By the 1380s the Ottomans had become by far the most powerful people on the Balkan peninsula, and by the end of the century they were poised to capture Constantinople and take over the Byzantine Empire.

Tamerlane temporarily delayed Ottoman expansion in the Byzantine realm. In 1402 Tamerlane's forces crushed the Ottoman army, captured the sultan, and subjected the Ottoman state to the conqueror's authority. After Tamerlane's death, Ottoman leaders had to reestablish their rule in their own realm. This undertaking involved both the repression of ambitious local princes who sought to build power bases at Ottoman expense and the defense of Ottoman territories against Byzantine, Venetian, and other Christian forces that sought to turn back the advance of the Turkish Muslims. By the 1440s the Ottomans had recovered their balance and began again to expand in the Byzantine Empire.

The Capture of Constantinople The campaign culminated in 1453 when Sultan Mehmed II captured the city of Constantinople, thus bringing to an end more than a thousand years of Byzantine rule. After subjecting it to a sack, he made the city his own capital under the Turkish name of Istanbul. With Istanbul as a base, the Ottomans quickly absorbed the remainder of the Byzantine Empire. By 1480 they controlled all of Greece and the Balkan region. They continued to expand throughout most of the sixteenth century as well, extending their rule to southwest Asia, southeastern Europe, Egypt, and north Africa. Once again, then, a nomadic people asserted control over a long-settled society and quickly built a vast empire.

during the late thirteenth and early fourteenth centuries carved a small state for himself in northwestern Anatolia. In 1299 Osman declared independence from the Seljuq sultan and launched a campaign to build a state at the expense of the Byzantine Empire. After every successful operation, Osman

CONCLUSION

This chapter has demonstrated that during the half millennium from 1000 to 1500 C.E., nomadic peoples of central Asia played a larger role than ever before in world history. In this period, they dominated affairs in most of Eurasia through their conquests and their construction of vast transregional empires. Turkish peoples built the most durable of the nomadic empires, but the spectacular conquests of the Mongols most clearly demonstrated the potential of nomadic peoples to project their formidable military power to settled agricultural societies. By establishing connections that spanned the Eurasian

landmass, the nomadic empires laid the foundation for increasing encounters and exchanges among peoples of different societies and traditions, thereby fostering the integration of the eastern hemisphere. As the example of Guillaume Boucher at the start of this chapter illustrates, beginning in the mid-thirteenth century, merchants, artisans, diplomats, and missionaries traveled frequently between lands as far removed as France and Central Asia. This rich interchange between social and cultural traditions on the one hand and dynamic encounters on the other allows us to speak, for the first time, about a truly Eurasian history. The age of nomadic empires from 1000 to 1500 C.E. thus foreshadowed the integrated world of modern times.

STUDY TERMS

Abbasid (346)

Chinggis Khan (347)

Ghaznavid Turks (347)

ilkhanate of Persia (353)

Jurchen (349)

Karakorum (342)

khan (346)

khanate of Chaghatai (350)

Khanbaliq (349)

khans of the Golden Horde (350)

Khubilai Khan (350)

Khwarazm shah (349)

kumiss (344)

Manichaeism (346)

Mongols (347)

Osman (359)

Ottoman Empire (358)

Seljuq Turks (346)

shamans (346)

sultan (346)

sultanate of Delhi (347)

Tamerlane (358)

Temüjin (347)

Uighurs (355)

Yuan dynasty (352)

yurts (344)

FOR FURTHER READING

Thomas T. Allsen. *Culture and Conquest in Mongol Eurasia.* Cambridge, 2001. Carefully studies the cultural exchanges sponsored by Mongol rulers, particularly those passing between China and Iran.

Thomas J. Barfield. *The Nomadic Alternative.* Englewood Cliffs, N.J., 1993. A sensitive study of nomadic societies in Africa and Eurasia by a leading anthropologist.

Carter Vaughn Findley. *The Turks in World History.* New York, 2005. A welcome volume that lucidly outlines the history of Turkish peoples and discusses relations between Turks and neighboring peoples.

Peter Jackson. *The Mongols and the West, 1221-1410.* London, 2005. Offers a comprehensive review of military, diplomatic, commercial, and cultural relations between Mongol and European societies.

Paul Kahn, ed. *The Secret History of the Mongols: The Origin of Chingis Khan.* Adapted from the translation of F. W. Cleaves. San Francisco, 1984. A translation of the Mongols' history of their own society, adapted for modern readers.

Adam T. Kessler. *Empires beyond the Great Wall: The Heritage of Genghis Khan.* Los Angeles, 1993. Well-illustrated survey of nomadic states in central Asia from the Xiongnu to the Mongols.

George Lane. *Daily Life in the Mongol Empire.* London, 2006. Explores the lives of ordinary people under the reign of Chinggis Khan, including dwellings, health, food, law, and culture.

Beatrice Forbes Manz. *The Rise and Rule of Tamerlane.* Cambridge, 1989. Scholarly analysis of Tamerlane's career and his empire.

David Morgan. *The Mongols.* 2nd ed. Oxford, 2007. Lucid and witty, this remains one of the best short works on the Mongols.

Morris Rossabi. *Khubilai Khan: His Life and Times.* Berkeley, 1988. Excellent scholarly study of the greatest of the great khans.

ZOOMING IN ON TRADITIONS

The Lion Prince of Mali

A remarkable oral tradition preserves the story of the lion prince **Sundiata,** thirteenth-century founder of the Mali Empire in west Africa. Oral traditions include folk stories, factual histories, genealogies, and other accounts transmitted by professional singers and storytellers known in west Africa as **griots.** Until scholars began to write down and publish west African oral traditions about the middle of the twentieth century, the story of Sundiata was available only when a griot recited it.

According to the oral tradition, Sundiata's father ruled a small kingdom in what is now the nation of Guinea in west Africa. Despite his royal parentage, Sundiata had a difficult childhood because a congenitally defective leg left him unable to walk well. When the old king died, his enemies invaded the kingdom and killed the royal offspring, sparing Sundiata only because they thought he was too weak to be a threat to them. But Sundiata overcame his disability, learned to use the bow and arrow, and mastered the arts of hunting and warfare. As Sundiata grew stronger, his enemies began to fear him, and they forced him into exile. While in exile, Sundiata distinguished himself as a warrior and leader and assembled a powerful cavalry force.

About 1235 Sundiata returned to his homeland to claim the throne. His cavalry slashed through the countryside and

Sundiata (soon-JAH-tuh)
griots (GREE-oh)

The magnificent mosque at Jenne, constructed in the fourteenth century, served as a principal center of Islamic education and scholarship in the Mali Empire.
Explorer/Science Source

defeated his enemies. Within a few years he had established the Mali Empire and consolidated his rule throughout a large portion of the valley of the Niger River. Although he respected traditional religious beliefs and magical powers, Sundiata was a Muslim and he welcomed Muslim merchants from north Africa into his realm. He built a capital city at Niani, which soon became a thriving commercial center. Indeed, as a result of its control of the trans-Saharan gold trade—and the political stability provided by Sundiata—the Mali Empire became one of the wealthiest lands in the world. For two centuries after Sundiata's death about 1260, the lion prince's legacy shaped the lives of west African peoples and linked west Africa with north Africa and the Mediterranean basin.

CHAPTER OVERVIEW

From the ancient era (500 B.C.E.–500 C.E.) forward, people from east Asia to the Mediterranean to the west African Savannah basin established extensive networks of trade and communication. Africans living south of the Sahara participated in the larger economy of Afro-Eurasia, though not so fully as their counterparts in north Africa. Geographic conditions help to explain why trade and communication networks did not embrace sub-Saharan Africa as readily as they did other regions: the Sahara poses a formidable challenge to overland travelers from the north, the African coastlines offer few good natural harbors, and cataracts complicate travel up some of the continent's major rivers.

Nevertheless, like their Eurasian and north African counterparts, peoples of sub-Saharan Africa built powerful states and participated in large-scale networks of communication, encounter, and exchange. Internal African processes drove much of that development. Between 1000 and 1500 C.E., in the wake of the Bantu and other migrations (discussed in chapter 3), peoples of sub-Saharan Africa continued to expand the amount of territory under cultivation and to establish agricultural societies. Further-more, as their population increased, they organized states, developed centers of economic specialization, and carried on interregional trade. Alongside these internal processes, relations with other peoples of Afro-Eurasia also profoundly influenced the development of African societies. From the early centuries C.E. to 1500 and later as well, trade with lands of the Mediterranean and the Indian Ocean basin encouraged African peoples to organize their societies to produce commodities desired by consumers throughout much of Afro-Eurasia. This trade promoted urban development, the organization of large states and empires, and the introduction of new food crops and new religious beliefs into sub-Saharan Africa.

CHRONOLOGY	
4th century C.E.	Introduction of bananas to Africa
11th to 13th century	Kingdom of Ghana
11th to 15th century	Swahili cities
12th to 15th century	Kingdom of Great Zimbabwe
12th to 16th century	Christian kingdom of Axum
13th to 15th century	Mali Empire
1230–1255	Reign of Sundiata
14th to 17th century	Kingdom of Kongo
1312–1337	Reign of Mansa Musa
1324–1325	Mansa Musa's pilgrimage to Mecca

EFFECTS OF EARLY AFRICAN MIGRATIONS

By 1000 C.E. Bantu-speaking peoples (originally from central Africa) had settled in most parts of Africa south of the equator, and Kushite, Sudanese, Mande, and other peoples had also established communities in lands far from their original homes. For the next several centuries, African people built societies on the foundation of small communities that the Bantu and other migrations had generated.

Agriculture and Population Growth

The principal early result of the Bantu and other migrations was to spread agriculture and herding to almost all parts of Africa except deserts and dense, equatorial rain forests. As they established agricultural societies, cultivators and herders displaced many of the hunting, gathering, and fishing peoples who previously inhabited sub-Saharan Africa and absorbed them into their societies. By about 500 B.C.E. most Bantu-speaking peoples had mastered the techniques of iron metallurgy, which enabled them to fashion iron tools like axes and hoes that facilitated further clearing of lands and extension of agriculture. By the early centuries C.E., cultivation and herding had reached the southernmost parts of Africa. Yams, sorghum, and millet were the dietary staples of many peoples in south Africa, and the indigenous Khoi people had adopted cattle raising even before Bantu-speaking people and Kushite herders moved into the region. Those developments resulted in increased agricultural production, rising population, and competition for fertile lands between different groups.

Bananas

First domesticated in southeast Asia, bananas probably entered Africa by way of sea lanes across the Indian Ocean. During the late centuries B.C.E., Malay seafarers from the islands that make up modern Indonesia sailed west beyond India, and by the early centuries C.E. they were exploring the east African coasts. Between about 300 and 500 C.E., they colonized the island of Madagascar and established banana cultivation there. (Apart from bananas, they brought Asian yams, taro, chickens, and southeast Asian cultural traditions. Malagasy, the language spoken on Madagascar even today, belongs to the Austronesian family of languages.) From Madagascar, bananas easily made the jump to the east African mainland. By 500 C.E. several varieties of bananas had become well established in Africa. They provided a nutritious supplement to Bantu diets and enabled the Bantu to expand into heavily forested regions where yams and millet did not grow well. Thus cultivation of bananas increased the supply of food available to the Bantu, enriched their diets, and allowed them to expand more rapidly than before.

Population Growth

The population history of sub-Saharan Africa clearly reflects the significance of iron metallurgy and bananas. In 400 B.C.E., before iron working had deeply influenced the continent's societies, the population of sub-Saharan Africa stood at about 3.5 million. By the turn of the millennium, human numbers exceeded 11 million. By 800 C.E., after banana cultivation had spread throughout the continent, the sub-Saharan population had climbed to 17 million. And by 1000, when the Bantu migrations had introduced agriculture and iron metallurgy to most regions of sub-Saharan Africa, the population had passed 22 million.

Bantu and Forest Peoples

The continuing **Bantu** migrations, the expansion of Bantu population, and the establishment of new Bantu communities contributed to changes in relationships between Bantu and foraging peoples such as the forest dwellers of central Africa (the peoples once referred to by the disparaging term "pygmies"). In earlier times, Bantu speakers had often regarded the forest peoples as useful guides to environments that were unfamiliar to them, and oral traditions suggest that they relied on foragers' expert knowledge to learn about the possibilities that new environments offered. As Bantu-speaking populations surged, however, it became increasingly difficult for foragers to flourish. Some forest peoples joined the cultivators and integrated into Bantu-speaking societies. Others retreated into the forests, where they were able to sustain small-scale societies by providing forest products such as animal skins in exchange for iron tools produced by neighboring Bantu communities.

Political Organizations

By 1000 C.E., after more than two millennia of migrations, Bantu-speaking people had approached the limits of their expansion. Because agricultural peoples already occupied most of the continent, migrating into new territories and forming new settlements was much more difficult than in previous centuries. Instead of migrating in search of new lands to cultivate, then, sub-Saharan African peoples developed increasingly complex forms of government that enabled them to organize their existing societies on larger scales.

Kin-Based Societies

Early Bantu-speaking societies did not depend on an elaborate hierarchy of officials or a bureaucratic apparatus to administer their affairs. Rather, Bantu-speaking peoples governed themselves mostly through family and kinship groups. Bantu-speaking peoples usually settled in villages with populations averaging about one hundred people. Older male heads of families constituted a village's ruling council, which decided the public affairs for the entire group. The most prominent of the family heads presided over the village as a chief and represented the settlement when it dealt with neighboring peoples. A group of villages might be linked by political and kinship ties, which became the principal individual focus of loyalties. Usually, there was no chief or larger government for the larger region. Instead, village chiefs negotiated on matters concerning two or more villages. Meanwhile, within individual villages, family and kinship groups disciplined their own members as necessary.

This type of organization lends itself particularly well to small-scale communities, but **kin-based societies** often grew to large proportions. Some networks of villages and districts organized the public affairs of several hundred thousand people. By the nineteenth century, for example, the Tiv people of Nigeria, numbering almost one million, conducted their affairs in a kin-based society built on a foundation of family and clan groups.

Early Cities: Jenne-jeno

Meanwhile, speakers of Niger-Congo languages also established a vibrant urban society in the middle stretches of the Niger River, where low-lying lands forced the river into an inland delta. Equipped with iron tools, settlers arrived in the region during the late centuries B.C.E., and by 400 C.E. the settlement of **Jenne-jeno** ("Ancient Jenne," located just south of the modern city of Jenne in Mali) was emerging as a center of iron production and trade as well as manufactured textiles. Merchants of Jenne-jeno handled iron products as well as the region's abundant supplies of rice, fish, and domesticated animals, including cattle, sheep, and goats. They participated in an extensive trade network that reached from north Africa and the Mediterranean to the savannas and forests of central Africa. By the eighth century C.E., Jenne-jeno had become the principal commercial crossroads of west Africa.

Seated figure, Mali, Inland Niger Delta region, Djenné peoples, 13th century.
The Metropolitan Museum of Art, New York, Purchase, Buckeye Trust and Mr. and Mrs. Milton F. Rosenthal Gifts, Joseph Pulitzer Be.

A bronze plaque from the kingdom of Benin depicts a local chief flanked by warriors and attendants.
Peter Horree/Alamy Stock Photo

Although the city declined as west African kingdoms and empires arose in later centuries, it left a legacy of urban development in the region by inspiring the foundation of Timbuktu and other cities.

Chiefdoms After about 1000 C.E., many kin-based societies faced challenges as they sought control over human labor or valuable trade routes. Conflicts between villages and regions became more frequent and more intense. Increased conflict encouraged many African communities to organize military forces for both offensive and defensive purposes, and military organization in turn encouraged the development of more formal structures of government. Many districts fell under the leadership of powerful chiefs, who imposed their own authority on their territories. Some of these chiefs conquered their neighbors and consolidated their lands into small kingdoms. These kingdoms emerged in several regions of sub-Saharan Africa after about 1000 C.E. The kingdoms of **Ife** and **Benin,** for example, arose in the forested regions of west Africa. Both realms were city-states in which the court and urban residents controlled the surrounding countryside through family relationships and political alliances. Both Ife and Benin also produced magnificent sculptures that put human faces and figures to the early history of sub-Saharan Africa. Small kingdoms appeared also in southern Africa and central Africa.

Kingdom of Kongo One of the most active areas of political development was the basin of the Congo River (previously known as the Zaire River), a region where brisk economic development supported the emergence of large as well as small kingdoms. After about 1000 C.E., economic and military challenges encouraged kin-based societies in the Congo region to form small states embracing a few villages each. By 1200 conflict between these small states had resulted in the organization of larger, regional principalities that could resist political and military pressures better than small kingdoms could. One of the more prosperous of the Congolese states was the **kingdom of Kongo,** which participated actively in trade networks involving copper, raffia cloth, and nzimbu shells from the Atlantic Ocean. During the fourteenth century the kingdom of Kongo comprised much of the modern-day Republic of the Congo and Angola.

The central government of Kongo included the king and officials who oversaw military, judicial, and financial affairs. Beneath the central government were six provinces administered by governors, each of whom supervised several districts

Ife (EE-fehy)
Benin (beh-NEEN)

administered by subordinate officials. Within regions, villages ruled by chiefs provided local government. Though not the only kingdom in sub-Saharan Africa, Kongo was perhaps the most tightly centralized of the early Bantu kingdoms. In most cases the king or other central administrators could appoint or replace local officials at will, and the central government maintained a royal currency system based on seashells that came from the Indian Ocean. The kingdom of Kongo provided effective organization from the fourteenth until the mid-seventeenth century, when Portuguese slave traders undermined the authority of the kings and the central government.

Kin-based societies did not disappear with the emergence of formal states. On the contrary, they survived into the nineteenth century in much of sub-Saharan Africa. Yet regional states and large kingdoms became increasingly prominent during the centuries after 1000 C.E. as African people responded to competition for control over scarce labor or trade networks.

AFRICAN SOCIETIES AND CULTURAL DEVELOPMENT

By the eleventh century C.E., there was enormous variation in the size and scale of African societies. The peoples of sub-Saharan Africa spoke some eight hundred different languages, and the continent supported a wide variety of societies and economies: mobile bands of hunting and gathering peoples, fishing peoples who lived alongside the continent's lakes and coasts, nomadic herders, subsistence farmers who migrated periodically to fresh lands, settled cultivators, and city-based societies that drew their livelihoods from mining, manufacturing, and trade. Although this diversity makes it difficult to speak of African society and cultural development in general terms, certain social forms and cultural patterns appeared widely throughout sub-Saharan Africa.

Social Classes

In kingdoms, empires, and city-states, such as Kongo, Mali, and Kilwa, respectively, African peoples developed complex societies with clearly defined classes: ruling elites, military nobles, administrative officials, religious authorities, wealthy merchants, artisans, business entrepreneurs, common people, peasants, and slaves. These societies resembled those found in other settled, agricultural lands of Eurasia organized by powerful states.

In the small states and kin-based societies of sub-Saharan Africa, however, social structures were different. Small states often generated an aristocratic or ruling elite, and they always recognized a class of religious authorities. Outside the larger states and empires, however, kinship, sex and gender expectations, and age groupings were the principal considerations that determined social position in sub-Saharan Africa.

An illustration from a seventeenth-century missionary account shows an African blacksmith (seated at right) working at his forge while an attendant (seated at left) uses a bellows to pump air into the furnace.
Fotosearch/Stringer/ Getty Images

Kinship Groups Extended families and clans served as the main foundation of social and economic organization in small-scale agricultural and foraging societies. Unlike their counterparts in north Africa and Eurasia, sub-Saharan African peoples mostly did not recognize the private ownership of land. Instead, communities claimed rights to land and used it in common. The villages of sub-Saharan Africa, where most of the population lived, generally consisted of several extended family groups. Male heads of families jointly governed the village and organized the work of their own groups. They allocated portions of the communal lands for their relatives to cultivate and were responsible for distributing harvests equitably among all members of their groups. Thus most villagers functioned in society first as members of a family or a lineage.

The Division of Labor Sex and gender relations also influenced the roles individuals played in society. Sex largely determined work roles. Indeed, men dominated some of the most prestigious trades. Leather tanning, for example, was the work of men who carefully guarded knowledge of their techniques and tanning compounds, which they passed down to their heirs. Men also dominated iron working, which was a highly valued skill in many African societies because blacksmiths knew the secrets of turning ores into useful objects such as knives, hoes, spearheads, and swords. Blacksmiths often served as community leaders, and like leather tanners, they passed knowledge of their craft down to their heirs. Women in blacksmith families often served as potters for their communities. They too enjoyed special prestige because of their ability to transform ingredients from the earth into useful pottery vessels. When it came to agricultural and family life, men usually undertook the heavy labor of clearing land and preparing it for cultivation. Women contributed most of the labor for the planting and harvesting of crops and also took primary responsibility for domestic chores and child rearing.

Women's Roles As in other societies, men largely monopolized public authority. Yet women in sub-Saharan Africa generally had more opportunities open to them than did their counterparts in other lands. Women enjoyed high honor as the sources of life. On at least a few occasions, women made their way to positions of power, and aristocratic women often influenced public affairs by virtue of their prominence within their families. Women merchants commonly traded at markets, and they participated actively in both local and long-distance trade in Africa. Sometimes women even engaged in combat and organized all-female military units.

Age Grades Apart from kinship and expectations based on sex and gender roles, African societies made a place for age groups that included all individuals within a given community born within a few years of one another. Historical linguistic analysis suggests that the recognition of those age grades, or age sets, arose in the early days of agricultural society in the Sudan, and it is clear that in many African societies the practice of grouping individuals into **age grades** has continued into recent times. Members of age grades performed tasks appropriate for their level of development, and they often bonded with one another to form tight circles of friends and political allies. Members of an age grade might provide labor for community projects, for example, or take joint responsibility for looking after village elders. They aided members who experienced adversities and helped one another at crucial junctures, such as marriage and the building of a new household. Thus age grades had the effect of establishing social ties that crossed the lines of family and kinship.

Slavery One class of individuals stood apart from the other social groups: slaves. As in other lands, the institution of slavery had a place in Africa since remote antiquity, and slave holding and slave trading were prominent features of sub-Saharan African society. Most enslaved people were captives of war. Others came from the ranks of debtors and criminals. Within Africa most enslaved people probably worked as domestic laborers, although many also worked as construction laborers, miners, or porters.

Slave ownership was a major form of personal wealth in sub-Saharan Africa. Since there was little if any private ownership of land, it was impossible for individuals to become wealthy through the accumulation of landholdings. On the basis of their slaves' labor, however, slaveholders were able to build wealth through increased agricultural production. Slaves also brought enhanced social status for their owners.

Slave Trading After about the ninth century C.E., the expansion of the trans-Saharan and Indian Ocean trade networks stimulated increased traffic in African slaves. Muslim merchants provided access to markets in India, Persia, southwest Asia, and the Mediterranean basin, where the demand for slaves outstripped the supply available from eastern Europe, previously the main source of slaves. As a result, merchants from northern lands traded in sub-Saharan Africa not only for gold, ivory, and exotic local products but also for slaves.

In response to that demand, rulers of large-scale states and empires began to make war on smaller states and kin-based societies in search of captives destined for northern slave markets. In some years, ten thousand to twenty thousand Africans were forced from their homes and sold into slavery. During the mid-fourteenth century, the Moroccan traveler Ibn Battuta crossed the Sahara in a caravan that included six hundred slaves bound for north Africa and the Mediterranean basin. King Mansa Musa of Mali set out on his pilgrimage to Mecca with five hundred slaves, many of whom he distributed along the way as gifts to his hosts. Other slaves were taken from the coastal cities of east Africa for destinations in Persia and India.

The Zanj Revolt Records of this slave trade are scarce, but a lengthy uprising known as the **Zanj revolt** throws light on the nature of African slavery. The term *Zanj* referred to black slaves from the Swahili coast. At least by the seventh century C.E., many Zanj slaves labored under extremely difficult conditions in southern Mesopotamia, where they worked on sugarcane plantations or cleared land of salt deposits to prepare it for cultivation. On several occasions they mounted revolts, which Muslim authorities promptly snuffed. Following a series of riots, in about 869 an enslaved man named Ali bin Muhammad organized about fifteen thousand Zanj slaves into an immense force that captured Basra, the most important city of southern Mesopotamia, and even established a rebel state in the region. Distracted by other threats, the Abbasid rulers of Mesopotamia turned their full attention to the rebellion only in 879, a full decade after it had begun. By 883 they had crushed the revolt, killed Ali bin Muhammad, and executed the other rebel leaders. Despite its ultimate collapse, the fourteen-year Zanj revolt clearly demonstrated both the determination of enslaved people to escape their brutal circumstances as well as the extreme desire of slaveholders to maintain the status quo.

Though smaller than the Atlantic slave trade of modern times, the **Islamic slave trade** was a sizable affair: between 750 and 1500 C.E., the number of African slaves transported to foreign lands may have exceeded ten million. The high demand led to the creation of networks within Africa for the purpose of capturing people and selling them as slaves. This economic system has the dubious distinction of serving as a foundation for the Atlantic slave trade in later centuries.

African Religions

Peoples of sub-Saharan Africa developed a wide range of languages, societies, and cultural traditions. Religious beliefs and practices in particular took many forms. The continent's peoples referred to their deities by different names, told different stories about them, and honored them with different rituals. Yet certain features were common to many religions of sub-Saharan Africa. In combination, those features offer considerable insight into the cultural and religious climate of sub-Saharan Africa in premodern times.

Creator God Many African peoples had recognized a single, dominant creator god from the early days of Sudanic agriculture. Through the centuries, their beliefs underwent considerable development as individual peoples learned about deities honored in other societies or as they sought their own improved understandings of the gods and their roles in the world. Nevertheless, many peoples recognized a single divine

force or male god as the agent responsible for setting the world in motion and providing it with order. Some peoples believed that this god also sustained the world, intervening indirectly, through spirits, to influence the course of human affairs. Some considered this deity to be all-powerful, others regarded him as all-knowing, and many considered him both omnipotent and omniscient.

Lesser Deities and Spirits Apart from the superior creator god, Africans recognized many lesser deities and spirits often associated with the sun, wind, rain, trees, rivers, and other natural features. Unlike the creator god, these lesser deities participated actively in the workings of the world. They could confer or withhold benefits and bring favor or injury to humans. Similarly, many Africans believed that the souls of departed ancestors had the power to intervene in the lives and experiences of their descendants: the departed

Masks such as this one from Congo were essential to the proper observance of religious rituals, which often involved communicating with natural or animal spirits. In what ways do the features of this mask associate the diviner with powers not accessible to normal humans?
De Agostini Picture Library/Getty Images

Zanj (zahn-jee)

could shape events to the advantage of descendants who behaved properly and honored their ancestors, and could bring misfortune as punishment for evil behavior and neglect of their ancestors' memory. Much of the ritual of African religions focused on honoring deities, spirits, or ancestors' souls to win their favor or regain their goodwill. The rituals included prayers, animal sacrifices, and ceremonies marking important stages of life—such as birth, circumcision, marriage, and death.

Diviners Like other peoples of the world, Africans recognized classes of religious specialists—individuals who by virtue of their innate abilities or extensive training had the power to mediate between humans and supernatural beings. Often referred to as diviners, they were usually men, although they were sometimes women who understood clearly the networks of political, social, economic, and psychological relationships within their communities. When afflicted by illness, sterility, crop failure, or some other disaster, individuals or groups consulted diviners to learn the cause of their misfortune. Diviners then consulted oracles; identified the causes of the trouble; and prescribed medicine, rituals, or sacrifices designed to eliminate the problem and bring about a return to normality.

For the most part, African religions were concerned not with matters of theology but, rather, with the more practical business of explaining, predicting, and controlling the experiences of individuals and groups in the world. Thus African religions strongly emphasized morality and proper behavior as essential to the maintenance of an orderly world. Failure to observe high moral standards would lead to disorder, which would displease deities, spirits, and departed ancestors and ensure that misfortune befell the negligent parties. Because proper moral behavior was so important to their fortunes, family and kinship groups took responsibility for policing their members and disciplining those who fell short of expected standards.

The Arrival of Christianity

Alongside religions that concentrated on the practical matter of maintaining an orderly world, two religions of salvation won converts in sub-Saharan Africa—Christianity and Islam. Both arrived in Africa as foreign faiths introduced by outsiders, though in time sub-Saharan adherents adapted both faiths to the needs and interests of their societies.

Early Christianity in North Africa Christianity reached Egypt and north Africa during the first century C.E., soon after its appearance. Alexandria in Egypt became one of the most prominent centers of early Christian thought, and north Africa was the home of St. Augustine, among many other leaders of the fledgling church. Yet for several centuries Christianity remained a Mediterranean tradition whose appeal did not reach sub-Saharan Africa.

The Christian Kingdom of Axum About the middle of the fourth century C.E., Christianity established a foothold in the kingdom of **Axum,** located in the highlands of modern Ethiopia. The first Axumite converts were probably local merchants who traded with Mediterranean Christians calling at the port of Adulis on the Red Sea. As missionaries visited Ethiopia, the kings of Axum also converted to Christianity, possibly in hopes of improving relations with their powerful neighbors to the north in Egypt. Indeed, the kings of Axum were some of the first royal converts to Christianity, which they adopted shortly after the Roman emperor Constantine himself. Missionaries later established monasteries, translated the Bible into the Ethiopian language, and worked to popularize Christianity throughout the kingdom.

In the late seventh century C.E., the ruling house of Axum fell into decline, and during the next several centuries the

---

Axum (AHK-soom)

What's Left Out? ■ ▬ ▬ ▬ ▬ ▬

Perhaps more than any other region of the world, the history of sub-Saharan Africa has been stereotyped as static, unchanging, and primitive. Why? In part it is because the discipline of history was itself being formed in the West just as Europeans—with their deeply racist assumptions about the primitive nature of people with darker skins—were in the process of conquering large portions of the region in the late nineteenth century. In part it is because sub-Saharan African history had largely been preserved in oral histories instead of textual archives, which were not valued by the Europeans who encountered them. As a result, Europeans were unable to access the rich and evolving histories of sub-Saharan Africans and assumed they did not exist. But the growth of African Studies in the twentieth century, practiced in many cases by people born in Africa, has demonstrated that such stereotypes are as false for sub-Saharan Africa as they are for anywhere else. At the same time, more recent academic comprehension of oral history as a complex and sophisticated means of recording the past has allowed historians to gain a much greater understanding of sub-Saharan African histories. Consider how much history remains untold when historians value only textual sources, in pre-modern sub-Saharan Africa or elsewhere.

Source: Jonathan Reynolds. "History and the Study of Africa." *Oxford University African Bibliographies.* Fall 2013.

The church of St. George at Lalibela, Ethiopia, (built in the 12th or 13th century) is a massive structure in the form of a cross. Workers excavated the surrounding earth and then carved the church itself out of a rock.

Gavin Hellier/robertharding/Getty images

expansion of Islam left an isolated island of Christianity in the Ethiopian highlands. During the twelfth century, however, a new ruling dynasty undertook a centralizing campaign and enthusiastically promoted Christianity as a foundation of cultural unity for the land. From the twelfth through the sixteenth century, Christianity enjoyed particular favor in Ethiopia. During the twelfth century, the Ethiopian kings ordered the carving of eleven massive churches out of solid rock—a monumental work of construction that required enormous resources and untold hours of labor. During the thirteenth century, rulers of Ethiopia's Solomonic dynasty claimed descent from the Israelite kings David and Solomon in an effort to lend additional biblical luster to their authority. The fictional work ***Kebra Negast*** (*The Glory of Kings*), which undertook to trace that lineage, in fact became popular in the twentieth century among Rastafarians and fans of reggae music in Ethiopia, Jamaica, and other places. Meanwhile, Christianity

retained its privileged status in Ethiopia until it fell out of favor following the socialist revolution of 1974.

Ethiopian Christianity For centuries after the introduction of Christianity to Ethiopia, Ethiopian Christians had little contact with Christians in other lands. As a result, although Ethiopian Christianity retained basic Christian theology and rituals, it increasingly reflected the interests of its African devotees. For example, Ethiopian Christians believed that a large host of evil spirits populated the world, and they carried amulets or charms for protection against these menacing spirits. The twelfth-century carved-rock churches themselves harked back to pre-Christian values because rock shrines had been a prominent feature in Ethiopian religion from the second or perhaps even third millennium B.C.E. The rock churches absorbed that tradition into Ethiopian Christianity. Not until the sixteenth century, when Portuguese mariners began to visit Ethiopia en route to India, did Ethiopians reestablish relations with Christians from other lands.

Kebra Negast (kee-brah NAH-gahst)

ISLAMIC KINGDOMS AND EMPIRES

In the seventh and eighth centuries, merchants from north Africa and southwest Asia introduced Islam to sub-Saharan Africa. Islam arrived in sub-Saharan Africa by two routes: it went to west Africa overland by trans-Saharan camel caravans, and it traveled to coastal east Africa over the sea lanes of the Indian Ocean in the vessels of merchant-mariners. After the eighth century C.E., Islam profoundly influenced the political, social, and economic development of both Saharan and sub-Saharan Africa as well as its cultural and religious development. At the same time, Africans in both west and east Africa adapted Islam to their own cultures, giving African Islam distinctly African characteristics.

Trans-Saharan Trade and Islamic States in West Africa

The Sahara has never served as an absolute barrier to communication between human societies. Small numbers of nomadic peoples have lived in the desert ever since the Sahara's formation about 5000 B.C.E. Those nomads migrated around the desert and had dealings with other peoples settled on its fringes. Even in ancient and classical times, merchants occasionally organized commercial expeditions across the desert, although the value and volume of trade was much smaller than in the Mediterranean and Red Sea basins.

Camels The arrival of the camel was instrumental to improving communication and transportation across the Sahara. **Camels** came to north Africa from Arabia, by way of Egypt and the Sudan, sometime in the first millennium B.C.E. and perhaps earlier. During the late centuries B.C.E., a special camel saddle, which took advantage of the animals' distinctive physical structure, also made its way to north Africa. Because a caravan took seventy to ninety days to cross the Sahara and because camels could travel long distances before needing water, they proved to be useful beasts of burden in an arid region. After about 300 C.E., camels increasingly replaced horses and donkeys as the preferred transport animals throughout the Sahara as well as in the deserts of central Asia.

When Arab conquerors introduced Islam into north Africa during the seventh and eighth centuries, they also integrated the region into a larger network of commerce and communication. Thus it was natural for Muslims in north Africa to explore the potential of trade across the Sahara. By the late eighth century, Islamic merchants in search of gold had trekked across the desert and established commercial relations with societies in sub-Saharan west Africa. There they found not only gold but a series of long-established trading centers such as Gao, a terminus of caravan routes across the Sahara that offered access to the Niger River valley, which was a flourishing market for copper, ironware, cotton textiles, salt, grains, and carnelian beads.

The Kingdom of Ghana The principal state of west Africa at the time of the Muslims' arrival there was the **kingdom of Ghana** (not related to the modern state of Ghana), situated between the Senegal and Niger rivers in a region straddling the border between the modern states of Mali and Mauritania.

Ghana (GAH-nuh)

Early-twentieth-century photograph of dromedary camels and their handlers in the Sahara. Note the special camel saddle and rigging that are specifically adapted to the animals' unique physical structure.
Michael Maslan/Corbis Historical/Getty Images

How the Past Shapes the Future ▶ ▶ ▶ ▶

The Diffusion of Technologies

Camels had been used for centuries by traders in Arabia and North Africa—thanks especially to the camel saddle invented in about 200 C.E.—before Muslim traders made their way across the Sahara to West Africa in the seventh and eighth centuries. Camels, although living beings, can be considered a technology because their use helped humans adapt the natural environment to their needs, making it possible to reliably and repeatedly traverse the vast Sahara. Think about the variety of ways that the diffusion of camels to sub-Saharan Africa—in terms of trade, urban growth, the accumulation of wealth, and the slave trade—affected the region over the very long term.

Gold Trade As trade and traffic across the desert increased, Ghana underwent a dramatic transformation. It became the most important commercial site in west Africa because it controlled the trade in **gold** that was mined and smelted nearby. Muslim merchants flocked to camel caravans traveling across the Sahara to Ghana in search of gold for consumers in the Mediterranean basin and elsewhere in the Islamic world. Ghana itself did not produce gold, but the kings procured nuggets from lands to the south—probably from the region around the headwaters of the Niger, Gambia, and Senegal rivers, which enjoyed the world's largest supply of gold available at the time. By controlling and taxing trade in the precious metal, the kings both enriched and strengthened their realm. Apart from gold, merchants from Ghana provided ivory and slaves for traders from north Africa. In exchange, they received horses, cloth, small manufactured wares, and salt—a crucial commodity but one that local sources could not supply in large quantities.

Koumbi-Saleh Integration into **trans-Saharan trade** networks brought enormous wealth and considerable power to Ghana. The kingdom's capital and principal trading site stood at **Koumbi-Saleh,** a small town today but a thriving commercial center with a population of some fifteen thousand to twenty thousand people when the kingdom was at its height, from the ninth to the twelfth century. Al-Bakri, a Spanish Muslim traveler of the mid-eleventh century, described

This west African terra-cotta sculpture from the thirteenth or fourteenth century depicts a helmeted and armored warrior astride a horse with elaborate harness and head protection.
Heritage Image Partnership Ltd/Alamy Stock Photo

Koumbi-Saleh as a flourishing settlement with buildings of stone and more than a dozen mosques. Koumbi-Saleh's wealth also supported a large number of *qadis* and Muslim scholars. From taxes levied on trade passing through Ghana, the kings financed a large army—al-Bakri reported that they could field two hundred thousand warriors—that protected the sources of gold, maintained order in the kingdom, kept allied and tributary states in line, and defended Ghana against nomadic incursions from the Sahara.

Islam in West Africa By about the tenth century, the kings of Ghana had converted to Islam. Their conversion led to improved relations with Muslim merchants from north Africa as well as Muslim nomads from the desert who transported trade goods across the Sahara. It also brought them recognition and support from Muslim states in north Africa. The kings of Ghana made no attempt to impose Islam forcibly on their society nor did they accept Islam exclusively even for their own purposes. Instead, they continued to observe traditional religious customs: al-Bakri mentioned, for example, that native religious specialists practiced what he believed to be magic and kept idols in the woods surrounding the royal palace at Koumbi-Saleh. Even in the absence of efforts to impose Islam on Ghana, however, the faith attracted converts, particularly among those engaged in trade with Muslim merchants from the north.

As the kingdom expanded to the north, it became vulnerable to attacks by nomadic peoples from the Sahara who sought to seize some of the kingdom's wealth. During the early thirteenth century, raids from the desert weakened the kingdom, and it soon collapsed. Several successor states took over portions of Ghana's territory, but political leadership in west Africa fell to the powerful **Mali Empire,** which emerged just as the kingdom of Ghana dissolved.

Sundiata As we saw in the introduction to this chapter, the lion prince Sundiata (reigned 1230–1255) built the Mali Empire during the first half of the thirteenth century after his return from exile. While away from home, he made astute alliances with local rulers, gained a reputation for courage in battle, and assembled a large army dominated by cavalry. By about 1235 he had

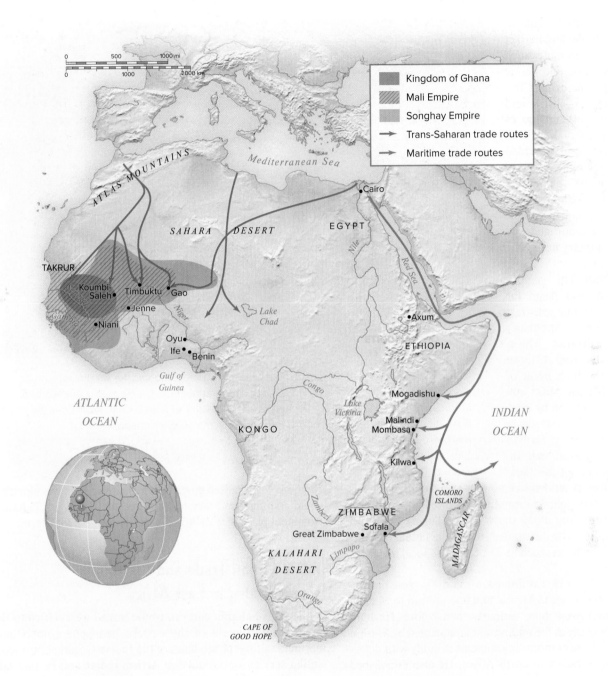

MAP 18.1 Kingdoms, empires, and city-states of sub-Saharan Africa, 800–1500 C.E.

After the emergence of Islam, trans-Saharan overland routes linked sub-Saharan west Africa with the Mediterranean region, and maritime trade routes linked sub-Saharan east Africa to the Indian Ocean basin.

How critical was the role of trade in the emergence of cities and states in sub-Saharan Africa?

consolidated his hold on the Mali Empire, which expanded to include Ghana as well as other neighboring kingdoms in the regions surrounding the Senegal and Niger rivers. The empire included most of the modern state of Mali and extended also to lands now known as Mauritania, Senegal, Gambia, Guinea-Bissau, Guinea, and Sierra Leone.

The Mali Empire and Trade Mali benefited from trans-Saharan trade on an even larger scale than Ghana did. From the thirteenth until the late fifteenth century, Mali controlled and taxed almost all trade passing through west Africa. Enormous caravans with as many as twenty-five thousand camels linked Mali to north Africa. The capital city of Niani attracted merchants seeking to enter the gold trade, and market cities on the caravan routes such as **Timbuktu,** Gao, and Jenne became prosperous centers featuring buildings of brick and stone. Like the earlier kings of Ghana, the rulers of Mali converted to Islam and provided protection, lodging, and comforts for Muslim merchants from the north. Although they did not force Islam on their realm, they encouraged its spread on a voluntary basis.

Mansa Musa The significance of trade and Islam for west Africa became clearest during the reign of Sundiata's grand-nephew **Mansa Musa,** who ruled Mali from 1312 to 1337, during the high point of the empire. Mansa Musa observed Islamic tradition by making his pilgrimage to Mecca in 1324–1325. His party formed a gargantuan caravan that included thousands of soldiers, attendants, subjects, and slaves as well as a hundred camels carrying satchels of gold. Mansa Musa bestowed lavish gifts on those who hosted him along the way, and during his three-month visit to Cairo, he distributed so much gold that the metal's value declined by as much as 25 percent on local markets.

Mansa Musa and Islam Mansa Musa drew great inspiration from his pilgrimage to Mecca, and upon return to Mali he took his religion even more seriously than before. He built mosques, particularly in the trading cities frequented by Muslim merchants, and he sent promising students to study with distinguished Islamic scholars in north Africa. He also established religious schools and brought in Arabian and north African teachers, including four descendants of Muhammad himself, to make Islam better known in Mali.

Yet within a century of Mansa Musa's reign, Mali was in serious decline: factions crippled the central government, provinces seceded from the empire, and military pressures came both from neighboring kingdoms and from desert nomads. By the late fifteenth century, the Songhay Empire had completely overcome Mali. Yet Mansa Musa and other Mali rulers had established a

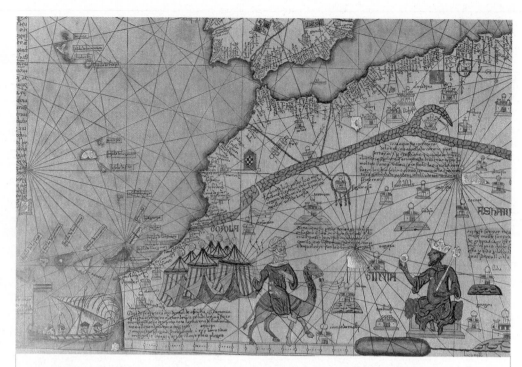

Mansa Musa, emperor of Mali, enjoyed a widespread reputation as the wealthiest king in the world. On this map, prepared in 1375 by a cartographer from the Mediterranean island of Majorca, Mansa Musa holds a gold nugget about the size of a grapefruit. What does this illustration reveal about the image of west Africa in the Mediterranean world?
Abraham Cresques/Getty Images

tradition of centralized government that the Songhay realm itself would continue, and they had ensured that Islam would have a prominent place in west African society over the long term.

Indian Ocean Trade and Islamic States in East Africa

While trans-Saharan caravan traffic linked west Africa to the larger trading world of the eastern hemisphere, merchant-mariners sailing the sea lanes of the Indian Ocean performed a similar service for coastal east Africa. Indian and Persian sailors had visited the east African coasts after about 500 B.C.E., and Hellenistic and Roman mariners sailed through the Red Sea en route to the same coasts. After the late centuries B.C.E., Malay seafarers also ventured into the western Indian Ocean from their island homelands in southeast Asia, and by the fourth and fifth centuries C.E. they had established colonies on the island of Madagascar.

By the second century C.E., Bantu-speaking peoples had populated much of east Africa. They introduced agriculture, cattle herding, and iron metallurgy to the region, and here, as elsewhere in sub-Saharan Africa, they founded complex societies governed by small, local states. As their population increased and merged with indigenous inhabitants, they founded settlements on the coasts and offshore islands as well as the interior regions of east Africa. Those coast dwellers supplemented their

---

Timbuktu (tim-buhk-TOO)

Gao (gou)

Jenne (jehn-neh)

Mansa Musa (MAHN-suh MOO-suh)

This Chinese vase was brought to East Africa as part of the Indian Ocean trade.

Heritage Image Partnership Ltd/Alamy Stock Photo

agricultural production with ocean fishing and maritime trade. They were the founders of **Swahili** society.

The Swahili *Swahili* is an Arabic term meaning "coasters," referring to those who engaged in trade along the east African coast. The Swahili dominated the east African coast from Mogadishu in the north to Kilwa, the Comoro Islands, and Sofala in the south. They spoke Swahili, a Bantu language supplemented with words and ideas borrowed from Arabic. Swahili peoples developed different dialects, but they communicated readily among themselves because individuals frequently visited other Swahili communities in their oceangoing crafts. Indeed, all along the east African coast, Swahili society underwent similar patterns of development with respect to language, religion, architecture, and technology.

By the tenth century, Swahili people increasingly adopted Islam and also interacted with Muslim traders from other places. From the interior regions of east Africa, the Swahili traded for

Swahili (swah-HEE-lee)

Gerezani Fortress on the east African coast at Kilwa, a testament to the wealth and military power of this major Swahili city on the Indian Ocean.

Ulrich Doering/Alamy Stock Photo

SOURCES FROM THE PAST

Ibn Battuta on Muslim Society at Mogadishu

During the fourteenth century the Muslim Moroccan jurist Ibn Battuta traveled throughout much of the eastern hemisphere. Twice he visited sub-Saharan Africa: in 1331, when he traveled along the Swahili coast, and in 1351–1352, when he visited the Mali Empire. His account of his visit to the Swahili city of Mogadishu offers insight into the mercantile and social customs of the city as well as the hospitality accorded to distinguished visitors.

[Mogadishu] is an exceedingly large city. The custom here is, that whenever any ships approach, the young men of the city come out, and each one addressing himself to a merchant, becomes his host. If there be a theologian or a noble on board, he takes up his residence with the Qadi [magistrate of shari'a law]. When it was heard that I was there, the Qadi came with his students to the beach: and I took up my abode with him. He then took me to the Sultan, whom they style Sheikh. Their custom is, that a noble or a theologian, must be presented to the Sultan, before he takes up his abode in the city. When, therefore, the Qadi came to the palace, one of the King's servants met him. . . . The servant then went to the Sultan, and informed him: but soon returned to us with a basket of vegetables, and some fawfel [areca] nut. These he divided among us, and then presented us with rose-water; which is the greatest honour done among them to any-one. He then said: It is the command of the King, that this person should reside in the student's house. The Qadi then took me by the hand, and conducted me to it. It was near the palace, was spread with carpets, and prepared for a feast. The servants then brought meats from the palace.

> **Why did Ibn Battuta's hosts treat him with such special care?**

Their meat is generally rice roasted with oil, and placed in a large wooden dish. Over this they place a large dish of elkushan, which consists of flesh, fish, fowl, and vegetables. They also roast the fruit of the plantain, and afterwards boil it in new milk: they then put it on a dish, and the curdled milk on another. They also put on dishes, some of preserved lemon, bunches of preserved pepper-pods salted and pickled, as also grapes, which are not unlike apples, except that they have stones. These, when boiled, become sweet like fruit in general, but are crude before this: they are preserved by being salted and pickled. In the same manner they use the green ginger. When, therefore, they eat the rice, they eat after it these salts and pickles. The people of [Mogadishu] are very corpulent: they are enormous eaters, one of them eating as much as a congregation ought to do.

> **Why do travelers so frequently comment on the food and eating habits of other people?**

The Sultan then sent for me and for each of my companions a [suitable] dress; after which I was presented to him. . . . I remained some days the King's guest, and then set out for the country of the Zanuj [it is not clear what place he refers to here], proceeding along the sea-shore.

For Further Reflection

■ From Ibn Battuta's report, how could you characterize the role of hospitality on the Swahili coast?

Source: Ibn Battuta, 1304–1377, and Samuel Lee. *The Travels of Ibn Battuta.* London: Printed for the Oriental translation committee, sold by J. Murray [etc.], 1829, 56–57.

gold, slaves, ivory, and local products such as tortoise shells and leopard skins, which they traded for pottery, glass, and textiles that Muslim merchants brought from Persia, India, and China. The rapidly increasing volume and value of trade had large repercussions for Swahili states and societies, just as the expansion of the trans-Saharan trade had for west African societies.

The Swahili City-States By the eleventh and twelfth centuries, coastal East Africans had grown wealthy through their trading activities. By controlling and taxing trade within their jurisdictions, local chiefs strengthened their own authority and increased the influence of their communities. Gradually, trade concentrated at several coastal and island port cities that enjoyed sheltered or especially convenient locations: Mogadishu, Lamu, Malindi, Mombasa, Zanzibar, Kilwa, Mozambique, and Sofala. Each of those sites developed into a powerful city-state governed by kings who supervised trade and organized public life in the region.

The cities themselves underwent an impressive transformation. Villages in the interior regions of east Africa had buildings made of wood and dried mud, the principal materials used even for prominent structures such as mosques. By about the twelfth century, however, Swahili peoples began to construct much larger buildings of coral, and by the fifteenth century the main Swahili towns boasted handsome stone mosques and public buildings. Meanwhile, the ruling elites and wealthy merchants of Swahili trading cities dressed in silk and fine cotton clothes, and they set their tables with porcelain imported from China.

Kilwa Travelers' reports and recent archaeological discoveries have thrown especially clear light on the development of **Kilwa,** one of the busiest city-states on the east African coast. The earliest Bantu inhabitants of Kilwa relied mostly on fishing and engaged in a limited amount of trade between about 800 and 1000 C.E. During the next two centuries, they imported pottery and stoneware from other regions in east Africa and began to rely more on agriculture to support their growing numbers. By

the early thirteenth century, Kilwans were prosperous enough to erect multistory stone buildings, and they used copper coins to facilitate economic transactions. Between 1300 and 1505, Kilwa enjoyed tremendous prosperity. The Moroccan traveler Ibn Battuta visited the city in 1331 and reported that Muslim scholars from Arabia and Persia lived at Kilwa and consulted regularly with the local ruler.

With a population of about twelve thousand, Kilwa was a thriving city that had many stone buildings and mosques. Residents imported cotton and silk textiles as well as perfumes and pearls from India, and archaeologists have unearthed a staggering amount of Chinese porcelain. Merchants of Kilwa imported those products in exchange for gold, slaves, and ivory obtained from interior regions. By the late fifteenth century, Kilwa exported about a ton of gold per year. Participation in Indian Ocean trade networks brought similar experiences to the other major Swahili cities.

Kilwa (KIHL-wah)

The massive stone complex of Great Zimbabwe, which featured very fine construction techniques, required the services of numerous expert masons and other crafts workers.
Georg Gerster/Science Source

In fact, the influence of long-distance trade passed well beyond the coasts to the interior regions of east Africa. Villagers in the interior did not enjoy the cosmopolitan lifestyles of the Swahili elites, but trade and the wealth that it brought underwrote the establishment of large and powerful kingdoms in east and central Africa.

Zimbabwe The best known of these kingdoms was **Zimbabwe.** The term *zimbabwe* refers simply to the dwelling of a chief. As early as the fifth and sixth centuries C.E., the region occupied by the modern states of Zimbabwe and Mozambique featured many wooden residences known throughout the land as *zimbabwe*. By the ninth century, chiefs had begun to build their *zimbabwe* of stone—indicating an increasingly complex society that could invest resources in expensive construction projects. About the early thirteenth century, a magnificent stone complex known as **Great Zimbabwe** began to arise near Nyanda in the modern state of Zimbabwe. Within stone walls 5 meters (16 feet) thick and 10 meters (32 feet) tall, Great Zimbabwe was a city of stone towers, palaces, and public buildings that served as the capital of a large kingdom situated between the Zambesi and Limpopo rivers. At the time of its greatest extent, during the late fifteenth century, up to eighteen thousand people may have lived in the vicinity of the stone complex at Great Zimbabwe, and the kingdom stretched from the outskirts of the Swahili city of Sofala deep into the interior of south-central Africa.

Zimbabwe (zihm-BAHB-way)

Kings residing at Great Zimbabwe controlled and taxed the trade between the interior and coastal regions. They organized the flow of gold, ivory, slaves, and regional products from sources of supply to the coast. Their control over those products enabled them to forge alliances with local leaders and to profit handsomely from commercial transactions. Just as the trans-Saharan trade encouraged the building of states and empires in west Africa, the Indian Ocean trade generated wealth that financed the organization of city-states on the coast and large kingdoms in the interior regions of east and central Africa.

Islam in East Africa In east Africa, again as in west Africa, trade brought cultural as well as political changes. Like their counterparts in west Africa, the ruling elites and the wealthy merchants of east Africa converted to the Islamic faith. They did not necessarily give up their religious and cultural traditions but, rather, continued to observe them for purposes of providing cultural leadership in their societies. By adopting Islam, however, they laid a cultural foundation for close cooperation with Muslim merchants trading in the Indian Ocean basin. Moreover, Islam served as a fresh source of legitimacy for their rule because they gained recognition from Islamic states in southwest Asia, and their conversion opened the door to political alliances with Muslim rulers in other lands. Even though the conversion of elite classes did not bring about the immediate spread of Islam throughout their societies, it enabled Islam to establish a presence in east Africa under the sponsorship of some particularly influential patrons. The faith eventually attracted interest in larger circles and became one of the principal cultural and religious traditions of east Africa.

CONCLUSION

States and societies of sub-Saharan Africa shared similarities with and also differed from societies in other parts of the eastern hemisphere. The foundations of most sub-Saharan societies were the traditions of agricultural economy and iron-working skills that spread throughout most of the African continent. As these peoples migrated to new regions and established new communities, at first they based their societies on kin groups. When different societies came into conflict with one another, however, they increasingly established formal political authorities to guide their affairs. African peoples organized states of various sizes, some very small and others quite large. When they entered into commercial relationships with Muslim peoples in southwest Asia and north Africa, they also built formidable imperial states in west Africa and bustling city-states in coastal east Africa. These states had far-reaching implications for sub-Saharan societies because they depended on a regular and reliable flow of trade goods—particularly gold, ivory, and slaves. Trade and the regular encounters it entailed also had cultural implications because it facilitated

the introduction of Islam, which together with native African traditions profoundly influenced the development of sub-Saharan societies. After the eighth century, many ruling elites in both west Africa and coastal east Africa—like Sundiata, King of Mali, who we encountered at the beginning of the chapter—accepted Islam and strengthened its position in their societies by building mosques, consulting Muslim advisers, and supporting Islamic schools. By 1500 C.E. African traditions and Islamic influences had combined to fashion a series of powerful, productive, and distinctive societies in sub-Saharan Africa that were increasingly integrated into wider networks of exchange and encounter in North Africa and Eurasia.

STUDY TERMS

age grades (367)	Benin (365)
Axum (369)	camels (371)
Bantu (364)	gold (372)

Great Zimbabwe (378)

griots (362)

Ife (365)

Islamic slave trade (368)

Jenne-jeno (364)

Kebra Negast (370)

Kilwa (377)

kin-based societies (364)

kingdom of Ghana (371)

kingdom of Kongo (365)

Koumbi-Saleh (372)

Mali Empire (372)

Mansa Musa (374)

Sundiata (362)

Swahili (375)

Timbuktu (374)

trans-Saharan trade (372)

Zanj revolt (368)

Zimbabwe (378)

FOR FURTHER READING

Ibn Battuta. *Ibn Battuta in Black Africa.* Ed. and trans. by Said Hamdun and Noel King. Princeton, 1998. Translations of travel accounts of visits to coastal east Africa and the empire of Mali by a famous fourteenth-century Moroccan traveler.

Christopher Ehret. *The Civilizations of Africa: A History to 1800.* Charlottesville, Va., 2002. An important contribution that views Africa in the context of world history.

Mary Anne Fitzgerald and Phillip Marsden, *Ethiopia: The Living Churches of an Ancient Kingdom.* Cairo, 2017. Beautifully illustrated volume that traces the history of the ancient churches of Ethiopia.

Bernd Heine and Derek Nurse. *African Languages: An Introduction.* Cambridge, 2000. A sophisticated treatment of the historical complexity of African languages by expert linguists.

J. F. P. Hopkins and N. Levtzion, eds. *Corpus of Early Arabic Sources for West African History.* Princeton, 2000. Translations of numerous important accounts by Muslim merchants and geographers who reported on conditions in west Africa before modern times.

Mark Horton and John Middleton. *The Swahili: The Social Landscape of a Mercantile Society.* Oxford, 2000. Useful survey that draws on both archaeological and written evidence.

John S. Mbiti. *African Religions and Philosophy.* 2nd ed. London, 1990. A thorough and systematic study of traditional African religions in their cultural context.

Roderick James McIntosh. *The Peoples of the Middle Niger: The Island of Gold.* Oxford, 1998. Fascinating volume emphasizing the environmental context of west African history.

D. T. Niane, ed. *Sundiata: An Epic of Old Mali.* 2nd ed. Trans. by G. D. Pickett. London, 2006. Translation of the story of Sundiata, founder of the Mali Empire, as preserved in African oral tradition.

Jan Vansina. *Paths in the Rainforests: Toward a History of Political Tradition in Equatorial Africa.* Madison, 1990. A brilliant synthesis of early African history by one of the world's foremost historians of Africa.

The Regional States of Medieval Europe

The Late Byzantine Empire

The Holy Roman Empire

Regional Monarchies in France and England

Regional States in Italy and Iberia

Economic Growth and Social Development

Growth of the Agricultural Economy

The Revival of Towns and Trade

Social Change

European Christianity during the High Middle Ages

Schools, Universities, and Scholastic Theology

Popular Religion

Reform Movements and Popular Heresies

The Medieval Expansion of Europe

Atlantic and Baltic Colonization

The Reconquest of Sicily and Spain

The Crusades

ZOOMING IN ON TRADITIONS AND ENCOUNTERS

From Venice to China and Back

In 1260 C.E. two brothers, Niccolò and Maffeo Polo, traveled from their native Venice to Constantinople. The Polo brothers were jewel merchants, and while in Constantinople, they decided to pursue opportunities farther east. They made their way to the great central Asian trading city of Bokhara, where they spent three years and received an invitation to join a diplomatic embassy going to the court of Khubilai Khan. They readily agreed and traveled by caravan to the Mongol court in China, where the great khan received them and inquired about their land, rulers, and religion.

Khubilai was especially interested in learning more about Roman Catholic Christianity so he asked the Polo brothers to return to Europe and request the pope to send learned priests who could serve as authoritative sources of information on Christian doctrine. They accepted the mission and returned to Italy in 1269 as envoys of the great khan.

Venice, home of Marco Polo and a legion of merchants, drew enormous prosperity from trade. This image depicts Marco Polo leaving Venice on his eastward journey.
Timewatch Images/Alamy Stock Photo

As it turned out, the Polo brothers were not able to satisfy the great khan's desire for expertise in Christian doctrine even though the pope had been willing to send priests to accompany them back to China. In fact, the pope designated two missionaries to accompany the Polos, and the party set out in 1271, together with Niccolò's seventeen-year-old son, **Marco Polo.** Soon, however, the missionaries became alarmed at fighting along the route, and they decided to abandon the embassy and return to Europe. Thus only the Polos completed the difficult and sometimes dangerous journey, arriving at the Mongol court of Shangdu three and a half years later, in 1274. Although they instead presented Khubilai with letters and presents from the pope—including a sample of lamp oil from the church of the Holy Sepulchre in Jerusalem—they did not bring the requested missionaries. The great khan nevertheless received the Polos warmly and welcomed them to his court. In fact, they remained in China in the service of the great khan for the next seventeen years. Their mission gave rise to Marco Polo's celebrated account of his travels, and it signaled the reintegration of Europe into the political and economic affairs of the larger eastern hemisphere.

CHAPTER OVERVIEW

As a result of the turmoil and disarray that plagued Europe during the half millennium from 500 to 1000 C.E., western Europeans practiced their own traditions and played little role in the development of a hemispheric economy during the era dominated by the Tang, Song, Abbasid, and Byzantine empires. But during the early middle ages, Europeans laid the foundations of a more dynamic and stable society. Regional states became the basis for a more enduring political order. New tools and technologies led to increased agricultural production and economic growth. The missionary efforts of the western Christian church brought cultural and religious unity to most of Europe. During the "high middle ages" of European history—the period from about 1000 to 1300 C.E.—European peoples built a vibrant society on the political, economic, and cultural foundations laid during the early middle ages.

Although the idea of empire continued to fascinate political thinkers and leaders, empire builders of the high middle ages did not manage to bring all of Europe under their control. Instead, local rulers organized strong regional states. Increased agricultural production fueled rapid population growth. Economic expansion led to increased long-distance trade, enriched cities, and supported the establishment of new towns. Cultural and religious affairs also reflected the dynamism of the high middle ages, as European philosophers and theologians reconsidered traditional doctrines in light of fresh knowledge.

Political organization, demographic increase, and economic growth pushed Europeans once again into encounters with the larger world. European merchants began to participate directly in the commercial economy of the eastern hemisphere, sometimes traveling as far as China—as we saw in the case of the Polo family—in search of luxury goods. Ambitious military and political leaders expanded the boundaries of Christendom by seizing Muslim-held territories in Spain and the Mediterranean islands, in the process expanding their encounters with new peoples and ideas. European forces even mounted a series of military crusades that sought to bring Islamic lands of the eastern Mediterranean basin under Christian control. While the Crusades ultimately failed, they clearly demonstrated that Europeans were beginning to play a much larger role in the world than they had for the previous half millennium.

CHRONOLOGY	
962	Coronation of Otto I as Holy Roman emperor
1056–1106	Reign of Emperor Henry IV
1066	Norman invasion of England
1073–1085	Reign of Pope Gregory VII
1096–1099	First crusade
1122–1204	Life of Eleanor of Aquitaine
1152–1190	Reign of Emperor Frederick Barbarossa
1170–1221	Life of St. Dominic
1182–1226	Life of St. Francis
1187	Recapture of Jerusalem by Saladin
1202–1204	Fourth crusade
1225–1274	Life of St. Thomas Aquinas
1271–1295	Marco Polo's trip to China
1453	Fall of Constantinople to Ottoman Turks

THE REGIONAL STATES OF MEDIEVAL EUROPE

Long after its collapse, the Roman Empire inspired European philosophers, theologians, and rulers, who dreamed of a centralized political structure embracing all of Christian Europe. The Byzantine Empire survived as the dominant power in the eastern Mediterranean region, where it flourished through the early eleventh century. By 1100 C.E., however, Byzantium experienced domestic social and economic difficulties as well as foreign pressure from both east and west. Even as Byzantium influenced the emergence of new states in Russia and eastern Europe, the empire itself gradually declined and in 1453 fell to Muslim Turkish invaders. As Byzantium weakened, western Europe underwent an impressive round of state building.

Beginning in the late tenth century, German princes formed the so-called **Holy Roman Empire,** which they viewed as a Christian revival of the earlier Roman Empire. Meanwhile, independent monarchies emerged in France and England, and other authorities ruled in the various regions of Italy and Spain. Thus medieval Europe became a political mosaic of independent and competing regional states.

The Late Byzantine Empire

Social and Economic Problems

For about three centuries, the *theme* system—which granted farm land to men who served as soldiers—served the Byzantine Empire well by supporting both a powerful army and a prosperous independent peasantry. About the eleventh century, however, wealthy

MAP 19.1   The regional states of medieval Europe, 1000–1300

Note the large number of states and the different kinds of states that claimed sovereignty in medieval Europe.

To what extent did the invasions of the ninth and tenth centuries (depicted in Map 16.3) influence the political development of medieval Europe?

During the sack of Constantinople in 1204, crusading forces seized and carted away Byzantine treasures of all sorts—including the great bronze horses that now reside in St. Mark's basilica in Venice.

Leemage/Universal Images Group/Getty Images

landowners increasingly undermined the *theme* system by acquiring the properties of independent peasants and accumulating them into large estates. That development transformed formerly free peasants into a class of dependent agricultural laborers while reducing incentives for individuals to serve in Byzantine military forces. It also led to diminished tax receipts for the central government.

Challenges from the West As domestic problems mounted, Byzantium also faced fresh foreign challenges. From the west came representatives of an increasingly dynamic western Europe, where rapid economic development supported a round of military and political expansion. During the early eleventh century, Norman adventurers—descendants of Vikings who had settled on the Norman peninsula in northern France—carved out a regional state in southern Italy and expelled the last

Byzantine authorities there. During the twelfth and thirteenth centuries, the Normans and other western European peoples mounted a series of crusades—vast military campaigns intended to recapture Jerusalem and other sites holy to Christians from Muslim rule—and took the opportunity to plunder the Byzantine Empire. Venetian merchants even managed to hijack the fourth crusade (1202–1204 C.E.) from its original mission in the eastern Mediterranean and targeted Constantinople instead. Venetians had become prominent in the commercial life of the eastern Mediterranean, and they viewed the fourth crusade as an opportunity to strengthen their position against Byzantine competition. In 1204 the crusaders conquered Constantinople, looted its art and treasure, and destroyed parts of the city. Byzantine forces recaptured the city in 1261, but the humiliating destruction of the imperial capital dealt the empire a blow from which it never completely recovered.

Fourteenth-century illustration of Pope Gregory VII receiving Henry IV at his fort at Canossa, after Henry showed his penitence by kneeling in the snow for three days.
Album/Alamy Stock Photo

Challenges from the East As Europeans advanced from the west, nomadic Turkish peoples invaded from the east. Most important among them were the Muslim Seljuqs, who, beginning in the eleventh century, sent waves of invaders into Anatolia, the agricultural heartland of the Byzantine Empire. Given the military and financial problems of Byzantium, the Seljuqs found Anatolia ripe for plunder. In 1071 they handed the Byzantine army a demoralizing defeat at the **battle of Manzikert.** Byzantine forces then turned on each other in civil war, allowing the Seljuqs almost free rein in Anatolia. By the late twelfth century, the Seljuqs had seized much of Anatolia, while crusaders from western Europe held most of the remainder.

The loss of Anatolia sealed the fate of the Byzantine Empire. A territorially truncated Byzantium survived until the mid-fifteenth century, but it enjoyed little autonomy and faced a series of challenges from Italian merchants, western European adventurers, and Turkish invaders. In 1453, following a long era of decline, the Byzantine Empire came to an end when Ottoman Turks, under the dynamic leadership of twenty-one-year-old Sultan Mehmed II, captured Constantinople and absorbed Byzantium's last remaining territories into their expanding realm.

The Holy Roman Empire

Otto I As the Carolingian Empire—which ruled over much of western Europe from 800–888—faded at the end of the ninth century, counts, dukes, and other local authorities took responsibility for providing order in their own regions. Gradually, some of them extended their influence beyond their own jurisdictions and built larger states. **Otto I** of Saxony was particularly aggressive. By the mid-tenth century, he had established himself as king in what is now northern Germany. He campaigned east of the Elbe River in lands populated by Slavic peoples (in what is now eastern Germany, western Poland, and the Czech Republic), and twice he ventured into Italy to quell political disturbances and protect the pope. In appreciation for his aid in protecting the papal states during a rebellion, Pope John XII proclaimed Otto Emperor of the Romans in 962 C.E., thus reviving the idea of the Holy Roman Empire born during the time of Charlemagne (r. 800–814).

The imperial title had considerable cachet, and on several occasions energetic emperors almost transformed the Holy Roman Empire into a hegemonic state that might have reintroduced imperial unity to Europe. Conflict with the papacy, however, prevented the emperors from building a strong and dynamic state. Although the popes crowned the medieval emperors, their relations were usually tense because both popes and emperors made large claims to authority in Christian Europe. Relations became especially strained when emperors sought to influence the selection of church officials, which the popes regarded as their own prerogative, or when emperors sought to extend their authority into Italy, where the popes had long provided political leadership.

Investiture Contest Neither the popes nor the emperors were strong enough to dominate the other, but the popes were able to prevent the emperors from building a powerful imperial state that would threaten the papacy as Europe's principal spiritual authority. The capacity of the papacy to weaken the empire became apparent during the **Investiture Contest,** a controversy over the appointment of church officials in the late eleventh and early twelfth centuries. From the earliest days of the Holy Roman Empire, imperial authorities had named important church officials to their positions because the higher clergy provided political as well as religious services. In an effort to regain control of the clergy and ensure that church officials met appropriate spiritual criteria, Pope Gregory VII (1073–1085 C.E.) ordered an end to the practice of lay investiture—the selection and installation of church officials by non-church rulers such as emperors. When Emperor Henry IV (1056–1106 C.E.) challenged the pope's policy, Gregory excommunicated him and released his subjects from their duty to obey him. The German princes then took the opportunity to rebel against the emperor. Henry eventually regained control of the empire but only after beseeching Gregory's mercy while standing barefoot in the snow. Because of the pope's intervention in imperial affairs, however, the German princes won concessions that enhanced their independence and diminished the emperor's authority.

Frederick Barbarossa Popes and emperors clashed over their conflicting interests in Italy as well as over the appointment of church officials. Among the most vigorous of the medieval emperors was Frederick I, known as **Frederick Barbarossa**—"the red beard"—a strong opponent of papal power who reigned from 1152 to 1190 C.E. Working from his ancestral lands in southern Germany, Barbarossa sought to absorb the wealthy and increasingly urban region of Lombardy in northern Italy. Integration of Lombardy with his German holdings might have provided Barbarossa with the resources to control the German princes, build a powerful state, and dominate much of Europe. That prospect did not appeal to the popes, who marshaled support from other European states on behalf of the Italian cities. By the end of Barbarossa's reign, the papal coalition had forced the emperor to relinquish his rights in Lombardy. Once again, papal policies forestalled the transformation of the Holy Roman Empire into a powerful state.

Voltaire, the eighteenth-century French writer, once quipped that the Holy Roman Empire was "neither holy, nor Roman, nor an empire." Indeed, the Holy Roman Empire was an empire principally in name. In reality, it was a regional state ruling Germany, though it also wielded influence intermittently in eastern Europe and Italy. In no sense, however, did the Holy Roman Empire restore imperial unity to western Europe.

Regional Monarchies in France and England

In the absence of an effective imperial power, regional states emerged throughout medieval Europe. In France and England, princes established regional monarchies on the basis of relationships between lords and their retainers (subjects or followers).

Capetian France The French monarchy grew slowly from humble beginnings. When the last of the Carolingians died, in 987 C.E., the lords of France elected a minor noble named Hugh Capet to serve as king. Capet held only a small territory around Paris, and he was in no position to challenge his retainers, some of whom were far more powerful than the king himself. During the next three centuries, however, his descendants, known as the **Capetian** kings, gradually added to their fortunes and expanded their political influence. Relying on relationships between lords and retainers, they absorbed the territories of retainers who died without heirs and established the right to administer justice throughout the realm. By the early fourteenth century, the Capetian kings had gradually centralized power and authority in France.

The Normans The English monarchy developed quite differently. Its founders were the **Normans** of what is now modern France. Though nominally subject to Carolingian and later to Capetian rulers, the dukes of Normandy in fact pursued their own interests with little regard for their lords. Within Normandy the dukes built a tightly centralized state in which all authority stemmed from the dukes themselves. The dukes also retained title to all land in Normandy, and in an effort to forestall conflicts of interest they strictly limited the right of their retainers to grant land to others. By the late tenth century, Norman lords had built a series of castles from which disciplined armies dominated their territories, and in the eleventh century they emerged as prominent political and military leaders throughout Europe and much of the Mediterranean basin as well.

Norman England In 1066 Duke William of Normandy assembled a fleet of ships carrying seven thousand men and two thousand horses, and sailed across the English Channel to invade England. At the time England was ruled by descendants of the Angles, the Saxons, and other Germanic peoples who had migrated there during the fifth and sixth centuries. The Duke, who became known as **William the Conqueror,** won a speedy military victory and quickly began to introduce

Capet (KAHP-ay)

The Bayeux tapestry, a magnificent mural of woven linen about 70 meters (230 feet) long, depicts the Norman invasion and conquest of England in 1066, led by William the Conqueror. In this section Norman warriors sail across the English Channel and disembark in southern England.

Hulton Archive/Getty Images

Norman principles of government and land tenure to England. While retaining many institutions of their Anglo-Saxon predecessors, the Norman kings of England ruled over a much more tightly centralized realm than did the Capetian kings of France.

Both the Capetians and the Normans faced challenges from retainers seeking to pursue independent policies or enlarge their powers at the expense of the monarchs. Both dynasties also faced external challenges: indeed, they often battled each other because the Normans periodically sought to expand their possessions in France. On the basis of relationships between lords and retainers, however, both the Capetians and the Normans managed to organize regional monarchies that maintained order and provided reasonably effective government.

Regional States in Italy and Iberia

Church Influence in Italy Regional states emerged also in other lands of medieval Europe, though not on such a large scale as the monarchies of France and England. In Italy, for

example, no single regime controlled the entire peninsula. Rather, a series of ecclesiastical (run by the church) states, city-states, and principalities competed for power and position. In central Italy the popes had provided political leadership since the Carolingian era. Indeed, although the papacy was a spiritual rather than a political post, the popes ruled a good-sized territory in central Italy known as the Papal State. In northern Italy, too, the church influenced political affairs because bishops of the major cities took much of the initiative in organizing public life in their regions. During the high middle ages, however, as the cities grew wealthy from trade and manufacturing, lay classes challenged the bishops and eventually displaced them as ruling authorities.

Italian States By about the twelfth century, a series of prosperous city-states—including Florence, Bologna, Genoa, Milan, and Venice—dominated not only their own urban districts but also the surrounding rural areas. Meanwhile, in southern Italy, Norman mercenaries—cousins of those who conquered

FIORENZA

The Italian city-state of Florence grew rapidly during the high middle ages. This portrait of the city concentrates on the space enclosed by walls completed in the early fourteenth century.
DEA PICTURE LIBRARY/DeAgostini/Getty Images

Anglo-Saxon England—invaded territories still claimed by the Byzantine Empire and various Muslim states. Normans first intervened in Italian affairs in the year 999, when a group of Norman pilgrims aided the people of Salerno as they fought off an attack by a Muslim army. Other Normans later aided the city of Bari in its struggle for independence from Byzantine authority (1017–1018). When they learned that opportunities might be available for ambitious adventurers in an unstable region, Norman mercenaries soon made their way to southern Italy in large numbers. With papal approval and support, they overcame Byzantine and Muslim authorities, brought southern Italy into the orbit of Roman Catholic Christianity, and laid the foundations for the emergence of the powerful kingdom of Naples.

Christian and Muslim States in Iberia As in Italy, a series of regional states competed for power in the Iberian peninsula. From the eighth to the eleventh century, a series of Muslim states ruled most of the peninsula. Only in northern Spain did small Christian states hold sway, mostly in mountainous regions. Beginning in the mid-eleventh century, though, Christians from those states began to attack Muslim territories and enlarge their own domains. As in southern Italy, political and military instability attracted the attention of Norman mercenaries, many of whom traveled to Spain and joined the armies of the Christian kingdoms as soldiers of fortune. By the late thirteenth century, the Christian kingdoms of Castile, Aragon, and Portugal controlled most of the Iberian peninsula, leaving only the small kingdom of Granada in Muslim hands.

With its Byzantine Empire, Holy Roman Empire, regional monarchies, ecclesiastical principalities, city-states, and new states founded on conquest, medieval Europe might seem to present a chaotic and confusing political spectacle, particularly when compared with a land such as China, which by this time had been reunified by centralized imperial rule. Moreover, European rulers rarely sought to maintain the current state of affairs but, rather, campaigned constantly to enlarge their holdings at the expense of their neighbors. As a result, the political history of medieval Europe was a complicated affair. Yet the regional states of the high middle ages effectively tended to public affairs in limited regions. In doing so, they fashioned alternatives to large, centralized empires as a form of political organization.

ECONOMIC GROWTH AND SOCIAL DEVELOPMENT

As regional states provided increasingly effective political organization, medieval Europe experienced dramatic economic growth and social development. The economic revival closely resembled the processes that in an earlier era had strengthened China, India, and the Islamic world. Increased agricultural production, urbanization, manufacturing, and trade transformed Europe into a powerful society and drew it once again into commercial relationships with distant lands, as the example of the Polo family's travel attests.

In this painting from the late fifteenth century, the lord of the manor (in robes) watches his laborers harvest hay and cut wood.

Photo 12/Archives Snark/Alamy Stock Photo

Growth of the Agricultural Economy

As in China, India, and the Islamic world during the early postclassical era, a dramatic increase in agricultural yields was the foundation of economic growth and social development in medieval Europe. Several developments help to account for this increased agricultural production: the opening of new lands to cultivation, improved agricultural techniques, the use of new tools and technologies, and the introduction of new crops.

Expansion of Arable Land Beginning in the late tenth century, as local lords pacified their territories and put an end to invasions, Europe began to experience population pressure. In response serfs and monks cleared forests, drained swamps, and increased the amount of land devoted to agriculture. At first, some lords opposed those efforts because they reduced the amount of land available for game preserves, where nobles enjoyed hunting wild animals. Gradually, however, the lords realized that expanding agricultural production would yield higher taxes and increase their own wealth.

By the early twelfth century, lords were encouraging the expansion of cultivation, and the process gathered momentum.

Improved Agricultural Techniques Meanwhile, reliance on improved methods of cultivation and better agricultural technology led to significantly higher productivity. During the high middle ages, European cultivators refined and improved their techniques in the interests of larger yields. They experimented with new crops and with different cycles of crop rotation to ensure the most abundant harvests possible without compromising the fertility of the soil. They increased cultivation especially of beans, which not only provided dietary protein but also enriched the land because of their property of fixing nitrogen in the soils where they grow. They kept more domestic animals, which not only performed crucial farm labor such as plowing the fields but also served as sources of food and enriched fields with their droppings. They dug ponds in which they raised fish, which provided yet another dietary supplement. By the thirteenth century, observation and experimentation with new crops and new techniques had vastly increased understanding of agricultural affairs. News of those discoveries circulated widely throughout Europe in books and treatises on household economics and agricultural methods. Written in vernacular languages for lay readers, these works helped to publicize innovations, which in turn led to increased agricultural productivity.

New Tools and Technologies During the high middle ages, European peoples expanded their use of water mills and heavy plows, which had appeared during the early middle ages, and also introduced new tools and technologies. Two items in particular—the horseshoe and the horse collar—made it possible to increase sharply the amount of land that cultivators could work. Horseshoes helped to prevent softened and split hooves on horses that tramped through moist European soils. Horse collars—which had been in use in China since the third century—placed the burden of a heavy load on an animal's chest and shoulders rather than its neck and enabled horses to pull heavy plows without choking. Thus Europeans

How the Past Shapes the Future

The Diffusion of Technologies

Scholars believe that the emergence of the horse collar in Europe was a complex phenomenon, with the collar itself coming to northern Europe via central Asia, and the breast strap arriving from north Africa via Islamic Iberia. The horse collar was key to the increased agricultural productivity of Europeans by the thirteenth century. Because we know that agricultural productivity was an important factor in allowing Europeans to engage more consistently with regions outside Europe, consider the role of technological innovations in shaping the long-term future of regions around the world.

Population Growth As in other lands, increased agricultural productivity supported rapid population growth in medieval Europe. In 800 C.E., during the Carolingian era, European population stood at about twenty-nine million. By 1000, when regional states had ended invasions and restored order, it had edged up to thirty-six million. During the next few centuries, as the agricultural economy expanded, population surged. By 1100 it had reached forty-four million; by 1200 it had risen to fifty-eight million, an increase of more than 30 percent within one century; and by 1300 it had grown an additional 36 percent, to seventy-nine million. During the fourteenth century, epidemic plague severely reduced populations and disrupted economies in Europe as well as Asia and north Africa—a development discussed in chapter 21. Between 1000 and 1300, however, rapid demographic growth helped stimulate a vigorous revival of towns and trade in medieval Europe.

The Revival of Towns and Trade

Urbanization With abundant supplies of food, European society was able to support large numbers of urban residents—artisans, crafts workers, merchants, and professionals. Attracted by urban opportunities, peasants and serfs from the countryside flocked to established cities and founded new towns at strategically located sites. Cities founded during Roman times, such as Paris, London, and Toledo, again became thriving centers of government and business, and new urban centers emerged from Venice in northern Italy to Bergen on the west coast of Norway. Northern Italy and Flanders (the northwestern part of modern Belgium) experienced especially strong urbanization. For the first time since the fall of the Western Roman Empire, cities began to play a major role in European economic and social development.

Textile Production The growth of towns and cities brought about increasing specialization of labor, which in turn resulted in a dramatic expansion of manufacturing and trade. Manufacturing concentrated especially on the production of wool

could hitch their plows to horses rather than to slower oxen and bring more land under the plow.

New Crops Expansion of land under cultivation, improved methods of cultivation, and the use of new tools and technologies combined to increase both the quantity and the quality of food supplies. During the early middle ages, the European diet consisted almost entirely of grains and grain products such as gruel and bread. During the centuries from 1000 to 1300, meat, dairy products, fish, vegetables, and legumes such as beans and peas became much more prominent in the European diet, though without displacing grains as staple foods. Spain, Italy, and other Mediterranean lands benefited also from widespread cultivation of crops that had earlier been disseminated through the Islamic world: hard durum wheat, rice, spinach, artichokes, eggplant, lemons, limes, oranges, and melons all became prominent items in Mediterranean diets during the high middle ages.

Genoese bankers change money and check the accounts of their clients in this fourteenth-century manuscript illustration.
Album/Alamy Stock Photo

basin. During the tenth century the cities of Amalfi and Venice served as ports for merchants engaged in trade with Byzantine and Muslim partners in the eastern Mediterranean. During the next century the commercial networks of the Mediterranean widened to embrace Genoa, Pisa, Naples, and other Italian cities. Italian merchants exchanged salt, olive oil, wine, wool fabrics, leather products, and glass for luxury goods such as gems, spices, silk, and other goods from India, southeast Asia, and China that Muslim merchants brought to eastern Mediterranean markets.

As trade expanded, Italian merchants established colonies in the major ports and commercial centers of the Mediterranean and the Black Sea. By the thirteenth century, Venetian and Genoese merchants maintained large communities in Constantinople, Alexandria, Cairo, Damascus, and the Black Sea ports of Tana, Caffa, and Trebizond. Caffa was in fact the first destination of the Venetian brothers Niccolò and Maffeo Polo when they embarked on their commercial venture of 1260. Those trading posts enabled them to deal with Muslim merchants engaged in the Indian Ocean and overland trade with India, southeast Asia, and China. By the mid-thirteenth century the Polos and a few other Italian merchants were beginning to venture beyond the eastern Mediterranean region to central Asia, India, and China in search of commercial opportunities.

The Hanseatic League Although medieval trade was most active in the Mediterranean basin, a lively commerce grew up also in the northern seas. The Baltic Sea and the North Sea were sites of a particularly well-developed trade network known as the **Hanseatic League,** or more simply as the Hansa—an association of trading cities stretching from Novgorod in Russia to London and embracing all the significant commercial centers of Poland, northern Germany, and Scandinavia. The Hansa dominated trade in grain, fish, furs, timber, and pitch from northern Europe. The fairs of Champagne and the Rhine, the Danube, and other major European rivers linked the Hansa trade network with that of the Mediterranean.

textiles. The cities of Italy and Flanders in particular became lively centers for the spinning, weaving, and dyeing of wool. Trade in wool products helped to fuel economic development throughout Europe. By the twelfth century the counts of Champagne in northern France sponsored fairs that operated almost year-round and that served as vast marketplaces where merchants from all parts of Europe compared and exchanged goods.

Mediterranean Trade The revival of urban society was most pronounced in Italy, which was geographically well situated to participate in the trade networks of the Mediterranean

Improved Business Techniques As in postclassical China and the Islamic world, a rapidly increasing volume of trade encouraged the development of credit, banking, and new forms of business organization in Europe. Bankers issued letters of credit to merchants traveling to distant markets, thus freeing them from the risk and inconvenience of carrying cash or bullion. Having arrived at their destinations, merchants exchanged their letters of credit for merchandise or cash in the local currency. In the absence of credit and banking networks, it would have been impossible for merchants to trade on a large scale.

Meanwhile, merchants devised new ways of spreading and pooling the risks of commercial investments. They entered into partnerships with other merchants, and they limited

Hanseatic (han-see-AT-ik)

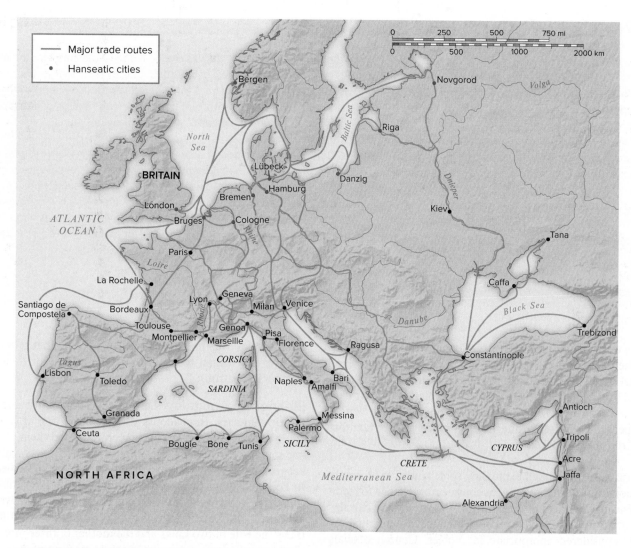

MAP 19.2 Major trade routes of medieval Europe.

By the eleventh century, overland, river, and maritime trade routes created a commercial network that linked all parts of Europe. These routes also facilitated trade between European Christians and Muslims in the Mediterranean basin and southwest Asia.

What does the proliferation of trading routes and cities suggest about the state of the medieval European economy?

the liability of partners to the extent of their individual investments. The limitation on individual liability encouraged the formation of commercial partnerships, thus further stimulating the European economy.

Social Change

The Three Estates Medieval social commentators frequently held that European society embraced **three estates** or classes: "those who pray, those who fight, and those who work." Those who prayed were clergy of the Roman Catholic church. From humble parish priests to bishops, cardinals, and popes, the clergy constituted a spiritual estate owing its loyalty

to the church rather than secular rulers. The fighters came from the ranks of nobles. They inherited their positions in society and received an education that concentrated on equestrian skills and military arts. Finally, there were those who worked—the vast majority of the population—who mostly cultivated land as peasants dependent for protection on lords, those who fought.

The formula dividing society neatly into three classes, though a simplification, captures some important truths about medieval Europe. It clearly reflects a society marked by political, social, and economic inequality: although they did not necessarily lead lives of luxury, those who prayed and those who fought enjoyed rights and honors denied to those who worked. Though bound by secular law, for example,

What's Left Out?

One of the things usually left out of surveys of most pre-modern histories is what life was like on a day-to-day basis for the majority of people. In the case of Europe during the Middle Ages (and in much of the rest of the world, too), by far the largest number of people were peasants and village-dwellers. Their lives were often difficult; full of hard work; and dependent on unpredictable things like the seasons, the weather, and the harvest. Because they were generally not literate, most left no records of their own. Historians can therefore only catch glimpses of them through sources like church records, which tell us when people were born, when they died, when they married, and when they had children. But some sources, such as coroner's records, can give us a taste of some of the everyday hazards of life in the Middle Ages. Coroners in England, for example, were required to investigate all unexpected deaths. A sample of coroners' records from one English county in the thirteenth century included multiple instances of accidental drowning in wells or rivers, lethal scalding after falling into vats of boiling water for laundry, and deaths when cooking fires caused houses to burn down. While these records do not tell us what people were thinking, they do allow us to get a sense for both the effort and the danger involved in performing even the simplest tasks—such as drinking, washing, and cooking—during the Middle Ages. Consider how much of the human experience is left out when we focus mainly on sources kept by the tiny minority of European people in the Middle Ages who were from literate, noble, or elite backgrounds.

Source: Emilie Amt, *Women's Lives in Medieval Europe: A Sourcebook* (Routledge, 2010).

---

clerics were members of an international spiritual society before they were subjects of a lord, and if they became involved in legal difficulties, they normally faced courts of law administered by the church rather than secular rulers. For their part the nobles mostly lived off the surplus production of dependent peasants and serfs, and lived in much greater comfort than "those who worked."

Chivalry Again though expressing some truths, the formula overlooks processes that brought considerable change to medieval European society. Within the ranks of the nobles, **chivalry** was an informal but widely recognized code of ethics and behavior considered appropriate for nobles. Church officials originally promoted the chivalric code in an effort to curb fighting within Christendom. By the twelfth century the ritual by which a young man became initiated into the nobility as a knight commonly called for the candidate to place his sword upon a church altar and pledge his service to God. Thus, rather than seeking wealth and power, the noble who observed the chivalric code was supposed to devote himself to the causes of order, piety, and the Christian faith.

Troubadours Aristocratic women found the chivalric code much to their liking. Instead of emphasizing the code's religious dimensions, however, they promoted refined behavior and tender, respectful relations between the sexes. Reflections of their interests survive in the songs and poems of the **troubadours,** a class of traveling poets, minstrels, and entertainers whom aristocratic women enthusiastically patronized. The troubadours, who were most active in southern France and northern Italy, drew inspiration from a long tradition of love poetry produced in nearby Muslim Spain. Many troubadours visited the expanding Christian kingdoms of Spain, where they heard love poems and songs from servants, slaves, and musicians of Muslim ancestry. Enchanted by that refined literature, they began to produce similar verses for their own aristocratic patrons.

Eleanor of Aquitaine During the late twelfth and thirteenth centuries, troubadours traveled from one aristocratic court to another, where noblewomen rewarded them for singing songs and reciting verses that celebrated passionate love between a man and a woman. Troubadours flocked especially to Poitiers, where **Eleanor of Aquitaine** (1122–1204) liberally supported romantic poets and entertainers. Eleanor was the wealthiest and most powerful woman of her day, at different times the wife of two kings and the mother of three more. She used her influence to encourage the cultivation of good manners, refinement, and romantic love. The troubadours' performances did not instantly transform rough warriors into polished courtiers. Over the long term, however, the code of chivalry and the romantic poetry and song presented at aristocratic courts gradually softened the rough manners of the nobility.

Independent Cities Social change also touched those who worked. By the twelfth century the ranks of workers included not only peasants but also increasing numbers of merchants, artisans, crafts workers, and professionals such as physicians and lawyers, who filled the growing towns of medieval Europe. The expansion of the urban working population promoted the development of towns and cities as jurisdictions that fit awkwardly in the framework of the medieval political order. Because of their military power, lords could dominate small towns and tax their wealth. As towns grew larger, however, urban populations were increasingly able to resist the demands of nobles and guide their own affairs. By the late eleventh century, inhabitants of prosperous towns were demanding that

Eleanor of Aquitaine on horseback, from a thirteenth-century fresco in the Chapel of St. Radegund, France.
De Agostini Picture Library/Getty Images

local lords grant them charters of incorporation that exempted them from political regulation, allowed them to manage their own affairs, and abolished taxes and tolls on commerce within the urban district. Sometimes groups of cities organized leagues to advance their commercial interests, as in the case of the Hansa, or to protect themselves against the encroachments of political authorities.

Guilds The cities of medieval Europe were by no means egalitarian societies: cities attracted noble migrants as well as peasants and serfs, and urban nobles often dominated city affairs. Yet medieval towns and cities also reflected the interests and contributions of the working people. Merchants and workers in all the arts, crafts, and trades organized **guilds** that regulated the production and sale of goods within their jurisdictions. By the thirteenth century the guilds had come to control much of the urban economy of medieval Europe. They established standards of quality for manufactured goods, sometimes even requiring members to adopt specific techniques of production, and they determined the prices at which members had to sell their products. In an effort to maintain a balance between supply and demand—and to protect their members' interests—they also regulated the entry of new workers into their groups.

Guilds had social as well as economic significance. They provided a focus for friendship and mutual support in addition to work. Guild members regularly socialized with one another, and prosperous guilds often built large halls where members held meetings, banquets, and sometimes boisterous drinking parties. Guilds came to the aid of members and their families

by providing financial and moral support for those who fell ill. They also arranged funeral services for their deceased and provided support for survivors. Quite apart from regulating work, then, guilds constituted a kind of social infrastructure that made it possible for medieval cities to function while also enhancing the welfare of their members.

Urban Women Women who lived in the countryside continued to perform the same kinds of tasks that their ancestors tended to in the early middle ages: household duties, weaving, and the care of domestic animals. But medieval towns and cities offered fresh opportunities for women as well as for men. In the patriarchal society of medieval Europe, few routes to public authority were open to women, but in the larger towns and cities women worked alongside men as butchers, brewers, bakers, candle makers, fishmongers, shoemakers, gemsmiths, innkeepers, launderers, money changers, merchants, and occasionally physicians and pharmacists. Women dominated some occupations, particularly those involving textiles and decorative arts, such as sewing, spinning, weaving, and the making of hats, wigs, and fur garments.

Most guilds admitted women into their ranks, and some guilds had exclusively female memberships. In thirteenth-century Paris, for example, there were approximately one hundred guilds. Six of them admitted only women, but eighty others included women as well as men among their members. Despite the persistence of patriarchal social structures, the increasing prominence of women in European society illustrates the significance of towns and cities as agents of social change in medieval Europe.

This painting from 1568 depicts a woman fishmonger working alongside her husband.
Peter Horree/Alamy Stock Photo

EUROPEAN CHRISTIANITY DURING THE HIGH MIDDLE AGES

Throughout the middle ages, Christianity guided European thought on religious, moral, and ethical matters—Eastern Orthodox Christianity in the Byzantine Empire and Roman Catholic Christianity in western Europe. Representatives of the Orthodox and Roman Catholic churches administered the rituals associated with birth, marriage, and death. Most of the art, literature, and music of the high middle ages drew inspiration from Christian doctrines and stories. Just as mosques and minarets defined the skylines of Muslim cities, the spires of churches and cathedrals dominated the landscape of medieval Europe, testifying visually to the importance of religion and the pervasive presence of the Eastern Orthodox and Roman Catholic churches.

Schools, Universities, and Scholastic Theology

During the early middle ages, European society was not stable and wealthy enough to support institutions of advanced education. Monasteries sometimes maintained schools that provided a rudimentary education, and political leaders occasionally supported scholars who lived at their courts, but very few schools offered formal education beyond an elementary level. In the absence of a widely observed curriculum or course of study, early medieval scholars drew their inspiration from the Bible and from major spokesmen of the early Christian church such as St. Augustine of Hippo.

Cathedral Schools During the high middle ages, economic development sharply increased the wealth of Europe and made more resources available for education. Meanwhile, an increasingly complex society created a demand for educated individuals who could deal with complicated political, legal, and theological issues. Beginning in the early eleventh century, bishops and archbishops in France and northern Italy organized schools in their cathedrals and invited well-known scholars to serve as master teachers. Schools in the cathedrals of Paris, Chartres, and Bologna in particular attracted students from all parts of Europe.

By the twelfth century the **cathedral schools** had established formal curricula based on writings in Latin, the official language of the Roman Catholic church. Instruction concentrated on the liberal arts, especially literature and philosophy. Students read the Bible and the writings of the church fathers, such as St. Augustine, St. Jerome, and St. Ambrose, as well as classical Latin literature and the few works of Plato and Aristotle that were available in Latin translation. Some cathedral schools also offered advanced instruction in law, medicine, and theology.

Universities About the mid-twelfth century, students and teachers organized academic guilds and persuaded political authorities to grant charters guaranteeing their rights. Student guilds demanded fair treatment for students from townspeople, who sometimes charged excessive rates for room and board, and called on their teachers to provide rigorous, high-quality instruction. Faculty guilds sought to vest teachers with the right to bestow academic degrees, which served as licenses to teach in other cities, and to control the curriculum in their institutions. These guilds had the effect of transforming cathedral schools into universities. The first universities were those of Bologna, Paris, and Salerno—noted for instruction in law, theology, and medicine, respectively—but by the late thirteenth century, universities had appeared also in Rome, Naples, Seville, Salamanca, Oxford, Cambridge, and other cities throughout Europe.

The Influence of Aristotle The evolution of the university coincided with the rediscovery of the works of Aristotle. Western European scholars of the early middle ages knew only a few of Aristotle's minor works that were available in Latin translation. Byzantine scholars knew Aristotle in the original Greek, but they rarely had any dealings with their Roman Catholic counterparts. During the high middle ages, as commerce and communication increased between Byzantine Orthodox and Roman Catholic Christians, western Europeans learned about Aristotle's thought and obtained Latin translations from Byzantine philosophers. Western European scholars also learned about Aristotle through Muslim philosophers who appreciated the power of his thought and had most of his works translated into Arabic. Christian and Jewish scholars in Sicily and Spain became aware of those Arabic translations, which they retranslated into Latin. Although the resulting works had their flaws—they filtered Aristotle's original Greek through both Arabic and Latin—they made Aristotle's thought accessible to Western European scholars.

Scholasticism: St. Thomas Aquinas During the thirteenth century, understanding of Aristotle's thought and Latin translations of his works spread throughout Europe, and they profoundly influenced almost all branches of thought. The most notable result was the emergence of **scholasticism,** which sought to synthesize the beliefs and values of Christianity with the logical rigor of Greek philosophy. The most famous of the scholastic theologians was **St. Thomas Aquinas** (1225–1274), who spent most of his career teaching at the University of Paris. While holding fervently to his Christian convictions, St. Thomas believed that Aristotle had understood and explained the workings of the world better than any other thinker of any era. St. Thomas saw no contradiction between Aristotle and Christian revelation but, rather, viewed them as complementary authorities: Aristotle provided the most powerful analysis of the world according to human reason, and Christianity explained the world and human life as the results of a divine plan. By combining Aristotle's rational power with the teachings of Christianity, St. Thomas expected to formulate the most truthful and persuasive system of thought possible.

Aquinas (uh-KWIY-nuhs)

In St. Thomas's view, for example, belief in the existence of God did not depend exclusively on an individual's faith. By drawing on Aristotle, St. Thomas believed, it was possible to prove rationally that God exists. Aristotle himself never recognized a personal deity such as the Jewish and Christian God, but he argued that a conscious agent had set the world in motion. St. Thomas borrowed Aristotle's arguments and identified the conscious agent with the Jewish and Christian God, who outlined his plan for the world in the Hebrew scriptures and the Christian New Testament. Thus, as expressed in the thought of St. Thomas Aquinas, scholastic theology represented the harmonization of Aristotle with Christianity and the synthesis of reason and faith.

A manuscript illustration depicts a professor, at top left, lecturing in a medieval German university. About half the students listen and take notes diligently, while the others catch up on their sleep or chat with friends.

Album/Oronoz/Newscom

Like the neo-Confucianism of Zhu Xi or the Islamic philosophy of Ibn Rushd, scholastic theology reinterpreted inherited beliefs in light of the most advanced knowledge of the time.

Popular Religion

St. Thomas and the other scholastic theologians addressed a sophisticated, intellectual elite, not the common people of medieval Europe. The popular masses neither knew nor cared much about Aristotle. For their purposes, Christianity was important primarily as a set of beliefs and rituals that gave meaning to individual lives and that bound them together into coherent communities. Thus formal doctrine and theology did not appeal to popular audiences as much as the ceremonies and observances that involved individuals in the life of a larger community—and that also brought benefits in the form of supernatural aid or protection for an individual's crops or family.

Sacraments Popular piety generally entailed observance of the sacraments and devotion to the saints recognized by the Roman Catholic church. Sacraments are holy rituals that bring spiritual blessings on the observants. The church recognized seven sacraments, including baptism, matrimony, penance, and the Eucharist. Most important was the Eucharist, during which priests offered a ritual meal commemorating Jesus' last meal with his disciples before his trial and execution by Roman authorities. In addition to preparing individuals for salvation and symbolizing their membership in a holy community, the Eucharist had mundane uses: popular beliefs held that the sacrament would

protect individuals from sudden death and advance their worldly interests.

Devotion to Saints Popular religion also took the form of devotion to the saints. According to church teachings, saints were human beings who had led such exemplary lives that God held them in special esteem. As a result, they enjoyed special influence with heavenly authorities and were able to intervene on behalf of individuals living in the world. Medieval Europeans constantly prayed for saints to look after their spiritual interests and to ensure their admission to heaven. Often, they also invoked the aid of saints who had reputations for helping living people as well as souls of the dead. Tradition held that certain saints could cure diseases, relieve toothaches, or guide sailors through storms to a port.

The Virgin Mary During the high middle ages, the most popular saint was always the Virgin Mary, mother of Jesus, who personified the Christian ideal of womanhood, love, and sympathy, and who reportedly lavished aid on her devotees. According to a widely circulated story, the Virgin once even spared a criminal from hanging when he called upon her name. During the twelfth and thirteenth centuries, Europeans dedicated hundreds of churches and cathedrals to the Virgin, among them the splendid cathedral of Notre Dame ("Our Lady") of Paris.

Saints' Relics Medieval Europeans went to great lengths to express their adoration of the Virgin and other saints through veneration of their **relics** and physical remains, widely believed to retain the powers associated with those holy individuals. Churches assembled vast collections of relics, such as clothes, locks of hair, teeth, and bones of famous saints. Especially esteemed were relics associated with Jesus or the Virgin, such as the crown of thorns that Jesus reportedly wore during his crucifixion or drops of the Virgin's milk miraculously preserved in a vial. The practice of assembling relics clearly opened the door to fraud, but medieval Europeans avidly continued to admire and venerate saints' relics.

Pilgrimage Some collections of relics became famous well beyond their own regions. Like Muslims making the hajj, pilgrims trekked long distances to honor the saints the relics represented. Throughout the high middle ages, streams of

SOURCES FROM THE PAST

Margery Kempe's Pilgrimage to Jerusalem

Margery Kempe (1373–1438) was the daughter of a five-time mayor of the bustling city of Bishop's (now King's) Lynn in Norfolk, England. She was not a noble, but a member of the growing urban elite of the time. She married John Kempe in 1393 and had fourteen children. Jesus Christ began to appear to her in visions shortly after the birth of her first child, and she continued to experience visions for much of her adult life. In 1414, she began the first of her many long-distance pilgrimages to Christian religious sites, visiting both Rome and Jerusalem over the course of a year. Although she was not literate, she wanted her story to be preserved and dictated her story to a priest before she died. Her Book of Margery Kempe *may be the first known autobiography in English. Below, Margery describes reaching the holy city of Jerusalem.*

And so they went forth into the Holy Land till they might see Jerusalem. And when this creature [Kempe] saw Jerusalem, riding on an ass, she thanked God with all her heart, praying him for his mercy that like as he had brought her to see this earthly city Jerusalem, he would grant her grace to see the blissful city Jerusalem above, the city of Heaven. . . .

Then they went to the Temple in Jerusalem, and they were let in that one day at evensong time [the time of evening prayers for Christians] and they abide there till the next day at evensong time. Then the friars lifted up a cross and led the pilgrims about from one place to another where our Lord had suffered his pains and his passions, every man and woman bearing a wax candle in their hand. And the friars always as they went about told them what our Lord suffered in every place. And the foresaid creature [Kempe] wept and sobbed so plentivously [sic] as though she had seen our Lord with her bodily eye suffering his Passion at that time. Before her in her soul she saw him verily by contemplation, and that caused her to have compassion. And when they came up onto the Mount of Calvary she fell down that she might not stand nor kneel but wallowed and wrested with her body, spreading her arms abroad, and cried with a loud voice as though her heart should 'a burst asunder, for in the city of her soul she saw verily and freshly how our Lord was crucified. Before her face she heard and saw in her ghostly sight the mourning of our Lady, of St. John and of Mary Magdalene, and of many other that loved our Lord. And she had so great compassion and so great pain to see our Lord's pain that she might not keep herself from crying and roaring. . .

> Note that Kempe is asking God to receive her in heaven after her death. What might this tell us about the concerns people in the Middle Ages might have had about mortality?

> Why did the friars' actions have such an effect on Kempe? What do you think she might have been trying to convey about her faith here?

> While it was not unusual for mystics to receive visions of god and the saints, Kempe was unusual in her loud prostrations. What might her companions have thought of her response?

For Further Reflection

■ Margery Kempe was one of a number of Christian mystical women in the Middle Ages who were neither nobles nor nuns. What does her experience as a traveler from England all the way to Jerusalem in 1414–1415 tell us about the increasing integration of Europeans with the wider world? What kinds of things can it tell us about European women in the Middle Ages?

Source: Joel Fredell, editor. *The Book of Margery Kempe*, folio 33. http://english.selu.edu/humanitiesonline/kempe/legal.php. Translated into modern English from the original.

---

pilgrims visited two European cities in particular—Rome in Italy and Compostela in Spain—and some ventured even farther to Jerusalem and the holy land of Christian origins. Rome was the spiritual center of western Christian society: apart from the popes and the central administration of the Roman Catholic church, the relics of St. Peter and St. Paul, the two most prominent apostles of early Christianity, rested in the churches of Rome. Compostela stood on the very periphery of Christian society, in a remote corner of northwestern Spain. Yet the relics of St. James preserved in the cathedral of Santiago

de Compostela exercised a powerful attraction for the pious, who made Compostela the second-most popular **pilgrimage** destination of medieval Europe. Some devoted pilgrims also visited Jerusalem and the sites associated with the origins of Christianity: spiritual as well as commercial interests called Europeans into the larger world.

The making of pilgrimages became so common during the high middle ages that a travel industry emerged to serve the needs of pilgrims. Inns dotted the routes leading to popular churches and shrines, and guides shepherded groups of

The cathedral of Notre Dame de Paris ("Our Lady of Paris"), viewed from the south. Built in the second half of the twelfth century, the cathedral is one of the triumphs of the Gothic style of architecture that became popular in western Europe during the medieval period. The cathedral suffered serious damage in a fire that broke out in April 2019.
Catherine Ursillo/Science Source

pilgrims to religious sites and explained their significance. There were even guidebooks that pointed out the major attractions along pilgrims' routes and warned them of difficult terrain and unscrupulous scoundrels who took advantage of visitors. Geoffrey Chaucer's well-known *Canterbury Tales* is, in fact, a collection of stories about a group of pilgrims traveling together to the English town of Canterbury during the fourteenth century.

Reform Movements and Popular Heresies

Although veneration of the saints and the making of pilgrimages indicated a deep reservoir of piety, popular religion also reflected the social and economic development of medieval Europe. Particularly in western Europe, as wealth increased, several groups of particularly devout individuals feared that European society was becoming excessively materialistic. Even the Roman Catholic church seemed tainted by materialism. Benedictine monasteries, in which monks originally observed the virtues of poverty, chastity, and obedience, had in many cases become comfortable retreats where privileged individuals led leisurely lives. Meanwhile, the central administration of the Roman church expanded dramatically as lawyers and bureaucrats ran the church's affairs and sought ways to swell its treasury.

Dominicans and Franciscans The devout responded to this state of affairs in several ways. Working within the Roman church, some individuals organized movements designed to champion spiritual over materialistic values. Most prominent of them were St. Dominic (1170–1221) and St. Francis (1182–1226). During the thirteenth century St. Dominic and St. Francis founded orders of mendicants (beggars), known as the Dominican and Franciscan friars, who would have no personal possessions and would have to beg for their food and other needs from audiences to whom they preached. Mendicants were especially active in towns and cities, where they addressed throngs of recently arrived migrants whose numbers were so large that existing urban churches and clergy could not serve them well. The **Dominicans** and the **Franciscans** also worked zealously to combat heretical (nonconforming) movements and to persuade heretics to return to the Roman Catholic church.

Popular Heresy Whereas the Dominicans and the Franciscans worked within the church, others rejected the Roman Catholic church altogether and organized alternative religious movements. During the twelfth and thirteenth centuries in particular, several popular movements protested the increasing materialism of European society. The Waldensians, who were most active in southern France and northern Italy, despised the Roman Catholic clergy as immoral and corrupt, and they advocated modest and simple lives. They asserted the right of the laity to preach and administer sacraments—functions that the church reserved exclusively for priests—and they did not hesitate to criticize the church on the basis of biblical teachings. Although church authorities declared them heretical, the Waldensians continued to attract enthusiastic participants: a few Waldensians survive even today.

Bogomils and Cathars Some popular heresies flourished in both the Byzantine Empire and western Europe. As long-distance trade networks linked Mediterranean lands, alternative religious ideas spread readily throughout the region. Reviving the dualistic views of the ancient Manichaeans, the **Bogomils** of Bulgaria and Byzantium viewed the world as a site of unrelenting, cosmic struggle between the forces of good and evil. In a quest for purity and spiritual perfection, they despised the material world and adopted an ascetic regime, renouncing wealth, marriage, and material pleasures.

St. Francis of Assisi was the son of a wealthy merchant in central Italy, but he abandoned the comforts that he inherited and pledged himself to a life of poverty and preaching. Stories represented in this fresco from the basilica of St. Francis at Assisi report that he preached to the birds and encouraged them to sing in praise of God.
The Print Collector/Heritage Images/Alamy Stock Photo

THE MEDIEVAL EXPANSION OF EUROPE

During the high middle ages, the relationship between western European peoples and their neighbors underwent dramatic change. Powerful regional states, economic expansion, and demographic growth all strengthened European society, and church officials encouraged the colonization of pagan and Muslim lands as a way to extend the influence of Roman Catholic Christianity. Beginning about the mid-eleventh century, Europeans embarked on expansive ventures on several fronts: Atlantic, Baltic, and Mediterranean. Scandinavian seafarers ventured into the Atlantic Ocean, establishing colonies in Iceland, Greenland, and even for a short time North America. In the Baltic region, Europeans conquered and introduced Christianity to Prussia, Livonia, Lithuania, and Finland. In the Mediterranean basin, Europeans recaptured Spain and the Mediterranean islands that Muslims had conquered between the eighth and the tenth centuries. Finally, knights from all over Europe mounted enormous campaigns designed to seize the holy land of Palestine from Muslims and place it under Christian authority. As military ventures, the crusades—as they were known—achieved limited success because they brought the holy land into Christian hands only temporarily. Nevertheless, the crusades signaled clearly that Europeans were beginning to play a larger role in the affairs of the eastern hemisphere than they had during the early middle ages.

Atlantic and Baltic Colonization

Vinland   When regional states began to emerge and protect western Europe from Viking raids during the ninth and tenth centuries, Scandinavian seafarers turned their attention to the islands of the North Atlantic Ocean. They occupied Iceland beginning in the late ninth century, and at the end of the tenth century a party led by Eric the Red discovered Greenland and established a small colony there. About 1000 C.E. his son Leif Ericsson led another exploratory party south and west of Greenland, arriving eventually at modern Newfoundland in Canada. There the party found plentiful supplies of fish and timber. Because of the wild grapes growing in the region, Leif called it Vinland ("Wine Land"). During the years following Leif's voyage, Greenlanders made several efforts to establish permanent colonies in Vinland.

Since the 1960s, archaeologists in northern Newfoundland have uncovered Scandinavian tools and building foundations dating to the early eleventh century. From this evidence and the stories of maritime ventures preserved in Scandinavian sagas, it is clear that the Greenlanders founded a colony in Newfoundland and maintained it for several decades. Ultimately, they left Vinland—or died there—since they did not have the resources to sustain a settlement over the stormy seas of the North Atlantic Ocean. Nonetheless,

Their movement grew rapidly in the late tenth century, and in the eleventh century the **Cathars** (sometimes called Albigensians) were promoting similar views in southern France and northern Italy. Bogomils and Cathars rejected official churches, which they considered hopelessly corrupt, along with their priests and sacraments.

Both in Byzantium and in western Europe, established authorities took a dim view of these popular movements, which they regarded as threats to cultural stability and religious orthodoxy. Beginning in the late eleventh century, government and church officials teamed up and mounted ruthless campaigns to destroy the Bogomils and the Cathars. By the fourteenth century, Bogomils and Cathars survived in only a few remote regions of Europe.

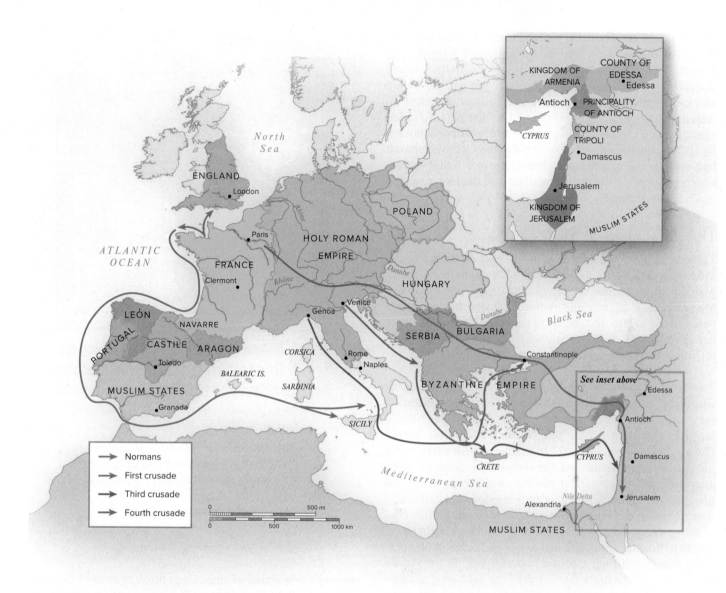

MAP 19.3   The medieval expansion of Europe, 1000–1250

Compare Map 19.3 with Map 16.3. How can you explain the differences between these two maps?

What does Map 19.3 suggest about the military and organizational capabilities, strategies, and aims of medieval Europe?

the establishment of even a short-lived colony indicated a growing capacity of Europeans to venture into the larger world.

Christianity in Scandinavia

While Scandinavians explored the North Atlantic, the Roman Catholic church drew Scandinavia itself into the community of Christian Europe. The kings of Denmark and Norway converted to Christianity in the tenth century. Conversion of their subjects came gradually and with considerable resistance because most held tightly to their inherited traditions. Yet royal support for the Roman Catholic church ensured that Christianity would

have a place in Danish and Norwegian societies. In 999 or 1000 the Norwegian colony in Iceland also formally adopted Christianity. Between the twelfth and the fourteenth centuries, Sweden and Finland followed their neighbors into the Christian faith.

Crusading Orders and Baltic Expansion

In the Baltic lands of Prussia, Livonia, and Lithuania, Christian authority arrived in the wake of military conquest. During the era of crusades, zealous Christians formed a series of hybrid, military-religious orders. The most prominent were the Templars, Hospitallers, and Teutonic Knights, who not only took religious vows but also pledged to devote their lives and efforts to the struggle against Muslims and pagans. The Teutonic Knights were most active in the Baltic region, where they waged military campaigns against the pagan Slavic peoples during the twelfth and thirteenth centuries. Aided by German missionaries, the Knights founded churches and monasteries in the territories they subdued. By the late thirteenth century, the Roman Catholic church had established its presence throughout the Baltic region, which progressively became absorbed into the larger society of Christian Europe.

The Reconquest of Sicily and Spain

The boundaries of Christian Europe also expanded in the Mediterranean basin. There, Europeans came into conflict with Muslims, whose ancestors had conquered the major Mediterranean islands and most of the Iberian peninsula between the eighth and the tenth centuries. As their society became stronger, Europeans undertook to reconquer those territories and reintegrate them into Christian society.

The Reconquest of Sicily Most important of the islands was Sicily, which Muslims had conquered in the ninth century. During the eleventh century, Norman warriors returned Sicily to Christian hands. The Norman adventurer Robert Guiscard carved out a state for himself in southern Italy while his brother Roger undertook the conquest of Sicily. By 1090, after almost twenty years of conflict, Roger had established his authority throughout the island. Missionaries and clergy soon appeared and reintroduced Roman Catholic Christianity to Sicily. Islam did not disappear immediately: Muslims continued to practice their faith privately, and Muslim scholars in Sicily introduced their Christian counterparts to the Arabic translations of Aristotle that inspired the scholastic philosophers. Over the longer term, however, as Muslims either left Sicily or converted to Christianity, Islam gradually disappeared from the island.

The *Reconquista* of Spain The reconquest of Spain—known as the ***reconquista***—took a much longer time than did the recapture of Sicily. Following the Muslim invasion and conquest of the early eighth century, the caliphate of Córdoba ruled almost all of the Iberian peninsula. A small Christian state survived in Catalonia in the far northeast, and the kingdom of León resisted Muslim advances in the far northwest. The process of *reconquista* began in the 1060s from those Christian toeholds. By 1085 Christian forces had pushed as far south as Toledo, and by 1150 they had recaptured Lisbon and established their authority over half of the peninsula. Their successes lured reinforcements from France and England, and in the first half of the thirteenth

The crusades involved brutal conflict and atrocities from all sides. In this twelfth-century manuscript illustration, crusaders lob severed enemy heads at Muslims defending a fortress.
The Picture Art Collection/Alamy Stock Photo

century a new round of campaigns brought most of Iberia as well as the Balearic Islands (off the coast of eastern Spain) into Christian hands. Only the kingdom of Granada in the far south of the peninsula remained Muslim. It survived as an outpost of Islam until 1492, when Christian forces mounted a campaign that conquered Granada and completed the *reconquista*.

The political, economic, and demographic strength of Christian Europe helps to explain the reconquests of Sicily and Spain as military ventures. Especially in the case of Spain, however, it is clear that religious concerns also helped to drive the *reconquista*. The popes and other leading clergy of the Roman Catholic church regarded Islam as a threat to Christianity, and they enthusiastically encouraged campaigns against the Muslims. When reconquered territories fell into Christian hands, church officials immediately established bishoprics and asserted Christian authority. They also organized campaigns to convert local populations. Dominican friars were especially active in Spain. They appealed to learned audiences by explaining Christianity in the terms of scholastic theology and arguments derived from Aristotle,

---

reconquista (ray-kohn-KEE-stah)

whom Muslim intellectuals held in high esteem. When addressing popular audiences, they simply outlined the basic teachings of Christianity and urged their listeners to convert. With the establishment of Christian rule, the Roman Catholic church gradually began to displace Islam in conquered Spain.

The Crusades

The term *crusade* refers to a holy war. It derives from the Latin word *crux,* meaning "cross," the device on which Roman authorities had executed Jesus. When a pope declared a crusade, warriors would "take up the cross" as a symbol of their faith, sew strips of cloth in the form of a cross on the backs of their garments, and venture forth to fight on behalf of Christianity. The wars that Christians fought against pagans in the Baltic and Muslims in the Mediterranean were crusades in this sense of the term, as was the campaign waged by Roman Catholic Christians against Cathar heretics in southern France. In popular usage, though, *crusades* generally refers to the huge expeditions that Roman Catholic Christians mounted in an effort to recapture Palestine, the land of Christian origins, and the holy city of Jerusalem from Muslim authorities.

Urban II **Pope Urban II** launched the crusades in 1095. Speaking at the Council of Clermont (in central France), Urban warned church leaders that Muslim Turks were threatening the eastern borders of Christendom. Indeed, the pope had recently received an urgent appeal from the Byzantine emperor, who requested military forces from western Europe to reinforce his own armies as Turkish invaders advanced toward Constantinople. Urban urged European princes to stabilize Christendom's borders and then go further to recapture Jerusalem and restore Christian rule to the holy land. He added emphasis to his appeal with the assertion that "Deus vult"—"God wills it!"

The First Crusade Shortly after Pope Urban announced the crusade, French and Norman nobles began to organize a military expedition to the holy land. In late 1096 the crusading armies began the long trek to Palestine. In 1097 and 1098 they captured Edessa, Antioch, and other strategic sites. In 1099 Jerusalem fell to the crusaders, who then proceeded to extend their conquests and carve conquered territories into Christian states.

Although the crusaders did not realize it, hindsight shows that their quick victories came largely because of division and disarray in the ranks of their Muslim foes. The crusaders' successes, however, encouraged Turks, Egyptians, and other Muslims to settle their differences, at least temporarily, in the interests of expelling European Christians from the eastern Mediterranean. By the mid-twelfth century, the crusader communities had come under tremendous pressure. The crusader

A fourteenth-century manuscript illustration depicts Muslims burning captured crusaders at the stake.
Album/Alamy Stock Photo

state of Edessa fell to Turks in 1144, and during the third crusade the Muslim leader Salah al-Din, known to Europeans as **Saladin,** recaptured Jerusalem in 1187. Crusaders maintained several of their enclaves for another century, but Saladin's victories sealed the fate of Christian forces in the eastern Mediterranean.

Later Crusades Europeans did not immediately concede Palestine to the Muslims. By the mid-thirteenth century, they had launched five major crusades, but none of the later ventures succeeded in reestablishing a Christian presence in Palestine. The fourth crusade (1202–1204) was a particularly demoralizing affair, as crusaders ravaged Constantinople, the seat of Eastern Orthodox Christanity. Nevertheless, even though the later crusades failed in their principal objective, the crusading idea inspired European dreams of conquest in the eastern Mediterranean until the late sixteenth century.

Consequences of the Crusades As holy wars intended to reestablish Roman Catholic Christianity in the eastern Mediterranean basin, the crusades were wars of military and political expansion. Yet in the long run, the crusades were much more important for their social, economic, commercial, and cultural consequences. Even as European armies built crusader states in Palestine and Syria, European

Saladin (SAHL-uh-din)

scholars and missionaries encountered Muslim philosophers and theologians, and European merchants traded eagerly with their Muslim counterparts. The result was a large-scale exchange of ideas, technologies, and trade goods that profoundly influenced European development. Through their sojourns in Palestine and their regular dealings with Muslims throughout the Mediterranean basin, European Christians became acquainted with the works of Aristotle, Islamic science and astronomy, "Arabic" numerals (which Muslims had borrowed from India), and techniques of paper production (which Muslims had learned from the Chinese). They also learned to appreciate new food and agricultural products such as spices, granulated sugar, coffee, and dates as well as trade goods such as silk products, cotton textiles, carpets, and tapestries.

In the early days of the crusades, Europeans had little to exchange for those products other than rough wool textiles, furs, and timber. During the crusading era, however, demand for the new commodities increased throughout western Europe as large numbers of people developed a taste for goods previously available only to wealthy elites. Seeking to meet the rising demand for luxury goods, Italian merchants developed new products and marketed them in commercial centers and port cities such as Constantinople, Alexandria, Cairo, Damascus, Tana, Caffa, and Trebizond. Thus Niccolò, Maffeo, and Marco Polo traded in gems and jewelry, and other merchants marketed fine woolen textiles or glassware. By the thirteenth century, large numbers of Italian merchants had begun to travel well beyond Egypt, Palestine, and Syria to avoid Muslim intermediaries and to deal directly with the producers of silks and spices in India, China, and southeast Asia. Thus, although the crusades largely failed as military ventures, they encouraged the reintegration of western Europe into the larger economy of the eastern hemisphere.

CONCLUSION

From 1000 to 1300, Europe underwent thorough political and economic reorganization. Building on foundations laid during the early middle ages, political leaders founded a series of independent regional states. But despite the establishment of the Holy Roman Empire, they did not revive central imperial authority in western Europe. Regional states maintained good order and fostered rapid economic growth, which fostered the development of regional traditions. Beginning in the tenth century, Agricultural improvements brought increased food supplies, which encouraged urbanization, manufacturing, and trade. By the thirteenth century, European peoples traded actively throughout the Mediterranean, Baltic, and North Sea regions encountering new people and ideas. As we saw in the case of Marco Polo and his family, a few plucky merchants even ventured as far away as China in search of commercial opportunities. In the high middle ages, as in the early middle ages, Christianity was the cultural foundation of European society. The church prospered during the high middle ages, and advanced educational institutions such as cathedral schools and universities reinforced the influence of Christianity throughout Europe. Christianity even played a role in European political and military expansion because church officials encouraged crusaders to conquer pagan and Muslim peoples in Baltic and Mediterranean lands. Thus between 1000 and 1300, western European peoples strengthened the traditions of their own society and began in various ways to have regular encounters with their counterparts in other regions of the eastern hemisphere. After a long period of relative isolation, by the end of the high middle ages Europe had become far more integrated with the wider world than in centuries past.

STUDY TERMS

battle of Manzikert (384)	Marco Polo (381)
Bogomils (397)	Normans (385)
Capetian (385)	Otto I (384)
Cathars (398)	pilgrimage (396)
cathedral schools (394)	Pope Urban II (401)
chivalry (392)	relics (395)
crusades (401)	*reconquista* (400)
Dominicans (397)	Saladin (401)
Eleanor of Aquitaine (392)	scholasticism (394)
Franciscans (397)	St. Thomas Aquinas (394)
Frederick Barbarossa (385)	three estates (391)
guilds (393)	*theme* system (382)
Hanseatic League (390)	troubadors (392)
Holy Roman Empire (382)	William the Conqueror (385)
Investiture Contest (385)	

FOR FURTHER READING

Thomas Asbridge. *The Crusades.* New York, 2010. A breezy narrative history of the early crusades.

Robert Bartlett. *The Making of Europe: Conquest, Colonization, and Cultural Change, 950–1350.* Princeton, 1993. A well-documented examination of European expansion from a cultural point of view.

Judith Bennett. *Medieval Europe: A Short History.* New York, 2010. An engaging survey of medieval Europe written by a pioneer in the field.

Rosalind Brooke and Christopher Brooke. *Popular Religion in the Middle Ages: Western Europe, 1000-1300.* London, 1984. Well-illustrated essays on the faith of the masses.

Caroline Walker Bynum. *Holy Feast and Holy Fast: The Religious Significance of Food to Medieval Women.* Berkeley, 1998. A pathbreaking book about the ways women shaped their relationships to religion in the medieval period.

J. R. S. Phillips. *The Medieval Expansion of Europe.* Oxford, 1988. Excellent survey of European ventures in the larger world during the high and late middle ages.

Daniel Power, ed. *The Central Middle Ages.* Oxford, 2006. Seven leading scholars discuss aspects of medieval European history.

Christopher Tyerman. *God's War: A New History of the Crusades.* Cambridge, Mass., 2006. A comprehensive review of crusades throughout Europe and the larger Mediterranean basin.

Elisabeth van Houts, ed. *The Normans in Europe.* Manchester, 2000. Presents English translations of sources illuminating Norman roles in medieval Europe.

Jeffrey Wigelsworth. *Science and Technology in Medieval European Life.* Westport, Conn, 2006. An introductory survey of medieval European technology and scientific thought that also explores the relationship between science and religion.

Worlds Apart: The Americas and Oceania

States and Empires in Mesoamerica and North America

    The Toltecs and the Mexica

    Mexica Society

    Mexica Culture

    Peoples and Societies of North America

States and Empires in South America

    The Coming of the Incas

    Inca Society

The Societies of Oceania

    The Nomadic Foragers of Australia

    The Development of Pacific Island Societies

ZOOMING IN ON TRADITIONS

The Aztec Capital at Its Height

In November 1519 a small Spanish army first encountered **Tenochtitlan,** capital city of the Aztec Empire. The Spanish forces came in search of gold, and they had heard many reports about the wealth of the Aztec Empire. Yet none of those reports prepared them adequately for what they saw.

Years later, Bernal Díaz del Castillo, a soldier in the invading Spanish army, described the city just before its conquest. Tenocthtitlan sat in the water of Lake Texcoco, connected to the surrounding land by three broad causeways, and as in Venice, canals allowed canoes to navigate to all parts of the city. Bernal Diaz recalled that the route to Tenochtitlan had been full of wonders even before reaching Tenochtitlan, confessing that he and his men "saw so many cities and villages built in the water and other great towns on dry land and that straight and level causeway going towards Mexico [Tenochtitlan], we were amazed . . . on account of the great towers and [temples] and buildings rising from the water, and all built of masonry." Once in Tenochtitlan, Bernal Diaz noted that the imperial palace included many large rooms and apartments while its armory was well stocked with swords, lances, knives, bows, arrows, slings, armor, and shields. The aviary of Tenochtitlan included eagles, hawks, parrots, and smaller birds, while jaguars, mountain lions, wolves, foxes, and rattlesnakes were noteworthy residents of the zoo.

Huitzilopochtli, the patron god of the Mexica people.
The History Collection/Alamy Stock Photo

To Bernal Díaz the two most impressive sights were the markets and the temples of Tenochtitlan. The markets astonished him because of their size, the variety of goods they offered, and the order that prevailed there. In the principal market at Tlatelolco, a district of Tenochtitlan, Bernal Díaz found gold and silver jewelry, gems, feathers, embroidery,

Tenochtitlan (teh-NOCH-tee-tlahn)

Texcoco (TEHS-ko-ko)

Tlatelolco (tl-tay-LOL-ko)

Huitzilopochtli (we-tsee-loh-POCK-tlee)

slaves, cotton, cacao, animal skins, maize, beans, vegetables, fruits, poultry, meat, fish, salt, paper, and tools. It would take more than two days, he said, to walk around the market and investigate all the goods offered for sale. His fellow soldiers compared the market of Tlatelolco favorably to those of Rome and Constantinople.

The temples also struck Bernal Díaz, though in a different way. Aztec temples were the principal sites of rituals involving human sacrifice. Bernal Díaz described climbing to the top of the main pyramidal temple in Tenochtitlan, where fresh blood lay pooled around the stone that served as a sacrificial altar. He described priests with hair entangled and matted with blood. Interior rooms of the temple were so encrusted with blood, Bernal Díaz reported, that their walls and floors had turned black, and the stench overcame even professional Spanish soldiers. Some of the interior rooms held the dismembered limbs of sacrificial victims, and others were resting places for thousands of human skulls and bones.

The contrast between Tenochtitlan's markets and its temples challenged Bernal Díaz and his fellow soldiers. In the markets they witnessed peaceful and orderly exchange of the kind that took place all over the world. In the temples, however, they saw signs of human sacrifice on a scale rarely matched, if ever, anywhere in the world. Yet by the cultural traditions of the Aztec Empire, there was no difficulty reconciling the commercial activity of the marketplaces with the human sacrifice of the temples. Both had a place in the maintenance of the world: trade enabled a complex society to function, while sacrificial rituals pleased the gods and persuaded them to keep the world going.

CHAPTER OVERVIEW

Although the peoples of Africa, Asia, and Europe interacted regularly before modern times, the indigenous peoples of the Americas had only sporadic dealings with their contemporaries across the oceans. Scandinavian seafarers established a short-lived colony in Newfoundland, and occasional ships from Europe and west Africa may have made their way to the western hemisphere. Before 1492, however, interaction between peoples of the eastern and western hemispheres was fleeting and random rather than a sustained and regular affair. During the period from 1000 to 1500 C.E., however, the peoples of North and South America, like their counterparts in the eastern hemisphere, organized large empires with distinctive cultural and religious traditions, and they created elaborate trade networks touching most regions of the American continents.

As in the Americas, the indigenous peoples of Australia and the Pacific islands had irregular and sporadic dealings with peoples outside Oceania. Asian trade networks extended to the Philippines, the islands of Indonesia, and New Guinea. They even touched a few regions of northern Australia and the Mariana Islands, including Guam, but they did not extend to the more distant island societies of the Pacific Ocean. Pacific islanders themselves often sailed over the open ocean, creating and sustaining links between the societies of various island groups. They also had some dealings with the inhabitants of Asian and American lands bordering the Pacific Ocean. But like their counterparts in the western hemisphere, the indigenous peoples of Australia and the Pacific islands built self-sufficient societies and developed unique traditions distinct from those in Afro-Eurasia. Even though they had extremely limited

CHRONOLOGY	
AMERICAS	
950–1150	High point of the Toltec empire
1175	Collapse of the Toltec empire
1250	Inca settlement near Cuzco
1345	Foundation of Tenochtitlan by the Mexica
1400	Emergence of the five Iroquois nations
1428–1440	Reign of the Aztec ruler Itzcóatl
1438–1471	Reign of the Inca ruler Pachacuti
1440–1469	Reign of the Aztec ruler Motecuzoma I
1502–1520	Reign of the Aztec ruler Motecuzoma II
1519	Arrival of Spanish conquerors in Mexico
OCEANIA	
11th century	Beginning of population growth in Pacific islands
12th century	Beginning of two-way voyages between Hawai`i and Tahiti and the Marquesas islands
13th century	Emergence of distinct social classes and chiefly states
14th century	Construction of fishponds in Hawai`i

amounts of land and other natural resources to work with, by the thirteenth century C.E. they had established well-organized agricultural societies and chiefly states throughout the Pacific islands. Until the fifteenth century for the Americas and the eighteenth century for Oceania, the world's oceans ensured that these two regions were truly worlds apart from the more interconnected regions of Africa, Asia, and Europe.

STATES AND EMPIRES IN MESOAMERICA AND NORTH AMERICA

Mesoamerica entered an era of war and conquest in the eighth century C.E. Great stores of wealth had accumulated in **Teotihuacan,** the largest early city in Mesoamerica (discussed in chapter 6). When Teotihuacan declined, it became a target for less-prosperous but well-organized forces from the countryside and northern Mexico. Attacks on Teotihuacan opened a long era of militarization and empire building in Mesoamerica that lasted until Spanish forces conquered the region in the sixteenth century. Most prominent of the peoples contesting for power in Mesoamerica were the Toltecs and the **Mexica,** the architects of the Aztec Empire.

The Toltecs and the Mexica

During the ninth and early tenth centuries, after the collapse of Teotihuacan, several regional states dominated portions of the high central valley of Mexico, the area surrounding Mexico City where agricultural societies had flourished since the late centuries B.C.E. Although these successor states and their societies shared the religious and cultural traditions of Teotihuacan, they fought relentlessly among themselves. Their capital cities all stood on well-defended hill sites, and warriors figured prominently in their works of art.

Toltecs With the emergence of the **Toltecs** and later the Mexica, much of central Mexico again came under unified rule. The Toltecs began to migrate into the area about the eighth century. They came from the arid land of northwestern Mexico, and they settled mostly at **Tula,** about 50 kilometers (31 miles) northwest of modern Mexico City. Though situated in a corner of the valley of Mexico that possesses thin soil and receives little rainfall, the Toltecs tapped the waters of the nearby River Tula to irrigate crops of maize, beans, peppers, tomatoes, chiles, and cotton. At its high point, from about 950 to 1150 C.E., Tula supported an urban population that might have reached sixty thousand people. Another sixty thousand lived in the surrounding region.

The Toltecs maintained a large and powerful army that campaigned periodically throughout central Mexico. They built a compact regional empire and maintained fortresses far to the northwest to protect their state from invasion by nomadic peoples. From the mid-tenth through the mid-twelfth

century, they exacted tribute from subject peoples and transformed their capital into a wealthy city. Residents lived in spacious houses made of stone, adobe, or mud and sometimes covered their packed-earth floors with plaster.

Tula The city of Tula became an important center of weaving, pottery, and obsidian work, and residents imported large quantities of jade, turquoise, animal skins, exotic bird feathers, and other luxury goods from elsewhere in Mesoamerica. The Toltecs maintained close relations with societies on the Gulf coast as well as with the Maya of Yucatan. Indeed, Tula shared numerous architectural designs and art motifs with the Maya city of Chichén Itzá (discussed in chapter 6) some 1,500 kilometers (932 miles) to the east.

Beginning about 1125 C.E. the Toltec empire faced serious difficulties as conflicts between different ethnic groups living at Tula led to civil strife. By the mid-twelfth century, large numbers of migrants—mostly nomadic peoples from northwestern Mexico—had entered Tula and settled in the surrounding area. By 1175 conflicts between the various groups, old and new, had destroyed the Toltec state. Archaeological evidence suggests that fire destroyed much of Tula about the same time. Large numbers of people continued to inhabit the region around Tula, but by the end of the twelfth century the Toltecs no longer dominated Mesoamerica.

The Mexica Among the migrants drawn to central Mexico from northwestern regions were people who called themselves the Mexica, often referred to as Aztecs because they dominated the alliance that built the **Aztec Empire** in the fifteenth century. (The term *Aztec* derives from *Aztlán,* "the place of the seven legendary caves," which the Mexica remembered as the home of their ancestors.) The Mexica arrived in central Mexico about the middle of the thirteenth century. They had a reputation for causing conflicts by kidnapping women from nearby communities and seizing land already cultivated by others. They were often expelled by the communities they encountered. For a century they migrated around central Mexico, jostling and fighting with other peoples and sometimes surviving only by eating fly eggs and snakes.

Tenochtitlan About 1345 the Mexica settled on an island in a marshy region of Lake Texcoco and founded the city that would become their capital—Tenochtitlan, on top of which Spanish conquerors later built Mexico City. Though inconvenient at first, the site offered several advantages. The lake harbored plentiful supplies of fish, frogs, and waterfowl. Moreover, the lake enabled the Mexica to develop the *chinampa* system of

---

Teotihuacan (teh-o-tee-WAH-kahn)

Mexica (MEHK-si-kah)

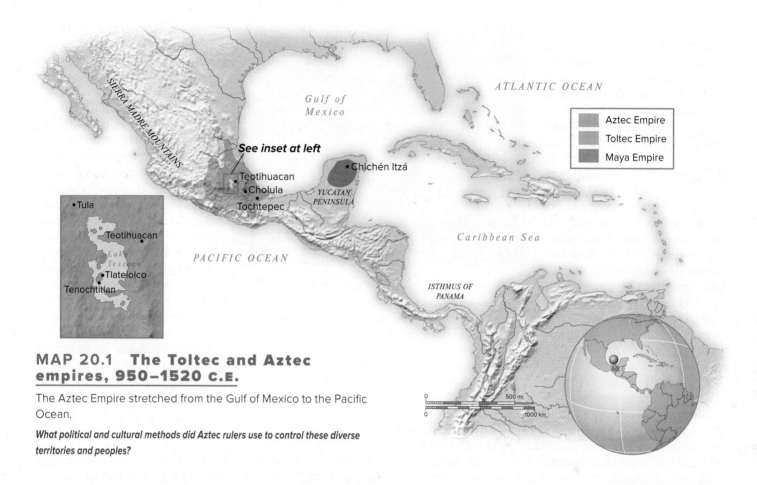

MAP 20.1   The Toltec and Aztec empires, 950–1520 C.E.

The Aztec Empire stretched from the Gulf of Mexico to the Pacific Ocean.

What political and cultural methods did Aztec rulers use to control these diverse territories and peoples?

agriculture. The Mexica dredged a rich and fertile muck from the lake's bottom and built it up into small plots of land known as *chinampas*. During the dry season, cultivators tapped water from canals leading from the lake to their plots, and in the temperate climate they grew crops of maize, beans, squashes, tomatoes, peppers, and chiles year-round. *Chinampas* were so fertile and productive that cultivators were sometimes able to harvest seven crops per year from their gardens. Finally, the lake served as a natural defense: waters protected Tenochtitlan on all sides, and Mexica warriors patrolled the three causeways that eventually linked their capital to the surrounding mainland.

The Aztec Empire By the early fifteenth century, the Mexica were powerful enough to overcome their immediate neighbors and demand tribute from their new subjects. During the middle decades of the century, prodded by the military elite that ruled Tenochtitlan, the Mexica launched ambitious campaigns of imperial expansion. Under the rule of "the Obsidian Serpent" **Itzcóatl** (1428–1440) and **Motecuzoma I** (1440–1469), also known as Moctezuma or Montezuma, they advanced first against Oaxaca in southwestern Mexico. After conquering the city and slaying many of its inhabitants, they populated Oaxaca with colonists, and the city became a bulwark for the emerging Mexica empire.

The Mexica next turned their attention to the Gulf coast, whose tropical products made welcome tribute items in Tenochtitlan. Finally, they conquered the cities of the high plateaus between Tenochtitlan and the Gulf coast. About the mid-fifteenth century, the Mexica joined forces with two neighboring cities, Texcoco and Tlacopan (modern Tacuba), to create a triple alliance that guided the Aztec Empire. Dominated by the Mexica and Tenochtitlan, the allies imposed their rule on about twelve million people and most of Mesoamerica, excluding only the arid northern and western regions and a few small pockets where independent states resisted the expanding empire.

Tribute and Trade The main objective of the triple alliance was to exact tribute from subject peoples. From nearby peoples the Mexica and their allies received food crops and manufactured items such as textiles, rabbit-fur blankets, embroidered clothes, jewelry, and obsidian knives. Tribute obligations were sometimes very oppressive for subject peoples. The annual tribute owed by the state of Tochtepec on the Gulf coast, for example, included 9,600 cloaks, 1,600 women's

Itzcóatl (tsee-ko-atl)
Motecuzoma (mo-tek-oo-ZO-mah)
Oaxaca (wah-HAH-kah)

garments, 200 loads of cacao, and 16,000 rubber balls, among other items. Ruling elites entrusted some of these tribute items to officially recognized merchants, who took them to distant lands and exchanged them for local products. These included luxury items such as translucent jade, emeralds, tortoise shells, jaguar skins, parrot feathers, seashells, and game animals. The tropical lowlands also supplied vanilla beans and cacao—the source of cocoa and chocolate—from which Mexica elites prepared tasty beverages.

Unlike imperial states in the eastern hemisphere, the Aztec Empire had no elaborate bureaucracy or administration. The Mexica and their allies simply conquered their subjects and assessed tribute, leaving local governance and the collection of tribute in the hands of the conquered peoples. The allies did not even maintain military garrisons throughout their empire. Nor did they keep a permanent, standing army. They simply assembled forces as needed when they launched campaigns of expansion or mounted punitive expeditions against insubordinate

An artist's depiction of *chinampas* agriculture, made by staking out and framing "fields" in shallow lake beds, then building them up until they were above the level of the lake. What made this technique worth the intensive work required to establish growing areas in the first place?

Alfredo Dagli Orti/Shutterstock

subjects. Nevertheless, the Mexica in particular had a reputation for military prowess, and fear of reprisal tended to keep most subject peoples in line.

At the high point of the Aztec Empire in the early sixteenth century, tribute from 489 subject territories flowed into Tenochtitlan, which as a result was an enormously wealthy city. The Mexica capital had a population of about two hundred thousand people, and three hundred thousand others lived in nearby towns and suburban areas. The principal market even had separate sections for merchants dealing in gold, silver, slaves, henequen and cotton cloth, shoes, animal skins, turkeys, dogs, wild game, maize, beans, peppers, cacao, and fruits.

Mexica Society

Mexica society was rigidly hierarchical and stratified between nobles and non-nobles. The Mexica looked upon all males as potential warriors, and public honors and rewards

What's Left Out?

More contemporary source material survives about the Mexica and their subjects than any other peoples of the pre-Columbian Americas. However, nearly all of the sources that survive are problematic in some way. For example, while there are some books written by the Mexica in their own language (Nahuatl), scholars do not agree about when these books were produced. Furthermore, many Mexica documents appear to have been destroyed either by Mexica kings prior to the Spanish arrival or by the Spanish who sought to eradicate Mexica beliefs after the conquest. Some Spanish conquistadores wrote letters and accounts of their initial contact with the Mexica, but these obviously tell the story from their point of view rather than from the Mexica point of view. In addition, some of these sources—including the one written by Bernal Diaz del Castillo that introduces this chapter—were only written decades after the conquest. Still others, such as the famous *Florentine Codex* from which the "Sources of the Past" for this chapter was taken, were the result of lengthy interviews in Nahuatl conducted by Spanish missionaries with Mexica priests, elders, and other leaders a few decades after the conquest. But even though sources like the *Florentine Codex* seem to be told from the point of view of the Mexica, scholars argue that it is unclear how free the Mexica were to tell their version of their past given the power differences between the Spanish and the Mexica. Not only that, the original manuscript (completed in 1555) did not survive, and thus we are left with summaries that have been revised and translated many times since the sixteenth century. Yet in spite of multiple problems with the existing sources, nearly all histories written about the Mexica to date have been based on them. Consider how different the histories we are able to tell might be if we had access to more pre-conquest Mexica sources. How might these alter our perceptions of the Mexica people and their culture?

Sources: Fray Bernardino de Sahagún. *Historia general de las cosas de Nueva España.* Known as the *Florentine Codex.* Edited by Francisco del Paso y Troncoso. 4 vols. Madrid: *Fototipia de Hauser y Menet,* 1905. English translation: Fray Bernardino de Sahagún. *General History of the Things of New Spain.* 2nd. ed., rev. 4 vols. Santa Fe, New Mexico: School of American Research, 1900.

were reserved mostly for the military elite. Although individuals of common birth could distinguish themselves on the battlefield and thereby improve their social standing, for the most part, the military elite came from the Mexica aristocracy. Men of noble birth received the most careful instruction and intense training in military affairs, and they enjoyed the best opportunities to display their talents on the battlefield.

Warriors

The Mexica showered wealth and privileges on the military elite. Accomplished warriors received extensive land grants as well as tribute from commoners for their support. The most successful warriors formed a council whose members selected the ruler, discussed public issues, and filled government positions. They ate the best foods—turkey, pheasant, duck, deer, boar, and rabbit—and they consumed most of the luxury items such as vanilla and cacao that came into Mexica society by way of trade or tribute. Even dress reflected social status in Mexica society. Sumptuary laws (laws that regulate consumption and dress) required commoners to wear coarse, burlaplike garments made of henequen (fibers made from the agave plant) but permitted aristocrats to drape themselves in cotton. Warriors enjoyed the right to don brightly colored capes and adorn themselves with lip plugs and eagle feathers after they captured enemies on the battlefield and brought them back to Tenochtitlan.

Mexica Women

Women played almost no role in the political affairs of a society so dominated by military values, but they wielded influence within their families and enjoyed high honor as mothers of warriors. Mexica women did not inherit property or hold official positions, and the law subjected them to the strict authority of their fathers or husbands. Women were prominent in the marketplaces, as well as in crafts involving embroidery and needlework. Yet Mexica society prodded them toward motherhood and homemaking.

With the exception of a few who dedicated themselves to the service of a temple, nearly all Mexica women married. Mexica traditions taught that the principal function of women was to bear children, especially males who might become distinguished warriors. In fact, society recognized the bearing of children as equal to a warrior's capture of enemy in battle, and women who died in childbirth won the same fame as warriors who died valiantly on the battlefield. Even among the elite classes, Mexica women had the responsibilities of raising young children and preparing food for their families.

Priests

In addition to the military aristocracy, a priestly class also ranked among the Mexica elite. Priests received a special education in calendrical and ritual lore, and they presided over religious ceremonies that the Mexica viewed as crucial to the continuation of the world. Priests read omens and explained the forces that drove the world, thereby wielding

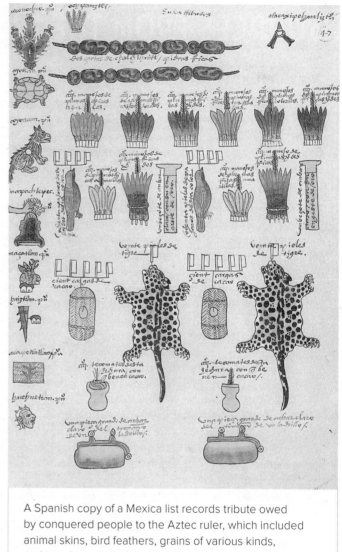

A Spanish copy of a Mexica list records tribute owed by conquered people to the Aztec ruler, which included animal skins, bird feathers, grains of various kinds, and jewelry.

Universal History Archive/Shutterstock

considerable influence as advisers to Mexica rulers. On a few occasions, priests even became supreme rulers of the Aztec Empire: the ill-fated Motecuzoma II (reigned 1502–1520), ruler of the Aztec empire when Spanish invaders appeared in 1519, was a priest of the most popular Mexica cult.

Cultivators and Slaves

The vast majority of the Mexica population consisted of commoners who lived in hamlets cultivating *chinampas* and fields allocated to their families by community groups known as **calpulli**. Originally, *calpulli* were clans or groups of families claiming descent from common ancestors. With the passage of time, ancestry became less important to the nature of the *calpulli* than the fact that

calpulli (kal-po-lee)

SOURCES FROM THE PAST

Mexica Expectations of Boys and Girls

Bernardino de Sahagún was a Franciscan missionary who worked to convert the native peoples of Mesoamerica to Christianity in the mid-sixteenth century. He interviewed Mexica elders and assembled a vast amount of information about what their society was like before the arrival of Europeans in what became known as the Florentine Codex. Although not unproblematic as sources (see the What's Left Out *feature in this chapter), his records include the speeches made by midwives as they delivered infants to aristocratic families. The speeches indicate clearly the roles men and women were expected to play in Mexica society.*

[To a newborn boy the midwife said:] "Heed, hearken: thy home is not here, for thou art an eagle, thou art an ocelot; thou art a roseate spoonbill, thou art a troupial [a bird like an oriole]. Thou art the serpent, the bird of the lord of the near, of the nigh. Here is only the place of thy nest. Thou hast only been hatched here; thou hast only come, arrived. Thou art only come forth on earth here. Here dost thou bud, blossom, germinate. Here thou becomest the chip, the fragment [of thy mother]. Here are only the cradle, thy cradle blanket, the resting place of thy head: only thy place of arrival. Thou belongest out there; out there thou hast been consecrated. Thou hast been sent into warfare. War is thy desert, thy task. Thou shalt give drink, nourishment, food to the sun, the lord of the earth. Thy real home, thy property, thy lot is the home of the sun there in the heavens. . . . Perhaps thou wilt receive the gift, perhaps thou wilt merit death [in battle] by the obsidian knife, the flowered death by the obsidian knife. . . ."

> What do the types of animals named here suggest about the expected nature of boys' lives?

And if it were a female, the midwife said to her when she cut her umbilical cord: "My beloved maiden, my beloved noblewoman, thou has endured fatigue! Our lord, the lord of the near, of the nigh, hath sent thee. Thou hast come to arrive at a place of weariness, a place of anguish, a place of fatigue where there is cold, there is wind. . . . Thou wilt be in the heart of the home, thou wilt go nowhere, thou wilt nowhere become a wanderer, thou becomest the banked fire, the hearth stones. Here our lord planteth thee, burieth thee. And thou wilt become fatigued, thou wilt become tired; thou art to provide water, to grind maize, to drudge; thou art to sweat by the ashes, by the hearth."

> Compared with the animals meant to represent boys, why are girls likened to banked fires and hearth stones? What do these images imply about expectations for their lives?

Then the midwife buried the umbilical cord of the noblewoman by the hearth. It was said that by this she signified that the little woman would nowhere wander. Her dwelling place was only within the house; her home was only within the house; it was not necessary for her to go anywhere. And it meant that her very duty was drink, food. She was to prepare drink, to prepare food, to grind, to spin, to weave.

For Further Reflection

■ How did gender roles and expectations of Mexica society compare with those of other settled, agricultural societies, such as China, India, the Islamic world, sub-Saharan Africa, and Europe?

Source: Bernardino de Sahagún. *Florentine Codex: General History of the Things of New Spain,* 13 vols. Trans. by Charles E. Dibble and Arthur J. O. Anderson. Salt Lake City: University of Utah Press, 1950–82, 171–73 (book 6, chapter 31).

groups of families lived together in communities, organized their own affairs, and allocated community property to individual families. Apart from cultivating plots assigned by their *calpulli,* Mexica commoners worked on lands awarded to aristocrats or prominent warriors and contributed labor services to public works projects involving the construction of palaces, temples, roads, and irrigation systems. Cultivators delivered periodic tribute payments to state agents, who distributed a portion of what they collected to the elite classes and stored the remainder in state granaries and warehouses. In addition to these cultivators of common birth, Mexica society included slaves, who usually worked as domestic servants. Most enslaved people were not foreigners, but Mexica. Families sometimes sold younger members into servitude out of financial distress, and other Mexica were forced into slavery because of criminal behavior.

Artisans and Merchants

Skilled artisans, particularly those who worked with gold, silver, cotton textiles, tropical bird feathers, and other items destined for consumption by the elite, enjoyed considerable prestige in Mexica society. Merchants specializing in long-distance trade occupied an important but somewhat insecure position in Mexica society. Merchants supplied the exotic products such as gems, animal skins, and tropical bird feathers consumed by the elites and provided political and military intelligence about the lands they visited. Yet they often fell under suspicion as greedy profiteers, and aristocratic warriors sometimes blatantly seized their wealth and goods because they knew most merchants did not have powerful protectors.

A Mexica manuscript known as the *Codex Borgia* depicts Quetzalcóatl (left) as the lord of life and Tezcatlipoca (right) as the god of death.
Biblioteca Apostolica Vaticana/Index S.A.S.

Mexica Culture

When they migrated to central Mexico, the Mexica already spoke the Nahuatl language, which had been the prevalent tongue in the region since the time of the Toltecs. The Mexica soon adopted other cultural and religious traditions, some of which dated from the time of the Olmecs (discussed in chapter 6), shared by all the peoples of Mesoamerica. Most Mesoamerican peoples played a ball game in formal courts, for example, and maintained a complicated calendar based on a solar year of 365 days and a ritual year of 260 days. The Mexica enthusiastically adopted the ball game, and they kept a sophisticated calendar, although it was not as elaborate as the Maya calendar.

Mexica Gods The Mexica also absorbed the religious beliefs common to Mesoamerica. Two of their principal gods—**Tezcatlipoca,** "the Smoking Mirror," and **Quetzalcóatl,** "the Feathered Serpent"—had figured in Mesoamerican pantheons at least since the time of Teotihuacan, although different peoples knew them by various names. Tezcatlipoca was a powerful figure, the giver and taker of life and the patron deity of warriors, whereas Quetzalcóatl had a reputation for supporting arts, crafts, and agriculture.

Ritual Bloodletting Like their predecessors, the Mexica believed that their gods had set the world in motion through acts of individual sacrifice. By letting their blood flow, the gods had given the earth the moisture it needed to bear maize and other crops. To propitiate the gods and ensure the continuation of the

world, the Mexica honored their deities through sacrificial bloodletting. Mexica priests regularly performed acts of self-sacrifice, piercing their earlobes or penises with cactus spines in honor of the primeval acts of their gods. The religious beliefs and bloodletting rituals clearly reflected the desire of the Mexica to keep their agricultural society going.

Huitzilopochtli Mexica priests also presided over the sacrificial killing of human victims. From the time of the Olmecs, and possibly even earlier, Mesoamerican peoples had regarded the ritual sacrifice of human beings as essential to the world's survival. The Mexica, however, placed much more emphasis on human sacrifice than their predecessors had. To a large extent the Mexica enthusiasm for human sacrifice followed from their devotion to the god **Huitzilopochtli.** Mexica warriors took Huitzilopochtli as their patron deity in the early years of the fourteenth century as they subjected neighboring peoples to their rule. Military success persuaded them that Huitzilopochtli especially favored the Mexica, and as military successes mounted, the priests of Huitzilopochtli's cult demanded sacrificial victims to keep the war god appeased.

Some of the victims were Mexica criminals, but others came as tribute from neighboring peoples or from the ranks of warriors captured on the battlefield during the many conflicts between the Mexica and their neighbors. In all cases, the Mexica viewed human sacrifice not as a gruesome form of entertainment but, rather, as a ritual essential to the world's survival. They believed that the blood of sacrificial victims sustained the sun and secured a continuing supply of moisture for the earth, thus ensuring that human communities would be able to cultivate their crops and perpetuate their societies.

Peoples and Societies of North America

Beyond Mexico the peoples of North America developed a rich variety of political, social, and cultural traditions. Many North American peoples depended on hunting, fishing, and collecting edible plants. In the arctic and subarctic regions, for example, diets included sea mammals such as whale, seal, and

Tezcatlipoca (tehs-cah-tlee-poh-cah)
Quetzalcóatl (keh-tzahl-koh-AHTL)

In this manuscript illustration an aide stretches a victim over a sacrificial altar while a priest opens his chest, removes the still-beating heart, and offers it to Huitzilopochtli. At the bottom of the structure, attendants remove the body of an earlier victim. *Library of Congress, Prints and Photographs Division [LC-USZC4-743].*

walrus supplemented by land mammals such as moose and caribou. Peoples in coastal regions consumed fish, but in interior regions (the North American plains, for example), they hunted large animals such as bison and deer. Throughout the continent nuts, berries, roots, and grasses such as wild rice supplemented the meat provided by hunters and fishers. Like their counterparts elsewhere, hunting, fishing, and foraging peoples of North America built societies on a relatively small scale because food resources in the wild would not support dense populations.

Pueblo and Navajo Societies In several regions of North America, agricultural economies enabled peoples to maintain settled societies with large populations. In what is

Navajo (NAH-vah-ho)

now the American southwest, for example, **Pueblo** and **Navajo** peoples tapped river waters to irrigate crops of maize, which constituted as much as 80 percent of their diets. They also cultivated beans, squashes, and sunflowers, and they supplemented their crops with wild plants and small game such as rabbit. The hot and dry environment periodically brought drought and famine. Nevertheless, by about 700 C.E. the Pueblo and the Navajo began to construct permanent stone and adobe buildings. Archaeologists have discovered about 125 sites where agricultural peoples built village communities.

Iroquois Peoples Large-scale agricultural societies emerged also in the woodlands east of the Mississippi River. Woodlands peoples began to cultivate maize and beans during the early centuries C.E., and after about 800 these cultivated foods made up the bulk of their diets. They lived in settled communities, and they often surrounded their larger settlements with wooden palisades, which served as defensive walls. By 1000, for example, the Owasco people

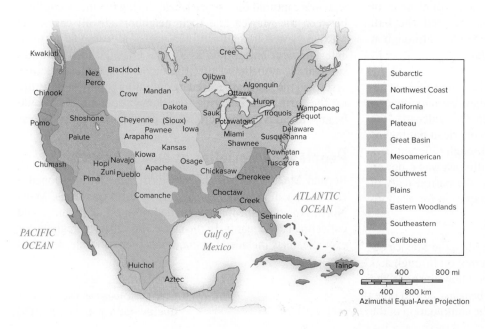

Subarctic
Northwest Coast
California
Plateau
Great Basin
Mesoamerican
Southwest
Plains
Eastern Woodlands
Southeastern
Caribbean

0   400   800 mi
0   400   800 km
Azimuthal Equal-Area Projection

MAP 20.2 North American cultural groups, ca. 1600

Selected cultural groups of North America around 1600. Note the great diversity of groups in every region from west to east.

Originally constructed about 1000 C.E., the Great Serpent Mound sits atop a ridge in modern Ohio. The serpent's coiled tail is visible at the left, while its open mouth holds an egg on the right. What purposes might a ridgetop mound like this have served?
Georg Gerster/Science Source

had established a distinct society in what is now upstate New York, and by about 1400 the five **Iroquois** nations (Mohawk, Oneida, Onondaga, Cayuga, and Seneca) had emerged from Owasco society. Women were in charge of Iroquois villages and longhouses, in which several related families lived together, and supervised cultivation of fields surrounding their settlements. Men took responsibility for affairs beyond the village—hunting, fishing, and war.

Mound-Building Peoples The most impressive structures of the woodlands were the enormous earthen mounds that dotted the countryside throughout the eastern half of North America. Woodlands peoples used those mounds sometimes as stages for ceremonies and rituals, often as platforms for dwellings, and occasionally as burial sites. Modern agriculture, road building, and real estate development have destroyed most of the mounds, but several surviving examples demonstrate that they sometimes reached gigantic proportions.

Cahokia The largest surviving structure is a mound at **Cahokia** near East St. Louis, Illinois. More than 30 meters (100 feet) high, 300 meters (1,000 feet) long, and 200 meters (650 feet) wide, it was the third-largest structure in the western hemisphere before the arrival of Europeans. Only the temple of the sun in Teotihuacan and the temple of Quetzalcóatl in Cholula were larger. When the Cahokia society was at its height, from approximately 900 to 1250 C.E., more than one hundred smaller mounds stood within a few kilometers of the highest and most massive mound. Scholars have estimated that during the twelfth century, fifteen thousand to thirty-eight thousand people lived in the vicinity of the Cahokia mounds.

Trade Because peoples north of Mexico had no writing, information about their societies comes almost exclusively from archaeological discoveries. Burial sites reveal that mound-building peoples recognized various social classes because they bestowed grave goods of differing quality and quantities on their departed kin. Archaeologists have shown, too, that trade linked widely separated regions and peoples of North America. An elaborate network of rivers—notably the Mississippi, Missouri, Ohio, and Tennessee rivers, along with their many tributaries—facilitated encounters and trade by canoe in the eastern half of North America. Throughout the eastern woodlands, archaeologists have turned up stones with sharp cutting edges from the Rocky Mountains, copper from the Great Lakes region, seashells from Florida, minerals from the upper reaches of the Mississippi River, and mica from the southern Appalachian mountains. Indeed, the community at Cahokia probably owed its size and prominence to its location at the hub of North American trade networks. Situated near the confluence of the Mississippi, Missouri, and Ohio rivers, Cahokia was most likely the center of trade and communication networks linking the eastern woodlands of North America with the lower Mississippi Valley and lands bordering the Gulf of Mexico.

Iroquois (EAR-uh-kwoi)
Cahokia (kuh-HOH-kee-uh)

STATES AND EMPIRES IN SOUTH AMERICA

South American peoples had no script and no tradition of writing before the arrival of Spanish invaders in the early sixteenth century. As a result, the experiences of early South American societies are much more difficult to recover than those of Mesoamerica, where writing had been in use since the fifth century B.C.E. Yet, from archaeological evidence and information recorded by Spanish conquerors, it is possible to reconstruct much of the historical experience of Andean South America, which had been the site of complex societies since the first millennium B.C.E. As in Mesoamerica, cities and secular government in South America began to overshadow ceremonial centers and priestly regimes during the centuries from 1000 to 1500 C.E. Toward the end of the period, like the Mexica in Mesoamerica, the Incas built a powerful state, extended their authority over a vast region, and established the largest empire South America had ever seen.

The Coming of the Incas

After the disappearance of the Chavín and Moche societies (discussed in chapter 6), a series of autonomous regional states organized public affairs in Andean South America. The states frequently clashed, but rarely did one of them gain a long-term advantage over the others. For the most part they controlled areas either in the mountainous highlands or in the valleys and coastal plains.

Chucuito After the twelfth century, for example, the kingdom of **Chucuito** dominated the highlands region around Lake Titicaca, which straddles the border between modern Peru and Bolivia at about 4,000 meters (13,000 feet) of elevation. Chucuito depended on the cultivation of potatoes and the herding of llamas and alpacas—camel-like beasts that were the only large domesticated animals anywhere in the Americas before the sixteenth century. In elaborately terraced fields built with stone retaining walls, cultivators harvested potatoes of many colors, sizes, and tastes. Like maize in Mesoamerica, potatoes served as the staple of the highlanders' diet, which revolved around a potato-based stew enlivened by maize, tomatoes, green vegetables, peppers, chiles, and meat from llamas, alpacas, or tender, domesticated guinea pigs.

Apart from meat, llamas and alpacas provided the highlanders with wool, hides, and dung, widely used as fuel in a land with few trees. In exchange for potatoes and woolen textiles, the highlanders obtained maize and coca leaves from societies in lower valleys. They used maize to enhance their diet and to brew a beerlike beverage, and they chewed the coca leaves, which worked as a mild stimulant and enhanced stamina in the thin air of the high Andes. (When processed, coca leaves yield a much more powerful stimulant with addictive properties—cocaine.)

Chucuito (CHEW-keeto)

MAP 20.3   The Inca Empire, 1471–1532

The Incas built the largest empire in the pre-Columbian Americas.

How were they able to maintain control over their extensive realm?

Chimu In the lowlands the powerful kingdom of **Chimu** (sometimes referred to as Chimor) emerged in the tenth century and expanded to dominate some 900 kilometers (560 miles) of the Peruvian coast for about a century before the arrival of the Incas in the mid-fifteenth century. Chimu governed a large and thriving society. Irrigation networks tapped the rivers and streams flowing from the Andes mountains, watered fields in the lowlands, and helped to generate abundant yields of maize and sweet potatoes. Judging from goods excavated at grave sites, Chimu society enjoyed considerable wealth and recognized clear distinctions between social classes.

Chimu's capital city, Chanchan, whose ruins lie close to the modern city of Trujillo, had a population that exceeded fifty thousand and may have approached one hundred thousand. Chanchan featured massive brick buildings, which indicated a capacity for mobilizing large numbers of people and resources for public purposes. The city's geography reflected a well-defined social order: each block belonged to an individual clan that supervised the affairs of its members and coordinated their efforts with those of other clans.

For several centuries, regional states such as Chucuito and Chimu maintained order in Andean South America. Yet, within a period of about thirty years, these and other regional states fell under the domination of the dynamic and expansive society of the Incas. The word *Inca* originally was the title of the rulers of a small kingdom in the valley of Cuzco, but in modern usage the term refers more broadly to those who spoke the Incas' **Quechua** language, or even to all subjects of the Inca Empire.

Quipu threads were different lengths and colors (though the colors in this example are faded). These designated the different items recorded: population, animals, textiles, weapons, and perhaps even rulers and notable events of their reigns. People needed an advanced education to record and "read" information by *quipu*.

Brendan Smialowski/AFP/Getty Images

their subjects. They routinely sought to encourage obedience among subject peoples by taking hostages from their ruling classes and forcing them to live at the Inca capital. When conquered peoples became restive or uncooperative, the Incas sent loyal subjects as colonists, provided them with choice land and economic benefits, and established them in garrisons to maintain order. When conquered peoples rebelled, Inca armies forced them to leave their homes and resettle in distant parts of the empire.

Inca Administration The vast Inca realm presented a serious administrative challenge to its rulers. The Inca administrative system was the invention of Pachacuti himself—the same Earthshaker who conquered the territories that made up the Inca Empire. Toward the end of his reign, about 1463, Pachacuti entrusted military affairs to his son and settled in the highland village of Cuzco, where he designed a system of government to consolidate his conquests. He implemented taxes to support Inca rulers and administrators, and he organized a system of state-owned storehouses to stock agricultural surpluses and craft products such as textiles. He also began construction on an extensive network of roads that enabled Inca military forces and administrators to travel quickly to all parts of the empire.

The Inca Empire After a long period of migration in the highlands, the Incas settled in the region around Lake Titicaca about the mid-thirteenth century. At first, they lived as one among many peoples inhabiting the region. About 1438, however, the Inca ruler Pachacuti (reigned 1438–1471) launched a series of military campaigns that vastly expanded the Incas' authority. Pachacuti ("Earthshaker") was a fierce warrior. According to Inca legends, he fought so furiously in one early battle that he inspired the stones in the field to stand up and combat his enemies. The campaigns of the Earthshaker were long and brutal. Pachacuti first extended Inca control over the southern and northern highlands and then turned his forces on the coastal kingdom of Chimu. Though well defended, Chimu had to submit to the Incas when Pachacuti gained control of the waters that supplied Chimu's irrigation system.

By the late fifteenth century, the Incas had built a huge empire stretching more than 4,000 kilometers (2,500 miles) from modern Quito to Santiago. It embraced almost all of modern Peru, most of Ecuador, much of Bolivia, and parts of Chile and Argentina as well. Only the tropical rain forests of the Amazon and other river valleys set a limit to Inca expansion to the east, and the Pacific Ocean defined its western boundary. With a population of about 11.5 million, the **Inca Empire** easily ranked as the largest state ever built in South America.

The Incas ruled as a military and administrative elite. They led armies composed mostly of conquered peoples, and staffed the bureaucracy that managed the empire's political affairs. But the Incas were not numerous enough to overwhelm

Quipu In the absence of any script or system of writing, Inca bureaucrats and administrators relied on a mnemonic aid (memory device) known as *quipu* to keep track of their responsibilities. *Quipu* consisted of an array of small cords of various colors and lengths, all suspended from one large, thick cord. Experts tied a series of knots in the small cords, which sometimes numbered a hundred or more, to help them remember certain kinds of information. Most *quipu* recorded statistical information having to do with population, state property, taxes, and labor services that communities owed to the central government. Occasionally, though, *quipu* also helped experts to remember historical information having to do with the establishment of the Inca Empire, the Inca rulers, and their deeds. Although much more unwieldy and less flexible than writing, *quipu* enabled Inca bureaucrats to keep track of information well enough to run an orderly empire.

Quechua (keh-CHUA)

quipu (KEE-poo)

Cuzco **Cuzco** served as the administrative, religious, and ceremonial center of the Inca Empire. When Pachacuti retired there, Cuzco was a modest village, but the conqueror soon transformed it into a magnificent capital that Incas considered "the navel of the universe." At the center was a huge plaza filled with glistening white sand transported from Pacific beaches to the high Andean city. Surrounding the plaza were handsome buildings constructed of red stone cut so precisely by expert masons that no mortar was necessary to hold them together. The most important buildings sported gold facings, which threw off dazzling reflections when rays of the Andean sun fell on them.

Since Cuzco was primarily a capital and a ceremonial center, the city's permanent population was sizable but not enormous—perhaps forty thousand—but some two hundred thousand Inca subjects lived in the immediate vicinity. Apart from high-ranking imperial administrators, the most prominent permanent residents of Cuzco proper included the Inca rulers and high nobility, the high priests of the various religious cults, and the hostages of conquered peoples who lived with their families under the watchful eyes of Inca guardians.

Inca Roads A magnificent and extensive road system enabled the central government at Cuzco to communicate with all parts of the far-flung Inca Empire and to dispatch large military forces rapidly to distant trouble spots. Two roads linked the Inca realm from north to south—one passing through the mountains, the other running along the coast. Scholars have estimated the combined length of those trunk routes at 16,000 kilometers (almost 10,000 miles). The combined length of the entire network of all Inca roads, including lesser thoroughfares as well as the major trunk routes, may have amounted to 40,000 kilometers (almost 25,000 miles).

Inca roads were among the best ever constructed before modern times. During the early sixteenth century, Spanish conquerors marveled at the roads—paved with stone, shaded by trees, and wide enough to accommodate eight horsemen riding abreast. A corps of official runners carried messages along the roads so that news and information could travel between Cuzco and the most distant parts of the empire within a few days. When the Inca rulers desired a meal of fresh fish, they dispatched runners from Cuzco to the coast, more than 320 kilometers (200 miles) away, and had their catch within two days. Like roads in empires in other parts of the world, the Incas' roads favored their efforts at centralization. Their roads even facilitated the spread of the Quechua language and their religious cult focusing on the sun, both of which became established throughout their empire.

Inca Society

Trade Despite those splendid roads, Inca society did not generate large classes of merchants and skilled artisans. On the local level the Incas and their subjects bartered surplus agricultural production and handcrafted goods among themselves. Long-distance trade, however, fell under the supervision of the central government. Administrators organized exchanges of agricultural products, textiles, pottery, jewelry, and craft goods, but the Inca state did not permit individuals to become independent merchants. In the absence of a market economy, there was no opportunity for a large class of professional, skilled artisans to emerge. Many individuals produced pottery, textiles, and tools for local consumption, and a few produced especially fine goods for the ruling, priestly, and aristocratic classes. But skilled crafts workers were much less prominent among the Incas than among the Mexica and the peoples of the eastern hemisphere.

Ruling Elites The main classes in Inca society were the rulers, the aristocrats, the priests, and the peasant cultivators of common birth. The Incas considered their chief ruler a god descended from the sun. In theory, this god-king owned all land, livestock, and property in the Inca realm, which he governed as an absolute and infallible ruler. Inca rulers retained their prestige even after death. Their descendants mummified the royal remains and regarded departed kings as intermediaries with the gods. Succeeding rulers often deliberated state policy in the presence of royal mummies so as to benefit from their counsel. Indeed, on the occasion of certain festivals, rulers brought out the mummified remains of their ancestors, dressed them in fine clothes, adorned them with gold and silver jewelry, honored them, and presented them with offerings of food and drink to maintain cordial relations with former rulers. Meanwhile, by way of tending to the needs of their living subjects, the Inca god-kings supervised a class of bureaucrats, mostly aristocrats, who allocated plots of land for commoners to cultivate on behalf of the state.

Aristocrats and Priests Like the ruling elites, Inca aristocrats and priests led privileged lives. Aristocrats consumed

Part of the Inca coastal road, here shown at Pachacamac Sanctuary.

Electra Kay-Smith/Alamy Stock Photo

fine foods and dressed in embroidered clothes provided by common subjects. Aristocrats also had the right to wear large ear spools that distended their lobes so much that Spanish conquerors referred to them as "big ears." Priests often came from royal and aristocratic families. They led celibate and ascetic lives, but they deeply influenced Inca society because of their education and their responsibility for overseeing religious rituals. The major temples supported hundreds of priests, along with attendants and virgin women devoted to divine service who prepared ceremonial meals and wove fine ritual garments for the priestly staff.

Peasants

The cultivators were mostly peasants of common birth who lived in communities known as *ayllu,* similar to the Mexicas' *calpulli,* which were the basic units of rural society. Ranging in size from small villages to larger towns, *ayllus* consisted of several families who lived together, sharing land, tools, animals, crops, and work. Peasants supported themselves by working on lands allocated to individual families by their *ayllu.* Instead of paying taxes or tribute, peasants also worked on state lands administered by aristocrats. Much of the production from these state lands went to support the ruling, aristocratic, and priestly classes. The rest went into state storehouses for public relief in times of famine and for the support of widows, orphans, and others unable to cultivate land for themselves. Apart from agricultural work, peasants also owed compulsory labor services to the Inca state. Men provided the heavy labor required for the construction, maintenance, and repair of roads, buildings, and irrigation systems. Women delivered tribute in the form of textiles, pottery, and jewelry. With the aid of *quipu,* Inca bureaucrats kept track of the labor service and tribute owed by local communities.

Descendants prepare a ritual meal for a mummified Inca ruler (depicted in the background).
Det Kongelige Bibliotek, Copenhagen.

A handsome llama fashioned from silver from Inca Peru.
Mark Dunn/Alamy Stock Photo

Inca Religion

Members of the Inca ruling class venerated the sun as a god and as their major deity, whom they called **Inti.** They also recognized the moon, stars, planets, rain, and other natural forces as divine. Some Incas, including the energetic ruler Pachacuti, also showed special favor to the god **Viracocha,** creator of the world, humankind, and all else in the universe. The cult of the sun, however, outshone all the others. In Cuzco alone some four thousand priests, attendants, and virgin devotees served Inti, whose temple attracted pilgrims from all parts of the Inca Empire. The first Spanish visitors to Cuzco reported that it took four hundred paces for them to walk around the temple complex, and they expressed amazement at its lavish decoration, including a golden sculpture of the sun encrusted with gems. Particularly astonishing to the visitors was an imitation garden in which grains of gold represented a field, which was planted with stalks of maize fabricated from gold and surrounded by twenty golden llamas with their attendants, also sculpted in gold. Priests of Inti and those serving other cults honored their deities with sacrifices, which in Inca society usually took the form of agricultural produce or animals such as llamas and guinea pigs rather than humans.

Moral Thought

In addition to sacrifices and ritual ceremonies, Inca religion had a strong moral dimension. The Incas taught a concept of sin as a violation of the established social or natural order, and they believed in a life beyond death, during which individuals would receive rewards or punishments based on the quality of their earthly lives. Sin, they believed, would bring divine disaster both for individuals and for their larger communities. The Incas also observed rituals of confession and penance by which

Inti (ihn-tee)

Viracocha (veer-rah-coh-chah)

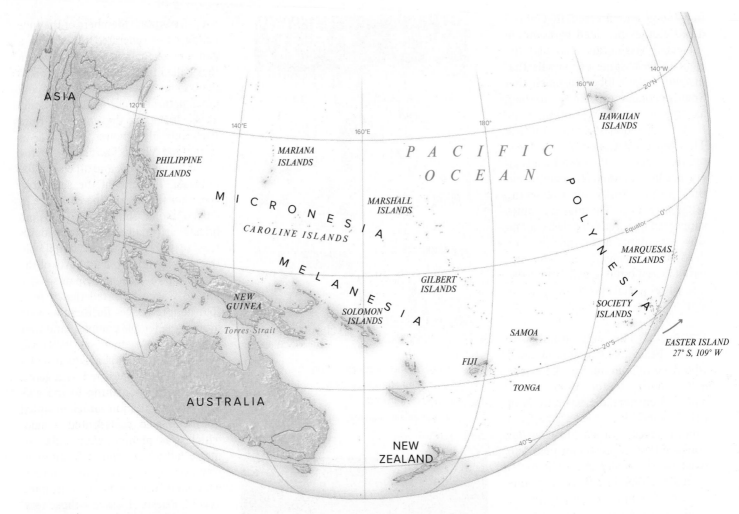

MAP 20.4 Oceania

Islands are much more numerous and much closer together in the western Pacific than in the eastern Pacific.

In what ways did proximity to or distance from other islands influence the development of Pacific island societies?

priests absolved individuals of their sins and returned them to the good graces of the gods.

THE SOCIETIES OF OCEANIA

Inhabitants of Oceania did not interact with peoples of different societies as frequently or systematically as did their counterparts in the eastern hemisphere, but they built and maintained flourishing traditions and societies of their own. The **aboriginal peoples** of Australia ventured over vast stretches of their continent and created networks of trade and exchange between hunting and gathering societies. Only in the far north, however, did they encounter peoples beyond Australia as they traded sporadically with merchants from New Guinea and the islands of southeast Asia. Meanwhile, throughout the Pacific Ocean, islanders built complex agricultural societies. By the time European mariners sailed into the Pacific Ocean in the sixteenth century, the larger island groups had sizable populations, hierarchical social

orders, and hereditary chiefly rulers. In the central and western Pacific, mariners sailed regularly between island groups and established elaborate trade networks. Islanders living toward the eastern and western edges of the Pacific Ocean also had occasional dealings with American and Asian peoples, sometimes with significant consequences for the Pacific island societies.

The Nomadic Foragers of Australia

After the aboriginal peoples of Australia learned how to exploit the resources of the continent's varied regions, they led lives that in some ways changed little over the centuries. Unlike their neighbors to the north, they did not turn to agriculture. The inhabitants of New Guinea began to herd swine and cultivate root crops about 5000 B.C.E., and the inhabitants of islands in the Torres Strait (which separates Australia from New Guinea) took up gardening soon thereafter. Although aboriginal peoples of northern Australia must have known about foods cultivated

A late-eighteenth-century sketch of priests traveling across Kealakekua Bay in Hawai`i wearing helmets made from gourds and foliage. Note the construction of the canoes. Using oceangoing vessels such as these, Polynesian peoples discovered and populated all the inhabitable islands of the vast Pacific Ocean. Historical Picture Archive/Corbis Historical/Getty Images

in neighboring lands, they maintained nomadic, foraging societies until European peoples migrated to Australia in large numbers during the nineteenth and twentieth centuries.

Trade As a result of their mobile and nomadic way of life, aboriginal Australians frequently encountered people from neighboring societies. Because Australia is a continent of enormous climatic and ecological diversity, different peoples enjoyed access to food and other resources unknown to others they encountered during their seasonal migrations. Even though as nomads they did not accumulate large quantities of material goods, groups regularly exchanged surplus food and small items when they met.

That sort of small-scale exchange eventually enabled trade goods to spread throughout most of Australia. Individuals did not travel along all the trade routes. Instead, trade goods passed from one aboriginal community to another until they came to rest in regions often distant from their origins. Baler and oyster pearl shells were among the most popular trade items. Archaeologists have turned up many of these shells fashioned into jewelry more than 1,600 kilometers (1,000 miles) from the waters where the oysters bred. From interior regions came stone axe heads, spears, boomerangs, furs, skins, and fibers.

Aboriginal peoples occasionally traded foodstuffs, but with the exception of some root vegetables, those items were generally too perishable for exchange. Peoples on the north coast also engaged in a limited amount of trade with mariners from New Guinea and the islands of southeast Asia. Australian spears and highly prized pearly shells went north in exchange for exotic items such as the striking flowers of the bird-of-paradise plant, stone clubs, decorative trinkets—and occasionally iron axes, much coveted by aboriginal peoples who had no tradition of metallurgy.

Cultural and Religious Traditions In spite of seasonal migrations, frequent encounters with peoples from other aboriginal societies, and trade over long distances, the cultural traditions of Australian peoples mostly did not diffuse much beyond the regions inhabited by individual societies. Aboriginal peoples paid close attention to the prominent geographic features of the lands around them. Rocks, mountains, forests, mineral deposits, and bodies of water were crucial for their survival, and they related stories and myths about those and other geographic features. Often, they conducted religious observances designed to ensure continuing supplies of animals, plant life, and water. Given the intense concern of aboriginal peoples with their immediate environments, their cultural and religious traditions focused on local matters and did not appeal to peoples from other regions.

The Development of Pacific Island Societies

By the early centuries C.E., humans had established agricultural societies in almost all the island groups of the Pacific Ocean. About the middle of the first millennium C.E., they ventured to the large islands of New Zealand—the last large, habitable region of the earth to receive members of the human species. After 1000 C.E., **Polynesians** inhabiting the larger Pacific islands grew especially numerous, and their surging population prompted remarkable social and political development.

Trade between Island Groups In the central and western regions of the Pacific, where several clusters of islands are relatively close to one another, mariners linked island societies. Regional trade networks facilitated exchanges of useful goods such as axes and pottery, exotic items such as shells and

How the Past Shapes the Future

The Diffusion of Technologies

Although the Polynesian islands were remote from other landmasses and from one another, between 1000 and 1500 C.E. Polynesian peoples nevertheless managed to diffuse technologies even to islands thousands of miles away. In the twelfth and thirteenth centuries, Tahitians who sailed to the Hawaiian islands introduced new ways of organizing society, new linguistic terms, and new technologies for constructing fishhooks—all of which were adopted by Hawaiian peoples. Given the importance of fish in the Hawaiian diet, how might new technologies for catching fish have impacted Hawaiian health and population over the long term? In the context of Polynesian societies, consider whether or not the diffusion of technologies that improved fishing techniques could be seen as being as important as the spread of gunpowder technologies or as the horse collar in Eurasia.

decorative ornaments, and sometimes even foodstuffs such as yams. Regional trade within individual island groups served social and political as well as economic functions because it helped ruling elites establish and maintain harmonious relations with one another. In some cases, trade crossed longer distances and linked different island groups. Inhabitants of the Tonga, Samoa, and Fiji islands traded mats and canoes, for example, and also intermarried, thus creating political and social relationships.

Long-Distance Voyaging Elsewhere in Polynesia, vast stretches of deep blue water made it much more complicated to travel between different island groups and societies. As a result, regular trade networks did not emerge in the eastern Pacific Ocean. Nevertheless, mariners undertook lengthy voyages on an intermittent basis, sometimes with momentous results. After the original settlement of Easter Island about 300 C.E., for example, Polynesian mariners probably ventured to the western coast of South America, where they learned about the cultivation of sweet potatoes. Between about 400 and 700 C.E., mariners spread sweet potatoes throughout Polynesia and beyond to New Caledonia and Vanuatu. The new crop quickly became a prominent source of food in all the islands it reached. Sweet potatoes were especially important for the **Maori** population of New Zealand because the staple crops of the tropical Pacific did not flourish in the temperate climes of New Zealand. Thus long-distance voyages were responsible for the dissemination of sweet potatoes to remote islands situated thousands of kilometers from the nearest inhabited lands.

Another case of long-distance voyaging prompted social changes in the Hawaiian Islands. For centuries after the voyages that brought the original settlers to the islands in the early centuries C.E., there was little travel or communication between Hawai`i and other Polynesian societies. During the twelfth and thirteenth centuries, however, a series of two-way voyages linked Hawai`i with Tahiti and the Marquesas Islands. Memories of those voyages survive in oral traditions that relate the introduction into Hawai`i of new chiefly and priestly lines from Tahiti. Evidence for the voyages comes also from Hawaiian adoption of fishhook styles from Tahiti and words from the Tahitian language.

Population Growth While undertaking regular or intermittent voyages over long distances, islanders throughout the Pacific Ocean also built productive agricultural and fishing societies. They cultivated taro, yams, sweet potatoes, bananas, breadfruit, and coconuts, and they kept domesticated chickens, pigs, and dogs. They also fed on abundant supplies of fish, which they caught by spear, net, and hook. After about the fourteenth century, as their population increased, the inhabitants of Hawai`i built ingenious fishponds that allowed small fry to swim from the ocean through narrow gates into rock-enclosed spaces but prevented larger fish from escaping. Fishponds enabled Hawaiians to harvest large quantities of mature fish with relative ease and thus contributed to the islanders' food supplies. The establishment of agricultural and fishing societies led to rapid population growth in all the larger Pacific island groups—Samoa, Tonga, the Society Islands (including Tahiti), and Hawai`i. In Hawai`i, the most heavily populated of the Polynesian island groups, the human population may have exceeded five hundred thousand when European mariners arrived in the late eighteenth century.

Nan Madol In other lands, dense populations promoted social organization on a scale never before seen in Oceania. On

A massive wall constructed of basalt rock protects a burial site at Nan Madol in Pohnpei.
Michael Runkel/Robert Harding World Imagery/Getty Images

Maori (MAU-ree)

SOURCES FROM THE PAST

Mo`ikeha's Migration from Tahiti to Hawai`i

A group of Polynesian oral traditions preserves memories of numerous two-way voyages between Tahiti and Hawai`i in the twelfth and thirteenth centuries. One of them has to do with Mo`ikeha, a high chief who left Tahiti because of domestic difficulties and migrated to Hawai`i, where he founded a new chiefly line. The legend recounts several voyages between Tahiti and Hawai`i. The following excerpts deal with Mo`ikeha's establishment as a chief in Hawai`i and the later arrival of his Tahitian son La`amaikahiki, who is credited with the introduction of Tahitian religious and cultural traditions to Hawai`i.

It was dark by the time they arrived [at the Hawaiian island of Kaua`i], so they did not land, instead, mooring their canoe offshore. Early the next morning the people saw this double-hulled canoe floating offshore with the kapu sticks of a chief aboard. The canoe was brought ashore and the travellers got off. Meanwhile the locals were gathering in a crowd to go surf-riding. . . . Among them were the two daughters of the ali`i nui [chief] of Kaua`i, Ho`oipoikamalanai and Hinauu.

> Does Mo`ikeha's reception on Kaua'i indicate that the people on the island saw him as an outsider or as a member of a common culture?

Mo`ikeha and his companions saw the crowd and followed along to take part in the morning exercise. Mo`ikeha was a handsome man with dark reddish hair and a tall, commanding figure.

When Ho`oipoikamalanai and her sister saw Mo`ikeha, they immediately fell in love with him, and they decided to take him for their husband. Mo`ikeha in the meantime was also struck with the beauty and grace of the two sisters, and he, too, fell in love with them and decided to take one of them to be his wife. After enjoying the surf for a time, Ho`oipoikamalanai and her sister returned home and told their father about the new arrival and said: "We wish to take that young chief as a husband for one of us." The father approved.

Orders were issued that Mo`ikeha be brought to the house of the two ali`i women. Mo`ikeha and his company were sent for and brought in the presence of the king [the ali`i nui of Kaua`i]. The love of these young people being mutual, Ho`oipoikamalanai and Hinauu took Mo`ikeha to be their husband. Mo`ikeha became ali`i nui of Kaua`i after the death of his father-in-law. . . .

> What might the fact that the two daughters of the chief were able to take the same man as their husband, and the fact that Mo`ikeha could take two more wives in addition to his first, say about marriage laws in Polynesia?

Mo`ikeha worked to make his two wives and five children happy, giving his undivided attention to the bringing up of his boys. He thought no more of Lu`ukia [his lover in Tahiti], but after a while, he began to feel a yearning desire to see his son La`amaikahiki, his child by his first wife Kapo. So he called his five sons together and said to them: "I'm thinking of sending one of you boys to bring your elder brother to Hawai`i." . . .

[After Mo`ikeha's son Kila sailed to Tahiti and found his elder half-brother] La`amaikahiki immediately prepared to accompany his brother to Hawai`i, as Mo`ikeha wished. La`amaikahiki took his priests and his god Lonoika`ouali`i, and set sail for Hawai`i with the men who had come with Kila. When they were approaching Kaua`i, La`amaikahiki began beating his drum. Mo`ikeha heard his drum and ordered everything, the land as well as the house, to be made ready for the reception of the chief La`amaikahiki. Upon the arrival of La`amaikahiki and Kila, the high priest of Kaua`i, Poloahilani, took La`amaikahiki and his god Lonoila`ouali`i ("Lono at the Chiefly Supremacy") to the heiau [temple]. It is said that La`amaikahiki was the first person to bring a god (akua) to Hawai`i. . . .

[After returning to Tahiti, then sailing again to Hawai`i, La`amaikahiki] set sail again, going up the Kona coast [of Hawai`i Island]. . . . It was on this visit that La`amaikahiki introduced hula dancing, accompanied by the drum, to Hawai`i. . . .

La`amaikahiki stayed a long time on Kaua`i teaching the people the art of dancing. From Kaua`i La`amaikahiki visited all the other islands of this group and thus the drum dance (hula ka`eke) spread to the other islands.

For Further Reflection

▪ How would you characterize the political, social, and cultural significance of two-way voyaging between Tahiti and Hawai`i?

Source: Teuira Henry and others. *Voyaging Chiefs of Havai`i.* Ed. by Dennis Kawaharada. Honolulu: Kalamaku Press, 1995, pp. 138–39, 144–46.

Pohnpei in the Caroline Islands, for example, the Sandeleur dynasty built a powerful state and organized construction of a massive stone palace and administrative center at **Nan Madol.** Built mostly during the period from 1200 to 1600, the complex included ninety-three artificial islets protected by seawalls and breakwaters on three sides.

Development of Social Classes

Beginning about the thirteenth century, expanding populations prompted residents of many Pacific islands to develop increasingly complex social and political structures. Especially on the larger islands, workers became more specialized: some concentrated on cultivating certain crops, and others devoted their efforts to fishing; producing axes; or constructing large, seagoing canoes. Distinct classes emerged as aristocratic and ruling elites decided the course of public affairs in their societies and extracted surplus agricultural production from those of common birth. The islands of Tonga, Tahiti, and Hawai`i had especially stratified societies with sharp distinctions between various classes of high chiefs, lesser chiefs, and commoners. Hawaiian society also recognized distinct classes of priests and skilled artisans, such as adze (a cutting tool similar to an axe) makers and canoe builders, ranking between the chiefly and common classes.

The Formation of Chiefly States

In addition to distinct social classes, island societies generated strong political leadership. Ruling chiefs generally oversaw public affairs in portions of an island, sometimes in an entire island, and occasionally in several islands situated close to one another. In Tonga and Hawai`i, high chiefs frequently launched campaigns to bring additional islands under their control and create large centralized states. Rarely, however, were these militant chiefs able to overcome geographic and logistic difficulties and realize their expansionist ambitions before the nineteenth century.

Nevertheless, high chiefs guided the affairs of complex societies throughout Polynesia. They allocated lands to families, mobilized labor for construction projects, and organized men into military forces. They commanded enormous respect within their societies. In Hawai`i, for example, the classes of high chiefs known as *ali`i nui* intermarried, ate the best fish and other foods that were *kapu* ("taboo") to commoners, and had the right to wear magnificent cloaks adorned with thousands of bright red and yellow bird feathers. Indeed, a *kapu* forbade commoners to approach or even cast a shadow on the *ali`i nui.*

Polynesian Religion

High chiefs often claimed that their power descended directly from the gods. They also worked closely with priests, who served as intermediaries between human communities and the gods. Gods of war and agriculture were common throughout the Pacific islands, but individual islands and island groups recognized deities particular to their own regions and interests. The most distinctive architecture of early Pacific societies was the ceremonial precinct and temple structure known as *marae* (or *heiau* in Hawaiian). *Marae* often had several terraced floors with a rock or coral wall designating the boundaries of the sacred space. In Tonga and Samoa, temples made of timber and thatched roofs served as places of worship, sacrifice, and communication between priests and the gods, whereas in eastern Polynesia religious ceremonies took place on platforms in open-air courtyards. The largest of those structures, the *marae* Mahaiatea on Tahiti, took the form of a step pyramid about 15 meters (49 feet) high with a base measuring 81 by 22 meters (266 by 72 feet).

Pacific island societies did not have access to the range of technologies developed by continental peoples until the sixteenth and later centuries. Yet Pacific islanders cleverly exploited their environments; established productive agricultural economies; built elaborate, well-organized traditions and societies; and reached out when possible to engage in trade with their neighbors. Their achievements testify anew to the human impulses toward densely populated communities and interaction with other societies.

CONCLUSION

The original inhabitants of the Americas and Oceania lived in societies that were considerably smaller than those of the eastern hemisphere. They did not possess the metallurgical technologies that enabled their counterparts to exploit more fully the natural environment, nor did they possess the transportation technologies based on wheeled vehicles and domesticated animals that facilitated trade and communication among peoples of the eastern hemisphere. Nevertheless, long before they entered into sustained encounters with European and other peoples, they built complex societies and developed sophisticated cultural and religious traditions. Indigenous peoples established foraging, fishing, and agricultural societies throughout the Americas, and they fashioned tools from wood, stone, and bone that enabled them to produce enough food to support sizable communities. In Mesoamerica and Andean South America, they also built imperial states that organized public affairs on a large scale. The cultural and religious traditions of these imperial societies reflected their concern for agricultural production and the maintenance of complex social structures.

The original inhabitants of Australia and the Pacific islands built societies on a smaller scale than did the peoples of the Americas, but they too devised effective means of exploiting the natural environment, developing strong traditions, and organizing flourishing communities. Australia was a continent of foraging nomadic peoples, whereas the Pacific islands supported densely populated agricultural societies. Although they had limited communication with peoples of the Americas or the eastern hemisphere, the peoples of Oceania had regular encounters with their neighbors, and inhabitants of the Pacific islands sometimes undertook lengthy voyages to trade with distant island groups. Although the peoples of the Americas and of Oceania were a world apart from their counterparts in Africa, Asia, and Europe, they built vigorous traditions and engaged in long-distance encounters within their own regions.

STUDY TERMS

aboriginal peoples (418)	*marae* (422)
ali`i nui (422)	Mexica (406)
ayllu (417)	Motecuzoma I (407)
Aztec Empire (406)	Nan Madol (422)
Cahokia (413)	Navajo (412)
calpulli (409)	Polynesians (419)
chinampa (406)	Pueblo (412)
Chimu (414)	Quechua (415)
Chucuito (414)	Quetzalcóatl (411)
Cuzco (416)	*quipu* (415)
Huitzilopochtli (411)	Tenochtitlan (404)
Inca Empire (415)	Teotihuacan (406)
Inti (417)	Tezcatlipoca (411)
Iroquois (413)	Toltecs (406)
Itzcóatl (407)	Tula (406)
kapu (422)	Viracocha (417)
Maori (420)	

FOR FURTHER READING

Inga Clendinnen. *Aztecs: An Interpretation.* Cambridge, 1991. A brilliant re-creation of the Mexica world, concentrating on cultural and social themes.

George A. Collier, Renato I. Rosaldo, and John D. Wirth, eds. *The Inca and Aztec States, 1400–1800: Anthropology and History.* New York, 1982. Seventeen well-focused essays represent approaches that scholars have taken to the Inca and Aztec empires.

Ross Hassig. *Aztec Warfare: Imperial Expansion and Political Control.* Norman, Okla., 1988. A solid scholarly study of Mexica military affairs and their role in the building of the Aztec Empire.

Peter Hiscock. *Archaeology of Ancient Australia,* London, 2008. Comprehensive overview of the current state of archaeological investigation into aboriginal culture and history.

Patrick V. Kirch. *On the Road of the Winds: An Archaeological History of the Pacific Islands before European Contact.* Berkeley, 2000. A valuable synthesis of recent scholarship by the foremost contemporary archaeologist of the Pacific islands.

Charles C. Mann. *1491: New Revelations of the Americas before Columbus.* New York, 2006. Summarizes a great deal of archaeological research on the pre-Columbian Americas.

Gordon McEwan. *The Incas: New Perspectives.* New York, 2008. Offers recent interpretations of Inca culture, politics, economics, and daily life.

Michael E. Moseley. *The Incas and Their Ancestors: The Archaeology of Peru.* Rev. ed. London, 2001. A comprehensive survey of Andean history through the era of the Incas.

Christina Thompson. *Sea People: The Puzzle of Polynesia.* New York, 2019. Engaging and fresh account about who settled Polynesia and how they got there.

Camilla Townsend. *Fifth Sun: A New History of the Aztecs.* Oxford, 2019. Revisionist history of the Aztec conquest told solely through documents produced by Mexica peoples themselves.

Expanding Horizons of Cross-Cultural Interaction

ZOOMING IN ON ENCOUNTERS
On the Road with Ibn Battuta

One of the great world travelers of all time was the Moroccan legal scholar **Ibn Battuta.** Born in 1304 at Tangier, Ibn Battuta followed family tradition and studied Islamic law. In 1325 he left Morocco to make a pilgrimage to Mecca [also called the hajj]. He traveled by caravan across north Africa and through Egypt, Palestine, and Syria, arriving at Mecca in 1326. After completing his hajj, Ibn Battuta spent a year visiting Mesopotamia and Persia, then traveled by ship through the Red Sea and down the east African coast as far south as Kilwa. By 1330 he had returned to Mecca, but then soon set off for India when he learned that the Muslim sultan of Delhi offered handsome rewards to foreign legal scholars. In 1333 he arrived in Delhi after following a long and circuitous land route that took him through Egypt, Syria, Anatolia, Constantinople, the Black Sea, and the great trading cities of central Asia—Bokhara and Samarkand.

For the next eight years, Ibn Battuta remained in India, serving mostly as a **qadi** (judge) in the government of the sultan of Delhi. In 1341 Ibn Battuta began his travels again, this time making his way around southern India, Ceylon, and the Maldive Islands before continuing to China about 1345. He

Ibn Battuta (ih-bun BAH-too-tah)
qadi (KAH-dee)

A giraffe from east Africa sent as a present by wealthy Swahili traders to China in 1414 and painted by a Chinese artist at a zoo in Ming dynasty China.
Barney Burstein/Corbis/VCG/Getty Images

visited the bustling southern Chinese port cities of Quanzhou and Guangzhou, where he encountered large communities of Muslim merchants, before returning to Morocco in 1349 by way of southern India, the Persian Gulf, Syria, Egypt, and Mecca.

But Ibn Battuta's travels were still not complete. In 1350 he made a short trip to the kingdom of Granada in southern Spain, and in 1353 he joined a camel caravan across the Sahara to visit the Mali Empire, returning to Morocco in 1355. During his travels Ibn Battuta visited the equivalent of forty-four modern countries and logged more than 117,000 kilometers (73,000 miles). His account of his adventures stands with Marco Polo's book as one of the classic works of travel literature and serves as a powerful historical record of the cultures he encountered.

CHAPTER OVERVIEW

Between 1000 and 1500 C.E., the peoples of the Eastern Hemisphere traveled, traded, communicated, and interacted more regularly and intensively than ever before. The large empires of the Mongols (discussed in chapter 17) and other nomadic peoples provided a political foundation for this cross-cultural interaction. When they conquered and pacified vast regions, nomadic peoples provided safe roads for merchants, diplomats, missionaries, and other travelers. Quite apart from the nomadic empires, improvements in maritime technology led to increased traffic in the sea lanes of the Indian Ocean and the South China Sea. As a result, long-distance travel became much more common than in earlier eras, which enabled individual travelers like Ibn Battuta and Marco Polo to venture throughout much of the Eastern Hemisphere.

Merchants and travelers exchanged more than trade goods. They diffused technologies and spread religious faiths. They also exchanged diseases that caused widespread and deadly epidemics. During the middle decades of the fourteenth century, bubonic plague traveled the trade routes from western China to central Asia, southwest Asia, north Africa, and Europe. During its initial, furious onslaught, bubonic plague caused death and destruction on a huge scale and interrupted long-distance trade networks.

By the early fifteenth century, however, societies had begun to revover from the plague. Chinese and western European peoples in particular restabilized their societies and had begun to renew cross-cultural encounters. In Europe, that effort had profound consequences for modern world history. As European mariners sought entry to the markets of Asia, they not only established direct connections with African and Asian peoples but also sailed to the Western Hemisphere and the Pacific Ocean. Their voyages brought the peoples of the Eastern Hemisphere, the Western Hemisphere, and Oceania into permanent and sustained interaction. Thus cross-cultural interactions of the period 1000 to 1500 had already laid the groundwork for global interdependence, a principal characteristic of modern world history.

LONG-DISTANCE TRADE AND TRAVEL

Travelers embarked on long-distance journeys for a variety of reasons. Nomadic peoples ranged widely in the course of migrations and campaigns of conquest. East European and African slaves were forced to travel to the Mediterranean basin, southwest Asia, India, and sometimes even southern China. Buddhist, Christian, and Muslim pilgrims undertook extraordinary journeys to visit holy shrines. Three of the more important motives for long-distance travel between 1000 and 1500 C.E. were trade, diplomacy, and missionary activity. The cross-cultural interactions that resulted helped spread technological innovations throughout the Eastern Hemisphere.

CHRONOLOGY	
1214	Creation of a Mongol artillery unit
1253–1324	Life of Marco Polo
1287–1288	Rabban Sauma's embassy to Europe
1291–1328	John of Montecorvino's mission to China
1304–1369	Life of Ibn Battuta
1304–1374	Life of Francesco Petrarca
1330s	First outbreaks of bubonic plague in China
1337–1453	Hundred Years' War
1347	Arrival of bubonic plague in the Mediterranean basin
1368–1644	Ming dynasty
1405–1433	Zheng He's expeditions in the Indian Ocean
1466–1536	Life of Desiderius Erasmus of Rotterdam
1488	Bartolomeu Dias's voyage around Africa
1492	Christopher Columbus's first voyage to the Western Hemisphere
1497–1498	Vasco da Gama's voyage to India

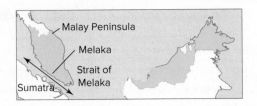

MAP 21.1 **Melaka and the Melaka Strait.**

Look at the position of Melaka relative to the strait. Why would the city have been such a strategic location for any power that ruled it?

Patterns of Long-Distance Trade

Merchants engaged in long-distance trade relied on two principal networks of trade routes. Luxury goods of high value relative to their weight, such as silk textiles and precious stones, often traveled overland on the Silk Roads used since classical times. Bulkier commodities, such as steel, stone, coral, and building materials, traveled the sea lanes of the Indian Ocean because it would have been unprofitable to transport them overland. The Silk Roads linked all of the

Eurasian landmass, and trans-Saharan caravan routes drew west Africa into the larger economy of the Eastern Hemisphere. The sea lanes of the Indian Ocean served ports in southeast Asia, India, Arabia, and east Africa while also offering access via the South China Sea to ports in China, Japan, Korea, and the spice-bearing islands of southeast Asia. Thus, in combination, land and sea routes touched almost every corner of the Eastern Hemisphere.

Trading Cities As the volume of trade increased, the major trading cities and ports grew rapidly, attracting buyers, sellers, brokers, and bankers from parts near and far. Khanbaliq (modern Beijing), Hangzhou, Quanzhou, Melaka, Cambay, Samarkand, Hormuz, Baghdad, Caffa, Cairo, Alexandria, Kilwa, Constantinople, Venice, Timbuktu, and many other cities had large quarters occupied by communities of foreign merchants. When a trading or port city enjoyed a strategic location, maintained good order, and resisted the temptation to levy excessive customs fees, it had the potential to become a major emporium serving long-distance trade networks. A case in point is **Melaka** (in modern Malaysia). Founded in the 1390s, within a few decades Melaka became the principal clearinghouse of trade in the eastern Indian Ocean. The city's

An illustration from a fourteenth-century French manuscript depicts Marco Polo tasting pepper as nearby laborers harvest it in southern India. Note that Polo is fully dressed and seems relaxed, while the laborers are clearly toiling in the sun.
DEA/J. E. Bulloz/Getty Images

authorities policed the strategic Strait of Melaka and maintained a safe market that welcomed all merchants and levied reasonable fees on goods exchanged there. By the end of the fifteenth century, Melaka had a population of some fifty thousand people, and in the early sixteenth century the Portuguese merchant Tomé Pires reported that more than eighty languages could be heard in the city's streets.

During the early and middle decades of the thirteenth century, the Mongols' campaigns caused economic disruption throughout much of Eurasia—particularly in China and southwest Asia, where Mongol forces toppled the Song and Abbasid dynasties (discussed in chapter 17). Mongol conquests inaugurated a long period of economic decline in southwest Asia

where the conquerors destroyed cities and allowed irrigation systems to fall into disrepair. As the Mongols consolidated their hold on conquered lands, however, they laid the political foundation for a surge in long-distance trade along the Silk Roads. Merchants traveling the Silk Roads faced less risk of banditry or political turbulence than in previous times. Meanwhile, strong economies in China, India, and western Europe fueled demand for foreign commodities. Many merchants traveled the whole distance from Europe to China in pursuit of profit.

Marco Polo The best-known long-distance traveler of Mongol times was the Venetian **Marco Polo** (1253–1324). Marco's father, Niccolò, and uncle Maffeo were among the

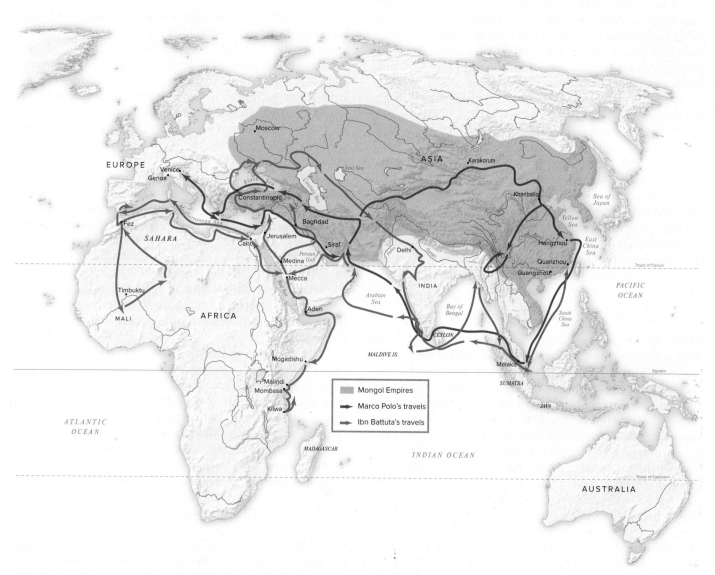

MAP 21.2   Travels of Marco Polo and Ibn Battuta.

Between them, Marco Polo and Ibn Battuta traveled across much of the Eurasian landmass, as well as parts of Africa and southeast Asia.

Compare the routes taken by Marco Polo and Ibn Battuta during their travels. How did the two men choose where to travel? What conditions made it possible for them to travel so far from their homes?

first European merchants to visit China. Between 1260 and 1269 they traveled and traded throughout Mongol lands, and they met Khubilai Khan as he was consolidating his hold on China. When they returned to China in 1271, seventeen-year-old Marco Polo accompanied them. The great khan took a special liking to Marco, who was a marvelous conversationalist and storyteller. Khubilai allowed Marco to pursue his mercantile interests in China and also sent him on numerous diplomatic missions, partly because Marco regaled him with stories about the distant parts of his realm. After seventeen years in China, the Polos decided to return to Venice, and Khubilai granted them permission to leave. They went back on the sea route by way of Sumatra, Ceylon, India, and Arabia, arriving in Venice in 1295.

A historical accident has preserved the story of Marco Polo's travels. After his return from China, Marco was captured and made a prisoner of war during a conflict between his native Venice and its commercial rival, Genoa. While imprisoned, Marco related tales of his travels to his fellow prisoners. One of them was a writer of romances, and he compiled the stories into a large volume that circulated rapidly throughout Europe.

In spite of occasional exaggerations and tall tales, Marco's stories deeply influenced European readers. Marco always mentioned the textiles, spices, gems, and other goods he observed during his travels, and European merchants took note, eager to participate in the lucrative trade networks of Eurasia. The Polos were among the first Europeans to visit China, but they were far from the last. Hundreds of others, mostly Italians, quickly followed the Polos. In most cases, their stories do not survive, but their travels helped to increase European participation in the larger economy of the Eastern Hemisphere.

Political and Diplomatic Travel

Marco Polo came from a family of merchants, and merchants were among the most avid readers of his stories. Marco himself most likely collaborated closely with Italian merchants during his years in China. Yet his experiences also throw light on long-distance travel undertaken for political and diplomatic purposes. Khubilai Khan and the other Mongol rulers of China did not entirely trust their Chinese subjects and regularly appointed foreigners to administrative posts. In his account of his travels, Marco reported that Khubilai appointed him governor of the large trading city of Yangzhou. There is no independent evidence to confirm that claim, but Marco may well have filled some sort of administrative position. In addition, he represented Khubilai Khan's interests on diplomatic missions. To support himself in China, then, Marco supplemented his mercantile ventures with various official duties assigned to him by his patron, the great khan.

Mongol-Christian Diplomacy The emergence of elaborate trading networks and the establishment of vast imperial states created great demand for political and diplomatic

representation during the centuries after 1000 C.E. The thirteenth century was a time of especially active diplomacy involving parties as distant as the Mongols and western Europeans, both of whom considered a military alliance against their common Muslim foes. As European Christians sought to revive the crusading movement and recapture Jerusalem from Muslim forces, the Mongols were attacking the Abbasid empire from the east. During the 1240s and 1250s, Pope Innocent IV dispatched a series of envoys who invited the Mongol khans to convert to Christianity and join Europeans in an alliance against the Muslims. The khans declined the invitation, proposing in reply that the pope and European Christians submit to Mongol rule or face destruction.

Rabban Sauma Although the early round of Mongol-European diplomacy offered little promise of cooperation, the Mongols later initiated another effort. In 1287 the Mongol ilkhan of Persia planned to invade the Muslim-held lands of southwest Asia, capture Jerusalem, and crush Islam as a political force in the region. In hopes of attracting support for the project, he dispatched **Rabban Sauma,** a Nestorian Christian priest born in the Mongol capital of Khanbaliq but of Turkish ancestry, as an envoy to the pope and European political leaders.

Rabban Sauma met with the kings of France and England, the pope, and other high officials of the Roman Catholic church. He enjoyed a fine reception, but he did not succeed in attracting European support for the ilkhan. Only a few years later, in 1295, Ghazan, the new ilkhan of Persia, converted to Islam, thus precluding any further possibility of an alliance between the Mongols of Persia and European Christians. Nevertheless, the flurry of diplomatic activity illustrates the complexity of political affairs in the Eastern Hemisphere and the need for diplomatic consultation over long distances.

The expansion of Islamic influence in the Eastern Hemisphere encouraged a different kind of politically motivated travel. Legal scholars and judges played a crucial role in Islamic societies because the **sharia** (Islamic law) prescribed religious observances and social relationships based on the Quran. Conversions to Islam and the establishment of Islamic states in India, southeast Asia, and sub-Saharan Africa created a demand for Muslims educated in Islamic law. After about the eleventh century, educated Muslims from southwest Asia and north Africa regularly traveled to recently converted lands to help instill Islamic values.

Ibn Battuta As we saw in the introduction to this chapter, the best known of the Muslim travelers was Ibn Battuta (1304–1369). Islamic rulers governed most of the lands Ibn Battuta visited—including India, the Maldive Islands, the Swahili city-states of east Africa, and the Mali Empire—but very few Muslims educated in the law were available in those lands. With his legal credentials Ibn Battuta had little

SOURCES FROM THE PAST

Ibn Battuta on Customs in the Mali Empire

Long-distance travelers often encountered unfamiliar customs in foreign societies. The Moroccan traveler Ibn Battuta—who is featured in the introduction to this chapter—approved heartily when staying with hosts who appeared to honor the values of his own Muslim society, but he had little tolerance for those whose practices differed from what he thought was acceptable behavior for Muslims. Here he describes his impressions of the Muslim-ruled Mali Empire (West Africa) when he visited the court of the sultan in the mid-fourteenth century.

Of all people, the blacks debase themselves most in presence of their king: for when any one of them is called upon to appear before him, he will immediately put off his usual clothing, and put on a worn-out dress, with a dirty cap; he will then enter the presence like a beggar, with his clothes lifted up to the middle of his legs; he will then beat the ground with both his elbows, and remain in the attitude of a person performing a prostration. When the Sultan addresses one of them, he will take up the garment off his back, and throw dust upon his head; and, as long as the Sultan speaks, everyone present will remain with his turban taken off. One of the best things in these parts is, the regard they pay to justice; for, in this respect the Sultan regards neither little nor much. The safety, too, is very great; so that a traveler may proceed alone among them, without the least fear of a thief or robber. Another of their good properties is, that when a merchant happens to die among them, they will make no effort to get possession of his property: but will allow the lawful successors to it to take it. Another is, their constant custom of attending prayers with the congregation; for, unless one makes haste, he will find no place left to say his prayers in. Another is, their insisting on the Koran's being committed to memory: for if a man finds his son defective in this, he will confine him till he is quite perfect, nor will he allow him his liberty until he is so. As to their bad practices, they will exhibit their little daughters, as well as their male and female slaves, quite naked. In the same manner will the women enter into the presence of the King, which his own daughters will also do. Nor do the free women ever clothe themselves till after marriage.

> Are there clues in Ibn Battuta's language that indicate whether or not he thought these practices of subservience to the sultan were positive or negative features of their customs?

> Thinking back to chapter 14 (The Expansive Realm of Islam), what was it about the teachings of Islam that made women's public nudity seem offensive to Ibn Battuta?

For Further Reflection

■ Think about the various ways in which Islamic influences and established local customs came together in the Mali Empire, and why this might have produced different results in Mali as compared to other places.

Source: Ibn Batuta, 1304–1377, and Samuel Lee. *The Travels of Ibn Batūta.* London: Printed for the Oriental translation committee, sold by J. Murray [etc.], 1829, 263–264.

difficulty finding government positions. As *qadi* and adviser to the sultan of Delhi, he supervised the affairs of a wealthy mosque and heard cases at law, which he strictly enforced according to Islamic standards of justice. On one occasion Ibn Buttuta sentenced a man to receive eighty lashes because he had drunk wine eight years earlier.

After leaving northern India, Ibn Battuta obtained a post as *qadi* in the Maldive Islands. There he heard cases at law and worked zealously to promote proper observance of Islam. He ordered lashings for men who did not attend Friday prayers, and he once sentenced a thief to lose his right hand in accordance with punishment prescribed by the sharia. He also attempted, unsuccessfully, to persuade island women to meet the standards of modesty observed in other Islamic lands by covering their breasts. In both east and west Africa, Ibn

Battuta consulted with Muslim rulers and offered advice about government, women's dress, and proper relationships between the sexes. Like many legal scholars whose stories went unrecorded, Ibn Battuta provided guidance in the ways of Islam in societies recently converted to the faith.

Missionary Campaigns

Sufi Missionaries Islamic values spread not only through the efforts of legal scholars but also through the missionary activities of Sufi mystics. As in the early days of Islam, **Sufis** in the period from 1000 to 1500 ventured to recently conquered or converted lands and sought to win a popular following for the faith in India, southeast Asia, and sub-Saharan Africa. Sufis did not insist on a strict, doctrinally literal understanding of Islam but, rather, emphasized piety and devotion to Allah. They even tolerated continuing reverence of traditional deities, whom the Sufis treated as manifestations of Allah and his powers. By taking a flexible approach to their missions, the Sufis spread Islamic values without facing the resistance that unyielding campaigns would likely have provoked.

Christian Missionaries Meanwhile, Roman Catholic missionaries also traveled long distances in the interests of spreading Christianity. Missionaries accompanied the crusaders and other forces to all the lands where Europeans extended their influence after the year 1000. In lands where European conquerors maintained a long-term presence—such as the Baltic lands, the Balkan region, Sicily, and Spain—missionaries attracted converts in large numbers, and Roman Catholic Christianity became securely established. In the eastern Mediterranean region, however, where crusaders were unable to hold their conquests permanently, Christianity remained a minority faith.

The most ambitious missions sought to convert Mongols and Chinese to Roman Catholic Christianity. Until the arrival of European merchants and diplomats in the thirteenth century, probably no Roman Catholic Christian had ever ventured as far east as China, although Nestorian Christians from central Asia had maintained communities there since the seventh century. As more Europeans traveled to China, their emigrant communities created a demand for Roman Catholic services. Many of the Roman Catholic priests who traveled to China probably intended to serve the needs of those communities, but some of them also sought to attract converts.

John of Montecorvino Most active of the Roman Catholic missionaries in China was **John of Montecorvino,** an Italian Franciscan who went to China in 1291, became the first archbishop of Khanbaliq in 1307, and died there in 1328. While serving the community of Roman Catholic Europeans in China, John worked energetically to establish Christianity in larger Chinese society. He translated the New Testament and the book of Psalms into Turkish, a language commonly used at the Mongol court, and he built several churches in China. He took in young boys from Mongol and Chinese families, baptized them, and taught them Latin and Roman Catholic rituals. He claimed to have baptized six thousand individuals by 1305, and he invited the great khan himself to convert to Christianity. Although popular and widely respected among Europeans, Chinese, and Mongols alike, John attracted few Asian peoples to Christianity.

Woodcut of John of Montecorvino (1246–1328).
Picture from History/Newscom.

Roman Catholic authorities in Europe dispatched many other priests and missionaries to China during the early fourteenth century, but like John of Montecorvino, they won few converts. Missions successfully established Christian communities in Scandinavia, eastern Europe, Spain, and the Mediterranean islands that European armies recaptured from Muslims during the centuries after 1000 C.E., but east Asia was too distant for the resources available to the Roman Catholic church. Moreover, east Asian peoples already possessed sophisticated religious and cultural traditions, so Christianity had little appeal. Nevertheless, Christian missions to China continued until the mid-fourteenth century, when the collapse of the Mongols' Yuan dynasty and the eruption of epidemic disease temporarily disrupted long-distance travel across Eurasia.

Long-Distance Travel and Cross-Cultural Exchanges

Cultural Exchanges Long-distance travel of all kinds, whether for commercial, political, diplomatic, or missionary purposes, encouraged cultural exchanges between peoples of different societies. Songs, stories, religious ideas, philosophical views, and scientific knowledge all passed readily among travelers who ventured into the larger world during the era from 1000 to 1500 C.E. The troubadours of western Europe, for example, drew on the poetry, music, and love songs of Muslim performers when developing the literature of courtly love. Similarly, European scientists avidly consulted their Muslim and Jewish counterparts in Sicily and Spain to expand their understanding of the natural world.

Large numbers of travelers also facilitated agricultural and technological diffusion during the period from 1000 to 1500. Indeed, technological diffusion sometimes facilitated long-distance travel. The magnetic compass, for example, invented in China during the Tang or the Song dynasty, spread throughout the Indian Ocean basin during the eleventh century, and by the mid-twelfth century European mariners used compasses in the Mediterranean and the Atlantic Ocean. Diffusion of the compass was a boon to maritime trade because it allowed mariners to sail over long stretches of deep water with confidence in their ability to find their destinations and return home safely.

Spread of Crops Long-distance journeys enabled Muslim travelers to introduce new food and commercial crops to sub-Saharan Africa. These crops included citrus fruits and Asian strains of rice, which enriched diets in west Africa after

SOURCES FROM THE PAST

John of Montecorvino on His Mission in China

The Franciscan John of Montecorvino (1247–1328) served as a Roman Catholic missionary in Armenia, Persia, and India before going to China in 1291. There he served as priest to expatriate European Christians, and he sought to attract converts to Christianity from the Mongol and Chinese communities. In a letter of 8 January 1305 asking for support from his fellow Franciscans in Italy, John outlined some of his activities during the previous thirteen years.

[After spending thirteen months in India] I proceeded on my further journey and made my way to China, the realm of the emperor of the Mongols who is called the great khan. To him I presented the letter of our lord the pope and invited him to adopt the Catholic faith of our Lord Jesus Christ, but he had grown too old in idolatry. However, he bestows many kindnesses upon the Christians, and these two years past I have gotten along well with him. . . .

I have built a church in the city of Khanbaliq, in which the king has his chief residence. This I completed six years ago; and I have built a bell tower to it and put three bells in it. I have baptized there, as well as I can estimate, up to this time some 6,000 persons. . . . And I am often still engaged in baptizing.

Also I have gradually bought one hundred and fifty boys, the children of pagan parents and of ages varying from seven to eleven, who had never learned any religion. These boys I have baptized, and I have taught them Greek and Latin after our manner. Also I have written out Psalters for them, with thirty hymnals and breviaries [prayer books]. By help of these, eleven of the boys already know our service and form a choir and take their weekly turn of duty as they do in convents, whether I am there or not. Many of the boys are also employed in writing out Psalters and other suitable things. His Majesty the Emperor moreover delights much to hear them chanting. I have the bells rung at all the canonical hours, and with my congregation of babes and sucklings I perform divine service, and the chanting we do by ear because I have no service book with the notes. . . .

> Since John of Montecorvino purchased these boys, how free do you think they would have been to choose their own religion?

Indeed if I had but two or three comrades to aid me, it is possible that the emperor khan himself would have been baptized by this time! I ask then for such brethren to come, if any are willing to come, such I mean as will make it their great business to lead exemplary lives. . . .

> According to John of Montecorvino, what has been his main limitation in converting Chinese people to Christianity?

I have myself grown old and grey, more with toil and trouble than with years, for I am not more than fifty-eight. I have got a competent knowledge of the language and script which is most generally used by the Tartars. And I have already translated into that language and script the New Testament and the Psalter and have caused them to be written out in the fairest penmanship they have, and so by writing, reading, and preaching, I bear open and public testimony to the law of Christ.

For Further Reflection

■ How did John of Montecorvino seem to regard the khan and his Chinese subjects? Does his tone sound hopeful about the eventual success of his Christian mission in China? Why or why not?

Source: Henry Yule and Henri Cordier, eds. *Cathay and the Way Thither,* 4 vols. London: Hakluyt Society, 1913–16, 3:45–50. (Translation slightly modified.)

---

the eleventh century. Muslims also introduced cotton to west Africa, and by 1100, cotton fabrics had become popular with the ruling elites and wealthy merchants of the west African kingdoms. Cotton grew well in the savannas, and by 1500 it was the principal textile produced in sub-Saharan Africa.

Sugarcane Muslims were also instrumental in the continuing diffusion of sugarcane. Muslim merchants and other travelers had begun large-scale cultivation of sugarcane in southwest Asia and north Africa during the Abbasid caliphate (750–1258 C.E.). They experimented with the plant in west Africa but had limited success because of adverse environmental conditions.

After the twelfth century, however, Muslims facilitated the westward spread of sugarcane by acquainting European crusaders with crystallized sugar refined from cane. Up to that time Europeans had little access to refined sugar, and they relied on honey and fruits as sweeteners. They immediately

An illustration from a manuscript of 1282 depicts a Christian (left) playing chess with a Muslim (right). Chess was one of many cultural elements that passed from Muslim to Christian societies during the crusading era.
Index/Heritage Images/ Heritage Image Partnership Ltd /Alamy Stock Photo

appreciated the convenience of refined sugar. Italian entrepreneurs began to organize sugarcane plantations on Mediterranean islands such as Sicily, Cyprus, Crete, and Rhodes. Rapidly increasing demand for refined sugar encouraged investors to seek suitable locations throughout the Mediterranean basin. The cultivation of sugarcane had deep social and economic implications. Besides influencing local economic development in lands where it spread, it touched distant societies. Like their Muslim predecessors, European sugar producers often used slave labor on their plantations, and the growth of plantations fueled an increasing demand for Muslim war captives and black Africans who could be forced into slavery.

Gunpowder Technologies Although Muslim merchants and travelers were especially prominent agents of diffusion,

Mongols also contributed to the process, notably by helping to spread gunpowder technologies west from China. Mongol invaders learned about gunpowder from Chinese military engineers in the early thirteenth century and soon incorporated gunpowder-based weapons into their arsenal: as early as 1214 Chinggis Khan's armies included an artillery unit. During the 1250s, as they campaigned in Persia and southwest Asia, the Mongols used catapults and trebuchets to lob gunpowder bombs into cities under siege. Muslim armies soon developed similar weapons in response.

By the mid-thirteenth century, gunpowder had reached Europe—possibly by way of Mongol-ruled Russia—and Europeans had begun to experiment with gunpowder-fueled rockets. By the early fourteenth century, armies from China to Europe possessed primitive cannons. Although not especially accurate, the weapons were powerful enough to blow holes in the defensive walls of cities under siege. Thus, with the assistance of Mongol warriors, gunpowder technology rapidly spread from its homeland in China across the entire Eurasian landmass.

Agricultural and technological diffusions of the era 1000 to 1500 C.E. were by no means unique processes in world history. For millennia, agricultural crops and technological skills had spread widely whenever peoples of different societies interacted with one another. Because of the particularly intense interactions of the period from 1000 to 1500 C.E., however, agricultural and technological diffusion profoundly influenced the lives of peoples throughout the Eastern Hemisphere. The spread of food crops enriched diets and supported increasing populations, and the spread of industrial crops such as cotton promoted economic development. The diffusion of the magnetic compass enabled mariners to sail the seas more safely and effectively, and the spread of gunpowder technology forever changed the nature of war.

CRISIS AND RECOVERY

As Eurasian peoples traveled over long distances, they not only exchanged trade goods, agricultural crops, and technological expertise but also unwittingly helped disease pathogens to spread. When diseases broke out among previously unexposed populations, they often caused deadly epidemics that severely disrupted whole societies. During the fourteenth century, **bubonic plague** erupted in epidemics that ravaged societies throughout most of Asia, Europe, and north Africa. Epidemic plague struck intermittently until the seventeenth century, but by the fifteenth century Chinese and European societies had begun to recover from its effects and wield their influence in the larger world.

Bubonic Plague

Climate Changes About 1300 C.E. a process of global climate change caused temperatures to decline significantly and abruptly throughout much of the world. For more than five hundred years, the earth experienced a **"little ice age,"** when temperatures were much cooler than in the era from 1000 to 1300 C.E. With markedly cooler temperatures and shorter growing seasons, agricultural production declined in many lands, leading to famine and sometimes even starvation. In some northerly lands, agriculture ceased to be a practical possibility: after the onset of the little ice age, Norse settlers abandoned the colonies they had occupied in Greenland since the tenth century.

Origins of Epidemic Bubonic Plague As they struggled to cope with the cooling climate, peoples in much of the Eastern Hemisphere suddenly encountered a new challenge in the form of devastating epidemic disease. Bubonic plague spread from the Yunnan region of southwestern China, where it probably had been endemic for centuries.

The plague bacillus infects rodents such as rats, squirrels, and prairie dogs, and fleas transmit the pathogen from one rodent to another. If rodent populations decline, fleas seek other hosts and sometimes spread the disease to human victims. In the early fourteenth century, Mongol military campaigns helped spread plague from Yunnan to China's interior: an epidemic in 1331 reportedly killed 90 percent of the population in Hebei province in northeastern China, near modern Beijing. During the 1350s epidemics broke out in widely scattered regions of China, and contemporaries reported that plague carried away two-thirds of the population in some afflicted areas.

Spread of Plague During the 1340s Mongols, merchants, and other travelers spread the disease along trade routes to points west of China. It thrived in the oases and trading cities of

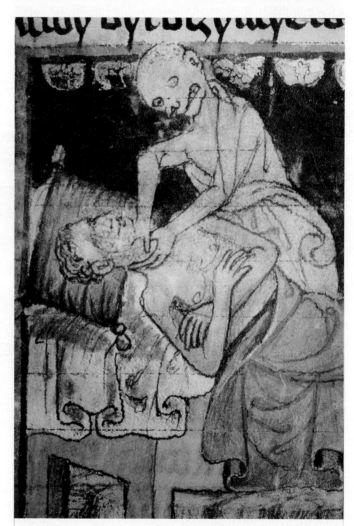

A painting from 1376 graphically communicates the horror felt by medieval Europeans when bubonic plague struck their communities. Here, death strangles a victim of the Black Death plague.

Werner Forman/Universal Images Group/Getty Images

central Asia, where domestic animals and rodents provided abundant breeding grounds for fleas and the plague bacillus. By 1346 it had reached the Black Sea ports of Caffa and Tana. In 1347, Italian merchants fled plague-infected Black Sea ports and unwittingly spread the disease throughout the Mediterranean basin. By 1348, following the trade routes, plague had sparked epidemics in most of western Europe.

Wherever it appeared, bubonic plague struck with frightful effects. Victims developed inflamed lymph nodes, particularly in the neck, armpit, and groin areas, and most died within a few days after the onset of symptoms. Internal hemorrhaging often discolored the inflammations known as buboes—which gave rise to the term *bubonic*—and because of the black or purple swellings, Europeans referred to the plague as the "Black Death." Bubonic plague typically killed 60 to 70 percent of its human victims and had the potential to ravage a society within a few months. In some small villages and towns, disease wiped out the entire population. A spate of new births generally followed outbreaks of plague as societies tried to replenish their numbers, but plague also returned and claimed new victims. In Europe plague erupted intermittently from the 1340s until the late seventeenth century.

Some parts of the Eastern Hemisphere did not suffer directly from plague epidemics. The long, cold winters of Scandinavia discouraged the proliferation of plague-bearing rodents and fleas, so the northernmost parts of Europe escaped the plague's worst effects. For reasons that are still poorly understood, India also seems to have avoided serious difficulties. In fact, the Indian population grew from 91 million in the year 1300 to 97 million a century later and 105 million in 1500. Epidemics also largely bypassed sub-Saharan Africa, even though plague had long been endemic in the Great Lakes region of east Africa.

Population Decline In lands hard hit by plague, however, it took a century and more to begin recovery from the demographic consequences of epidemic disease. In 1300 China's population, already reduced by conflicts with the Mongols since the early thirteenth century, stood at eighty-five million. In 1400, after about seventy years of epidemic plague, Chinese numbers amounted to only seventy-five million. A century later demographic recovery was under way, and China's population rebounded to one hundred million.

European society also reeled from the effects of bubonic plague. From seventy-nine million in 1300, Europe's population dropped by almost 25 percent to sixty million in 1400. As in China, demographic recovery in Europe was under way in 1500 when the European population climbed to eighty-one million. Islamic societies in southwest Asia, Egypt, and north Africa also suffered devastating population losses, and demographic recovery took much longer there than in China and Europe. In Egypt human population probably did not reach preplague levels until the nineteenth century.

Social and Economic Effects Because of the heavy demographic toll that it levied, bubonic plague disrupted societies and economies throughout Eurasia and north Africa. Epidemics killed the young, the weak, and the old in especially high numbers, but they spared no group. Peasants and laborers, artisans and crafts workers, merchants and bankers, priests and nuns, rulers and bureaucrats all fell before the plague's onslaught. The disease caused severe labor shortages, which in turn generated social unrest.

In western Europe, for example, urban workers demanded higher wages, and many left their homes in search of better conditions. Political authorities responded by freezing wages and forbidding workers to leave their homes. For their part, peasants in the countryside also sought to improve their circumstances by moving to regions where landlords offered better terms. Landlords responded to that challenge by restricting the freedom of peasants to move and by reimposing labor requirements: in effect, the lords sought to reinstate conditions of serfdom (in which peasants are tied to the land) that they had allowed to lapse before the arrival of plague. As a result of sharply conflicting interests, disgruntled workers and peasants mounted a series of rebellions that rocked both the towns and the countryside of western Europe. Authorities eventually extinguished the revolts but only after considerable social disruption and loss of life.

By the seventeenth century the plague had lost much of its ferocity. Epidemics occurred more sporadically, and they did not seriously diminish human populations. Since the 1940s, antibiotic drugs have brought the disease largely under control among human populations, although it survives in rodent communities throughout much of the world.

Ming artisans won worldwide fame for their blue-and-white porcelain, which inspired the founders of the Delft porcelain factory in the Netherlands. This porcelain bottle dates from the seventeenth century.
Gift of Martin A. Ryerson/ Art Institute of Chicago.

Recovery in China: The Ming Dynasty

By the mid-fourteenth century, the Mongols' Yuan dynasty was experiencing very difficult times. Financial mismanagement led to serious economic difficulties, and political conflicts led to assassinations and factional fighting among the Mongols. In 1368, with bubonic plague raging, the Chinese forces toppled the Yuan dynasty, and the Mongols departed China en

What's Left Out? ▨ ▨ ▨ ▨ ▨

Royal and imperial states utilized the services of eunuchs to administer their realms since antiquity. In China, we know the Ming emperors believed eunuchs were less likely than other men to threaten their rule because they were unable to build their own dynasties. As a result, the imperial family employed several thousand eunuchs at any given time. But few histories explore the reasons men chose to become eunuchs, not to mention the difficulties and dangers of the procedure itself. In fact, although some males in imperial China were castrated as a means of punishment, most eunuchs voluntarily chose to undergo castration as adults. Motivations varied but included poverty, the desire for a more comfortable life, or the desire to gain access to the imperial court and to serve the imperial family. The rewards could be significant as some eunuchs gained considerable power and influence at the imperial court. But the costs were high: Ming medical manuals indicated that complications from the procedure included infection, hemorrhage, and even death; that the healing time was about 100 days; and that eunuchs could suffer negative health effects for the remainder of their lives. Does the enormous personal sacrifice involved in becoming a eunuch help explain the trust Ming emperors placed in them?

Source: Shih-shan Henry Tsai, *The Eunuchs in the Ming Dynasty* (New York: SUNY Press, 1995).

masse and returned to the steppes, leaving China in a state of both demographic and political turmoil. An increasing birthrate soon helped to replenish human numbers. Political recovery accompanied the demographic rebound.

Hongwu When the Yuan dynasty fell, the governance of China returned to Chinese hands. The new emperor came from a family so poor that he spent much of his youth as a beggar. Orphaned, he entered a Buddhist monastery to assure himself of food, clothing, and shelter. Because of his size and strength, he came to the notice of military commanders, and he made his way through the ranks to lead the rebellious forces that toppled the Yuan dynasty. In 1368 he became Emperor **Hongwu,** and he proclaimed the establishment of the **Ming** ("brilliant") **dynasty,** which lasted until 1644.

Ming Centralization Hongwu immediately set about eliminating all traces of Mongol rule and establishing a government on the model of traditional Chinese dynasties. Like the founders of several earlier Chinese dynasties (discussed in chapter 8), Hongwu had little interest in scholarly matters, but he reestablished the Confucian educational and civil service systems to ensure a supply of talented officials and bureaucrats. At the same time, he moved to centralize authority more tightly than ever before in Chinese history. In 1380, when he suspected his chief minister of involvement in a treasonous plot, Hongwu executed the minister and his bureaucratic allies and also abolished the minister's position altogether. From that time forward the Ming emperors ruled directly, without the aid of chief ministers, and they closely supervised imperial affairs.

Mandarins and Eunuchs The Ming emperors insisted on absolute obedience to the policies and initiatives of the central government. They relied heavily on the **mandarins,** a special class of powerful officials sent out as emissaries of the central government to ensure that local officials

implemented imperial policy. The Ming emperors also turned to **eunuchs** (castrated males) for governmental services. Earlier Chinese emperors, as well as rulers of other lands, had long relied on eunuchs because they could not generate families and build power bases that might challenge ruling houses. In keeping with their centralizing policy, however, the Ming emperors employed eunuchs much more extensively than any of their predecessors, in the expectation that servants whose fortunes depended exclusively on the emperors' favor would work especially diligently to advance the emperors' interests.

The employment of mandarins and eunuchs enhanced the authority of the central government. The tightly centralized administration instituted by the early Ming emperors lasted more than five hundred years. Although the dynasty fell in 1644 to Manchu invaders, who founded the **Qing dynasty,** the Manchus retained the administrative framework of the Ming state, which largely survived until the collapse of the Qing dynasty in 1911.

Economic Recovery While building a centralized administration, the Ming emperors also worked toward economic recovery from nomadic rule and epidemic disease. The new rulers conscripted laborers to rebuild irrigation systems that had fallen into disrepair during the previous century, and agricultural production surged as a result. At the same time, they promoted the manufacture of porcelain, lacquerware, and fine silk and cotton textiles. Ming rulers did not actively promote trade with other lands, but private Chinese merchants eagerly sought commercial opportunities and conducted a thriving business marketing Chinese products in ports and trading cities from Japan to the islands of southeast Asia. Meanwhile, domestic trade surged within China, reflecting increasing productivity and prosperity.

---

eunuchs (YOO-nihks)

Qing (ching)

Connecting the Sources

Individual experiences of the bubonic plague

The problem   The rapid spread of bubonic plague from China to most of Eurasia in the four-teenth century was a disaster that had profound and lasting effects on historical developments in China, central and southwest Asia, north Africa, and Europe, from massive population decline to economic disruption to social and political unrest. Although historians and scientists continue to dispute exact mortality rates, it is clear that the plague killed many millions of people, reducing populations wherever it struck by at least 25 percent, and sometimes much more. When explor-ing the history of disasters like the plague, it can be easy to forget that each individual who lived through the event—or died from it—had his or her own story, feelings, and family. In world history, while it is important to understand the "big picture," it is also important to remember that the "big picture" is always composed of millions of individual stories. These individual stories remind us that experiencing terrible events was not easier for individuals just because many suffered similar fates or because they occurred a long time ago.

The following documents are only two examples—one from Italy and the other from Syria—of how individuals experienced the plague as it tore through Europe and southwest Asia in 1348.

The documents   Read the documents below, and consider carefully the questions that follow.

Document 1:

Francesco Petrarca (1304–1374) was an Italian scholar and early humanist who lived through the plague that struck Italy in 1348. Scholars believe he wrote the following letter, known as the Met-rica, to himself in about 1348.

> *O what has come over me? Where are the violent fates pushing me back to? I see passing by, in headlong flight, time which makes the world a fleeting place. I observe about me dying throngs of both young and old, and nowhere is there a refuge. No haven beckons in any part of the globe, nor can any hope of longed for salvation be seen. Wherever I turn my frightened eyes, their gaze is troubled by continual funerals: the churches groan encumbered with biers, and, without last respects, the corpses of the noble and the commoner lie in confusion alongside each other. The last hour of life comes to mind, and, obliged to recollect my misfortunes, I recall the flocks of dear ones who have departed, and the conversations of friends, the sweet faces which suddenly vanished, and the hallowed ground now insufficient for repeated burials. This is what the people of Italy bemoan, weakened by so many deaths; this is what France laments, exhausted and stripped of inhabitants; the same goes for other peoples, under whatever skies they reside. Either it is the wrath of God, for certainly I would think that our misdeeds deserve it, or it is just the harsh assault of the stars in their perpetually changing conjunctions. . . . Dense shadows have covered me with fear. For whosoever thinks they can recall death and look upon the moment of their passing with fearless face is either mistaken or mad, or, if he is fully aware, then he is very courageous.*

> What must it have been like for Petrarca to see so many friends, neighbors, and fellow city dwellers die in such great num-bers from the plague?

Document 2:

Ibn al-Wardi (ca. 1290–1349) was a Muslim writer who lived and worked in Aleppo (modern Syria). He wrote the following "Essay on the Report of the Pestilence" after the plague struck his region in the spring of 1348. The next year, in March 1349, al-Wardi himself died of the plague.

This plague is for the Muslims a martyrdom and a reward, and for the disbelievers a punishment and a rebuke. . . . I take refuge in God from the yoke of the plague. Its high explosion has burst into all countries and was an examiner of astonishing things. Its sudden attacks perplex the people. The plague chases the screaming without pity and does not accept a treasure for ransom. Its engine is far-reaching. The plague enters into the house and swears it will not leave except with all of its inhabitants. . . . Among the benefits of this . . . is the removal of one's hopes and the improvement of his earthly works. It awakens men from their indifference for the provisioning of their final journey. . . . Come then, seek the aid of God Almighty for raising the plague, for He is the best helper. Oh God, we call You better than anyone did before. We call You to raise from us the pestilence and plague. . . . We plead with You, by the most honored of the advocates, Muhammad, the Prophet of mercy, that You take away from us this distress. Protect us from the evil and the torture and preserve us.

> What role did God play in the outbreak of the plague, according to al-Wardi?

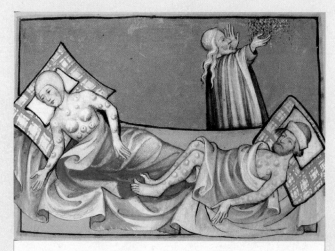

This 1411 illustration of plague-infected people is taken from the Toggenburg Bible.
Fine Art/Corbis Historical/Getty Images

Questions

1. What can these sources definitively tell you about the lives of the people who produced them? What **facts** can be gleaned from these sources?

2. In Document 1, what is Petrarca's state of mind? How does he describe the effects of the plague on himself and his loved ones? Do you think his reaction to the plague would have been shared by others in Italy, or might others have reacted differently?

3. In Document 2, what is the cause of the plague, according to al-Wardi? How does he describe the effects of the plague on those around him? What kinds of advantages does he argue that the plague has brought?

4. For both documents, how do each of the men view God's role in the plague? What are the similarities between the two excerpts? What are the differences? Finally, do you think their experience of the plague is representative, given that both were highly educated men? Why or why not? How useful are individual stories in interpreting and understanding world historical events?

Source Citations: **Document 1:** http://www.brown.edu/Departments/Italian_Studies/dweb/plague/perspectives/petrarca2.php
Document 2: John Aberth, *The First Horseman: Disease in Human History* (Upper Saddle River, N.J.: Pearson Prentice Hall, 2007), pp. 42–43.

English forces besiege a French citadel during the Hundred Years' War (1337–1453). Note that the besiegers on the left side of this manuscript illustration employ small firearms that launch gunpowder bombs. Although essentially a dynastic conflict between two European ruling houses, the series of conflicts that constituted the Hundred Years' War had a significant impact on military technology and strategy and were a major influence on developing notions of French and English patriotism.

Album/Alamy Stock Photo

Cultural Revival In addition to political and economic recovery, the Ming dynasty sponsored a kind of cultural revival in China. Emperor Hongwu tried to eradicate all signs of the recent nomadic occupation by discouraging the use of Mongol names and the wearing of Mongol dress. Ming emperors actively promoted Chinese cultural traditions, particularly the Confucian and neo-Confucian schools. Hongwu's successor, **Yongle,** organized the preparation of a vast encyclopedia that compiled all significant works of Chinese history, philosophy, and literature. This *Yongle Encyclopedia* ran to almost twenty-three thousand manuscript rolls, each equivalent to a medium-size book. The government originally planned to issue a printed edition of the encyclopedia but abandoned the project because of its enormous expense. Nevertheless, the *Yongle Encyclopedia* was a remarkable anthology, and it signaled the Ming rulers' interest in supporting native Chinese cultural traditions.

Recovery in Europe: State Building

Demographic recovery strengthened states in Europe as it did in China. In Europe, however, political authority rested with a series of regional states rather than a centralized empire. By the late fifteenth century, states in Italy, Spain, France, England, and Russia had devised techniques of government that vastly enhanced their power.

During the later middle ages (1300–1500), internal problems as well as bubonic plague complicated European political

Yongle (YAWNG-leh)

Portrait of the first Hongwu emperor (r. 1368–1398).
Pictures from History/Newscom.

and subjects, which supplemented the income that rulers received from their subordinates. The second was the maintenance of large standing armies, which, particularly since the Hundred Years' War, were often composed of mercenary forces and equipped with gunpowder weapons, supported by state funds.

Italian States The state-building process began in Italy, where profits from industrial production and trade enriched the major cities. The principal Italian states—the city-states of Milan, Venice, and Florence, the papal state based in Rome, and the kingdom of Naples—needed large numbers of officials to administer their complex affairs. They also needed ready access to military forces that could protect their interests. Beginning as early as the thirteenth century, the Italian city-states financed those needs by levying direct taxes and issuing long-term bonds that they repaid from treasury receipts. With fresh sources of finance, the principal Italian states strengthened their authority within their own boundaries and between them controlled public affairs in most of the Italian peninsula.

France and England During the fourteenth and fifteenth centuries, Italian administrative methods made their way beyond the Alps. Partly because of the enormous expenses they incurred during the Hundred Years' War, the kings of France and England began to levy direct taxes and assemble powerful armies. The French kings taxed sales, hearths, and salt; their English counterparts instituted annual taxes on hearths (the number of fireplaces within each home), individuals, and plow teams. Rulers in both lands asserted the authority of the central government over the nobility. The English kings did not establish a standing army, but they were able to raise powerful forces when rebellion threatened public order. In France, however, King Louis XI (reigned 1461–1483) maintained a permanent army of about fifteen thousand troops, many of them professional mercenary soldiers equipped with firearms. Because the high expense of maintaining such forces was beyond the means of the nobility, Louis and his successors enjoyed a decisive edge over ambitious subordinates seeking to challenge royal authority or build local power bases.

affairs. The Holy Roman Empire survived in name, but after the mid-thirteenth century effective authority lay with the German princes and the Italian city-states rather than the emperor. In Spain descendants of Muslim conquerors held the kingdom of Granada in the southern portion of the Iberian peninsula. The kings of France and England sparred constantly over lands claimed by both. Their hostilities eventually resulted in the **Hundred Years' War** (1337–1453), a protracted series of intermittent campaigns in which the warring factions sought control of lands in France. Russia had even more difficult problems. In the late 1230s Mongol armies conquered the flourishing commercial center of Kiev, and descendants of Chinggis Khan extracted tribute from Russia for almost 250 years thereafter. In the fifteenth century, however, the Mongol states fell into disorder, giving rise to a vast power vacuum in Russia.

Taxes and Armies By the late fifteenth century, however, regional states in western Europe had greatly strengthened their societies, and some had also laid the foundations for the emergence of powerful monarchies. The state-building efforts of the later middle ages involved two especially important elements. The first was the development of fresh sources of finance, usually through new taxes levied directly on citizens

Spain The process of state building was most dramatic in Spain, where the marriage in 1469 of Fernando of Aragon and Isabel of Castile united the two wealthiest and most important Iberian realms. Receipts from the sales tax, the primary source of royal income, supported a powerful standing army. Under Fernando and Isabel, popularly known as the Catholic Kings, Christian forces completed the *reconquista* (the reconquering of the Iberian peninsula from Muslim kingdoms) by conquering the kingdom of Granada and absorbing it into their state in 1492. The Catholic Kings also projected their authority beyond Iberia. When a French army threatened the kingdom of Naples in 1494, they seized southern Italy, and by 1559 Spanish forces had established their hegemony throughout most of the Italian peninsula. Fernando and Isabel also sought to make a place for Spain in the markets of Asia by sponsoring Christopher Columbus's quest for a western route to China.

Russia State building took place in Russia as well as in western Europe. After the fourteenth century, as Mongol power waned, Russian princes sought to expand their territories. Most successful among them were the grand princes of Moscow. As early as the mid-fourteenth century, the princes began the process of "gathering the Russian land" by acquiring territories surrounding their strategically located commercial town of Moscow on the Volga River. In 1480 Grand Prince Ivan III (reigned 1462–1505), later known as Ivan the Great, stopped paying tribute to the Mongol khan. By refusing to acknowledge the khan's supremacy, Ivan in effect declared Russian independence from Mongol rule. He then made Moscow the center of a large and powerful state. His territorial annexations were impressive: Muscovy, the principality ruled from Moscow, almost tripled in size as he brought Russian-speaking peoples into his realm. The most important addition to his possessions came with the acquisition of the prosperous trading city of Novgorod. A hub of the lucrative fur trade and a member of the Hanseatic League of Baltic commercial cities, Novgorod was an autonomous city-state that governed its affairs through a town council. The city's merchants had strong ties to Poland and Lithuania to the west, and Ivan wanted to make sure that Novgorod's prosperity did not benefit neighboring states. Thus he demanded that the city acknowledge his authority. After crushing a futile uprising organized by Novgorod's merchants, he ended the city's independence in 1478 and absorbed it into the expansive Muscovite state. With the aid of Novgorod's wealth, Ivan was then able to build a strong centralized government modeled on the Byzantine Empire. Indeed, Ivan went so far as to call himself *tsar* (sometimes spelled *czar*)—a Russianized form of the term *caesar,* which Byzantine rulers had borrowed from the classical Roman Empire to signify their imperial status.

Competition between European states intensified as they tightened their authority in their territories. This competition led to frequent small-scale wars between European states, and it encouraged the rapid development of military and naval technology. As states sought technological advantages over their neighbors, they encouraged the refinement and improvement of weapons, ships, and sails. When one state acquired powerful weapons—such as personal firearms or ships equipped with cannons—neighboring states sought more advanced devices in the interests of security. Thus technological innovations vastly strengthened European armies just as they began to venture again into the larger world.

Recovery in Europe: The Renaissance

Demographic recovery and state-building efforts in Europe coincided with a remarkable cultural flowering known as the **Renaissance.** The French word *renaissance* means "rebirth," and it refers to a period of artistic and intellectual creativity that took place from the fourteenth to the sixteenth century and that reflected the continuing development of a sophisticated urban society, particularly in western Europe. Painters, sculptors, and architects of the Renaissance era drew inspiration from classical Greek and Roman artists rather than from their medieval predecessors. They admired the convincing realism of classical sculpture and the stately simplicity of classical architecture. In their efforts to revive classical aesthetic standards, they transformed European art. Meanwhile, Renaissance scholars known as humanists looked to classical rather than medieval literary models, and they sought to update medieval moral thought and adapt it to the needs of a bustling urban society.

Italian Renaissance Art Just as they pioneered new techniques of statecraft, the Italian city-states also sponsored Renaissance innovations in art and architecture. In search of realistic depictions, Italian artists studied the human form and represented the emotions of their subjects. Italian painters such as Masaccio (1401–1428) and **Leonardo da Vinci** (1452–1519) relied on the technique of linear perspective to represent the three dimensions of real life on flat, two-dimensional surfaces. Sculptors such as Donatello (1386–1466) and **Michelangelo Buonarotti** (1475–1564) sought to depict their subjects in natural poses that reflected the actual workings of

Brunelleschi's magnificent dome on the cathedral of Florence dominates the city's skyline even today.
Adam Sylvester/Science Source

Renaissance (ren-uh-SAHNS)

Leonardo da Vinci (lee-uh-NAHR-doh duh-VIHN-chee)

Michelangelo Buonarotti (mik-uhl AN-juh-low baw-nahr-RAW-tee)

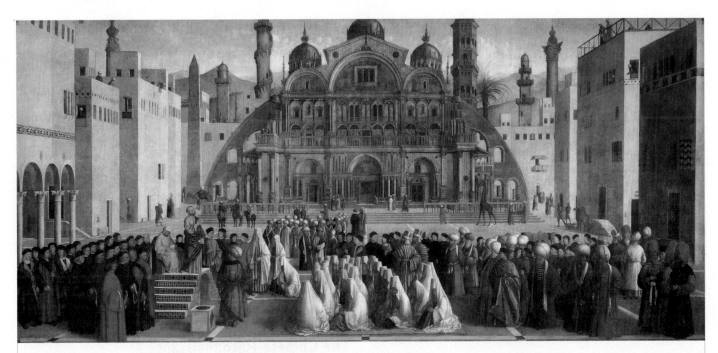

A painting by Venetian artists Gentile and Giovanni Bellini reflects Renaissance interests in the Muslim world. The painting depicts St. Mark (standing in the pulpit, left) preaching in Alexandria, Egypt. The audience includes Egyptians, Berbers, Turks, Persians, Ethiopians, and Mongols. Note also the technique of linear perspective to depict figures in realistic relationship to one another and their surroundings. How does linear perspective lend a sense of depth to this scene?
Alinari Archives/Getty Images

human muscles rather than in the awkward and rigid postures often found in earlier sculptures.

Renaissance Architecture Renaissance architects designed buildings in the simple, elegant style preferred by their classical Greek and Roman predecessors. Their most impressive achievement was the construction of domed buildings—awesome structures that enclosed large spaces but kept them open and airy under massive domes. Roman architects had built domes, but their technology and engineering did not survive the collapse of the Roman Empire. Inspired by the Pantheon, a handsome Roman temple constructed in the second century C.E., the Florentine architect Filippo Brunelleschi (1377–1446) reinvented equipment and designs for a large dome. During the 1420s and 1430s, he oversaw the construction of a magnificent dome on the cathedral of Florence. Residents of Florence took Brunelleschi's dome as a symbol of the city's wealth and its leadership in artistic and cultural affairs.

The Humanists Like Renaissance artists and architects, scholars and literary figures known as humanists also drew inspiration from classical models. The term *humanist* referred to scholars interested in the humanities—literature, history, and moral philosophy. They had little to do with the secular and often antireligious interests of movements that go under the name humanism today: on the contrary,

Renaissance humanists were deeply committed to Christianity. Several humanists worked diligently to prepare accurate texts and translations of the New Testament and other Christian writings. Most notable of them was **Desiderius Erasmus** of Rotterdam (1466–1536), who in 1516 published the first edition of the Greek New Testament along with a revised Latin translation and copious annotations. Other humanists drew inspiration from the intense spirituality and high moral standards of early Christianity and promoted those values in their society.

Humanists scorned the dense and often convoluted writing style of the scholastic theologians (discussed in chapter 19). Instead, they preferred the elegant and polished language of classical Greek and Roman authors and the early church fathers, whose works they considered more engaging and more persuasive than the weighty tomes of medieval philosophers and theologians. Thus humanists such as the Florentine **Francesco Petrarca,** also known in English as Petrarch (1304–1374), traveled throughout Europe searching for manuscripts of classical works. In the monastic libraries of Italy, Switzerland, and southern France, they found hundreds of Latin writings that medieval scholars had overlooked. During the fifteenth century, Italian humanists

Desiderius Erasmus (des-i-DEER-ee-uhs ih-raz-muhs)
Francesco Petrarca (frahn-CHES-koh PEE-trahrk-a)

became acquainted with Byzantine scholars and enlarged the body of classical Greek as well as Latin works available to scholars.

Humanist Moral Thought Classical Greek and Latin values encouraged the humanists to reconsider medieval ethical teachings. Medieval moral philosophers had taught that the most honorable calling was that of monks and nuns who withdrew from the world and dedicated their lives to prayer, contemplation, and the glorification of God, but the humanists drew inspiration from classical authors such as Cicero, who demonstrated that it was possible to lead a morally virtuous life while participating actively in the affairs of the world. Renaissance humanists argued that it was perfectly honorable for Christians to enter into marriage, business relationships, and public affairs, and they offered a spirited defense for those who rejected the cloister in favor of an active life in society. Humanist moral thought thus represented an effort to reconcile Christian values and ethics with the increasingly urban and commercial society of Renaissance Europe.

Renaissance Europe and the Larger World Quite apart from their conscious effort to draw inspiration from classical antiquity, Renaissance art and thought also reflected increasing European participation in the affairs of the Eastern Hemisphere. As merchants linked Europe to the larger hemispheric economy, European peoples experienced increased prosperity that enabled them to invest resources in artistic production and support for scholarship. Renaissance painters filled their canvases with images of silk garments, ceramic vessels, lacquered wood, spice jars, foreign peoples, and exotic animals that had recently come to European attention. Princes and wealthy patrons commissioned hundreds of these paintings that brought a cosmopolitan look to their palaces, residences, and places of business.

This enchantment with the larger world extended also into the realm of ideas. The Italian humanist Giovanni **Pico della Mirandola** (1463–1494) perhaps best reflected the enthusiasm of Renaissance scholars to comprehend the world beyond western Europe. In his exuberant *Oration on the Dignity of Man* (1486), Pico made a spirited effort to harmonize the divergent teachings of Plato, Aristotle, Judaism, Christianity, and Islam, not to mention Zoroastrianism and various occult and mystical traditions. His ambitious endeavor was ultimately unsuccessful: Pico had limited information about several of the traditions he sought to reconcile, and he sometimes offered superficial interpretations of doctrines that he imperfectly understood. Nevertheless, his *Oration* gave eloquent voice to the burning desire of many European scholars to understand the larger world. It is not surprising that just as Pico and other Renaissance humanists were undertaking that effort, European mariners were organizing expeditions to explore the lands and seas beyond Christendom.

Zheng He (jung ha)

EXPLORATION AND COLONIZATION

As peoples of the Eastern Hemisphere recovered from demographic collapse and restored order to their societies, they also sought to revive the networks of long-distance trade and communication that epidemic plague had disrupted. Most active in that effort were China and western Europe—the two societies that recovered most rapidly from the disasters of the fourteenth century. During the early Ming dynasty, Chinese ports accommodated foreign traders, and mariners mounted a series of enormous naval expeditions that visited almost all parts of the Indian Ocean basin. Meanwhile, Europeans ventured from the Mediterranean into the Atlantic Ocean, which served as a highway to sub-Saharan Africa and the Indian Ocean basin. By the end of the fifteenth century, Europeans not only had established sea lanes to India but also had made several return voyages to the American continents, thus inaugurating a process that brought all the world's peoples into permanent and sustained interaction.

The Chinese Reconnaissance of the Indian Ocean Basin

Having ousted the Mongols, the early Ming emperors were not eager to have large numbers of foreigners residing in China. Yet the emperors permitted foreign merchants to trade in the closely supervised ports of Quanzhou and Guangzhou, where they obtained Chinese silk, porcelain, and manufactured goods in exchange for pearls, gems, spices, cotton fabrics, and exotic products such as tortoise shells and animal skins. The early Ming emperors also refurbished the large Chinese navy built during the Song dynasty, and they allowed Chinese merchants to participate in overseas trading ventures in Japan and southeast Asia.

Zheng He's Expeditions Moreover, for almost thirty years, the Ming government sponsored a series of seven ambitious naval expeditions designed to establish a Chinese presence in the Indian Ocean basin. Emperor Yongle organized the expeditions for two main purposes: to impose imperial control over foreign trade with China and to impress foreign peoples with the power and might that the Ming dynasty had restored to China. Indeed, he might well have hoped to extend the tributary system, by which Chinese dynasties traditionally recognized foreign peoples, to lands in the Indian Ocean basin.

The expeditions took place between 1405 and 1433. Leading them was the eunuch admiral **Zheng He,** a Muslim from Yunnan in southwestern China who rose through the ranks of eunuch administrators to become a trusted adviser of Yongle. Zheng He embarked on each voyage with an awesome fleet of vessels complemented by armed forces large enough to overcome resistance at any port where the expedition called. On the first voyage, for example, Zheng He's fleet consisted of 317 ships accompanied by almost twenty-eight thousand armed troops. Many of these vessels were mammoth,

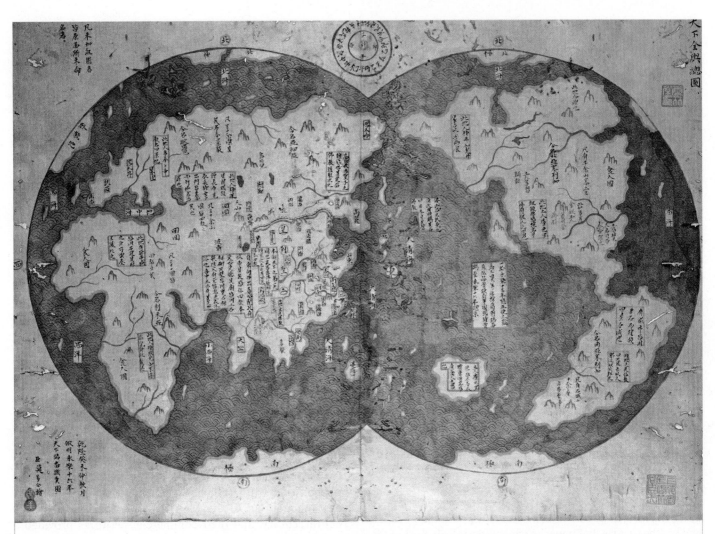

The Kangnido Map (1470) is one of the few surviving large-scale maps from east Asia before modern times. Produced in Korea, it draws on Chinese and Muslim sources, while exaggerating the size of the Korean peninsula.

Universal History Archive/Universal Images Group/Getty Images

nine-masted "treasure ships" with four decks capable of accommodating five hundred or more passengers, as well as huge stores of cargo. Measuring up to 124 meters (408 feet) long and 51 meters (166 feet) wide, these treasure ships were by far the largest marine craft the world had ever seen.

On the first three voyages, Zheng He took his fleet to southeast Asia, India, and Ceylon. The fourth expedition went to the Persian Gulf and Arabia, and later expeditions ventured down the east African coast, calling at ports as far south as Malindi in modern Kenya. Throughout his travels, Zheng He liberally dispensed gifts of Chinese silk, porcelain, and other goods. In return he received rich and unusual presents from his hosts, including African zebras and giraffes, which ended their days in the Ming imperial zoo. Zheng He and his companions paid respect to the local deities and customs they encountered, and in Ceylon they erected a monument honoring Buddha, Allah, and Vishnu.

Chinese Naval Power Zheng He generally sought to attain his goals through diplomacy. For the most part, his large contingents of armed troops overawed his hosts, and he had little need to engage in hostilities. But a contemporary reported that Zheng He walked like a tiger, and he did not shrink from violence when he considered it necessary to impress foreign peoples with China's military might. He ruthlessly suppressed pirates who had long plagued Chinese and southeast Asian waters. He also intervened in a civil disturbance to establish his authority in Ceylon, and he made displays of military force when local officials threatened his fleet in Arabia and east Africa. The seven expeditions established a Chinese presence and reputation in the Indian Ocean basin. Returning from his fourth voyage, Zheng He brought envoys from thirty states who traveled to China and paid their respects at the Ming court.

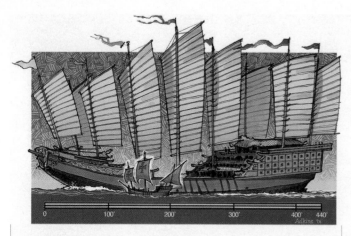

An artist's impression of the comparative size of one of the great treasure ships of Ming dynasty admiral Zheng He and one of the much smaller ships in the fleet in which Columbus sailed from Europe to the Americas.
Jan Adkins.

End of the Voyages Yet suddenly, in the mid-1430s, the Ming emperors decided to end the expeditions. Confucian ministers, who mistrusted Zheng He and the eunuchs who supported the voyages, argued that resources committed to the expensive expeditions would go to better uses if devoted to agriculture. Moreover, during the 1420s and 1430s the Mongols mounted a new military threat from the northwest, and land forces urgently needed financial support.

Thus in 1433, after Zheng He's seventh voyage, the expeditions ended. Chinese merchants continued to trade in Japan and southeast Asia, but imperial officials destroyed most of the nautical charts that Zheng He had carefully prepared and gave up any plans to maintain a Chinese presence in the Indian Ocean. The decommissioned treasure ships sat in harbors until they rotted away, and Chinese craftsmen forgot the technology of building such large vessels. Yet Zheng He's voyages demonstrated clearly that China could exercise military, political, and economic influence throughout the Indian Ocean basin.

European Exploration in the Atlantic and Indian Oceans

As Chinese fleets reconnoitered the Indian Ocean, European mariners were preparing to enter both the Atlantic and the Indian Ocean basins. Unlike Zheng He and his companions, Europeans did not venture onto the seas in the interests of diplomacy or in hopes of establishing a political and military reputation in foreign lands. Instead, they acted on two different but complementary motives: the desire to expand the boundaries of Roman Catholic Christianity and the desire to profit from commercial opportunities.

Portuguese Exploration The experience of Portugal illustrates that mixture of motives. Though Portuguese merchants were not especially prominent in trading circles, Portuguese fishermen had a long tradition of seafaring in the stormy Atlantic Ocean. Building on that experience, Portuguese mariners emerged as the early leaders in both Atlantic exploration and the search for a sea route to Asian markets through the Indian Ocean. During the fifteenth century Prince Henrique of Portugal, often called **Prince Henry the Navigator,** embarked on an ambitious campaign to spread Christianity and increase Portuguese influence on the seas. In 1415 he watched as Portuguese forces seized the Moroccan city of **Ceuta,** which guarded the Strait of Gibraltar from the south. He regarded his victory both as a blow against Islam and as a strategic move enabling Christian vessels to move freely between the Mediterranean and the Atlantic.

Colonization of the Atlantic Islands Following the capture of Ceuta, Henrique encouraged Portuguese mariners to venture into the Atlantic. During their voyages they discovered the Madeiras and Azores Islands, all uninhabited, which they soon colonized. They also made an unsuccessful effort to occupy the Canary Islands, inhabited by indigenous peoples but claimed since the early fifteenth century by the kingdom of Castile. Later discoveries included the Cape Verde islands, Fernando Po, São Tomé, and Principe off the west African coast. Because these Atlantic islands enjoyed fertile soils and a Mediterranean climate, Portuguese entrepreneurs soon began to cultivate sugarcane there, often in collaboration with Italian investors. Italians had financed sugar plantations in the Mediterranean islands since the twelfth century, and their commercial networks provided a ready means to distribute sugar to Europeans, who were rapidly developing a taste for sweets.

Slave Trade During the middle decades of the fifteenth century, a series of Portuguese fleets also explored the west African coast, each expedition proceeding a bit farther than its predecessor. Originally, the Portuguese traded guns, textiles, and other manufactured items for African gold and slaves. Portuguese traders took full advantage of the long-established African commerce in slaves, but they also changed the nature of the **slave trade** by dramatically increasing its volume and by sending slaves to new destinations. By the mid-fifteenth century, the Portuguese forced thousands of slaves annually to their forts on islands off the African coast. They sent most of their human cargo to recently founded sugar plantations in the Atlantic islands, where enslaved people worked as laborers, although some worked as domestic servants in Europe. The use of African slaves to perform heavy labor on commercial plantations soon became common practice, and it fueled the development of a huge, Atlantic-wide trade that would eventually deliver as many as twelve million enslaved Africans to destinations in North America, South America, and the Caribbean region.

Ceuta (SYOO-tuh)

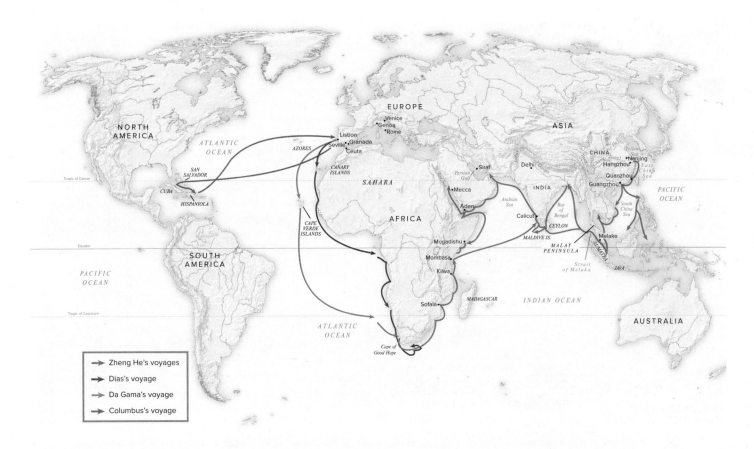

MAP 21.3   Chinese and European voyages of exploration, 1405–1498.

Although they followed different routes, all the voyagers represented on this map were seeking destinations in the Indian Ocean basin.

Why did Chinese and Iberian mariners want to establish a presence in the Indian Ocean during the fifteenth century?

Indian Ocean Trade While some Portuguese mariners traded profitably in west Africa, others sought to enter the lucrative trade in Asian silk and spices. A sea route to Asian markets would enable Portuguese merchants to avoid Muslim and Italian intermediaries in the Mediterranean and over land. Almost all Asian luxury goods reached European markets through such intermediaries, which prevented the Portuguese (and others) from participating directly in the flourishing commercial world of the Indian Ocean basin. Toward the end of the fifteenth century, Portuguese mariners began to search seriously for a sea lane from Europe around Africa and into the Indian Ocean. By 1488 **Bartolomeu Dias** had sailed around the Cape of Good Hope and entered the Indian Ocean. Restless because of the long journey and distance from home, the crew forced Dias to return immediately to Portugal, but his voyage proved that it was possible to sail from Europe to the Indian Ocean. In 1497 Vasco da Gama departed Portugal with the intention of sailing to India. After rounding the Cape of Good Hope, he cruised up the east African coast and found a Muslim pilot who showed him how to take advantage of the seasonal monsoon winds to sail across the Arabian Sea to India. In 1498 he arrived at Calicut,

and by 1499 he had returned to Lisbon with a hugely profitable cargo of pepper and spices.

During the following century, Portuguese merchants and mariners dominated trade between Europe and Asia. Indeed, they attempted to control all shipping in the Indian Ocean. Their ships, armed with cannons, were able to overpower the vessels of Arabs, Persians, Indians, southeast Asians, and others who sailed the Indian Ocean. They did not have enough ships to police the entire Indian Ocean, however, so most merchants easily evaded their efforts to control the region's commerce. Nevertheless, the entry of Portuguese mariners into the Indian Ocean signaled the beginning of European attempts to dominate commerce in Asia.

Christopher Columbus While Portuguese seafarers sought a sea route around Africa to India, the Genoese mariner Cristoforo Colombo, known in English as **Christopher Columbus,** conceived the idea of sailing west to reach Asian markets. Because geographers in the Eastern Hemisphere knew nothing of the Americas, Columbus's notion made a certain amount of sense, although many doubted that his plan could lead to profitable trade because of the long distances

Although Christopher Columbus believed that he had sailed into Asian waters, later mariners soon realized that the Americas were continents unknown to geographers of the eastern hemisphere. This map, prepared in 1565 by Paulo Forlani, shows that by the mid-sixteenth century, European geographers had acquired a rough but accurate understanding of South America and the Atlantic coastline of North America.
Everett Collection Historical/Alamy Stock Photo

How the Past Shapes the Future

The Diffusion of Technologies

When European mariners set out to spread Christianity and explore commercial possibilities in the Atlantic and Indian ocean basins, they employed a combination of technologies that had been diffused over the centuries from east and southwest Asia. One particularly effective combination was the use of technologies of transportation such as the compass (and later the astrolabe) along with technologies of warfare—especially cannons mounted on the sides of their ships. These diffused technologies allowed Europeans the ability to travel effectively by sea and to compel—using deadly force—vessels from other regions to comply with their desire to dominate trade. While Europeans were not able to dominate maritime trade completely, consider how important their use and adaptation of a variety of diffused technologies to suit their own goals were in their ability to explore the world's oceans between the fifteenth and the eighteenth centuries and how much these innovations changed the world once Europeans made contact with the Americas in the late fifteenth century.

involved. After the king of Portugal declined to sponsor an expedition to test Columbus's plan, the Catholic Kings, Fernando and Isabel of Spain, agreed to underwrite a voyage. In 1492 Columbus set sail. After a stop in the Canary Islands to take on supplies and make repairs, his fleet of three ships crossed the Atlantic Ocean, reaching land at San Salvador (Watling Island) in the Bahamas.

Columbus returned to Spain without the gold, silk, and spices that he had expected to find, but he persistently argued that he had reached islands near the Asian mainland and the markets of China and Japan. Although he made three more voyages to the Caribbean region, Columbus never acknowledged that his expeditions had not reached Asia. News of his voyages spread rapidly, however, and by the end of the fifteenth century other mariners had explored the Caribbean and the American continents enough to realize that the Western Hemisphere constituted a world apart from Europe, Asia, and Africa.

CONCLUSION

For millennia, peoples of different societies had traded, communicated, and interacted. But between 1000 and 1500 C.E., the intensity of these interactions increased dramatically as technologies of transportation improved. By 1500 the Indian Ocean served as a highway linking peoples from China to east Africa, and overland traffic kept the Silk Roads busy from China to the Mediterranean Sea, allowing people like Ibn Battuta and Zheng He to travel many thousands of miles. Trade goods, diplomatic missions, religious faiths, technological skills, agricultural crops, and—unfortunately for many—disease pathogens all moved readily over the sea lanes and the Silk Roads, and they profoundly influenced the development of societies throughout the Eastern Hemisphere.

By the year 1500, the world stood on the brink of a new era in the experience of humankind. As a result of European oceanic voyages across the Atlantic, peoples of the world's three major geographic zones—the the Eastern Hemisphere, the Western Hemisphere, and Oceania—were poised to enter into permanent and sustained interaction. The results of their engagements were profitable and beneficial for some peoples but difficult and even disastrous for others. The formation and reconfiguration of global networks of power, communication, and exchange that followed from those interactions rank among the most prominent themes of modern world history, and it is impossible to comprehend them except in context of the acceleration of cross-cultural interaction in the era 1000 to 1500.

STUDY TERMS

Bartolomeu Dias (445)	mandarin (435)
bubonic plague (433)	Marco Polo (427)
Ceuta (444)	Melaka (426)
Christopher Columbus (445)	Michelangelo Buonarotti (440)
Desiderius Erasmus (441)	Ming dynasty (435)
eunuch (435)	*qadi* (424)
Francesco Petrarca (441)	Qing dynasty (435)
Hongwu (435)	Pico della Mirandola (442)
humanist (441)	Prince Henry the
Hundred Years' War (439)	Navigator (444)
Ibn Battuta (424)	Rabban Sauma (428)
John of Montecorvino (430)	Renaissance (440)
Leonardo da Vinci (440)	sharia (428)
little ice age (433)	slave trade (444)

Sufis (429)	*Yongle Encyclopedia* (438)
tsar (440)	Zheng He (442)
Yongle (438)	

FOR FURTHER READING

John Aberth. *The First Horseman: Disease in Human History.* London, 2006. Global exploration of the dramatic effects disease has had on human communities over time.

Janet L. Abu-Lughod. *Before European Hegemony: The World System, A.D. 1250-1350.* New York, 1989. An important study of long-distance trade networks during the Mongol era.

Jerry H. Bentley. *Old World Encounters: Cross-Cultural Contacts and Exchanges in Pre-Modern Times.* New York, 1993. Studies cultural and religious exchanges in the Eastern Hemisphere before 1500 C.E.

Timothy Brook. *The Troubled Empire: China in the Yuan and Ming Dynasties.* Cambridge, MA, 2010. Well-written overview of the values, ecology, and interstate connections of China in this period.

Jerry Brotton. *The Renaissance Bazaar: From the Silk Road to Michelangelo.* Oxford, 2002. A provocative and well-illustrated study arguing that encounters in the larger world deeply influenced Renaissance cultural development in Europe.

K. N. Chaudhuri. *Asia before Europe: Economy and Civilisation of the Indian Ocean from the Rise of Islam to 1750.* Cambridge, 1990. Controversial and penetrating analysis of economic, social, and cultural structures shaping societies of the Indian Ocean basin.

Ross E. Dunn. *The Adventures of Ibn Battuta: A Muslim Traveler of the 14th Century: With a New Preface.* Berkeley, 2012. Fascinating reconstruction of Ibn Battuta's travels and experiences.

Brian Fagan. *The Little Ice Age: How Climate Made History, 1300-1850.* New York, 2000. Popular account of the little ice age, with emphasis on its effects in Europe and North America.

Monica Green, ed. *Pandemic Disease in the Medieval World: Rethinking the Black Death.* Amsterdam, 2015. Series of essays written by historians and scientists on the history and significance of the Black Death in global perspective.

John Larner. *Marco Polo and the Discovery of the World.* New Haven, Conn., 1999. Excellent study of Marco Polo and his significance, based on a thorough review of both textual evidence and recent scholarship.

Louise L. Levathes. *When China Ruled the Seas: The Treasure Fleet of the Dragon Throne, 1405-1433.* New York, 1994. Excellent popular account of Zheng He's voyages.

Karen Raber. *A Cultural History of Women in the Renaissance.* London, 2015. Explores the way the social and scientific changes of the Renaissance affected ideologies of gender and the lived experiences of women.

Glossary & Pronunciation Guide

AH *a* sound, as in *car, father*
IH short *i* sound, as in *fit, his, mirror*
OO long *o* sound, as in *ooze, tool, crew*
UH short *u* sound, as in *up, cut, color*
A short *a* sound, as in *asp, fat, parrot*
EE long *e* sound, as in *even, meet, money*
OH long *o* sound, as in *open, go, tone*
EH short *e* sound, as in *ten, elf, berry*
AY long *a* sound, as in *ape, date, play*
EYE long *i* sound, as in *ice, high, bite*
OW diphthong *o* sound, as in *cow, how, bow*
AW diphthong *a* sound, as in *awful, paw, law*

Note on emphasis: Syllables in capital letters receive the accent. If there is no syllable in capitals, then all syllables get equal accent.

Abbasid dynasty (ah-BAH-sihd) Cosmopolitan Arabic dynasty (750–1258) that replaced the Umayyads; founded by Abu al-Abbas and reached its peak under Harun al-Rashid.

Abdül Hamid II Reigned 1876–1909 C.E. Sultan of the Ottoman Empire whose despotic style of rule led to the creation of many opposition groups and to his deposition by dissidents in 1909.

Abolitionism Antislavery movement.

Absolutism Political philosophy that stressed the divine right theory of kingship: the French king Louis XIV was the classic example.

Abu Bakr (ah-BOO BAHK-uhr) First caliph after the death of Muhammad.

Achaemenid empire (ah-KEE-muh-nid) First great Persian empire (558–330 B.C.E.), which began under Cyrus and reached its peak under Darius.

Adam Smith 1723–1790. Scottish philosopher and founder of modern political economy, and a key figure in the Scottish Enlightenment. Best known for *An Inquiry into the Nature and Causes of the Wealth of Nations,* published in 1776.

Adolf Hitler 1889–1945 C.E. German politician and leader of the Nazi Party, who came to power in 1933. He initiated the European theater of World War II by invading Poland in 1939 and oversaw the establishment of death camps that resulted in more than ten million deaths.

Adwa 1896 Battle in which the Ethiopians badly defeated would-be Italian conquerors.

Aegean Sea Sea located between the mainlands of modern Greece and Turkey.

Aeschylus (ES-kuh-luhs) Greek tragedian, author of the *Oresteia*.

Afonso d'Alboquerque 1453–1515 C.E. Commander of the Portuguese forces in the Indian Ocean in the early sixteenth century. He was responsible for seizing Hormuz, Goa,

and Malacca, which allowed the Portuguese to control Indian Ocean trade.

African National Congress South African political party formed in 1912 that provided consistent opposition to the apartheid state, and eventually became the majority party at the end of the apartheid era in 1994.

Age grades Bantu institution in which individuals of roughly the same age carried out communal tasks appropriate for that age.

Ahimsa (uh-HIM-suh) Jain term for the principle of nonviolence to other living things or their souls.

Ahura Mazda (uh-HOORE-uh MAHZ-duh) Main god of Zoroastrianism who represented truth and goodness and was perceived to be in an eternal struggle with the malign spirit Angra Mainyu.

Akbar 1542–1605 C.E. The third Mughal emperor who ruled from 1556–1605 and was known for his religious tolerance.

Al-Andalus (al-ANN-duh-luhs) Islamic Spain.

Albert Einstein 1879–1955 C.E. German-born physicist who developed the theory of relativity and whose ideas had profound influence on the development of science in the twentieth century.

Alexander of Macedon Also known as Alexander the Great, Macedonian conqueror who defeated the Achaemenid Persian Empire and created an enormous empire in the mid-fourth century B.C.E.

Alexandria An important city of the ancient world, founded by Alexander on the Mediterranean coast of Egypt during the fourth century B.C.E.

Ali'i nui Hawaiian class of high chiefs.

Allah (AH-lah) God of the monotheistic religion of Islam.

al-Qaeda Militant Islamist organization founded by Osama bin Laden in 1988, which was responsible for the September 11, 2001, attacks in the United States.

Amon-Re (AH-muhn RAY) Egyptian god, combination of the sun god Re and the air god Amon.

Analects A collection of the sayings and teachings of the fifth century B.C.E. Chinese philosopher Confucius, collected by his students.

Anastacio Somoza Garcia 1896–1956. Brutal leader of the U.S.-trained Guarda Nacional in Nicaragua who became president and dictator in 1934.

Ancien Régime Meaning "old order," and refers to the period prior to the French Revolution in 1789.

Angkor (AHN-kohr) Southeast Asian Khmer kingdom (889–1432) that was centered on

the temple cities of Angkor Thom and Angkor Wat.

Anti-Semitism Term coined in the late nineteenth century that was associated with a prejudice against Jews and the political, social, and economic actions taken against them.

Antigonid empire The smallest of the three states that split from Alexander the Great's massive empire in 275 B.C.E. The Antigonid empire occupied Greece and Macedon.

Antonianism African syncretic religion, founded by Dona Beatriz, that taught that Jesus Christ was a black African man and that heaven was for Africans.

Antonio López de Santa Anna 1794–1896 C.E. Mexican army officer and politician best known for his efforts to prevent Spain from recapturing Mexico. Served as president of Mexico several times.

Ao One of the six Shang dynasty (1766–1122 B.C.E.) capitals near the modern city of Zheng-zhou.

Apartheid (ah-PAHR-teyed) South African system of "separateness" that was implemented in 1948 and that maintained the black majority in a position of political, social, and economic subordination.

Appeasement British and French policy in the 1930s that tried to maintain peace in Europe in the face of German aggression by making concessions.

Arianism Early Christian heresy that centered on teaching of Arius (250–336 C.E.) and contained the belief that Jesus was a mortal human being and not coeternal with God; Arianism was the focus of the Council of Nicaea.

Armenian Genocide Campaign of extermination undertaken by the Ottomans against two million Armenians living in Ottoman territory during World War I.

Artha Hindu concept for the pursuit of economic well-being and honest prosperity.

Arthashastra (AR-thah-sha-strah) Ancient Indian political treatise from the time of Chandragupta Maurya; its authorship was traditionally ascribed to Kautalya, and it stressed that war was inevitable.

Aryans (AIR-ee-anns) Indo-European migrants who settled in India after 1500 B.C.E.; their union with indigenous Dravidians formed the basis of Hinduism.

Asceticism (uh-SET-uh-siz-uhm) The practice of severe self-discipline and avoidance of all forms of indulgence, typically for religious reasons.

Ashoka (ah-SHOW-kuh) Powerful ruler of the South Asian Mauryan Dynasty, who reigned from 268–232 B.C.E.

Association of Southeast Asian Nations (ASEAN) Regional organization established in 1967 by Thailand, Malaysia, Singapore, Indonesia, and the Philippines; the organization was designed to promote economic progress and political stability; it later became a free-trade zone.

Assyrians (uh-SEAR-ee-uhns) Southwest Asian people who built an empire that reached its height during the eighth and seventh centuries B.C.E.; it was known for a powerful army and a well-structured state.

Astrolabe Navigational instrument for determining latitude.

Ataturk 1881–1938 C.E. Meaning "Father of the Turks," his real name was Mustafa Kemal. He was a Turkish army officer, reformer, and the first president of the modern Republic of Turkey after the Ottoman defeat in World War I.

Aten Monotheistic god of Egyptian pharaoh Akhenaten (r. 1353–1335 B.C.E.) and a very early example of monotheism.

Athens Important city-state of ancient Greece, located in the Attica region.

Attica The region surrounding the ancient city of Athens.

Attila the Hun Warrior king of the Huns, who ruled the confederation from 434–453.

Audiencias Spanish courts in Latin America.

Augusto César Sandino 1893–1934. Nationalist and liberal general of Nicaragua who fundamentally opposed U.S. intervention. He was murdered in 1934 by Anastacio Somoza Garcia's forces.

Augustus Grandnephew and protégé of Julius Caesar, who served as de facto ruler of the Roman state from 27 B.C.E. until his death in 14 C.E.

Aung San Suu Kyi 1945–. Burmese politician and author who received the 1991 Nobel Peace Prize for her opposition to Burmese military rule. Leads the National League for Democracy party.

Aurangzeb 1618–1707 C.E. The sixth Mughal emperor, who ruled for forty-nine years over almost all of the Indian subcontinent.

Auschwitz Camp established by the Nazi regime in occupied Poland, which functioned both as a concentration camp and an extermination camp. Approximately one million Jews were killed there.

Australopithecus (ah-strah-loh-PITH-uhkuhs) "Southern ape," oldest known ancestor of humans; it lived from around four million down to around one million years ago, and it could walk on hind legs, freeing up hands for use of simple tools.

Austronesians People who as early as 2000 B.C.E. began to explore and settle islands of the Pacific Ocean basin.

Avesta Book that contains the holy writings of Zoroastrianism.

Axum African kingdom centered in Ethiopia that became an early and lasting center of Coptic Christianity.

Aztec empire Central American empire constructed by the Mexica and expanded greatly during the fifteenth century during the reigns of Itzcoatl and Motecuzoma I.

Babur (BAH-ber) 1483–1530 C.E. Central Asian descendant of Chinggis Khan and Tamerlane who founded the Mughal dynasty in northern India in 1526.

Bakufu The military government of Japan from 1192 to 1868 C.E., headed by a shogun.

Balfour Declaration British declaration from 1917 that supported the creation of a Jewish homeland in Palestine.

Ban Zhao 45–115 C.E. Renowned female historian and scholar of the Han dynasty, and author of the Book of Han.

Bantu (BAN-too) African peoples who originally lived in the area of present-day Nigeria; around 2000 B.C.E. they began a centuries-long migration that took them to most of sub-Saharan Africa; the Bantu were very influential, especially linguistically.

Barack Obama 1961–. Forty-fourth president of the United States, who served from 2009 to 2017. Obama was the first U.S. president of African heritage.

Baron de Montesquieu 1689–1755 C.E. French political philosopher who advocated the separation of legislative, executive, and judicial government powers.

Battle of Gaugamela October 1, 331 B.C.E. The final meeting between Alexander of Macedon and King Darius III of Persia, in which Alexander was victorious.

Battle of Marathon A battle fought in 490 B.C.E. between Greek and Persian forces, from which the Greeks emerged victorious.

Bedouins (BEHD-oh-ihnz) Nomadic Arabic tribespeople.

Benazir Bhutto 1953–2007 C.E. Pakistani politician who served twice as Pakistani prime minister: in 1988–1990 and then again in 1993–1996. She was assassinated in 2007.

Benefice Grant from a lord to a vassal, usually consisting of land, which supported the vassal and signified the relationship between the two.

Benito Juárez (beh-NEE-toh HWAHR-ez) 1806–1872 C.E. Mexican lawyer of indigenous origins who served as president of Mexico on five occasions.

Benito Mussolini 1883–1945 C.E. Italian politician and journalist who led the National Fascist Party and ruled as prime minister from 1922 to 1943.

Berlin Conference Meeting organized by German chancellor Otto von Bismarck in 1884–1885 that provided the justification for European colonization of Africa.

Bezant Byzantine gold coin that served as the standard currency of the Mediterranean basin from the sixth through the twelfth century.

Bhagavad Gita (BUH-guh-vahd GEE-tuh) "Song of the Lord," an Indian short poetic work drawn from the lengthy *Mahabharata* that was finished around 400 C.E. and that expressed basic Hindu concepts such as karma and dharma.

Bhakti movement (BAHK-tee) Indian movement that attempted to transcend the differences between Hinduism and Islam.

Black Hand Pre–World War I secret Serbian society; one of its members, Gavrilo Princip, assassinated Austrian archduke Francis Ferdinand and provided the spark for the outbreak of the Great War.

Blitzkrieg German style of rapid attack through the use of armor and air power that was used in Poland, Norway, Denmark, Belgium, the Netherlands, and France in 1939–1940.

Bloodletting rituals Ritual involving the shedding of human blood as a form of sacrifice to the gods, practiced by the Maya and Aztecs amongst many other societies.

Bodh Gaya Town southwest of Pataliputra in which Gautama (Buddha) received enlightenment while sitting under a bo tree.

Bodhisattvas (BOH-dih-SAT-vuhs) Buddhist concept regarding individuals who had reached enlightenment but who stayed in this world to help people.

Bogomils Bulgarian group active in the tenth and eleventh centuries that believed in rejecting the material world and extreme ascetisicm.

Bolshevik (BOHL-shih-vehk) Russian communist party headed by Lenin.

Book of Songs The oldest existing collection of Chinese poetry, dating from the eleventh to the seventh centuries B.C.E.

Bourgeoisie Middle class in modern industrial society.

Brahman Central concept of classical Vedic religion, the name of the "universal soul" at the heart of the cosmos.

Brahmins (BRAH-minz) Hindu caste of priests.

Brezhnev doctrine Policy developed by Leonid Brezhnev (1906–1982) that claimed for the Soviet Union the right to invade any socialist country faced with internal or external enemies; the doctrine was best expressed in the Soviet invasion of Czechoslovakia.

BRICs Acronym for the fast-growing and developing economies of Brazil, Russia, India, and China.

Buddha (BOO-duh) The "enlightened one," the term applied to Siddhartha Gautama after his discoveries that would form the foundation of Buddhism.

Buddhism (BOO-diz'm) Religion, based on Four Noble Truths, associated with Siddhartha Gautama (563–483 B.C.E.), or the Buddha; its adherents desired to eliminate all distracting passion and reach nirvana.

Bunraku (boon-RAH-koo) Japanese puppet theater.

Bush doctrine A set of policies during the administration of American president George W. Bush (2001-2009) that advocated preemptive strikes by the United States against potential enemies instead of containment or deterrence.

Byzantine empire (BIHZ-ann-teen) Long-lasting empire centered at Constantinople; it grew out of the end of the Roman empire, carried the legacy of Roman greatness, and was the only classical society to survive into the early modern age; it reached its early peak during the reign of Justinian (483-565).

Caesaropapism Concept relating to the mixing of political and religious authority, as with the Roman emperors, that was central to the church-versus-state controversy in medieval Europe.

Cahokia (kuh-HOH-kee-uh) Large structure in modern Illinois that was constructed by the mound-building peoples; it was the third largest structure in the Americas before the arrival of the Europeans.

Caliph (KAL-ihf) "Deputy," Islamic leader after the death of Muhammad.

Cambyses (kam-BIE-sees) Son of Cyrus and second ruler of the Achaemenid Persian Empire, reigned 530-522 B.C.E.

Camillo di Cavour 1810-1861 C.E. Prime Minister to King Vittorio Emmanuel II of Piedmont and Sardinia, and key figure in bringing about the unification of Italy.

Capetian (cah-PEE-shuhn) Early French dynasty that started with Hugh Capet.

Capitalism An economic system with origins in early modern Europe in which private parties make their goods and services available on a free market.

Capitulation Highly unfavorable trading agreements that the Ottoman Turks signed with the Europeans in the nineteenth century that symbolized the decline of the Ottomans.

Captain James Cook 1728-1779 C.E. British explorer, navigator, and cartographer who served in the British Royal Navy. Famous for his expeditions to the Pacific Ocean in the eighteenth century.

Carolingians Germanic dynasty that was named after its most famous member, Charlemagne.

Carthage Northern African kingdom, main rival to early Roman expansion, that was defeated by Rome in the Punic Wars.

Caste A system of social distinction that emerged in South Asia late in the second millennium B.C.E., which divides the population into a series of "classes" or varnas.

Çatal Hüyük Important Neolithic settlement in Anatolia (7250-6150 B.C.E.).

Cathars Medieval heretics, also known as the Albigensians, who considered the material world evil; their followers renounced wealth and marriage and promoted an ascetic existence.

Catherine the Great 1729-1796 C.E. Catherine II was the longest-serving female ruler of Russia (from 1762 to 1796). She came to power by overthrowing her husband, Peter III, in a coup.

Catholic Reformation Sixteenth-century Catholic attempt to cure internal ills and confront Protestantism; it was inspired by the reforms of the Council of Trent and the actions of the Jesuits.

Caudillos (KAW-dee-ohs) Latin American term for nineteenth-century local military leaders.

Cave paintings Paintings made on the walls and ceilings of caves by early human artists.

Central Powers World War I term for the alliance of Germany, Austria-Hungary, and the Ottoman empire.

Chaghatai One of Chinggis Khan's sons, whose descendants ruled central Asia through the Chaghatai khanate.

Chan Buddhism (CHAHN BOO-diz'm) Influential branch of Buddhism in China, with an emphasis on intuition and sudden flashes of insight instead of textual study.

Chanchan (chahn-chahn) Capital of the pre-Incan, South American Chimu society that supported a large population of fifty thousand.

Chandragupta Maurya (chuhn-dra-GOOP-tah MORE-yuh) Founding ruler of the South Asian Mauryan Dynasty, who reigned from 321 to 297 B.C.E.

Chang'an (chahng-ahn) Capital city for various early Chinese dynasties, including the Qin, Han, and Tang.

Charlemagne Ruler of the European Carolingian Empire from 748-814 C.E.

Charles V Reigned 1519-1556. Emperor who inherited the Hapsburg family's Austrian territories as well as the Kingdom of Spain. When he became emperor in 1519, his empire stretched from Austria to Peru.

Chavín culture Mysterious but very popular South American religion (1000-300 B.C.E.).

Chichén Itzá (chee-CHEN eet-SAH) Major Mayan city located in the northern Yucatan Peninsula of modern Mexico.

Chimu Pre-Incan South American society that fell to the Incas in the fifteenth century.

Chinampas Agricultural gardens used by Mexica (Aztecs) in which fertile muck from lake bottoms was dredged and built up into small plots.

Chinggis Khan (CHIHN-gihs Kahn) 1162-1227 C.E. Founder and first Kahn (emperor) of the Mongol Empire, which became the largest contiguous land empire in the history of the world up to that time.

Chivalry European medieval code of conduct for knights based on loyalty and honor.

Chola kingdom Southern Indian Hindu kingdom (850-1267), a tightly centralized state that dominated sea trade.

Christopher Columbus 1451-1506 C.E. Italian explorer and navigator who made four transatlantic voyages to the islands off North America, which in turn opened the way for European colonization of the Americas.

Chu Autonomous state in the central Yangzi region of China during the Zhou dynasty (1122-256 B.C.E.).

Chucuito Pre-Incan South American society that rose in the twelfth century and fell to the Incas in the fifteenth century.

City-state Urban areas that controlled surrounding agricultural regions and that were often loosely connected in a broader political structure with other city-states.

Civil Code Civil law code promulgated by Napoleon Bonaparte in 1804.

Civil service examinations A battery of grueling tests given at the district, provincial, and metropolitan levels that determined entry into the Chinese civil service during the Ming and Qing dynasties.

Cixi 1835-1908 C.E. Former imperial concubine who established herself as effective ruler of the Qing dynasty in the fifty years prior to the end of Qing rule in 1908. She was hated by millions for her lavish spending, corruption, and resistance to reform.

Cohong Specially licensed Chinese firms that were under strict government regulation.

Collectivization of agriculture Process beginning in the late 1920s by which Stalin forced the Russian peasants off their own land and onto huge collective farms run by the state; millions died in the process.

Colossal human heads Large carved heads made of basalt, produced by the Olmec during the late-second and early-first millennia B.C.E.

COMECON The Council for Mutual Economic Assistance, which offered increased trade within the Soviet Union and eastern Europe; it was the Soviet alternative to the United States' Marshall Plan.

Comfort women Mainly Korean, Taiwanese, and Manchurian women who were forced into service by the Japanese army to serve as prostitutes to the Japanese troops during World War II.

Communalism A term, usually associated with India, that placed an emphasis on religious rather than national identity.

Communism Philosophy and movement that began in middle of the nineteenth century with the work of Karl Marx; it has the same general goals as socialism, but it includes the belief that violent revolution is necessary to destroy the bourgeois world and institute a new world run by and for the proletariat.

Confucianism (kuhn-FYOO-shuhn-iz'm) Philosophy, based on the teachings of the Chinese philosopher Kong Fuzi (551-479 B.C.E.), or Confucius, that emphasizes order, the role of the gentleman, obligation to society, and reciprocity.

Congress of Vienna Gathering of European diplomats in Vienna, Austria, from October 1814 to June 1815. The representatives of the "great powers" that defeated Napoleon—

Britain, Austria, Prussia, and Russia—dominated the proceedings, which aimed to restore the prerevolutionary political and social order.

Conquistadores (kohn-KEE-stah-dohrayz) Spanish adventurers such as Cortés and Pizarro who conquered Central and South America in the sixteenth century.

Constantine Roman emperor who reigned from 306 to 337 C.E. and who moved the capital of the empire from Rome to Constantinople.

Constantinople The purpose-built capital of the late-Roman and Byzantine empires from the fourth to the fifteenth centuries. The name translates as "city of Constantine," the Roman emperor who founded the city.

Constitutionalism Movement in England in the seventeenth century that placed power in Parliament's hands as part of a constitutional monarchy and that increasingly limited the power of the monarch; the movement was highlighted by the English Civil War and the Glorious Revolution.

Containment Concept associated with the United States and specifically with the Truman Doctrine during the cold war that revolved around the notion that the United States would contain the spread of communism.

Corporation A concept that reached mature form in the 1860s in England and France; it involved private business owned by thousands of individual and institutional investors who financed the business through the purchase of stocks.

Corpus iuris civilis (KOR-puhs yoor-uhs sih-VEE-lihs) *Body of the Civil Law,* the Byzantine emperor Justinian's attempt to codify all Roman law.

Council at Nicaea (nahy-SEE-uh) An assembly of leading theologians that convened in the city of Nicaea in 325 to determine the orthodox position of the Church on a range of contentious theological matters.

Council of Trent 1545–1563. Assembly of high Roman Catholic church officials which met over a period of years to institute reforms in order to increase morality and improve the preparation of priests.

Crimean War 1853–1856 C.E. War fought on the Crimean peninsula between Russia on one side and Great Britain, France, the Ottoman Empire, and Sardinia on the other.

Criollos (kree-OH-lohs) Creoles, people born in the Americas of Spanish or Portuguese ancestry.

Cross staff Device that sailors used to determine latitude by measuring the angle of the sun or the pole star above the horizon.

Crystal Palace Glass and iron structure that housed an exhibition in London in 1851 to display industrial products.

Ctesiphon (TES-uh-phon) Capital city of the Sasanian Empire from the mid-third to mid-seventh centuries C.E.

Cult of Dionysis Devotees of the god of wine in ancient Greece. By the fifth century B.C.E. the cult had gone from wild, emotional displays to reserved, thoughtful tributes.

Cuneiform Written language of the Sumerians, probably the first written script in the world.

Cyrus Founder and first ruler of the Persian Achaemenid Empire, who reigned from 548 to 530 B.C.E.

Daimyo (DEYEM-yoh) Powerful territorial lords in early modern Japan.

Dao Key element in Chinese philosophy that means the "way of nature" or the "way of the cosmos."

Daodejing (DOW-DAY-JIHNG) Book that is the fundamental work of Daoism.

Daoism (DOW-i'zm) Chinese philosophy with origins in the Zhou dynasty; it is associated with legendary philosopher Laozi, and it called for a policy of noncompetition.

Dar al-Islam The "house of Islam," a term for the Islamic world.

Darius Third ruler of the Achaemenid Persian Empire, who reigned 521–486 B.C.E.

Dasas Ancient Aryan Indian term for enemies or subject peoples.

Declaration of Independence Drafted by Thomas Jefferson in 1776; the document expressed the ideas of John Locke and the Enlightenment, represented the idealism of the American rebels, and influenced other revolutions.

Declaration of the Rights of Man and the Citizen Document from the French Revolution (1789) that was influenced by the American Declaration of Independence and in turn influenced other revolutionary movements.

Decolonization Process by which former colonies achieved their independence, as with the newly emerging African nations in the 1950s and 1960s.

Deer Park of Sarnath Park near the city of Benares where the Buddha publicly announced his doctrine in the year 528 B.C.E.

Deism (DEE-iz'm) An Enlightenment view that accepted the existence of a god but denied the supernatural aspects of Christianity; in deism, the universe was an orderly realm maintained by rational and natural laws.

Deng Xiaoping (duhng show-ping) 1904–1997 C.E. Chinese politician who led the People's Republic of China from 1978 to his retirement in 1992.

Descamisados "Shirtless ones," Argentine poor who supported Juan and Eva Perón.

Détente A reduction in cold war tension between the United States and the Soviet Union from 1969 to 1975.

Devshirme Ottoman requirement that the Christians in the Balkans provide young boys to be slaves of the sultan.

Dharma (DAHR-muh) Hindu concept of obedience to religious and moral laws and order; also, the basic doctrine of Buddhism.

Dhimmi (dihm-mee) Islamic concept of a protected people that was symbolic of Islamic toleration during the Mughal and Ottoman empires.

Dhow Indian, Persian, and Arab ships, one hundred to four hundred tons, that sailed and traded throughout the Indian Ocean basin.

Diaspora People who have settled far from their original homeland but who still share some measure of ethnic identity.

Diocletian (dah-yuh-KLEE-shuhn) Roman emperor who reigned from 284 to 305 C.E.

Dionysus Greek god of wine, also known as Bacchus; Greek plays were performed in his honor.

Domingo Faustino Sarmiento 1811–1888 C.E. Argentine intellectual, writer, and activist who became the seventh president of Argentina.

Dominicans An order of mendicants founded by St. Dominic (1170–1221 C.E.) whose purpose was to live in poverty and serve the religious needs of their communities.

Dona Beatriz 1684–1706 C.E. Kongo prophet and religious leader who founded her own Christian movement, Antonianism, which taught that Jesus was from the Kongo.

Dravidians A family of languages spoken in southern India and Sri Lanka, or the peoples who speak them. Some scholars believe Dravidians were the original inhabitants of India prior to Aryan settlement, though this is controversial.

Dreadnoughts A class of British battleships whose heavy armaments made all other battleships obsolete overnight.

Duma Russian parliament, established after the Revolution of 1905.

Dunhuang Oasis in modern western China that became a site of Buddhist missionary activity by the fourth century C.E.

Durham Report Report issued in 1839 by the British Earl of Durham and recent governor-general of Canada, which advocated significant self-government for a united Canada.

Dutch learning European knowledge that reached Tokugawa Japan.

East India Company British joint-stock company that grew to be a state within a state in India; it possessed its own armed forces.

Economic nationalism Economic policies pursued by many governments affected by the Great Depression in which the nation tries to become economically self-sufficient by imposing high tariffs on foreign goods. The policy served to exacerbate the damaging effects of the Depression around the world.

Eight-legged essay Eight-part essays that an aspiring Chinese civil servant had to compose, mainly based on a knowledge of Confucius and the Zhou classics.

Eleanor of Aquitaine 1122–1204 C.E. Aristocratic woman from the city of Poitiers, modern France, who supported poets and entertainers known as troubadours.

Eleusinian mysteries Cult in ancient Greece that encouraged initiates to observe high moral standards.

Emancipation Manifesto Manifesto proclaimed by the Russian Tsar Alexander II in 1861 that abolished the institution of serfdom and freed 23 million serfs.

Emiliano Zapata (eh-mee-LYAH-no zuh-PAH-tuh) 1879–1919 C.E. Mexican revolutionary and leader of the peasant revolution during the Mexican Revolution whose followers were called Zapatistas.

Emilio Aguinaldo (eh-MEE-lyoh AH-gee-NAHL-doh) 1869–1964 C.E. Filipino revolutionary who declared independence from Spain and then fought against the United States during its war of occupation.

Emporia Commercial establishments that specialize in products and services on a large scale, vital to the conduct of transregional trade.

Encomienda (ehn-KOH-mee-ehn-dah) System that gave the Spanish settlers (*encomenderos*) the right to compel the indigenous peoples of the Americas to work in the mines or fields.

Engenho Brazilian sugar mill; the term also came to symbolize the entire complex world relating to the production of sugar.

English Civil War 1642–1649. A series of armed conflicts between the English crown and the English Parliament over political and religious differences.

Enlightenment Eighteenth-century philosophical movement that began in France; its emphasis was on the preeminence of reason rather than faith or tradition; it spread concepts from the Scientific Revolution.

Epicureans (ehp-ih-kyoo-REE-uhns) Hellenistic philosophers who taught that pleasure—as in quiet satisfaction—was the greatest good.

Equal-field system Chinese system during the Tang dynasty in which the goal was to ensure an equitable distribution of land.

Essenes Jewish sect that looked for the arrival of a savior; they were similar in some of their core beliefs to the early Christians.

Etruscans (ih-TRUHS-kuhns) Northern Italian society that initially dominated the Romans; the Etruscans helped convey Greek concepts to the expanding Romans.

Eugenics A late nineteenth- and early twentieth-century movement that sought to improve the gene pool of the human race by encouraging those deemed fit to have more children, and by discouraging those deemed unfit from reproducing. The movement was deeply tied to racism, and was eventually adopted by the German Nazi regime to justify the extermination of "undesirable" populations.

Eunuchs (YOO-nihks) Castrated males, originally in charge of the harem, who grew to play major roles in government; eunuchs were common in China and other societies.

European Community (EC) Organization of European states established in 1957; it was originally called the European Economic Community and was renamed the EC in 1967; it promoted economic growth and integration as the basis for a politically united Europe.

European Union Established by the Maastricht Treaty in 1993, a supranational organization for even greater European economic and political integration.

Fascism Political ideology and mass movement that was prominent in many parts of Europe between 1919 and 1945; it sought to regenerate the social, political, and cultural life of societies, especially in contrast to liberal democracy and socialism; fascism began with Mussolini in Italy, and it reached its peak with Hitler in Germany.

Ferdinand Magellan (FUR-dih-nand muh-JEHL-uhn) 1480–1521 C.E. Portuguese explorer famous for organizing the first circumnavigation of the globe, by ship, from 1519 to 1522.

Five Pillars of Islam The foundation of Islam: (1) profession of faith, (2) prayer, (3) fasting during Ramadan, (4) almsgiving, and (5) pilgrimage, or hajj.

Five-year plans First implemented by Stalin in the Soviet Union in 1928; five-year plans were a staple of communist regimes in which every aspect of production was determined in advance for a five-year period; five-year plans were the opposite of the free market concept.

Foot binding A practice that involved the tight wrapping of young girls' feet with strips of cloth that prevented natural growth of the bones and resulted in tiny, malformed curved feet.

Four Noble Truths The foundation of Buddhist thought: (1) life is pain, (2) pain is caused by desire, (3) elimination of desire will bring an end to pain, (4) living a life based on the Noble Eightfold Path will eliminate desire.

Franciscans An order of mendicants founded by St. Francis (1182–1226 C.E.) whose purpose was to live in poverty and serve the religious needs of their communities.

Franciso Pizarro 1478–1541 C.E. Spanish conquistador whose military expeditions led to the fall of the Inca Empire.

Franklin Delano Roosevelt 1882–1945 C.E. American politician who served as the thirty-second president of the United States from 1933 until his death.

Franks Germanic peoples who founded a successful dynasty in France, which went on to rule a substantial European empire in the eighth and ninth centuries.

Frederick Barbarossa 1152–1190 C.E. Medieval emperor with lands in modern southern Germany who tried and failed to conquer Lombardy in modern Italy.

Friedrich Engels 1820–1895 C.E. German socialist philosopher who, with Karl Marx, founded modern communism and co-authored *The Communist Manifesto* (1848).

Front de Libération Nationale (FLN) The Algerian organization that fought a bloody guerrilla war for freedom against France.

Fu Hao Favorite consort of King Wu Ding of the Shang dynasty (thirteenth century B.C.E.), whose richly appointed tomb remained intact until the modern era.

Fukuzawa Yukichi 1835–1901. Prominent Japanese who traveled around Europe and North America after the Meiji Restoration to evaluate foreign administrative systems and constitutions.

Fulani (foo-LAH-nee) Sub-Saharan African people who, beginning in the seventeenth century, waged a series of wars designed to impose their own strict interpretation of Islam.

Funan Southeast Asian state that ruled the lower reaches of the Mekong River (including parts of modern Cambodia and Vietnam) between the first and sixth centuries C.E.

Galileo Galilei 1564–1642 C.E. Italian astronomer, engineer, and physicist from the town of Pisa, whose observations had a huge impact on the development of modern science.

Gamal Abdel Nasser 1918–1970 C.E. Second president of Egypt who led the overthrow of the monarchy in 1952 and served from 1954 until his death.

Gandhara Kingdom in modern Pakistan and Afghanistan established by the Persian emperor Darius in about 520 B.C.E.

Gathas (GATH-uhs) Zoroastrian hymns believed to be compositions by Zarathustra.

Gauchos (GOW-chohz) Argentine cowboys, highly romanticized figures.

Gaul Name of the region of modern France during the ancient Greek and Roman period.

General Agreement on Tariffs and Trade (GATT) Free-trade agreement first signed in 1947; by 1994 it had grown to 123 members and formed the World Trade Organization (WTO).

Ghana (GAH-nuh) Kingdom in west Africa during the fifth through the thirteenth century whose rulers eventually converted to Islam; its power and wealth was based on dominating trans-Saharan trade.

Ghazi (GAH-zee) Islamic religious warrior.

Ghaznavids Turkish tribe under Mahmud of Ghazni who moved into northern India in the eleventh century and began a period of greater Islamic influence in India.

Gilgamesh Legendary king of the Mesopotamian city-state of Uruk (ca. 3000 B.C.E.), subject of the *Epic of Gilgamesh,* world's oldest complete epic literary masterpiece.

Glasnost (GLAHS-nohst) Russian term meaning "openness" introduced by Mikhail Gorbachev in 1985 to describe the process of opening Soviet society to dissidents and public criticism.

Global warming The emission of greenhouse gases, which prevents solar heat from escaping the earth's atmosphere and leads to the gradual heating of the earth's environment.

Globalization The breaking down of traditional boundaries in the face of increasingly global financial and cultural trends.

Glorious Revolution 1688-1689. The events that led to the replacement of the Catholic English King James II by his Protestant daughter Mary II and her Dutch husband William of Orange.

Golden Horde Mongol tribe that controlled Russia from the thirteenth to the fifteenth century.

Gracchi Brothers Tiberius and Gaius, brothers in the Roman Republic who worked to limit the amount of land individuals could hold in order to alleviate social conflict during the second century B.C.E.

Grand Canal A huge network of canals that linked the Yangzi and Huang He river systems, and that eventually extended 2000 kilometers (1200 miles).

Great Game Nineteenth-century competition between Great Britain and Russia for the control of central Asia.

Great Zimbabwe Large sub-Saharan African kingdom in the fifteenth century.

Greater East Asia Co-Prosperity Sphere Japanese plan for consolidating east and southeast Asia under their control during World War II.

Greek fire Devastating incendiary weapon used mainly at sea by Byzantine forces in the seventh and eighth centuries C.E.

Greenpeace An environmental organization founded in 1970 and dedicated to the preservation of earth's natural resources.

Griots Professional singers, historians, and story-tellers in sub-Saharan Africa.

Guomindang (GWOH-mihn-dahng) Chinese nationalist party founded by Sun Yatsen (1866-1925) and later led by Jiang Jieshi; it has been centered in Taiwan since the end of the Chinese civil war.

Gupta (GOOP-tah) Indian dynasty (320-550 C.E.) that briefly reunited India after the collapse of the earlier Mauryan dynasty.

Guru Kabir 1440-1518 C.E. A blind weaver who became the most important teacher in the bhakti movement, which sought to harmonize Hinduism and Islam.

Hacienda (HAH-see-ehn-dah) Large Latin American estates.

Hadith A collection of sayings of the Prophet Muhammad and accounts of his deeds.

Hagia Sophia (HAH-yah SOH-fee-uh) Massive Christian church constructed by the Byzantine emperor Justinian and later converted into a mosque.

Hajj (HAHJ) Pilgrimage to Mecca.

Hammurabi's Code (hahm-uh-RAH-beez) Sophisticated law code associated with the Babylonian king Hammurabi (r. 1792-1750 B.C.E.).

Han Feizi (hahn fay-zi) Third-century B.C.E. scholar credited as one of the founders of the ideology of Legalism.

Han Wudi One of the most important emperors of the Early Han Dynasty, who reigned from 141 to 87 B.C.E.

Hangzhou Capital of the Southern Song dynasty in the late thirteenth century.

Hannibal Barca Carthaginian general who devastated the Italian peninsula during the Second Punic War, 218-201 B.C.E.

Hanseatic League (han-see-AT-ik) A commercial confederation of merchant guilds and market towns in northwestern Europe that dominated Baltic trade from the thirteenth to the fifteenth centuries.

Harappan (hah-RAP-puhn) Early brilliant Indian society centered in Harappa and Mohenjo-daro.

Harijans "Children of God," Gandhi's term for the Untouchables.

Harsha Ruler of northern India from 606 to 648 C.E.

Harun al-Rashid Powerful ruler of the Abbasid Caliphate who reigned from 789 to 809 C.E.

Hebrews Semitic-speaking nomadic tribe influential for monotheistic belief in Yahweh.

Heian (HAY-ahn) Japanese period (794-1185), a brilliant cultural era notable for the world's first novel, Murasaki Shikibu's *The Tale of Genji.*

Hellenistic Era Phase in Greek history (328-146 B.C.E.), from the conquest of Greece by Philip of Macedon until Greece's fall to the Romans; this era was a more cosmopolitan age facilitated by the conquests of Alexander the Great.

Helots Servants to the Spartan state, who were neither chattel slaves nor free.

Hernán Cortés 1485-1587 C.E. Spanish conquistador whose military expeditions led to the fall of the Aztec Empire.

Hieratic Simplified writing script that was used for day-to-day administration in Egypt.

Hieroglyphics (heye-ruh-GLIPH-iks) Ancient Egyptian written language.

Hijra Muhammad's migration from Mecca to Medina in 622, which is the beginning point of the Islamic calendar and is considered to mark the beginning of the Islamic faith.

Hinayana (HEE-nah-yah-nuh) Branch of Buddhism known as the "lesser vehicle," also known as Theravada Buddhism; its beliefs include strict, individual path to enlightenment, and it is popular in south and southeast Asia.

Hinduism Main religion of India, a combination of Dravidian and Aryan concepts; Hinduism's goal is to reach spiritual purity and union with the great world spirit; its important concepts include dharma, karma, and samsara.

Hiroshima bombing Bombing of the Japanese city on August 6, 1945 by an American bomber, which—along with the bombing of Nagasaki on August 9—led the Japanese to surrender and end World War II.

Hittites Indo-European-speaking peoples who constructed a powerful empire in Anatolia and Mesopotamia in the mid-second millennium B.C.E.

Ho Chi Minh 1890-1969 C.E. North Vietnamese revolutionary and politician who first fought the French and then the Americans, and then became the first prime minister of North Vietnam in 1945.

Holocaust German attempt in World War II to exterminate the Jews of Europe.

Home front Term made popular in World War I and World War II for the civilian "front" that was symbolic of the greater demands of total war.

Homer Supposed author of the ancient Greek epic poems the *Iliad* and the *Odyssey.*

Hominid (HAWM-ih-nihd) A creature belonging to the family Hominidae, which includes human and humanlike species.

Homo erectus (HOH-MOH ee-REHK-tuhs) "Upright-walking human," which existed from two million to two hundred thousand years ago; *Homo erectus* used cleavers and hand axes and learned how to control fire.

Homo sapiens (HOH-MOH SAY-pee-uhns) "Consciously thinking human," which first appeared around two hundred fifty thousand years ago and used sophisticated tools.

Hongwu 1328-1398 C.E. Personal name Zhu Yuanzhang, was the founding emperor of the Ming dynasty in China. Reigned 1368-1398.

Huitzilopochtli (wee-tsee-loh-pockt-lee) Sun god and patron deity of the Aztecs.

Hundred Days of Reform Chinese reforms of 1898 led by Kang Youwei and Liang Qichao in their desire to turn China into a modern industrial power.

Hundred Years' War 1337-1453 C.E. Series of intermittent wars between France and England over the control of modern France.

Huns A militarized confederation of Central Asian nomads whose westward migration helped precipitate the collapse of the Western Roman Empire.

Hyksos (HICK-sohs) Invaders who seized the Nile delta and helped bring an end to the Egyptian Middle Kingdom.

Ibn Battuta (ih-bun BAH-too-tah) Born 1304 in Morocco. Was the greatest Muslim traveler of his time. He covered 75,000 miles and visited almost every Muslim country and China.

Ibn Rushd (IB-uhn RUSHED) Known as Averroes in the West, he was an important Islamic philosopher whose intellectual contributions were also appreciated by many European scholars. He lived from 1126 to 1198 C.E.

Iconoclasts (eye-KAHN-oh-klasts) Supporters of the movement, begun by the Byzantine Emperor Leo III (r. 717-741), to destroy religious icons because their veneration was considered sinful.

Ilkhanate (EEL-kahn-ate) Mongol state that ruled Persia after abolition of the Abbasid empire in the thirteenth century.

Imperialism Term associated with the expansion of European powers and their conquest and colonization of African and Asian societies, mainly from the sixteenth through the nineteenth century.

Inca empire Powerful South American empire that would reach its peak in the fifteenth century during the reigns of Pachacuti Inca and Topa Inca.

Indentured labor Labor source for plantations; wealthy planters would pay the laboring poor to sell a portion of their working lives, usually seven years, in exchange for passage.

India Act 1935 British Act that transferred to India the institutions of a self-governing state.

Indian Partition Period immediately following Indian and Pakistani independence in 1947, in which millions of Muslims sought to move to Pakistan from India, and millions of Hindus sought to move from Pakistan to India. It was marked by brutal sectarian violence, and the deaths of between one half million and a million people.

Indian Rebellion of 1857 Ultimately unsuccessful rebellion in North and Central India by a large portion of the Bengal Army and the civil population against British rule.

Indira Gandhi 1917–1984 C.E. Indian politician and daughter of Jawaharlal Nehru who became the first Indian female prime minister in 1966.

Indo-Aryans Indo-European-speaking peoples who migrated from Central Asia into the Indus Valley and India subcontinent during the second millennium B.C.E.

Indo-Europeans Tribal groups from southern Russia who, over a period of millennia, embarked on a series of migrations from India through western Europe; their greatest legacy was the broad distribution of Indo-European languages throughout Eurasia.

Indra Early Indian god associated with the Aryans; Indra was the king of the gods and was associated with warfare and thunderbolts.

Intifada Palestinian mass movement against Israeli rule in the Gaza Strip and other occupied territories.

Investiture (ihn-VEHST-tih-tyoor) One aspect of the medieval European church-versus-state controversy, the granting of church offices by a lay leader.

Iron metallurgy The adoption and use of iron for weapons and tools.

Iroquois (EAR-uh-kwoi) Eastern American Indian confederation made up of the Mohawk, Oneida, Onondaga, Cayuga, and Seneca tribes.

Isaac Newton 1643–1727 C.E. English mathematician, physicist, and astronomer who played a key role in the Scientific Revolution.

Isfahan Capital city of the Safavid Empire (modern Iran), founded by Shah Abbas in the early seventeenth century.

Islam Monotheistic religion announced by the prophet Muhammad (570–632); influenced by Judaism and Christianity, Muhammad was considered the final prophet because the earlier religions had not seen the entire picture; the Quran is the holy book of Islam.

Ismail. Reigned 1501–1524. Founder of the Safavid dynasty in modern Iran.

Israelites A branch of the Hebrews who settled in Palestine (modern-day Israel) after 1200 B.C.E.

Jainism (JEYEN-iz'm) Indian religion associated with the teacher Vardhamana Mahavira (ca. 540–468 B.C.E.) in which every physical object possessed a soul; Jains believe in complete nonviolence to all living beings.

Janissaries Highly respected, elite infantry units of the Ottoman Empire, who formed the first modern standing army in Europe.

Jati Indian word for a Hindu subcaste.

Java An island in modern Indonesia, and formerly home to the capital of the Dutch East Indies at the city of Batavia (modern Jakarta), founded 1619.

Jawaharlal Nehru 1889–1964 C.E. Indian activist and politician who fought for decades for Indian independence and became the first prime minister of India.

Jenne-jeno Settlement in the middle Niger River region in Africa that flourished from the fourth to the eighth centuries C.E. Known for iron production.

Jesus of Nazareth A charismatic Jewish teacher who lived from 4 B.C.E. to the early 30s C.E, recognized as the founder of the religion of Christianity.

Jews A member of the people and cultural community whose traditional religion is Judaism and who trace their origins through the ancient Hebrew people of Israel to Abraham.

Jiang Jieshi (jyahng jeh-she) 1887–1975 C.E. Also known as Chiang Kai-Shek. Chinese nationalist revolutionary, military leader, and politician who led the Republic of China from 1928 to 1975, first in mainland China and then in Taiwan after the communist party won the civil war between them in 1949.

Jihad An Arabic term that literally translates as "struggle," and which has various meanings to Muslims, each of which refer to the imperative to spread Islam throughout the world.

Jizya (JIHZ-yuh) Tax in Islamic empires that was imposed on non-Muslims.

John of Montecorvino 1247–1328 C.E. Franciscan missionary who traveled to China in 1291 in order to win converts to Christianity.

Joint-stock companies Early forerunner of the modern corporation; individuals who invested in a trading or exploring venture could make huge profits while limiting their risk.

Jomo Kenyatta 1891–1978 C.E. Kenyan independence leader and politician who governed Kenya from its independence in 1963 until his death.

Joseph Stalin 1878–1953 C.E. Soviet revolutionary who led the Soviet Union from the mid-1920s to his death, whose policies resulted in the deaths of twenty million people.

Julius Caesar Major late-Republican Roman ruler who served as consul and later as dictator of the Roman state, assassinated in 44 B.C.E.

Junks Ships used by merchants and others in the seas off China and Southeast Asia to carry commercial cargo.

Justinian Important early emperor of the Byzantine Empire, who reigned from 527 to 565 C.E.

Ka'ba (KAH-buh) Main shrine in Mecca, goal of Muslims embarking on the hajj.

Kabuki (kah-BOO-kee) Japanese theater in which actors were free to improvise and embellish the words.

Kama Hindu concept of the enjoyment of physical and sexual pleasure.

Kamikaze (KAH-mih-kah-zee) A Japanese term meaning "divine wind" that is related to the storms that destroyed Mongol invasion fleets; the term is symbolic of Japanese isolation and was later taken by suicide pilots in World War II.

Kangxi (kahng-shee) 1654–1722 C.E. Fourth emperor of China's Qing dynasty, whose sixty-one-year rule was the longest in Chinese history.

Kanun (KAH-noon) Laws issued by the Ottoman Süleyman the Magnificent, also known as Süleyman Kanuni, "the Lawgiver."

Kapu Hawaiian concept of something being taboo.

Karl Marx 1818–1883 C.E. German philosopher and socialist revolutionary who founded, with Friedrich Engels, the modern communist movement and co-authored *The Communist Manifesto* (1848).

Karma (KAHR-mah) Hindu concept that the sum of good and bad in a person's life will determine his or her status in the next life.

Khoikhoi South African people referred to pejoratively as the Hottentots by Europeans.

Khubilai Khan (KOO-bih-lie Kahn) 1215–1294 C.E. Grandson of Chinggis Khan and founder of the Yuan dynasty in China in 1271.

Khwarazm Shah Ruler of Afghanistan and Persia in 1218, when Chinggis Khan sought to trade with his realm. After Khwarazm shah murdered Chingiss Khan's envoys, Chinggiss' forces devastated Persia in 1219.

King Kashta Circa 750 B.C.E. Kushite king who Egyptianized Nubia and conquered Upper Egypt.

King Nzinga Mbemba (Afonso I) (N-zinga MEHM-bah) 1456–1543 C.E. Ruler of Kongo in the first half of the sixteenth century, who became the first vassal king to Portugal.

Knossos City on the island of Crete that flourished during the Minoan period during the third millennium B.C.E.

Kong Fuzi 551–479 C.E. Original name of Confucius, Chinese philosopher and teacher of ethics.

Kongo Central African state that began trading with the Portuguese around 1500; although their kings, such as King Affonso I (r. 1506–1543), converted to Christianity, they nevertheless suffered from the slave trade.

Koumbi-Saleh Important trading city along the trans-Saharan trade route from the eleventh to the thirteenth century.

Krishna One of the incarnations of the Hindu god Vishnu, who appears in the Bhagavad-Gita as the teacher of Arjuna.

Kshatriayas (KSHAHT-ree-uhs) Hindu caste of warriors and aristocrats.

Kulaks Land-owning Russian peasants who benefited under Lenin's New Economic Policy and suffered under Stalin's forced collectivization.

Kumiss An alcoholic drink of the nomadic groups of Central Asia made of fermented mare's milk.

Kush Nubian African kingdom that conquered and controlled Egypt from 750 to 664 B.C.E.

Kushan empire Major Eurasian empire that controlled much of Central Asia and modern Pakistan and India during the first three centuries of the Common Era.

Kwame Nkruhmah (KWAH-mee en-KROO-mah) 1909–1972 C.E. Ghanaian politician and revolutionary who led the Gold Coast to independence in 1957 and served as the new country of Ghana's first prime minister.

La Reforma Political reform movement of Mexican president Benito Juárez (1806–1872) that called for limiting the power of the military and the Catholic church in Mexican society.

Lamaist Buddhism (LAH-muh-ihst BOOdiz'm) Branch of Buddhism that was similar to shamanism in its acceptance of magic and supernatural powers.

Laozi Semi-legendary sixth-century B.C.E. Chinese philosopher traditionally recognized as the founder of the ideology of Daoism.

Lapita Earliest known Austronesian migrants to sail out into the Pacific Ocean and establish settlements on Pacific Islands.

Latifundia (LAT-ih-FOON-dee-uh) Huge state-run and slave-worked farms in ancient Rome.

Lawbook of Manu Circa 500 B.C.E. Book of verses in the Hindu canon that spells out the norms of religious, domestic, and social life in ancient India.

Lázaro Cárdenas 1895–1970. President of Mexico who nationalized the oil industry in 1938.

League of Nations Forerunner of the United Nations, the dream of American president Woodrow Wilson, although its potential was severely limited by the refusal of the United States to join.

Lebensraum (LAY-behnz-rowm) German term meaning "living space"; the term is associated with Hitler and his goal of carving out territory in the east for an expanding Germany.

Lech Walesa (LEHK WAH-lehn-sah) Leader of the Polish Solidarity movement.

Legalism Chinese philosophy from the Zhou dynasty that called for harsh suppression of the common people.

Leonardo da Vinci 1452–1519 C.E. Noted Italian painter, sculptor, architect, and engineer of the Renaissance period.

Levée en masse (leh-VAY on MASS) A term signifying universal conscription during the radical phase of the French revolution.

Lex talionis (lehks tah-lee-oh-nihs) "Law of retaliation," laws in which offenders suffered punishments similar to their crimes; the most famous example is Hammurabi's Laws.

Li (LEE) Confucian concept, a sense of propriety.

Li Bai 701–761 C.E. One of the most popular poets of the Tang era, famous for his commentary on Chinese social life.

Lili'uokalani 1838–1917 C.E. The first and only queen of Hawaii, and the last Hawaiian sovereign to rule the islands prior to Hawai'i's annexation by the United States in 1898.

Lin Zexu 1785–1850 C.E. Chinese scholar and official appointed by the Qing government to destroy the illegal opium trade conducted by the British and other European and American traders.

Linear A Minoan written script.

Linear B Early Mycenaean written script, adapted from the Minoan Linear A.

Little Ice Age Period beginning in about 1300 C.E. when global temperatures declined for about 500 years.

Louis Riel 1844–1885 C.E. Leader of metis and indigenous people who organized the unsuccessful Northwest Rebellion against Canadian settlement in 1885. Riel was executed by Canadian authorities.

Louis the Pious 814–840 C.E. Only surviving son of Charlemagne, who held his father's empire together until his sons split it up after his death in 843.

Louis XIV (LOO-ee) 1638–1715 C.E. Also known as the Sun King, his seventy-two-year reign was the longest of any monarch in European history.

Louis XVI 1754–1793 C.E. The last king of France before the end of the French monarchy during the French Revolution, who was executed by guillotine.

Luddites Early-nineteenth-century artisans who were opposed to new machinery and industrialization.

Machismo (mah-CHEEZ-moh) Latin American social ethic that honored male strength, courage, aggressiveness, assertiveness, and cunning.

Madrasas (MAH-drahs-uhs) Islamic institutions of higher education that originated in the tenth century.

Magi Member of a priestly caste in ancient Persia.

Magyars (MAH-jahrs) Hungarian invaders who raided towns in Germany, Italy, and France in the ninth and tenth centuries.

Mahabharata (mah-hah-BAH-rah-tah) Massive ancient Indian epic that was developed orally for centuries; it tells of an epic civil war between two family branches.

Mahayana (mah-huh-YAH-nah) The "greater vehicle," a more metaphysical and more popular northern branch of Buddhism.

Maize A plant whose domestication was crucial to the emergence of complex states in early Mesoamerica.

Majapahit (MAH-ja-PAHT) Southeast Asian kingdom (1293–1520) centered on the island of Java.

Mali (MAH-lee) West African kingdom founded in the thirteenth century by Sundiata; it reached its peak during the reign of Mansa Musa.

Malintzin 1500–1529 C.E. Nahua woman who acted as interpreter and advisor for Hernan Cortes.

Manchus Manchurians who conquered China, putting an end to the Ming dynasty and founding the Qing dynasty (1644–1911).

Mandarin A Chinese bureaucrat-scholar who worked for the government in Imperial China.

Mandate of heaven Chinese belief that the emperors ruled through the mandate, or approval, of heaven contingent on their ability to look after the welfare of the population.

Mandate system System that developed in the wake of World War I when the former colonies ended up mandates under European control, a thinly veiled attempt at continuing imperialism.

Manichaeism (man-ih-KEE-iz'm) Religion founded by the prophet Mani in the third century C.E., a syncretic version of Zoroastrian, Christian, and Buddhist elements.

Manila City in modern Phillipines, and formerly capital of the Spanish colony of the Philippines, founded in 1565.

Manor Large estates of the nobles during the European middle ages, home for the majority of the peasants.

Mansa Musa (MAHN-suh MOO-suh) Reigned 1312–1337 C.E. Ruler of the wealthy and powerful Mali Empire in West Africa.

Mao Zedong 1893–1976 C.E. Chinese communist revolutionary who ruled China as the chairman of the Communist Party from 1949, when the communists defeated the nationalist Guomindang Party and forced its leaders to flee to Taiwan, until his death.

Maori (mow-ree) Indigenous people of New Zealand.

Marae Polynesian temple structure.

Marathon Battlefield scene of the Athenian victory over the Persians in 490 B.C.E.

Marco Polo 1254-1324 C.E. Italian merchant whose account of his travels to China and other lands became legendary.

Maroons Runaway African slaves.

Marshall Plan U.S. plan, officially called the European Recovery Program, that offered financial and other economic aid to all European states that had suffered from World War II, including Soviet bloc states.

Martin Luther 1483-1546. German monk and Catholic priest who became a critical figure in what became known as the Protestant Reformation after challenging the corruption of the church in his *Ninety-Five Theses,* published 1517.

Mary Wollstonecraft 1759-1797. English writer, philosopher, and advocate of women's rights, who wrote *A Vindication of the Rights of Woman* in 1792.

Matteo Ricci (maht-TAY-oh REE-chee) 1552-1610 C.E. Italian Jesuit who was one of the founders of the Jesuit China missions.

Mauryan empire Indian dynasty (321-185 B.C.E.) founded by Chandragupta Maurya and reaching its peak under Ashoka.

May Fourth Movement Chinese movement that began 4 May 1919 with a desire to eliminate imperialist influences and promote national unity.

Maya ball game Game in which Maya peoples used a hard rubber ball to propel through a ring without using their hands. Often used for ritual and ceremonial purposes.

Maya (Mye-uh) Brilliant Central American society (300-1100) known for math, astronomy, and a sophisticated written language.

Mecca Important city in modern Saudi Arabia, in which the hajj is conducted annually.

Medes (meeds) Indo-European branch that settled in northern Persia and eventually fell to another branch, the Persians, in the sixth century B.C.E.

Medina A city 345 kilometers (214 miles) north of Mecca, to which the Prophet Muhammad and his followers migrated in 622 C.E. Medina means "the city," as in "the city of the prophet."

Meiji Restoration (MAY-jee) Restoration of imperial rule under Emperor Meiji in 1868 by a coalition led by Fukuzawa Yukichi and Ito Hirobumi; the restoration enacted western reforms to strengthen Japan.

Melaka (may-LAH-kah) Southeast Asian kingdom that was predominantly Islamic.

Mencius (MEN-shi-us) Late-fourth/early-third century BCE Chinese philosopher recognized as one the most important followers of Confucius.

Menes (mee-neez) Egyptian conqueror who, according to tradition, unified Upper and Lower Egypt c. 3100 B.C.E. (sometimes identified with Narmer).

Mesoamerica (mez-oh-uh-MER-i-kuh) Another term for Central America.

Mesopotamia Term meaning "between the rivers," in this case the Tigris and Euphrates; Sumer and Akkad are two of the earliest societies.

Mestizo (mehs-TEE-zoh) Latin American term for children of Spanish and native parentage.

Métis (may-TEE) Canadian term for individuals of mixed European and indigenous ancestry.

Mexica (MEHK-si-kah) Nahuatl-speaking people from the Valley of Mexico who were the rulers of the Aztec Empire.

Michaelangelo Buonarotti 1475-1564 C.E. An Italian painter, sculptor, and architect of the Renaissance whose worked shaped the development of western art.

Mikhail S. Gorbachev 1931-. Soviet politician who served as the last leader of the Soviet Union from 1985 until 1991, when the Soviet Union dissolved.

Millet An autonomous, self-governing community in the Ottoman empire.

Ming Chinese dynasty (1368-1644) founded by Hongwu and known for its cultural brilliance.

Minoan (mih-NOH-uhn) Society located on the island of Crete (ca. 2000-1100 B.C.E.) that influenced the early Mycenaeans.

Missi dominici (mihs-see doh-mee-neechee) "Envoys of the lord ruler," the noble and church emissaries sent out by Charlemagne.

Missionaries People who travel on religious missions to help spread their faith.

Mithradates I (mihth-rah-DAY-teez) Powerful ruler of the Parthian Empire, who reigned from 171 to 132 B.C.E.

Mithraism (MITH-rah-iz'm) Mystery religion based on worship of the sun god Mithras; it became popular among the Romans because of its promise of salvation.

Moche (moh-CHEE) Pre-Incan South American society (300-700) known for their brilliant ceramics.

Modu 210-174 B.C.E. Highly successful leader of the Xiongnu peoples of the Central Asian steppes.

Mohandas Karamchand Gandhi 1869-1948 C.E. Indian nationalist, politician, and lawyer who led the campaign against British rule by employing methods of nonviolent confrontation.

Mohenjo-daro Set of ancient cities in modern southeast Pakistan, near the Indus River, that flourished in the third millennium B.C.E.

Moksha Hindu concept of the salvation of the soul.

Monotheism (MAW-noh-thee-iz'm) Belief in only one god, a rare concept in the ancient world.

Monroe Doctrine American doctrine issued in 1823 during the presidency of James Monroe that warned Europeans to keep their hands off Latin America and that expressed growing American imperialistic views regarding Latin America.

Monsoon system Seasonal winds that blow across the Indian subcontinent and Indian Ocean Basin that facilitated maritime trade during the early Silk Roads eras.

Motecuzoma I (mo-tek-oo-ZO-mah) c. 1397-1468. Fifth Aztec ruler whose conquests significantly extended Aztec rule beyond the Valley of Mexico.

Motecuzoma II (mo-tek-oo-ZO-mah) 1466-1520 C.E. Aztec emperor at the time of Hernan Cortes' invasion.

Mughals (MOO-guhls) Islamic dynasty that ruled India from the sixteenth through the eighteenth century; the construction of the Taj Mahal is representative of their splendor; with the exception of the enlightened reign of Akbar, the increasing conflict between Hindus and Muslims was another of their legacies.

Muhammad Ali Jinnah (moo-HAHM-ahd ah-lee JIN-uh) 1876-1948 C.E. Politician and independence fighter who led the All-India Muslim League from 1913 until the founding of Pakistan in 1947 and then served as the first leader of independent Pakistan until his death.

Muhammad Ali Reigned 1805-1848. Egyptian general who built a powerful army on the European model and became the effective ruler of Egypt in spite of its official status as an Ottoman territory.

Muhammad (muh-HAH-mehd) Prophet of Islam (570-632).

Mujahideen Meaning "Islamic warriors," a group who fought against Soviet intervention in Afghanistan in 1979. They were supplied and trained by United States CIA operatives, which helped lead to a Soviet withdrawal in 1989.

Munich Conference 1938 meeting between Germany, Great Britain, Italy, and France in which attendees agreed to German expansion in Czechoslovakia. The conference is considered part of the policy of appeasement that led Adolf Hitler to believe he had a free hand in Europe.

Muslim A follower of Islam.

Mutsuhito (MOO-tsoo-HEE-taw) 1852-1912 C.E. The first Meiji emperor of Japan who reigned from 1867 until his death. During his reign Japan transformed from a feudal to an industrial economy.

Mycenaean (meye-seh-NEE-uhn) Early Greek society on the Peloponnese (1600-1100 B.C.E.) that was influenced by the Minoans; the Mycenaeans' conflict with Troy is immortalized in Homer's *Odyssey.*

Nam Viet Early Chinese name for the modern nation of Vietnam.

Napoleon Bonaparte (nuh-POH-lee-uhn BOH-nuh-pahrt) 1769–1821 C.E. French military leader during the French Revolution who later seized power and crowned himself emperor from 1804 to 1814, and again in 1815 until he was defeated and exiled.

Nara era Japanese period (710–794), centered on the city of Nara, that was the highest point of Chinese influence.

National Policy Nineteenth-century Canadian policy designed to attract migrants, protect industries through tariffs, and build national transportation systems.

NATO The North Atlantic Treaty Organization, which was established by the United States in 1949 as a regional military alliance against Soviet expansionism.

Ndongo (n'DAWN-goh) Angolan kingdom that reached its peak during the reign of Queen Nzinga (r. 1623–1663).

Neandertal (nee-ANN-duhr-tawl) Early humans (100,000 to 35,000 years ago) who were prevalent during the Paleolithic period.

Nebuchadnezzar (neb-uh-kud-NEZ-er) King of the Babylonian Empire who reigned between 600 and 550 B.C.E.

Negritude (NEH-grih-tood) "Blackness," a term coined by early African nationalists as a means of celebrating the heritage of black peoples around the world.

Nelson Mandela 1918–2013 C.E. South African revolutionary and politician who consistently fought against the apartheid state until its demise in 1994. He became the first black president of South Africa, and served from 1994 to 1999.

Neo-Confucianism (nee-oh-kuhn-FYOO-shuhn-iz'm) Philosophy that attempted to merge certain basic elements of Confucian and Buddhist thought; most important of the early Neo-Confucianists was the Chinese thinker Zhu Xi (1130–1200).

Neolithic New Stone Age (10,000–4000 B.C.E.), which was marked by the discovery and mastery of agriculture.

Nestorian (neh-STOHR-ee-uhn) Early branch of Christianity, named after the fifth-century Greek theologian Nestorius, that emphasized the human nature of Jesus Christ.

New Economic Policy (NEP) Plan implemented by Lenin that called for minor free-market reforms.

Nicholas II Reigned 1894–1917. Russian tsar who was first deposed and then executed, along with his family, in the Russian Revolution.

Nicolaus Copernicus 1473–1543 C.E. Polish astronomer who theorized that the Sun, rather than the Earth, lay at the center of the universe.

Nile River The world's longest river, it flows 6695 km (4160 mi) from Lake Victoria through Egypt to the Mediterranean Sea.

Nirvana (nuhr-VAH-nuh) Buddhist concept of a state of spiritual perfection and enlightenment in which distracting passions are eliminated.

Noble Eightfold Path Final truth of the Buddhist Four Noble Truths that called for leading a life of balance and constant contemplation.

Nonaligned Movement Movement in which leaders of former colonial states sought to assert their independence from either Soviet or U.S. domination. The initial meeting was held in 1955 in Bandung, Indonesia.

North American Free Trade Agreement (NAFTA) Regional accord established in 1993 between the United States, Canada, and Mexico; it formed the world's second largest free-trade zone.

Nubia (NOO-bee-uh) Area south of Egypt; the kingdom of Kush in Nubia invaded and dominated Egypt from 750 to 664 B.C.E.

Nubians a member of one of the group of peoples that formed a powerful empire between Egypt and Ethiopia from the sixth to the fourteenth centuries.

Oceania Term referring to the Pacific Ocean basin and its lands.

Odoacer Germanic general who deposed Romulus Augustus in 476 C.E., thus bringing about the end of the western Roman Empire.

Olaudah Equiano (oh-LAU-duh eh-kwee-AHN-oh) 1745–1797 C.E. Writer and abolitionist from the Kingdom of Benin who was sold into slavery but purchased his freedom in 1766.

Olmecs Early Mesoamerican society (1200–100 B.C.E.) that centered on sites at San Lorenzo, La Venta, and Tres Zapotes and that influenced later Maya.

Olympe de Gouges 1748–1793 C.E. French feminist who authored the Declaration of the Rights of Woman and the Female Citizen at the start of the French Revolution in 1789, which advocated for equal rights for women. De Gouges was later executed by the Jacobins during the Terror.

Olympic Games A Pan-Hellenic festival in which competitors from all over ancient Greece competed in athletic competitions, founded according to tradition in 776 B.C.E.

Oracle bones Chinese Shang dynasty (1766–1122 B.C.E.) means of foretelling the future.

Organization of African Unity (OAU) An organization started in 1963 by thirty-two newly independent African states and designed to prevent conflict that would lead to intervention by former colonial powers.

Organization of Petroleum Exporting Countries (OPEC) An organization begun in 1960 by oil-producing states originally for purely economic reasons but that later had more political influence.

Osama bin Laden 1957–2011 C.E. Saudi Arabian-born founder of the militant pan-Islamic organization al-Qaeda responsible for planning the September 11, 2001, attacks in the United States.

Osiris Ancient Egyptian god that represented the forces of nature.

Osman (os-MAHN) 1258–1326 C.E. Also known as Osman Gazi. Founder of the Ottoman dynasty and the Ottoman state.

Otto von Bismarck 1815–1898 C.E. Conservative German statesman who engineered the unification of Germany and then served as its first chancellor until 1890.

Ottoman empire Powerful Turkish empire that lasted from the conquest of Constantinople (Istanbul) in 1453 until 1918 and reached its peak during the reign of Süleyman the Magnificent (r. 1520–1566).

Paleolithic Old Stone Age, a long period of human development before the development of agriculture.

Palestinian Liberation Organization (PLO) Organization created in 1964 under the leadership of Yasser Arafat to champion Palestinian rights.

Papacy The office or authority of the pope.

Paris Peace Accords Agreement reached in 1973 that marked the end of the United States' role in the Vietnam War.

Parsis (pahr-SEES) Indian Zoroastrians.

Parthians Persian dynasty (247 B.C.E.–224 C.E.) that reached its peak under Mithradates I.

Pataliputra (pah-tal-ih-puh-tra) Purpose-built capital city of the South Asian Mauryan and Gupta Empires.

Paterfamilias (PAH-tur fuh-MEE-lee-ahs) Roman term for the "father of the family," a theoretical implication that gave the male head of the family almost unlimited authority.

Patriarch (PAY-tree-ahrk) Leader of the Greek Orthodox church, which in 1054 officially split with the pope and the Roman Catholic church.

Patricians Roman aristocrats and wealthy classes.

Paul of Tarsus Christian apostle who sought converts in the first-century Roman Empire and was executed for being a threat to peace and stability.

Pax romana (pahks roh-MAH-nah) "Roman Peace," a term that relates to the period of political stability, cultural brilliance, and economic prosperity beginning with unification under Augustus and lasting through the first two centuries C.E.

Peloponnesian War Bitter and destructive "civil war" fought between Sparta and her allies, and Athens and her allies, between 431 and 404 B.C.E.

Peninsulares (pehn-IHN-soo-LAH-rayz) Latin American officials from Spain or Portugal.

Perestroika (PAYR-eh-stroy-kuh) "Restructuring," a Russian term associated with Gorbachev's effort to reorganize the Soviet state.

Pericles Athenian statesmen who ruled his city from 461–429 B.C.E.

Period of the Warring States Last centuries of the Zhou dynasty (403–221 B.C.E.) when wars divided the region until the establishment of the Qin dynasty ended the disunity.

Persian Royal Road A long-distance road, partly paved with stone, built by the Persian Achaemenid Empire. It stretched for 2575 km (1600 mi) from the Mediterranean coast to the Persian heartland in modern Iran.

Peter the Great Reigned 1682-1725. Russian tsar of the Romanov family who sought to modernize Russia based on the model established by western European states.

Pharaohs (FARE-ohs) Egyptian kings considered to be gods on earth.

Philip of Macedon King of Macedon who reigned from 359 to 336 B.C.E. Responsible for bringing all of Greece under his control in 338 B.C.E.

Phoenicians Semitic-speaking peoples who settled on a narrow coastal strip between the Lebanon Mountains and Mediterranean Sea and established a series of successful commercial maritime states in the second and first millennia B.C.E.

Pico Pico della Mirandola, 1463-1494 C.E. Italian humanist who sought to harmonize the various religions and philosophies of the world.

Plato Athenian Greek philosopher, a pupil of Socrates, who lived from 430 to 347 B.C.E.

Plebians (plih-BEE-uhns) Roman common people.

Pogrom Yiddish word meaning "devastation," referring to an organized massacre of a particular ethnic group—especially Jews in Eastern Europe.

Polis (POH-lihs) Greek term for the city-state.

Pope Gregory I Important pope whose papacy lasted from 590 to 604, well known for his prolific writings.

Popol Vuh (paw-pawl vuh) Mayan creation epic.

Porcelain A very light, thin and adaptable type of pottery that, when fired with glazes, became a highly valuable export commodity during the Tang and Song dynasty.

Porfirio Díaz (pohr-FEER-eeo DEE-ahs) 1830-1915 C.E. Mexican general and politician who served seven terms as president, for a total of thirty-one years.

Potosí (paw-taw-SEE) City in the central highlands of modern-day Bolivia that became the world's largest silver-producing area after silver was discovered in 1545.

Prague Spring Period in 1968 in which the communist leader of Czechoslovakia, Alexander Dubcek, launched a reform movement aimed at softening Soviet-style rule. The movement was crushed when Russian forces invaded.

Prehistory The period before the invention of writing.

Proletariat Urban working class in a modern industrial society.

Protestant Reformation Sixteenth-century European movement during which Luther, Calvin, Zwingli, and others broke away from the Catholic church.

Protoindustrialization Also called the "putting-out system," in which entrepreneurs delivered raw materials to families in the countryside, who would then spin and weave the materials into garments. The entrepreneurs would then pick up the garments, pay the families, and sell them on the market.

Ptolemaic (TAWL-oh-may-ihk) Term used to signify both the Egyptian kingdom founded by Alexander the Great's general Ptolemy and the thought of the philosopher Ptolemy of Alexandria (second century C.E.), who used mathematical formulas in an attempt to prove Aristotle's geocentric theory of the universe.

Ptolemaic empire (TAWL-oh-may-ihk) Empire that ruled Egypt during the Hellenistic era.

Punic Wars A series of three wars fought between the Roman Republic and Carthage between 264 and 146 B.C.E.

Punt Land that traded with the ancient kingdoms of Egypt, whose exact whereabouts are unknown but may be in or near modern Eritrea.

Putting-out system Method of getting around guild control by delivering unfinished materials to rural households for completion.

Qadi Islamic judge.

Qanat (kah-NAHT) Persian underground canal.

Qi (chee) Chinese concept of the basic material that makes up the body and the universe.

Qianlong (chyahn-lawng) 1711-1799 C.E. Sixth emperor of China's Qing dynasty and grandson of Kangxi.

Qin Shihuangdi (chihn she-huang-dee) First emperor of the short-lived but highly influential Qin Dynasty, who reigned from 221 to 210 B.C.E.

Qin (chihn) Chinese dynasty (221-207 B.C.E.) that was founded by Qin Shihuangdi and was marked by the first unification of China and the early construction of defensive walls.

Qing (chihng) Chinese dynasty (1644-1911) that reached its peak during the reigns of Kangxi and Qianlong.

Qizilbash (gih-ZIHL-bahsh) Term meaning "red heads," Turkish tribes that were important allies of Shah Ismail in the formation of the Safavid empire.

Queen Hatshepsut Female pharaoh of ancient Egypt, who reigned from 1473 to 1458 B.C.E.

Queen Nzinga (N-zinga) 1583-1663 C.E. Seventeenth-century queen of the Ndongo and Matamba kingdoms in modern-day Angola.

Quetzalcoatl (keht-zahl-koh-AHT'l) Aztec god, the "feathered serpent," who was borrowed originally from the Toltecs; Quetzalcoatl was believed to have been defeated by another god and exiled, and he promised to return.

Quinto (KEEN-toh) The one-fifth of Mexican and Peruvian silver production that was reserved for the Spanish monarchy.

Quipu (KEE-poo) Incan mnemonic aid comprised of different-colored strings and knots that served to record events in the absence of a written text.

Quran (koo-RAHN) Islamic holy book that is believed to contain the divine revelations of Allah as presented to Muhammad.

Raja Sanskrit term for "king."

Ram Mohan Roy 1772-1833 C.E. Bengali intellectual who sought to harmonize aspects of European society with those of Indian society with the goal of reforming India along progressive lines.

Ramayana (rah-mah-yah-nah) Ancient Indian masterpiece about the hero Rama that symbolized the victory of *dharma* (order) over *adharma* (chaos).

Rape of Nanjing Japanese conquest and destruction of the Chinese city of Nanjing in the 1930s.

Re Sun god in ancient Egypt, and the chief deity among Egyptian gods.

Realpolitik (ray-AHL-poh-lih-teek) The Prussian Otto von Bismarck's "politics of reality," the belief that only the willingness to use force would actually bring about change.

Reconquista (ray-kohn-KEE-stah) Crusade, ending in 1492, to drive the Islamic forces out of Spain.

Reconstruction System implemented in the American South (1867-1877) that was designed to bring the Confederate states back into the union and also extend civil rights to freed slaves.

Relics Physical remains of saints or religious figures assembled by churches for veneration.

Rhapta Port that emerged as a principal commercial center in East Africa in the centuries around the turn of the millennium.

Roman Empire An empire that succeeded the Roman Republic during the reign of Augustus, which dates from 27 B.C.E. to 395 C.E.

Roman republic Period of Roman society from 509 B.C.E. to 27 B.C.E. characterized by republican form of government.

Romanov dynasty (ROH-mah-nahv) Russian dynasty (1610-1917) founded by Mikhail Romanov and ending with Nicholas II.

Ronald Reagan 1911-2004. Fortieth president of the United States, who served from 1981 to 1989. Reagan was noted for his anti-communism.

Rubaiyat (ROO-bee-aht) "Quatrains," famous poetry of Omar Khayyam that was later translated by Edward Fitzgerald.

Saddam Hussein 1937-2006 C.E. The fifth president of Iraq, who served from 1979 to 2003 until he was ousted by a coalition led by the United States.

Safavid empire (SAH-fah-vihd) Later Persian empire (1501-1722) that was founded by Shah Ismail and that became a center for Shiism; the empire reached its peak under Shah Abbas the Great and was centered on the capital of Isfahan.

Sakk Letters of credit that were common in the medieval Islamic banking world.

Saladin 1137-1193 C.E. Muslim leader and crusader who recaptured Jerusalem from the Christians in 1187.

Saljuqs (sahl-JYOOKS) Turkish tribe that gained control over the Abbasid empire and fought with the Byzantine empire.

Samsara (sahm-SAH-ruh) Hindu term for the concept of transmigration, that is, the soul passing into a new incarnation.

Samurai (SAM-uhr-eye) A Japanese warrior.

Sanskrit Original and "sacred" language of the Indo-Aryans.

Sappho Poetess who wrote around 600 B.C.E., known for writing about physical attraction between women.

Sargon of Akkad Ruler of the Mesopotamian city of Akkad who conquered most of the other city-states of the region to establish the first empire in world history.

Sasanians (suh-SAHN-iens) Powerful empire that ruled much of Central Asia and Mesopotamia from 224 to 651 C.E.

Sati (SUH-TEE) Also known as *suttee*, Indian practice of a widow throwing herself on the funeral pyre of her husband.

Satrapies System of provincial government in the Persian Empire, in which administration is divided into provinces, each of which was called a satrapy.

Satraps (SAY-traps) Persian administrators, usually members of the royal family, who governed a satrapy.

Satyagraha (SAH-tyah-GRAH-hah) "Truth and firmness," a term associated with Gandhi's policy of passive resistance.

Schism Mutual excommunication of the Roman pope and Byzantine patriarch in 1054 over ritual, doctrinal, and political differences between the two Christian churches.

Schlieffen plan (SHLEE-fn) The name of German war plans to deal with a war in which battles would have to be fought on two fronts. The plan was implemented at the start of World War I, when it was clear that Germany would go to war with Russia and France.

Scholasticism Medieval attempt of thinkers such as St. Thomas Aquinas to merge the beliefs of Christianity with the logical rigor of Greek philosophy.

Scientific racism Nineteenth-century attempt to justify racism by scientific means; an example would be Gobineau's *Essay on the Inequality of the Human Races.*

Scramble for Africa Period between about 1875 and 1900 in which European powers sought to colonize as much of the African continent as possible.

Seleucids (sih-LOO-sihds) Persian empire (323–83 B.C.E.) founded by Seleucus after the death of Alexander the Great.

Self-determination Belief popular in World War I and after that every people should have the right to determine their own political destiny; the belief was often cited but ignored by the Great Powers.

Self-Strengthening Movement Chinese attempt (1860–1895) to blend Chinese cultural traditions with European industrial technology.

Semitic (suh-miht-ihk) A term that relates to the Semites, ancient nomadic herders who spoke Semitic languages; examples of Semites were the Akkadians, Hebrews, Aramaics, and Phoenicians, who often interacted with the more settled societies of Mesopotamia and Egypt.

Sepoys Indian troops who served the British.

Serfs Peasants who, though not chattel slaves, were tied to the land and who owed obligation to the lords on whose land they worked.

Sergei Witte (SAYR-gay VIHT-tee) Late-nineteenth-century Russian minister of finance who pushed for industrialization.

Sericulture The cultivation of silkworms for the production of silk.

Shah Abbas the Great 1571–1629 C.E. Fifth Safavid Shah of Iran who is generally considered the strongest of the Safavid rulers.

Shah Jahan 1592–1666 C.E. Fifth Mughal emperor who commissioned the building of the Taj Mahal for his wife, Mumtaz.

Shamanism (SHAH-mah-niz'm) Belief in shamans or religious specialists who possessed supernatural powers and who communicated with the gods and the spirits of nature.

Shang dynasty Dynasty of ancient China that ruled, according to tradition, from 1766–1122 B.C.E.

Shang Yang 390–338 B.C.E. Minister to the Duke of Qin state in Western China, and important developer of the political philosophy of Legalism.

Sharia (shah-REE-ah) The Islamic holy law, drawn up by theologians from the Quran and accounts of Muhammad's life.

Shia (SHEE-ah) Islamic minority in opposition to the Sunni majority; their belief is that leadership should reside in the line descended from Ali.

Shintoism (SHIHN-toh-iz'm) Indigenous Japanese religion that emphasizes purity, clan loyalty, and the divinity of the emperor.

Shiva (SHEE-vuh) Hindu god associated with both fertility and destruction.

Shogun (SHOH-gun) Japanese military leader who ruled in place of the emperor.

Shudras (SHOO-druhs) Hindu caste of landless peasants and serfs.

Siberia Region to the east of Russia in north-eastern Europe, which was conquered by the Russians between 1581 and 1639.

Siddhartha Gautama (sih-DHAR-tuh GOW-tau-mah) Indian *kshatriya* who achieved enlightenment and became known as the Buddha, the founder of Buddhism.

Sikhs (SIHKS) Adherents of an Indian syncretic faith that contains elements of Hinduism and Islam.

Silk Roads An extensive network of trade routes that linked much of Eurasia with North Africa during the Classical Period.

Silla dynasty Important early Korean dynasty that flourished during the seventh and eighth centuries.

Sima Qian Major ancient Chinese historian who lived during the second and early first centuries B.C.E. and wrote the first complete history of China to that point, the *Shiji.*

Simón Bolívar (see-MOHN boh-LEE-vahr) 1783–1830 C.E. Venezuelan military and political leader who led a number of Latin American states to independence from the Spanish.

Sinicization Process by which non–Han Chinese people come under the cultural or political domination of Han Chinese.

Sino-Japanese War War between China and Japan from 1897 to 1901, over the status of Korea. The Chinese were badly defeated.

Social Darwinism Nineteenth-century philosophy, championed by thinkers such as Herbert Spencer, that attempted to apply Darwinian "survival of the fittest" to the social and political realm; adherents saw the elimination of weaker nations as part of a natural process and used the philosophy to justify war.

Socialism Political and economic theory of social organization based on the collective ownership of the means of production; its origins were in the early nineteenth century, and it differs from communism by a desire for slow or moderate change compared with the communist call for revolution.

Socrates (SAHK-rah-teez) Athenian Greek philosopher who lived from 470 to 399 B.C.E.

Solidarity Polish trade union and nationalist movement in the 1980s that was headed by Lech Walesa.

Solon Aristocrat in Athens in the sixth century B.C.E. who forged a compromise between wealthy aristocrats and discontented common and landless classes who threatened rebellion.

Song Taizu (sawng tahy-zoo) First emperor of the Chinese Song dynasty who reigned from 960 to 976 C.E.

Song (SOHNG) Chinese dynasty (960–1279) that was marked by an increasingly urbanized and cosmopolitan society.

Soviets Russian elected councils that originated as strike committees during the 1905 St. Petersburg disorders; they represented a form of local self-government that went on to become the primary unit of government in the Union of Soviet Socialist Republics. The term was also used during the cold war to designate the Soviet Union.

Spanish Inquisition Institution organized in 1478 by Fernando and Isabel of Spain to detect heresy and the secret practice of Judaism or Islam.

Sparta Important city state of ancient Greece, located in the Peloponnesus region.

Srivijaya (sree-VIH-juh-yuh) Southeast Asian kingdom (670–1025), based on the island of Sumatra, that used a powerful navy to dominate trade.

St. Augustine 354–430 C.E. Bishop of the North African diocese of Hippo, and one of the leading intellectuals of the Late Roman Empire.

St. Basil 329–379 C.E. Byzantine Christian reformer who prepared regulations for monasteries emphasizing poverty, charity, and chastity.

St. Ignatius Loyola 1491–1556 C.E. A Basque nobleman and soldier who later devoted his life to religion and founded the missionary Society of Jesus (the Jesuits).

St. Thomas Aquinas (uh-KWIY-nuhs) 1225–1274 C.E. An Italian Dominican friar and Catholic priest whose religious writings became enormously influential in the school of Scholasticism.

Stateless societies Term relating to societies such as those of sub-Saharan Africa after the Bantu migrations that featured decentralized rule through family and kinship groups instead of strongly centralized hierarchies.

Stoics (STOH-ihks) Hellenistic philosophers who encouraged their followers to lead active, virtuous lives and to aid others.

Strabo (STRAH-boh) Greek geographer (first century C.E.).

Strategic Arms Limitation Talks (SALT) Agreement in 1972 between the United States and the Soviet Union.

Stupas (STOO-pahs) Buddhist shrines.

Sufis (SOO-fees) Islamic mystics who placed more emphasis on emotion and devotion than on strict adherence to rules.

Sui dynasty (SWAY) Chinese dynasty (589–618) that constructed the Grand Canal, reunified China, and allowed for the splendor of the Tang dynasty that followed.

Sui Yangdi (sway yahng-dee) Second emperor of the Chinese Sui Dynasty, responsible for the construction of the Chinese Grand Canal system, who reigned from 604–618 C.E.

Süleyman (SOO-lee-mahn) Ottoman Turkish ruler Süleyman the Magnificent (r. 1520–1566), who was the most powerful and wealthy ruler of the sixteenth century.

Sultan Selim III Reigned 1789–1807. Ottoman sultan whose efforts at reform threatened his elite fighting corps (the Jannissaries), who revolted and locked him up.

Sumerians (soo-MEHR-ee-uhns) Earliest Mesopotamian society.

Sun Yatsen 1866–1925 C.E. Chinese physician and politician who founded the Chinese nationalist Guomindang Party and then briefly served as the first president of the Republic of China.

Sundiata (soon-JAH-tuh) Founder of the Mali empire (r. 1230–1255), also the inspiration for the *Sundiata,* an African literary and mythological work.

Sunni (SOON-nee) "Traditionalists," the most popular branch of Islam; Sunnis believe in the legitimacy of the early caliphs, compared with the Shiite belief that only a descendant of Ali can lead.

Suu Kyi, Aung San (SOO KEY, AWNG SAHN) Opposition leader (1945–) in Myanmar; she was elected leader in 1990 but she was not allowed to come to power; she was a Nobel Peace Prize recipient in 1991. She was finally released from house arrest in November 2010.

Swahili (swah-HEE-lee) East African city-state society that dominated the coast from Mogadishu to Kilwa and was active in trade. Also a Bantu language of East Africa, or a member of a group who speaks this language.

Sykes-Picot Treaty Secret 1917 treaty between the British and French, with the agreement of Russia, to divide the modern Middle East between them after the end of World War I.

Taíno (TEYE-noh) A Caribbean tribe who were the first indigenous peoples from the Americas to come into contact with Christopher Columbus.

Taiping rebellion (TEYE-pihng) Rebellion (1850–1864) in Qing China led by Hong Xiuquan, during which twenty to thirty million were killed; the rebellion was symbolic of the decline of China during the nineteenth century.

Tale of Genji Japanese literary work written during the Heian Period (794–1185 C.E.) by the aristocratic woman Murasaki Shikibu.

Taliban Strict Islamic organization that ruled Afghanistan from 1996 to 2002.

Tamerlane (TAM-er-lane) 1336–1405 C.E. Also known as Timur. Founder of the Timurid Empire in modern-day Iran and Central Asia.

Tang dynasty Powerful and wealthy Chinese dynasty that ruled a vast East Asian empire from 618 to 907 C.E.

Tang Taizong (TAHNG TEYE-zohng) Chinese emperor (r. 627–649) of the Tang dynasty (618 to 907).

Tanzimat era "Reorganization" era (1839–1876), an attempt to reorganize the Ottoman empire on Enlightenment and constitutional forms.

Temüjin (TEM-oo-chin) Mongol conqueror (ca. 1167–1227) who later took the name Chinggis Khan, "universal ruler."

Tenochtitlan (the-NOCH-tee-tlahn) Capital of the Aztec empire, later Mexico City.

Teotihuacan (tay-uh-tee-wah-KAHN) Central American society (200 B.C.E.–750 C.E.); its Pyramid of the Sun was the largest structure in Mesoamerica.

Terra australis incognita Meaning "unknown southern land," it refers to land that European explorers had speculated must exist in the world's southern hemisphere from the second to the eighteenth centuries.

Terra Nullius Concept meaning "land belonging to no one" used frequently by colonial powers who sought to justify the conquest of nomadic lands.

Teutonic Knights Crusading European order that was active in the Baltic region.

Theodor Herzl 1860–1904 C.E. Jewish Austro-Hungarian writer and journalist who founded the modern Zionist movement.

Theodora Wife of the Emperor Justinian, who played a key role in the success of his reign.

Third Rome Concept that a new power would rise up to carry the legacy of Roman greatness after the decline of the Second Rome, Constantinople; Moscow was referred to as the Third Rome during the fifteenth century.

Three estates The three classes of European society, composed of the clergy (the first estate), the aristocrats (the second estate), and the common people (the third estate).

Three Principles of the People Philosophy of Chinese Guomindang leader Sun Yatsen (1866–1925) that emphasized nationalism, democracy, and people's livelihood.

Thucydides Athenian historian who wrote a history of the Peloponnesian war in the fifth century B.C.E.

Tian (TEE-ehn) Chinese term for heaven.

Tikal (tee-KAHL) Maya political center from the fourth through the ninth century.

Timbuktu (tim-buhk-TOO) City in the Mali Empire known for its large population, wealth, and places of learning.

Timur-i lang (tee-MOOR-yee LAHNG) "Timur the Lame," known in English as Tamerlane (ca. 1336–1405), who conquered an empire ranging from the Black Sea to Samarkand.

Tokugawa bakufu Feudal style of government that ruled Japan under the direction of shoguns from 1603 until the Meiji Restoration in 1868.

Tokugawa Ieyasu (TOH-koo-GAH-wah) 1543–1616 C.E. Founder and first shogun of the Tokugawa dynasty in Japan.

Tokugawa (TOH-koo-GAH-wah) Last shogunate in Japanese history (1600–1867); it was founded by Tokugawa Ieyasu who was notable for unifying Japan.

Toltecs Central American society (950–1150) that was centered on the city of Tula.

Toussaint Louverture (too-SAHNT loo-vehr-TOOR) 1743–1803 C.E. Haitian general and leader of the Haitian Revolution against the French until his death in a French prison.

Trail of Tears Forced relocation of the Cherokee from the eastern woodlands to Oklahoma (1837–1838); it was symbolic of U.S. expansion and destruction of indigenous Indian societies.

Treaty of Nanjing 1842 Treaty forced on China by Great Britain after Britain's victory in the first Opium War, which forcibly opened China to western trade and settlement.

Treaty of Versailles 1919 treaty between the victorious Entente powers and defeated Germany at the end of World War I, which laid the blame for the war on Germany and exacted harsh reparations.

Treaty of Waitangi Treaty between British government and indigenous Maori peoples of New Zealand in 1840 that was interpreted differently by both sides and thus created substantial Maori opposition to British settlement.

Triangular trade Trade between Europe, Africa, and the Americas that featured finished products from Europe, slaves from Africa, and American products bound for Europe.

Tribunes Officials elected by plebians (commoners) in the Roman Republic to represent their interests in the Roman government.

Triple Alliance Pre–World War I alliance of Germany, Austria-Hungary, and Italy.

Triple Entente (ahn-TAHNT) Pre–World War I alliance of England, France, and Russia.

Troubadors A class of traveling poets and entertainers enthusiastically patronized by Medieval aristocratic women in modern southern France and northern Italy.

Truman Doctrine U.S. policy instituted in 1947 by President Harry Truman in which the United States would follow an interventionist foreign policy to contain communism.

Tsar Alexander II 1818–1881 C.E. Emperor of Russia from 1855 until his assassination, best known for his emancipation of the serfs in 1861.

Tsar (ZAHR) Old Russian term for king that is derived from the term *caesar*.

Tula Original region of the Toltec people, located to the northwest of modern Mexico City.

Twelve Tables Rome's first set of laws, established in 449 B.C.E.

Twelver Shiism (SHEE'i'zm) Branch of Islam that stressed that there were twelve perfect religious leaders after Muhammad and that the twelfth went into hiding and would return someday; Shah Ismail spread this variety through the Safavid empire.

Uighurs (WEE-goors) Turkish tribe.

Ukiyo Japanese word for the "floating worlds," a Buddhist term for the insignificance of the world that came to represent the urban centers in Tokugawa Japan.

Ulaanbaatar (OO-lahn-bah-tahr) Mongolian city.

Ulama Islamic officials, scholars who shaped public policy in accordance with the Quran and the *sharia*.

Umayyad (oo-MEYE-ahd) Arabic dynasty (661–750), with its capital at Damascus, that was marked by a tremendous period of expansion to Spain in the west and India in the east.

Umma (UM-mah) Islamic term for the "community of the faithful."

United Nations (UN) Successor to the League of Nations, an association of sovereign nations that attempts to find solutions to global problems.

Untouchables Lowest caste (or varna) in the South Asian caste system.

Upanishads (oo-PAHN-ee-shahds) Indian reflections and dialogues (800–400 B.C.E.) that reflected basic Hindu concepts.

Urdu (OOR-doo) A language that is predominant in Pakistan.

Uruk (OO-rook) Ancient Mesopotamian city from the fourth millennium B.C.E. that was allegedly the home of the fabled Gilgamesh.

Utopian socialism Movement that emerged around 1830 to establish ideal communities that would provide the foundation for an equitable society.

Vaishyas (VEYES-yuhs) Hindu caste of cultivators, artisans, and merchants.

Vaqueros (vah-KEHR-ohs) Latin American cowboys, similar to the Argentine gaucho.

Varna (VAHR-nuh) Hindu word for caste.

Varuna (vuh-ROO-nuh) Early Aryan god who watched over the behavior of mortals and preserved the cosmic order.

Vedas (VAY-duhs) "Wisdom," early collections of prayers and hymns that provide information about the Indo-European Aryans who migrated into India around 1500 B.C.E.; *Rig Vedaf* is the most important collection.

Velvet revolution A term that describes the non-violent transfer of power in Czechoslovakia during the collapse of Soviet rule.

Venta, La (VEHN-tuh, lah) Early Olmec center (800–400 B.C.E.).

Venus figurines Small Paleolithic statues of women with exaggerated sexual features.

Vernacular (ver-NA-kyoo-lar) The language of the people; Martin Luther translated the Bible from the Latin of the Catholic church into the vernacular German.

Versailles (vehr-SEYE) Palace of French King Louis XIV.

Viet Minh North Vietnamese nationalist communists under Ho Chi Minh.

Vietnamization President Richard Nixon's strategy of turning the Vietnam War over to the South Vietnamese.

Vijayanagar kingdom (vee-juh-yah-NAH-gahr) Southern Indian kingdom (1336–1565) that later fell to the Mughals.

Vikings A group that raided the British Isles from their home at Vik in southern Norway.

Vishnu (VIHSH-noo) Hindu god, preserver of the world, who was often incarnated as Krishna.

Vladimir Ilyich Lenin (VLAD-uh-meer IL yich LEHN-in) 1870–1954 C.E. Russian revolutionary and politician who led the Bolshevik Revolution in November 1917 and became the first head of state of the Soviet Union until his death.

Vo Nguyen Giap 1912–2013. Vietnamese general who served as Ho Chi Minh's right-hand man and is credited with the strategy behind the Vietnamese victory at the battle of Dien Bien Phu.

Volksgeist (FOHLKS-geyest) "People's spirit," a term that was coined by the German philosopher Herder; a nation's volksgeist would not come to maturity unless people studied their own unique culture and traditions.

Volta do mar (VOHL-tah doh MAHR) "Return through the sea," a fifteenth-century Portuguese sea route that took advantage of the prevailing winds and currents.

Voltaire (vohl-TAIR) 1712–1778 C.E. French Enlightenment writer and philosopher famous for his wit and criticism of the Catholic church. His real name was Francois-Marie Arouet.

Voudou (voh-DOW) Syncretic religion practiced by African slaves in Haiti.

W. E. B. DuBois 1868–1963. African American activist and intellectual who championed the movement of American blacks back to Africa.

Waldensians Twelfth-century religious reformers who criticized the Roman Catholic church and who proposed that the laity had the right to preach and administer sacraments; they were declared heretics.

Wanli (wahn-LEE) Chinese Ming emperor (r. 1572–1620) whose refusal to meet with officials hurried the decline of the Ming dynasty.

War chariots An ancient horse-drawn two-wheeled vehicle used in war.

War Communism The Bolshevik policy of nationalizing industry and seizing private land during the civil war.

Warsaw Pact Warsaw Treaty Organization, a military alliance formed by Soviet bloc nations in 1955 in response to rearmament of West Germany and its inclusion in NATO.

White Huns A nomadic people from Central Asia who occupied Bactria (modern Afghanistan) in the fourth century C.E. and eventually crossed the Hindu Kush mountains into India.

William the Conqueror Reigned 1066–1087. William I, the first Norman king of England after the Norman invasion in 1066.

Wind wheels Prevailing wind patterns in the Atlantic and Pacific Oceans north and south of the equator; their discovery made sailing much safer and quicker.

Winston Churchill 1874–1965 C.E. British politician who was prime minister of the United Kingdom from 1940 to 1945, during which time he led the British to victory.

Witch hunts Period in the sixteenth and seventeenth centuries in which about 110,000 people (mainly women) were tried as witches in western Europe.

Woodrow Wilson 1856–1924. President of the United States during World War I and author of the "Fourteen Points," one of which envisioned the establishment of the League of Nations.

World Health Organization (WHO) United Nations organization designed to deal with global health issues.

World Trade Organization (WTO) An organization that was established in 1995 with more than 120 nations and whose goal is to loosen barriers to free trade.

Wu Zhao 626–706 C.E. Concubine of Emperor Tang Taizong, who seized imperial power for herself in 690 after Taizong became debilitated.

Wuwei (woo-WAY) Daoist concept of a disengagement from the affairs of the world.

Xia (shyah) Early Chinese dynasty (2200–1766 B.C.E.).

Xianyang (SHYAHN-YAHNG) Capital city of the Qin empire.

Xiao (SHAYOH) Confucian concept of respect for one's parents and ancestors.

Xinjiang (shin-jyahng) Western Chinese province.

Xuanzang (SHWEN-ZAHNG) Seventh-century Chinese monk who made a famous trip to India to collect Buddhist texts.

Xunzi (SHOON-dzuh) Third-century B.C.E. Chinese philosopher and administrator recognized as one the most important followers of Confucius.

Yahweh (YAH-way) God of the monotheistic religion of Judaism that influenced later Christianity and Islam.

Yang Jian (yahng jyahn) First emperor of the short-lived but effective Sui Dynasty which united China after centuries of division, reigned from 589 to 604 C.E.

Yangshao (YAHNG-show) Early Chinese society (2500–2200 B.C.E.).

Yangzi (YAHNG-zuh) River in central China.

Yellow Turban Uprising Major peasant revolt that broke out in the last decades of the Later Han Dynasty and was partly responsible for that dynasty's collapse.

Yin One of the six Shang dynasty (1766–1122 B.C.E.) capitals near the modern city of Anyang.

Yongle (YAWNG-leh) Chinese Ming emperor (r. 1403–1424) who pushed for foreign exploration and promoted cultural achievements such as the *Yongle Encyclopedia.*

Young Turks Nineteenth-century Turkish reformers who pushed for changes within the Ottoman empire, such as universal suffrage and freedom of religion.

Yu (yoo) Legendary founder of the Xia dynasty (ca. 2200 B.C.E.).

Yuan dynasty (yoo-AHN) Chinese dynasty (1279–1368) that was founded by the Mongol ruler Khubilai Khan.

Yucatan (yoo-kuh-TAN) Peninsula in Central America, home of the Maya.

Yurts (yuhrts) Tents used by nomadic Turkish and Mongol tribes.

Zaibatsu (zeye-BAHT-soo) Japanese term for "wealthy cliques," which are similar to American trusts and cartels but usually organized around one family.

Zambos (ZAHM-bohs) Latin American term for individuals born of indigenous and African parents.

Zamudio, Adela (ZAH-moo-dee-oh, ah-DEH-lah) Nineteenth-century Bolivian poet, author of "To Be Born a Man."

Zarathustra (zar-uh-THOO-struh) Persian prophet (ca. sixth century B.C.E.) who founded Zoroastrianism.

Zemstvos (ZEHMST-voh) District assemblies elected by Russians in the nineteenth century.

Zen Buddhism Japanese version of Chinese Chan Buddhism, with an emphasis on intuition and sudden flashes of insight instead of textual study.

Zhang Qian (jung-chen) Han Dynasty explorer and ambassador who was dispatched by Emperor Wudi during the late-second century B.C.E. to establish relations with states to the west of China.

Zheng He (jung ha) 1371–1433 C.E. Chinese mariner, explorer, and admiral during the early Ming Dynasty who traveled as far as Malindi in East Africa.

Zhou dynasty (JOH) Chinese dynasty (1122–256 B.C.E.) that was the foundation of Chinese thought formed during this period: Confucianism, Daoism, Zhou Classics.

Zhu Xi (ZHOO-SHEE) Neo-Confucian Chinese philosopher (1130–1200).

Ziggurats (ZIG-uh-rahts) Mesopotamian temples.

Zimbabwe (zihm-BAHB-way) Former colony of Southern Rhodesia that gained independence in 1980.

Zoroastrianism (zohr-oh-ASS-tree-ahn-iz'm) Persian religion based on the teaching of the sixth-century-B.C.E. prophet Zarathustra; its emphasis on the duality of good and evil and on the role of individuals in determining their own fate would influence later religions.